SOMETHING *in the* ETHER

....

Lunder Building

SOMETHING *in the* ETHER

· ·

A Bicentennial History of
Massachusetts General Hospital,
1811–2011

Webster Bull and Martha Bull

With a Foreword by
Peter L. Slavin, MD, and David F. Torchiana, MD

MEMOIRS UNLIMITED
Beverly, Massachusetts

Library of Congress Cataloging-in-Publication Data
Bull, Webster, 1951–, author.
Something in the ether : a bicentennial history of Massachusetts
General Hospital, 1811 / 2011 / Webster Bull and Martha Bull;
with a foreword by Peter L. Slavin and David F. Torchiana.
p.; cm.
Includes bibliographical references and index.
ISBN 978-0-9830988-0-5 (alkaline paper)
1. Massachusetts General Hospital—History. 2. Hospitals—
Massachusetts—History. I. Bull, Martha, 1986–, author. II. Title.
[DNLM: 1. Massachusetts General Hopital. 2. Hospitals, General—his-
tory—Boston. 3. History, 19th Century—Boston. 4. History, 20th
Century—Boston. 5. History, 21st Century—Boston. wx 28 AM4]
RA 982.B72M373   2011
362.1109744'61—dc22   2010045054

All photos courtesy Massachusetts General Hospital,
unless otherwise noted.
Front cover photo: Early operation using ether, 1847, from a
whole-plate daguerreotype by Southworth and Hawes
Cover design by Arch MacInnes
Interior design by Joyce C. Weston
Printed in the United States of America

Published by Memoirs Unlimited, Beverly, Massachusetts
Distributed to the trade by Applewood Books, Carlisle, Massachusetts

CONTENTS

· · · · · · · · · · · ·

Human Face of the Outpatient Department • Walter Bauer and the Rise of the Physician-Scientist • Infectious Diseases from Syphilis to HIV/AIDS • Dermatology from Syphilology to Molecularly Targeted Therapies

FOREWORD

. . . .

WHAT IS IT ABOUT THIS PLACE THAT IS SPECIAL? What unique qualities of Massachusetts General Hospital captured the attention of a young internist and a heart surgeon, encouraging them to spend their careers here, to grow and serve side by side? What is "in the ether" here?

Academic medical centers change the course of human history, and each has its stories of breakthrough and achievement, of lives saved and improved. At Mass General since 1846, we have proudly pointed to the first public demonstration of ether in surgery, but our annual Ether Dinner is more remarkable in some ways than the event it commemorates.

Once a year the hospital hosts a dinner for employees who have reached milestones of service: 20, 25, 30 years, and so on to up to half a century and longer. Because this is a big place, the Ether Dinner fills a very large ballroom. Employees are encouraged to invite family members. Most impressive about this annual event is that everyone is honored, and equally: heart surgeons and members of our Environmental Services Department, Nobel Prize–winning scientists and receptionists. If you've been here 30 years, you get the same recognition as the next person. It is an evening of happiness and pride. You can feel it in the air.

Surgical colleagues at Mass General experience the same sort of togetherness. In other institutions, surgeons often have their own dressing rooms and lounges; for the surgical services at MGH, by contrast, there is one common lounge for all personnel—surgeons, nurses, technicians, everyone—and the locker rooms are segregated only by gender. This is clearly an egalitarian tradition, and perhaps it is an old, parsimonious Yankee tradition as well. If so, it is like many good things about Mass General, which is not only the first Harvard teaching hospital, but also the first Boston one. Many of the good things about this hospital have Boston roots.

There is not only an intellectual commitment but also an emotional attachment that comes over those of us who work here. It is a bit like being part of a military mission, like what the trauma surgeon Susan Briggs and her IMSuRT (International Medical Surgical Response Team) colleagues feel anytime they are called to provide emergency medical assistance at disaster sites around the globe. You know you are part of something important, thrilling, maybe even dangerous.

You know you may not be a hero yourself, but you are part of a team that has a chance to be heroic. That feeling can come over you whether you're visiting an Asian village devastated by a tsunami or greeting a frightened child and her family on the curb in front of the Yawkey Building. Then you realize that the disaster victim and the little girl are, in their own ways, more heroic than you are.

The first three jobs of any leader here are not to mess things up. Massachusetts General Hospital has been working pretty well for 200 years now, and we should not be too heavy-handed in trying to change it. Still, to carry the torch forward, to advance the mission, we need to understand the institution we have inherited—as administrators, as nurses and physicians, and as new employees for whom English is a second language. We need to understand what it is about this place that commands such loyalty and sense of purpose.

We trust that the stories of achievement, of trial, and of humanity in this book will help us all to understand the mission collectively, so we can advance it.

Peter L. Slavin, MD, President, Massachusetts General Hospital
David F. Torchiana, MD, CEO and Chairman, Massachusetts
General Physicians Organization

AUTHOR'S NOTE

·············

THIS BOOK MUST STAND OR FALL AS A COLLECTION OF STORIES. It was never meant to be an encyclopedic history. The mission assigned in 2007 was to capture the spirit of Massachusetts General Hospital. I can only hope that most of what the reader finds here serves that mission—from the evocative title to more than 100 interviews with MGH personnel and observers. Even the chapters about the nineteenth century, whose characters were unavailable for interviews, are focused on the personal side of this remarkable enterprise; they draw on memoir and anecdote as much as on official records.

With my coauthor, I aimed to tell the story of the hospital in a continuous 200-year arc—while also chronicling developments in all major departments, from the large, catchall units of Medicine and Surgery to the Emergency Department and Patient Care Services. But how could we do so without creating an overly detailed chronology? We decided that within each chapter we would include several long sections to tell the departmental stories. Each of these sections takes off from a meaningful moment within that chapter's main narrative.

For example, chapter 2 tells the iconic story of the first public demonstration of ether in surgery, which occurred at Massachusetts General Hospital on October 16, 1846. Following this, the main narrative breaks off for an account of the Department of Anesthesia, from Ether Day to the present. Then the story returns to 1846. I hope this makes the book more readable, but if the reader finds that this structure detracts from enjoyment of the main narrative, skimming is permitted!

This book doesn't mention every achievement or achiever. Doing so would require a longer or drier work. Consequently, many who turn to the index to find their names will be disappointed. What this book seeks to do is to suggest the astounding breadth and depth of Massachusetts General Hospital. We approached this project as lay writers following our noses. The stories you read here are stories we bumped into, stories that inspired us, wowed us, taught us something. I hope they do justice to a great institution.

Some things are missing, or underexposed:

- There is little about the nonmedical, nonadministrative staff of Mass General, the everyday workers who deliver breakfast trays to patients, who keep the floors clean, who greet cars at the curb—and always, it seems, with courtesy and pride. This is not a "people's history" of Mass General. It is largely a doctors' history, with significant input from trustees, administrators, and nurses.

- There is not enough about the educative mission of the place; but there are allusions to Harvard Medical School and to house officers (interns and residents) and fellows all the way along. The reader will have to imagine medical students and doctors in training at the elbows of all the staff physicians mentioned.

- There is only scattered evidence of clinical brilliance, and devotees of arts like vascular surgery and laparoscopy will find little to entertain them. One egregious omission will serve as an example. Whereas the topic of world health gets a long, climactic section in chapter 8, the revered Hermes Grillo and a whole cadre of brilliant thoracic surgeons get little more than a bullet point. The only excuse for this is story. As a nonmedical writer, I found the world health stories—of refugee medicine, disaster relief, and health care for the homeless—particularly gripping. I'm sure there are good stories about thoracic surgery, too.

- There is not enough about women here, although that is a function of the times since 1811. The first woman surgeon at MGH did not join the Harvard faculty until the 1970s, and Harvard was typical, or perhaps typically conservative. The last chapter makes amends, because in recent years the hospital staff has diversified in every way possible, and since the 1980s some of the most impressive stories are women's stories.

So that's the caveat: not everything is here. For all that is here, there can only be thanks. Among the many allies who encouraged and supported this project, the following must be mentioned:

Trustees, administrators, and doctors—More than 100 MGH personnel and observers sat for interviews, some more than once. Leading the list were Chairwoman of the Board Cathy Minehan, MGH President Peter Slavin, and MGPO (Massachusetts General Physicians Organization) CEO and Chairman David Torchiana. Most generous with his time was W. Gerald "Jerry" Austen, former chief of surgery and founding chairman of the MGPO. (This book dispenses with honorifics like MD and PhD in order to avoid pages of "alphabet soup." An index of names in the back fills in the missing degrees.)

The book committee—I was hired while planning was afoot for the MGH bicentennial year of 2011. Lynn Dale and her boss, Peggy Slasman, hired me and cheered me on, while a book committee offered valuable advice. Foremost among the committee members were the senior physicians Paul Russell and John Stoeckle. If this book has any academic backbone, that is due to two others on the book committee, the coordinator for Reference Services at Treadwell Library, Martha Stone, and MGH's archivist, Jeff Mifflin, who together checked facts and picked apart references. Jeff doubled as photo researcher, seconded by the tireless Catherine MacDonald. The MGH photo lab, particularly Sam Riley and Michelle Rose, provided camera-ready images. Michelle Marcella provided help with captioning, indexing, and other matters.

Collaborators—Gary Larrabee provided entrée to this project and helped with early outlining. Anna Kasabian jumped in for six months when I most needed it. Every book could use a doctor, and Stephanie Schorow is a good one. She did a read-through at the eleventh hour and made some important improvements to several sections at 11:45. Ann Twombly is my longtime, indispensable project manager and copy editor. With the cover designer Arch MacInnes and interior designer Joyce Weston, Ann deserves final credit for this book's clean look and content. Without Carol Mendoza, nothing got done in my office during the three years of writing and editing. Carol had the unenviable task of checking every footnote.

A whole paragraph is due the one person without whom this book would not have been delivered on time or with as much style and integrity. That is Martha McNiff Bull, a PBK graduate of the University of Chicago and at this writing an MFA candidate at Columbia University. In between, she worked smartly and tirelessly with her father. Martha researched and wrote the first 90 years of the main narrative (the first two chapters) and several of the department histories. This book is the longest project I have ever worked on and, with Martha's name beside mine, the proudest.

It did not seem appropriate to post a formal dedication by two outside authors on an institutional history like this one, but if anyone had asked me for one, I would have had a dedication ready: *In homage to Richard Clarke Cabot*. From this innovative, selfless, heartbreaking paragon of Boston Brahmanism, a distinctive line of medical *service* passed through Howard Means to John Stoeckle and Jim O'Connell, two living doctors whose stories jumped out at me, as I hope they will at you.

Webster Bull
Beverly, Massachusetts

SOMETHING *in the* ETHER

. . . .

This Hospital has always inspired the fervid attachment of those holding any relation to it whatsoever,—whether as citizens, proud of its benevolent services; as pupils, grateful for its teachings; or as medical officers, who have put their own work into its comprehensive fields of usefulness. It has universally fostered a feeling of affection, such as is cherished for an Alma Mater.
—Oliver Wendell Holmes

You're amongst the tigers, as you know.
—Paul S. Russell

PROLOGUE

. . . .

EMERGENCY

A STORM IS BREAKING IN THE TRAUMA-ACUTE UNIT of the Emergency Department (ED) at Massachusetts General Hospital. In a triangular area no bigger than a classroom, with eleven stretcher bays on the periphery and a nurses' station forming an inner triangle, at least fifty people are moving about like Brownian particles in a small pot: doctors, nurses, technicians, ambulance drivers and EMTs, worried family members, a crying mother. The sound track is a rhythm of beeping monitors and a chaos of voices, mostly female. A cry goes up for a pediatric anesthesiologist, and then it is repeated: "Has anyone called a pediatric anesthesiologist?!" A little girl in bay no. 3 is fighting for breath.

Alasdair Conn looks out of the corner of his eye at a first-time observer and says with a gentle smile and an accent that was once Scottish, "Welcome to my world!"

This should be a relatively quiet time in the ED: 11:15 in the morning. The 47 stretcher bays that make up the full department don't usually fill until after lunchtime, causing overflows into hallways. Friday and Saturday nights aren't any busier than the middle of a weekday, although the arc of alcohol-related injuries overtakes that of workplace heart attacks, strokes, and construction accidents.

Since 1988 Conn has been the director of the Department of Emergency Medicine at Mass General, and he says today's activity in acute is nothing. Conn is a silver-haired Sean Connery, and he speaks with the drama of a professional actor, letting his voice rise and fall and come to sudden stops as he reaches the climax of a story. He talks soberly of a man once brought to the ED straight from street racing his car along Revere Beach and crashing into a ball of flames. "He was burned over 100 percent of his body. It was one or two in the morning. It took them a long time to douse the fire and get him out. There was nothing that wasn't burnt. His ears were gone, his hair was gone, his eyes were burnt. He had fourth-degree burns, when the burn is through muscle and down to bone. He was like a little stick man covered with char. He was sitting up in the bed in the burn bay, no. 5, contracted, in shock. He had a pulse and that was it. The burn guys came in and looked at him and said, 'We're done.' He did not survive. It was awful."[1]

Conn leads what he calls a Cook's Tour of the department. He heads to the ambulance entrance, which in 2010 abuts the construction site of the Lunder Building. (The name recognizes a $35 million gift from Peter and Paula Lunder and the Lunder Foundation.) This $680 million structure (including the building and its contents), due to open in the MGH bicentennial year of 2011, is the latest pile of steel, concrete, and glass to overshadow the Bulfinch Building, the hospital's first structure, opened to patients in September 1821. It will expand Mass General's inpatient capacity roughly from 900 to 1,050.

The Bulfinch received its first patient within days of opening, and subsequent patients trickled in slowly over the coming weeks. If statistics prove out, and Conn says they are uncanny predictors, the ED will receive between 250 and 300 visits today alone. Of these, roughly a quarter will be admitted to inpatient beds, accounting for nearly half of all hospital admissions. Estimated MGH totals for 2010 were 50,000 inpatient admissions overall, 25,000 of them from the ED. Conn says, "We're very predictable. I need 70 beds a day upstairs." The third oldest general hospital in the country and the grandfather of Harvard-affiliated academic medical centers, MGH is known for its "quaternary" care, the treatment of the most complex and often rare diseases; thus, it can be the ultimate referral point on a worldwide health care network. But the ED is open to everyone, and since a law change in 2009, no one can be turned away.

At the end of this book is the story of the Boston Health Care for the Homeless Program, headed by a remarkable Harvard-trained MGH physician. Jim O'Connell says that though the Boston homeless who use shelters tend to visit Boston Medical Center in the South End more often because it is closer to a majority of shelters, street people (the homeless who prefer not to use shelters) gravitate to the ED at Mass General in the West End: "It took me a long time to figure this out, but when you get to folks who stay out on the street under bridges, they tend to use Mass General. I think it's not only a geographic thing, but I think Mass General is more accessible to street people. A bunch of people feel it's dignified to be cared for at Mass General, and they're very proud of that."

In 1821 a single surgeon, John Collins Warren, and a single physician, James Jackson, had full privileges at Mass General, and their start-up institution treated the poor—street people, along with manual laborers, domestic workers, and transients like sailors. Today the ED alone has 45 "attendings" (dedicated full-time physicians, two at a time overnight, six to seven at peak hours). They treat everyone from the homeless to a wealthy businessman flown in by helicopter from vacation in New Hampshire.

A BIT OF HISTORY

In the nineteenth century the ED was known as the "accident room" and was located on the first floor of Bulfinch East. A horse-drawn ambulance brought patients along a drive to the rear of the building. In 1903 the accident room was moved to the Operating Building and in 1916 to the basement of the Moseley Building. The move to current quarters in the White Building came in 1939, although this space has undergone renovations in 70 years and is soon to undergo another, when the Lunder Building opens. Long known as the Emergency Ward and the Overnight Ward, Emergency became a "department" sometime after Earle W. Wilkins Jr. wrote his short history of the service about 1980.[2]

Wilkins, known as The Pope, was on the MGH search committee that recruited Conn in 1988. Still standing at the entrance of his department, Conn talks excitedly about the new ambulance bays that will line the ground floor of the new building: "Ambulances will drive up and into the building and turn around inside the building. In actual fact, the ambulance bay will have another function, as an enormous decontamination facility. We occasionally get somebody who has been exposed to a chemical, but what happens if we get a hundred people at once? What happens if somebody goes to the Boston Garden and drops a chemical agent designed for mischief? In that event, we'll be able to convert the entire ambulance bay to a decontamination unit."

In the admitting area behind the ambulance entrance, nurses like Dianne Farley initiate physician-led triage, a system developed under Conn. About 25 percent of patients who visit the ED will be admitted to the hospital. About 8 percent of these will have a life-threatening event in the ensuing 24 hours. The trick is knowing which ones. In most hospitals an emergency visitor is seen first by a triage nurse, then waits in the sitting room to be seen by a physician. Conn said, "I get frustrated waiting 10 minutes in a supermarket checkout line. Imagine if your child had abdominal pain and you had to wait two hours!"

Conn wondered how to speed the process and looked for a hospital where triage was handled by physicians, not nurses. He found one in rural Ontario—too small to be relevant—and one at Vanderbilt University Medical Center. He sent a team to Nashville to study the Vanderbilt system; then they implemented it at MGH with modifications. Farley and others at the front desk now take basic information—name, age, Social Security number—and look for the patient's file among over four million electronic records kept on previous visitors to MGH. Depending on these data and presenting symptoms, Farley makes a call—to send the patient to acute, urgent, pediatric, acute psychiatric, or "fast track" for relatively minor injuries such as a broken wrist. Fast track sees about 70 to 80 patients per day, but some patients may be sicker than they know. Conn tells the story of a walk-in with apparently minor symptoms, a woman with a pain in her leg and a sudden inability to write. ("I went to the supermarket this morning, doctor, picked up my pen, and couldn't use it.") Conn ordered a CT scan of her head and found a brain tumor. A chest X-ray revealed a previously undiscovered tumor of the lung that had metastasized to the brain.

In the screening area behind admitting, an attending physician, Vicki Noble, sits at a computer monitor that shows her the status of each bay in the department, including an observation area on the 12th floor of the Bigelow Building. Today Noble is the doctor overseeing triage efforts throughout the ED. Each bed on her monitor lights up red, yellow, or green, like a stoplight, to indicate the status of the patient occupying it. Noble is an appealing, good-humored woman in her thirties who is unimpressed by an author writing a history of Mass General. She says, "We were on TV a couple of days ago, so this is no big deal. I'd rather have a big-screen movie contract."

Mission control for triage used to be code-named Orbit, as in "patient orbiting ED waiting for bed." The system has become much more efficient and is now called START, for "selective triage and rapid treatment." Noble points out a complication of maximizing efficiency: "We're a referral hospital, but we're also a teaching hospital, so there's a twofold mission. One of those missions is to educate people—so you can't be too efficient. You have to actually learn and see and experiment, and have the time to do that. It's a push-pull. We have to keep the teaching mission, but we also have to provide regular medical care. Everyone's really smart here and works hard, so it's a pleasure to work as part of this team. But it's stressful."

There are two "urgent" units, A and B, for adults who "aren't going to die in the next few hours," according to Conn. Just about every acute trauma patient is admitted to the hospital. For the urgent units, the percentage falls to about 50. In each an attending physician like Leslie Milne manages a team of professionals— three surgical residents, a physician assistant, and a medical resident. Before Conn took over the department, MGH emergency services were resident-run. Now a full-time staff member (also known in the Harvard hospital system as a "faculty member") is in charge on rotating shifts 24/7.

The Pediatric Unit is small, smaller than Conn would like it to be, but an original design had to be modified to accommodate the building's alarm system, and three bays were sacrificed. Conn looks forward to the redesigned "pedi" unit in the new layout. Though small, the unit has a soothing atmosphere here, with walls painted like a Maurice Sendak story.

The Acute Psychiatric Unit has seclusion rooms monitored by video surveillance. "Not all these patients are cooperative," Conn says—suicides, depressives, people brought in by police exhibiting bizarre behavior, "walking naked down the street." Nurse Mark Dirschel—sporting tattoos, elaborate neck jewelry, a full beard, and studded biker boots—is a match for any of them. His demeanor says: I don't take guff from you. Beside him sits a psychiatrist, a policeman, and a second security man. If one of the patients in isolation chambers shown on the video bank in front of them becomes violent, there's little question who will control the encounter.

The MGH Emergency Department once had a single computed tomography (CT) scanner, which Conn claims was the busiest in the world. "To me," he said, "that was an indication we needed more than one." Today the ED has three plain-vanilla X-ray rooms, two CT scanners (16-slice and 64-slice), and one magnetic resonance imaging (MRI) system—"probably the first MRI in an ED to my knowledge in the country. There are relatively few indications for an emergency MRI (acute stroke, spinal cord compression), but when you need it, you need it."

In the nearby interpretation room, Laura Avery, a radiologist, sits in the glimmering dark surrounded by 15 or 20 video screens. As Conn enters, she is examining the X-rays of the little girl in bay no. 3. "There's nothing blocking her airway," she says. "Probably viral." The young emergency patient will be fine.

In the simulation lab down the hall, full-size mannequins lie on beds. Using one of them, a technician teaches a student how to put intravenous lines into the chest. Simulation exercises are often run in which students must determine which course of treatment to follow given a set of presenting symptoms. The mannequins (aided by a "puppet master" in a control room) respond to treatments with falling blood pressure, rising temperature, and other symptoms of trouble. Conn boasts about the clinical research efforts of people like Jim Gordon, who heads the simulation lab at Harvard Medical School (HMS) and is also on the MGH ED staff;

Jeff Cooper, a professor of anesthesia and bioengineering, who directs the MGH Center for Medical Simulation; and Steve Dawson, a radiologist whose team is creating a mannequin that will die if you don't treat it right. Together, these efforts illustrate the traditional third leg of the stool that is an academic medical center, where patient care, education, and research jointly support the mission. According to Conn and to many others interviewed for this book, a fourth leg has emerged in recent decades: community or world health.

Somewhere in all this maze, the indispensable nurse manager Maryfran Hughes is keeping the ED on track. Hughes doubles as director of the Conference of Boston Teaching Hospitals Disaster Committee, charged with emergency preparedness. If, following Conn's imaginary scenario, a chemical agent is dropped in the Garden, Hughes will be responsible for coordinating the linkage of hospitals, emergency medical services, fire departments, and police that respond.

FROM SCOTLAND TO MARYLAND TO MASSACHUSETTS

Both of Alasdair Conn's parents were from Aberdeen, Scotland. His father studied physics at Cambridge University before World War II and spent time developing radar. His mother was a friend of the wife of the Nobel laureate Hans Krebs. The distinguished Dr. Krebs had a theory that, when looked back on, the twentieth century would divide into three parts represented by the disciplines of chemistry, physics, and biochemistry. Therefore, he advised a young Alasdair Conn in the 1960s to read biochemistry along with his medicine.

Conn went to medical school at the University of Edinburgh, and although he was invited to work toward a PhD in biochemistry, a chance conversation in 1971 led to a one-year postgraduate hitch in Baltimore, Maryland. He overstayed his visit to the States by 40 years and initially helped develop a groundbreaking shock trauma unit that included emergency transport by helicopter. Conn says, "I decided I wanted to stay on this side of the pond, went to Toronto for surgery, came back to the States, and became interested in what happens to the patients before they get to the hospital." He eventually was named emergency medical services director for the state of Maryland. "I was running all the ambulances and the protocols and the helicopter programs, as well as doing trauma surgery."

When Boston decided it wanted an emergency helicopter program of its own in the early 1980s, Conn says he was "the fool" they chose to run it. He had all the qualifications for a politically sticky climate: he was a trauma surgeon who knew helicopters, and better yet, he had never been to Boston, so he would not favor one hospital over another. From the start, in 1985, Boston MedFlight flew trauma patients to the hospital that best served their needs. Conn's time was split evenly between helicopter work and trauma surgery at Boston City Hospital (now Boston Medical Center). The chairman of the board of the nonprofit organization was The Pope himself, MGH's Earle Wilkins. When Wilkins stepped down at MGH in 1988, Conn was his logical successor. Today MedFlight is run by Conn's wife, Suzanne Wedel.

To revitalize the Emergency Department at Mass General, Conn told Wilkins and the search committee that he would need a decade: three years to renovate the physical plant and hire full-time attending staff for the first time in the department's history; three years to create a residency program in emergency medicine; three years to jump-start a research program; and one year for slippage. The committee said, "You've got the job."

When the Blake Building was constructed at MGH in the early 1990s, Conn led the charge to place a helipad on the roof. The structure would have to be sound enough to sustain the weight of a 10,000-pound helicopter in 500-foot freefall (a regulation) or the weight of the 22,000-pound helicopter used by President George H. W. Bush when he summered in Kennebunkport, Maine. The helipad was financed in part by a $1 million gift from a businessman flown to MGH and treated successfully by its world-class burn unit after an accident on Lake Winnepesaukee. The helipad has proved to be a lifesaver, most notably in February 2003, when nine survivors from The Station nightclub fire in West Warwick, Rhode Island, were MedFlighted to Mass General.

Scratch Conn the trauma surgeon and emergency director and you'll find a Scottish boy in love with flying, naval warcraft, and locomotives. The shelves in his office at Mass General are filled with models of helicopters (AH-1 Cobra, CH-53 Super Stallion), fighter planes (Spitfire, Raptor), bombers (the B-17 "Flying Fortress"), battleships (the HMS *Dreadnought*), and even a locomotive (the Union Pacific "Big Boy"). He is surely the only unit chief at MGH who would say, "If I could be any plane in the world, it would be an A-10 Warthog."

From his office Conn looks back over the history of emergency medicine, and toward its future.

> Not in my lifetime, but 50 years from now, emergency medicine will be the most powerful service in the hospital. Because the way that health care is moving is that the hospital is transitioning. The hospital, by and large, will decrease in size. In the future, treatment is not going to be in the hospital, either. If you don't need intensive care, treatment will be done at home or in an outpatient facility. When people become sick, they'll have their blood pressure and pulse measured through the Internet and we'll be monitoring it. Why will the ED be monitoring it? Because we're here 24/7, and we're very accustomed to speaking to nonphysicians about health care. We already direct paramedics, EMS, flight nurses about what to do in certain situations. So we'll be the connection.
>
> The hospital of the future will have a big ED with an adjacent diagnostic center. It will have an observation unit, as we do now, for those who need to stay additional hours for testing or observation. It will have an ICU and a suite of ORs and an ambulatory care center and that will be it.

Conn's thesis has an economic rationale as well: "If we're 50 percent of the visits to the hospital, the real savings to health care will be avoiding those admissions that are inappropriate. How many people admitted through the ED could be managed elsewhere?"

It's a far cry from the accident room in the old Bulfinch Building, an afterthought for MGH doctors of the nineteenth century. Somewhere, no doubt, John Collins Warren and James Jackson are scratching their heads at all this, or cheering.

· · · · · · · · · · · ·

CHAPTER I

A GENTLEMEN'S AGREEMENT,
1811–1845

*It was designed by Charles Bulfinch,
and he intended it to endure. It has endured.*
—James Howard Means

THE IDEALISM AND COMMERCIAL MIGHT *that shaped the city of Boston in the post-Revolutionary period also led to the founding of Massachusetts General Hospital. A charter for a city hospital was approved by the Commonwealth of Massachusetts in 1811, but the inspiration goes back further. The family of the Revolutionary War hero Joseph Warren, who died in the Battle of Bunker Hill, played a major role in advocating for a hospital established in association with the fledgling Harvard Medical School—a necessity if Harvard was to compete with schools in Philadelphia and New York. Wealthy philanthropists supported a facility that would serve the city's poor, who were otherwise left to waste away in the almshouse. Backers of the hospital believed that they were fulfilling their responsibilities to community and God.*

By 1817 the trustees had purchased land in Boston and Charlestown for a hospital and an asylum for the mentally ill, respectively. The renowned architect Charles Bulfinch, designer of the Massachusetts State House and the U.S. Capitol Building, was charged with creating a facility with an eye to grandeur and patient care. (The "it" in Means's statement above is the Bulfinch Building—and, more broadly, the hospital as a whole, since the Bulfinch Building once was the hospital.)

Lofty goals and unforgettable characters marked MGH's early history. One of the founders, James Jackson, wore two watches so he would never be a moment late; his colleague John Collins Warren could amputate a leg in forty seconds flat, a mercy in the days before anesthesia. Rufus Wyman, the first superintendent of what would become the McLean Hospital for the Mentally Ill, ate his dinner with inmates. Such men, motivated by scientific curiosity as well as compassion, and driven by both personal ambition and humanitarian fervor, helped lay the foundation for a world-class medical institution.

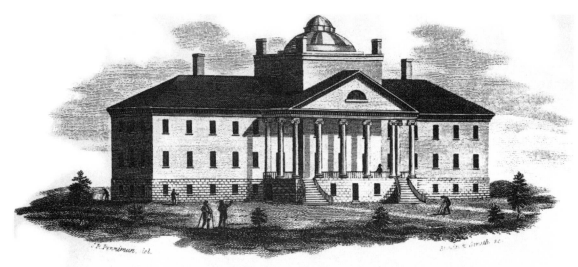

MASSACHUSETTS GENERAL HOSPITAL.

Early engraving of the Bulfinch Building.

BOSTON IN 1811 was an old town and a new city. Settled nearly two centuries before, the venerable village with its narrow, winding streets was aware of both its Puritan heritage and its more recent political past. It was serious, sober, and set in its ways. But the city of Boston was also less than 30 years old, the fourth-largest city in an upstart nation,[1] trying out brand-new principles of democracy and flexing its economic muscle on the world stage for the first time, a community eager, energetic, with something to prove.

Boston in 1811 was a combination of conservatism and revolution, of religious tradition and economic ambition. It had bought both silver and teeth from Revere; then it had answered his call to rebellion. It had chased British ships from its harbor on principle and was now sending American ships around the globe for profit. Home to Cotton Mather, it would soon hear Ralph Waldo Emerson's first sermon, but it also would transplant the Industrial Revolution to north-lying towns named for some of its own first families, Lawrence and Lowell, using plans stolen from the British.

Sited on a narrow peninsula topped by three prominent hills, Boston was still in some ways the biblical "City upon a hill" envisioned by its founder, John Winthrop, a Puritan minister; but already it was leveling its hills to fill inlets and estuaries, to expand its commercial potential, to stretch its wharves toward the world. In 1811 the Back Bay was still just a bay, but it would soon be a neighborhood combining Congregational principles and capitalist prosperity. In 1811 the Massachusetts State House, built before the turn of the century to plans by Charles Bulfinch, stood on the one hill that would remain. Topped with copper to reflect the morning sunlight, it would be gilded a half century later, by which time Boston itself would have earned its pot of gold. In 1811 Boston was dominated by white males, but the city would soon stand tall for abolitionism, foster notable female leaders, and welcome, albeit grudgingly, immigrant masses that would power its economy and politics.

THE FAMILY WARREN

John Collins Warren was a grandchild of Boston and a nephew of the American Revolution. He was a cofounder of the Massachusetts General Hospital.

The Warrens were landowners who had made their first American livings as mariners, carpenters, and farmers. John C. Warren's uncle Joseph Warren was a respected Boston doctor and a famous patriot who died at the battle of Bunker Hill. Handsome and charismatic, Joseph Warren had advocated for the controversial practice of smallpox inoculation credited to Cotton Mather and stressed the importance of quality medical education for aspiring doctors. Although he loved medicine, Joseph Warren loved Boston more. He turned down the post of surgeon in chief of the Continental Army to be an officer in the fighting army mustered to defend the town and countryside he had grown up in.

Joseph Warren was memorialized in poems that quoted his dying words on Bunker Hill in Charlestown, just across the river from the future site of the Massachusetts General Hospital: "'Tis sweet for our country to die." His adoring younger brother John Warren, twelve years his junior, set out at two in the morning following the battle to determine Joseph's condition and learned after a frantic two-day search that his brother had died. Two weeks later, Joseph's death was confirmed by the silversmith Paul Revere, who positively identified the false teeth he had made for the hero.

John Warren, the father of John Collins Warren, though less handsome and vivacious than his older brother Joseph, shared his love of medicine and anatomy. As a student at Harvard College, from which he graduated in 1771, John was a member of the Spunkers, a club Joseph had cofounded for the illicit procurement and dissection of corpses. Autopsy was illegal; it was thought of as desecration. The Spunkers often risked their lives in a search for the remains of forsaken criminals, foreigners, or lost souls. When friends of a criminal guarded his body, or when similar societies caught wind of the same corpse, the Spunkers often put themselves in danger.

Even as a young doctor, John Warren had the largest private practice in the city of Boston. He lived just east of the Boston Common, in what is now Downtown Crossing. As both physician and surgeon, Warren attended patients in their homes and sometimes assisted at childbirths, as male midwifery was coming to be accepted. In 1780 prominent Boston doctors, including John Warren, met at the Green Dragon Tavern, a meeting place for patriots during the Revolution, to set a fee scale for private practice. That group became the Boston Medical Society (distinct from the Massachusetts Medical Society, founded the next year). Some of the problems

John Warren, first professor of anatomy and surgery at Harvard Medical School.

the society faced were widespread quackery, conspicuous and heated rivalries among physicians, and public distrust of physicians.

At a later meeting of the society on November 30, 1781, John Warren was asked to repeat a course of lectures in anatomy that he had held at the military hospital for the Continental Army. At these lectures he dissected unclaimed bodies of soldiers for colleagues and students whom he trusted enough to invite. Although the lectures began illegally, the Boston Medical Society soon voted to sponsor them. When Harvard College professors and later Harvard President Joseph Willard began to attend Warren's lectures, the need for secrecy dwindled.

On May 16, 1782, Willard met with the Fellows of Harvard College to discuss the need for a medical professorship. In September the appointed committee reported in favor and asked Warren to draft a curriculum. Twelve years earlier, Ezekiel Hersey, a Harvard alumnus of the class of 1728, had laid the cornerstone for a medical professorship when he bequeathed £1,000 for a professor of anatomy and physic, whenever such a position would be created.

John Warren was named the medical school's first professor of anatomy and surgery at age 29, on November 22, 1782. Benjamin Waterhouse, John Warren's bitter rival, became professor of the theory and practice of physic on December 24. On May 22, 1783, Aaron Dexter was appointed to teach chemistry and *materia medica* (pharmacology). The Medical Institution of Harvard University officially opened on October 7, 1783. The first medical lectures were given in the basement of Harvard Hall, in what is now Harvard Yard, although John Warren's anatomical demonstrations were probably held nearby in Holden Chapel. Harvard's addition of medical education elevated it from college to university status.

The Professor's Son

John Collins Warren was the eldest son of the 19 children born to the first Harvard professor of surgery and his wife, Abigail, daughter of the wealthy Governor John Collins of Rhode Island. He caused his father some concern. John C. Warren graduated from Harvard in 1797 at the top of his class, more from love of excelling than of study per se. During his first year out of college, he studied French language and culture, but he showed no interest in medicine. His father, understanding the hardships of the medical profession, sought a position as a merchant for his son. Not finding one, John Warren took his son on as an apprentice during his second year out of Harvard.

Medical apprenticeships, the prototype of residencies, lasted for between one and five years. Apprentices compounded medicines, made home visits, acted as nurses, and looked after a doctor's records and accounts.[2] Such training was often the only practical experience that a young man had before beginning to practice medicine on his own.

The life of a medical apprentice bored John C. Warren, who was much more captivated by the young girl with whom he fell in love. He lacked the professional security to support a family, and she lacked the family wealth that Abigail Collins had brought to her union with John Warren Sr., so both families discouraged the marriage. Seeing his son heartbroken and despondent, John Warren prescribed a remedy for depression, a grand tour of Europe. John C. Warren sailed for London on

June 16, 1799, to study medicine. He served for a year as the senior dresser of William Cooper, the senior surgeon of Guy's Hospital in London. Warren paid Cooper $250 for the privilege of filling the position. When William Cooper retired, his nephew Astley Cooper took over his uncle's practice and teaching to became one of London's most respected medical men.

John Collins Warren, founding surgeon of Massachusetts General Hospital.

Warren lived a solitary, austere life in London. He visited patients and dressed their wounds in the morning, attended lectures at noon, dissected in the afternoon, and made notes at night. His landlady brought him his meals in his room. Breakfast and supper were bread and tea, and his midday meal, for which he allowed 10 minutes, consisted of a mutton chop and potato. He never touched alcohol. The young Warren took very little time out from his studies for socializing. He wrote to his father from London on January 24, 1800: "I neither eat, drink, nor sleep much: for one sound is singing in my ears; keeps me waking at night, and rouses me in the morning,—'There is no time to lose.' My anxiety to return home is very great; but my anxiety to return with proper improvements, with such acquisitions as shall make me respectable in my own and in the eyes of others, and shall raise me a little above the common herd, is much greater than that."[3] He was an ambitious young man of distinctly Puritan disposition.

Warren did make time on weekends to dine out, often at the house of Christopher Gore, later the governor of Massachusetts. His idealism sometimes got the better of him, as when once he began haranguing in behalf of a hungry mob that he chanced to encounter en route to Gore's. The mob began to cheer for their well-dressed and eloquent advocate, until a passing army officer advised Warren to desist.[4]

After London, Warren studied in Edinburgh, then in Paris. In each city the aspiring doctor was exposed to the latest medical ideas and methods. He accessed the "clinical material," dead and alive, that European hospitals provided.

A Friendship Resumed

While in London, John Collins Warren often met with an old friend from Harvard, James Jackson. Jackson's father, Jonathan, was a prominent merchant of Newburyport, Massachusetts, who had founded a shipping firm with two brothers-in-law only to see it fail during the Revolution. Jonathan Jackson was forced to take a series of jobs whose salaries were insufficient to fund so long an overseas stay for his son James as John C. Warren enjoyed.

Although Jackson was not a teetotaler like Warren, he also practiced self-discipline. At Harvard Jackson had severely restricted his intake of food to combat the fatigue that obstructed his studies.[5] Before his overseas voyage, James Jackson had served for two years as an apprentice to Edward Augustus Holyoke of Salem, one of the most prominent and respected American physicians of his era. (Holyoke would live to celebrate his 100th birthday in 1828.) Jackson arrived in London shortly after Warren, and the two attended the same series of lectures by Henry Clive (surgeon at St. Thomas's Hospital) and William Cooper (surgeon at Guy's Hospital).

The demands that Jackson placed on himself fueled his medical career in later years. He always wore two watches so that he would never be a moment late for an appointment. After writing a prescription for a patient, Jackson would lay it aside and double-check it later before handing it over to the patient. Jackson, like his Brahmin successor of a century later, the physician Richard C. Cabot, was said to be quite suspicious of the medicines of his day, believing that rest, diet, and hygiene could contribute as much or more to a patient's cure.[6] Jackson's attention to detail extended beyond the medical realm, as one of his domestic attendants would remember: "Before retiring he always took a foot-bath. The tub had to be carried to his dressing-room at 8:30 and placed on a certain flower on the carpet. He had two pitchers brought, one containing hot water and the other cold, and these were placed on certain flowers on either side of the foot-bath. Both basin and pitchers had patterns of large flowers upon them, and they had to be arranged so that the flowers would seem to grow away from him. He never excused any one for being late. He lived by rule, but was very good and kind, although exacting."[7]

Of the two hospital founders, Jackson would be the friendly doctor with comforting bedside manner, whereas Warren developed a stern, professorial air. Oliver Wendell Holmes, a student of Jackson and later one of Boston's foremost medical men, wrote of Jackson, "With his patients he was so perfect at all points that it is hard to overpraise him. . . . His smile was itself a remedy better than . . . potable gold. . . . He was very firm, with all his kindness. He would have the truth about his patients."[8] Holmes later remembered that John C. Warren "commanded allegiance and obedience where Jackson inspired love and confidence."[9]

As a practicing surgeon in later years, John C. Warren would appear grim, composed, and more removed from his patients than Jackson, according to the exigencies of contemporary surgery. Whereas his father, John Warren, had been the students' beloved professor of anatomy, the surgeon John C. Warren was revered and feared, and not without reason. Before surgical anesthesia, which Warren himself would help pioneer in 1846, surgery guaranteed excruciating pain. H. H. A. Beach, a visiting surgeon at MGH before the advent of anesthesia, would recall "many a bloody struggle between operators, patients, and assistants . . . that commonly occurred before the days of anaesthesia."[10] According to a latter-day historian, these were a "terrible experience for the patient and put a great strain upon the surgeon and his assistants. The patient's cries of suffering were heard in the corridors and wards, as well as in the operating room, until he became too weak to utter them."[11]

Little wonder that surgeons like Warren developed a thick skin. A surgeon who had witnessed MGH operations before 1846 later told Warren's grandson that when he was about to amputate: "Your grandfather would stand behind [the patient's] back and say to the patient, 'Will you have your leg off, or will you not have it off?' If the patient lost his courage and said 'No,' he had decided not to have the leg amputated, he was at once carried to his bed in the ward. If, however, he said 'Yes,' he was immediately taken firmly in hand by a number of strong assistants and the operation went on regardless of what he might say thereafter. If his courage failed him *after* this crucial moment, it was too late and no attention was paid to his cries of protest."[12]

Warren was said to have amputated a leg in as little as forty seconds.[13] His colleagues, though they respected him immensely, did not necessarily like him. Henry I. Bowditch, son of the legendary navigator Nathaniel Bowditch and brother of Nathaniel I. Bowditch, historian of the early days of Massachusetts General Hospital, praised "the neat, curt and *effective incisiveness* of the Doctor's own *rapid hand* when wielding the knife or lancet." Bowditch's words regarding John C. Warren's personality were less laudatory. He referred to Warren as "an autocrat '*enragé*,' as the French say. His own will was law for all, not only those immediately in contact with him."[14] The rate of attrition among Warren's assistants was said to be high.[15]

The two young doctors, though different in personality, shared the same firm dedication to the improvement and practice of their profession. Their willingness to collaborate benefited the world of medicine for years after their deaths. Jackson wrote a note to Warren in his *Letters to a Young Physician*, in which he explained, "We often differed in opinion. But we have always agreed to differ. . . . We have continued to this day on terms of intimacy and friendship."[16]

BEYOND THE ALMSHOUSE

The friendship between John C. Warren and James Jackson eventually dominated Harvard Medical School and was indispensable to the founding of Massachusetts General Hospital. At its inception in the 1780s, the medical school had been stabilized by opposing forces: the elder John Warren and Benjamin Waterhouse, who had played an important role in implementing the smallpox vaccination in America. A third professor, Aaron Dexter, remained neutral in a balance of power that did not last for long after the young doctors John Collins Warren and James Jackson returned to Boston from Europe.

The faculty of the Harvard Medical School grew from three to six. In 1806 John C. Warren was named adjunct professor of surgery. Shortly after, John Gorham, fiancé of John C. Warren's sister Mary, became adjunct professor of chemistry. When Warren's ally James Jackson was appointed adjunct professor of clinical medicine, the Warren faction crossed over into Waterhouse's professional territory, and the younger Warren effectively stood at the nexus of control.

Waterhouse wrote a newspaper article mocking "Captain Squirt" and his son, "Young Squirt," clear references to the Warrens. Waterhouse knocked at John Warren's door in Boston to show off his work. Having already read Waterhouse's insult, John Warren cried out, "You damned rascal, get off my steps or I'll throw you off!" Waterhouse then spent the afternoon strutting down State Street, showing the article to every passerby, relating Warren's reaction, and asking coyly, "Now, *what* do you suppose Dr. Warren meant by *that*?"[17]

Most students of Harvard Medical School and five of its six professors lived in Boston. Only Waterhouse resided in Cambridge. Students and faculty desired better access to lectures, demonstrations, and the Boston almshouse, the only thing that passed for a clinic in the city in the first years of the nineteenth century, so professors wrote a petition to the Harvard Corporation to move the Harvard Medical School from Cambridge to Boston. Waterhouse reluctantly signed it. In July 1810 the Harvard Corporation consented, and the medical school moved to 49 Marlborough Street in Boston (now 400 Washington Street).[18]

The situation came to a head when a group of doctors, notably Waterhouse and Samuel Danforth, another rival of John Warren, drew up and signed a petition to the Massachusetts legislature for the creation of a new Boston medical school unaffiliated with any university—a clear competitor and threat to Harvard Medical School. The professors and administrators of the new medical school would hold unchecked authority to admit and graduate any student they pleased (at a time when students' fees went directly into the professors' pockets). The professors of the Harvard Medical School felt that both their careers and the esteem of their profession were at stake.

The Massachusetts legislature voted against the new medical school, 211–195. Whether the prominent Warren family had any influence on the vote is unknown. The Warrens and their allies cited a number of "particulars" against Waterhouse in a petition that they submitted to the Harvard Corporation. Waterhouse's "Vindication," which took 20,000 words to establish, served him little. In May 1812 he was shown the door. James Jackson was elected professor of the theory and practice of physic. The excision of Waterhouse left a unified body whose descendants and associates would intermarry and lead Harvard Medical School and Massachusetts General Hospital for the next century.

On February 25, 1811, by another act of the legislature, the Massachusetts General Hospital was chartered. It was the first general hospital in Boston and only the third in America. (The Boston Dispensary, founded 1796 and an ancestor of today's Tufts Medical Center, functioned as a walk-in clinic for the poor.) Its two predecessors were, like MGH, teaching hospitals affiliated with schools of medicine. In 1751 Benjamin Franklin and Thomas Bond cofounded the Pennsylvania Hospital. The College of Philadelphia (now the University of Pennsylvania) expanded to include the School of Medicine, affiliated with the hospital. In 1767 King's College (now Columbia University) opened a medical school. The affiliated New York Hospital was founded in 1771 by a royal charter from King George III.

Boston needed a hospital if its medical school was to compete with the medical schools already established in Philadelphia and New York. The scope of cases that came into doctors' paths while they made the rounds of their private practices was limited; likewise, aspiring doctors, who attended lectures and apprenticed to practicing physicians, were limited in their practical training. A hospital would expose doctors and medical students to more cases while improving medical care for all—not just those patients, mostly impoverished or homeless, who had to

The Boston Almshouse on Leverett Street.

resign themselves to care at the hands of strangers in a public facility. A Boston hospital would also add to the city's eminence, placing it in the medical ranks of Philadelphia and New York.

A few previous institutions had provided care for the Boston sick and insane. During a smallpox epidemic in 1717, the Massachusetts General Court commissioned a quarantine hospital on Spectacle Island in Boston Harbor. Another quarantine hospital on Rainsford Island was so magnificent in appearance that it was dubbed "The Greek Temple." A few ad hoc inoculation hospitals appeared during other epidemics. There the uninfected could "take the pox" and be attended during the mild ensuing infection. A military hospital for the Continental Army had provided critical relief for sick and wounded soldiers during the Revolutionary War. In 1790 the Boston Marine Society convened at the Bunch of Grapes Tavern on State Street to plan a marine hospital to care for the sick and injured members of their perilous trade. Nine years later, such a marine hospital was ordered built on Castle Island. It was moved to the Charlestown Navy Yard in 1804.

Those with a family, responsible employer, or local friend usually received medical or surgical care in a private home. The destitute who had none of these were consigned to an almshouse. The Boston almshouse was located on Leverett Street in the city's West End, not far from the current location of Mass General.[19] A philanthropic organization, the Overseers of the Poor, was responsible for this institution, which provided a mere eight beds for the city's paupers and abandoned sick. Among the gentlemen serving as Overseers were Thomas Handasyd Perkins, Joseph Coolidge Jr., and Edward Tuckerman, all future trustees of Mass General.[20] Convalescent patients acted as nurses to pay for their stays. In the winter, almshouse patients often died for want of sufficient heat and nourishment. Birthing prostitutes, syphilitic seamen, and the abandoned insane crowded into the beds of this den for the down and out.

The Circular Letter

Boston needed a middle ground between the almshouse and expensive private medical care in an appropriately clean, warm environment. In 1801 William Phillips bequeathed $5,000 for the creation of a general hospital, whenever the appropriate parties would take up the task. Phillips's dream was realized 10 years later. On March 3, 1810, the Reverend John Bartlett, chaplain of the almshouse, held a meeting at Vila Hall on Court Street to discuss a Boston hospital. Bartlett enlisted Warren and Jackson to draw up a circular letter soliciting donations from potential hospital benefactors.

In the circular letter, printed and distributed to many of the city's wealthiest citizens on August 20, 1810, Warren and Jackson answered two principal questions: whether a hospital would provide better care for the sick than any alternative, and whether there were enough poor Bostonians to warrant such an institution. They answered both in the affirmative, emphasizing that without a hospital a deserving, industrious, but impecunious person would be deprived of proper care. Highest on the list of worthy sufferers were the mentally ill. The authors called on readers' sense of Christian stewardship, reminding them of the "obligation of succoring the poor in sickness."[21] The creation of a hospital, and with it an asylum for the insane, was not just a civic duty, but a religious obligation.

Though they took pains to prove that many patients would be upstanding citizens of modest means, pushed to desperation through ill fortune, Warren and Jackson asserted that all were worthy objects of charity: "When in distress, every man becomes our neighbor, not only if he be of the household of faith, but even though his misfortunes have been induced by transgressing the rules both of reason and religion."[22] In fact, the moral rectitude of patients would weigh in admissions decisions for years.

Warren and Jackson cited improved medical education as a primary benefit of a hospital. All Bostonians would profit from such improvement, they asserted. The authors explained that young doctors undertook the care of all their patients "with very little knowledge, except that acquired from books;—a source whence it is highly useful and indispensable that they should obtain knowledge, but one from which alone they never can obtain all that is necessary to qualify them for their professional duties. With such deficiencies in medical education, it is needless to show to what evils the community is exposed."[23]

The State Charter

That winter, at the meeting of the General Court of Massachusetts (the official name for the state legislature), the legion of hospital advocates petitioned for permission to execute what the circular letter had proposed. Many affluent Bostonians would readily donate, they assured the court. The petitioners suggested that the General Court grant the old Province House to the new hospital. Built as a home for a seventeenth-century merchant, used as a British military headquarters during the Revolution, and subsequently turned into a government house for Massachusetts officials, the Province House stood about 50 feet back from today's Washington Street, near the corner of Milk Street. The legislature was influenced

BOSTON, AUGUST 20, 1810.

SIR,

It has appeared very desirable to a number of respectable gentlemen, that a hospital for the reception of lunatics and other sick persons should be established in this town. By the appointment of a number of these gentlemen, we are directed to adopt such methods, as shall appear best calculated to promote such an establishment. We therefore beg leave to submit for your consideration proposals for the institution of a hospital, and to state to you some of the reasons in favour of such an establishment.

It is unnecessary to urge the propriety and even obligation of succouring the poor in sickness. The wealthy inhabitants of the town of Boston have always evinced that they consider themselves as " treasurers of God's bounty" ; and in Christian countries, in countries where Christianity is practised, it must always be considered the first of duties to visit and to heal the sick. When in distress every man becomes our neighbour, not only if he be of the household of faith, but even though his misfortunes have been induced by transgressing the rules both of reason and religion. It is unnecessary to urge the truth and importance of these sentiments to those, who are already in the habit of cherishing them ; to those, who indulge in the true luxury of wealth, the pleasures of charity. The questions, which first suggest themselves on this subject, are whether the relief afforded by hospitals is better than can be given in any other way ; and whether there are in fact so many poor among us, as to require an establishment of this sort.

The relief to be afforded to the poor, in a country so rich as ours, should perhaps be measured only by their necessities. We have then to inquire into the situation of the poor in sickness, and to learn what are their wants. In this inquiry we shall be led to answer both the questions above stated.

There are some, who are able to acquire a competence in health and to provide so far against any ordinary sickness, as that they shall not then be deprived of a comfortable habitation, nor of food for themselves and their families ; while they are not able to defray the expenses of medicine and medical assistance. Persons of this description never suffer among us. The Dispensary gives relief to hundreds every year ; and the individuals who practice medicine gratuitously attend many more of this description. But there are many others among the poor, who have, if we may so express it, the form of the necessaries of life, without the substance. A man may have a lodging, but it is deficient in all those advantages, which are requisite to the sick. It is a garret, or a cellar, without light and due ventilation, or open to the storms of an inclement winter. In this miserable habitation he may obtain liberty to remain during an illness ; but, if honest, he is harassed with the idea of his accumulating rent, which must be paid out of his future labours. In this wretched situation the sick man is destitute of all those common conveniences, without which most of us would consider it impossible to live, even in health. Wholesome food and sufficient fuel are wanting ; and his own sufferings are aggravated by the cries of hungry children. Above all, he suffers from the want of that first requisite in sickness, a kind and skilful nurse.

But it may be said that instances are rare among us, where a man, who labours with even moderate industry, when in health, endures such privations in sickness as are here described. They are not however rare among those, who are not industrious ; and who, nevertheless, when labouring under sickness, must be considered as having claims to assistance. In cases of long protracted disease, instances of such a description do occur amongst those of the most industrious class. Such instances are still less rare among those women, who are either widowed, or worse than widowed. It happens too frequently that

Page one of the circular letter dated August 20, 1810, used to raise funds for a new hospital.

in its decision by both the Overseers of the Poor and a committee report on the expense of a lunatic asylum. The Lower House voted 132–126 for the hospital, which would include an asylum for the mentally ill.

On February 25, 1811, the Massachusetts Legislature released the charter for the Massachusetts General Hospital, which granted James Bowdoin, a prominent philanthropist and statesman, and 55 other eminent Bostonians "power to hold real and personal estate of the yearly value of $30,000."[24] The Board of Visitors, which would monitor the hospital and its patients, included the governor, lieutenant-governor, president of the senate, Speaker of the house, and chaplains of

The state charter dated February 25, 1811, authorizing
56 prominent Bostonians to found a hospital.

both houses. The Board of Visitors would choose four of the 12 trustees. To this day, four members of the Mass General board are state appointees, although the board now numbers 16. Few conflicts of interest arose between the trustees and the Board of Visitors, as bonds of family and friendship united them.

The new hospital was granted the Province House, to be used for the institution or sold for money, at the trustees' discretion. A condition of the grant was that the trustees raise an additional $100,000 from private donors within a period of five years. Initially, the charter required the hospital to support 30 of the city's sick and insane residents. The requirement was later repealed to eliminate unnecessarily long patient stays that were said to encourage pauperism.

Fund-Raising

The War of 1812 dashed hopes of quick fund-raising success. A national trade embargo dampened the economy, and potential donors had less to spare. The period for raising $100,000 was extended an additional five years in June 1813.

The trustees of Massachusetts General Hospital held their first meeting on February 23, 1813, at the home of a trustee, Thomas Handasyd Perkins. The former U.S. president John Adams moderated. The first order of business was to draft an address to the public requesting donations. It took until January 9, 1814, for a draft to be approved by the Overseers of the Poor and again approved by the trustees. "A suitable circular letter to every clergyman in the Commonwealth" was to be attached to the address, which was published in pamphlet form.[25]

Probably because of a depressed postwar economy, the trustees suspended the fund drive in January 1815. Less than a month earlier, British and American authorities had signed the Treaty of Ghent, restoring the relationship of the two countries to *status quo ante bellum*. Because transatlantic news traveled slowly, Americans did not learn of the treaty until mid-February 1815.

One thousand copies of a new address to the public were distributed in April 1816. This second pamphlet was brief, referring to the first address. The trustees were again ready to receive subscriptions. This time, benefactors could choose whether the general hospital or the asylum received their donations. The drive had the backing of Protestant clergymen, who emphasized the religious duty that donations to the hospital would fulfill. The trustees often appealed to the public's sense of Christian charity, as in this article from the *Boston Daily Advertiser*:

> The Roman Catholic and the Greek, the Lutheran and the Calvinist, the Presbyterian and the Quaker, have all united in considering this one of the peremptory Christian duties; and shall the Congregational scion alone be barren of the sweetest fruits which the tree of Christianity has produced? Shall this metropolis give a colour to the aspersions which have been cast upon its religious principles, and afford reason to believe that its inhabitants are devoid of vital piety, that their religion is that of the lips and not of the heart. . . . it is not a gift which we ask, we demand the payment of a debt. We are all stewards of God's bounty, and we are bound and directed to distribute it.[26]

The fund-raising committees always advanced the idea that a donation to the hospital satisfied a personal responsibility to one's community and to God. To shirk that responsibility was to publicly display indifference to America, to Boston, to one's fellow Christian countrymen, and thus to God.

Granted four acres of land in what was known as Prince's Pasture, west of the Leverett Street almshouse, the board officially launched its fund-raising drive on December 26, 1816. In three days donations came to $78,802. By January 5, 1817, the sum reached $93,969. When the drive ended on March 1, the 1,047 subscriptions exceeded $107,000. The largest gift was that of William Phillips Jr., who quadrupled his father's bequest of 1797, donating $20,000. The smallest donation was 25 cents, given by a poor black man. More than $100,000 having been raised, the hospital met the requirement for a grant of the old Province House. The trustees briefly entertained, then quickly abandoned, the idea of using it as temporary hospital. David Greenough, a developer, paid MGH a lump sum of $33,000 to lease the Province House for 99 years.

Twenty thousand dollars was allocated to purchase the Prince's Pasture site, and the deal was finalized on October 6, 1817. Choosing a site for an asylum involved other criteria. A revolution in the treatment of mental illness had begun in 1793, when Philippe Pinel was appointed director of Le Bicêtre, France's largest and most infamous insane asylum. Previously, the mentally ill had been treated like animals. Asylum guards were instructed to beat patients to scare them out of their insanity. One asylum in Germany lowered its patients into a pit of snakes. Even King George III was thrashed to treat his mental illness.

Pinel unshackled Le Bicêtre's inmates and gave them decent food, clean air, and activities to occupy their minds and bodies. His book *Traité médico-philosophique sur l'aliénation mentale, ou la manie* introduced a new method for the treatment of mental illness called "moral management." It emphasized the importance of environment in curing mental illness. Patients responded most sympathetically to treatment at asylums in pastoral settings that separated the more severe cases from the milder ones.[27] The influence of the Tuke family and the example of their Quaker Retreat in York, England, were also instrumental in the development of "moral treatment."[28]

After consulting with doctors versed in these new, enlightened ways, the trustees decided to purchase the Barrell mansion, across the river in Charlestown. Joseph Barrell, a wealthy merchant and horticultural enthusiast, had hired Charles Bulfinch, Boston's foremost architect, to design a country home on the eighteen-acre property just before the turn of the nineteenth century. Less than 10 years later, in 1804, Barrell died in debt. The bucolic setting of the Barrell mansion was thought ideal for moral management of the insane. The trustees purchased the estate for $15,650 in 1816 and officially acquired the deed on March 16, 1817. One of the earliest photographs of the hospital, taken apparently from Beacon Hill, shows the Charles River just beyond it and the Barrell estate-turned-asylum on the far shore. Thus, it seems that from the State House a trustee could look down proudly on both sites.

The Architect

As plans moved forward for the asylum, trustees focused intensely on the general hospital facility. Charles Bulfinch played a key role in developing the Federal style of architecture, which dominated the early nineteenth-century urban landscape with domes and columns. By 1816 he had designed not only the Massachusetts State House but also University Hall at Harvard, from which he had graduated in 1781.

On December 29, 1816, three days after the hospital fund-raising drive opened, the trustees sent Bulfinch to the hospitals in Philadelphia and New York to study their designs and, upon his return, to provide suggestions for the hospital and asylum buildings. On March 2, 1817, Bulfinch presented his ideas before the Board of Trustees. Two weeks later he submitted a ground plan for the expansion of the Barrell mansion. He was subsequently commissioned to turn the country home he had built for Joseph Barrell almost two decades earlier into an insane asylum. Bulfinch's design joined a three-story wing to each side of the existing mansion by means of a covered archway. One wing housed the male patients, the other the female patients, for a total of 100 inmates.

The architect Charles Bulfinch.

After they purchased the North Allen Street property in 1817, the trustees called on Bulfinch to make suggestions for the main hospital building that were based on his findings in New York and Philadelphia. The architect proposed that the hospital be divided into a number of small wards, each with small rooms, to ensure privacy. Although Bulfinch may have been their choice from the outset, the trustees held an open competition for a hospital design to accommodate 150 patients, with amenities including kitchens, laundry, heat, water, and ventilation.[29] The winning architect would receive $100 in prize money.

Charles Bulfinch took a personal interest in institutional architecture and new amenities like interior heating and sanitation, so he accepted the challenge with enthusiasm. He specified gray Chelmsford granite as building stone. His design for the first floor included wards for moribund cases, as well as a morgue, laundry, small sickroom, and kitchen-scullery. The two upper stories of the three-story building were dedicated to the care of the sick. The design provided comfortable living quarters for hospital staff members who boarded at the hospital. When Bulfinch officially won the competition, he worked closely with John C. Warren and James Jackson to perfect plans for the building's interior.

Though practical considerations—including a rudimentary method for removing human waste from indoor toilets—drove the interior design, the Greek Revival–style exterior is imposing and impressive. In at least one case, however, Bulfinch allowed function to trump appearance. Some critics have claimed that the building's four chimneys destroy the aesthetic of Bulfinch's signature portico-mounted dome, but those chimneys were essential to warming the wards that housed the sick. The original Bulfinch design and structure were much narrower than the present-day structure, as wings were added east and west in 1845–1847.

Bulfinch's practical innovations would be touted in an 1824 brochure, "Some Account of the Medical School in Boston and of the Massachusetts Hospital." The brochure boasted that "The Massachusetts General Hospital . . . is justly considered the finest building in the state. . . . The whole house is supplied with heat by air-flues from furnaces in the cellar, and with water by pipes and a forcing pump. Various modern improvements in domestic economy, conducive to cleanliness and comfort, are introduced, together with such auxiliary apparatus for the sick as is found useful in the management of their diseases."[30]

Stones for the construction of the hospital building were shaped by convicts at the state prison in Charlestown.[31] The cornerstone of the North Allen Street building was laid on July 4, 1818, with a Masonic ceremony by the Grand Lodge of Massachusetts. The cornerstone contains several coins and an engraved tablet describing the benefactors of the hospital and citing the generosity of the people of Massachusetts. Grand Master Francis J. Oliver spoke as he handed building tools to the master builder: "This building is not to be a temporary pavilion for the display of opulence, splendor, and pride, but a temple dedicated to humanity, a lazar-house built by enlightened Compassion, where Charity and Philosophy are to walk a perpetual round to alleviate misery, and to combat with and destroy disease and pain. . . . [It will be] a sort of mile-stone on the journey of civilization, to show how far the Christian spirit had advanced in this age, in ameliorating the condition of man."[32]

Bulfinch was called to Washington, D.C., before his Boston hospital building was erected, so that he could supervise the construction of a still grander and nationally prominent edifice, the U.S. Capitol. The Bulfinch Building, still the centerpiece of Massachusetts General Hospital, was completed by Alexander Parris, one of Bulfinch's former students.[33]

THE ASYLUM OPENS

On March 23, 1818, the trustees of Massachusetts General Hospital unanimously elected Rufus Wyman to fill the joint positions of physician and superintendent of the asylum, for which he received a salary of $1,500. Wyman was born on July 6, 1778, and graduated from Harvard College in 1799. Only later did he earn a medical degree, after studying medicine under John Jeffries (a prominent Boston doctor who accompanied Jean-Pierre Blanchard in the first hot-air balloon flight across the English Channel in 1785) and attending with him at the Leverett Street almshouse. Unlike Warren and Jackson, who had private residences, private practices, and personal assistants to attend to rudimentary tasks, Wyman worked, ate, and slept at the asylum. There was hardly any job at the asylum for which he was not responsible. The trustees' annual report of 1832 stated that Wyman had spent only five nights away in his 14 years of service.

The asylum opened on October 6, 1818. Applications for admission were

McLean Asylum for the Insane, as it looked upon opening in 1818
(engraving by Abel Bowen).

submitted to Wyman, along with a notarized statement of facts. A visiting committee had the power to review Wyman's admissions and to set rates. The first asylum
patient was dragged in by his father, who claimed that his son was "possessed with
a devil." When Wyman asked the father if he had undertaken any treatment on
his own, the father replied that he often whipped his son. The boy was admitted,
quickly cured, and released. Away from his father's lash, the young man became a
peddler, amassing more than $10,000, thanks to his "Yankee shrewdness."[34]

Rufus Wyman adhered to the new ideas in psychiatry. He insisted that insanity was treatable, and he encouraged recreation and exercise as therapy. The large,
idyllic property in Charlestown was perfect for long walks, and patients were often
treated to off-site carriage rides. Wyman avoided the use of force and restraints on
patients unless necessary. By the end of 1821, 146 patients had entered the asylum, and 118 had left. Of those 118 patients, 6 "eloped" (escaped), 9 died, 29 were
removed by request of the administration, 23 were discharged as "improved," 19
as "much improved," and 32 as "cured."[35]

For the inmates' tranquility and speedy convalescence, Wyman separated the
severe cases of insanity from the milder cases. In 1822 he had five strong rooms
built for "raging" women. In 1826 began the three-year construction of "The
Lodge," a two-story brick building that stood apart from the mansion and contained strong rooms for "idiotics," epileptics, and violent males.

In November 1823 the trustees created the position of steward of the asylum
to relieve Wyman of some of his duties, including apothecary work. John Goodwin was elected to fill the post. After Goodwin resigned, the trustees appointed
George William Folsom as steward in 1825. Folsom, a graduate of Phillips Exeter
Academy and Harvard College, was a part-time Harvard Medical School student
during his tenure at the asylum.

A fragile young man, Folsom is remembered today for the journal he kept, in which he detailed daily life at the asylum. Upon arriving at the Charlestown institution, surprised by the almost sociable atmosphere, Folsom wrote, "Find crazy people much more pleasant than I expected."[36] The inmates ate supper with Wyman, his family, and Folsom; read with them; and went for walks with them. A few patients even tutored Wyman's children and gave Folsom dancing lessons.

Work at the asylum consumed Folsom's life. He wrote, "Time goes—minutes, hours, days, months pass away, and I have little other evidence of the fact but the callender."[37] The "heaviness" and "stupor" of which Folsom complained in his journal may have been indicative of something more serious than fatigue. After repeated attempts to cure himself with the purgatives and emetics he prepared for patients, Folsom died in 1827 at the age of 24.

Major Bequests

Two large gifts secured the asylum financially and allowed it to keep abreast of patients' needs as the institution grew. John McLean was a Boston merchant who had once been ruined by ships lost at sea. Shortly after he filed for bankruptcy, one of his ships returned, restoring his wealth. He held a dinner party for all his creditors. Under each guest's plate McLean slipped a check for the sum he owed the man, plus interest.[38] In November 1823 John McLean bequeathed $25,000 to the Corporation of the Massachusetts General Hospital, payable upon the death of his widow. He made the institution his residuary legatee, which eventually increased his donation to more than $120,000, by far the largest that the institution had received.

The trustees commissioned Gilbert Stuart, George Washington's portraitist, to paint their most opulent benefactor. On June 12, 1826, the trustees decided to rename the asylum the McLean Asylum for the Insane.[39] It bears John McLean's name to this day, although in 1892 the name was changed to the McLean Hospital for the Mentally Ill, in light of new ideas in psychiatry.[40] McLean's widow thought the entire MGH corporation should be renamed in his honor, but the trustees felt that potential donors would be more inclined to fund an institution bearing the name of the state than one named after an individual.[41]

In August 1830 Mary Belknap informed the trustees of her late brother Jeremiah's bequest of $10,000. The trustees gave her charge of a free bed for life. (A free bed was the right to admit one patient; employers of domestic servants as well as factory owners paid for such beds to assure care for their ill or injured

John McLean, *whose large gift secured the asylum financially.*

workers.) Belknap made the corporation her residuary devisee, and when she died in 1833, the value of her bequest exceeded $100,000. Thanks to Belknap's gift, the trustees were able to commission a new building for female asylum patients in 1837. It was named Belknap House in honor of its benefactor.

There had long been a public concern that the asylum would be an institution only for the wealthy. Both the hospital and the asylum had significant operating costs, and most hospital patients were too poor to pay their board in full. The average annual rate of board at McLean in 1828 was $90.32, far more than a working-class family could afford. There were, however, plenty of wealthy people with mentally ill family members, whom they sent to McLean. Partial-pay patients were accepted, but those who could pay in full were preferred. With so many wealthy inmates, McLean soon generated the main stream of income for the hospital corporation. The concentration of wealth at McLean grew after Dorothea Dix persuaded the Massachusetts legislature in 1841 to expand the Worcester Public Asylum. The McLean Asylum thereafter catered to more affluent patients.[42] McLean boasted a "rest cure" in a country club atmosphere and offered activities such as literary discussions, bowling, and gardening.[43]

When Wyman fell ill in 1832, he tendered his resignation. To retain his services, the trustees separated the posts of physician and superintendent, and they elected Wyman physician. The trustees maintained Wyman's salary at $1,500, "a price greater than they believed those of any other person could be worth who should fill both situations."[44] Captain Luke Bigelow was appointed superintendent and allotted a salary of $700.

Wyman retired fully on May 1, 1835. The trustees elected him to their board, but he declined the offer. His assistant, Thomas G. Lee, was promoted to the position of physician. Upon his appointment, the trustees urged Lee to avoid bearing the responsibilities of his post quite as heavily as Wyman had. They instructed him "not to confine himself too strictly to his duties, or debar himself from the enjoyment of social intercourse with his friends, or to neglect that occasional relaxation by which his health may be improved and preserved."[45]

Lee's brief tenure as physician was fruitful for McLean: with the help of the trustees, he procured a piano and a billiard table for recreation, began a library for asylum patients, opened a carpentry shop for the male patients, and, with the help of his wife, created the Belknap Sewing Society for female patients. Lee acted as patriarch of the McLean family, and he expected his assistants to fill their roles with appropriate decorum. Of his assistants he wrote, "We will not continue any male or female attendant whom we cannot invite into our family, seat at our table, and with whom we could not confidently place our own wives, sisters, and brothers. We do not consider their service as servile: they are the companions of the unfortunate, engaged in the same employments as ourselves; they shall command our friendship and respect."[46] Lee's tenure was as short as it was productive: he fell ill and died on October 29, 1836.

The Asylum Grows

After Lee, Luther Bell was appointed superintendent and physician. Bell's duties were much lighter than Wyman's had been in 1818: in 1837 there were

Luther Bell, superintendent of McLean Asylum, 1836–1855.

32 asylum employees in addition to the professional staff. Like his predecessors, Bell was open to the new ideas of his profession. In 1840 he abolished treatments such as bleeding and purging. Four years later he cofounded the Association of Medical Superintendents of American Institutions for the Insane, forerunner of the American Psychiatric Association.

By the end of 1847 McLean had admitted 2,864 patients. In that year alone 343 were treated, of whom 87 recovered and 33 died. By that time three railroads skirted the asylum grounds, and another was being applied for. Industry was encroaching on the bucolic setting. That summer saw a great outbreak of dysentery at the asylum. Seventy of about 170 patients fell ill. The casualties included 10 patients and two of Bell's children, a 10-year-old girl and a five-year-old boy.

On January 1, 1851, there were 100 female patients and 100 male patients, numbers that both the trustees and Bell agreed "should be deemed its full capacity." Wealthy patients were charged rates over cost, poorer patients charged much less, and the poorest sometimes did not pay at all. The year 1850 saw a surplus of nearly $4,000 at the asylum; by contrast, at the general hospital, in the same year, only $4,226.27 was defrayed by patient fees of a cost total of $29,024.[47] The asylum was the cash engine of the enterprise.

At the end of 1855 Bell retired. More than 4,000 patients had been admitted since the asylum's opening in 1818, and Bell had cared for about 65 percent of them. When his successor fell ill two years later, Bell temporarily returned to take charge of the asylum until John Tyler was elected in February 1858. Tyler held the post of asylum physician and superintendent until 1871, when he resigned on the grounds of ill health. He was succeeded by George Jelly.

MGH trustees, unconcerned that the asylum was now surrounded by busy railroad tracks, purchased five acres of adjoining land in 1860, before the Civil War erupted. The asylum added cottages for "highly excited female patients" in 1863 and for "highly excited male patients" in 1865. The corporation also purchased the remaining portion of the adjoining Barrell farm in 1867 and built a chapel in 1870. By 1872 however, MGH trustees began discussing the feasibility of relocating McLean to a larger, quieter tract of land that lacked the distractions caused by passing trains. Tracks now all but surrounded the asylum. The board found a new property in Waverley (now part of Belmont) in 1875 and purchased the 114-acre parcel from the Waverley Company for $75,000. Ground was not broken until 1892 for new asylum structures. The new McLean (with its name significantly changed from "asylum" to "hospital") was formally opened in 1895, displaying a "cottage plan" around a large central administration building.

SLOW START FOR THE GENERAL HOSPITAL

On September 3, 1821, the general hospital in Boston, equipped with 60 beds, admitted its first patient, a 30-year-old saddler with syphilis. Boston memory, tinged with Puritan pride, has always held that the man caught his affliction in that den of depravity, New York City. The second patient did not arrive until three weeks later, a sailor with prolapsed hemorrhoids. It was not a pretty sight:

> In 1821 there were no true anesthetic agents; alcohol and opium merely served to dull the pain. But, as happened in this case, four strong men held the patient on his knees on his bed with his head down and the dirty operative field close to the surgeon's face. With a few quick strokes of the scalpel, the piles were removed. Convalescence required three weeks; and every day the patient had a rectal irrigation with a highly irritating copper sulfate solution. At the end of the period, he was discharged cured.[48]

Before the end of the year, an additional 18 patients were admitted, an average of one patient every six days. In 1822, 122 patients followed. On at least one occasion in 1823, for the first time, all hospital beds were occupied.

During its first years the hospital had a limited staff. Unlike Wyman at the asylum, John C. Warren and James Jackson restricted their hospital duties to patient care, often with students in tow. Although they provided their services to patients free of charge, the doctors had two of the largest and most lucrative private practices in Boston and lectured extensively at the medical school, where students continued to pay fees directly into their pockets.

On April 1, 1821, the trustees appointed Nathaniel Fletcher and his wife as superintendent and matron of the hospital. Fletcher was a retired ship's captain from Newburyport who had amassed some wealth, then lost it to a trade embargo during the War of 1812. Husband and wife worked, ate, and slept at the hospital. Like Wyman, Fletcher often hosted patients at his dinner table and saw to their general well-being.

Rest, nourishing food, warmth, and clean air were considered important components of hospital care, especially since medical knowledge of the day had limited power to cure. The superintendent and matron attempted to maintain an atmosphere conducive to healing, or at least to tranquility, an environment combining well-ventilated air, quiet, and sound morality. Patients were prohibited from spitting, drinking, smoking, or swearing. Failure to comply with hospital decorum resulted in dismissal.

After Fletcher's death in May 1825, the trustees unanimously elected Nathan Gurney to the post of superintendent. His wife assumed the role of matron for four years, until her death. A year later, in 1830, Gurney announced his engagement to another woman, and the couple were married at the hospital. According to Nathaniel I. Bowditch, "The wedding was subsequently celebrated in fine style; the House Physicians, &c., officiating as groomsmen. Many patients were present at the wedding visit. It was a gay scene,—one seldom witnessed in a Hospital."[49]

Before Florence Nightingale helped elevate its status in the latter half of the nineteenth century, nursing was an undesirable occupation, staffed mostly by lower-class women. No certification was required, although the hospital, unlike the almshouse, where ambulatory patients worked as nurses to pay for their stay, did pay its nurses. Some senior nurses at MGH, like Rebecca Taylor, proved their competence and dedication to the institution. Taylor retired in 1860 as a highly valued employee after serving as head nurse for 34 years. James Jackson wrote of her upon her retirement with words suggesting that she had pulled herself up by her own shoelaces, without benefit of schooling or high breeding:

Rebecca Taylor, a senior nurse who retired in 1860.

> There is not any comparison to be made between our good nurse and Miss Nightingale. The latter is a lady of education, and in a different rank of life. She sees how important is the office of a nurse. She has studied the duties, I may say the high duties of a nurse for the sick. She has brought science to her aid. . . . My friend is one of much humbler pretensions. She has been a hired nurse. She sought an employment for her living. Having gained an appointment, she gave herself to her duties. Filled with a sense of duty, she brought all her faculties into exercise, without bustle, and without parade.[50]

Joshua Green was appointed apothecary of the hospital on October 11, 1821. A week earlier, James Jackson had nominated Walter Channing as his assistant. The brother of the famed Unitarian theologian William Ellery Channing, Walter Channing would distinguish himself as first professor of obstetrics and midwifery, as well as medical jurisprudence, at Harvard Medical School and as an early editor of the *New England Journal of Medicine*. The medical staff that supported the chief physicians and surgeons (initially Jackson and Warren only) would grow steadily over the years. Ambitious young medical students scrambled to fill the positions of house physician and house surgeon, unpaid underlings who lived at the hospital and worked ceaselessly in the hopes of someday being the next Warren or Jackson.

The nomination and appointment of medical assistants to the physicians and surgeons was one of the points of tension between the hospital administration and the doctor-professors. Who could work at the hospital, which students could have access to its wards, and what became of its records and cadavers were topics of heated dispute. A great fear for many hospital patients in the early nineteenth century was to be subjected to the indiscreet eyes and prodding tools of curious medical students, or to have one's body dissected postmortem. Medical professionals fought to increase student access to ward patients for the general improvement of the medical profession, and in the name of scientific progress; the trustees countered the doctors with their own opposing force, defending the individual's right to respectful treatment and personal dignity in life and death.

Hospital Finances

Securing private donations was critical to keeping the young institution alive. On October 23, 1825, the trustees instituted an effective measure to encourage donations: in return for a gift of $100, a donor would control a free bed for one year. The trustees instituted a successful free bed drive. The hospital needed more money to keep up with costs.

A few eccentric gifts were accepted with surprise, though not without gratitude. On behalf of Jacob Van Lennep and Company, Bryant Tilden and Robert Edes donated a mummy from Thebes in May 1823. The mummy, said to be that of a stonecutter named Padihershef, was taken on a tour of American cities, and the admission charged for its viewing brought the hospital about $1,200. In his *History of the Massachusetts General Hospital*, Nathaniel I. Bowditch noted that the mummy "is now an appropriate ornament of the operating room at the hospital."[51] (As this book went to press in 2011, Padihershef remained on duty in the same "operating room," the Ether Dome on the fourth floor of the Bulfinch Building, a National Historic Landmark now used for lectures and rounds.) In April 1824 the trustees thanked Gorham Parsons for his gift of "a sow of an uncommonly fine breed." The sow weighed 273 pounds—and is no longer in evidence.[52]

Although Bostonians were generous, the cost of maintaining both hospital and asylum combined with the dearth of paying patients eventually created an

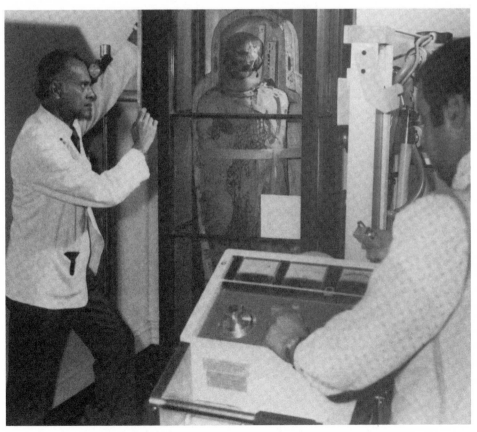

Padihershef, the MGH mummy, was studied with X-rays in 1976.

A midcentury engraving shows the Bulfinch Building with new wings added in the foreground and, across the river to the left, the McLean Asylum.

"embarrassed state of the finances." The trustees issued a report on the "unexampled difficulties of the times" in December 1838. The report included financial figures for that year: "total receipts (of which $6,740 was capital), $16,081; current expenses, $17,506.24; excess of expenditures, $1,425.24; due to Massachusetts Hospital Life Insurance Company, $50,000;—and the completion of the Belknap Ward."[53]

Donors did not respond sufficiently to the financial crisis. At the beginning of 1843 the trustees announced that they had received only two donations in the previous five years. On December 31, 1843, they voted to ask the hospital doctors what improvements might be most useful.[54] Following the doctors' advice, the trustees commissioned the addition of wings on the east and west ends of the Bulfinch Building. To fund this project, the trustees organized the largest fundraising drive since 1816. A 14-page pamphlet soliciting donations for the new wings recalled the participation of many Bostonians in the last drive. Although the majority of those benefactors had since died, the pamphlet held that "the fountain which their benevolence caused to gush forth still continues to flow on in an uninterrupted stream of health and comfort to many a suffering being."[55] It further explained that Boston fell short in its provision for the needy ill. Paris boasted one hospital bed for every 250 inhabitants, whereas Boston had only one bed for every 1,666. The pamphlet concluded with an assurance that each donor would "leave a memento of himself, that shall outlive his generation, and be dear to the hearts of his children and of every true man."[56] The cost of the Bulfinch wings was estimated at $50,000; the drive raised $62,550.

The need for added space clearly reflected a growing patient count; but the list of patients was also diversifying. In the spring quarter of 1822 there had been 27 new patients. Aside from a scrivener, a baker, and a confectioner, the patient group consisted entirely of laborers and farmers. In the spring quarter of 1826, 139 new patients were admitted, some of whom were skilled laborers and students, although unskilled laborers and farmers still constituted the majority. In the spring of 1832 the hospital took in a clergyman, a silversmith, a jeweler, and a mercantile tailor. The public was gradually becoming less afraid of entering a hospital, but a long road still lay ahead before hospitals were considered the best location for treatment and convalescence.

WARREN'S AND JACKSON'S LEGACIES

On October 13, 1837, James Jackson submitted his resignation as physician of the hospital. Seven years earlier, his eldest son, James Jackson Jr., had sailed for Europe to study medicine, as Jackson senior had done three decades earlier. Father and son loved each other dearly, and they communicated often while the younger Jackson was overseas:

> From the moment of his son's leaving home, Dr. Jackson began to look forward eagerly to the day of his return, so intense was his affection for him, and with such fervor had he accustomed himself to picture his future career and to see himself living again and with redoubled interest under the glow of this fresh life. Letters passed between them by every packet, and it was with eager interest that he followed every step of his progress, and longed to hear of the acquaintances that he made, the books he read, and the cases that he observed.[57]

Their written correspondence continued until the son returned home in 1833, after four years of medical study in Europe. No sooner was he home than he was seized by typhoid fever and, immediately after, by dysentery. Apparently recuperating, James Jackson Jr. attended a dinner party with friends, where he relapsed and died. The elder Jackson was crushed by his son's death. While continuing his medical practice, Jackson wrote his son's memoir, which he published privately in 1836. One year later he retired from his hospital duties. The trustees took the opportunity to express their regret at Jackson's decision, and to extol his contributions to the hospital: "Under his constant attention, together with that of the professional friends assembled around him, the system on which the Hospital is conducted has been perfected, till it seems, at length, admirably adapted to the purposes for which the institution was founded, and promises to insure its utility during all its future existence." The board requested that Jackson "sit for his portrait to some artist of talent, that it may adorn the walls which have so often been the witnesses of his disinterested labors."[58]

James Jackson, a founding physician of Massachusetts General Hospital.

At the annual meeting of the corporation on January 24, 1838, Jackson was elected a consulting physician, along with George C. Shattuck, John Randall, and John Ware. The hospital physicians were the same, minus Jackson: Jacob Bigelow, Enoch Hale, and Walter Channing, whom Jackson had named as his first assistant at the hospital, and who, as a leading Boston obstetrician, had cofounded the Boston Lying-In Hospital for women in 1832, now part of Brigham and Women's Hospital. But the Jackson name did not disappear from the roster of MGH's practicing physicians: Jackson's nephew, John Barnard Swett Jackson, was reelected as the hospital's assistant or admitting physician. J. B. S. Jackson would become

Harvard Medical School's first professor of pathological anatomy and first curator of the Warren Anatomical Museum, founded by John C. Warren.

Warren retained his post as hospital surgeon, along with George Hayward. Warren had always held Jackson in high regard, as evidenced in his autobiographical notes, written after Jackson's retirement: "[Jackson's] frankness of character, as well as clearness of judgment, acquired the confidence of his professional brethren to an almost unexampled extent. . . . He has prolonged his life and intellectual powers beyond the usual period; and this prolongation is attributable not only to a well-directed system of living, but to the means he has employed for preserving mental equanimity in the various trying events he has been called to experience."[59]

Warren and Jackson's friendship continued until Warren's final illness. Jackson served as Warren's physician until the latter's death in May 1856.

Like Jackson, Warren had hopes that his sons would continue what he had begun. One of them, J. Mason Warren, followed in his footsteps. Mason was a fragile young boy and almost died of dyspepsia at age 16. The younger Warren graduated from the medical school in 1832 and sailed for Paris to continue his medical studies.

The elder Warren was eager to hand over his practice to his son. He was ambitious for Mason's medical reputation, and he broke rules in the hopes of securing and elevating it. Henry I. Bowditch, Mason's friend and Harvard Medical School classmate, recalled how, when he referred a friend to John C. Warren for surgery, the elder Warren arrived with Mason in tow, presumably to assist. At the last minute, John C. Warren handed Mason the scalpel and instructed him to perform the surgery. Bowditch was appalled by the stunt, and he privately noted that Mason would never have agreed in advance to such underhandedness.[60] In 1837 the trustees issued a statement (after the story had been published in a newspaper) censuring John C. Warren for allowing "the employment of Dr. J. Mason Warren, a young man not connected with the Hospital, during the absence of his father, whose turn it was to officiate."[61] Mason Warren rose above this paternal pressure to achieve some eminence in the surgical theater; he was one of the first plastic surgeons in America and performed the first rhinoplasty; but his health proved too delicate to bear the weight of a medical professorship on top of a private practice, to his father's disappointment.

Mason's older brother, John, does not appear in most Warren genealogies. He drank too much and suffered from severe depression. In 1840 he was taken to the McLean asylum, where he attempted suicide. John C. Warren disavowed his son John, whose name does not appear in the elder Warren's biography.

The Warren name survived in the annals of MGH surgery despite these familial strains. Mason's son, J. Collins Warren, known as Coll, would take up the family business. Oliver Wendell Holmes, noting the city's medical nepotism, wrote in 1881: "There has hardly been a year for more than a century in which 'Dr. Warren' or 'Dr. Jeffries' could not be called upon by his Boston fellow-citizens for his services as surgeon or physician. Dr. Jackson [Holmes's mentor] is represented by his grandchildren and other blood relations."[62]

Although MGH would advance medicine and especially surgery in the coming years, it became ever more ingrown as a medical institution over the remaining course of the nineteenth century. Son succeeded father in the operating room; add sons-in-law, cousins, and Harvard classmates to the mix, and the entire professional roster for the first hundred years had no more than two degrees of separation. Not until 1908 did the name Warren, for one example, disappear from the roster of physicians privileged to practice at MGH (and it would reappear later). It took a medical outsider from Philadelphia in 1912 to open MGH to the outside world and begin to infuse Boston's flagship hospital with non-Brahmin blood.

. . . .

CHAPTER 2

SURGERY EMERGES FROM THE DARK AGES, 1846–1900

We must remember that the thought of painless surgery did not burst upon the world de novo in the year 1846, when the first public demonstration of ether anaesthesia was given. Running through all medical history, there is a constant reference to the abolishing of pain, and even among the ancients many fairly successful attempts were made in that direction.

—James Gregory Mumford,
A Narrative of Medicine in America

O F ALL THE BREAKTHROUGHS *at Massachusetts General Hospital, the foremost occurred on Ether Day. Before October 16, 1846, patients had to endure excruciating pain under a surgeon's knife, often with fatal results. Yet the 1846 discovery that ether could safely put surgical patients temporarily to sleep was marred by fierce arguments between a distinguished doctor and a dentist with questionable credentials over who deserved credit for the innovation.*

The nineteenth century saw other milestones in surgery and the work of brilliant, sometimes iconoclastic pioneers. Chief among these at MGH was the contentious Henry Jacob Bigelow, who devised new ways of removing bladder stones and treating dislocated hips. Such early operators, wearing stained black frocks, often worked in rooms that had not been cleaned, let alone sterilized, using instruments only perfunctorily washed. Eventually, the importance of antisepsis was realized, and with the institution of asepsis, or sterile operating rooms, surgeons could conduct increasingly invasive procedures without losing patients to postoperative infections.

This was a time of expansion at MGH; new buildings for an operating theater, patient wards, student nurse housing, and a mortuary were added around the Bulfinch cornerstone. When the Civil War broke out, MGH surgeons and physicians went to the front to assist, and some did not return; meanwhile, wounded Union soldiers were treated at the hospital. During the Spanish-American War,

The Bulfinch Building with Harvard Medical School in front of it, circa 1855.
The buiding to the left of Bulfinch is "The Brick," also known as the Foul Ward. Between
Bulfinch and the Medical School building are sheds covering the MGH wharf.

soldiers suffering from malaria and typhoid fever were treated in tents set up on the lawn as ad hoc contagious wards.

McLean Hospital was relocated to a bucolic setting in Belmont and a convalescent hospital was instituted nearby. A Harvard president shook up the medical school with stricter standards; no longer would a well-known surname alone be grounds for admission. Women continued to be barred from the medical school, but nurses achieved new respect as a nursing school began to graduate well-trained, professional caregivers.

Three short departmental histories in this chapter lead the reader from past to present in anesthesiology, pathology, and orthopaedics.

CHARLES T. JACKSON was born to Brahmin privilege but achieved distinction on his own merits. He took the Boylston Prize for a medical essay upon graduating from Harvard Medical School in 1829 and then studied medicine and geology in Europe. After his return to the United States, Jackson began an eminent career as a chemist, geologist, and physician. For almost a decade he was the state geologist for Maine, New Hampshire, and Rhode Island, and as the brother-in-law of Ralph Waldo Emerson, he no doubt occupied a minor niche in New England's social-cultural pantheon. He was, however, no relation to James Jackson, cofounder of MGH.

Charles Jackson was well versed in the medical publications of his day. Humphry Davy, a brilliant British chemist, had engaged in extensive personal experimentation with nitrous oxide in the company of friends and patients. In

1800 Davy published a 500-page opus on "laughing gas" entitled *Researches, Chemical and Philosophical; Chiefly concerning Nitrous Oxide*. The widely read book, of which Charles Jackson owned a copy, suggested that nitrous oxide might be useful in surgery. This advice went unheeded, and nitrous oxide cured only the ennui of the bourgeois, who began to serve laughing gas at dinner parties as a replacement for wine.

Charles T. Jackson.

It was well known that inhaling ether caused a state akin to intoxication, demonstrated in experiments by scientists on laboratory animals and by medical students on themselves at infamous "ether frolics" (all in the name of science, of course). Most considered this state of intoxication to be harmful and potentially fatal, however, so the compound's nepenthean properties were not researched carefully. Despite the danger associated with ether inhalation, it was prescribed as a remedy for respiratory discomfort following accidental inhalation of chlorine gas.[1]

When Charles Jackson accidentally inhaled chlorine gas in 1842, he inhaled ether to relieve irritation in his respiratory tract. The next day Jackson again took ether vapors to calm his throat and entered a relaxed and dreamy state, from which he emerged unharmed. He concluded that ether use was safe and subsequently encouraged his students to carry out experiments with ether on patients. Respecting the public's fear of ether, no one followed Jackson's suggestion, and the anesthetic potential of ether during surgery remained untapped.[2]

William T. G. Morton, son of a farmer from Charlton, Massachusetts, embarked on a variety of schemes and fraudulent business practices shortly after leaving home at the age of 17. Having worn out his welcome in Rochester, Baltimore, Cincinnati, St. Louis, and New Orleans, he returned to Massachusetts in 1842 and entered into the practice of dentistry under the tutelage of a Hartford-based dentist, Horace Wells. By 1843 Wells and Morton had started a dental partnership, opening an office in Boston, to be run by Morton. Wells had developed a technique for using nitrous oxide to dull pain during tooth extraction and passed this knowledge on to his partner. Morton resolved to marry Elizabeth Whitman, daughter of a wealthy former congressman and prominent Connecticut lawyer, Lemuel Whitman, who frowned on Morton's lowly dentistry practice. To appease him, Morton entered Harvard Medical School in 1844, where he studied chemistry under Charles Jackson. He and Elizabeth Whitman were married the same year.[3]

More likely than not, Jackson mentioned the anesthetic potential of ether in one of his lectures. He may even have recounted his own experience inhaling the compound. Morton latched onto the idea, and began extensive personal research on the use of ether to dull or prevent pain during tooth extraction.

William T. G. Morton.

Morton kept his experiments secret from the scientists and doctors who entered his office, as well as those whose advice he sought. In the summer of 1846 Morton called at the office of Joseph Wightman, a respected scientist who would serve as mayor of Boston from 1861 until 1863. He inquired whether a bag of India rubber would hold ether. Wightman replied that the bag would have to be treated, and suggested that Morton seek Jackson's advice.

Following Wightman's recommendation, Morton rang at Jackson's office. He and Jackson had a conversation at which two of Jackson's students were present. Morton made a vague inquiry about ether. Jackson recommended that Morton use pure rectified sulphuric ether to dull pain during tooth extraction and assured him of its safety. He instructed Morton to spatter or pour it on a handkerchief and hold the handkerchief over the patient's mouth, being sure the patient inhaled well. Morton feigned ignorance, and asked, "Sulphuric ether, what is that? Is it a gas?" Jackson fell for Morton's act and directed him to the office of a Dr. Metcalf to procure some ether, which Morton did.

After making two experiments with ether on himself (lapsing into total unconsciousness on the second occasion), Morton persuaded a patient to undergo etherization for a tooth extraction. Afterward, the patient reported that she had felt no pain. Morton advertised his painless dental technique in local newspapers and attracted much attention, including the interest of a 28-year-old MGH surgeon named Henry Jacob Bigelow, who observed successful pain-free extractions in Morton's office and used his influence to convince John Collins Warren to allow a trial use of ether during surgery. Warren consented and, on October 16, 1846, performed the first successful surgery under ether anesthesia beneath the dome of the Bulfinch Building at MGH, known afterward as the Ether Dome. Morton arrived late, having been busy overseeing the preparation of an inhalation device (a handheld glass globe equipped with valves). Warren removed a tumor from the neck of the patient, Gilbert Abbott, who reported no pain whatsoever when he awoke. Warren famously exclaimed, "Gentlemen, this is no humbug!"[4] (Horace Wells had been allowed to demonstrate ether at MGH the year before, and when it didn't work, onlookers had jeered, "Humbug!") Word of the ether breakthrough spread through the medical community, reaching Australia within eight months in those days of slow mails. Surgery could be performed painlessly from this time forward.

A battle between Morton and Jackson ensued over who had made the key discovery of ether's properties, each trying to tarnish the other's credibility. Morton tried to take out a patent on his preparation, which he called Letheon (diethyl ether adulterated with oil of orange). In an attempt to win over Jackson, Morton promised him one-tenth of the profits from the patent. The hospital trustees and later a congressional committee made separate investigations into the matter, and both came to the firm conclusion that Morton had discovered ether as a surgical anesthetic. Jackson had given Morton advice without which Morton might never have pursued his investigations, but the information that Jackson provided was no more than Morton could have gleaned from the medical and scientific publications of the day.

The trustees and the congressional committee both expressed displeasure that Morton would try to take out a patent on a discovery that relieved suffering. No self-respecting doctor of the 1840s would have thought of patenting a breakthrough. Quack doctors regularly patented medicines and devices, but to patent such a discovery was to withhold relief from those in pain.[5] Morton explained that he had invested private funds and had lost dental business during his experiments with ether. The hospital eventually awarded Morton a commemorative box with $1,000 inside, and the French Academy gave Morton (and Jackson) a ribbon and a cash award. Morton's patent on the Letheon, U.S. No. 4848, expired in 1860. When Morton sued the New York Eye Infirmary in 1862, effectively claiming that any institution that had used ether without his permission owed him money, the judge ruled that the patent had always been void, as it did not protect a new invention, but rather a novel use for an old compound.[6]

If everyone had realized that ether had already been used successfully as an anesthetic in surgery before 1846, perhaps there would not have been such a tempest in the local teapot. An MGH anesthesiologist, Bucknam McPeek, cited two such attempts, and there may have been others.[7]

In January 1842 William E. Clark, a medical student at Berkshire Medical College in Pittsfield, Massachusetts, inspired by ether parties, administered ether to a woman before pulling her tooth. Clark's professor claimed that the patient's unconsciousness was mere hysteria. Clark accepted his professor's assurance and never publicized his finding, though he went on to a distinguished medical career. In March 1842 Crawford Long, a country doctor in Georgia and an alumnus of Jefferson Medical College at the University of Pennsylvania, performed the first of a series of minor operations using ether. Only in December 1849 did Long publish the records of these experiments in *Southern Medical Journal,* in an article titled "An Account of the First Use of Sulfuric Ether by Inhalation as an Anesthetic in Surgical Operations." By that time, findings at MGH had already been reported. The first Mass General article on ether was written by Henry J. Bigelow in late 1846. In the 15 months between Ether Day and the start of 1848, 132 operations were performed at MGH using ether. On May 12, 1851, the trustees reported that since January 1, 1848, an additional 350 operations had used some anesthetic, including 186 with sulfuric ether, 138 with chlorate ether, 25 with chloroform, and 1 with nitrous oxide gas.[8]

Charles Jackson could never get past the feeling that his ingenious idea had been stolen from him. The incident was not isolated: Jackson also claimed that he had suggested the electric telegraph to Samuel Morse and assured the world that he was responsible for the discoveries of guncotton (generally attributed to Christian Schönbein), the stomach's digestive process (William Beaumont), and the potential to mine copper from Lake Superior's deposits (Douglass Houghton).

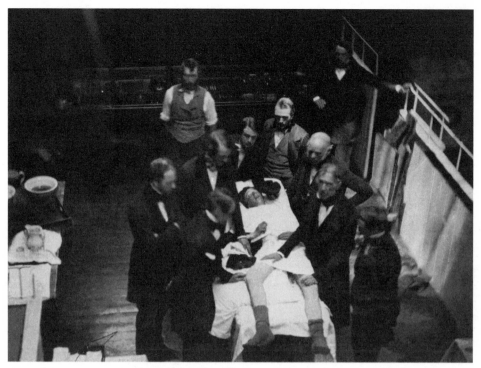

An early operation using ether. John Collins Warren stands second from right, with his hands on the patient's legs. The image is from a whole-plate daguerreotype by Southworth and Hawes.

Ralph Waldo Emerson's brother-in-law wound up in the same facility as Emerson's two biological brothers, the McLean Asylum, where Jackson was sent in 1873 and died in 1880. Jackson was laid to rest in Mount Auburn Cemetery in Cambridge, which Henry Jacob Bigelow's father, Jacob Bigelow, had helped design. Morton had been buried there 12 years earlier.[9]

ANESTHESIA SINCE ETHER DAY

The 165-year time line of anesthesiology at MGH begins on October 16, 1846, which through the years has assumed iconic importance. Following Ether Day was a long period of low interest. Until the twentieth century, anesthesia was administered with a frankly nonprofessional approach: the youngest surgical house officer was the designated "etherizer," who had just enough time to learn the job before passing it on to the next pup.[10] "The etherizer learned in the hard school of experience," one historian wrote, undoubtedly eliding some tragedies.[11] Such a loose approach would be unthinkable today, but it was the norm in medicine a century ago, with some variations. (The British favored chloroform over the highly flammable ether.)

J. M. T. Finney was one pup thrown into the surgical wars at MGH in the late 1880s. He would recall his first experience of administering anesthesia:

> Later on that same day I was called upon to anesthetize a patient. It was my first anesthetic, and I was scared. I had had no instruction whatever in the

administration of anesthetics, and had only seen from a distance its administration by the internes or externes who were the regular anesthetists. In those days they used a big cone made out of toweling, which fitted tightly over the patient's face. A bunch of gauze was put in the apex of the cone. Ether was poured on this gauze until it was pretty well saturated. Then the cone was applied to the patient's face and held there until he became unconscious. The patient had been strapped previously to the stretcher on which he was lying while the ether was being given. Often it took two orderlies or doctors to hold the patient on the table. What happened in this barbarous method of administering the ether was that the patient was practically asphyxiated; hence the violent struggles. It was a pretty trying ordeal for all concerned.[12]

A circular letter sent by the MGH Committee on Anaesthesia[13] in 1909 to 26 other "prominent hospitals" found that "most hospitals used house officers for the giving of anaesthesia," that "there was very little instruction of house officers or students," and (since many anesthetics are potent depressants of respiration and circulation in sick patients) that "the method was unsatisfactory."[14]

The 1909 letter found that several prominent hospitals had hired nurses as anesthetists as a safety upgrade over amateur house-officer etherizers. That year Mass General hired two nurses for this role, Helen Altimus and Grace Perkins. In 1911 Perkins wrote a report:

During the past two years I have anesthetized in the vicinity of 1800 patients at the Massachusetts General Hospital without serious mishap at the time of operation. Neither has there been a serious case of ether pneumonia resulting. . . . All adult patients are given morphia grains 1/6 and atropine grains 1/100 s.c., from half an hour to 15 minutes before they are anaesthetized. . . .

The following anaesthetics are in use at the present time: ether, nitrous oxide, gas and oxygen, anaesthol, novocaine, stovaine or tropocaine.

The first and commonest of these is ether. Ether is administered by the open, semi-open and closed methods; the open being called the "drop method." . . . The semi-open is the method that is most commonly used, and is by far the most satisfactory in the majority of cases.

By holding the cone a short distance from the patient's face and working it down by degrees, one is enabled to put the patient under the influence of ether in from eight to ten minutes, with little or no excitement.[15]

It was the nurse anesthetist's responsibility not only to

The ether inhaler designed by William T. G. Morton.

assure and comfort the patient but also to monitor the patient's color, respiration, and other vital signs during surgery.

As late as the 1930s another intern-anesthetist, Francis D. Moore, found it "shocking . . . that I was suddenly confronted late at night with an anesthesia machine, valves, cranks, and canisters of nitrous oxide and oxygen, and was expected to proceed, untutored, to induce anesthesia and put the patient 'to sleep.' At night, hurried, harried, and tired, with no help. That I and my fellows got through this without causing any deaths (at least none of which I was aware) was pure luck."[16]

Henry Knowles Beecher

There was no anesthesia department at MGH until after the arrival of Freeman Allen as consulting anesthetist, an unpaid position, in 1903. Until MGH opened Phillips House for private patients in 1917 and Allen could charge private patients directly for his services, he earned his income off-campus by treating private patients in their homes and, as the practice of surgery became more complex, in small, freestanding, private facilities like St. Margaret's Hospital and the L. C. Elliot Private Hospital, both on Beacon Hill.[17] Born in Stockbridge, Massachusetts, in 1870, Allen was the son of an Episcopal minister and a grandson of Harriet Beecher Stowe, author of *Uncle Tom's Cabin*. After Harvard College and Harvard Medical School, he was appointed a surgical house pupil at MGH in 1899. Following 18 months with the army in Cuba during the Spanish-American War, Allen returned to Boston, where J. Collins Warren, grandson of the founding surgeon John Collins Warren, convinced him to specialize in anesthesia.

No one replaced Freeman Allen for three years after his death in 1930. Then Howard H. Bradshaw was appointed anesthetist. Bradshaw returned to the practice of surgery in 1936, but not before leaving behind a manifesto for the future organization of an MGH anesthesia service: "We believe that a department of anesthesia should be under the direct supervision of a graduate in medicine. This individual should have been trained more in the surgical than in the medical field, because it is well to know just what a given surgical procedure demands from anesthesia. He should be trained in the physiology of respiration, and in gas exchange in general, and be familiar with the pharmacology of pain-relieving and sleep-producing drugs. He should also be teacher, organizer, and investigator."[18]

The hospital got all this and more in Henry Knowles Beecher, appointed instructor in anesthesia at the Harvard Medical School, April 27, 1936; assistant anesthetist at MGH, May 1, 1936; and anesthetist, September 1, 1936. In 1941 the academic status of the chief of anesthesia would be fully assured when Beecher was appointed the first Henry Isaiah Dorr professor of teaching and research in anesthesia and anesthetics at the medical school, activating a bequest made in 1917.[19] Beecher was a legend during and after his time. At his death, the *Harvard Gazette* wrote: "In science he was a Cyclops; in social life, a Bacchus."[20] As another associate put it, "Almost everything about HKB was larger than life, and often seemed unique."[21]

Why did Beecher accept the proposal of Edward "Pete" Churchill, chief of surgery, that he abandon surgery for anesthesia at a time (1936) when anesthesia had virtually no academic standing, when it was, in the words of a latter-day practitioner, "a low-prestige, low-paying, empiric field limited to operating room activities and almost completely lacking a scientific basis"? [22] Churchill may have urged Beecher into anesthesia because he needed an expert to advance his initiatives in surgery, especially in thoracic surgery, which involves opening the chest cavity and collapsing the lungs. (Maintaining or supplementing lung function would become a major focus of anesthesiology.) Churchill was "very much aware of Dr. Beecher's unusual intellectual abilities."[23] Whether Beecher would have made the coolest surgeon is also a matter Churchill might have considered. According to an associate: "[Beecher] was not a smooth, natural or graceful anesthetist. He was by nature impatient and quick; if anything went wrong, he might have the operating room in a mild uproar. . . . An IV infiltration in Beecher's room might cause almost as much excitement as an arrest in anyone else's. Most . . . had worked with him in the operating room for many years and wrote off the *Sturm und Drang* simply as part of the fabric of the institution . . . like the pillars on the front of the Bulfinch Building."[24]

Despite these eccentricities, Beecher was a safe, effective clinician, according to his colleague Bucknam "Jack" McPeek: "I cannot recall a single instance

of a patient being really hurt by Beecher. . . . There is something of a perception today, especially among those who were not close to [him], or were envious of his reputation, that he was an inadequate or poor clinician. I think this is largely a bum rap."[25]

Beecher had come to Harvard Medical School from an unlikely feeder in those days, the chemistry department at the University of Kansas. A native of a tiny (pop. 300) Kansas town and raised in modest circumstances, he may have been driven by a farm boy's ambition to make it in Metropolis. In moving from the farm to the university to Harvard, Beecher refashioned his own image. At the University of Kansas, a biographer notes that "he savored a foppish side."[26] After his graduation in 1926, he abandoned his awkward surname, Unangst, and assumed the maiden name of his maternal great-grandmother, Beecher. This may have been his way of

Henry Knowles Beecher.

distancing himself from his father, from whom Beecher was estranged. He entered Harvard Medical School as Henry Knowles Unangst Beecher and left as Henry Knowles Beecher.

By the time he graduated he had won the first of his two Warren Triennial Prizes—the 1931 prize for two articles about respiration, a central concern in anesthesia. In 1937 he won again for the monograph "Physiology of Anesthesia." Recognizing Beecher's academic promise, Churchill arranged for him to take a fellowship in Copenhagen in 1935–1936 working with a Nobel Prize winner, the physiologist August Krogh.

A big fish in the small pond of academic anesthesia, Beecher set about enlarging the pond. He founded an anesthesia lab in 1936, partly to get out from under the thumb of surgery. Previous papers in anesthesia from MGH had been headed "from the Department of Surgery," with no reference to anesthesia. In its first 21 years, his lab published 200 papers "from The Anesthesia Laboratory of the Harvard Medical School at the Massachusetts General Hospital."[27]

Recruiting would be a problem. Because of the poor standing of anesthesia, most of Beecher's recruits were foreign-born. McPeek commented that as late as 1959, when he graduated from HMS, "almost everyone went into the larger, more popular specialties like internal medicine, general surgery, psychiatry, pediatrics. Smaller fields got very few students from the class." When the German-born Edward Lowenstein joined the Cardiac Surgery Unit of the Anesthesia Department in 1965, he jokingly referred to the Brahmin-born anesthesiologist Phillips Hallowell as "our token American."[28]

Like many other patriotic personnel at MGH, the hospital's chief of surgery dropped everything to serve his country. Churchill became a surgical consultant to the European Theater of Operations in 1943, and Beecher followed, leaving Julia Arrowood as acting chief of anesthesia in his place. Beecher was tried in the crucible of Anzio beachhead, where Allied troops were pinned against the Italian shoreline by German artillery for a week in February 1944, but even under the German guns he thought of the medical implications. Why did injured soldiers often require less morphine than nonmilitary casualties? Beecher speculated that the soldiers considered themselves lucky to be alive and going home. This led to a crucial report and a key postwar investigative theme: pain.

Beecher was the same intellectual dynamo after 1945. He made major contributions in anesthesia while branching out into the wider field of medical ethics. His achievements in the lab included the first efforts to quantify pain, pioneering studies of the placebo effect, and work on LSD a decade before Timothy Leary. In 1954 he and Donald P. Todd published a landmark study of the results of more than half a million applications of anesthesia in 10 university hospitals over a five-year period. It showed the death rate from anesthesia to be one in 1,650.[29] McPeek explained colorfully: "Post-operative patients in the morgue do not have tattoos on their foreheads saying, 'My surgeon's knife slipped' or 'My anesthetist let the oxygen run out' or 'My internist didn't control my insulin.' Beecher and Todd set up committees of anesthetists, surgeons, internists, etc., to carefully review each patient's record to determine an accurate cause of death."

The Beecher-Todd findings carried one misinterpretation, which had repercussions for the rest of Beecher's career. The investigators wrote: "When the muscle relaxants enter the situation, the anesthesia death rate increases nearly 6-fold [from one in 2,100 to one in 370]. . . . These data suggest that the widespread custom of using curare for many trivial purposes is not justified."[30] Beecher and Todd were right about the higher incidence of death associated with curare, but they were wrong to suggest that there was something inherently toxic about muscle relaxants. This angered some colleagues, and the flap helped establish Beecher as a lightning rod for controversy. Today muscle relaxants are safely used as a cornerstone of anesthetic practice.

More important, however, was the positive outcome of the ambitious, wide-ranging Beecher-Todd study, which was all the more remarkable for having been tabulated and analyzed without computers. The study is remembered today as "the first serious attempt to learn the incidence of mortality attributable to anesthesia" and as "one of the few pivotal events responsible for the dramatic success in promoting anesthesia patient safety."[31] Warren Zapol, chief of anesthesia from 1994 to 2008, noted that by the time he stepped down, the death rate from anesthesia had improved from Beecher's 1954 benchmark of one in 1,600 to one in 250,000.

Beecher's 1966 article "Ethics and Clinical Research" was arguably his greatest moment as an agent provocateur—infuriating many even as he changed the way medical research was practiced in the world.[32] The article reviewed 22 recently published clinical experiments (several in the *New England Journal of Medicine*). Beecher did not name names, although the names must have been obvious to insiders. "Evidence is at hand," Beecher wrote, "that many of the patients in [these experiments] never had the risk satisfactorily explained to them, and it seems obvious that further hundreds have not known that they were the subjects of an experiment although grave consequences have been suffered as a direct result of experiments described here." Beecher's point was not that clinical research, even using double blinds and placebos, is wrong. His point was that patients must be informed of the risks and give their consent. Postmortem analysis of the article did name names, so that even the uninformed reader can appreciate Beecher's brass.[33]

A commentator wrote: "Beecher's extreme defensiveness about his position on ethics in experimentation and his prickly replies to critics were to be characteristic of his exchanges on the topic."[34] Even some of his colleagues in anesthesia at MGH sided against him. Henrik Bendixen maintained that informed consent was "impossible; rather, admission to a teaching hospital should be taken as tacit consent."[35] Ordinary medical practitioners, without a personal stake in research, generally supported Beecher, because he was attempting to raise the standards of his profession. "The response Beecher received in letters from the lay public was wildly enthusiastic, but often demonstrated a lack of understanding of the specific point Beecher had been trying to make."[36]

Beecher soldiered on through praise and outrage. In the 1960s organ transplantation was becoming more feasible (see chapter 6). A transplanted organ must be harvested from a donor, but not before the donor's life has ended. When does life end? To answer this question, Beecher prepared his last great paper in 1968, "A Definition of Irreversible Coma," originally published in the *Journal of the American Medical Association* as "A Definition of Irreversible Coma: Report of the

Ad Hoc Committee of the Harvard Medical School to Examine the Definition of Brain Death."[37] Here again, Beecher drew controversy, as some concluded that his work was meant to justify and facilitate organ harvesting. Two of Beecher's successors at MGH would see it differently.

Ed Lowenstein, who became the Dorr professor in 1998, wrote, "Beecher was probably motivated primarily by the urge to relieve suffering and avoid medical technology intrusion, somewhat by the wish to use scarce, expensive intensive care resources ethically and efficiently, but little by a wish to increase supply of organs for transplantation." Lowenstein argued that the criteria for brain death have remained "robust" for the 40 years since Beecher and are likely to "remain the standard for the foreseeable future."[38]

Warren Zapol did not deny the key application of Beecher's paper to transplantation ethics, commenting, "Doctors did not want to be seen as vultures hovering over patients, waiting for them to die to take out their kidneys and other organs." But, Zapol added, "Beecher's work was very wise: he never mentioned transplantation, he just said, 'This is what it takes to call a person dead.' His criteria allowed end-of-life withdrawal of care."

Harry's Boys

After World War II Beecher's recruitment efforts in anesthesia at MGH began to bear fruit, a tribute to his professional standing though probably not his finesse. McPeek recalled: "His lack of political skill amounted almost to a character defect. He seemed regularly to involve himself in expensive battles that were not central to his real concerns, and that he hadn't a hope of winning."[39]

Building a department in a major academic medical center is partly a matter of money, and here Beecher seemed to know just what he was doing. Whereas other anesthetists on staff were paid as salaried employees of the hospital, he arranged with Churchill in 1937 to offer a private, fee-for-service practice, almost exclusively in Phillips House, the MGH building for private patients opened in 1917. Beecher became the anesthetist to the carriage trade in Boston, a lucrative market. For these private patients there was no standard fee for anesthesia; the rule was to charge what the market would bear. Beecher's work in Phillips House, however, benefited not his own bank account so much as "an anesthesia fund," according to MGH's one-time director Nathaniel Faxon.[40] This financed the growth of his department. McPeek would call Beecher "without a doubt the biggest private contributor to anesthesia research funds during the 1950s and perhaps one of the larger in

Edward Lowenstein.

the 1960s." Beecher also befriended a great benefactor of MGH, Edward Mallinck-rodt, whose St. Louis–based chemical company was the leading maker of ether.

Some credit for his recruiting successes should be given to Beecher's social skills. Accounts of his colleagues suggest that Beecher possessed personal charms that attracted others, male and female. These skills were on display in the clinic, where he was "naturally kind and thoughtful. . . . Little old ladies loved him. By the time I knew him," wrote McPeek, "at the end of the 1950s, he . . . had a large number of grateful patients who would not consider letting anyone else give them an anesthetic."[41]

Any listing of distinguished anesthesiologists who had populated Beech-er's department by the time of his retirement in 1968 would have to include Henrik Bendixen, William Brewster, John Bunker, Bennie Geffin, Joachim (Nick) Gravenstein, Arthur Keats, Henning Pontoppidan, Myron Laver, Edward Low-enstein, and Donald Todd. Their accomplishments were many, but perhaps the greatest can be appreciated only in relation to surgery.

Chief of Surgery Edward Churchill was one of the last generalists to head a surgical service at a major teaching hospital, and he held the line against special-ization until his retirement in the early 1960s (for more on Churchill, see chapter 4). Specialization did arrive in anesthesia by the mid-1950s, however, largely as a result of the polio epidemic of 1952–1955. After the war, and in part inspired by his war experience, Beecher had formed an oxygen therapy unit. A few years later, lured by Thorkild W. Andersen, a Danish member of the MGH anesthesia staff, another foreign recruit joined up. Henning Pontoppidan recalled: "Even without the usual libation of Scotch I was invited by Dr. Beecher, after a fifteen-minute-long interview, to commence as a first year resident [in December 1953] . . . at the grand salary of $1,000 per year."[42] A major polio epidemic had hit Scandinavia the year before, and Pontoppidan brought with him to Boston the latest techniques for maintaining respiration in patients whose lungs had failed, as happens in bulbar polio.

Since the 1920s polio victims had been kept alive in iron lungs, or tank res-pirators, airtight tin cans that enclosed patients' entire bodies below their necks, including both legs and arms, and forced their lungs to inflate and deflate by alter-ing the air pressure in the tank. Giving a patient in an iron lung a bedpan or, worse, changing the sheets, could be terrifying, since a side door had to be opened and the operation completed swiftly and the door closed again before the patient suffered severe cyanosis.[43] In an emergency, a Danish doctor in 1952 had treated a dying girl by intubating her and creating positive pressure in her lungs. Pontop-pidan learned this technique: "I served my internship in 1952 in a county hospi-tal in northern Denmark, and most of my medical rotation was spent manually bag-breathing children and adults with paralytic poliomyelitis. Most survived, but many died despite heroic efforts. It was an experience that is hard to forget."[44] In 1954 Pontoppidan was joined at MGH by another Scandinavian import, Henrik Bendixen, and when the polio epidemic came to a devastating climax in New England a year later, Beecher fortunately had his team in place, including the original Scandinavian import, Andersen.

The ninth floor of the White Building was transformed into a polio ward with

44 tank respirators provided by the March of Dimes. The polio epidemic sub-sided and new outbreaks were prevented by the Salk vaccine, but many patients continued to suffer from respiratory failure—from diverse causes including Guil-lain-Barré syndrome, myasthenia gravis, and drug overdose. The polio ward was later discontinued, and these patients were spread around the MGH campus. A problem with this arrangement was that on three floors of White, in Bulfinch, in Phillips House, and in Baker Memorial (a 1930 structure for middle-income patients), those on life-sustaining respiratory equipment could not be monitored satisfactorily, as there were not yet the necessary alarm systems to alert staff if, say, a patient's oxygen supply ran out. Furthermore, there was a lack of concen-trated nursing care. Floor nurses could not devote sufficient time at the bedsides of patients dependent on mechanical ventilation to keep them out of trouble or detect trouble promptly when it occurred. Said Pontoppidan, "On several occa-sions I had the sad experience of entering a room during rounds and finding the patient unattended and dead in bed."[45]

These tragedies finally gave the impetus to establish the MGH Respiratory Intensive Care Unit (RICU) in 1961, the first such unit in the United States. Pontoppidan, who had traveled to Toronto General Hospital to observe a respira-tory unit there, directed the original five-bed unit in Phillips House. The MGH RICU, with its central nursing station from which respiratory patients were moni-tored, demonstrated the benefits of dedicated and specially trained medical and nursing staffs working together to provide care to patients who were among the sickest in the hospital. The RICU was moved to a 10-bed unit on Jackson 4 in 1969. In 1984 Pontoppidan stepped down as director and was succeeded by Roger S. Wilson, who led the unit until 1991. In the late 1990s the hospital opened the RACU (respiratory acute care unit) on Bigelow 9, dedicated to treating patients requiring prolonged ventilatory support. In 2000 the 10-bed RICU and the 10-bed GRACU (a surgical postoperative intensive care unit in the Gray Building) com-bined and moved to Ellison 4 to be merged into the Surgical Intensive Care Unit (SICU) under the direction of the anesthesiologist William Hurford and nurse manager Susan Tully. Luca Bigatello succeeded Hurford as medical director of the SICU, and today Ulrich Schmidt holds that position and Tully continues as nurs-ing director. Though MGH no longer has a dedicated RICU, the term is still used for calls to the "RICU consult," that is, the anesthesiologist who responds to all emergency airway calls in the hospital.

Beecher and his Scandinavian team had started something. By the 1970s the RICU had begotten a whole family of intensive care units at MGH driven by the specialized anesthesia and respiratory care required by each. In 2011 MGH has nine separate intensive care units, most pronounced to rhyme with the first: rick-you. These are the PICU (pediatric), NICU (neonatal), SICU (surgical), MICU (medical), Neuro ICU, Transplant ICU, Burn ICU, CSICU (cardiac surgery), and CICU (cardiac medical).

Life after Beecher

Brilliant recruiting and specialized anesthesia services helped Beecher reap his final harvest in 1968, when anesthesia was extricated from the clutches of surgery

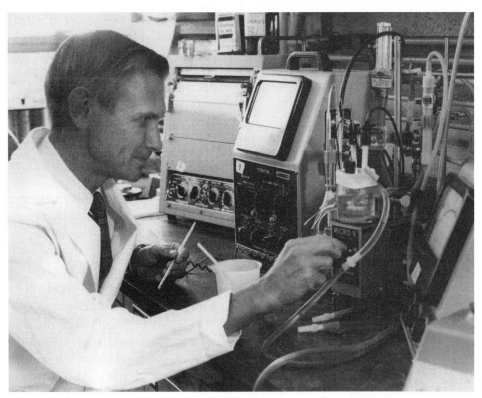

Richard Kitz.

at MGH and given its own departmental status, a move Churchill had always opposed. An independent Department of Anesthesia at Harvard Medical School, for which Beecher had lobbied, was established after his retirement, on October 17, 1969, 123 years and one day after Ether Day. In this academic recognition of anesthesia, HMS was well behind the times; 48 of the four-year medical schools in the United States already had anesthesia departments.[46]

Leroy Vandam once described the MGH Anesthesia Department under Beecher as "happy anarchy,"[47] a trait McPeek lauded and believed continued under Beecher's immediate successors, Richard Kitz (1969–1994) and Warren Zapol (1994–2008). In such conditions, individual contributions were encouraged and the cream rose to the top. Like many MGH chiefs, Beecher wanted to name his own successor, but instead the hospital and its new chief of surgery, W. Gerald "Jerry" Austen, reached outside, to perhaps the preeminent anesthesia department in the country, at Columbia Presbyterian Hospital in New York, and tapped Richard J. Kitz, a student of the noted anesthesiologist Emanuel M. "Manny" Papper. In the Papper era, Columbia Presbyterian was "a hot-bed of anesthesia research,"[48] and Kitz was just back from a sabbatical in the toxicology labs of the Department of Pharmacology at the prestigious Karolinska Institute in Stockholm. If there is a downside to "happy anarchy," Kitz was the corrective. He is credited by all as a highly effective administrator. Clinical care, research, and education in anesthesia all made strides under his leadership.

Kitz reportedly found the MGH program inferior to that at Columbia Presbyterian—although Lowenstein would note that a multitude of professors, department chairmen, and clinical leaders had been produced under Beecher's leadership. Residents were overworked; they had no sleeping quarters, instead catching a few winks "on the floor, gurneys and an OR table in what was then the cystoscopy room."[49] In all, Kitz calculated that he was short about 10 anesthetists for the workload in the ORs of MGH—which were spread over the campus haphazardly. The 1969 opening of the Gray Building, with its brand-new operating suites, would have "a major positive effect on morale and our staffing plans."[50] Not only would it concentrate surgery in one place, but it would also relieve the terrible shortage of operating space that caused cases to run into the evening hours and be scheduled all day on Saturday.

Since the Beecher-Todd study of 1954, a primary focus of MGH's Anesthesia Department had been patient safety. A set of criteria for monitoring patients was pushed by the department under Kitz and formalized by the Anesthesia Department at Harvard Medical School. New rules were developed, along with new monitors for carbon dioxide, blood oxygen saturation (pinkness), and other vital signs. According to Zapol, "Kitz carried the safety banner to the Harvard chiefs, then they wrote the safety criteria." A prime pioneer for safety at MGH was David Cullen. As a result of improved monitoring and therefore patient safety, the malpractice insurance rates for anesthesiologists plunged between the 1970s and the first years of the new century. Another key contributor was Hassan Ali. Recruited by Kitz from Liverpool, he brought "his knowledge of clinical measurements of neuromuscular transmission, the innovative 'train-of-four.'"[51] Ali's work standardized the monitoring of paralyzing drugs.

In the research arena, Kitz answered some of Beecher's questions about muscle relaxants by developing shorter-acting drugs in collaboration with John Savarese. Meanwhile, the anesthesiologist Nathaniel M. Sims, working in bioengineering, led the development of smart monitors and pumps. Subsequently, there was a move to "distributed monitoring," moving monitors with patients, instead of unplugging a patient each time he or she was moved. Jeffrey B. Cooper, another bioengineer, started a critical incidents study, getting people to tell him about things that occurred that might have caused grievous harm or death but didn't—and analyzing the circumstances that led to them.[52] His work resulted in establishment of both the Anesthesia Patient Safety Foundation by the American Society of Anesthesiologists and the National Patient Safety Foundation by the American Medical Association. Cooper's contributions were noted by medical writer Atul Gawande in an "Annals of Medicine" piece in the *New Yorker* as "the first in-depth, scientific look at errors in medicine."[53]

The Hospital's Southernmost Operating Room

Warren Zapol replaced Dick Kitz upon the latter's retirement in 1994. Zapol's father was a New York City businessman who had studied medicine in Germany during "an unfortunate period of time." Zapol, an only child, said, "I'm sure a lot of the reason for my interest in medicine was that his efforts had been frustrated in Germany in the 1930s." Zapol's mother was an elementary school teacher in Brooklyn, where Zapol was born. He attended New York's public schools, graduating from Stuyvesant High at the age of 16. Zapol's science bent led him to

MIT, where he "got seduced by some very smart physiologists who worked in pain, including [Patrick D.] Pat Wall, a strange, wonderful man." (Upon Wall's death in 2001, the International Association for the Study of Pain would eulogize Wall as the "major figure and dominant personality" in the field.)[54] As chairman of anesthesia at MGH, Zapol would make pain an important investigative focus, highlighted by his recruitment of Clifford Woolf, a leading pain researcher then in the United Kingdom and a protégé of Wall's.

Following graduation from medical school at the University of Rochester, Zapol did a surgical internship at Boston City Hospital, and then, selected to join the Public Health Service at the height of the Vietnam War, Zapol said, "I thought the NIH [National Institutes of Health] would be more fun than combat." At the NIH he worked with Theodor Kolobow, a pioneering inventor of extracorporeal membrane oxygenation (ECMO), a novel disposable device that looks like a three-foot length of four-inch-diameter PVC pipe and functions as a lung (or heart-lung) bypass machine, oxygenating blood outside the subject's body, buying time for an injured lung to heal. The first experimental subjects were sheep, preferred over other animals, Zapol said, because they don't bark and don't bite. Zapol took the device for trials on critically wounded soldiers in Danang, Vietnam, where he served as a medical research consultant.

Back home and now married to Nikki Kaplan, Zapol joined the MGH residency program in August 1970, where ECMO was beginning to be used with critically ill adults and then with blue, or cyanotic, babies. ECMO devices were the next step in mechanical assistance of the human lung, following the use of mechanical ventilators brought to MGH from Denmark by Henning Pontopiddan during the polio epidemic. To use ECMO to assist the respiration of a newborn, it was necessary to thin the baby's blood with heparin, an anticoagulant, and in about 15 percent of cases this led to severe hemorrhaging. But, Zapol said, since 50 percent of blue babies would die without any intervention, "we hoped to achieve a net gain. Pediatricians, however, hated ECMO because you had to perform major cannulation surgery and anticoagulate, and you needed a team to run one of these things. The ECMO device was never loved." Another, simpler solution to aid the respiration of infants born blue was needed.

Nitric oxide (NO) is poisonous. Tanks of this pollutant gas have skulls and crossbones printed on their labels. But in the mid-1980s three scientists teamed up to demonstrate the surprising fact that this poisonous molecule is actually an important signaling agent produced in the human body from the amino acid arginine, regulating blood pressure by causing blood vessels to dilate. The scientists— Robert Furchgott, Ferid Murad (formerly a medical house officer at MGH), and Louis Ignarro—won the 1998 Nobel Prize in Physiology or Medicine for their discovery of nitric oxide as a physiological signaling molecule. Coincidentally, that was also the year of the commercial release of a blockbuster drug that relies on NO for its properties. That drug is Viagra (sildenafil citrate).

In 1989, on a trip to Los Angeles, where he was being recruited by UCLA as chief of anesthesia, Zapol happened to see a newspaper article showing levels of pollutants in the LA atmosphere: CO, SO_2, NO_2. Suddenly, it occurred to him: since NO_2 (nitrous oxide) is created by oxidizing NO, there must be NO in the atmosphere as well, and people must be breathing it all the time! Thus began a 10-year crusade to prove that nitric oxide could be inhaled safely at low doses and could effectively relieve respiratory distress, acting as a potent and selective pulmonary vasodilator by dilating the lung's circulation without dilating other blood vessels in the body. The obstacles to approval were substantial; it took 10 years for the Food and Drug Administration to give NO the green light as a treatment for cyanotic term infants. Zapol recalled the seminal early trials: "I'll never forget the first baby we used it on successfully with colleague neonatologist-anesthesiologist Jesse (Jay) Roberts. We had to cover the skull and crossbones on the tank label because the parents would have freaked out. The baby turned pink before our eyes, even at 20 parts per million, 40, 80—as we came up from low levels of nitric oxide, the baby got pinker and pinker. It's the coolest thing that ever happened to me."

Zapol has a letter in his office from one of the first children saved by nitric oxide. Assisted by a grateful parent, the child wrote: "Dear Dr. Zap, Hi I just want to thank you and all those other people who do experiments and stuff. I was very sick when I was born (PPHN,[55] my dad says) and that NO stuff helped me get better. Now I am three and play with trucks and cars and everything. Love, Zeke."[56]

Though nitric oxide worked on only about one-third of children when it was first used on newborns in the mid-1990s, the percentage is now 60 to 70 percent, because the gas is used earlier, before pulmonary damage can occur. Mass General obtained patents on the technique, and the licensing royalties, shared with the inventors, Zapol and Claes Frostell (who worked with Zapol on NO as a research fellow), continue to come in at this writing.

Warren Zapol (center) on sea ice off McMurdo Station, Antarctica, with Roger D. Hill (left) and Robert C. Schneider (right). Zapol called it the southernmost branch of the MGH (courtesy Warren M. Zapol).

Zapol is a traveler. When interviewed for this book, he was on his way to Alaska with his family to do some salmon fishing and to attend meetings of the U.S. Arctic Research Commission, on which he serves as a presidentially appointed commissioner. He was in Moscow in the midst of the Cold War, saving the life of the daughter of a prominent Soviet heart surgeon. He did research over a span of two decades at McMurdo Station in Antarctica (79 degrees south latitude), where, with sponsorship from the National Science Foundation, he opened what he called the MGH's southernmost operating room. In an investigative career often focused on hemoglobin (the molecule in the blood that picks up oxygen from the lungs), Zapol and the teams of scientists he has assembled have gone to great lengths to study prodigious mammalian divers by developing "diving microcomputers." They studied Weddell seals of the Antarctic, which can remain submerged for as much as 90 minutes hunting Antarctic codfish on the ocean floor, and Korean and Japanese *haenyo*, or "sea women," who traditionally "breath-hold" dive for shellfish for as long as three or four minutes without artificial breathing apparatus. Zapol's team learned key physiological secrets that enable the seals to use and distribute oxygen more efficiently than humans.

Back home, the 14 years of Zapol's leadership in anesthesia were highly productive ones for the department. Both the staff and their anesthetic caseload doubled (to 148 and 41,000 per year, respectively). During this time the Anesthesia Department formally assumed the leadership role in operating rooms at MGH—a dramatic change from the early Churchill-Beecher days, when the anesthetist was the humble handmaiden of the domineering surgeon. Leaders of the department played a central role in designing the OR suites in the new 10-story Lunder Building, which was being built as this book was written in 2009–2010. Under Zapol the department developed a computerized intraoperative record, then the only such system at a major Boston medical center. Simulation for team training and individual testing, begun by Jeff Cooper under Dick Kitz, has continued to develop.

In addition to the work of Zapol's lab (wherever located), research has grown and prospered in anesthesiology. Lowenstein credited Zapol with increasing federally funded research in the department by an order of magnitude in his years as chief. With the addition of four chairs that Zapol established (the Kitz, Morton, Zapol, and Beecher chairs) to the preexisting Dorr, Mallinckrodt, and Jenney chairs, MGH has more furniture in its anesthesiology department than in all the other Harvard hospitals combined, ensuring continued research excellence in future.

Pat Wall's old protégé Clifford Woolf, brought in by Zapol from University College London, has developed new drugs to block pain before it occurs. Lowenstein said that Woolf is "perhaps the leading conceptual thinker about pain in the world now." Woolf is the first holder of the Richard J. Kitz Chair in Anesthesiology. Ken Bloch came from MGH cardiology as the first incumbent of the William T. G. Morton Chair and continued to lead important work in molecular biology of the heart and lung. Emery Brown, a talented mathematician and anesthesiologist, was honored with the first Warren Zapol Chair, upon Zapol's retirement. Said Zapol, "It's a relief that I don't have to be dead. Retirement from chiefdom is

Jeanine Wiener-Kronish (courtesy MGH Department of Anesthesia, Critical Care and Pain Medicine).

sufficient to have a Harvard chair named after you!"

Zapol's replacement, Jeanine Wiener-Kronish, arrived from the University of California, San Francisco (UCSF), in 2008. Wiener-Kronish had trained in internal medicine, pulmonary medicine, and critical care before training in anesthesia at UCSF. Her career has included basic research on bacterial-induced acute lung injury, and she has worked to develop an antibody to block a virulence system in *Pseudomonas aeruginosa*. Her 31-year tenure at UCSF included administration of a laboratory, being vice chair of the Department for Research Efforts, and working as an intensivist. She came to MGH to maintain and strengthen the department, by further developing the OR clinicians, the critical care specialists, and the pain physicians as well as maintaining top-level basic and clinical research. Her department has been renamed the Department of Anesthesia, Critical Care and Pain Medicine, the DACCPM.

To help accomplish this vision, Wiener-Kronish first recruited J. Perren Cobb, a world-famous intensivist interested in creating a national network for critical care clinical research. Cobb has initiated a strategy for the development and increase of critical care services at MGH. Searches for division chiefs of clinical OR services were under way in 2010. Faculty in the DACCPM are collaborating with MIT to develop models that evaluate staffing of the faculty in the operating room; other collaborations are evaluating care processes in the preoperative clinic. A new joint fellowship with MIT that teaches process assessment to anesthesiologists interested in directing operating rooms has been developed; the first fellow started in July 2010.

Others in the DACCPM are collaborating with the Harvard Computing Group to develop anesthesiologists and computer scientists with research interests in analysis of data from the ORs and the ICUs. This has led to another new fellowship, beginning in July 2010, that involves working collaboratively with Harvard computer scientists and DACCPM faculty to develop and analyze data in the departmental electronic database streaming from the operating rooms.

Henry Knowles Beecher would relish knowing that many of these developments effectively started with him.

THE CONTROVERSIAL DR. BIGELOW

We return now to the mid-nineteenth century and another Henry B. in the MGH pantheon: Henry Jacob Bigelow, who was central to the advance of surgery at Mass General during the second half of the nineteenth century. We can date his tale from October 16, 1846, when Bigelow assisted beside John Collins Warren at the first operation under ether anesthesia. Before the year was out, as previously noted, Bigelow would write the first professional paper on the surgical uses of ether.

Like the Warren family story, Bigelow's really begins at the time of the American Revolution and with his grandfather the Reverend Jacob Bigelow. A member of the Harvard class of 1776, Bigelow became a beloved country clergyman who ministered to the same congregation for more than 40 years "without schism or division among his parishioners."[57] His grandson Henry Jacob Bigelow would inherit his name—but not his universal appeal. Though beloved by his friends and respected by his colleagues, Henry Jacob Bigelow always had his opponents.

Henry Jacob's father, Jacob Bigelow (1786–1879), became an eminent Boston physician. He spent 50 of his 92 years as a professor of *materia medica* (pharmacology) at Harvard Medical School. Jacob Bigelow was also a respected botanist, a collaborating designer of Mount Auburn Cemetery, and president of the American Academy of Arts and Sciences. His "Discourse on Self-Limited Diseases" was one of the most important medical works of its day.[58] The starkly realistic paper highlighted the inability of contemporary medicine to change the course of many diseases: "This deficiency of the healing art is not justly attributable to any want of sagacity or diligence on the part of the medical profession. It belongs rather to the inherent difficulties of the case, and is, after abating the effect of errors and accidents, to be ascribed to the apparent fact, that certain morbid processes in the human body have a definite and necessary career, from which they are not to be diverted by any known agents, with which it is in our power to oppose them."[59]

Jacob's son, Henry Jacob, would grow to share his father's practical, conservative sensibility. The son knew from a young age that he wished to pursue a medical career, which earned him the playground nickname "Doctor." He entered Harvard College in 1833, at age 15. A renaissance man like his father, Bigelow played the French horn with the Pierian Sodality (now the Harvard-Radcliffe Orchestra) and assumed an active role in the Rumford Chemical Society, manufacturing nitrous oxide for the society's annual romp, when its members inhaled laughing gas under the supervision of the professor of chemistry.[60] During his freshman year at Harvard, Bigelow took part in a student rebellion. When his father scolded him, Henry Jacob pointed out that his father had been involved in a similar demonstration during his own Harvard career. The father replied that he later saw the folly of his action. The son quipped, "Well, I want to see the folly of it, too."[61]

Bigelow yearned to see everything for himself, as evidenced by his early love of the microscope. During studies in Europe he became an adept operator of the new tool that would animate the field of pathology. Even in his youth there was no finer microscopist in the country. He focused on facts he observed himself and had no patience for ungrounded theorizing. As a professor, Bigelow later said to his students, "You can see more with a critical eye than with a naked eye, but with no eye so much as the eye of faith. Now, gentlemen, you may look for these grafts with the naked eye; I will look with a critical eye; and we will let Mr. —— look with the eye of faith. Then we will compare notes."[62] Believing only his own critical eye, Bigelow rarely did background research before carrying out his experiments. Disappointment ensued if he subsequently realized that another man had already made the same discovery.

Henry Jacob Bigelow as a young man.

His father was a physician, and the dynastic world of early Boston medicine dictated that the younger Bigelow should be a physician as well. James Jackson, the MGH cofounder and dear friend to the Bigelow clan, tried to divert the ambitious Henry Jacob from the surgical path. Jackson chided the aspiring surgeon: "Your father is a medical, not a surgical practitioner. You want to forsake your best chance, and try to practice in *that* corner of the room, when all your interests and opportunities are with him, over in the other corner!" In response to the eminent doctor's well-meant advice, the youth exclaimed, "I'll be damned if I won't be a surgeon!"[63]

In 1838, at the age of 20, Henry Jacob was appointed house surgeon at Massachusetts General—what today would be termed a surgical intern or resident. After graduating from Harvard Medical School in 1841, Henry Jacob continued his studies abroad, alongside his longtime friend Samuel Cabot, a budding surgeon himself. Bigelow studied primarily in Paris, where he boarded in the Latin Quarter with his friend Jeffries Wyman, son of the first superintendent of the McLean Asylum, Rufus Wyman. Bigelow returned to a Boston mired in its old ways, but the young doctor was determined to make his presence felt. Oliver Wendell Holmes and Reginald Fitz wrote of their friend and colleague:

> He had little respect for tradition. He intended to be the founder of his own fortune, and to be dependent upon no one but himself for promotion. He made no concealment of his aspirations. His restless energy soon manifested itself, and he may perhaps have seemed imperious and masterful; but he was recognized, among those who knew him, as one mapping out his own path by sheer force and independence of character, undeterred by the fear of seniors or rivals, and undisturbed by criticism. "If he does not become a distinguished man," Dr. James Jackson is declared to have said of Dr. Bigelow, "it will be because Boston is not a large enough field for his ability."[64]

Bigelow and his medical school classmate Henry Bryant, who had also recently returned from Paris, where he had been an extern in its hospitals, established a Charitable Surgical Institution that offered the poor free surgical treatments in the basement of the First Church on Chauncy Place in Boston. The circular issued by Bigelow and Bryant promised not only free treatment, but also to forward a diagnosis, prognosis, and suggested treatment to any other doctor, and to attend the patient in his or her home if necessary. They would also distribute free vaccines to physicians and give cardiac and pulmonary examinations.

There was much chatter around Boston about the young surgeons with big ideas, and quickly a cutting spoof on the circular surfaced:

> DEAR SIR,—You are respectfully informed that the subscribers have opened a Medical and Surgical establishment for the purpose of furnishing gratuitous professional assistance to all applicants, together with medicines, surgical apparatus, board, lodging, good clothes, and whatever else the circumstances of the patient may require. . . . We are happy to add that we have recently obtained a stethoscope of six thousand ordinary stethoscope power, by which means cerebral auscultation can be practised at a great distance, and many things heard which do not in reality exist. . . . The advantages of early application are obvious: it will at once insure to patients the full ardor of our professional zeal, and demonstrate our superiority to all old practitioners and country physicians, and prove that we are illustrious men.
>
> FESTINANS BIGBLOW, equal to two Surgeons
MR. EXTERNUS, recently from abroad[65]

MEDICAL EDUCATION IN THE NINETEENTH CENTURY

In the mid-nineteenth century a young man from Massachusetts could work through Harvard Medical School's curriculum in two years. Provided that he could pay for tickets to professors' lecture series (the fees went straight to the professor) and pass what James C. White called "a final and farcical examination," he could obtain a Harvard medical degree.[66] Each student had to sign up for the seven subjects offered (though attendance was not monitored) in at least one of the two years of his medical education. The other year could be spent at a medical school with comparable courses. There was no gradation of classes: all students attended the same lectures, regardless of their various levels of knowledge.

The students, most of whom lacked a college degree, visited MGH a few times a week: two clinical medical visits, one surgical, and an opportunity to observe an operation under the dome on Saturdays. They followed a physician or surgeon around his ward en masse, listened to him confer with the nurse about changes in cases, and watched him treat patients. Some of the only hands-on experience a medical student received was in dissection. Each aspiring doctor was expected to dissect the "three parts" during his course of studies: an arm, a leg, and a head. No microscope or test tube enlightened these crude forays into morbid anatomy.[67]

In 1838 some of Boston's senior physicians, including Jacob Bigelow (the father) and Oliver Wendell Holmes, felt that the Harvard Medical School's curriculum left something to be desired. Many of them Harvard Medical School professors, they banded together to create the Tremont Street Medical School. The institution provided a series of lectures as well as recitations and demonstrations throughout the year, which were best attended when Harvard lectures were not in session. Tremont offered high-quality lectures, but its curriculum was limited:

sufficient clinical and laboratory courses were lacking.[68] Although the school did not offer a degree (only a supplementary medical education), it maintained its autonomy for 20 years, until 1858, when Harvard Medical School took Tremont under its wing as a summer medical school. When HMS finally established a graded course of instruction in 1871, the Tremont Street Medical School disappeared entirely into Harvard.[69]

The young upstart surgeon Henry Jacob Bigelow, not yet a Harvard professor, was given a chair at his father's institution on Tremont Street. In 1844 he began teaching as the Tremont Street Medical School's instructor in surgery and chemistry. His zeal and energy, along with his detailed diagrams, dissections, and case studies, made his lectures popular among medical students.

In February 1846 John C. Warren wrote a letter to the MGH Board of Trustees, asking their opinion of a potential relocation of the Harvard Medical School from the Marlborough Street location to the vicinity of the hospital. The board voted "that they cannot perceive any advantage to this institution to arise therefrom."[70] Nonetheless, the medical school moved to North Grove Street the next year, on the long front lawn, as it were, of the Bulfinch Building. The institutions' new proximity strengthened the de facto link that had existed since the hospital's founding, and it permitted medical students to move quickly between lectures and hospital rounds.

After Harvard Medical School moved to North Grove Street, Henry Jacob Bigelow found his own institution's location on Tremont Street inconvenient to the newly neighboring MGH and HMS. The retirement of HMS Professor of Surgery George Hayward was imminent, and Bigelow was known to be a likely candidate to succeed him. The resourceful young surgeon invented a brilliant solution: he bought a house adjacent to the North Grove Street HMS building, knocked down a wall, and used the newly enlarged space to hold his own series of lectures. Bigelow eked out only two or three lectures before the popular series was moved to the Chauncy Place Infirmary, but he was not punished for his audacity. When Hayward retired in 1849, Bigelow was appointed Harvard's professor of surgery.[71]

Murder at the Med School

Later that year the Harvard Medical School was the site of a great scandal. George Parkman was one of the wealthiest, most powerful, best connected of Bostonians. He entered Harvard College at age 15 and graduated in the class of 1809. From a young age, Parkman took an interest in the treatment of mental illness and in the work of Philadelphia's illustrious Benjamin Rush. Parkman received his medical degree from the University of Aberdeen in Scotland and later studied in Paris with Philippe Pinel, a visionary behind psychiatric moral management (see chapter 1).

In 1816, with plans for an asylum in the works, Parkman contacted the MGH trustees to inform them that they could purchase the Magee property on 16 acres of land in Roxbury for $16,000. Parkman offered to supply $11,000 if the trustees would raise the remaining $5,000. The trustees accepted and appointed Parkman superintending physician of the asylum. The trustees quickly realized that Parkman already ran a private institution for the insane on that property and planned merely to transfer funds subscribed by his friends for his private asylum to the MGH asylum, and in doing so to receive a promotion. So the board declined to purchase the Magee property and instead named Rufus Wyman superintendent of the embryonic asylum, subsequently located in Charlestown.[72]

Parkman maintained an interest in the treatment of insanity. He visited the patients at the asylum, gave items for their comfort and recreation, and donated to Harvard the North Grove Street plot on which the new medical school was built. Despite his philanthropy, Parkman was not universally liked and withdrew from the active pursuit of medicine to concentrate on managing his extensive real estate holdings, which included many decrepit tenement buildings. Parkman was also a part-time usurer. Though he was worth half a million dollars in 1849, he was notoriously ruthless with his debtors. Park-

A sketch of George Parkman,
the murder victim.

man's tall, lean silhouette, with its protruding chin, was a daily fixture on Boston streets, along which he paraded, collecting rent and loans.

One man to whom Parkman lent significant sums was HMS Professor John Webster. The short, stocky, bespectacled Webster taught chemistry, mineralogy, and geology to students who would always consider him tolerable and respectable, but not brilliant. Webster's income from lecturing and publishing chemistry books did not approach the amount he spent to maintain the lifestyle his family came to expect. He had four daughters, two of debutante age. The exasperated man resorted to borrowing money from friends and acquaintances.

In financial straits, Webster put up a valuable collection of minerals as collateral for two separate loans: one from Parkman and another from Robert Gould Shaw Sr. Learning of Webster's two-timing maneuver just before Thanksgiving 1849, the enraged Parkman marched to the Harvard cashier and tried to collect Webster's lecture fees as partial repayment of the debt. On Friday, November 23, Webster knocked at the Parkmans' door and suggested that the two men meet at the North Grove Street school building that afternoon at one-thirty. Parkman never returned home for his two o'clock lunch.

The medical school's janitor, Ephraim Littlefield, reported that he found Webster's laboratory locked from the inside that afternoon and heard the water running continuously. Littlefield grew increasingly suspicious of Webster's uncharacteristically erratic behavior. The police thoroughly searched the medical school building on Monday and Tuesday, to no avail. On Thanksgiving Day, November 29, Littlefield cut a hole through the brick wall into Webster's privy. Peering in, he discerned human remains scattered about. Police subsequently found additional body parts in a tea chest and some half-calcined bones in the lab's furnace. Further investigation showed that the parts were from the same body.

The 12-day trial that began on March 19, 1850, was one of the first celebrity trials in American history. A number of expert witnesses testified, including William T. G. Morton of ether fame, and Jeffries and Morrill Wyman, whose father had been appointed director of the asylum in Parkman's stead. The jury found Webster guilty, and he was sentenced to death. Webster then wrote a confession of guilt, stating that Parkman had provoked him to a rage, in which state Webster struck Parkman only once. Attempts to save Webster from the gallows were in vain, and on August 30 he was hanged at the Leverett Street Jail.[73]

FIRST SERVICE IN WARTIME

Though geographically removed from Civil War battles, Massachusetts General Hospital felt the war's effects within its own walls, as the staff attended the needs of injured and disabled soldiers. In 1862, when the cost to keep a patient for one week was $6.04, the trustees voted to admit any invalid soldier for whom there was an available bed at a weekly fee of $4.50.[74] (Of 7,668 total patients treated at MGH from 1861 through 1865, only 1,601 paid anything at all, and very few of those covered their own cost.)[75] Once a government military hospital was established in Boston, MGH admitted soldiers to its own wards free of charge. In 1863, 212 such soldiers were treated as inpatients.[76]

The war claimed the services of a number of MGH surgeons and physicians, some temporarily, others permanently. In October 1862 the trustees granted Benjamin Shaw of MGH a leave of absence to act as an army hospital inspector for the United States Sanitary Commission, an organization that furnished what little medicine and surgery could provide to ailing and injured soldiers. Shortly afterward, McLean's Superintendent John Tyler was permitted to do the same. Both men were asked to furnish appropriate temporary replacements for the duration of their absence.[77]

Tyler's predecessor, the longtime McLean superintendent Luther V. Bell, willingly offered his medical services to the Union Army. The cofounder of the American Psychiatric Association was deeply patriotic and gave his life for his country. On February 4, 1862, Bell wrote home: "I do not contemplate leaving the service (health of myself and children continuing) until this wicked Rebellion is for ever quelled." The next night Bell was overcome with an illness that proved fatal within a week.[78]

Henry Jacob Bigelow, too, contributed his services to the medical war effort. At the age of 45, Bigelow was exempt from compulsory military service, but he nevertheless provided a substitute to fight in his stead. Just after war broke out in 1861, Bigelow was requested to give a series of free lectures on surgery to young assistant surgeons who would operate in the war with limited skill or knowledge. The invitation to lecture was extended on a Saturday, and Bigelow gave his first lecture the following Monday, having prepared a talk as well as cadavers for his demonstrations.[79]

Had J. Collins Warren, grandson of the MGH founder, been a few years older, he might have attended Bigelow's wartime lectures. In June 1864 Warren enlisted as an acting assistant surgeon and joined many young men who had only "the

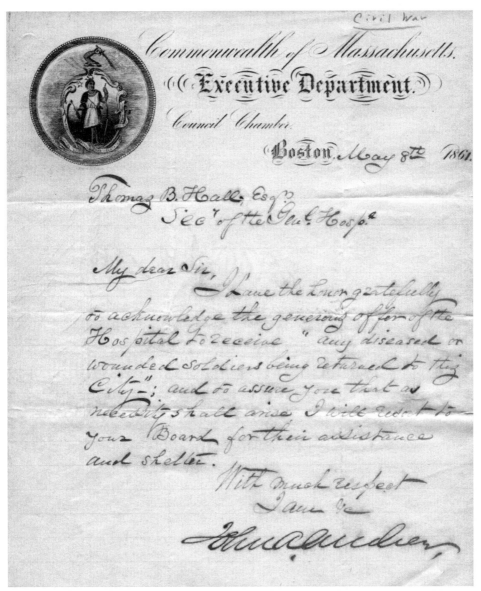

A letter from Massachusetts Governor John A. Andrew acknowledging the hospital's offer to care for "any diseased or wounded soldiers being returned to this City" during the Civil War.

slender preparation that was characteristic of so many an army surgeon."[80] Warren was ferried to the White House on the Pamunkey River, 20 miles from Richmond, Virginia. There he witnessed the abysmal conditions that Union soldiers suffered. Warren recalled the military camps, whose distasteful types committed "reckless and not entirely nonalcoholic actions,"[81] nestled next to the "promiscuously [grouped] hospital tents and their gruesome neighbors—improvised graveyards."[82] Warren detailed the surgical conditions that caused many an injured soldier to be moved from the former to the latter: "Chloroform was the only anesthetic used in the army on account of its smallness of bulk as compared with that of ether. Operations were performed with great rapidity and often seemed crude and ill planned in our eyes. A total resection of the lower jaw was done for gunshot injury; the hunt for the bullet in each case seemed relentless and often involved very extensive laying open of the tissues. The remedy seemed to us in many cases worse than the disease."[83]

Another deficiency of Union military hospitals was the "almost entire absence of women." He described the one exception, a nurse who lacked the feminine manners that might soothe the afflicted. Warren wrote, "She seemed to be enacting a role not altogether in keeping with the attributes of her sex . . . [and] to exemplify the brutalizing influences of the life to which she had been exposed and of which she formed a component part."[84] The need for the calming effects of womanly virtue and maternal instinct was simultaneously felt back home, within the walls of Mass General.

TRAINING NURSES

Before the young women educated at the Boston Training School for Nurses became a permanent fixture at Mass General, starting in the 1870s, there were no trained female medical professionals at the hospital. The hospital matron was sometimes the superintendent's wife, who served as the mother figure for patients and house pupils. Early nurses, like the respected Rebecca Taylor (see chapter 1), helped create and maintain a healing ambiance in the hospital, at a time when atmosphere and diet contributed as much to patient recuperation as crude medical science. Nurses were valued for their attitudes, not their intelligence or education. In *History of the Massachusetts General Hospital Training School for Nurses,* Sara Parsons noted that in early days "many of the nurses were of the poorest grade, women such as one would not have admitted to one's own household," and that there were "occasional cases of drunken nurses, and accidents arising therefrom."[85]

In 1862 Georgia Sturtevant arrived at Mass General as an assistant nurse. Six years later the matron, Mary Colesworthy, passed away, and Sturtevant took over her position, which she held until retiring in 1894.[86] She also served for many years as the overseer of the Treadwell Library. Dating to 1847, the library was named for John Treadwell, who in 1858 left 2,500 medical books and $5,000 for the purchase of more books. When Sturtevant was hired, nurses were paid $7.50 per month. Their shifts, which included much serving, washing, ironing, and mending, lasted from 5 A.M. until 9:30 P.M., "with an occasional hour off, if the work could be so arranged as to make it expedient."[87] The women shared a building with contagious and delirious patients and slept two to a bed (more accurately, a folding cot) in rooms between wards. They dined in a dimly lit, dingy room with an empty fireplace. Sturtevant remembered with respectful regret:

> I would not for a moment question the wisdom or large-heartedness of those men who devised and perfected such a wonderful scheme. . . . But that these men—I would speak reverently, for they are not here to defend themselves— should so strangely forget to provide for the health and comfort of those who were to be the chief instruments in carrying out their charitable designs, seems almost beyond belief. For example, while the patients, no matter of what nationality, or in what station of life, reposed on dainty, dimity-curtained

Boston Training School for Nurses, class of 1886.

beds, and used only solid silver (spoons), the nurses, after being on duty for sixteen hours, were shut up in little boxes of rooms between two wards, and sipped their "souchong"—or whatever brand it might have been—from pewter teaspoons, and drank their ice-water, when they were allowed that luxury, from pewter tumblers.[88]

Sarah Cabot, sister of an MGH surgeon, Samuel Cabot, was the first to suggest a training school for nurses in Boston. She had support from friends, including the former MGH trustee Martin Brimmer and her own brother. Another ally of Sarah Cabot in her campaign for a nursing school was Mary Parkman, wife of the longtime MGH doctor Samuel Parkman. Mrs. Parkman had met Florence Nightingale in England and was impressed by the nursing school associated with St. Thomas's Hospital that Nightingale had founded. She spoke with the famous nurse about founding a school of nursing in Boston based on similar principles. Cabot procured a copy of Nightingale's book of rules and regulations from her cousin, who was associated with the nurses' training school at Bellevue Hospital in New York, which also followed the Nightingale plan. In 1873 the Boston Training School for Nurses became the third nurses' training school in the country founded on Nightingale principles, though its administrators engaged in "altering, cutting out and rearranging the Nightingale book to suit the American need."[89]

For all the support it enjoyed, the Boston Training School for Nurses (BTSN) also received strenuous opposition, most notably from Henry Jacob Bigelow. Bigelow shared his unsavory opinion of the school with Mrs. Parkman. She let Bigelow finish, then replied, "Verily, verily, this is the hand of Esau, but I think I hear the voice of — Henry Jacob" (a reference to the biblical Jacob who outwitted

Anna Maxwell, an early superintendent of the Boston Training School for Nurses.

his twin brother, Esau, and deceived his father, Isaac).[90] After heated debate, the MGH trustees consented to the training school's being associated with the hospital. On November 1, 1873, the school opened its doors to its first four students. Not until 23 years later would the trustees officially incorporate the school and give it the Massachusetts General name. The school's Board of Directors, headed by Martin Brimmer, included men and women. Two superintendents, a Mrs. Billings, whose first name has been lost to history, and Mary Phinney von Olnhausen, quickly came and went. The third, Linda Richards, stayed on as superintendent for three years after her appointment in November 1874.[91]

The MGH annual report for 1875 acknowledged the success of the school and the service its students provided the hospital: "The Training School for Nurses has been continued with gratifying success under the superintendence of Miss Linda Richards, and an arrangement has been made to extend its usefulness, by gradually placing all the wards in the charge of the School, under the Regulations and the pleasure of the Trustees."[92] The building known as "The Brick," originally built as an isolation ward for contagious diseases, was renovated for $3,700 in 1876 and began to serve as nurses' housing. Trustees and doctors were beginning to see the value of a well-educated nursing staff living on-site.[93] In 1879 another story was added to the building, and nurses' accommodations were enhanced.[94]

More living quarters for nurses were provided in 1883 with the construction of the three-story Thayer Building, named for MGH's vice president and benefactor Nathaniel Thayer. Thayer's wife established the Thayer Library in the building, giving nurses access to 726 books and some periodicals for their education and recreation. "The Thayer" added a fourth story in 1887 and a new wing in 1900. By the turn of the century, nurses benefited from an elevator, fire escapes, a basement gymnasium, and a rooftop sunning area in their own quarters.[95]

Uniform dress for nurses, so much a part of the image of nursing, was introduced at the Training School in 1881. The first uniform simply consisted of "caps, cuffs, and aprons with wide strings tied in a big bow at the back."[96] Before Anna Maxwell resigned as superintendent of the training school in 1889, she instituted a full uniform. The MGH historian Grace Whiting Myers wrote that Maxwell "chose a very pretty blue and white gingham. But, alas! it proved not to be serviceable, for the lovely color—the joy of all the blond nurses, but the bane of the brunettes—stood neither wear nor laundering, and about a year later it found a substitute in the fine black and white check, still worn."[97]

The new nurses were of a different caste and character than the early ones, although some time had to pass before the stigma associated with nursing faded. Sophia F. Palmer graduated from the Boston Training School for Nurses in 1878. A Milton native and direct descendant of *Mayflower* passengers, Palmer lived with her family on Beacon Hill when she enrolled at the school. Ashamed of their daughter's career path, her family refused to visit her at MGH. The training school alumna went on to a career in private nursing and became the first nurse to cross the Rockies for a patient, the daughter of the Union general Irvin McDowell. Later she cofounded the *American Journal of Nursing* with several former classmates, which she edited until her death in 1920.[98]

Nursing at McLean

The committee on admitting patients at the McLean Asylum issued a report in 1877 on the potential benefit of having its own female nursing staff. After stating the financial advantages of employing women, the report continued: "All danger of harsh treatment would be avoided. The influence of the nurses would be a soothing one much needed by irritable nerves. Our men patients come to us from the care of women, their mothers, sisters or wives. From their arrival at the Asylum, they hardly see a woman's face."[99]

In 1881 McLean employed "ward maids," whose calming presence, even in the male wards, proved beneficial for patients. Two years later the world's first training school for nurses at an asylum was established at McLean. In a 1921 centennial history of MGH, C. Macfie Campbell, an HMS professor of psychiatry and director of the Boston Psychopathic Hospital, recalled the role of McLean's Superintendent Edward Cowles: "In establishing this training school, Dr. Cowles made a very important contribution to the whole movement of mental hygiene, and to the development of public opinion. He raised the prestige of the work; he emphasized the fact that nursing the mentally sick is simply one technical branch of nursing, as psychiatry is one branch of medicine."[100]

The psychiatric branch of nursing required special flexibility. A longtime McLean nurse once told Cowles, "In a general hospital, the patient must please the nurse; with the insane the nurse must please the patient."[101] The training school at McLean graduated its first class of 16 in 1886.

Opposition to the formal training of a nursing force gradually dwindled. In their annual report of 1893, 20 years after they had ambivalently agreed to an affiliation with the BTSN, the MGH trustees called it an "admirable and successful institution."[102] On the first day of 1896 the training school's directors officially transferred management of the school to the MGH trustees. The Boston Training School for Nurses became the Massachusetts General Hospital Training School for Nurses.

Although the ancillary role of the educated nurse in the hospital continued to grow, the scientific grounding of her education was limited. Sylvia Perkins, the former assistant director and historian of the training school, described the limitations of a nurse's activity and understanding in the early twentieth century as medical research at MGH was beginning to grow:

Her functions [in assisting researchers] included collecting specimens, recording, and assisting at tests. She lacked the knowledge which could have led to more involvement, to greater understanding and accuracy, and to better care and more fruitful investigation. "This is the way we do it" is a poor substitute for comprehension of purpose and method. Despite significant improvements in the School's curriculum, science courses continued to be limited, and they were not taught by instructors who had the sound preparation of a college faculty member. Even so, there were doctors who decried the number of hours students were off the wards attending class, as well as what they considered the tendency to "over-educate" nurses.[103]

In 1895, in an attempt to weed out unqualified nurses in hospitals, the Boston Training School formed its Alumnae Association, to which all graduates of the training school would belong. The following year saw the creation of the Nurses' Associated Alumnae of the United States and Canada.[104] In less than a century since the founding of MGH, professional training was beginning to transform nursing from inept care provided by convalescent patients and women of questionable character to the educated ministration of a uniformed, trained, and nationally organized force.

The Institute of Health Professions

Flash forward to the mid-twentieth century, when Ruth Sleeper directed the school and the hospital nursing staff (for more on Sleeper and other recent nursing leaders, see chapter 8). By this time, and especially after World War II, women were demanding a liberal arts education to complement the vocational training offered at nursing schools like that at MGH. Nearby institutions, such as Boston University, offered both nursing and liberal arts, and though Mass General offered incomparable clinical training, it could never compete in liberal arts. Sleeper recognized this and in 1964 suggested that MGH consider developing a freestanding, degree-granting institution.[105] General Director John Knowles would come to agree, suggesting that the hospital develop something he called MGH University, offering advanced programs for all non-physician professionals. Charles Sanders, general director in the 1970s, took up the idea, supported by Henry Mankin, chief of orthopaedic surgery and chair of the MGH Committee on Teaching and Education, and John Lawrence, chairman of the MGH trustees. In 1975 the hospital formally petitioned the Massachusetts Board of Higher Education for degree-granting authority. At a public hearing local colleges and universities voiced opposition to the notion of a freestanding school at a local hospital; nevertheless, two years later, the petition was granted.

The official transition could now begin. In 1981 the MGH School of Nursing closed, and the Institute of Health Professions (IHP), formally commissioned the year before, became a reality. By this time IHP students had enrolled in certificate programs in physical therapy, social work, and dietetics. The first nursing students were enrolled in an IHP degree program in 1982, and the following year the IHP awarded its first advanced degree, a master's in physical therapy, then soon added a program in speech-language pathology. No longer a function of the nursing department, the IHP took on its own nonprofit corporate identity and received its first formal accreditation from the Commission on Institutions of Higher Education of the New England Association of Schools and Colleges in 1985. Over the next two decades the IHP's continued growth created the need for larger quarters, and in late 2001 the school moved from its previous quarters at 101 Merrimac Street in Boston into Building 36 at the old Charlestown Navy Yard, near MGH's Charlestown research facilities. In June 2002, on the 25th anniversary of the institute, the Catherine Filene Shouse Building—named for the foundation that made it possible with a $2 million gift—was formally dedicated.

Along with other nursing tracks and degrees, the IHP now offers a doctor of nursing practice (DNP) degree, a clinically oriented alternative to the more research-oriented PhD in nursing, focusing on advanced practice, application of clinical research, and leadership. MGH's Chief Nurse and Senior Vice President for Patient Care Services Jeanette Ives Erickson studied for her DNP at the IHP. The story of how nursing became Patient Care Services, and how an MGH nursing leader became a full-fledged member of the hospital leadership team 130 years after the Boston Training School was founded, will be taken up in chapter 8.

THE "CULT" OF ASEPSIS

After the advent of surgical anesthesia, the scene of an operating room became less grim. The outlook in the recovery room, however, was as bleak as ever. Outbreaks of infection could wipe out whole wards. When Mass General suffered an epidemic of virulent hospital gangrene in the 1860s, all surgical wards were closed. Bed sores were considered an inevitability. Surgeons and dressers, surrounded by infection as they were, often suffered from infection themselves. Death hovered around every surgical patient, and medicine lacked the means to keep it at bay.

A surgeon's ideal was to heal "by first intention," or directly following surgery, but this was the exception rather than the rule. After surgery, wounds were almost always "doing badly." Dressings were most often made of lint from used cotton or linen that had been picked to pieces by convalescent patients for that purpose. After a few days, surgical patients were generally reported to display "constitutional disturbances." The dressings would then be removed

Henry P. Bowditch (left) and J. Collins Warren.

and a large flaxseed poultice applied, at which point a "creamy" pus would ooze forth. If no erysipelas, pyemia, or septicemia occurred, the wound was reported to be doing well and would "heal from the bottom" over a course of six weeks or so.[106] Patients with wounds so rank as to offend the nostrils of other patients were moved to isolation rooms in "The Brick."

J. Collins Warren, grandson of the MGH founder and known as Coll, recalled the unhygienic practices of a *fastidious* surgeon, hastily performing a minor surgery on an unanesthetized patient: "The visiting surgeon on inspection of a wound would laconically say 'Knife!' and a fluctuating spot would be lanced or a few sinuses sliced open without further ceremony. I remember on one such occasion handing a knife from my pocket case to Dr. Hodges, who after one glance flung it on the bed and demanded contemptuously a 'clean' instrument."[107]

Any nineteenth-century surgery was life-threatening, even though surgeons rarely dug into the body's inner cavities. The most common surgeries treated dislocations, fractures, and bladder stones. Henry Jacob Bigelow was highly successful in the reduction of hip dislocations, devising a simple and bloodless method that would bear his name;[108] and he innovated the procedure of litholapaxy, or the rapid crushing and removal of bladder stones. According to a younger surgeon who watched him perform the procedure, Bigelow "devised an instrument which he could pass into the bladder through the urethra, crush the stone into small fragments, and then completely evacuate them by means of a suction apparatus without the use of the knife."[109] The current chief of urology, Scott McDougal, confirmed this: "Bigelow's genius was to learn how to evacuate stones from the bladder. With an irrigation device, he put water in and pulled water back out. An instrument with jaws was inserted blind, a screw turned, the stone crushed. The problem was, you couldn't always get the fragments out." This clever technique notwithstanding, the abdomen was terra incognita to even the most intrepid surgeon because of the extremely high incidence of postoperative infection. Only strangulated hernia usually justified abdominal surgery.[110] Until 1869 not a single MGH patient (of at least six) who had undergone ovariotomy (incision into an ovary) survived.

Starting from the work of Louis Pasteur in France and then Joseph Lister in England, the phrase "germ theory of disease" began to infiltrate medical literature, but the mainstream was slow to fathom its far-reaching implications. If a surgeon noted the radical theory, he did not change his operating habits accordingly. Before operating, surgeon and assistants would don frock coats, not surgical scrubs. Washing up was a *post*-surgical activity. Likewise, surgical instruments were cleaned after, not before surgery, and they were stored in plush cloth cases. Ward tenders used sea sponges "as clean as soap and water could make them," then tucked them away for use with the next open wound.[111]

After a few years as a house pupil at MGH, Coll Warren graduated from Harvard Medical School in 1866. Afterward, Warren spent time in Vienna, Berlin, London, and Paris. Over the course of his travels, he began to hear rumors about the use of carbolic acid. Warren admitted that at the time even the name of the substance that would revolutionize surgery was unknown to him.[112] The meeting that most impressed Warren was with Joseph Lister at the surgeon's home in

Glasgow. Lister showed the rising young American his methods for using carbolic acid as an antiseptic agent in the healing of wounds after surgery. At the time, Lister separated his carbolized plaster dressings from direct contact with wounds using a protective layer of waterproof material permeable to the acid's vapors. At one point during the interview, Lister turned to the young Warren and said, "I do not expect my contemporaries to accept all my doctrines, but I look to the coming generation to adopt and perfect them."[113]

When Warren, a member of that coming generation, returned home bearing the Lister dressings he was so eager to introduce to his hometown, the established surgeons of Boston met Lister's expectations. They spurned the "cult" of antisepsis, to which many claimed the young hotspurs accorded excessive importance. Warren was quickly informed that "the 'carbolic acid treatment' had already been tried and discarded."[114] The "germ theory of disease" was still regarded as speculative medicine.

Twenty years would pass before the Lister approach was fully incorporated into Boston surgical practice. J. M. T. Finney was assigned to the West Surgical Service at MGH in 1888 at a time when the three visiting surgeons, members of the old guard, were Charles Burnham Porter, John Homans, and Arthur T. Cabot. A mentor would tell Finney: "Well, that is an excellent combination, Dr. Porter, Dr. Cabot, and Dr. Homans. From Dr. Porter you will learn how to operate, from Dr. Cabot you will learn how to take care of your patients after operation, and from Dr. Homans you will learn what not to do—and I fancy you will probably learn more from him than from either of the others."[115] Finney would remember one other interesting figure in the MGH OR: "Old Jim Mains, the head orderly in the operating room, had an advanced case of paralysis agitans (shaking palsy), but he could do more with a struggling, half-etherized patient than anyone I ever saw."[116]

Finney recognized the late 1880s and early 1890s as a transition period for surgery:

> The antiseptic solutions, carbolic acid and bichloride of mercury, were used freely in irrigating the wounds, which were closed in nearly every case with drainage tubes. They were usually needed, as infections, blood poisoning and septicemia, were of common occurrence. The healing of a wound by primary union (that is, without pus formation) was always a matter of comment. . . .
>
> The technique then employed in preparing for an operation was to shave the skin of the patient in the region to be operated upon, wash the skin with soap and water, apply bichloride solution 1:1000, protect the area around the field of operation with towels and then proceed with the operation. The hands of the surgeon and the assistants had first been washed not too vigorously with soap and water and rinsed in bichloride or carbolic acid solution. The operating surgeons were not dressed in clean white suits, as they are now. Instead the style was black Prince Albert coats buttoned up tight. These were kept in a closet in the operating amphitheater and rarely, if ever, cleaned, and showed ample evidence of previous hard service in the spots of dried blood and pus that covered them. . . . No wonder then that drainage tubes and suppuration were the order of the day in practically all operative wounds.[117]

Antiseptic dressings were not the only development that surgeons in Boston and elsewhere hesitated to use. The microbiology of the physician Robert Koch paved the way for the "rule of scrubbing" in German operating rooms. Only slowly did basic hygienic practices become commonplace in Boston's hospital wards and operating rooms. Rubber glove use was long dismissed as frivolous. In 1898, prompted by a large number of septic cases, surgeons and surgical assistants began using rubber gloves.[118]

The advent of antisepsis and then asepsis, the maintenance of a sterile operating environment, opened up a new world to surgeons: the abdominal cavity. Samuel Cabot performed the first successful ovariotomy at MGH on May 30, 1869. He used cotton soaked in carbolic oil to cover the incision.[119] In the 1870s John Homans, brother of the MGH visiting surgeon Charles D. Homans, made a name for himself as the leading ovariotomist of Boston. The senior surgeons of MGH still considered the surgery dubious. (Cabot's patient was the only survivor among the nine ovariotomy patients in MGH history to that point.) When John Homans finally received an appointment as a visiting surgeon at MGH (he had been denied once before on the grounds that two surgeon brothers simultaneously practicing at the same hospital were one too many), he was required to forgo admitting any of his ovariotomy patients to the hospital.[120] The question of abdominal surgery at the hospital arose again, and was again dismissed, this time because the new surgical procedures required new operating rooms and surgical wards, and the existing surgical facilities were not suited to such invasive surgery. To keep up with new developments in medicine and surgery, Mass General would need to modernize its facilities.

ORTHOPAEDICS FROM EARLY SPECIALTY TO MULTIPLE SUBSPECIALTIES

Until the middle of the twentieth century, most surgical leaders at MGH frowned on specialization; a surgeon, they believed, should be able to meet any crisis and treat any part of the body. Specialization was seen as a sort of youthful rebellion, or as the way an outsider could break into the club. But a Boston surgeon was born a surgeon—a Brahmin who inherited steady hands from his surgeon father.

Some specialties did develop, however slowly. The practice of orthopaedic surgery at MGH has a curious history. Early surgeons with an interest in what we know today as orthopaedics included the enigmatic Henry Jacob Bigelow, who otherwise decried specialization. Bigelow pioneered a method of reducing traumatic hip dislocations. But it was a father-son team that is credited with getting the discipline of orthopaedics off the ground. John Ball Brown, a consulting surgeon at MGH, founded the Boston Orthopedique Infirmary in 1838, the first American hospital with an orthopaedic focus. Brown's son, Buckminster Brown, is widely considered the first American orthopaedic surgeon. He endowed the first American professorship in orthopaedic surgery at Harvard in 1892.[121]

In June 1887, 35 charter members convened in New York to form the American Orthopaedic Association (AOA). In the same year E. H. Bradford, Robert Lovett, and Buckminster Brown established a discrete Department of Orthopaedic

Pavilion wards erected southwest of Bulfinch beginning in 1873.

Surgery at Boston Children's Hospital. Thirteen years later the MGH trustees created the position of consulting orthopaedic surgeon and appointed Joel E. Goldthwait. A new Outpatient Department Building on Fruit Street opened in 1903, and four years later orthopaedics achieved department status at MGH, with an outpatient clinic in the basement of the Outpatient Building. Goldthwait was named surgeon of the new department.[122] Carter Rowe remembered, "It seemed as if the orthopaedic clinic was always 'in the basement.'"[123] Thornton Brown recalled that in the late 1920s and 1930s the space was "limited and gloomy. . . . Its stall-like examining rooms, separated by partial partitions of darkened varnished oak, provided little in the way of privacy and comfort."

Goldthwait meanwhile raised $70,000 to build an orthopaedic ward. Ward I (the letter, not the numeral) opened on November 6, 1907, and featured a total of 18 beds, nine for men and nine for women. (As the following section explains, Ward I was one of a series of freestanding, pavilion-style wards built of brick and sprawling on the grounds southwest of Bulfinch in the late nineteenth century.) Here the sexes were separated by a room with four cribs. The basement housed its operating, sterilizing, and plaster rooms. Ward I served as the headquarters for the Orthopaedic Department until 1940, when the department moved to the fifth floor of the new White Building. Ward I, most recently used by the Physical Therapy Department, was the last standing brick ward on the MGH campus, torn down in 1990 to create space for the Ellison Tower.[124] The ward cost $40,000 to build, and the balance of Goldthwait's money was used to establish the Orthopaedic Fund, whose income would be used for orthopaedic research.[125]

Physical therapy at MGH began during this period, with the establishment in 1907 of the Zander Room (or Medico-Mechanical Department) for "electrotherapy, hydrotherapy, massage and gymnastics."[126] The room was located in the basement of the new outpatient building and held 36 apparatuses for resistance exercise designed by the Swedish doctor Gustav Zander, as well as "numerous hot air baths for limbs."[127] During World War I MGH discontinued its use of the Zander system. Physical therapy at MGH did not resume until 1940, when Arthur Watkins, a recent graduate of the MGH neurological residency, was appointed chief of physical therapy. Watkins instituted a physical therapy training program in collaboration with Simmons College, Children's Hospital, and Brigham and Women's Hospital.

The MGH Brace Shop (or the Surgical Appliance Shop) opened in 1908 in the basement of the new Bradlee Surgical Building. In 1916 the shop included a smithy, a leather room, a finishing room, and a nickel-plating room. Its staff comprised a blacksmith, a harness maker, and two "finishers."[128] In 1937 the brace shop moved to a site adjacent to the Charles Street Jail,[129] where it served both the hospital and Beacon Hill patients until it was relocated to the first floor of the Gray Building in 1980. Paul Norton and Thornton Brown developed an important lumbar spine brace called the Norton-Brown brace, which was constructed at the Brace Shop.

In 1922 the surgical laboratory moved, vacating space in the main operating room. Orthopaedic surgical procedures, which until then had been conducted in the basement of Ward I, across the hall from the conference room, were thereafter performed in the same building as general surgery.

Goldthwait was succeeded as orthopaedic surgeon by Elliott Brackett. Brought over from Children's Hospital, Brackett in 1911 became the first chief of orthopaedics at MGH. He served as chief until 1919, when Robert Osgood took over. In 1917 Osgood and his fellow MGH orthopaedic surgeon Charles Scudder cofounded the MGH Fracture Clinic, the first of its kind in the country and possibly the world. When Osgood left MGH in 1922 to head orthopaedics at Children's Hospital, the department recruited Nathaniel Allison from Barnes Hospital and Washington University in Saint Louis to serve as its new chief.

A Boston Original

One of the most controversial—and brilliant—MGH surgeons in this early period, with no small expertise in orthopaedics, was Ernest Amory Codman, an innovator whose career was nearly ruined by his stubbornness and a provocative cartoon. Born a Brahmin in 1869, he graduated from Harvard Medical School in 1895 and became a surgical trainee and then a surgical staff member at MGH. He was a pioneer in six fields: anesthesiology, radiology, duodenal ulcer surgery, orthopaedic oncology, shoulder surgery, and the study of medical outcomes.[130]

Codman and a fellow medical student, Harvey Cushing (a pioneer of neurosurgery who had a distinguished career at Johns Hopkins and especially at the Peter Bent Brigham Hospital), were the first to keep careful records on administration of anesthesia, on what they called "ether charts." Fascinated by the new field of X-rays, Codman became one of the nation's first "skiagraphers" (radiologists), and he published the first atlas of normal skeletal radiographs. He founded the Registry of Bone Sarcoma at MGH.[131] Codman's textbook, *The Shoulder: Rupture of the Supraspinatus Tendon and Other Lesions in or about the Subacromial Bursa*, published in 1934, became a classic of orthopaedic literature. He was the first to describe benign chondroblastoma of the shoulder, later known as Codman's Tumor.

Ernest Amory Codman.

Codman's greatest legacy, however, was his passionate insistence that physicians and hospitals track and acknowledge errors to improve outcomes. "Much of [Codman's] professional life was dedicated to convincing his surgical colleagues that the proof of success of a surgical procedure depended on the follow-up of the patient, and not on the reputation of the surgeon, or his seniority on the staff of this hospital."[132] Codman emphasized that every hospital should follow up with each of its patients to determine the success of treatment. He himself kept "End Result Cards" stored in an elaborate filing system.[133]

Codman also argued that resistance to specialization dampened scientific progress at MGH. As he noted in a minority report to the trustees, "Our ideal should be to have some one member of the Hospital Staff doing as good work as any one in the community or in fact in the country, in each of the special branches of surgery. . . . At present, we do not see correctly where our individual interests lie and rather than allow the Massachusetts Hospital to advance in stomach surgery, for instance, we each prefer to take our individual try at it."[134]

Angered by what he saw as Mass General's reluctance to study end results, Codman resigned in 1911. He opened his own 12-bed hospital at 15 Pinckney Street on Beacon Hill, publishing a promotional brochure entitled "Medical Ethics of the Codman Hospital."[135] He published his outcomes and promised to refund fees if outcomes were bad. In January 1915, while chairing a meeting of the Suffolk District Surgical Society, Codman unveiled a three-foot-by-six-foot-eight-inch cartoon drawn on brown wrapping paper depicting an ostrich with its head in the sand kicking golden eggs (patient fees) to Boston physicians, while the MGH trustees and President Lowell of Harvard looked on. One of the captions reads: "If we let her know the results of our patients do you suppose she would still be willing to lay?" The cartoon caused an uproar; Codman was ostracized and his practice suffered.[136]

After treating soldiers during World War I and victims of the 1918 influenza pandemic, Codman struggled to keep up his Boston practice. He and his wife never had children, and he died in 1940 of melanoma, possibly caused by repeated exposure to X-rays. He received little appreciation during his lifetime. "In fact," wrote Bill Mallon in his biography of Codman, "his efforts to reform medical science by starting the field of outcome studies brought him mostly ridicule, censure and poverty."[137]

Today Codman is acknowledged as a pioneer in outcomes study; the committee on hospital standards that he founded and led for the American College of Surgeons later evolved into the Joint Commission for Accreditation of Hospital

Organizations. The commission's most prestigious quality award bears his name. Codman "would have been the most important person in American surgery in that era if he had had an ounce of diplomacy, but he was not inclined to compromise," noted David Torchiana, chairman and chief executive officer of the Massachusetts General Physicians Organization.

Into the Modern Era

In the early twentieth century orthopaedic surgeons could do much less to help their patients than they can today. Orthopaedic treatment was largely supportive. Before the advent of the polio vaccine, many patients crippled by the disease needed tendon transfers, braces, and casts. Osteomyelitis, a bacterial infection of bone or bone marrow, could be drained but was dangerous. The stainless steel used in open reductions was high in iron and corroded easily. As the range of technology, materials, and surgical methods broadened in the latter half of the 1930s, however, "orthopaedic surgery began to change gradually from a strap-and-buckle service to a surgical one, as surgeons were becoming expertly trained."[138]

Marius N. Smith-Petersen, a giant in the field whose name became synonymous with orthopaedics at MGH, served as chief from Nathaniel Allison's departure for the University of Chicago in 1929 until 1947. Smith-Petersen was an innovator. His development of the three-flanged hip nail was one of the single most important innovations in orthopaedic surgery. The high mortality rate associated with hip fractures earned them the moniker "old lady's friend." The nail obviated the Whitman plaster hip spica, a large cast from mid-torso to knee that caused many complications, most significantly deep-vein thrombosis, which could lead to a fatal pulmonary embolism. Smith-Petersen's invention paved the way for orthopaedic surgeons to develop a wide range of nails, many still used today.

The hip spica did not fall entirely out of use, however. One night in the 1930s an inebriated resident returned to the resident quarters and

Nathaniel Allison (left) and Marius Smith-Petersen.

awoke his overworked, sleeping colleagues, a violation he had committed many times. The unfortunate resident passed out on the pool table and woke the next morning hung over and immobilized in a plaster hip spica. His fellow residents informed him that he had fallen four stories from a window the previous night and had fractured his femur. The spica was removed later that day and the prank revealed.[139]

In 1916, during his orthopaedic residency at Children's Hospital, Smith-Petersen had assisted at an open reduction of a child's congenital hip dislocation. He later recalled: "The hip was exposed through a Kocher incision; it was bloody. It was brutal. The patient survived by a very narrow margin. . . . I said to my senior, Dr. Roy Abbott, 'There must be some other way of exposing the hip.' 'Why don't you figure it out?' was his answer."[140]

Smith-Petersen accepted the challenge, and to practice his "bloodless" method, procured a "nice lean hip" from Harvard Medical School, which he tucked away in a basement room of Ward I. The new method of incision that he developed came to be known as the anterior Smith-Petersen incision. His work between 1937 and 1939 led to the first successful hip arthroplasty, a biologic restoration of diseased or arthritic joints, with a cup inserted between the ball and the socket of the hip to allow cartilage to grow. Vitallium, a lightweight, corrosion-resistant alloy developed in 1932, was an ideal material for orthopaedic surgery, as it rarely caused reactions. The vitallium cup or mold arthroplasty proved to be one of the twentieth century's key innovations in orthopaedic surgery.

Otto Aufranc, Smith-Petersen's longtime associate, would succeed him in leading hip surgery at MGH. In so doing, Aufranc ushered in the subspecialization of MGH orthopaedics, according to the latter-day orthopaedist and historian of the department James Herndon.[141] Aufranc made innumerable advances in cup arthroplasty, and after his departure, William Harris took up the torch. Harris was among the first to adopt the total hip replacement technique in lieu of cup arthroplasty. His Harris Hip Rating method is internationally accepted as the standard method of hip evaluation.[142]

Another technique pioneered by Smith-Petersen was spinal osteotomy, to correct severe spinal curvature. Perhaps his most daring innovation, the procedure involves breaking the patient's neck or lumbar spine and realigning it; the threat of paralysis always looms. Spinal osteotomy is still a highly selective and risky surgery.

Smith-Petersen was exacting with himself, with his coworkers and residents, and with his patients. His three orthopaedic residents at MGH, Otto Aufranc, Carroll Larson, and Carter Rowe, benefited from his mentorship, and all became significant contributors in the field. Smith-Petersen refused overweight patients for elective surgery. In his view, a patient who lacked the discipline to maintain a healthy weight would also fail to follow through with the necessary postoperative physical therapy. Nevertheless, Smith-Petersen had a remarkable bedside manner, and he endeared himself to his patients. Henry Beecher remembered him in the operating room as "a brilliant, intuitive improviser."[143]

From the founding of the Fracture Clinic within the Department of Surgery in 1919, MGH had been a hub for fracture care. In 1947 Edwin Cave became the first orthopaedic surgeon with sole responsibility for the Fracture Clinic. Phil Wilson Sr., an early leader of the Fracture Clinic, instituted the MGH Fracture Course, a monthlong course in fractures taught by MGH orthopaedic and general surgeons. The teaching model was adopted by the American College of Surgeons, which set up training courses in conjunction with its annual meetings. In turn, the American Academy of Orthopaedic Surgeons employed the teaching method established in the MGH Fracture Course in its annual lecture series, which thousands of orthopaedic surgeons attend every year.

Raising the Barr

Following Smith-Petersen, Joseph Seaton Barr served as chief of the Orthopaedic Service from 1946 until 1964. In collaboration with the neurologist Jason Mixter (see chapter 7), Barr discovered that sciatica was due to a herniated disc. Barr broadened the scope of the department, expanded clinical activity, and established a basic science research laboratory in orthopaedics. Barr's close relationship with the chief of orthopaedics at Children's Hospital, William Green, benefited both departments. Barr was appointed the John B. and Buckminster Brown professor of orthopaedic surgery at HMS in 1948, and he was elected president of the American Academy of Orthopaedic Surgeons in 1951.

Melvin Glimcher served as chief of the Orthopaedic Service from 1965 to 1970. After his residency in orthopaedics, Glimcher had taken additional training at MIT, where he investigated the process of bone formation from collagen. Glimcher would establish one of the world's first orthopaedic research labs using new techniques of molecular biology and contributing to basic science as few orthopaedists anywhere had done before him. Appointed the first Edith M. Ashley professor of orthopaedic surgery in October 1965, Glimcher saw his department publish more than 100 scholarly papers during his tenure.

In 1969, under Glimcher's leadership, William H. Harris established a basic science research lab, which continues to operate 42 years later as the Harris Orthopaedics Laboratories (HOL). Although focused today primarily on biomechanics and biomaterials research, the lab's guiding philosophy has always been "to go wherever the problem takes us." This philosophy has led to groundbreaking work on preventing fatal pulmonary emboli. Wide-ranging efforts aimed at combating these problems resulted in record low rates of infection, of mortality, and of loosening of components. Over 40 years, HOL has continued to study the erosion of bone around the prosthesis. It was discovered that this erosion was caused by a macrophage response to tiny wear particles of polyethylene. HOL was first to establish the key aspects of the molecular biology of this adverse reaction and followed that critical observation with the creation of a new polyethylene that dramatically reduced both wear and bone erosion. Now, more than 2 million total-hip and total-knee patients worldwide walk on this new material. Currently under the direction of Orhun Muratoglu and Henrik Malchau, HOL continues to develop better polyethylenes and hydrogels for human implantation.

A blood relative of John Ball and Buckminster Brown, Thornton Brown joined the MGH orthopaedic staff in 1958, after his residency there. He served

twice as interim chief of the Orthopaedic Service: once before Melvin Glimcher,
1964–1965, and a second time, 1970–1972,
before Henry Mankin took over. Brown
served as editor in chief of the *Journal of
Bone and Joint Surgery*, following in the
footsteps of William Rogers, an associate of
Smith-Petersen from MGH.[144]

When Henry Mankin arrived at MGH
in 1972 to become the new chief of the
Orthopaedic Service, he expanded the
department's subspecialties of pediatric
orthopaedics, hand surgery, and orthopaedic oncology. A bone oncologist himself,
Mankin brought several orthopaedic sur-

Henry Mankin.

geons from the Hospital for Joint Diseases in New York, including Richard Smith
in hand surgery, Michael Ehrlich in pediatric orthopaedics, and Robert Leffert in
upper extremity problems. Orthopaedic oncology, headed by Mankin for many
years, is now led by Francis Hornicek. The MGH Center for Sarcoma and Connective Tissue Oncology is one of the largest in the world, having treated more
than 25,000 patients with a vast array of disorders, and it accomplishes important
research in limb-sparing procedures, often using allograft replacement. The unit
has performed more than 1,500 such procedures. The hospital boasts one of the
world's largest bone banks, established by Mankin and later run by William Tomford.[145] Today basic research in orthopaedic oncology includes the development
of a fresh frozen tumor tissue bank, containing more than 1,000 specimens used
in research.

For years the establishment of a children's orthopaedic service at MGH had
seemed unnecessary because of close collaboration between the orthopaedic
departments at MGH and Children's Hospital. Michael Ehrlich was recruited
to become the first chief of the MGH Pediatric Orthopedic Unit, a position he
held from 1972 to 1989. While establishing a dedicated clinical unit for children,
Ehrlich was also noted for being a dedicated teacher of residents and medical students. His research contributions included studies in the enzymology of cartilage
metabolism. David Zaleske joined the pediatric unit in 1981. His research interests were in growth plate reconstruction and transplantation as well as the developmental biology and tissue engineering of joints. When Ehrlich was recruited
to Brown University in 1989, Zaleske was appointed chief of the MGH Pediatric
Orthopedic Unit. In 2001 Brian Grottkau became chief of the service, and he
along with Maurice Albright reestablished the unit's clinical volume and increased
the service's outpatient and surgical volume. Additionally, Grottkau established
the Pediatric Orthopaedic Laboratory for Tissue Engineering and Regenerative
Medicine, a translational research laboratory, at MGH.

In hand surgery, Richard J. Smith led the way, beginning from his appointment by Mankin in the early 1970s until his untimely death in 1987. After these

initial years of growth, Smith was succeeded as chief by Richard Gelberman and then, in 1995, by Jesse Jupiter. Robert Leffert, a leader in shoulder problems, together with Jupiter in hand surgery, made MGH a world-class center for care of patients with upper-extremity problems. Jupiter has been an innovator in the field of hand surgery for more than three decades. He has contributed numerous operative techniques and implants for complex fractures and reconstructive dilemmas of the hand and upper extremity.

Today the Hand and Upper Extremity Service receives more than 11,000 outpatient visits and performs more than 2,000 surgical procedures per year. Clinical problems treated cover a spectrum including congenital deformities, arthritic conditions, nerve injuries and compressions, and microvascular repair and reconstructive surgery. Traumatic and reconstructive problems in the elbow and wrist account for a large proportion of regional referrals. An annual lectureship named for Smith brings world-renowned hand and upper-extremity surgeons to MGH.

In addition to growth in the clinical arena, the MGH Orthopaedic Service became a center for teaching. Mankin held a daily breakfast with residents at 6:30 A.M. and instituted the annual Thesis Day, at which each graduating resident would present a paper on a special interest before the department. He established a journal club, which served as a forum for informal discussion of current important articles in orthopaedic literature; two courses for orthopaedic residents at hospitals throughout New England (Pathology and Basic Science, and Prosthetics and Orthotics); heavy weekly teaching rounds; and the Robert Bayley Osgood Lecture in the spring and the Richard Jay Smith Lecture in the fall.[146]

Sports Medicine

The 1960s and 1970s saw the emergence of another orthopaedic specialty, sports medicine, a development that not only benefited the elite athlete and the weekend warrior, but also had an influence on games themselves by fostering new protective gear and safety protocols for athletes. These developments can be traced

Bert Zarins.

to the foresight of the general surgeon Augustus Thorndike, who joined the staff in 1921. As a physician for Harvard University's athletic department, he became alarmed by the injuries he treated, particularly football injuries. So in addition to developing treatments like the Thorndike shoulder brace, he improved taping and bandaging techniques to better protect joints and ligaments from injury. He also helped develop the suspension helmet for football players and first suggested that a physician be on hand at every athletic contest. Though it would take several more decades for sports medicine to be recognized as its own field, Thorndike raised awareness that a game could produce lifelong health problems, which could be avoided with the right equipment and treatment.[147]

Carter Rowe, a shoulder specialist, carried on Thorndike's work. In the 1960s Rowe and MGH physicians forged a relationship with the Boston Bruins, serving as the hockey team's orthopaedic consultants and operating on such NHL legends as Bobby Orr and Phil Esposito.

Bertram Zarins joined the MGH sports medicine unit in 1976 and, with Dinesh Patel, was among the first to use arthroscopy, a technique allowing surgeons to look inside the knee or other joint and to operate without making a major incision. Zarins was hired as team orthopaedist for the

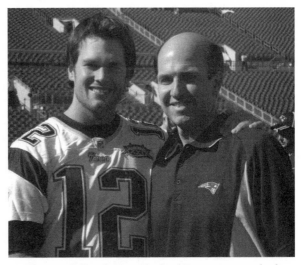

Thomas Gill with New England Patriots quarterback Tom Brady. Gill treated Brady after his season-ending knee injury in 2008.

Boston Bruins and started the first Sports Medicine Clinic at MGH, adding a Runner's Clinic in 1979. In 1982 he became team physician for the New England Patriots football team as well as for the Boston Bruins, and in 1984 he was appointed head physician for the U.S. Olympic Team at the Winter Olympics in Sarajevo. As the media reported on the astonishingly rapid recovery of prominent athletes from potentially career-ending injuries, the general public took notice. "The pros were getting arthroscopic surgery and it was in the news and other people were demanding it," Zarins recalled. In 1982 Zarins was appointed chief of the newly established Sports Medicine Service, one of the few such units in the country.

Arthur Boland, who joined the MGH staff in 1986, is a distinguished contributor to the Sports Medicine Service. Boland had been appointed surgeon for the Harvard Athletic Department in 1969 and head team physician for Harvard University in 1975. Elected president of the American Orthopaedic Society for Sports Medicine (AOSSM), Boland in 2000 was the recipient of this organization's Mr. Sports Medicine Award. In 2005 Boland was inducted into the AOSSM's Hall of Fame, the society's highest honor.

Thomas Gill IV joined the MGH Sports Medicine staff in 1999 and soon became the team physician for the Boston Breakers professional women's soccer team. Appointed medical director for the World Champion Boston Red Sox baseball team in 2005 and head team physician for the New England Patriots in 2006, Gill has continued to conduct a research-based practice of sports medicine, thereby expanding the service's investigative mission. The Sports Medicine Research Program works closely with the Orthopaedic Bioengineering Laboratory, under the direction of Guoan Li, and with the Laboratory for Musculoskeletal Tissue Engineering, under the direction of Mark Randolph. In June 2007 Zarins stepped down after 25 years as chief of the service, and Gill was named his successor.

Today, MGH continues to strengthen its commitment to sports medicine care. In September 2006 MGH opened its state-of-the-art Sports Medicine Center at 175 Cambridge Street in Boston. The new center enables the service to offer comprehensive care to people at all levels of activity, with space for orthopaedic surgeons and primary care physicians. With satellites in Foxboro and Waltham, Massachusetts, the service continues to provide care for the Boston Red Sox, New England Patriots, Boston Bruins, and New England Revolution professional teams, as well as several local colleges and high schools and amateur athletes of all ages and abilities.

Orthopaedics Today

In 1996 Henry Mankin retired as chief of the department after more than two decades of leadership, although he continued to be chief of the Orthopaedic Oncology Service until 2000. Harry E. Rubash, who had trained at the University of Pittsburgh, MGH, and Rechts der Isar Hospital in Munich, Germany, became chief of the Department of Orthopaedic Surgery in 1998. As director of the Joint Replacement Service at the University of Pittsburgh, Rubash had performed more than 3,500 total joint arthroplasties, fueling his interest in the biomechanics and failure mechanisms of total joint arthroplasty in the hip and knee. He developed several new reconstructive techniques for acetabular fractures, acetabular and femoral hip component revisions, primary and revision knee surgeries, and periprosthetic osteolysis.

With the support and encouragement of James Herndon, chairman of the Department of Orthopaedic Surgery for Partners HealthCare (see chapter 7), Rubash has led the MGH Orthopaedic Service into new areas both clinically and in the laboratory. In 1999 the Orthopaedic Trauma Service got off to a flying start when the internationally renowned traumatologist Mark Vrahas was hired as Partners' chief of Orthopaedic Trauma Services to develop the service from one run

by chief residents to one directed by specialists. The mission was to develop a combined clinical trauma service across the Brigham and Women's Hospital and MGH. Vrahas held dual roles from 1999 to 2001 as both Partners' and MGH's Orthopaedic Trauma Service chief. In 2001 he recruited Malcolm Smith from the St. James's University Hospital (Leeds, U.K.) as chief of the MGH service. In addition to his extraordinary clinical skills, Smith brought with him a reputation as a highly regarded educator. Today, Vrahas, Smith, and David Lhowe constitute the full-time MGH orthopaedic trauma faculty. Under their leadership, several Harvard combined orthopaedic residents have chosen to subspecialize in trauma, and the fellowship program in orthopaedic trauma has become one of the most popular in the field, attracting top talent.

Harry Rubash.

Three new laboratories have opened during the first years of Rubash's leadership:

- The Orthopaedic Bioengineering Laboratory was established in 1998 by Guoan Li, who now has joint faculty appointments at the Harvard Medical School and Massachusetts Institute of Technology. Notably, Li has focused on the novel application of robotic technology to the in vitro motion simulation of the human upper and lower extremity. Using this robotic technology, the laboratory pioneered the investigation of human knee function in high-flexion angles and revealed many factors that hinder deep flexion after total knee arthroplasty. Additionally, the laboratory was the first to generate a new conceptual technology for ACL reconstruction—the single-tunnel double-bundle ACL reconstruction.

- The Laboratory for Musculoskeletal Tissue Engineering was founded in 2002 under Mark Randolph and Thomas Gill to focus on cartilage repair and regeneration in the knee. Cartilage has a limited capacity to heal because of its innate lack of vascular supply, which prevents a normal inflammatory process and healing response. Developing the use of chondrocytes to promote a healing response in cartilage lesions, the lab's research team received the 2004 Hughston Award for the best paper published in the *American Journal of Sports Medicine*. The group also focuses on developing new photochemically cross-linked hydrogels for articular cartilage repair and regeneration. Working with the Wellman Center of Photomedicine, the group has developed a novel means to photo-cross-link collagen gel for use as an encapsulation gel for chondrocytes and neocartilage formation. The laboratory continues to expand into new areas of musculoskeletal tissue engineering and regeneration.

- In 2010 the Laboratory for Musculoskeletal Research and Innovation was established under the direction of S. Adam Hacking to address critical issues in orthopaedics and to develop technologies for improving patient care. Hacking brings in vivo and in vitro expertise in bone tissue engineering, biomaterials development and analysis, fracture and graft healing, and implant osseointegration. His work at MGH focuses on novel methods to fight implant infection; methods to enhance implant fixation; the use of noninvasive techniques to assess skeletal integrity and implant fixation; methods to improve defect healing, fracture healing, and allograft incorporation; and the use of microfabrication techniques to generate bone from its fundamental unit, the osteon. The Laboratory for Musculoskeletal Research and Innovation collaborates with the Wyss Institute for Biologically Inspired Engineering, Draper Laboratories, the Department of Physics at the University of Helsinki, and researchers at Harvard-MIT Health Sciences and Technology (HST).

In 2004 the MGH Orthopaedics Department moved to the newly opened Yawkey Center for Outpatient Care, increasing its clinical space from 16,000 square feet in five locations to 32,000 square feet in a single contiguous one. Orthopaedic services continued to expand, including the Orthopedic Ambulatory

Surgery Center in the Mass General West building in Waltham in 2006; the Mass General North Shore Medical Center for Outpatient Care in Danvers in 2009; and MGH's Orthopaedic and Rehabilitation Services at the Brigham and Women's/Mass General Health Care Center at Patriot Place, a multispecialty ambulatory health care center in Foxboro, Massachusetts. In 2010 MGH was designated a "Blue Distinction Center" for spine surgery and knee and hip replacement by Blue Cross and Blue Shield, a designation given to medical facilities demonstrating consistent, reliable care and better overall outcomes.

With world-class specialists in hands, feet and ankles, shoulders, arthroplasty, orthopaedic oncology, orthopaedic trauma, orthopaedic spine, pediatric orthopaedics and sports medicine, the department has been consistently ranked as the best in New England and one of the top four in the country by *U.S. News and World Report.*

"Many great orthopaedic surgeons have graced the halls of the MGH and their legacy is reflected in the work we continue today," Rubash told colleagues in his annual message in the *Orthopaedic Journal* at the Harvard Medical School in 2003. "As a Department, we continue to take tremendous pride in providing our patients with the highest quality of orthopaedic care and in training orthopaedic surgeons who contribute to both basic and translational research."[148]

A GROWING CAMPUS

The surgical boom that followed the introduction of ether and the advent of antisepsis generated a need for more operating space and facilities to accommodate new procedures. In 1868 a new operating theater was completed at MGH, featuring rooms for surgical preparation, etherization, recovery, sulfur baths, and outpatient surgery; a private operating room; and personal offices for physicians and surgeons.[149]

After much prodding from physicians to increase patient accommodations, the trustees commissioned two new wards in 1873, at a projected cost of $15,000. Ward A, named the Warren Ward for the recently deceased J. Mason Warren, was to be an open ward. Ward B, known as the Jackson Ward in honor of the late James Jackson, would serve two purposes: half the rooms were reserved for private patients, the other half were for isolation cases.

Wards A and B were one-story buildings constructed according to the pavilion plan advocated by Florence Nightingale. Proper ventilation and heating were essential to these buildings, which stood southwest of Bulfinch and just west of the operating room, on land that extended to Charles Street and the Charles River just beyond. They were built of temporary materials. Common medical wisdom of the day indicated that the wards would become "hospitalized" (contaminated) in six or seven years, after which time they would no longer be fit for use. The new wards, something like army field hospitals, were applauded for their construction and ventilation.[150]

The following year doctors recommended that the Jackson Ward be used exclusively for private patients at the cost of $35 per week and that a new ward be

Ward A, the first of the pavilion wards, 1885.

built for isolation. The trustees consented, and Ward C (the Bigelow Ward) was built.[151] It stood directly west of Bulfinch and formed the peak of a triangle with Wards A and B to its south. In 1875 an additional ward for isolated patients went up and was named Ward D, or the Townsend Ward, in honor of the late MGH surgeon Solomon D. Townsend. Ward D stood directly west of Ward C. Like A and B, both C and D followed the pavilion plan.

In 1874 construction began of a new autopsy building that would double as a mortuary. The Allen Street House, as it came to be known, was a brick building north of Bulfinch West that also provided offices for the staff attending the pathological cabinet (about which more below).[152] This inaugurated a more than 60-year period at MGH when the words *Allen Street* had a morbid connotation.[153] The addition of a new pathology building alongside in 1896 only heightened the associations for some. As Claude Welch would recall graphically from the perspective of the 1920s: "The street side of the pathology building was essentially a solid red brick wall. There were only two openings, a small door through which the workers passed and a larger one, which accommodated hearses and periodically opened to disgorge them and their resident corpses. To me, the rear end of the hospital suggested a set of thrombosed hemorrhoids and the attendant discharge of effluvia. To 'go to Allen Street' therefore meant to be covered with a sheet and taken to the morgue."[154]

Edgar Allan Poe might have taken to Allen Street, but it was Lewis Thomas who finally took up the quill. The 1937 edition of the HMS yearbook, the *Aesculapiad*, contains his ode to Allen Street, of which we offer here Cantos I and II:

Canto I: Prelude

Oh, Beacon Street is wide and neat, and open to the sky—
Commonwealth exudes good health and, never knows a sigh—
Scollay Square, that lecher's share, is noisy but alive—
While sin and domesticity are blended on Park Drive—
And he who toils on Boylston Street will have another day
To pay his lease and live in peace, along the Riverway—
A thoroughfare without a care is Cambridge Avenue
Where ladies fair let down their hair for passers-by to view—
Some things are done on Huntington, no sailor would deny,
Which can't be done on battleships, no matter how you try—
Oh, many, many roads there are, that leap into the mind
(Like Sumner Tunnel, that monstrous funnel, impossible to find!)
And all are strange to ponder on, and beautiful to know
And all are filled with living folk, who eat and breathe and grow.

Canto II

But let us speak of Allen Street—that strangest, darkest turn,
Which squats behind a hospital, mysterious and stern.
It lies within a silent place, with open arms it waits
For patients who aren't leaving by the customary gates.
It concentrates on end results and caters to the guest
Who's battled long with his disease and come out second best.
For in a well-run hospital, there's no such thing as death.
There may be stoppage of the heart, and absence of the breath—
But no one dies! No patient tries this disrespectful feat.
He simply sighs, rolls up his eyes, and goes to Allen Street.
Whatever be his ailment—whate'er his sickness be,
From "Too, too, too much insulin" to "What's this in his pee?"
From "Gastric growth," "One lung (or both)," or "Question of Cirrhosis"
To "Exitus undiagnosed," or "Generalized Necrosis"—
He hides his head and leaves his bed, and covered with a sheet,
He rolls through doors, down corridors, and goes to Allen Street.
And there he'll find a refuge kind, a quiet sanctuary,
For Allen Street's that final treat—the local mortuary.[155]

In 1882 MGH construction along Allen Street (now part of Blossom Street) continued, when the long-felt need for adequate accommodations for student nurses was recognized, and the Thayer Building was built exclusively for them, at a cost of $35,000.[156]

Another addition to MGH real estate was a convalescent hospital, which opened in Waverley, now part of Belmont, Massachusetts, in 1882. In 1879 Mary Russell had donated $1,000 to begin a fund for such an establishment, which MGH sorely needed. Providing for chronic and convalescent patients in the main wards had long tied up beds and funds. The convalescent hospital was a boon to those who needed a stay in a quiet, recuperative environment before reentering the world.

Hospital funds were consistently drained by patients who could afford to pay something but took advantage of free services. From 1875 until 1877, a box for voluntary donations was placed in each room. Beginning in 1877 the Outpatient Department instituted routine interrogations of every incoming patient. Patients were asked to give what they could, but donations under 25 cents were discouraged. If a patient could spare more than a dollar, he or she was told to seek medical advice at a doctor's office. An investigation later that year revealed that many patients were lying about their means to avoid hiring a private doctor. Some were even comfortable homeowners.[157]

Abuse of the Outpatient Department continued in spite of attempts to control admissions. The department needed larger facilities to accommodate all the patients seeking treatment. In 1882 the trustees received an anonymous gift of $25,000 as a memorial to the late George H. Gay. These funds were allocated

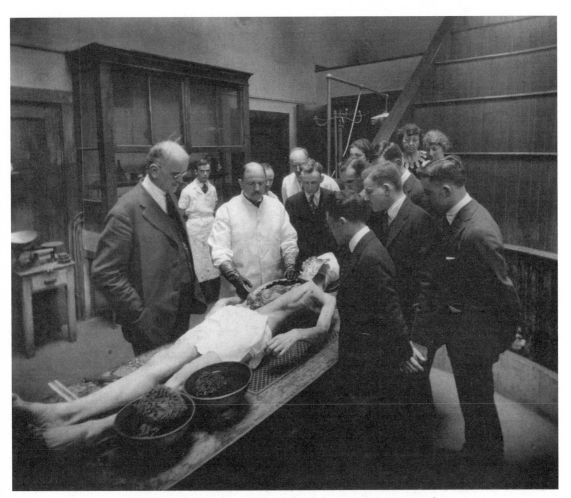

Chief of Medicine David Edsall (left) observes an autopsy in the Allen Street House, about the time of World War I.

to the construction of an outpatient ward. The Gay Ward opened on January 1, 1884, at the south end of the operating theater. In the ward's first year, 14,824 outpatients were treated, by far the largest number of outpatients seen in any year of MGH history to that date.[158]

In January 1888 Helen Bradlee donated $50,000 as a memorial to her late brother, J. Putnam Bradlee. After much deliberation, the trustees heeded the long-time behest of visiting surgeons and opted to use the money to build a ward for abdominal surgery. Ward E, the Bradlee Ward, opened in 1889 for clean abdominal surgery. It stood between Ward D and Charles Street. The MGH surgeon Maurice H. Richardson wrote: "Abdominal surgery is now a field where the most brilliant successes are to be attained. No branch of surgery can compare with it for a moment. . . . It is from the work we are now doing, and hope to do in abdominal surgery (and I would include cerebral surgery as well) that the Hospital must gain its position among the Hospitals of the world at the end of the next ten years. We have the chance now to take the lead, and I do not see how there can be, for a moment, any hesitation whatever."[159]

The MGH trustees asked in their annual report of 1890, "Who will imitate the liberal giver of the Bradlee Ward, and provide the Hospital with a ward for contagious diseases?"[160] Although most contagious cases had theretofore been ushered along to Boston City Hospital, Ward F was completed in 1894 and named the Gardner Ward, in thanks to George A. Gardner for his gift of $50,000 in 1893. The Gardner, set apart at the far southwest corner of the campus, contained six single isolation rooms, as well as a nursery with three or four cribs. The ward catered to "accidental and unavoidable cases of contagious disease [and to patients] who, from the nature of their maladies other than contagious, might be disturbing to patients in the general wards."[161]

Massachusetts General Hospital treated 221 soldiers from the Spanish-American War in 1898. Most suffering from malaria or typhoid fever, the emaciated men stayed in tents that served as ad hoc contagious wards on the lawn of the campus. When it was possible to move them, these war patients were released to their homes to be treated there.[162] This war effort was predominantly medical, whereas Civil War care had been largely surgical.[163]

In 1899 the philanthropic Charles G. Weld, who also made significant donations to the Museum of Fine Arts in Boston and what is now the Peabody Essex Museum in Salem, offered to fund a new ward building for the treatment of "skin and other diseases, in connection with the out-patient department." Although the surgeons of MGH, led by Henry J. Bigelow, had decried the creation of a ward for skin diseases, Ward G opened at the southwest corner of the operating theater in 1902.[164]

The Massachusetts Charitable Eye and Ear Infirmary (familiarly, "Mass Eye and Ear"), not officially part of MGH, opened a new building that abutted the southwest corner of the MGH campus in 1899. The medical board at MGH discussed dissolving their own Ophthalmological Department, but decided to put off doing so until a tighter link was established between the two institutions. Mass Eye and Ear relied on MGH's new Allen Street plant for its light, heat, and power.

MCLEAN MOVES TO BELMONT

The McLean Asylum's need for new and bigger facilities was as dire as that of the general hospital. With railroad tracks almost completely encircling and even cutting through the asylum grounds in Somerville (which had incorporated the section of Charlestown where McLean was situated), the once bucolic campus found itself an island in an industrial wasteland. The asylum had long been operating at capacity, and in 1872 MGH trustees acknowledged the pressing need for relocation. Three years later, they purchased 114 acres of land on Wellington Hill in what is now Belmont from the Waverley Company for $75,000.[165] Frederick Law Olmsted, the renowned landscape architect responsible for Boston's system of public parks known as the Emerald Necklace, advised on the site selection, development, and planning. The new McLean layout would feature a number of comfortable, sturdy cottages. Some years elapsed before building began at the new site, though doctors and administrators alike regularly acknowledged the need. In 1880 parcels of land on the outskirts of the Somerville property were sold to create funds for construction at the new site.[166]

By 1882 cramped quarters constrained McLean Superintendent Edward Cowles to house patients with varying degrees of mental illness together. Such a situation had long been considered undesirable, as patients grouped by type of case seemed more likely to recover quickly.[167] Additional plots of 40 acres and 28 acres adjoining the Waverley property were purchased in 1885 and 1886, respectively.[168]

Construction in Belmont began in 1892, the year the asylum was renamed the McLean Hospital for the Mentally Ill. The trustees initially commissioned two buildings: Belknap House (housing 30 female patients and some offices) and the Appleton Ward (accommodating eight female patients). George P. Upham offered to build an equivalent of the Appleton Ward for males, to be named the

Rear view of McLean Asylum, 1890s, before the move to Belmont.

Upham Memorial Building, in honor of his late son, George P. Upham Jr. William Peters, architect of many Back Bay residences, designed the august colonial giant of red pressed Somerville brick with white Georgia marble details, still standing but no longer in use.[169]

In 1894 the first two cottage residences were built in Belmont, and Cowles prepared to move patients. Belmont residents and McLean patients alike were anxious about the move. When the time came to relocate in October 1895, patients were invited out in groups for carriage rides. The carriages stopped at the Waverley property, and the patients disembarked to find their belongings in order at their new home, some perhaps unaware of the relocation. Though many Belmont residents had expressed anxiety about the notion of an insane hospital in their neighborhood, they read of the move in the papers only after the fact.[170]

The standard of living of the "improved class of sufferers" (Luther Bell's phrase) remained high, even luxurious, at the new McLean property. Patients benefited from on-site amenities such as a riding stable, gymnasiums, art collections, a chapel, a working farm, a bakery, two piggeries, a beef and a dairy barn, flower gardens, an apiary, apple and pear orchards, and a spring for freshwater. In 1896 the first of several single-residence cottages went up, each of them a two-story, five-bedroom colonial-style home (three bedrooms for servants) with a terraced garden and spectacular views.[171] No surprise, then, that when Frederick Law Olmsted became senile at age 76 in 1898, he took up residence in one of the McLean cottages that he had helped design. In more lucid moments he was overheard complaining, "They didn't carry out my plans, confound them."[172]

(Though McLean remains part of the Massachusetts General Hospital, this volume will leave the old asylum at its new address in Belmont and follow the story of MGH alone from here on.)

PATHOLOGY FROM MICROSCOPE TO MOLECULES

Until 1896, when James Homer Wright arrived at MGH to run the new pathological laboratory, pathology at MGH was limited largely to autopsy and the study of gross anatomy. Laboratory work was conducted in a small, dark room measuring six by ten feet, in the basement of the Bulfinch Building. The trustees voted in 1847 to allow the admitting physician to spend no more than $50 on the hospital's first microscope. Four years later they instituted a new position for a chemist-microscopist, who would run all the laboratory tests for hospital physicians and surgeons, attend and assist at all autopsies, and keep careful records of these. John Bacon Jr. filled the position until 1855, when the trustees created the Pathological Cabinet.

Nineteenth-century surgeons like John Collins Warren and Henry Jacob Bigelow took pride in their personal collections of morbid specimens. Bigelow often said, "No single branch of education is more essential to the medical student than pathological anatomy, the corner stone of medicine."[173] Warren donated his collection to Harvard Medical School upon retirement from teaching in 1847, along with $5,000 to maintain it. The collection of anatomical and pathological specimens, wax figures, drawings, photographs, prints, and medical and surgical instruments and machines formed the foundation of the Warren Anatomical Museum, to which other doctors, such as Oliver Wendell Holmes and J. B. S. Jackson, would contribute their own collections. Warren stipulated that his own skeleton be displayed as part of the anatomical collection to serve as "a lesson useful, at the same time, to morality and science."[174] At this writing, Warren's skeleton is in storage at the Warren Museum, which has become part of the Center for the History of Medicine at Harvard Medical School. The skeleton is not on display, however, despite the donor's express wishes.

The MGH Board of Trustees appointed Calvin Ellis first curator of the Pathological Cabinet in 1855. In that role Ellis collected instructive morbid specimens following surgery or, more commonly, autopsy, and arranged them for study and observation. In 1864 the hospital added its first staff artist, Lucius Manlius Sargent Jr., to draw pathological specimens. Benjamin Joy Jeffries founded the Eye Pathology Laboratory at the Massachusetts Eye and Ear Infirmary in 1868.

Ellis was succeeded in 1871 by Reginald Fitz, who had recently returned from his post-HMS medical tour of Europe with a passion for pathological anatomy. On June 18 Fitz made a presentation before the Association of American Physicians on his groundbreaking article, "Perforating Inflammation of the Vermiform Appendix; With Special Reference to Its Early Diagnosis and Treatment." The course and symptoms of appendicitis were mapped out and a radical operation suggested as the only solution. Fitz apparently invented the term *appendicitis* as early as 1881. Fitz's findings, in tandem with the opening of the new ward for clean abdominal surgery, turned appendectomy into something of a fad, the procedure being performed by feisty and ambitious young surgeons. In 1889 Fitz also clarified the nature of acute pancreatitis.

Harvard's professor of pathological anatomy beginning in 1878, Fitz hoped that his position as pathologist would serve as a springboard onto the visiting hospital staff. When openings for visiting physicians were repeatedly filled by others, Fitz tendered his resignation. Not wanting to lose his valuable services, the hospital trustees implored him to remain at the hospital and appointed him visiting physician in 1892. By this time, as is explained further in chapter 3, important competition had appeared on the national scene, most notably Johns Hopkins Hospital in Baltimore. To keep up with the competition, Harvard Medical School poached the pathologist William Thomas Councilman from Johns Hopkins, and he was appointed to its new pathology chair. Councilman suggested that the MGH trustees establish a pathological department and hire a full-time, salaried pathologist (as opposed to a professor–private practitioner, like the rest of the MGH staff). When asked to weigh in, doctors expressed resounding support for a pathological department and laboratory. Maurice Richardson recommended that the new facilities include a laboratory for the study of bacteriology.

Reginald Fitz.

James Homer Wright.

The trustees agreed to the proposals, and in the spring of 1894 a temporary laboratory was set up at the Allen Street House. In 1895 the trustees announced their intention to raise $100,000 to build a new pathological and bacteriological laboratory according to the plans prepared by physicians and surgeons, and they ordered building to begin at once. James Homer Wright was hired from Boston City Hospital to work full-time as a pathologist and oversee the intended clinical-pathological laboratory. Wright went overseas in March 1896 to observe European pathological departments and laboratories and returned for the official opening of the new laboratory on October 16, the fiftieth anniversary of the first public use of ether as a surgical anesthetic at the hospital. Although Wright and a technical assistant were the laboratory's only staff members, 16 benches were available for doctors, who paid $25 a year to rent a bench beside Wright.

The first report of the Clinical-Pathological Laboratory in 1898 stated that the "chief purpose of this laboratory has been to give to the Hospital the benefit of those modern microscopical, bacteriological and chemical methods which are of such great importance in the diagnosis and study of disease."[175] Twenty-two articles had already been published from findings in the laboratory. In 1899 a new lab for photomicrography was outfitted in the same building, and a Mass General trustee, Francis Blake, designed the microtome, which could cut sections to 1/25,000 of an inch.

The laboratory that ran tests for the private patients in Phillips House from 1917 to 1927 occupied a small room on that building's second floor and was operated by a single, unsupervised technician.[176] Baker Memorial, the MGH hospital for middle-income patients, opened with its own laboratory in 1930. The Baker lab was also responsible for testing and listing professional blood donors. To consolidate laboratory work and save time and money, the tests in the Phillips House laboratory were moved to the Baker lab in 1933, and the former was abandoned as a pathological laboratory. By the end of 1936 the personnel of the Baker laboratory had grown from one technician to a full staff of a physician, a diener (mortuary worker), a secretary, and eight full-time technicians.

The Mallory and Castleman Years

In 1926 Tracy B. Mallory succeeded Wright as chief of pathology. Upon his arrival at the Massachusetts General from Boston City Hospital, Mallory instituted a residency program in pathology, which survives today as one of the world's leading pathology residency programs. In 1942 Mallory and Edward Gall published a pioneering paper on the histological classification of lymphomas. Mallory's service as chief consultant of pathology in the Mediterranean theater during World War II would result in important work on traumatic shock and acute tubular necrosis.

From 1926 until 1935 the annual number of autopsies increased from 177 (35 percent of hospital deaths) to 436 (60 percent). The number of microscopic slides processed rose from 3,830 in 1926 to 21,312 in 1935. In 1928 the interior of the old Allen Street House was gutted and rebuilt to include a modern postmortem amphitheater, a small auxiliary autopsy room, an enlarged morgue, photographic and dark rooms, and a small laboratory for research in bacteriology.

Several forces served to connect the pathology laboratory with clinical services as the pathological department grew. First were the clinical-pathological conferences developed by Richard C. Cabot, which maintained the dialogue between the two (see chapter 3). Second, medical students were assigned exercises in the pathological laboratory corresponding to their medical specialty. Growth in research at the hospital, especially in allergies, gastrointestinal disease, pulmonary pathology, and diseases of the thyroid, served as a third tie between pathology and clinical medicine.

Benjamin Castleman became chief of pathology at Massachusetts General in 1953 after Mallory's death two years earlier, and he took over editing the

Tracy B. Mallory.

clinicopathological case reports. "Castleman of the CPCs" (clinicopathological conferences) prepared and edited about 1,200 manuscripts comprising approximately 2,000 case reports over a period of 23 years. In addition to his own research, notably on diseases of the parathyroid, the thyroid, and the mediastinum, Castleman accorded great importance to his roles as teacher and department head. He said, "The entire staff meets every morning at 8:15 and for up to one hour I personally check all the gross material of the autopsies of the day before. . . . Every afternoon from 2 to 3, I personally check the interesting and problem microscopic slides of the surgical pathology specimens that have come through that day. . . . This personal teaching of the house staff has paid off in that applications for appointments come in droves."[177]

The MGH Pathology Department maintained its commitment to its role in patient care. Castleman remembered his mentor, Tracy Mallory, as one who reinforced that link. Mallory, he said, "instilled in me certain principles of conservatism in pathology—being sure that when you say something, you're *sure* of it; if you're not, to *say* so, and always to act conservatively, in the interest of the patient. . . . Because at the end of that slide is what the physician or surgeon is going to *do* to that patient." Castleman maintained the departmental emphasis on, in his own words, "the responsibility of patient care and thus the necessity of expert knowledge of anatomic pathology." He focused on what the radiologist Richard Schatzki referred to as "the whole patient and the whole abnormal process, not restricted solely to the pathological findings."[178]

By the 1950s pathology staff attended 15 to 20 weekly meetings with other

Benjamin Castleman.

departments, at which they presented gross and microscopical material relevant to that department. The first specialties with which pathology at MGH was closely linked were neurology and dermatology, as well as the otolaryngology department at Mass Eye and Ear. Charles S. Kubik founded the Neuropathology Laboratory in 1926 and oversaw it until his retirement in 1951. A decade later it was renamed the Charles S. Kubik Laboratory for Neuropathology in his honor; from the 1960s through the 1990s the laboratory was directed by E. P. Richardson Jr. Dermatopathology first emerged at MGH in the 1940s under Walter Lever. Wallace H. Clark expanded the unit when he arrived at MGH from Tulane University in 1962. An alumnus of both the Dermatology and Pathology departments, Martin

C. Mihm further expanded the division after Clark. In 1962 the MGH Pathology Department arranged to process the surgical specimens of the Otolaryngological Department at Mass Eye and Ear. Karoly Balogh served as pathologist there until 1968, when he was succeeded by Max Goodman.

When the Warren Building was constructed in the early 1950s, Castleman secured ample space in it for the Pathology Department. New labs were named the James Homer Wright Pathology Laboratories. In 1950 the Pathology Department incorporated the Cytology Laboratory, which moved into the Pathology Department's Warren Building quarters seven years later. Leonard Atkins instituted a bone marrow bank in 1957 for use in case of atomic bomb casualties; it was funded by the Atomic Energy Commission. The country escaped a nuclear attack and the work in bone marrow culture led to chromosome preparations, and subsequently to the establishment of the Cytogenetics Laboratory in 1959.

Robert T. McCluskey succeeded Castleman as chief of pathology in 1974, though Castleman continued to work and lecture until a few weeks before his death in 1982. (He would also serve as interim general director of MGH in 1972, between the administrations of John Knowles and Charles Sanders; and with David C. Crockett and S. B. Sutton, he edited the official history of the hospital spanning the years 1955–1980.)

An expert in inflammation and renal disease, McCluskey proved an administrative pioneer. Specialty areas in pathology had grown up in relationship to medical specialties. For example, as the Infectious Disease Division grew (see chapter 5), it began to run its own labs. But under regulatory changes of the 1970s and 1980s it became undesirable for doctors to be both clinicians *and* laboratory directors. Early on, McCluskey perceived the need to centralize all specialty labs under pathology, and toward the end of his career he did so, hospital-wide. Consolidation of clinical labs doing fluid-based analyses took a few years and extended into the tenure of McCluskey's successor, Robert B. Colvin.

Recent Years in Pathology

During the McCluskey years the department grew tremendously in faculty, trainees, and cases. Well-known surgical pathologists included the gynecological and genitourinary pathologist Robert E. Scully, whose work includes the pathological classification of tumors of the female reproductive system used today. In papers published in the 1970s, Scully and his associates linked in utero exposure to diethylstilbestrol (DES), a synthetic form of estrogen prescribed to pregnant women to prevent miscarriage, to clear cell adenocarcinoma, a rare type of vaginal cancer.

In 1991 Robert B. Colvin, an expert on renal diseases, became the chief of pathology. To accommodate the rapid expansion of clinical services at MGH, Colvin oversaw the complete subspecialization of pathology, complete by 1996. Today all MGH pathologists are specialists: gynecological pathologists, neuropathologists, and so on. Colvin also secured significant space for pathology in Building 149 of the Charlestown Navy Yard, where the department continues its research today. Though its initial focus was immunopathology, investigative pathology was concentrated on cancer research after Colvin appointed David N. Louis as founding director of the new Division of Molecular Pathology and Research.

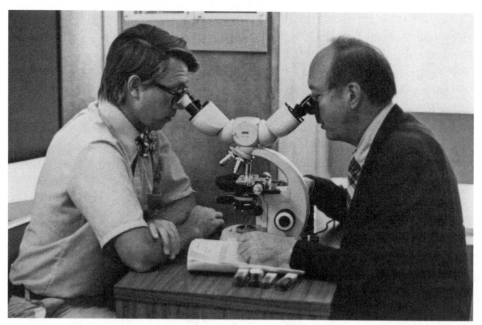

Chief of Pathology Robert McCluskey (right) and his successor-to-be, Robert Colvin, confer about a research project.

Louis, an expert on nervous system tumors and molecular genetics, became the sixth chair of the Pathology Department at MGH in 2006, 110 years after its founding. Louis has worked to unify anatomic pathology, laboratory medicine, and molecular pathology and research. The department continues to grow, with emphasis on the cancer research center in Charlestown, molecular diagnostic laboratories, and a new program of pathology informatics.

In contrast to early pathologists who relied on autopsy and resected organs and limbs to glean information about a patient, alive or dead, today's pathologists perform only 250 autopsies a year—and more than 10 million laboratory tests. Although much of the pathologist's work is behind the scenes (from the patient's point of view), 70 percent of decisions made in a hospital are based on laboratory tests. The Pathology Department also runs the Blood Bank, including the donor center, and blood storage and distribution.

During surgery the naked eye often doesn't suffice to determine the type of tumor, or whether the surgeon has removed it entirely. While operating, surgeons send a piece of a tumor into the pathology lab that adjoins the operating room. Within five minutes, pathologists prepare a frozen section to observe under a microscope and call the surgeon with the results, so that he or she may continue surgery with a better understanding of the patient's needs.

The scale of the sample that a pathologist can analyze is growing ever smaller. Early in the hospital's history, pathological services were divided into small side (biopsies) and large side (amputations and resections) analyses. The advent of new technology has added cytology and molecular diagnostics to the pathologist's toolkit, which once included only the microscope. Pathologists not only interpret the slides that lab technicians prepare, but also correlate the outcome of one test with previous relevant information from the patient's medical history. One promise of a new system of pathology informatics is that one day every patient's entire medical history will be available in a standardized format. Computer algorithms will permit high-level analysis of a quantity of data that even a very intelligent doctor could not synthesize and interpret.

The other major focus of pathology informatics is the development of computer systems to recognize patterns in laboratory samples—whether a tumor is benign or malignant, for example. MGH pathologists are now working with technology companies to develop recognition algorithms

David N. Louis.

that can make the distinctions that pathologists now make using a microscope. For example, Pap smears were always screened by a human; a technologist would circle suspicious areas, which would go to a pathologist for review. Today a computer takes pictures of all the cells and identifies cell patterns as good or bad, which a pathologist will then examine.

The surgical pathology staff, 2010. Back row, from left: Eugene J. Mark, Gregory Y. Lauwers, Nancy L. Harris, Robert H. Young, David C. Wilbur. Front row: W. Stephen Black-Schaffer, Jennifer L. Hunt, Andrew E. Rosenberg, E. Tessa Hedley-Whyte, Judith A. Ferry.

The computer has proven to be more sensitive in identifying abnormalities a technician might miss. At least 90 percent of liquid-based specimens are not seen by a human. Quality control of computer systems depends heavily on human input, however, and the question of where to draw the line between normal and abnormal is left to human interpretation. Though computers are commonly used for liquid samples, developing recognition algorithms for tissue sections is a greater challenge. All tissue samples continue to be examined directly by the human eye. MGH pathologists are working to facilitate the process of capturing images of tissue digitally and building algorithms to help pathologists do their interpretive work.

Education at all levels is a central element of the MGH Pathology Department. Robert H. ("Robin") Young is a leader in creating courses for other pathologists, of which the department holds 10 to 15 annually through Harvard Continuing Medical Education. Pathology has 35 residents, who follow a track of anatomical or clinical pathology, or both. Twelve to 15 pathology fellowships are in the clinic, and many more are in research. The department also trains laboratory technicians to perform tasks like cutting sections and running tests. As tests are increasingly controlled by machines, the need to train bright, young pathologists in the ever-growing number of subspecialties is felt and met at MGH.

DR. BIGELOW RETIRES

Henry Jacob Bigelow was both an innovator and a traditionalist. His new methods for the reduction of hip dislocations and for litholapaxy were milestones in surgery. He constantly strove to reinvent and perfect medical apparatuses, including a surgical chair that earned him renown. But he spurned any man who actively sought to attach his name to an improvement in medical instruments. And as we have seen, he also resisted specialization in surgery.

In other words, Bigelow was a paragon of nineteenth-century surgery. In addition to possessing remarkable mechanical and imaginative faculties, he was revered for his manual dexterity and presence of mind in the operating room. Holmes and Fitz praised their colleague's artisanship: "He was alert and active in every movement, full of life and animation. In the jargon of medical students, he was a 'brilliant operator'; to see him 'manipulate,' as they said, was worth the sacrifice of duties usually deemed imperative."[179]

Bigelow loathed the idea of causing more pain with his treatment than the patient was already enduring, an attitude that endeared him to his patients. Bigelow himself often said, "Dying is nothing, but pain is a very serious matter."[180] In 1871 Bigelow averred that during the 25 years during which he had practiced medicine, he had "never intentionally given a patient, unless by his own choice, any pain without narcotization . . . [or] allowed a patient to die a painful death when opium would lull him into his long sleep."[181] The larger-than-life surgeon would go far beyond the call of duty in the service of his patients, according to Holmes and Fitz: "In the days before abdominal surgery and antisepsis were understood, he once spent an entire night, sitting on the floor, oblivious of his constrained and painful attitude, in unremitting compression with his finger of a bleeding abdominal artery, which had been divided by a stab,—its ligature being perilous, and digital pressure being the only way in which fatal hemorrhage could then be safely averted."[182]

Henry Jacob Bigelow in later years.

Although Bigelow was not regarded as a humble man by his contemporaries, he treated his patients as sentient beings rather than interesting medical data. He sought to expand medical understanding, but never at the expense of curing or comforting the individual. In his "Fragments of Medical Science and Art," Bigelow made his values clear: "Do not identify surgery with the knife,—with blood and dashing elegance. Distrust surgical intrepidity and boldness. If such epithets have any meaning, they are in bad taste, and tend to give wrong impressions of scientific excellence. . . . Surgery is not operative surgery. Its province is to save, not to destroy; and an operation is an avowal of its own inadequacy."[183]

Bigelow vehemently opposed many reforms that he felt would strip the medical profession of its integrity. He had a strong sense of right and wrong, which his colleagues did not always share. Bigelow spoke bluntly about his distaste for the use of medicine as a means to financial gain. He believed that the honor of association with such a fine institution as MGH was compensation enough for any surgeon. When many doctors advocated the right to accept fees for their services at the hospital, Bigelow deeply opposed the movement. In April 1889 he wrote:

> A public hospital is a trust, originally set apart as a charity for the sick, and not for the pecuniary benefit of their attendants. Whatever, in a charitable institution, is practiced for any other end leads to its gradual, insidious deterioration. Whatever diverts the property, the resources, or the conveniences of a charity trust—or even the patients who apply for them—to the private advantage of its officers, is a form of the spoils system. . . . If a hospital is dependent upon legacies and charitable subscriptions, it should be able to go to the community with clean hands. No appeal in its behalf would excite much sympathy were it known that a portion of the money given was to enable medical men to collect fees more conveniently.[184]

The esteemed surgeon often refused payment from patients in financial straits. He seemed immune to flattery and bribery, and he held a straight course in the direction he perceived as right. Because his professional opinions were so highly regarded, Bigelow often received gifts from manufacturers or retailers who hoped the surgeon might tout their wares. To a foreign-born dealer of medicinal wines who had repeatedly sent Bigelow large quantities of his product, Bigelow wrote a pointed letter: "Don't send me any more wine. We have a code of medical ethics here, which I wrote myself, prohibiting any medical man from publicly puffing any such thing, [which would] weaken the distinct line between the regular practice of medicine and the practice of quackery. . . . Your system of advertisement is a liberal one, and I am a conservative."[185]

Bigelow's retirement from clinical practice in 1886, shortly after that of the closely associated MGH surgeon Richard Hodges, marked the end of an era of surgery at MGH that had begun on Ether Day. Upon retirement, Bigelow was invited to become the first-ever surgeon emeritus at the hospital, with five beds at his disposal to treat which patients he pleased. Unofficially assured that the position would also entail the right to attend and vote at hospital staff meetings, Bigelow accepted the honor. At their final meeting before they bestowed the title on Bigelow, the trustees reneged, omitting the right to attend and vote at staff meetings. Bigelow's dear friend Oliver Wendell Holmes remembered how this turn soured Bigelow's feelings toward MGH:

> The offer as thus modified Dr. Bigelow at once declined; and his sense of the indignity put upon him, and of the false position in which he was placed by this remarkable change of attitude on the part of the trustees, coupled with his knowledge of the causes by which it had been brought about [namely, his fierce opposition to a new rule that would allow doctors to collect fees from hospital patients], embittered for the remainder of his life his relations with the Hospital upon which he had shed so much lustre, and for which he had labored with such diligence, fidelity, and affection during his entire professional career.[186]

Disgruntled as he was, Bigelow retired to a bucolic estate in Newton, Massachusetts. The property reflected the surgeon's lifelong interest in botany and horticulture: wild rosebushes, brambles, and barberry bushes lined the avenue that led to the rhododendrons, exochordias, and flower beds opening onto the house that Henry Hobson Richardson, the noted architect of Boston's Trinity Church, had designed for Bigelow in 1885. The shingled house with a circular tower is one of the few remaining private residences designed by Richardson, although it was restored and divided into five condominiums in 1981 on the PBS television show *This Old House*.

Even in retirement, the enigmatic surgeon's idiosyncrasies were as evident as ever. Botany was just another field for his contrary ways. A friend wrote to Bigelow's son William Sturgis Bigelow: "Your father spends his time trying to make plants grow on the top of a hill in New England which the Lord intended should grow in a swamp in the tropics; and the curious part of it is that he seems to succeed."[187]

In the third year of his residence at his Newton estate, Bigelow flipped his carriage while driving home and suffered a serious head injury, followed by a long illness. Finally, unable to eat and ever weakening, Bigelow died on October 30, 1890. His friends Holmes and Fitz noted his dignity during the final days of his life: "His mind remained bright and clear till very near the close of life. With unclouded judgment he noted the indications of approaching dissolution. Uncomplaining, quietly demonstrative to those about him, and with a placid composure, slowly and serenely he ceased to live." [188]

CHAPTER 3

. . . .

MEDICINE ENTERS THE MODERN ERA, 1901–1930

In its early history, when it was the only Boston hospital,
a position upon its staff was essential for a doctor who expected
to make his name known in medicine or surgery. Today the
Hospital must meet the keen competition of other teaching
hospitals: the Peter Bent Brigham Hospital, the
Boston City Hospital, the Beth Israel Hospital, the
Massachusetts Memorial Hospitals.
— *Frederic A. Washburn,* The Massachusetts
General Hospital

A N ACADEMIC MEDICAL CENTER *is often likened to a three-legged stool,*
standing on three key missions: patient care, teaching, and research. But
for decades after its founding, Massachusetts General Hospital balanced
on just two; research did not factor in. MGH's Brahmin founders may have been
visionary, but they resisted change while more academically driven institutions like
Johns Hopkins began to woo top talent. There was competition in Boston, too,
as other hospitals sprang up to serve a growing population. (In 1912 the following
Boston-area hospitals were affiliated with Harvard Medical School: MGH, Bos-
ton City Hospital, Boston Lying-In Hospital, the Boston Dispensary, Children's
Hospital, McLean Hospital, Boston State Hospital for the mentally ill, Massa-
chusetts Eye and Ear Infirmary, Long Island Hospital in Boston Harbor, Car-
ney Hospital, and the Free Hospital for Women.)[1] *Eventually, as Boston itself*
changed—its economic and political structure irrevocably altered by immigrants
from Ireland and eastern Europe—Mass General began to change as well.

Led by Boston-born Richard Clarke Cabot, the hospital established a Social
Service Department in 1905, just one of Cabot's innovations. But it took an
outsider from Philadelphia and St. Louis, David L. Edsall, to push MGH into
the modern era of clinical research during his tenure as chief of medicine (1912–
1923). One of Edsall's legacies was the legendary Ward 4. His successor,
James Howard Means, maintained the momentum; the medical leaders Means
recruited would be the foundation for clinical and investigative successes in the

The lobby of Phillips House.

latter half of the twentieth century. Meanwhile, MGH staff faced stiff challenges treating World War I casualties and victims of the devastating Spanish flu epidemic. The hospital also built new inpatient facilities that catered to the wealthy (Phillips House) and those of moderate means (Baker Memorial).

A section in this chapter documents the growth of radiology at MGH, beginning with the inspiring but tragic story of the "roentgenologist" Walter James Dodd. Another section examines the Cardiology Department, and a third looks at endocrinology, with a visit to Ward 4.

IF JOHN COLLINS WARREN AND JAMES JACKSON tower over the early history of the Massachusetts General Hospital, that is partly because they wanted it that way. From the state charter of 1811 until 1828, the professional medical staff of MGH was one surgeon (Warren), one physician (Jackson). The pair enjoyed the hospital's only privileges. Boston's charity hospital served them as a personal clinic for teaching and as a showcase for their professional reputations. Though they volunteered their time at Mass General, off-campus their admiring private patients paid them top dollar. If others had not objected to this monopoly, Warren and Jackson would have had little reason to change it.

A "board of consulting physicians" existed from the start, but as one of their number, John G. Coffin, wrote to the trustees in 1824, they seemed "to be little more than cyphers, to meet occasionally to preserve appearances." Coffin called the MGH staff "somewhat like monopoly,"[1] as opposed to the personnel at hospitals in New York, Philadelphia, London, Edinburgh, and Paris, each of which had three or more staff members working in rotation. Coffin wondered, what if Dr. Warren should fall ill, what if an accident befell Jackson?

In 1828 Warren was prevailed on to add two assistant surgeons, but he held firm against sharing his leadership position. He wrote:

> First because it must interrupt & disturb an arrangement well established, which has stood the experiment of nearly ten years, and under which the Institution has attained a very decided character in this department. Second, because it is perfectly obvious & certain to my mind, and every day's experience confirms me in it, that the surgical practise there is not more than sufficient to keep one surgeon in operative practise, and I think it better to have one industrious well experienced, than a number partially so. Third, there should be a head to everything. . . . For these and other reasons I could quote, I hope such a system will never be adopted, and I do not think it will.[2]

A new system was adopted seven years later. In 1835 the setup was changed to three physicians of equal rank (Jackson, Walter Channing, and John Ware) and two surgeons (Warren and George Hayward). A third surgeon (Solomon D. Townsend) was added in 1839. With this division of duties began a system of rotations that would last into the twentieth century. Each surgeon and each physician was responsible for covering the entire hospital for a limited term each calendar year. When his rotation was completed, a doctor's entire caseload was passed along to the next member of the relay team. House officers (newly trained, unpaid interns living on the grounds) provided continuity of care and did most of the hands-on doctoring.

This new organization lasted longer than it should have. The drawbacks were obvious long before 1908, when Frederick Shattuck, Elbridge Cutler, and James Minot wrote a letter to the trustees:

> This system was certainly a wise one in the past when Boston was a small city, the Massachusetts General the only hospital, and that an experiment. Boston is now a large city. There are several other large general hospitals and many special hospitals, and hospitals have left the experimental stage far behind them.
>
> An obvious and very serious objection to the divided service is, that it offers great impediment to the advance of knowledge, in that no one member of the Staff has the chance to follow out an investigation in pathology or therapeutics.[3]

The world had changed since the heyday of Warren and Jackson, and in fundamental ways Massachusetts General Hospital had failed to change with it. In the 1820s MGH had a double mission: to care for the sick poor and, in cooperation with Harvard, to educate the community's doctors. By the late nineteenth

Maurice Howe Richardson.

century a third leg had been added to the stool: medical research. On this, the three doctors wrote in 1908, "the reputation of a hospital depends."[4] Yet the very system of rotations prevented serious, sustained clinical research, the advancement of medical knowledge by the observation and treatment of live patients. In a hospital still staffed by part-time, volunteer generalists working in rotation, how could a doctor follow through on anything but the most limited clinical experimentation?

By 1900 other large general hospitals were stealing a march on Mass General. Shattuck, Cutler, and Minot's letter referred to competition within Boston, beginning with Boston City Hospital, founded in 1858 and affiliated as MGH was with Harvard Medical School. Later in their letter, they would make mention of the two biggest elephants in the room: Johns Hopkins Hospital of Baltimore (opened May 7, 1889) and the Mayo brothers of Rochester, Minnesota (who performed their first surgery at St. Mary's Hospital, also in 1889, effectively founding the Mayo Clinic). Johns Hopkins Hospital and the medical school directly associated with it were organized on principles different from those at MGH. Hospital and university worked hand-in-glove; all major appointments at the hospital were made only with the approval of the medical school. Hospital chiefs were department chairmen at Johns Hopkins Medical School. Furthermore, Hopkins appointments were full-time appointments. In Baltimore one did not find privileged doctors descending from their Beacon Hill aeries three or four months out of the year to do charitable work in the spirit of Christian stewardship. In Baltimore as in Rochester, the institution paid its physicians and surgeons full-time salaries, expecting full-time effort and world-class results in return. Clinical expertise and biomedical research surged ahead.

One young doctor had a perfect opportunity to compare the old world of MGH with the brave new one represented by Johns Hopkins. J. M. T. Finney was trained in surgery on MGH's West Service but in 1890 was hired away by the Baltimore upstart. Fifty years later he would write:

> Coming from the Massachusetts General Hospital, rich in traditions and closely linked with names and events prominent in the medical and surgical

annals not only of Boston and New England, but of the whole world of medicine, to the Johns Hopkins Hospital, with no traditions and no past, looking only to the future, was like stepping out of one world into another. The transition from the old order to the new was taking place in surgery just at the time of my transfer. The aseptic method of sterilization by heat was just beginning to replace antiseptic solutions and the spray in the practice of certain members of the staff, but it had not as yet been universally adopted. At the Massachusetts General Hospital, which represented the best in the pre-antiseptic period, tradition and precedent were just beginning to be questioned by the rising young advocates of the new order of surgical procedure, while at the Johns Hopkins Hospital the leaders were all young men to start with, imbued with modern ideas and trained in modern methods, not unmindful of the lessons of the past, but looking steadfastly into the future for the solution of the problems as yet unsolved.[5]

At least since the 1870s, when Harvard's President Charles Eliot began reorganizing the medical school along modern, professional lines, Harvard Medical School had sought some say in appointments to the MGH staff; but the hospital resisted, maintaining its autonomy from the university. Even Eliot's sensible suggestion that house officers at MGH be appointed on the basis of a competitive examination was rejected. Personal references and oral interviews would suffice very well, thank you, Mr. Eliot. The old Brahmin network knew just who the best chaps were likely to be.

When space became too cramped in the medical school quarters adjoining the hospital grounds in December 1883, Eliot moved the Harvard medical campus away from MGH to a site at the intersection of Boylston and Exeter streets in Boston's newly filled Back Bay. Still, since a professor of medicine needed a clinic in which to demonstrate his art and since Mass General remained the premier, though not the only, Harvard-affiliated clinic in Boston, many Harvard professorships continued to be filled from the ranks of the up-and-coming MGH staff. This and aristocratic Boston's penchant for inbreeding and nepotism meant that the talent pool for Harvard faculty and MGH staff was inevitably limited compared with meritocratic operations like Hopkins and the Mayo Clinic.

In 1893 the surgeon Maurice H. Richardson lamented: "We hear of nothing but the John [sic] Hopkins Hospital and what they do there. Some of our hospital graduates are now working at John Hopkins, and we are sending on to them to find out what they are doing. . . . Now I for one want John Hopkins to sent [sic] to the Massachusetts Hospital to find out what we are doing.[6]

As long as fathers, grandfathers, and benefactors made the appointments at MGH, however, that was unlikely to happen. Writing in 1881, Dr. Oliver Wendell Holmes noted:

> There has hardly been a year for more than a century in which "Dr. Warren" or "Dr. Jeffries" could not be called upon by his Boston fellow-citizens for his services as surgeon or physician. [MGH's founder] Dr. [James] Jackson is represented by his grandchildren and other blood relations; Dr. Bigelow, Dr. Hayward, Dr. Channing, Dr. Putnam, Dr. Shattuck, Dr. Homans, are names

as familiar to the young people of to-day as they were to their parents and grandparents. The memories of the past yet survive in our two honored medical brethren—the venerable Dr. Edward Reynolds, and the indefatigable Dr. David Humphreys Storer, who still attends to his professional duties as he did in the youthful period of the century.[7]

When J. Collins Warren, grandson of the founding surgeon, retired early in the twentieth century, it was the first time in nearly 100 years that a Warren had not been on the hospital staff. When Phillips House, the MGH private hospital for the well-to-do, opened in 1917, its first patient was none other than J. Collins Warren.

Why could even such an inbred staff not devote full-time efforts to MGH, to allow persistent, serious research to blossom, as was happening in Baltimore and Rochester? Because the same Brahmin sensibility that dictated the path to professional advancement at Mass General—from the best families, through the best schools, including Harvard—insisted that Mass General adhere to its charitable mission. Mass General had been founded to serve the poor, at a time when no self-respecting citizen of any means would have undergone the humiliation of entering a charity ward.

But medicine had changed. Boston had changed. And Boston medicine was changing too, with or without Mass General.

BOSTON IN 1900

At the start of the twentieth century Boston was powered by old money and new masses. The city's great dynastic fortunes had been established between the American Revolution and the Civil War, particularly in ocean trade and manufacturing. One of the first Bostonians to enter the China trade after the Revolution, Thomas Handasyd Perkins, a founder of Mass General Hospital, became the city's undisputed merchant prince, trading slaves in Haiti, furs between the Pacific Northwest and China, and opium from Turkey to China. His massive fortune helped finance the hospital and other worthy Boston endeavors like the Museum of Fine Arts and the Perkins School for the Blind, which would educate Annie Sullivan, teacher of Helen Keller.[8] Perkins married his daughter into the Cabot family, thus augmenting another dynastic fortune that had started in privateering during the Revolution. Eliza Perkins Cabot's grandson was Samuel Cabot, a leading surgeon at MGH in the mid-nineteenth century (see chapter 2).

As Perkins and others sent their sailing ships around the globe, other Boston fortunes were built by local watermills. In 1810, the year before MGH was chartered, Francis Cabot Lowell visited England and returned with pirated designs for power looms; not permitted to copy these designs, he had memorized them instead. In 1813 he formed the Boston Manufacturing Company with Nathan Appleton and Patrick Tracy Jackson (that family name again). The following year they built their first water-powered plant in Waltham, on the Charles River west of Boston; success bred success, and soon whole towns dedicated to mass production were named for their founding Boston families, Lowell and Lawrence. New rail lines, financed partly by Perkins's trading profits, connected these Merrimack River towns with the hub of the New England economy, Boston. (It is to MGH and Harvard's own Oliver Wendell Holmes that Boston owes its nickname, "The Hub," although originally Holmes said, with consummate humility, only that the Massachusetts State House on Beacon Hill was "the hub of the solar system.")

"Colonel" Perkins passed from the scene in 1854 at the age of 90, declaring that he had always intended to die sitting up in his chair, whereupon he did. We can arbitrarily mark this year, 1854, as a watershed in Boston history. For by this time the doors to the highest levels of Boston society were closing. As Cleveland Amory noted in *The Proper Bostonians*, for a Boston family to be first-rate socially, "somewhere along the line—there must be the merchant prince, the real Family-founder. . . . Whether in shipping, in railroading, in textiles, in mining, or in banking, he is the stout trunk of almost every First Family tree."[9] Boston dynasties founded after the Civil War are, by the rule of Amory, nouveaux riches. But if the doors to the aristocracy were slamming, others were being forced open: by the 1850s the docks and old neighborhoods of Boston were flooded with refugees from the Irish potato famine. Jewish refugees from Germany and eastern Europe would soon follow. From the 1830s to 1900, the city's population grew 450 percent, from under 100,000 to more than 550,000.

The footprint of the city expanded. The fetid Back Bay was filled, beginning two years after Perkins's death, creating a new, upscale neighborhood to pair with Beacon Hill. Further landfill projects in the South Bay and elsewhere added to the urban surface area, as did the annexation of neighboring towns in 1868 (Roxbury), 1870 (Dorchester), and 1873 (Charlestown). Boston's old money created new cultural institutions, including the Museum of Fine Arts (1876), the Boston Symphony Orchestra (1881), and the Boston Public Library, which moved to its current location in Copley Square in 1895. Meanwhile, the pioneering landscape designer Frederick Law Olmsted was commissioned in 1878 to join the city's disjointed green spaces into a glittering "Emerald Necklace."

For all that Brahmin families did to enhance The Hub, immigrants kept coming, and power, political and economic, began shifting. One could begin the tale with the West End's Martin Lomasney, nicknamed "the Mahatma." A forerunner to better-known Boston Irish politicians like James Michael Curley and John Fitzgerald Kennedy, Lomasney developed a power base as boss of Boston's Ward 8, the West End. As the Bulfinch Building is squarely sited in this ward, the advent of Irish political power in Boston must have been particularly striking to MGH doctors named Warren, Jackson, Cabot, and Shattuck. At

Frederick Shattuck.

the turn of the century Curley would begin his extraordinary reign over the imagination, if not always the polity, of Boston, first in the Massachusetts State House (1902), then in the U.S. House of Representatives (1910), followed by four intermittent terms as mayor (1914–1950), one as governor (1934), and two more in the U.S. House (1943–1947), where he surrendered his seat to a young Harvard grad and PT boat captain named Kennedy. Throw in two jail terms and you have the bare bones of the Curley résumé.[10]

While the Irish began to dominate politics, Jewish immigrants would make inroads in other arenas. Louis Dembitz Brandeis, a Boston lawyer, became the first Jewish justice on the U.S. Supreme Court, where he served from 1916 to 1939. A major university would be founded in his honor in Waltham in 1947. (Its president, Samuel Thier, would become the first Jewish president of Mass General in 1994.) Meanwhile, Edward A. Filene (1860–1937) developed his family clothing business into nothing less than the largest department store in the world. Well might the WASP doctors of MGH cling to their power in medicine and surgery. The entire world was at the gates—and grabbing for just about everything else.

Dramatic changes in Boston's demographics in the latter half of the nineteenth century and into the twentieth were reflected in Boston medicine, as were the increasing number of medical specialties, which the old guard at MGH held off as long as possible. Dispensaries, or outpatient clinics, had existed before 1811. The Massachusetts Eye and Ear Infirmary opened as the Boston Eye Infirmary in 1824, and in 1832 one of the nation's first maternity hospitals, Boston Lying-In, opened as well. But it was in 1858, not long after Colonel Perkins's death, that the first competing general hospital was chartered in Boston. Boston had grown, and the city needed more hospital beds, which MGH, with 140, could not or would not supply; furthermore, much of the city's growing population was increasingly remote from the Bulfinch Building of the West End.[11] Boston City Hospital, in the South End, was the result. The staff of Mass General opposed such competition, and when the groundswell of support for Boston City proved unstoppable, West End voices said, well then, BCH should treat a lower class of patient than MGH. But the founders of Boston City stood against its becoming a place for paupers, and affiliated with Harvard Medical School, as it soon was, the "City" inevitably provided competition for the oldest hospital in the city. In 1864 Mass Eye & Ear also began an affiliation with Harvard Medical School. Competition took another form, too. "From the beginning," wrote Morris J. Vogel, a student of Boston hospitals of the period, "Boston City—in contrast to Massachusetts General—had selected its house officers from applying medical students by competitive oral examination."[12]

In the next half century numerous hospitals, both general and specialty, would open, many serving immigrant groups. In 1863 the Carney Hospital, the first Catholic hospital in New England, began caring for a largely Irish-born patient population in South Boston. Nursing was provided by the Daughters of Charity of St. Vincent de Paul. Five years later St. Elizabeth's Hospital, founded by five laywoman members of the third order of St. Francis, opened for the care of South End women. In 1869 a group of Harvard Medical School graduates under Dr. Francis Henry Brown established Boston Children's Hospital in the South End. Again, the patients were predominately Irish immigrants, at least initially; nursing was by the Anglican Order of the Sisters of St. Margaret.

By the 1890s improvements in surgical techniques had led to several private hospitals for surgery. These included the L. C. Elliot Private Hospital (the most successful of the group) as well as the Pirlot Private Hospital, the F. A. Rein-hard Hospital, the Laing Dispensary, and the Dr. Phillips Private Hospital.[13] The final decade of the nineteenth century also saw the opening of the Boston Emergency Hospital (1891); Deaconess Hospital, founded by Methodist deaconesses (1896); and Faulkner Hospital in Jamaica Plain (1900). In 1902 Mt. Sinai Hospital opened in the West End, providing outpatient care and a home lying-in service for the city's Jewish population. Hospital literature was available in both English and Yiddish.[14] In 1916, the year Mt. Sinai was effectively folded into it, Beth Israel Hospital was established as a general hospital in Roxbury, underwritten, staffed, and patronized by the Jewish community. The kitchen served only kosher food. Vogel wrote, "As the Irish hospitals had done for Catholic practitioners, Beth Israel offered Jewish doctors opportunities for hospital affiliation otherwise generally denied them. And soon after it opened, Beth Israel began a nurses training school, opening to Jewish girls, a career from which they had been excluded."[15]

Against this background of hospitals opening right and left, another major change threatened the generalist grandees at MGH: specialization. This began in outpatient departments and dispensaries, where younger, newly trained specialists earned their spurs before some were granted admission to inpatient staffs. At Boston City, early specialties included dermatology (1868), otology (1869), gynecology (1873), neurology (1877), and laryngology (1877). Mass General was slower to act. A ward exclusively for the care of skin diseases was opened in 1870 but closed by a vote of the trustees two years later. Outpatient clinics opened for ophthalmology in 1873 and otology in 1884.[16] Change took time. Vogel noted:

> The growing influence of specialists, and thus also of scientific medicine, in hospital affairs was institutionalized at Massachusetts General in 1898 when the trustees installed the senior practitioner in each of the outpatient departments as a regular voting member of the visiting staff. Nathaniel Faxon, later administrator of the hospital, remembered the growing influence of the specialties while he was an intern in 1905–6. They brought "new men with new ideas" into positions of power and played a significant role in reshaping the hospital in the early years of the twentieth century.[17]

Arguably the greatest change in the Boston medical landscape at the beginning of the twentieth century was the founding of the Peter Bent Brigham Hospital, opened on Longwood Avenue in Brookline in 1913. Like Mass General, Boston City Hospital was affiliated with Harvard Medical School; also like Mass General, the City insisted on controlling its own appointments. At the turn of the century, then, Harvard boasted relations with the region's two largest and most important general hospitals, but it had no final control over either one. Try as Harvard's President Charles Eliot and others might to reform the medical curriculum at Harvard, opportunities for clinical training for its students remained tightly in the grip of these two independent-minded general hospitals. To remedy this, in

1889 Harvard began to consider the founding of its own university hospital. Here is where Brigham came into the picture.

Peter Bent Brigham, a Boston millionaire with interests in railroads and real estate, died in 1877 and left a large fortune in trust, the capital to be used 25 years after his death to found a hospital. Harvard's leadership began to eye the Brigham bequest, which would grow to $4.3 million by 1902. Forcing Harvard's hand was the fact that the medical school was already running out of room on Boylston Street, where it had moved from in front of Bulfinch in 1883. Vogel explained the attraction of a Harvard-controlled hospital built with this sizable gift: "A school controlling appointments in a great new hospital would no longer be operating on only the local scene. It would be a national institution reaching beyond Boston for a distinguished staff."[18]

With such a powerhouse in the offing, organizers raised close to $5 million more for an enhanced medical school associated with the new hospital, drawing contributions from Morgan, Rockefeller, and Huntington interests. Leading the charge for a new Harvard-controlled hospital was none other than J. Collins Warren, who considered that his grandfather had made a mistake by putting MGH under the control of its own trustees rather than Harvard. The younger Warren would also lead the fund-raising charge for the Collis P. Huntington Memorial Hospital for cancer patients (folded into MGH in 1941) and for Vanderbilt Hall, a dormitory for HMS students. Heading up the search committee for Brigham hospital leadership was the very same William T. Councilman, late of Johns Hopkins, who had hired J. Homer Wright as an MGH pathologist in 1896. Councilman's first loyalty was to Harvard Medical School, and he pushed the hiring of Hopkins-affiliated doctors, the best and the brightest, for leadership positions at the Brigham, including the surgeon in chief, Harvey Cushing (Johns Hopkins Hospital by way of Harvard Medical School), and the physician in chief, Henry A. Christian (Boston City Hospital by way of Johns Hopkins Medical School).

In fact, the Peter Bent Brigham Hospital, which finally opened in 1913, was not the first Boston hospital to be completely under the control of Harvard Medical School. That distinction fell to Children's Hospital and then Infants' Hospital (founded as the West End Nursery in 1881). But it was a major shot across the bow of MGH, and for the next 80 years—or until MGH and the Brigham merged to form Partners HealthCare in 1994—it would be the Avis to Mass General's Hertz.

RADIOLOGY FROM X-RAY TO fMRI

A nineteenth-century surgeon operated in a cave plunged in darkness. Until 1846 that cave was guarded by two monsters, one at the entrance, another at the exit. At the entrance stood pain, a monster slain by ether. At the exit of the cave, after surgery, stood infection, a monster defanged by Lister and his successors. But even in 1890, after the advent of anesthesia and asepsis, the cave of surgery was dark, and notwithstanding diagnostic guesses, the surgeon seldom knew what he would find until he mucked around. Then, just before the turn of the century, a small boy appeared with a torch, took the surgeon by the hand, and showed him the way: there's the fracture, there the abscess, there the deadly tumor. The name of the small boy was Wilhelm Conrad Roentgen, and the name of his torch the X-ray.

Roentgen, a German who would win the first Nobel Prize in physics in 1901, took his first "medical X-ray" on December 22, 1895, and titled it *Hand mit Ringen,* "Hand with Rings." It was an image of his wife's left hand. Whether the MGH photographer Walter James Dodd or Harvey Cushing, a house officer, was first to apply Roentgen's technique in Boston is a matter of dispute, though never as acrimonious as the Morton-Jackson ether spat. Dodd's is the compelling story, although Cushing would have a stellar career as a pioneer brain surgeon at Peter Bent Brigham Hospital.

Walter Dodd.

Who better to experiment with X-ray technology than the MGH "photographer"? After all, roentgenology, as it was grandly known, "was at first a matter only of taking pictures, though by a hitherto unknown method."[19] Who better than the self-made Dodd, when many of the hospital's professional staff initially looked askance at the X-ray? The early X-ray images were murky, and even with improved technology, interpreting the chiaroscuro patterns was a challenge for the radiologist. X-rays "take a picture" of everything in their path, from the front of the body to the back, collapsing the depth of field and putting everything on one plane, making interpretation a hard-won art.

Born in London in 1869, the son of a "worker in metal roofing," Walter Dodd came to America at age 10 to live with a sister. He went to work at 13, eventually snagging a job in Harvard's chemistry lab as an assistant janitor. He impressed the professors with his curiosity and mental abilities and obtained permission to audit classes and participate in lab work. In 1893 he became the assistant apothecary at MGH, qualified as a registered pharmacist, and doubled as the hospital's photographer for purposes of pathology. After reading accounts of Roentgen's X-ray technology, he rigged his own apparatus and started using it at MGH in 1896. Physicians were impressed by the potential of X-rays and made frequent use of Dodd's services. A second set of X-ray equipment was given to MGH by Charles G. Weld in 1897.

Dodd and his assistant, Joseph Godsoe, were forever tinkering to improve their machines. The MGH administration continually moved them from room to room; they were never granted a permanent space that would indicate that their work was highly esteemed. When George A. Waterman was a house officer in 1900, he would recall:

> [The] X-ray room was . . . in the little room under the arch, at the left of the main entrance of the old, original building. It was in this room that Dr. Putnam first started the Department of Neurology, when he came back from Europe in 1872. Dr. Shattuck used to picture Dr. Putnam as sitting in this little room under the arch with an electric battery. They used to send to him all cases that nobody understood. On account of the appearance of the arch

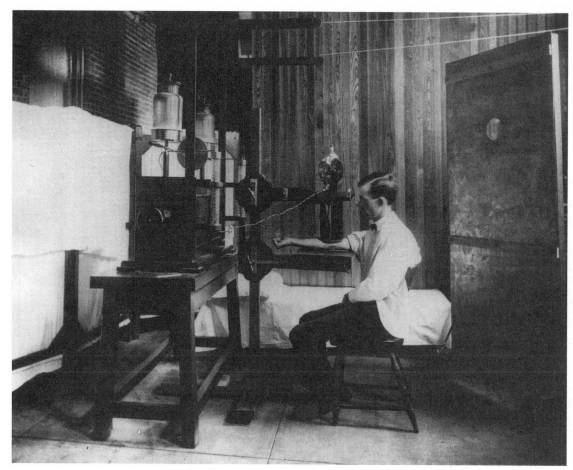

Walter Dodd demonstrates early X-ray equipment.

and the inflow of patients not understood, and not desirable for this reason, Dr. Shattuck said they used to call it the "*cloaca maxima.*"[20]

To translate loosely from the Latin, the X-ray Department was tucked in the rear end of the hospital.

Although his lab moved several times, Dodd did not move until 1908. He usually resided at Mass General, and Frederic Washburn's account of the early days of radiology in his history covering 1900–1935 suggests that Dodd seldom left the grounds. From its first days the department had "constant service," according to Washburn, day, night, Sundays, and holidays, which "meant much devotion on the part of the staff of the Department."[21] Only the crudest abnormalities within the body could be made out in the early X-ray images: a fracture, a bullet lodged near a lung, a coin or whistle caught in the throat. Dodd became a master at interpreting these shadowy images. He finally earned a medical degree in 1908, not from Harvard but from the University of Vermont. The following year he was promoted to skiagrapher (from the Greek for "shadow painting") "and thus received the official title to the job he had done from the beginning, fourteen years before," according to Washburn.[22] With his new medical standing, he moved out of the hospital, opened a Back Bay office for private practice, and worked mornings at MGH. George W. Holmes was made assistant roentgenologist, and Godsoe became apothecary and photographer.

Like many who experimented with early X-rays, Dodd was burned badly by radiation. Otha W. Linton, a historian of the MGH Radiology Department, explained why: "The common way to tell when a tube was ready to make a patient exposure was for the operator to hold his hand between the tube and the face of a fluoroscope. When the bones of his hand became visible, the tube was ready for use. This meant that the operator's hand received the most radiation."[23]

No one knew how many X-rays were too many. Linton noted, "At first, most physicians worked with what was termed the 'erythema dose' or the length of exposure required to make the skin redden—much like observing a sunburn."[24] Tumors became Dodd's constant companions. First admitted to MGH as a patient in 1898, he "submitted to operation after operation until he finally died, a martyr to x-ray, in 1916. His sufferings were intense."[25] He underwent at least 50 surgical excisions on his hands, until he had to wear gloves to hide the maimed and missing knuckles. As a final act of heroism, Dodd joined the Harvard Medical Unit in June 1915 and went with it to France, before the United States entered World War I. He had a major operation on his arm before leaving. He was driven by ambulance to a train, which took him to New York, from which he embarked on a boat.[26] "His death, shortly after his return, cast a gloom over the Hospital," according to Washburn.[27] George C. Shattuck would recall that Dodd's "never failing good humor, helpfulness and heroism made a deep impression upon us all."[28]

We are left to imagine one sweet spot in Dodd's last years: in 1910, past the age of 40 and finally free to keep a place of his own, he married an MGH nurse, Margaret Lea, and together the couple enjoyed homes in Boston and on the shore for the last six years of his life.[29] A tribute in the 1917 annual report must have been some consolation to Mrs. Dodd. Alluding to her husband's Horatio Alger–like success, it read in part: "Starting with nothing but high character and ability, he worked his way to a position of leadership and great usefulness. . . . His cheerful bearing of pain and his devotion to science are an inspiration to all the hospital."[30]

The Holmes and Hampton Years

Since the days of Dodd the Radiology Department at MGH has experienced a century of growth. A brief overview suggests that, unlike some departments that have grown by fits and starts, radiology has been blessed by the leadership it needed at each phase in its development to assure a relatively smooth growth curve. For 55 years, from Dodd's death in 1916 until the arrival of Juan M. Taveras in 1971, the department had just three chiefs, George W. Holmes, Aubrey O. Hampton, and Laurence L. Robbins; Holmes and Robbins served all but 18 months during that period. Such continuity would persist, as at this writing Taveras has had only one successor, James Thrall, who followed him in 1988.

Beginning in 1916, the year of Dodd's death, fourth-year Harvard medical students were instructed in the use of X-rays. By the end of the war, when Holmes was made roentgenologist, X-rays were commonplace. A machine was placed in one of the operating rooms to help in the setting of fractures. When Phillips House opened in 1917, it was equipped with its own X-ray machine,

George W. Holmes.

and when Baker Memorial Hospital opened 13 years later, it had its own radiology service as well. This divided the radiology staff more or less along class lines. Holmes did his work for the high-paying patients of Phillips, Aubrey Hampton (before he became chief) and James Lingley focused their work on the middle-income patients of Baker, and Richard Schatzki was assigned the charitable wards of Bulfinch.

Walter Dodd had been interested by the apparent ability of X-rays to reduce pain, and early on radiation was used with moderate success against inoperable cancers. Through 1971 Holmes, Hampton, and Robbins would insist that radiologists be trained in both diagnosis and treatment, and the addition of Milford Schulz to the staff during World War II was a boost to radiation medicine, what we now call radiation oncology. It was not until Taveras took over that radiation medicine split off from radiology and became its own discipline at MGH. (For more on radiation medicine, see the discussion of cancer in chapter 7 and the proton beam in chapter 8.)

The department's odyssey from one hole in the wall to the next paused in the Gay Ward in the 1920s, then moved again to temporary quarters before finally settling into the White Building when it opened in 1939. By this time radiology had been reassigned to the Department of Medicine from its initial status as a subset of surgery. The residency program was extended to three years to meet board requirements.[31] Radiology was on a dramatic growth curve, at Mass General and everywhere, but it would remain a chancy and sometimes dangerous pursuit, especially in proximity of the million-volt Van de Graaff machine installed for radiation treatment in 1939:

> In December of 1944 a serious accident occurred in the Department when several people ventured into the cathode-ray beam from the million-volt machine. That injuries could occur from this source was essentially unknown and totally unpublished at that time. Fortunately, all five people who were involved in the accident survived, although it must be recognized that at least one of them might not have had it not been for the availability of recently available antibiotics. That this was a new event was appropriately recognized, and publicized, and thus was of value in determining the unanticipated effect of atomic bomb radiation which was to follow in the near future.[32]

George Holmes retired twice. Aubrey O. Hampton replaced him early in 1941, but after the attack on Pearl Harbor, Hampton entered military service at

Walter Reed Army Hospital and Holmes emerged from retirement to oversee the department for the duration of the war. For his service before becoming chief as much as for his brief term as leader, Hampton would be remembered as "one of the most intuitive radiologists in the country. One trainee reported memorably, 'He could look at a film and tell you what color suit the patient had worn to the hospital.' "[33]

After his second retirement at war's end, Holmes was remembered as "the builder, the consolidator, the teacher, and the manager of the 'busiest department in the hospital.' "[34] He had enjoyed a distinguished academic career and by the time of his retirement was a national figure. Everyone makes mistakes, and Holmes seems to have overlooked the future of nuclear medicine: the use of radioactive isotopes for diagnosis and treatment. But this specialty would return under his successor, Laurence L. Robbins.

The Robbins and Taveras Years

Born in Burlington, Vermont, the son of a Methodist minister, Robbins earned his medical degree from Walter Dodd's alma mater, the University of Vermont. He was named acting chief in 1945 and assumed permanent status in February 1946, at the age of 35. He would serve for 25 years and become the first professor of radiology at Harvard Medical School. According to a colleague, Robbins had "an uncanny eye for an abnormal X-ray pattern and established a reputation for diagnostic accuracy that made him a legend in his own department. He could dazzle staff conferences by spotting the pathology from a distance of 15 feet at a 45-degree angle to the view box and then finish his bravura performance by referring to similar cases he had seen ten or 15 years earlier—even remembering the names of patients."[35] Robbins was a genial father figure besides, with an open office door, one of those leaders who would be forgotten too easily but for the many brilliant radiologists who developed under his leadership; meanwhile, the department exploded, from more than 30,000 annual examinations just before World War II to five times that in 1971, Robbins's last year as chief. Peers recognized his stature: he was awarded gold medals by the Radiological Society of North American and the American College of Radiology.

Three other radiologists formed the Big Four of MGH radiology in the Robbins era: Milford Schulz (radiation medicine); Stanley Wyman, who developed the specialty of angiography; and Edward "Ted" Webster, who pushed forward the academic study of radiation physics. Other key contributors included Majic Potsaid (nuclear medicine), Paul F. New (neuroradiology, the first true radiological subspecialty at MGH), and Lucy Squire, a legendary teacher. The 1960s were a challenging decade, however, as the advent of Medicare, not to mention the presence of the charismatic general director John Knowles, threatened

Laurence L. Robbins.

Juan Taveras.

comfortable payment patterns for radiologists; and the department was drawn into the first skirmish of an ongoing turf battle with the Cardiology Division over who would "own" catheterization techniques. Stanley Wyman did all in his power to develop these, but the high-profile Cardiology Division, where the after-image of the legendary Paul Dudley White still shimmered (more on him later in this chapter), was not about to cede control to radiology. Stanley Baum, who would pick up the torch from Wyman in the 1970s, encountered more of the same, according to Linton: "Dr. Baum was aggressive about pushing for radiologists to perform all elements of angiography. . . . Charles Sanders, chief of the catheter laboratory and later hospital director, said he saw no reason why radiologists should learn catheter placement skills. Dr. Baum replied that he had devised many of the procedures he used and intended to teach them to radiology fellows, and he did."[36]

By the time Juan Taveras took over in 1971, MGH had established a tradition that would have been unthinkable in the nineteenth century, of looking outside Boston for its chiefs. Born and first trained in the Dominican Republic and most recently head of the Mallinckrodt Institute of Radiology at Washington University in St. Louis, Taveras was such an outsider. He was highly esteemed, having 234 papers and 11 books eventually to his credit, including the standard reference in his specialty, *Diagnostic Neuroradiology*, coauthored in 1964 with Ernest H. Wood.

Linton summarized the situation in MGH radiology that faced Taveras upon his arrival: "Most of the equipment was old and worn. Some units dated to the opening of the department in the White Building in 1939. Salaries were low by comparison with private practice or some other academic centers. The examination volume had increased in 1971 to 164,671 procedures in 29 rooms. The residency program was strong. Generally speaking, morale of radiologists was good. 'For a radiologist, MGH was the most exciting place in Boston,' recalled one junior member of the staff."[37]

According to Linton, Taveras was an early subspecialist in neuroradiology, and under his leadership a trend toward specialization begun under Robbins came into full flower. Majic Potsaid became director of nuclear medicine, and by the end of Taveras's first year, there were 10 other subspecialties within radiology: gastrointestinal, genitourinary, bone, neuro, angio, pediatric, cardiovascular, ultrasound, body CT, and mammography—a list that remained pretty much intact as late as 2009. In addition, Ted Webster headed up a new division of radiologic sciences, where he was joined by Gordon Brownell, who had headed the physics research lab since the 1950s. Brownell's team did groundbreaking work on positron emission (PET) scanning.[38]

As a neuroradiologist, Taveras was notably ahead of the curve on computed tomography, called CT or "cat" scanning. At his urging, MGH bought one of the first two units in existence in 1973. The first-generation CT machine took pictures of the brain by rotating around the head; a second generation in 1976 had the capacity to image the entire body. Ultrasound was added to the radiological armamentarium in the 1970s, at MGH as elsewhere. Then came the development of magnetic resonance imaging (MRI), where again Taveras was among the first to see the potential. When H. William Strauss replaced Majic Potsaid as head of nuclear medicine in the mid-1970s, the radio-cardio turf battle continued over this new technology. Strauss and the cardiologist Gerry Pohost joined the fight over cardiac applications of MRI. According to Linton, "Dr. Taveras was able to preserve radiology's control of MRI, but at the compromise of some domain over nuclear cardiac imaging."[39] When Thomas J. Brady arrived in 1980 for a nuclear medicine fellowship—then stayed (in 2011 he was still on board as vice chairman of MGH radiology research and director of nuclear medicine)—MRI work at MGH leapt ahead, and the overall radiology research program was placed on a stronger footing.

Enter James Thrall

By the mid-1980s Taveras had reached retirement age, but replacing him was no easy task. Although he had led the way into new scanning technologies, much of the equipment in the department was aging, as Taveras had not marshaled the financial resources to keep it up. There was a 15 or 20 percent vacancy rate among radiation technologists, although, according to James Thrall, who would replace Taveras, "the quality of the radiation professionals was good." The search committee sought someone with the demonstrated ability to run a large department, but many top candidates declined the opportunity because the radiation facilities at MGH were below par. Thrall noted that if the committee had looked at him when beginning their search in 1985, "I would not have been a candidate."

Trained at University of Michigan Medical School, Thrall had served a hitch at Walter Reed in Washington, where he worked in nuclear medicine, before his appointment to the chairmanship at Henry Ford Hospital in Detroit in 1983. His track record as chairman was only two years long by 1985, but the MGH search dragged on into 1988. Finally Tom Brady, a former fellow under Thrall, recommended his old boss. Barbara O'Neill, a member of the search committee, called Thrall and asked him to look at Mass General. He recalled: "What attracted me was not the condition of

James Thrall.

the department but the quality of the radiologists in the department, that and the idea that if others had been successful in this environment, there was no reason I couldn't be successful. I perceived in the MGH and Harvard Medical School environments one of the very few places in the country where you could build a world-class research program."

Research, which before Taveras had "commanded very little support from outside funding agencies," according to Linton,[40] had grown to somewhere between $3 million and $4 million. That represented a small percentage of the hospital's $90 million annual research budget. Growth would explode. In 2009 the total radiology research budget was $75 million, or 15 percent of the $500 million research total at MGH. The number of radiologists on staff had more than tripled under Taveras, from 42 to 153, though not without some organizational and financial stresses, some of which were addressed by the formation of a radiology group practice, MGH Radiology Associates, in 1985. Under Thrall in 2009 the department had about 460 faculty and trainees, including 115 radiologists, 95 MD trainees, and 250 PhD scientists, another tripling.

A chronic problem, shortage of space, was addressed upon Thrall's arrival in 1988. MGH was making the biggest move in its history—branching off the main West End campus into half a million square feet of new research space in the old Charlestown Navy Yard across the Charles River, a story that is developed fully in chapter 7. Here, in a massive, 10-story structure, the Radiology Department had not only space but two other important features needed for its high-tech equipment: lofty ceilings and strong floors: perfect for siting heavy MRI units. Juan Taveras had already made a move, getting an initial 9,000 square feet for his department there. But Thrall pushed the envelope, adeptly negotiating another 35,000 square feet for radiology as one condition of his hiring. This included three imaging bays for MRI scanners. There was a hitch, as Thrall recalled:

> MGH realized we had regulatory authority for only one MRI. I pointed out that if an opportunity came up for another MRI system, it would be disruptive to the original system to unbutton the facility and construct a second bay, and more expensive; so we built three bays even though we had authorization for only one MRI, a great case of the institution betting on itself. Within six months of the facility's completion, General Electric approached us about placing a state-of-the-art echoplanar MRI system (very rapid imaging) in one of the bays, and it was precisely on that system that the first images for functional MRI (fMRI) were obtained. I can break out into a cold sweat thinking how close we came to not having the space for that critical installation.

fMRI

Arguably the most dramatic achievement during Thrall's tenure has been the development of functional magnetic resonance imaging, or fMRI. Simply put, all earlier radiologic imaging, from X-ray through PET and CT to MRI itself, took pictures of static anatomy. A radiologist could not, and still cannot, tell by looking at an X-ray whether the subject is alive or dead. Functional MRI, pioneered at

MGH and developed elsewhere from the mid-1980s onward, shows life itself—an organ system in action.

Bruce Rosen has been in the catbird seat since fMRI's first mention at MGH. There is a long line of astronomers who became radiologists (both interpret images), and Rosen is one of them, a self-described "propeller head" who built a telescope in his backyard as a boy. A Harvard College mentor counseled Rosen that jobs in astronomy would be nonexistent in the years following his thesis. An advisor at MIT demonstrated how radioastronomy could be used to detect breast tumors—deducing gradients in tissue temperature from radio waves emitted back by the tissue ("thus combining several of my greatest interests," according to Rosen). Rosen discovered MGH's first MRI machine in the sub-basement of the Gray Building only to be rebuffed by the cardiologist Gerry Pohost, who still wanted MRI for himself. Rosen heard a lecture by an MGH radiologist, Jeff Newhouse, about MRI and thought, "This is cool." By this time Rosen had his own fellowship money and could pursue the interest if it pleased him. It did.

Ian Pykett, the resident nuclear magnetic resonance (NMR) physicist, left MGH to start his own company, Advanced NMR Systems, and Rosen, a grad student, suddenly became the hospital's NMR physicist. Rosen had a simple explanation: "I was the only one who knew how to fix the machine." Working with a radiology fellow, Arno Villringer, Rosen began exploring ways to measure blood flow in order to measure function. The technique involved injecting a contrast agent in the bloodstream and taking MRI images of the brain in two states: at rest and in activity. By subtracting one image from another, it was possible to deduce the areas of the brain that were fired by the activity. Originally, Rosen worked with gerbils and rats.

Jack Belliveau, a grad student, came into the story here, in about 1986. Belliveau began using this subtraction technique to study stroke in gerbils—leading to one of the all-time nutty names for a rock and roll band (Belliveau's). The band was called Gerbil Stroke Model. To this day, evaluating stroke victims is arguably the most important clinical application of fMRI. Using a high-speed MRI machine developed by Ian Pykett's successful start-up, studies moved from gerbils to humans the day Bruce Rosen himself was injected with contrast agent and imaged. "I sacrificed myself for science," Rosen said, still functioning quite well nearly 20 years later. In November 1991 Belliveau was lead author of a cover story on fMRI in *Science,* which marked one of the signature achievements in the history of MGH radiology.[41] Belliveau won a Young Investigator Award from the Society of Magnetic Resonance Imaging for his first demonstration of human brain activity using MRI.

Important as this method was, it required injection of an agent and subtracting one picture from another. Ken Kwong, an MGH fellow at the time, was building on early work of Keith Thulborn and exploring how to image blood flow and brain function *without* a contrast agent. Then a resident in radiology at MGH and now director of the MR research program at the University of Illinois at Chicago, Thulborn found that deoxyhemoglobin molecules (found in deoxygenated blood returning to the heart) acted like small magnets disturbing the MR field

Bruce Rosen (foreground) and Ken Kwong with an image of their 1991 cover story in Science (courtesy MGH REMS).

and showed up on an MRI. Thulborn did his work in test tubes; Kwong realized that it might work in humans. Another investigator, Seiji Ogawa, was doing related work at AT&T and had published papers on it, but Kwong credits his insight to Thulborn and Robert Turner, whose critical animal imaging experimental result changed the thinking on how blood flow change and the MR signal should be linked. Turner is now director of neurophysics at the Max Planck Institute for Human Cognitive and Brain Sciences in Germany.

Kwong and his team were able to image blood flow in the brain without a contrast agent in the very first experiment he ran one evening in early May 1991. "My immediate reaction," said Kwong, "was, this could be MR signal noise." Where some might have rushed to publish a finding, any finding, Kwong spent another two or three months verifying his observations—just in time for an annual conference of the Society of Magnetic Resonance in Medicine, or so he thought. His paper for the conference, submitted in time but in a strange twist delayed in the mail, was ruled out of the conference. Kwong's überboss, Tom Brady, asked Kwong if he would like the finding presented in a plenary session that Brady was heading. Without any record yet of publishing to prove that the finding was his, Kwong agreed without a second thought. Said Kwong, "It was great science. I said, 'Let's get it out there.'" It surprised no one that there was a mad scramble after the conference to publish papers based on Brady's presentation on the amazing images of brain activation mapping. It was Kwong, however, who had both the intellectual honesty and the confidence of his results to make his discovery available to the world, without promise of reward. Rosen acknowledged Kwong's achievement: "That changed the way we study and understand the brain. Now without any contrast agent we can observe the human brain in real time. We use activation mapping all the time now when we have patients we are going to operate on. The MRI may show where the tumor is but it doesn't show where the functional parts of the brain are. The surgeon needs to know what part of the brain is controlling motion, language or memory, to avoid cutting into that."

The applications of fMRI are countless, 20 years after the methodology was first deduced at MGH. Rosen added, "We have more neurologists and psychiatrists using this tool now than radiologists. We are beginning to study Alzheimer's, autism, schizophrenia. How about neuroeconomics? With fMRI we think we can study the brain when it is making irrational economic decisions!"

Other Recent Developments in MGH Radiology

The MRI operation in Charlestown evolved into the Martinos Center for Biomedical Imaging thanks to a gift from a Greek shipping family. In 2009 Bruce Rosen was director of the NMR center at Martinos. By then more than 200 investigators from all over MGH were using the center's machines and technologies. Anesthesiologists, for example, were trying to understand consciousness. Gastroenterologists were using it to understand irritable bowel syndrome. Why do people overeat? MRI-based techniques may help understand even this question at some not-so-distant date.

Molecular imaging   Beyond fMRI, the MGH Radiology Department was among the earliest proponents of molecular imaging, establishing the Center for Molecular Imaging Research at MGH in 1994, long before most peer institutions or commercial organizations were using the term. Under Ralph Weissleder's direction, MGH has what may be the leading program in the country and perhaps the world. Weissleder and other pathfinders recognized that the basic imaging paradigm of nuclear medicine could be replicated at the molecular level, as he explained in the September 1999 issue of *Radiology*: "Most traditional cross-sectional imaging techniques such as MRI, CT, and ultrasonography are reliant on physical (e.g., absorption, scattering, proton density, relaxation rates) and physiologic (e.g., blood flow) properties as the main source of contrast for the purposes of disease detection and characterization. Molecular imaging is built on these and other imaging techniques (nuclear, optical imaging) and is aimed at the exploitation of specific molecules as the source of image contrast."[42]

What Weissleder characterized as a "paradigm shift" created the potential for earlier detection of disease at the molecular level. We have come a long way from Walter Dodd's fuzzy shadow pictures. In 2007 Weissleder was tapped to head the new Center for Systems Biology in the Richard B. Simches Research Center on the main campus (see chapter 8).

3-D imaging   In the late 1990s Gordon J. Harris established a major effort to use advanced computer programming to resolve CT, MRI, PET, and other images into three dimensions. Walter Dodd's old chest X-ray collapsed everything from the front of the chest to the back into one plane. With 3-D imaging, MGH radiologists can focus on any unique location within the body.

Quality management   Thrall can boast of "a quality management program in the department that no one else has." Radiology at MGH even has its own industrial engineer. "Hospitals traditionally are like groupings of cottage industries on the same campus, with nonstandard processes," said Thrall. At MGH the Radiology Department led the way in coordinating digital record keeping and record retrieval. One example: if today a doctor decides to order a CT scan of a patient's head, the order-entry system will prompt the doctor if a scan has been run in any hospital in the MGH network, thus avoiding duplication of work and cost.

In Thrall's view, radiology has led the way for the entire hospital: "When I arrived in 1988 there was not a single computer terminal where we could look up a patient's record number. We still had rotary telephones! Institutionally we were very far behind, but especially in the past 15 years [1994–2009] we have gone from laggards to leaders. We probably have the best hospital information systems, and the only one I know of with an ontology search engine—like a systemwide Google search but with criteria rank-ordered."

Using computerized order entry of every patient and procedure, Thrall estimated that the MGH Radiology Department had eliminated 400,000 phone calls per year. Monitoring this and so many other variables is the MGH Institute for Technology Assessment, founded within the Radiology Department in 1997 and headed by Scott Gazelle. Now an institution-wide program, it applies decision science, economics, clinical epidemiology, statistics, and outcomes analysis to investigative and clinical endeavors.

The MGH Department of Radiology in 2009 performed 650,000 exams per year on the main campus, at two outside hospitals (Martha's Vineyard and Saints Memorial in Lowell), and at eight imaging centers in the surrounding community. MGH had 14 MRI systems (each worth an estimated $2.5 million, not counting $1 million–$3 million in building overhead for each) and 12 CT scanners (high-end machines go for $1.5 million apiece). One measure of the department's prominence nationally and internationally was Thrall's position as chairman of the American College of Radiology Board of Chancellors. So dominant was MGH radiology on the national research landscape that in 2009 Thrall was selected to serve as a member of the advisory committee to the director of the National Institutes of Health (NIH). The success of MGH, Thrall says, is due not to machines or buildings but to people, "and in radiology we have had some of the most outstanding clinicians and scientists in the country. I would like to be remembered most for nurturing personal and professional growth in our department, from the top-level physician and scientist to the entry-level employee."

Looking beyond radiology, Thrall saw what he considered an overarching theme of success at Massachusetts General Hospital: "From time to time great institutions do things that are not obvious to everyone else and thereby distinguish themselves. The institutions that bubble to the top do more of the nonobvious." The decision to build three bays in Charlestown, instead of one, was such a nonobvious decision, Thrall believed. He also thought that the Bulfinch Building was another: "It was not obvious that Boston in 1811 needed a hospital." Other examples cited by Thrall include the move to Charlestown and the building of a proton beam facility (see chapter 8).

"MGH," said Thrall, "is a magnet for people who want to accomplish things in their lives, and they perceive in the environment the tools to let them do that. It's a meritocracy that builds on itself. Excellence begets further excellence. When I first arrived, my first impression of the department and of the entire institution was *creative anarchy*. I thought, We need to keep the creativity piece and get rid of the anarchy. Under President Peter Slavin and MGPO [Massachusetts General Physicians Organization] CEO David Torchiana, we have achieved discipline while retaining individual creativity."

Walter Dodd would smile.

REORGANIZING THE STAFF

As late as 1908, when Dodd earned his medical degree from the University of Vermont, the time-honored MGH model was firmly in place: Dodd took an office on Beacon Hill, where he charged fees to private clients, and served part-time at MGH, mostly pro bono in the charity wards of Bulfinch. It was a model that, however benevolent it appeared, was holding the hospital back. The system of rotations meant discontinuity of care; moreover, it prevented the full flowering of clinical research, since few doctors were around long enough each year to pursue ongoing investigations.

By the first decade of the twentieth century, agents of change were afoot. The Shattuck-Cutler-Minot letter of 1908 recommended a new hybrid system to test the effectiveness of a continuous service. Elbridge Cutler and Reginald Fitz, two of the three rotating physicians on one service, were retiring, and the letter suggested that instead of these positions' being refilled, Shattuck be appointed full-time visiting physician for the service. Meanwhile, the service would remain on the rotation system, and the two systems would be compared. A minority report was filed by Whiteworth Gannett and Herman Vickery against this plan, on the grounds that "for nearly a hundred years, the present system has proved satisfactory."[43] Trustees accepted the proposed change, however, and Shattuck was made visiting physician on the continuous service and Richard C. Cabot was appointed his assistant and presumably heir apparent, since Shattuck's own retirement was nearing.

Surgeons were slower to change, "but the spirit of the times was irresistible," according to Washburn. The "forward-looking" Ernest Amory Codman (see chapter 2) was one voice for change: "Our ideal should be to have some one member of the Hospital Staff doing as good work as any one in the community or in fact in the country, *in each of the special branches of surgery.* . . . At present, we do not see correctly where our individual interests lie and rather than allow the Massachusetts Hospital to advance in stomach surgery, for instance, we each prefer to take our individual try at it."[44] Here was the added issue of medical and surgical specialties, which MGH was slow to accept. Specialization was a young man's game, a way for the newly trained doctor to break into the generalist ranks of established practitioners. Much of the old guard stood against it.

Surgeons finally decided to reorganize in 1911 "after much discussion";[45] the South Surgical Service was discontinued; and Maurice H. Richardson was installed as surgeon in chief—though when Richardson retired, the position would lapse. Chiefs of the East and West Surgical Services were authorized and the two men with most seniority, Francis B. Harrington and Samuel J. Mixter, were installed.

With this reorganization came the first "residents," although they were originally called house physicians and house surgeons—to distinguish them from the "resident physician," the title used by the hospital director. This reflected "the experience of other hospitals, notably Johns Hopkins. These men were graduate House Officers, appointed as a reward for outstanding work, to guide the House Officers, to take more responsibility than the latter were ready for, to participate in teaching and research where they were fitted, and to supply the public with a more highly trained group of doctors."[46] Paid small salaries beginning in 1913 and "given maintenance" at the hospital, residents increased in number dramatically; by 1935 there were 24.

In 1912 the General Executive Committee was organized to smooth relations between medical staff and administration. The first meeting was held April 30 in the Treadwell Library. Members of the GEC since that date have included top administrators and chiefs of medical and surgical services and departments. The charter members in 1912 were Maurice Richardson, Francis Harrington, Samuel Mixter, Algernon Coolidge, Richard C. Cabot, Director Frederic Washburn, and the new chief of medicine, David L. Edsall.

Meanwhile, however, the reorganized Surgical Service treaded water. Richardson died only a few months after taking over as chief,[47] and Harrington and Mixter retired, giving way to a succession of others in the next 15 years. Not until 1923 was a new overall surgical chief appointed, Edward P. Richardson, son of Maurice, but this position again lapsed with his retirement.

Upon Richardson's retirement, Washburn reported, "The majority of the General Executive Committee (GEC) recommended that an invitation be given to an eminent surgeon in another city [to replace Richardson]. . . . [But] the minority of the General Executive Committee . . . felt that just as good material could be found at home. The Surgical Staff felt also that payment of a continuous Chief was unnecessary."[48] In March 1930 Richardson's successor, Edward Delas "Pete" Churchill, returned to MGH from Boston City Hospital. Churchill began as an associate surgeon, but he was made chief of the West Service and Homans professor of surgery in 1931. At that time the West Service included all full-time surgical staff, while the East was "under the forceful leadership of Arthur Allen. . . . As the [1930s] drew to a close, however, it was apparent that instead of the services drawing apart, the East and West, in defiance of Kipling's dictum, did in fact meet on common ground"[49]—allowing Churchill to assume the title of chief of the surgical service, a single leader at last. Churchill, a dominant figure, will be profiled in detail in chapter 4.

PHILLIPS HOUSE AND BAKER MEMORIAL

One final puzzle piece was needed before the MGH staff could become fully focused: noncharity wards where patients of major to moderate means paid for the services of physician and surgeon. For the hospital's first 100 years any fees (and they were small) for a doctor's attentions inside the hospital walls were paid to the hospital, and the doctor saw none of the proceeds. Since the doors opened to patients in 1821 there had been a few private rooms in Bulfinch. When the single-story wards began sprawling southwest of Bulfinch after the Civil War, Jackson Ward B was set aside for private patients as well. Still, during the nineteenth century takers for private rooms were few among Boston residents; most were out-of-towners who had no family home in which to receive care. In 1876 a notice in the society newspaper, the *Boston Evening Transcript*, carried the following advertisement for private service at MGH, its publication suggesting that such service needed promoting:

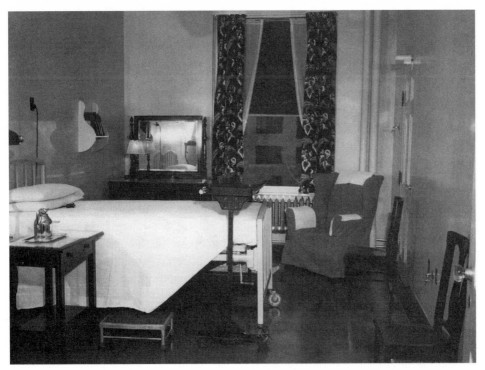

A patient's room in Phillips House.

It may not be generally known to the community that there are in the hospital some very elegant and luxurious private apartments for the reception and treatment of a class of patients, whether citizens or strangers, who, for peculiar reasons or circumstances would find special advantages here. If a visitor to the city, without relatives or intimate friends, became ill, or met with an accident while transiently staying at one of our hotels, and wished to enjoy all the care and luxuries to which an easy lot may have accustomed him, he would find in one of these apartments, with its attendant resources and accompaniments, a most desirable and privileged refuge.[50]

Better-heeled Bostonians continued to say "no, thank you" to hospital care until the turn of the century. Washburn cogently reviewed the innovations that changed their minds:

After Morton's demonstration of anaesthesia, Pasteur's discovery of the germ theory of disease, and Lister's application of it to surgery, it began to be apparent that something better in the way of facilities was needed for successful surgery. With the discovery of the X-ray and its application in surgery and medicine to diagnosis and treatment, and with the better knowledge of pathology and the use of the microscope on frozen specimens removed at the time of the operation, it became impossible to duplicate in the home the hospital facilities. The well-to-do discovered that in hospitals the poor were getting better opportunities for diagnosis and treatment than were available to them in their homes. They began to demand that this be changed so that their chances should be at least equal to those of the poor.[51]

In his 1910 report as resident physician, Washburn noted:

A private hospital built in close connection with the General Hospital is much to be desired. From the point of view of the community, this is needed because there is now in Boston no place where people of moderate means and the well-to-do can go to a hospital and pay their doctor and get all the advantages which they could have in a hospital connected with such an institution as ours. We have here the high traditions of a hundred years, well equipped laboratories and their accrued knowledge and recognized standing, the X-ray, Electrical, Hydrotherapeutic and Medico-Mechanical Departments with their skilled and experienced operators. From the point of view of the Hospital, a private hospital would be of value in the training of our nurses, in furnishing us a revenue to help support the charity wards, and in bringing to our doors people of means who, we would hope, would become interested in the work done by the institution. It would concentrate the work of the Staff and enable them to spend more of their time at the Hospital to the advantage of the patients.[52]

Before World War I, a committee of trustees took a fact-finding tour of other hospitals with private wards, including the New York, Roosevelt, and St. Luke's hospitals in New York, as well as Johns Hopkins, and in 1914 Director Frederic Washburn visited large hospitals in Europe.

Phillips House finally opened in 1917, at the edge of MGH land along Charles Street; it was a win-win proposition for doctors and the wealthy patients they previously had seen on the side. Named for the first great family of MGH benefactors, Phillips provided luxury accommodations for those who could afford them, and its patients paid not only the hospital for these but also the doctor for his care. *Luxury accommodations* is not hyperbole: adjoining many patient rooms were smaller chambers for live-in servants brought from home; butlers were sent ahead to set fires for the master's or mistress's arrival. Food from S. S. Pierce was custom-cooked in the Phillips House kitchen and served on silver and china, accompanied by fresh-cut flowers on the side. Phillips House had its own telephone exchange. Call it the Ritz with MDs. We might chuckle at the extravagance and exclusivity, but the doctor benefited, the patient benefited, and MGH began to assemble a true full-time staff for the first time, just in time. There is evidence that a brain drain was already under way, that other great hospitals were luring doctors with the promise of full-time duty.[53]

The eight-story Phillips House had room for 102 patients.[54] Patients could choose their own physicians, "provided they are members of our staff or our alumni,"[55] a list later supplemented by "a small invited list of doctors on the staffs of other hospitals that had no private wards."[56] MGH had no obstetricians on staff (nor would it for another 76 years), so a portion of Phillips House was set aside for maternity services, where outside OBs could bring their patients, thus increasing hospital occupancy. A nurse-assistant to the director of the hospital, Pauline Dolliver, was put in charge of the entire Phillips operation. Dolliver had been superintendent of nurses and principal of the nursing school from 1897 to 1909. She took ill in 1920 and was replaced by Alvira Stevens, who had served as

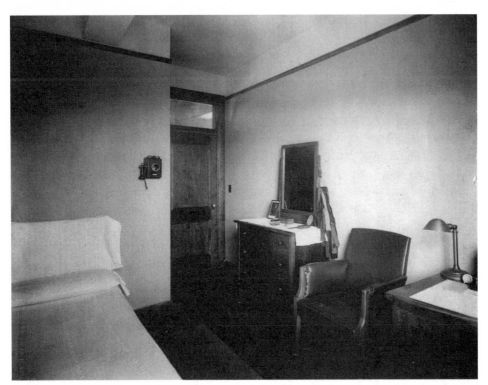
A patient's room in Baker Memorial.

assistant superintendent at McLean and seen service overseas during World War I with British General Hospital No. 22. "Her patience, tact, and fine personality have made her eminently successful,"[57] wrote Washburn, her former boss, in 1938.

Six years after its opening the trustees could boast that the ward for the wealthy "has fulfilled the need in the community for a high-class hospital in Boston, where people who can afford to pay for it may go and receive the advantages of treatment at an institution where all the appliances and knowledge demanded today by medical science can be found."[58] Phillips House would be followed in 1930 by the 11-story Baker Memorial for patients of moderate means. This larger facility was made possible by a $1 million gift from Mary Rich Richardson in memory of her parents. Eventually, the Richardson bequest proved insufficient to cover construction expenses, and a public fund-raising effort added $900,000.[59] A commitment from the Julius Rosenwald Fund helped cover operating expenses. Old Wards C and D, directly west of Bulfinch, were destroyed to make way for Baker, which itself would be destroyed in 1991 to make way for the Blake Building. Like Phillips, Baker was largely self-contained, with its own operating rooms, X-ray and anesthesia services, offices, and kitchen.

Baker Memorial was for patients caught in the middle, according to Haven Emerson, a historian of the facility. Such patients were too proud for charity, too impecunious for Phillips House:

> It was generally recognized by 1914 that people of moderate means were receiving less efficient care in case of sickness than were other classes of the community. Self-respect prevented their applying for free ward care, and

their resources were not sufficient to meet the very considerable charges in a private hospital which must be self-supporting, with the result that when sick they had generally to remain at home, where their physicians could not provide necessary laboratory and other scientific examinations and certain forms of treatment available in a general hospital.[60]

Dedicated February 27, 1930, Baker opened with 189 beds and 31 bassinets: "Several floors were used by the General Hospital for ward patients, resident physicians, and nurses, until with the increased demand for space for middle-rate patients the bed capacity was enlarged, from year to year, to 242 beds and 40 bassinets in 1936 and thereafter through 1939. In 1940 there were 271 beds available for the first six months and 284 in the second half of the year. It seems likely that within the present Baker Memorial building the maximum bed capacity will be 303 beds and 40 bassinets."[61]

Baker offered MGH-quality care at reasonable rates: $6.50 per day for a single room, $5.50 for a double, $4.50 for a quad, and $4.00 for a cubicle. Further surgery, lab, and anesthesia fees were added, and the physician collected what he could. An upper limit of $150 per stay was set on "medical or surgical attending and consultant services."[62] Early patients were classified as follows: professional (28 percent), mercantile (29 percent), artisan (32 percent), retired or unspecified (11 percent).[63] It is probably fair to say that there were few "artisans" in Phillips House and few "professionals" in Bulfinch. The class structure held. For the staff, this maximized potential income. No longer was a surgeon forced to operate on a well-to-do person as an act of charity. No longer did the physician miss the middle-income patients who were too proud to accept charity but unable to afford Phillips House. The demand curve for hospital services (on which a select few *wanted* high-priced services, a larger number could afford medium-range pricing, and the masses needed free care) was in full play.

Third-party insurance would arise in the 1930s, with the advent of Blue Cross, and the applecart would tip again. Baker Memorial's run would last until 1991, but after relocating from its original building to the top three floors of the Ellison Building, Phillips House continues to accommodate well-to-do patients and others in private rooms. (Some patients are placed there not because of their financial circumstances but for medical need—for example, to provide privacy to the family of a dying patient.) The current facility (59 beds) affords spectacular views of the city and the Charles River. Old ways die hard, especially in Boston.

RICHARD C. CABOT

It is tempting to equate the Boston Brahmin with stodgy conservatism, and it would take a non-Boston, non-Harvard physician named David L. Edsall to shake up the old MGH aristocracy and push it, kicking and screaming, into the twentieth-century world of full-time clinical research, specialization, and biomedical scientific investigation. But before moving on to Edsall, who arrived in 1912, let's pause to consider the case of Richard Clarke Cabot. No one had bluer Boston blood. Cabot was a paragon of all things good about Boston medicine, and as controversial as he was gifted.

Richard C. Cabot.

A nephew of Samuel Cabot and a cousin of Arthur Tracy Cabot, both men MGH mainstays in their times, he was a great-grandson of Thomas Handasyd Perkins, a founding benefactor of the hospital. His family was closely related to other Boston dynasties, including the Jacksons, Higginsons, Dudleys, Lowells, and Lees. His mother, Elizabeth Dwight Cabot, was a cousin of Harvard's President Charles W. Eliot. His father, James Elliot Cabot, was a personal friend and biographer of Ralph Waldo Emerson, and the younger Cabot cherished personal memories of the frail, elderly Concord philosopher visiting his boyhood home.[64] Though he thought he might have a career as a Unitarian minister or philosopher (the Emerson influence, surely), Richard Cabot credited a meeting with Edward Trudeau, the founder of the Saranac Lake tuberculosis colony, with his decision to become a physician. A graduate of the Noble and Greenough School and Harvard College, where he was summa cum laude in philosophy (1889), Cabot was the first Dalton Scholar in 1894–1895 and wrote a paper titled "Diagnostic and Prognostic Importance of Leucocytosis."[65]

Hematology became one of his strengths, and he began his medical practice by opening a blood lab in his home at 190 Marlborough Street in Boston.[66] By the time he was invited to join the staff of MGH in 1898, he had already published his first book, *A Guide to the Clinical Examination of the Blood for Diagnostic Purposes* (1897), which became a standard work on the subject and went through five editions. Imagine how hard it must have been for an outsider to crack the Boston-bred MGH staff at the turn of the century if Cabot, with such a pedigree and record of accomplishment, had to wait *five years* from his graduation from Harvard Medical School (1893) to earn appointment to the outpatient staff of MGH, what we would call an entry-level position. Cabot even enjoyed the support of his uncle Edmund Dwight, chairman of the hospital board.

Richard Cabot rose through the ranks at Harvard Medical School as lecturer (1899), instructor (1903), assistant professor (1908), and professor of clinical medicine (1918). His October 24, 1914, article on heart disease for the *Journal of the American Medical Association* was called "a landmark in medical history" by no less an authority than Paul Dudley White, the father of American cardiology.[67] With the Brahmin call to duty encoded in his genes, Cabot paused once in his career to serve on a troop ship treating patients with infectious diseases in the Spanish-American War and then again in 1917–1919, when he served as chief of medicine at U.S. Base Hospital No. 6 in France. Like Cabots before and after him, he recognized that his singular gifts, genetic and financial, obliged him to do more than most men of his time. "I feel that not to do something really great will be for me to have failed entirely. I have never heard or read of anyone with such advantages," he wrote in his notebook.[68]

Despite his scientific bona fides, Cabot saw medicine as something more than identifying and rooting out a microorganism from a diseased organ. He saw it in what today we might call holistic terms; his senior paper at Harvard Medical School was "The Medical Bearing of Mind-Cure," in which he analyzed the newly minted phenomenon of Christian Science and discussed the medical value of faith. Elsewhere he called for physicians to broaden their approach: "In the practice of medicine outside of the hospital, psychical elements are everywhere present and often paramount, while in the laboratory they are reduced to a minimum."[69] Too much time in the lab would make physicians view patients as experimental objects and not as human bodies with souls.

He saw medicine in broad terms, just as he saw his personal role and duty. Richard Cabot took teaching seriously. Beginning from his own case notebooks, which stretched to 36 bound volumes by the time of his retirement from active clinical work in the 1920s, he developed and promoted the Clinical-Pathological Conferences, or Cabot Case Records, a "substantial contribution" to teaching, according to Washburn.[70] Beginning in about 1900 at Harvard Medical School, Cabot developed the pedagogical technique of describing for students the patient's symptoms and lab results; asking the students to provide differential diagnoses (to list all possible conditions that might have caused the symptoms); then delivering the definitive diagnosis himself, based on a surgical finding or autopsy, the results of which he had withheld until then. Cabot published the first 78 of these cases, with questions about each, in 1906, two years before the opening of the Harvard Business School, where the "case method" was enthusiastically embraced and became the principal means of instruction.[71] Beginning in 1910 Cabot held exercises with house officers and visitors in the MGH wards. In 1911 he published another 100 case histories, followed later by another 385, as *Differential Diagnosis, Volume I*, and another 317, as *Volume II*. Cabot's cases became regular features in the *Boston Medical and Surgical Journal* starting in 1924, and each week similar case studies continue today in the *Journal's* successor, the *New England Journal of Medicine*.

Still, Richard Cabot is perhaps best known for another innovation. In 1905 he founded the Social Service Department at Mass General, the first affiliated with an American hospital. Social service was an outgrowth of his work with outpatients; he understood that the mostly impoverished people who dropped in without appointments came from environments that might be detrimental to their health. These patients, he noted eloquently, "shoot by us like comets, crossing for a moment our field of vision, then passing out into oblivion."[72] Why "cure" them only to release them back into unhealthy families, homes, and neighborhoods? With the support of influential friends, including the chief of neurology, James J. Putnam, and Mrs. Nathaniel Thayer, the wife of a trustee and later a trustee herself, Cabot set about training social service workers who would follow up by visiting patients at home and better assuring their continuing health.[73] Ida M. Cannon, a sister of the legendary HMS physiologist Walter B. Cannon, was a social service bulwark and MGH legend. She became chief social worker in 1907 and director of the Social Service Department in 1914. In his biography of

Ida Cannon and Richard C. Cabot of the MGH social service department.

David Edsall, Joseph Aub also credits Peggy Reilly, a nurse, for her work in the early Social Service Department. Aub wrote, "She deserves a chapter herself for her great spirit and her gift of laughter."[74] Reilly told Aub that Cabot personally underwrote the cost of 13 social service workers to get his department up to speed.

Cabot founded the Social Service Department at MGH the old-fashioned way, with private funds, and he had to fight for formal institutional standing. In 1909 Cabot published *Social Service and the Art of Healing*. The following year he raised the hackles of colleagues with a paper arguing that "the unacceptably high percentage of diagnostic errors seen in hospitalized clinic patients was often caused by the failure of physicians to take adequate social histories. This work, along with his public exhortations for prepaid medical practice, nearly led to his expulsion from the Massachusetts Medical Society in 1915."[75] Cabot continued to publish on social work: *What Men Live By* (1914), *Social Work: Essays on the Meeting-Ground of Doctor and Social Worker* (1919), and *The Goal of Social Work*, papers edited by Cabot (1927). Social work gained departmental status in 1919. That same year Cabot shifted fields, accepting an appointment as a professor of social ethics at Harvard College. He maintained his private practice on Marlborough Street and a limited clinical presence at Mass General, but he retired from Harvard Medical School at age 52.

In his ongoing work on ethics, Richard Cabot continued to anger former medical colleagues with his critiques. A lab scientist by training, he did not believe in the miracle of pharmacology, at least not as it was practiced in his day. In 1906 he had written in his article "The Physician's Responsibility for the Nostrum Evil" in the *Journal of the American Medical Association:* "I believe that we not only feed public demand for useless and harmful drugs, but also go far to create that very demand. We educate our patients and their friends to believe that every or almost every symptom and disease can be benefited by a drug."[76]

In the same article Cabot railed against "placebo giving," by which he meant physicians prescribing drugs that they knew were unlikely to work organically. In this, in his pointed criticism of doctors who failed to take account of patients' social circumstances, and in cautioning fellow doctors against using patients for experimental purposes, Cabot seems a forerunner to another ethical gadfly, Henry Knowles Beecher. It is perhaps not surprising that Cabot's generally laudatory obituary, written by Paul Dudley White and published in the *New England Journal of Medicine*, took one good dig, citing Cabot's "militant bluntness and precipitate desire to correct the errors of the practice of medicine."[77]

If sympathy for a wealthy Brahmin from "cold-roast Boston" comes hard, consider the terrible burden Cabot bore throughout his adult life. In 1893, when Cabot was just 25, his beloved older brother Ted lay dying of diabetes, at a time when insulin was still three decades from discovery. Newly educated at Harvard Medical School, Cabot was called home by his parents to care for Ted. Richard Cabot revealed what happened in his brother's bedroom 43 years later in biographical interviews with Ada McCormick, who was helping him organize his papers.[78] Cabot euthanized Ted with chloroform, not because Ted had asked him to do so (he hadn't), but because Richard wanted to put Ted out of his misery. The tragedy did not end there, as McCormick described it:

> It was an awkward and ugly event in his memory of it. He recalled that after he thought that Ted was dead, he began to speak about him in the past tense, when suddenly a whispered voice rose up to him: "Richard gave up too soon—I wasn't dead," his brother said. Even reported from the distance of forty intervening years the words were chilling. They seemed not so much to be directed at Cabot as to be about him, a gentle rebuke from the elder to the younger brother. Cabot told McCormick that it had not been easy to finish what he had begun and, in his words, "to crush out his struggling life with chloroform." Finally, his brother's misery was ended. Cabot had been equal to the task after all, although he agonized to McCormick on that August day that one had to consider "how much you are doing it for the other person & how much to relieve your suffering at their suffering."[79]

Well might Cabot have wondered about medical ethics.

We feel again for Richard C. Cabot when reading that David L. Edsall arrived from St. Louis in 1912 and snatched the prestigious Jackson Professorship that by all rights should have been Cabot's. The outgoing Jackson professor, Frederick Shattuck, had endorsed Cabot, at least for a time, but 1912 was not the moment for a broad-minded philosopher of medicine to lead Massachusetts General Hospital forward into the brave new world of biomedical science. Two years before, Abraham Flexner's epochal report on medical education in the United States, sponsored by the Carnegie Foundation for the Advancement of Teaching, had pointed a finger at Harvard and MGH for letting medicine be ruled by old families and old ways and thereby falling behind in investigation. Flexner wrote, in part: "While the university is free to secure laboratory men wherever it chooses, it is practically bound to make clinical appointments by seniority, in accordance with the custom prevailing in the hospital which it uses, or to leave its professor without a hospital clinic. In general it follows that the heir to the hospital service is heir to the university chair. In consequence there is a noticeable lack of sympathy between the laboratory and the clinical men. They do not represent the same ideals."[80] The Boston powerhouses were not the only institutions cited by Flexner, who recommended closing fully half of all American medical schools. This in fact happened; in 1901 there were 155, in 1943 about 60.[81]

Cabot was a good sport about Edsall's appointment and supported him publicly. But in private and in later years he let his true feelings be known. Missing out on the Jackson Professorship was one of the great disappointments of his life. One can only speculate on how the MGH Department of Medicine might have been different if a philosopher and medical ethicist had been in control. T. Andrew Dodds wrote, "The life of Richard Cabot reminds us that the growing emphasis of laboratory-based science to clinical medicine was not inevitable."[82]

But Edsall came, Edsall conquered, and biomedical research arrived at Mass General.

A WIND FROM THE WEST

To understand the implications of Edsall's arrival, consider the professional dress of Frederick Shattuck, Edsall's predecessor, as recalled by a future chief of medicine, James Howard Means, who was a house officer under Shattuck: "He wore a garment which was morphologically like a morning coat but it was made out of tweed so it wasn't black like a morning coat. It was quite a fancy looking garment and with it he almost invariably wore a red necktie and a fancy waistcoat and spats etc. so he was quite a dressy looking figure in those days. . . . His coachman drove him down every day in his private turnout and left him at the east end of the Bulfinch Building."[83]

Edsall "was a totally new breed of cat," according to Means.[84] He wore a white lab coat, and an inelegant ill-fitting one at that, according to Aub: "He did not even appear on the wards well dressed, but got into a white surgical gown, very loose and shapeless. His heavy, enormous figure appeared even stranger in the white gown, and it was always too small for him, so his long arms would stick out from the sleeves, while the ribbons which tied the gown in the back fluttered in the breeze. The Boston doctors looked on rather puzzled."[85]

The lab coat makes us think at once of Edsall as a scientist and technician, but the brilliant young doctors Edsall brought along in

David L. Edsall.

his wake—like Aub, like the legendary cardiologist Paul Dudley White, like the Nobel Prize–winner George Minot—saw Edsall first as a teacher. He ushered in a new era at MGH not because he was the best lab scientist but because he found other men with the abilities to be the best in their fields and nurtured their development. Edsall's gift for teaching and mentoring is one that should never be forgotten when listing the virtues of leading contributors at MGH. Massachusetts General Hospital is a *teaching* hospital, uniquely associated with arguably the most distinguished medical school on the planet, and its true leaders—since John Collins Warren and James Jackson—have been clinicians, investigators, *and teachers*. Edsall would one day leave MGH to become dean of Harvard Medical School.

Edsall had the stature and presence of a leader. He stood six feet, four inches, and had a deep voice, as described by Aub and his collaborator Ruth K. Hapgood, writers of the primary Edsall biography, *Pioneer in Modern Medicine*.[86] Edsall was "built to scale, which caused inevitable comparisons with Barnum's famous elephant Jumbo."[87] A native of New Jersey, he entered Princeton College with the intention of studying classics. But his first taste of lab work, in a sophomore course on zoology and botany, was decisive, according to Edsall himself: "That little piece of work, on the development of a chick's ear, was one of the really significant things in my training as it gave me some idea, early in my life, as to what it meant to work and think independently and to make an effort in an elementary way to arrive at a scholarly judgment on some subject, even though it was a small one."[88]

Edsall developed an intense interest in pure research, especially chemistry. Inspired in part by his older brother's career in medicine, he enrolled in 1890 at the University of Pennsylvania's medical school, at a time when Penn, Harvard, and Columbia's College of Physicians and Surgeons were arguably the three leading medical schools in the United States; Johns Hopkins Medical School was only just building steam. Medicine was discovering new methods in Philadelphia then as in Boston. Edsall would recall that he and his Penn roommate were "the only students among the six or seven hundred then in the whole of that school who had ever counted blood or examined stained specimens of blood."[89] A couple of years after Edsall's 1893 graduation from medical school, Richard Cabot would open his hematology clinic in the Back Bay.

After interning at Mercy Hospital in Pittsburgh, a choice he later called a mistake, Edsall went abroad for a year of medical studies in London, Vienna, and Graz (Austria). The miracle of diphtheria antitoxin, just coming into use, opened his eyes, as did the emerging German dominance in biomedical investigation, where William Osler would note "the paramount importance of knowledge for its own sake. . . . The presence in every medical center of a class of men devoted to scientific work gives a totally different aspect to professional aspirations."[90] Edsall returned to Pittsburgh, hung out a shingle, and waited for patients. He persevered for six months, then moved back to known turf, Philadelphia. Here he had the good fortune to land an assistantship to the great professor of medicine William Pepper. From Pepper's lab in 1897 he published his first paper, a case study of a patient with tuberculosis and cancer. This and subsequent work from the young Edsall concentrated on the analysis of gastric contents. As Aub and Hapgood noted: "The papers dealt with patients, using the relatively new techniques of the chemical laboratory to study their diseases. This represented a new approach to clinical medicine; in America, not even counting of blood was yet indulged in by pioneers like Richard Cabot. It was an active and exciting period."[91]

By the end of the decade Edsall was an instructor in clinical medicine at Penn and a key contributor in Pepper's lab. He had practiced medicine at both the Home for Incurables and St. Christopher's Hospital for Children and held the position of pathologist at the Methodist Hospital—while helping write the annual summary of medical advances in *The American Year-Book of Medicine and Surgery*, which required him to know everything worth knowing about the cutting edge of medical practice and investigation. A prodigy, he was 12 years from Boston.

Nine more years in Philadelphia, 1900–1909, included marriage to his beloved Margaret Harding Tileston, a Boston native, and the birth of their three sons, as well as charter memberships in the Interurban Clinical Club, the Society for Experimental Biology and Medicine, and the American Society for Clinical Investigation. Edsall became a recognized authority in everything from pediatrics (he was first president of the Philadelphia Pediatric Society and subsequently a president of the American Pediatric Society) to industrial diseases (soon to be an important theme at MGH). He began an association with Harvard Medical School in 1904, when Penn sent him north to study the new Harvard "concentration method" of teaching. It was through this connection that Edsall's name first came into play as a possible successor to Frederick Shattuck as head of the East Medical Service at MGH, although for a long time Richard Cabot would be considered the heir apparent.

In the academic year 1909–1910 Washington University in St. Louis, motivated by the same Carnegie-Flexner report that had criticized Harvard, sought to upgrade its medical school by calling Edsall west. But Edsall's proposed plan for Washington University was too grandiose for the school's limited budget, and at the last minute Edsall was offered the chairmanship of medicine at Penn so that he could effect a Flexner-spurred reorganization at *that* institution. University politics in Philadelphia, including a reaction by the old guard, frustrated Edsall's plans for reform there, and by the middle of academic year 1910–1911 he was entertaining a revised offer from St. Louis, to become Washington University's professor of preventive medicine. It was a step back from a central leadership role, but it was a new discipline.

Edsall's first assignment in St. Louis was to take a year off, for research and study. He chose to spend the year in eastern Massachusetts—for Margaret, for a summer on Cape Cod, for Harvard, and for the Carnegie Nutrition Laboratory in Cambridge, where he began work on metabolism that would spill over to MGH. Before the winter meeting of the Aesculapian Club he delivered what may have reverberated as a sort of manifesto, clearly defining and calling for a new era of clinical research in medicine:

> It is especially important that clinicians be trained into the judicial and inquiring spirit . . . for no one is more constantly an investigator than any thoughtful practicing physician and no one has more important or more complex problems to solve, and his mind must be trained to meet these. . . . I

think all thoughtful clinicians will agree with me that [a clinician's] greatest struggle is in avoiding the danger of falling into the habit of deciding all things upon an empirical basis. While a hypercritical attitude makes a man ineffective, there is nothing more dangerous perhaps in practical medicine than an uncritical attitude.[92]

It is hard to appreciate today what a challenging perspective this was at the time. Medical research was in the very first stages of explosive growth, but clinically based physicians, including much of the MGH staff, had yet to embrace it. Years later Edsall would recall that "serious devotion to research in medicine was looked at askance by very many of the medical profession itself. . . . [The] purely clinical viewpoint was almost wholly dominant."[93]

Edsall was poised to upset tradition. Back in St. Louis, a tempest was rising in the teapot again. MGH and Harvard partisans can take comfort that theirs was not the only medical community held back by an old guard at the cusp of the modern era. Edsall's efforts in Philadelphia had been stalled by politics and tradition, and now in St. Louis factions of "jealous alumni" and "a variety of trustees" were digging in their heels against the substantive changes Edsall felt called to effect.[94] Things in St. Louis went from bad to worse as the academic year played out, but Washington University's loss proved to be Harvard's gain. By the spring of 1912 the groundswell of support for Edsall as Jackson professor at Harvard and new chief of the East Medical Service at MGH had grown to a torrent. Even Richard Cabot was willing to fall on his sword for the man from the west. He magnanimously wrote an introduction for Edsall to the *Boston Transcript*:

> He does not represent a clearly defined new order of things, with a division so sharp as that which Lister brought into the practice of surgery; yet in a very real way he does stand for that new combination of chemical and pharmacological research which is the most striking and most promising movement in the medical world of today. Boston has until very lately had no adequate inducements to offer to a man like Dr. Edsall. The archaic organization of our hospitals gave no adequate opportunity for such work as Dr. Edsall's until the staff of the Massachusetts General generously sacrificed their own personal interests to a reorganization which made it possible to offer Dr. Edsall an adequate place.[95]

As Aub and Hapgood note, "This was really very handsome of Cabot."[96]

Edsall got a surprisingly warm welcome from cold-roast Boston and particularly noted "the pleasant spirit of general affection for Harvard" that seemed to animate the medical community. What Edsall lacked was not the support of his new community but laboratories and the funds to put full-time men in them.

James Howard Means would recall that Edsall "did not try to accomplish too much at once. To find a man here, a salary there, and now and then a bit of space in which research could be done was in the beginning enough for him."[97] Means called early lab space under Edsall "perhaps bizarre, and certainly disseminated."[98] The metabolic lab was sited in a small triangular room under the Outpatient Department amphitheater, and others were on the third floor of the so-called power house, which contained the generator. In 1917 the hospital built the Moseley Memorial Building to absorb administration offices from the ground floor of Bulfinch East, leaving space in Bulfinch that, following a 1925 remodeling, became the pioneering Ward 4 (more on this below). In 1930 the top floor of Bulfinch West would be remodeled for surgical research.

An eyewitness wrote: "Edsall wanted more assistants, so he picked three of the interns he found on duty at the time of his arrival [Paul Dudley White, James Howard Means, and George Minot] and sent them off in various directions for training in research methods." This was generous and courageous of Edsall: these promising young men might have chosen not to return. But all of them did return and "formed the original nucleus of his full-time teaching and investigative medical clinic."[99] If this trio had been Edsall's only legacy to MGH, it would have been enough. Means would head the Medical Service at MGH for nearly three decades, and Minot would win a Nobel Prize for diagnosing and curing pernicious anemia. Paul Dudley White would become one of America's first celebrity physicians, called in to care for President Eisenhower following a heart attack. As an American goodwill ambassador around the globe throughout his career, he was nominated for the Nobel Peace Prize in 1970.

CARDIOLOGY FROM PAUL DUDLEY WHITE

Two MGH physicians, Richard Eustis and Joseph Pratt, began a cardiac "class" for adults and children with heart conditions in the Outpatient Department in 1913, when blood pressure was beginning to be taken regularly and heart X-rays were used more frequently. In the same year David Edsall decided to send a promising young doctor to study cardiology and electrocardiography in London, and to bring back a prototype electrocardiogram (ECG) machine known as an Einthoven string galvanometer. Happily for the future of cardiology at MGH and cardiac care worldwide, Paul Dudley White, the short, slender, magnetic young man who had studied under Pratt as a fourth-year medical student and graduated from Harvard Medical School in 1913, was the "promising young doctor." White had assured Richard Smith, a brilliant young pediatrician, that he could assist him in his practice after graduation. Nevertheless, with Smith's blessing, White accepted Edsall's offer, moved in part by the recent death of his little sister Dorothy from rheumatic heart disease.

For several years to come, most doctors would feel that "the field of cardiology and its name were beneath the dignity of a young physician trained in internal medicine."[100] White himself recalled, "My former medical school teachers or hospital chiefs would warn me that I was entering an insignificant special field and would never be heard from again. Even the nurses would advise me not to study such a difficult part of the body as the circulation, which was customarily relegated to a few back pages of the medical textbooks of the early years of the twentieth century."[101] With some trepidation, White sailed for England in July 1913 to study cardiology with James Mackenzie, who demonstrated the efficacy of digitalis in treating cardiac arrhythmias, and Mackenzie's student Thomas Lewis, who pioneered ECG use in the clinic and in the laboratory on human and animal

Paul Dudley White (left) with President Dwight Eisenhower, whom he treated following a heart attack.

specimens alike. Lewis, a dedicated researcher, eventually took White under his wing. White often assisted Lewis into the early morning hours, accompanied Lewis on his walk home, and went back to the laboratory to accomplish a few hours' additional work.

Upon his return to MGH, White founded the country's first dedicated cardiac unit in June 1916. The medical world was not sympathetic to White's enthusiasm. Most doctors regarded the ECG as "a troublesome toy, always getting out of order and of little or no clinical usefulness,"[102] "little better than the clumsy old mechanical pulse tracing machine called the sphygmograph."[103] The newly acquired Einthoven machine found its home in the basement of the ward for skin diseases, next to the syphilitic bathroom. Cardiology would be headquartered in this dark corner until it moved to the former apothecary shop under the stairs near the central entrance of the Bulfinch Building. The department was allotted more adequate quarters in Bulfinch East in 1925, though its tenure there was bookended by stopovers in its old haunt, the skin ward basement.

White's initial efforts to develop the discipline of cardiology at MGH were interrupted by his service in World War I. Daniel Fiske Jones, a senior MGH surgeon, invited White to join his Harvard unit, to serve at Base Hospital No. 22, near Boulogne, France. After a brief reprise of his duties at home during the first half of 1917, White shipped off to war again, this time with the MGH unit, led by its commanding officer, Col. Frederic Washburn and, as chief of the Medical Service, Lt. Col. Richard C. Cabot.

In January 1919 White led a small unit of medical officers on relief work in Eastern Macedonia and the Greek Islands under the Red Cross. White's unit worked with Greek doctors to help victims of a typhus epidemic that had devastated the Balkans. He recalled forcibly escorting 24 gypsies with the help of a gendarme to a public bath for a compulsory delousing. Passing an entourage of priests in the street warding off disease with candles and relics, White thought the priests must be doing at least as much good as the doctors, who could offer the sick people little relief.

After World War I Paul White took over the Outpatient Department and the adult heart clinic at MGH and later added the children's heart clinic, as well. Richard Cabot's influence was again evident: in 1925 the clinic employed a full-time social worker, Edith Terry, who instituted programs for pediatric patients, such as the "In-Bed Club," arts and crafts, and tutoring in school subjects. She also made follow-up medical-social home visits to the young patients. By 1936 the Cardiac Clinic had one part-time and two full-time social workers.[104] In his speech at the hospital in honor of Ether Day in 1936, White emphasized, "Optimism and the improvement of the home care of heart patients have been keynotes."[105]

Though not most widely known for his publications, Paul White accomplished significant original work in cardiological research. He pioneered electrocardiograph use and published more than 700 articles, as well as 12 books, including his textbook, *Heart Disease*, first published in 1931, which served as the standard in cardiology for several decades. White was also immortalized by his work in electrophysiology with Louis Wolff and John Parkinson. The three men discovered a condition of uncontrolled rapid heartbeat, now called Wolff-Parkinson-White syndrome.

In the course of his international travels, White met many young physicians, whom he encouraged to come to MGH for a postgraduate year. A spiritual descendant of White, Roman DeSanctis, recalled how, on July 1 each year, young doctors would appear from nobody knew where, having been invited by Paul White. To create a formal program for the young talent he attracted, White founded a nine-month postgraduate course in cardiology. After White left the hospital, the subsequent chief of cardiology, Edward Bland, took charge of the postgraduate program, and later DeSanctis did the same. The course ended in 1964 when Bland retired as chief of cardiology.

White cultivated professional relationships and personal friendships with men and women from around the world. He organized collaborative studies with Soviet cardiologists and was a member of the first group of doctors to venture behind the Iron Curtain after World War II. Later he joined a second group of physicians who went to China after the Bamboo Curtain fell. After the Chinese Cultural Revolution ended in 1976, leading Chinese cardiologists visiting the United States made a trip to MGH a top priority, to pay their respects to Paul White.

DeSanctis recalled sitting in a Hong Kong airport, en route from Tokyo to Thailand in 1971, when White unexpectedly appeared. Mao Zedong had been ill, and reporters eager for a story nearly knocked down the octogenarian doctor to learn if he had seen the Chinese premier. He had not; he was on his way to make a house call on the Shah of Iran. Medicine was an international language that everyone could share, White believed, and one he helped promulgate. His work for world peace, which he named irenology, or the science of peace, was in line with his dedication to preventive heart medicine: the health and well-being of people, today and tomorrow, were the ultimate goals of his life's work.

White often described his work as preventive heart medicine; to an American public suffering from an epidemic of cardiovascular disease he advocated an active lifestyle with regular exercise, a healthy and moderate diet, and abstinence from tobacco. Owing in large part to White's influence, long-term prevention of heart disease became fashionable. White practiced what he preached. DeSanctis recalled meeting White for lunch one day at the latter's Beacon Hill office. White had ordered a chicken salad sandwich for DeSanctis; when lunch was brought in, White made his own lunch out of four saltine crackers arranged on a plate.

On the national scene, White helped found the American Heart Association in 1924. He resigned as chief of cardiology at MGH in 1949 to become the executive director of the committee that founded the National Heart Institute of the National Institutes of Health. He later encouraged heart health through a series of lectures initially entitled "Hearts of Husbands," referring to the high rate of heart disease among middle-aged men. The program began in Oregon in 1964, where citizens were worried about the growing discrepancy in life expectancy between men and women. Women were invited to seminars on heart health, with the hopes that they might be able to create the necessary changes in their husbands' daily habits. White encountered some resistance to his program. A woman writing to *Reader's Digest* accused White and other doctors of joining wives against husbands. She presented the following example: "John comes home from work in the evening and asks his wife 'What's for dinner?' She replies, 'Soup and fish and vegetables.' 'And what's for dessert?' he asks. She says there is no dessert. 'Why not?' he demands, for like most men he enjoys rich desserts. 'Because Dr. White says, "No,"' she answers. Whereupon John slams out of the house to get his dessert somewhere else."[106] In response to this and other objections, White changed the title of the preventive cardiology meetings to "Hearts of Husbands, Wives, and Their Children," with emphasis on children, whose habits are still malleable.

When President Eisenhower suffered a heart attack in 1955, White was called in to attend him. On one trip to Washington for a subsequent checkup, White walked the four or five miles to the White House from what is now the Reagan Washington National Airport because the weather was good. He used the fame that was thrust upon him after Eisenhower's heart attack to promote awareness of heart health and fund-raising for heart programs. The city of Boston would later honor White, an avid cyclist, by naming the 17-mile bicycle route around the Charles River the Paul Dudley White Bike Path. Paul White died on October 31, 1973, at the age of 87 years.

The Years after White

When Paul Dudley White left MGH in 1949, Edward Bland, who performed classic studies on rheumatic fever, succeeded him as the second chief of cardiology. That year, after New York doctors André Cournand and Dickinson Richards developed cardiac catheterization as a minimally invasive diagnostic method, a cardiac catheterization lab opened on the second floor of the George Robert White Building at MGH. The first cardiac catheterization studies were performed by Allan Friedlich and Gordon Myers. These doctors used the "cath lab" to study pulmonary hypertension, especially in patients with rheumatic valvular heart disease and congenital heart disease.[107] The data provided by these heart catheters helped open the field of intracardiac surgery to doctors.

By the 1960s the department's leading clinicians were Edward Bland, Conger Williams, Gordon Myers, Allan Friedlich, Howard Sprague, and Edwin Wheeler. In 1962 Roman DeSanctis was appointed as a junior staff member and took over some of the cath lab duties until a permanent director was chosen. There were three cardiac fellows, no research labs, and no research grants.[108] Clinical treatments, including drugs such as digitalis and quinidine, and physical methods such

Edward Bland.

as special beds and Southey's tubes, received particular attention. But when Edgar Haber succeeded Bland as the third chief of cardiology in 1964, cardiovascular research took off at MGH.

Walter Bauer, chief of medicine from 1951 until his death in 1963, had spotted Haber when the latter was only an assistant resident. On a fast track in his late twenties, Haber went from residency to the National Institutes of Health, where he worked with Christian Anfinsen, a biochemist whose work on ribonuclease won him a share of the 1972 Nobel Prize in Chemistry. After a year of clinical cardiology in England, Haber returned to MGH and succeeded Bland as chief in 1964.

During his years as a resident, Haber had become alarmed by the number of patients who died suddenly from myocardial infarction, or heart attack. Out of spare parts he built an apparatus for monitoring the electrocardiogram and detecting heart arrhythmias. Haber's heart monitor, the first of its kind, administered drugs according to the activity of the monitored heart. The new device planted the seed for the Coronary Care Unit, where patients with heart attacks were concentrated for highly specialized care. The MGH unit opened in 1971 with six beds on Phillips House 2, under the direction of DeSanctis, who was later assisted by Adolph Hutter. When DeSanctis became director of clinical cardiology 10 years later, Hutter directed the Coronary Care Unit for more than two decades. Subsequent Coronary Care Unit directors were Michael Fifer and James Januzzi.

Haber was one of the first basic scientists in a field that had until then focused almost exclusively on whole-animal physiological research (instrumenting a dog or a cat, for example, and observing changes). Haber emphasized the importance of both clinical and basic science research in cardiology, and he personally focused on immunochemistry and biochemistry, on which much of today's cardiology research is centered. Haber accomplished a vast body of work, including his pioneering studies on digoxin (digitalis) toxicity with Tom Smith. The two men developed a digoxin antibody to combat digoxin toxicity and a digoxin radioimmunoassay (a sensitive technique for measuring concentrations of antigens), which permitted the determination of blood levels of digoxin. These methods are still used today. Though somewhat formal and aloof, Haber was said to be a tremendous leader. In

Edgar Haber.

discussions with colleagues Haber would often appear to doze off until his inter-locutor stopped talking, at which point, Haber would look up and say, "Go on." He trained many young doctors at MGH who went on elsewhere to continue his tradition of basic science research in cardiology.

Under Haber MGH provided space for research projects funded by the National Institutes of Health, notably the Myocardial Infarction Research Unit (MIRU), established in 1967. Before the foundation of the MIRU, doctors and scientists had always approached the NIH with their own proposals for research. The MIRU was the first of many research projects that resulted from centralized management and direction of national research on a disease. Among the MGH doctors chosen for the MIRU, Herman "Chip" Gold and Robert Leinbach accom-plished critical work on dissolving clots in patients with acute myocardial infarc-tion. The MIRU was succeeded at MGH by the Specialized Center for Research in Ischemic Heart Disease.

Charles Sanders led the cardiac cath lab from 1965, when its primary focus was the evaluation of valvular or congenital heart disease. Though heart surgery (see chapter 6) was beginning to succeed with valve replacement, patients with the relevant condition were limited. The advent of coronary artery bypass surgery greatly widened the pool of potential patients who needed the diagnostic tech-niques of the catheterization lab. Sanders would become general director of MGH in 1972 (see chapter 6), and Peter Block assumed direction of the cath lab. He brought percutaneous coronary artery dilation to MGH, whereby a balloon is used to open narrowed coronary arteries, relieving symptoms of coronary artery disease without coronary bypass surgery. Block was responsible for the use of angioplasty (the widening of a blocked or obstructed blood vessel) at MGH in the 1970s, when the annual number of angioplasties quickly leapt from a few dozen to 1,500.

Working in the catheterization lab, J. Warren Harthorne was a pioneer in the development of pacemakers. He was elected first president of the Pacemaker Society and led the Pacemaker Laboratory from 1974. MGH hosted early work in implantable defibrillators used to treat patients at risk for sudden death. Studying ventricular dysrhythmia, Jeremy Ruskin led the electrophysiology lab from 1977, where doctors determined efficacy of various (sometimes dangerous, sometimes experimental) antiarrhythmic drugs, and developed the new field of cardiac elec-trophysiology. Ruskin still served in 2010 as the director of the very busy Cardiac Arrhythmia Service, which now treats all kinds of arrhythmias and has trained more than 30 of the leaders in this field now working around the world.

By 1980 techniques in cardiac catheterization had developed dramatically. In the new lab on Gray 3A, MGH cardiologists discovered that a heart catheter and coronary angiography could be performed in patients just after coronary occlusion without great risk of death. That lab was also home to the innovation of the intra-aortic balloon pump that kept low-cardiac-output patients alive while they recov-ered from major heart attacks or surgery or awaited definitive therapy. The devel-opment of balloon pump technique involved collaboration between cardiology, particularly Gold and Leinbach, and cardiac surgery, notably Mortimer Buckley.

The state-of-the-art Knight Catheterization Laboratory opened in 1999 in the Blake Building under the direction of Igor Palacios. Palacios, also director of

Roman DeSanctis.

the Structural Heart Disease Program, has pioneered techniques such as opening valves with balloons, closing heart defects with catheters, and using angioplasty and stents on narrowed coronary arteries. As one of the most respected interventional cardiologists in the world, he also has developed an international referral practice for several kinds of cardiac problems, such as rheumatic mitral valve disease and nonsurgical closure of intracardiac defects. While Palacios directs the lab's interventional program, Michael Fifer is its medical director, and Kenneth Rosenfield directs the Vascular Medicine Section.

In 1980 the Cardiac Division had 42 staff physicians and scientists, 37 clinical or research fellows, and 153 administrative and technical personnel. By 2010 it comprised approximately 450 physicians, scientists, nurses, and fellows in training, including more than 70 full-time clinical cardiologists and 15 part-time cardiologists. The Cardiac Division's fellowship training program is among the most prestigious in the world. Peter Yurchak directed the program for more than three decades, beginning in 1976. In 2007, as Yurchak was planning to partially retire and transfer responsibilities to his replacement, he became sick with pancreatic cancer and died within six months. Calum MacRae led the fellowship program until July 1, 2009, when Douglas Drachman was appointed its director.

The senior staff of the Cardiac Division place great importance on their interaction and collaboration with the fellows. Valentine Fuster, chief of cardiology at MGH in the early 1990s, instituted the Morning Report, a biweekly colloquium for fellows and senior cardiologists to meet and discuss cases. Roman DeSanctis, who still participated in the Morning Report in 2010 with Adolph Hutter, Eric Isselbacher, and James Januzzi, emphasized how essential the training component is to the Cardiology Division. "My greatest interest," said DeSanctis, "is training outstanding young people."

Valentine Fuster.

The Last Twenty Years

When Edgar Haber retired as chief in 1988, DeSanctis served as acting chief until Valentine Fuster arrived in 1991. Fuster, a renaissance man and one of the world's top cardiologists, led the division for three years, after which he returned to Mount Sinai Hospital in New York. He developed a faculty practice and expanded research mechanisms of atherosclerosis. Arthur Weyman came from his job as chief of the Echocardiography Laboratory in 1994 to become the fifth chief of cardiology.

Mark Fishman succeeded Weyman in 1998 as the division's sixth chief. From 1990 to 1998 Fishman had founded and directed the MGH Cardiovascular Research Center (CVRC). Fishman recruited a number of young world-class scientists to work at the CVRC, focusing on zebrafish as a model system to connect genes with the form and function of the cardiovascular system. In 1998, when Fishman was appointed chief of cardiology, he brought the CVRC under the Cardiac Division.

After an interim period as acting chief from 2002 to 2003, William Dec, a noted clinician and clinical investigator, became the seventh chief of cardiology at MGH. Dec had arrived at MGH as an intern in 1978, then trained in cardiology. He served as medical director of the MGH Heart Failure and Cardiac Transplant Program from its founding in 1984 until 2004. (It is now run by Marc Jay Semigran.) In 2004 Dec initiated the Vascular Medicine Section, a clinical service that Rosenfield now directs.

With the opening of the new Yawkey Center for Outpatient Care on Fruit Street in October 2004, care of cardiac outpatients was centralized. Whereas patients once had to travel from building to building to get their echocardiograms and blood work done and then go see the doctor, they can now make all of those appointments in the Yawkey Center.

The MGH Heart Center was created in 2006 under Dec's leadership, as a new organizational, administrative, and research framework for a number of cardiology programs at MGH. Eleven multidisciplinary clinical programs include the Thoracic-Aortic Center, the Cardiac Prevention Center, and the Structural Heart Center.

A three-year search for a new director of the CVRC following Fishman's departure led to Kenneth Chien's hiring as scientific director. Chien says it was the "unequivocally peerless world-class clinical cardiovascular medicine and clinical care, and the outstanding training in clinical cardiology," in addition to its high-level cardiovascular science in animal models, that attracted him to MGH from the Salk Institute at the University of California, San Diego.

Cardiovascular research at MGH goes back a long way. It was the primary focus when Paul Dudley White helped establish the Framingham Heart Study in 1948. More than 5,000 residents of Framingham, Massachusetts, between the ages of 30 and 62 who had not yet developed cardiovascular disease were examined and tracked every two years. The researchers hoped to identify some of the important factors that contribute to cardiovascular disease. The children and spouses of the 1948 participants were examined in the study's second round in 1971. Their grandchildren joined the third generation of participants in 2002. The Framingham Study continues to produce important information on the prevention and the natural history of cardiovascular diseases.

William Dec.

Genome-wide association studies (GWAS) using MGH patients, Framingham data, and international scientific collaborations assess the aggregate effects of thousands of genes on the development of certain, primarily cardiovascular, diseases in hundreds of patients. Now that powerful tools with which to analyze cardiovascular disease have been developed on animal models, cardiovascular research is returning to the arena of clinical medicine. Thomas Wang, Christopher O'Donnell, Christopher Newton-Cheh, and Sekar Kathiresan are spearheading these collaborations.

The heart is a mosaic of cell types, which raises the question: How are heart cells differentiated and coordinated during their very short period of development in utero? In 2009 CVRC scientists identified the master heart stem cell in the embryo that forms the three major distinct cell types in the heart: endothelial (blood lining), smooth muscle, and heart muscle. They subsequently discovered the father cell, the cell that gives rise to the master heart cell. On July 2, 2009, the discoveries were announced in the leading scientific journal, *Nature*.[109]

Thanks to a recent advance called cell reprogramming, an investigator can

Kenneth Chien.

take a skin cell from a patient and convert it to an embryonic stem cell, from which the master heart progenitor cell, responsible for the formation of all other heart cells, can be isolated. If the patient has a heart defect, the master heart progenitor cell can be used to form all the types of heart cells. Instead of studying a mouse with the same heart condition as a patient, doctors will now be able to study a patient's heart in a petri dish and directly develop drugs to treat the patient's problem.

This advancement will allow doctors to screen new drugs against diseased cells, improve those drugs, and eliminate their side effects. Patients who are at highest risk for cardiovascular disease from specific genetic disorders will be identified earlier and their treatments improved. Another future possibility is the treatment of heart disease with human master heart stem cells from embryonic stem cells or reprogrammed skin cells. Doctors may soon be able to implant reprogrammed cells and generate strips of muscle to replace bad muscle. As cardiological studies are integrated with other disciplines, heart science is moving closer to the patient, which has always been the driving force behind heart science at MGH.

ENDOCRINOLOGY AND THE STORY OF WARD 4

Even with a mandate to jump-start research at MGH, David L. Edsall found research funds hard to come by. The Dalton Scholarships had been available since 1891, and in 1910 Frederick Shattuck had endowed the Walcott Fellowship. MGH funded one resident per year, "but even by the time Edsall left the hospital in 1923, he had only $13,000 to support all the work that was being done. By contrast, the MGH research budget exceeded $10 million per year in the mid-1960s and $500 million 40 years later.

What credit does David Edsall deserve for research taking off during his 12-year tenure at MGH? Francis M. Rackemann wrote: "There is no doubt that it was Dr. Edsall who did more than any other man to promote clinical research at the Massachusetts General Hospital. It was he who wanted to extend and improve the training and experience of his young men. It was he who helped to start their investigations and who encouraged them, and finally it was he who 'sold' the idea to the Director and to the Trustees of the Hospital, so that his young scientists could find little places here and there to set up their laboratories and have a little money for apparatus and supplies."[110]

Edsall faced personal hardship at MGH (his beloved Margaret died of pneumonia in his first year), and he was not triumphant in everything he undertook at the hospital. In the mid-1910s, while war was raging overseas, he had a battle of his own trying to engineer a Johns Hopkins–like accord with the medical school that would have speeded the development of full-time positions at MGH. This would have allowed doctors to forgo the financial benefits of private practice on the side and turn their attention more completely to clinical research. His initiatives were squelched, initially by the surgical staff, then by others. For decades to come private practice would be a factor in MGH economics and, in some respects, an obstacle to progress. Still, extraordinary first steps were taken in clinical research, beginning with endocrinology.

In important ways the Department of Medicine is the intellectual center of any academic medical center, and at MGH for the better part of a century the Endocrine Division has been at or near the intellectual heart of the Department of Medicine. Nowhere else at the hospital has there been a greater commitment to investigative careers, and the research dollars pouring into endocrine at MGH in the early twenty-first century dwarfed those for any other department. The Mayo Clinic's Endocrine Division has sometimes outpointed MGH in the *U.S. News and World Report* rankings, largely on the strength of the Mayo's clinical reputation. But the endocrine research effort at MGH is second to none. More subjective has been the prodigiousness of the influence of MGH training on endocrine scientists worldwide. The list of presidents of the Endocrine Society and the list of heads of endocrine divisions nationwide are dominated by MGH-trained endocrinologists. Said Henry Kronenberg, chief of the Endocrine Division at MGH in 2008: "It's a well-kept secret in the Endocrine Society that a third or more of the officers of the society have been through the MGH program."

How did the Endocrine Division at MGH grow? Give ample credit to Fuller Albright and John Potts, but don't forget the Benedict Universal Respiration Apparatus. When David Edsall arrived at MGH in 1912, he brought a Benedict apparatus with him. Like Roentgen's X-ray apparatus, this was one of the new appliances transforming clinical and investigative medicine in the early twentieth century. The Benedict machine measured a subject's intake of oxygen and output of carbon dioxide. When Edsall proved too busy to pursue his own research with the apparatus, one of his acolytes, James Howard Means, adopted it, using it to study respiratory disorders. But Means soon became more interested in studying a patient's metabolic rate by measuring the transformation of gases. Observations of abnormal metabolism led Means to the thyroid gland, the regulator of metabolism, and in 1913 a modest thyroid clinic sprang up. The clinic was put on firmer footing after World War I, and in 1920 weekly case-study sessions began. This was an early prototype of the clinical approach at MGH, bringing together physicians and surgeons, lab technicians and nurses, to focus on a specific problem by observing and treating real patients.

When David Edsall left full-time duty at MGH to become dean of Harvard Medical School in 1923, he left behind a vision: to create a small ward used for clinical research by anyone on the hospital staff. That vision was realized in what became known as Ward 4, under the leadership of Edsall's replacement as chief of medicine, James Howard Means. As a physician came upon an investigative puzzle that could be solved only by observing patients and treating them experimentally, that staff member could make use of one or more beds in Ward 4. The overhead cost of research was initially covered by a hospital budget item of $15,000 for board, lodging, medicine, and nursing for 10 patients. Ward 4 had its own diet kitchen and dietitian. After World War II a private benefactor, Edward Mallinckrodt Jr., began to make significant gifts, and on August 20, 1948, the MGH trustees voted to name Ward 4 for him.[111]

In his history of Ward 4 from 1925 to 1958, Means defined three types of research. The first, method-centered, was inspired by a new diagnostic technology. When Roentgen developed X-ray technology, investigators were soon using it to explore every corner of the body. The second type of research, object-centered, is focused on a condition; one example is research in the MGH Thyroid Clinic. The third type of research Means defined as free research, starting not with a technique or a condition but with an investigator. It amounts to saying, "Here is a worker of high promise—let's give him an opportunity to make best use of his talents." This statement could have been the motto for Ward 4—and it has become *the* motto of research at MGH since Edsall's day.

Ward 4, Edsall's brainchild, Means's mission, admitted its first patient, suffering from lead poisoning, on November 4, 1925. Joe Aub's work was financed by the Lead Industries Association. "These studies," wrote Washburn, "were the beginning of a line of research, founded and guided by Aub, which has continued in the hands of his pupils, Drs. Walter C. Bauer and Fuller Albright, through nearly every aspect of calcium and phosphorus metabolism, its relation to all sorts of chronic bone and joint disease, on the one hand, and the endocrines and endocrine diseases, on the other."[112] Lead is chemically like calcium. Both respond to the hormone secreted by the parathyroid gland, known as parathyroid hormone, or PTH. PTH became a major focus of Ward 4.

The Strange Case of Captain Martell

In 1919 Capt. Charles Martell of the U.S. Merchant Marine began to shrink. A strapping six-foot, one-inch, specimen, he lost seven inches of height over the next six years. His neck shortened and thickened, requiring a brace. He became "pigeon-breasted" and began to pass "fine white gravel" in his urine. Eugene DuBois of Bellevue Hospital in New York City correctly diagnosed what was then called von Recklinghausen's disease of bone, a degeneration of the skeleton due to the loss of calcium.[113] DuBois deduced that the cause might be an overactive parathyroid gland, possibly caused by an adenoma, or tumor. Extra PTH would cause calcium loss in the skeleton and gravel in the urine.

Martell was transferred to MGH in April 1926 for further study, where he was the "most colorful occupant" of Ward 4. Unfortunately, this kindly soul beloved by the MGH staff walked into a surgical nightmare. Studies confirmed DuBois's

Capt. Charles Martell,
an early Ward 4 patient.

diagnosis of adenoma. But where was the tumor? X-rays disclosed nothing. Edward P. Richardson twice operated, twice removing a normal parathyroid gland (the human body usually has four at the base of the neck), and nothing changed in Martell's condition. Martell was discharged, then readmitted to Bellevue. A gauntlet of treatments included traction, which helped temporarily. He was put on a high-calcium diet to compensate for the loss of calcium, and eventually the other two parathyroid glands were removed. An MGH surgeon, Oliver Cope, who became something of a legend hunting for wayward parathyroid glands, took over, but he found no tumor even after three more surgeries. Finally, MGH Chief of Surgery Edward Churchill split Martel's sternum and removed a tumor deep in the patient's chest. This demonstrated that the parathyroidectomies had been incomplete, as a gland (the body sometimes has five) had migrated into the chest cavity, bearing an adenoma. With the tumor gone, Martell began to improve, even standing on his own for the first time in years, when a by-product of calcium in his diet caught up with him: a kidney stone lodged in his ureter, requiring surgery. Complications ensued and death followed.

Fifty people had teamed up in Ward 4 to study Martell and other cases of hyperparathyroidism (too much PTH) and its opposite, hypoparathyroidism (too little). Together the conditions became a focus of work in the ward. For it was about this time that Fuller Albright came into his own, and the parathyroid gland would be just one of the endocrine subjects that fascinated him.

The Finest Early Endocrinologist

Albright was a certified legend whose memory is cherished by all who knew him. Henry Kronenberg noted: "Lots of MGH people are fond of the importance of Aub, Means, and others, but if you polled endocrinologists elsewhere for the important endocrinologists of the first half of the twentieth century, just about the only name people would mention is Albright." Alexander Leaf, chief of medicine after Walter Bauer, wrote a personal remembrance: "His tastes were simple. He was never so happy as when casting a trout fly in an Adirondack lake, unless it was when talking shop with a colleague. He loved a good game of bridge. He had a good eye for color and form, but no ear at all for music. He and his wife Claire were both fond of travel and did a good deal of it in this country, in Europe, and in South America. His dress reflected his lack of self-consciousness: Who can forget the old tweed jacket, the baggy trousers, and the jaunty bow tie?"[114]

Albright was a model of clinical re-search for all who came after him at MGH, an ideal blend of research and practice. He established two ambulatory clinics "for the double purpose of providing clinical material for his investigations and of serving a professional function valuable to the clientele of the hospital."[115] These were the Ovarian Dysfunctions Clinic, which primarily treated menstrual disorders, and the Stone Clinic, a legacy of Captain Martell. Albright's interest eventually took in the pituitary-adrenocortical axis—the linkage between the adrenal glands in the abdomen and the master gland that regulates so much in the endocrine system, the pituitary, nestled deep within the skull. In a study of the pituitary's relations with both the gonads and the adrenal gland, Albright asked whether an abnormality was caused by the master pituitary or a subordinate gland. Means wrote: "Albright was a past master at unraveling the endocrine enigmas that came to him through his clinics and practice. He went at it with gusto and in somewhat

Fuller Albright.

the manner one might use in solving a picture puzzle."[116] Diagnostic tools included bedside observation, hormone assays on blood and urine, blood chemistry and balance studies, X-rays, and biopsies.

Few accounts of MGH legends include the statement made about Albright by Means, that he was "very fond of his ovarian dwarfs."[117] Previous investigators had thought this condition the result of a hormonal shortage; Albright showed that in fact the patient's pituitary was *over*producing gonadotropic (gonad-stimulating) hormones to make up for missing ovaries. Other abnormalities of growth interested him equally, including pituitary and hypothyroid dwarfs. Albright was fascinated by sexual abnormalities, including eunuchoidism, sexual precocity, and what Means referred to as "feminization of males" and "masculinization of females."[118]

A key assistant to Albright from 1939 on was Anne P. "Nan" Forbes, a brilliant and outgoing physician and investigator. By this time Albright was already experiencing the effects of the Parkinson's disease that would cut short his brilliant career. During the war Albright would write of Parkinson's, "This condition does not come under my special medical interests, or else I am sure I would have had it solved long ago. . . . The condition has its compensations: one is not yanked from interesting work to go to the jungles of Burma . . . one avoids all kinds of deadly committee meetings, etc."[119] Those statements reflect Albright's self-confidence, desire to investigate every medical mystery, impish sense of humor, and courage. In 1956, frustrated with his ineffectiveness, Albright prevailed on a New York surgeon to try an experimental procedure injecting alcohol into the thalamic region of his brain. The procedure was performed on one side of his brain, bringing some relief from his symptoms. When the same procedure was performed on the other side, Albright suffered a cerebral hemorrhage. He never worked or spoke again. He lived from 1956 to 1969 as a patient at Massachusetts General Hospital.

A Ward without Limits

Fuller Albright was only the most brilliant and wide-ranging of investigators using Ward 4 during the Means and Bauer years. The gastroenterologist Chester Morse Jones studied bile by feeding a tube down a subject's alimentary canal until it reached the duodenum, where a flow of bile was encouraged by a release of Epsom salts. Benjamin V. White explored from the other end of the alimentary canal—"looking up the rectum into the lower colon through a sigmoidoscope," according to Means, and observing "the action of certain drugs and irritants, and of emotions, both in normal persons and those suffering from a common disease called mucous colitis. On one occasion a medical student was acting as subject; his colon was being observed through the instrument when an attractive young nurse entered the room. In this embarrassing situation, the subject's mucous membrane was observed to turn a bright red—the first observed example of the rectal blush!"[120]

Walter Bauer's work on connective tissue diseases (notably arthritis) would result in the Robert W. Lovett Memorial Group for the Study of Diseases Causing Deformities, named for the orthopedic surgeon who cared for President Franklin D. Roosevelt. After Bauer became Jackson professor and chief of medicine, succeeding Means in 1951, Evan Calkins took over the Lovett Group, and in 1961 Stephen M. Krane replaced him. John Talbott's studies of gout spilled over into Ward 4, as did Bernard Jacobson's studies of pernicious anemia, and Harriet Hardy's studies of workers in a fluorescent bulb factory who were being poisoned by beryllium. Hardy's work led to the establishment of a beryllium case registry at MGH in 1952; more than 500 cases were recorded in the first four years.

In his study *Ward 4*, Means illustrated the extraordinary "fecundity" of the Mallinckrodt facility in a final chapter called "Ward Round." Writing in 1957, he took the reader on a visit to each of the 10 beds. The patients observed represented the range of work that still occupied Ward 4 more than three decades after it opened:

> In bed #1 was a "feeble-minded cretinous dwarf"[121] being attended and studied by the thyroid group under Dr. John Stanbury. Next up was Albert J., a chef suffering from malformation of the bones in his legs and skull, possibly suffering from Paget's disease. In bed #3 was Fred D., a surgical patient suffering from cirrhosis. Next was Maria A., "a scion of the Spanish aristocracy of a Central American country,"[122] whose growth had stopped at age ten. Margaret S. was a widow under the care of Nan Forbes showing a "complete destruction and calcification of both her ovaries and adrenal glands."[123] In bed #6 was a Canadian woman with a kidney stone. In beds #7–9 were patients being studied by the cancer group—one with breast cancer, one with prostate cancer, and one without any cancer at all. Rounding out Ward 4 on this day in 1957 was Bruce E., a fifty-eight-year-old suffering from steatorrhea, or fatty diarrhea.[124]

In 1958 Bauer appointed Lloyd Hollingsworth "Holly" Smith Jr. to head up the endocrine unit. This appointment was typical of Bauer: Smith had no clinical training in endocrinology. It was Bauer's belief that a department of medicine grew best and fastest when led by investigators, and Smith had investigative experience to burn, having worked in succession in biochemistry at Harvard, at the Public Health Research Institute in New York, at the Karolinska Institute in Stockholm, and at the Huntington Laboratories with Paul Zamecnik. Recalled Smith: "Bauer called me in one day and said I'm going to make you head of endocrinology. I never had a day's training in endocrine. He said, 'I think you can make it in academic medicine.' Then he looked me in the eye and said, 'I'm going to really support you for the next five years, and if you don't make it, I'll kick your ass out of here.' I thought that was a sporting proposition."

Very quickly a stellar endocrine group formed around Smith, including Daniel D. Federman, Steve Krane, and Mitchell Rabkin. In 1963 Robert Ebert was appointed chief of medicine, to replace Walter Bauer, who had died. Smith went to Oxford as a research fellow in 1963–1964. While there he was recruited to become chief of medicine at the University of California, San Francisco (UCSF). Under his leadership as chief and later as dean, UCSF became arguably the finest public academic medical center in the country and a formidable competitor with MGH for recruiting residents and interns in medicine.

The staff of the Endocrine Unit on the steps of the Bulfinch Building, circa 1962. In the front row, from left, are department secretary Kay Boling (Bander), Daniel Federman, Chief Lloyd Hollingsworth "Holly" Smith, Janet McArthur, Nan Forbes, and an unidentified woman. In second row, second from right, is Mitchell Rabkin, later CEO of Boston's Beth Israel Hospital (courtesy Lloyd Hollingsworth Smith).

A Second Golden Age

The Endocrine Division had rotating leadership for several years, as Dan Federman replaced Smith in 1964 and Bernard Kliman took over for a year only in 1967, when Federman became assistant chief of medicine. Federman is credited with setting up the first endocrine fellowship program at MGH. Kliman was known for innovation in the measurement of steroid hormones and metabolites.

Meanwhile, the methodology of endocrinology was undergoing sea change. With the invention of the radioimmunoassay an investigator could measure a hormone, and the field of protein chemistry staged a revolution. A young investigator at the National Institutes of Health, John Potts, was recruited back to MGH to bring this revolution to the MGH Endocrine Division in 1968, and the second golden age of endocrinology at MGH was on. The link between Fuller Albright and John Potts can be expressed in three letters: PTH. The case of Captain Martell, beginning 1927, had illustrated for the investigators of Ward 4 how a tumor on the parathyroid, causing overproduction of PTH, could lead to bone loss. Why then, two years later, did rats show bone *gain* when given PTH? Forty years on, Potts would pick up this question and run with it.

Potts enjoyed saying with mock self-deprecation that he had chosen to work on an endocrine system "so undistinguished it doesn't even have its own name. It's only named for what it's next to." But he also enjoyed saying that the parathyroid remained a "pretty hot topic," even in the twenty-first century. As an undergraduate, Potts had double-majored in biology and English. "I began to get interested in science," he recalled, "and I imagined myself practicing medicine near my hometown of Moorestown, New Jersey." But as a med student at the University of Pennsylvania, Potts met a professor and distinguished surgeon, Brooke Roberts, whose interest in endocrinology was infectious. Potts wrote a paper on parathyroid hormone, about the time in the mid-1950s when Fuller Albright's radical surgery for Parkinson's was ending his ability to investigate PTH.

John Potts.

A nascent interest in PTH and calcium metabolism was fired by Potts's two years as an intern and assistant resident at MGH (1957–1959). Albright may have been out of commission, but Bauer, Aub, and the endocrine surgeon Oliver Cope were still in action. In 1959 Potts began a nine-year hitch at the NIH, starting out in the National Heart Institute labs of Christian Anfinsen, who would share the 1972 Nobel Prize in Chemistry. Six years after the discovery of DNA by Crick and Watson, Anfinsen was studying ribonuclease, one of the first enzymes to be analyzed. "Anfinsen was a great Pied Piper," Potts recalled. "I worked with him for a couple of years on the structure of ribonuclease, then the NIH gave me my own lab." Potts sought to apply to the structure of PTH the principles of protein chemistry that were being elucidated in Anfinsen's lab.

Anfinsen worked on ribonuclease because it is plentiful and easily isolated and analyzed. PTH is far harder to collect—but medically more important. Gerald Aurbach, working elsewhere at the NIH, had already accomplished the laborious task of isolating PTH, using strong solvents that allowed the purification of the protein without breaking it up. Applying Anfinsen's techniques, Potts collaborated with Aurbach for a decade. The investigators began with bovine PTH, then moved to human. Eventually, they identified the structure of PTH and synthesized the polypeptide, proving the structure—after Potts had returned to MGH with his first grant in hand. Sounding very much like Walter Bauer, Chief of Medicine Alexander Leaf had invited Potts to head up the MGH endocrine unit although Potts had no formal clinical training in endocrinology. Potts had a simple explanation that goes to the heart of the MGH approach: "The place goes for the person—and the talent they see in him or her."

One might wonder why, in this case, the person went for the place. Leaf didn't promise Potts a big budget or formal institutional support as Potts started out to build an endocrine unit. "When I first came here," Potts recalled, "they didn't give me very much, they just gave me the chance to be here. It was like having an empty hot-dog concession, but in Yankee Stadium. It was up to me to get on with it." Potts said that MGH leaders are "self-selecting." Some people like being part of a large, supportive, sheltering organization. Those people who self-select for MGH like the opposite: a chance to prove themselves, not only as scientist-clinicians but also as entrepreneurs.

Henry Kronenberg.

Colleagues from the NIH came along with Potts, including Hugh Niall, who brought an automated technique for protein analysis he had learned in Australia; Leonard Deftos, who was doing studies of calcitonin, a thyroid hormone that opposes the action of PTH; and Henry Keutmann, a premier peptide chemist who would eventually determine the entire sequence of human PTH. Other contributors in the 1970s included Geoffrey Tregear, an Australian colleague of Niall; Michael Rosenblatt, who worked out much of the biological activity of PTH by synthesizing fragments of the polypeptide; Joel Habener, who first isolated messenger RNA encoding the precursor of parathyroid hormone; and Gino Segre and Henry Kronenberg, who would carry on Potts's work with PTH in important ways after Potts was appointed chief of medicine in 1981.

Kronenberg's story is illustrative of the way an entire generation of endocrine physician-scientists came to the fore under Potts. Kronenberg had first arrived at MGH as an intern in 1970, then returned as an endocrine fellow in 1974 after some time at the NIH. In 1975, as he would recall years later:

> I needed to start doing some research and wanted to study molecular biology. The only group in endocrine doing molecular biology at the time was John Potts's group, which is why I got interested in PTH. John had paid Joel Habener to go over to MIT to work with Alex Rich isolating the messenger RNA for PTH. In 1975 Habener came back here to set up his own lab, and I picked up the baton and went to the Rich lab at MIT. I had good timing, because recombinant DNA had just been invented by Stanley Cohen and Herbert Boyer in 1972–1973, and by 1975 their discovery had filtered from Stanford to MIT—though not to the MGH.

Until Howard Goodman brought molecular biology to MGH in a big way in 1981 (see chapters 6–8), the hospital did not allow work with recombinant DNA, as there were initial concerns about the dangers of gene mutation. No one was quite sure these new labs wouldn't be creating dangerous new life-forms. Kronenberg observed:

> The wonderful thing John did (and it's still done in our division) was that he paid me with a training grant from NIH to work in someone else's lab. He was effectively supporting Alex Rich's work at MIT, and he had no guarantee that I would want to come back to MGH. It was a gamble, and it is the reason we still get the best fellows in endocrine: we tell them they can do their research anywhere in Boston. This is a brilliant approach bred from confidence, caring more about the training of a fellow than building your own group. Of course,

John Potts was savvy and he read me right. He figured he would get me back here with smoke, mirrors, and charisma—and he did.

In 1982 Kronenberg returned to MGH from MIT, where he had cloned the DNA that encodes PTH—a job, he said, that "any college student could do now in two months with kits you can buy off the shelf. But there were no kits then. Recombinant DNA was being done in a handful of places in the world at that time and I was in one of them. In that lab at MIT, we had to wear caps and gowns, sign in through an airlock, everything was autoclaved going in and out, and there were no sinks. Today this work is done on an open bench."

"When I came back from MIT," Kronenberg continued, "John Potts gave me a little money and a lab in the basement of the Bulfinch Building." The room's ceiling leaked, there were no windows, it was a bit depressing, but Kronenberg had his own hot-dog concession, grandly titled the Endocrine Genetics Unit.

When John Potts became chief of medicine in 1981, succeeding Alexander Leaf, Michael Rosenblatt was named head of the Endocrine Division, but after three years Rosenblatt left unexpectedly to assume an important investigative position at Merck. Kronenberg was tapped to replace him. "My job," the new chief said, "was to bring molecular biology to endocrine at MGH. We had a bunch of investigators here that John had trained who were great physiologists and cell biologists; I taught them to do molecular biology." In the years ahead, Kronenberg and his team, in collaboration with Gino Segre and his team, would continue work in PTH, especially as it relates to osteoporosis. Investigative developments included cloning of the PTH receptor and using gene-knockout technology in mice to further understand how the receptor works. Meanwhile, a major clinical research effort headed by Robert Neer used PTH (more recently in its commercial form of Forteo, manufactured by Eli Lilly) to improve pharmaceutical treatment of osteoporosis. Neer had come to the Endocrine Unit in 1968, the same year John Potts arrived, and together they championed the use of PTH to treat osteoporosis for more than two decades before this culmination of their work.

"Today," Kronenberg said in 2008, "the group of scientists in the endocrine unit think of ourselves not just as molecular biologists but as translational physician-scientists—people going full blast advancing basic discovery in bone and PTH research on one hand while trying hard to apply it in the clinical setting. And," Kronenberg added with a grin, "they're paying me to do this! It's an amazingly privileged life."

Today the Endocrine Unit is just one of six in the Endocrine Division (just one example of how complex the MGH organization chart is). Here follows a brief account of work in the other five units.

Thyroid

The first true specialty unit in medicine at MGH was the thyroid clinic, founded in 1913 under the mentorship of David Edsall. In part because Means, the clinic's first chief, had been chief of medicine from 1923 to 1951, work on the thyroid and its "poor neighbors," the parathyroid glands, remained the focus of most endocrine work at MGH into the 1960s. Endocrine surgery, again largely focused on the thyroid and parathyroid, formally became a subspecialty of the Surgical Service in 1972—the year the ne plus ultra of endocrine surgery at MGH, Oliver Cope, retired, and Chiu-An Wang replaced him.

Farahe Maloof was an outstanding leader for many years, but he died of an unusual and debilitating disease of the brain and was replaced by E. Chester "Chip" Ridgeway. Ridgeway left to become chief of the Endocrine Division at the University of Colorado, however, and his replacement, J. Larry Jameson, also departed to become head of endocrine at Northwestern University. Another promising thyroid investigator, William W. ("Bill") Chin, moved across town to Brigham and Women's Hospital to head their Genetics Department before moving on to Eli Lilly, where he investigated nuclear receptors. After Jameson's departure, the Thyroid Unit was folded into the Neuroendocrine Unit; ultimately thyroid came back under the umbrella of the main Endocrine Division. Remarked Kronenberg, "I think there is a lot of exciting thyroid science still to be done. The way we will grow a thyroid unit is from young people staying and flourishing."

Though thyroid has effectively disappeared as a stand-alone area of investigation, a thriving Thyroid Associates practice, perhaps the biggest in New England, is run by Gilbert Daniels and Douglas Ross. Meanwhile, other investigative specialties have proliferated.

Diabetes

As chief of endocrine until 1981 and then as chief of medicine, Potts recruited and nurtured the careers of young leaders in molecular endocrinology, reproductive endocrinology, neuroendocrinology, and lipids disorders. Each of these will be discussed below. One unit Potts did not create was diabetes, a specialty set apart in the 1950s by Walter Bauer, who picked Richard Field as its first chief. Field's focus became ever more clinical, as he treated patients with diabetes while leaving the investigative work to others, and Donald B. Martin was appointed by Alex Leaf to replace him in 1966. Martin was committed to understanding insulin regulation of metabolism and attracted several enthusiastic junior colleagues. He left for a senior position at the University of Pennsylvania in 1979 and was replaced by one of these colleagues, Joseph Avruch. Impelled by the evidence that defective insulin action on cells predisposes a person to type-2 diabetes, Avruch and his colleagues sought to uncover the biochemical basis for insulin's actions within the cell; these mechanisms, the understanding of which emerged over several decades, proved to have implications for a surprising variety of diseases.

While Avruch's work moved increasingly toward the molecular biology laboratory, the diabetes unit proved yet again the wisdom of Walter Bauer's strategy: units directed by physician-scientists committed to investigative excellence will attract superb clinicians and clinical investigators. In the case of the MGH diabetes unit, the lead clinical researcher has been David Nathan.

Nathan trained in endocrinology at MGH in the 1970s because of the strength of the Endocrine Division. He said, "You saw everything here—many rare diseases as well as all the common ones." He did a year in Don Martin's lab, whereupon Martin left the hospital. Nathan recalled:

Joe Avruch took over and saw me in the lab where I had been breaking things for about a year. As a bench scientist he recognized that there were exciting things about to happen in diabetes. He tapped me on the shoulder and said, "How would you like a job?" He said we needed clinical research in diabetes, and asked me to take over the clinic and establish a clinical research program. That night I called my mother and told her I had been offered an exciting opportunity at Mass General. She asked what any mother would ask: "What are they paying you?" I hadn't asked. Then as now, you were expected to fund yourself.

It was, Nathan said, "a terrifically exciting, fertile time in diabetes." He became one of the 21 investigators on a major $200 million national research effort, the Diabetes Control and Complications Trial (1983–1993), and when the landmark report of the trial's findings was written, the young MGH investigator was the lead author and editor. The DCCT is considered the single most important contribution to diabetes care in the insulin era.

In the MGH Diabetes Center of the twenty-first century, clinical research has become so tightly integrated with the treatment of patients that each patient is effectively considered part of the research enterprise. With from 800 to 1,000 patients coming and going at any one time, the center not only treats type-1 and type-2 diabetes with the latest therapies and techniques but also leads the way in developing such innovations as an artificial pancreas. Although type-1 patients are just 5 percent of the total diabetes population, 35 percent of those seen at the MGH clinic suffer from this life-threatening form of the disease. "We may have 15 studies going on at any one time," said Nathan, "and as soon as we learn new methodologies, we're able to filter them back to patients, who are always getting the most advanced, scientifically informed care possible."

Said Avruch: "David has established himself as the preeminent clinical investigator in diabetes in the world today." Nathan's children had a different perspective. Realizing that while their father was on duty at Mass General, diabetes had exploded to epidemic proportions in the United States, they suggested that it might have been better if he had stayed home from work!

An early sponsor of Avruch's work was the Howard Hughes Medical Institute, endowed by the late eccentric tycoon of aviation. With Hughes's support, Avruch established his first lab in 1978 on the site of an old medical intensive care unit on Bulfinch 3. Sharing space with him was Joel Habener, who since 1976 had been pursuing pioneering work in molecular biology, particularly as it pertains to the endocrine system. As the two investigators moved forward, their labs were often contiguous (both moved to the Wellman Building, now Thier, in the early 1980s) and their work moved on parallel tracks, as each focused on problems related to diabetes. While Avruch was studying the interaction between insulin and the cells affected by it, Habener studied how insulin itself is created.

The most recent wave of work in the diabetes unit has been the search for the genes responsible for type-2 diabetes. Leading this effort at MGH has been David Altshuler, whom Avruch characterized as "one of the most important human geneticists in the world today."

Molecular Endocrinology and Neuroendocrinology

Joel Habener's work since the 1970s—and that of the Department of Molecular Endocrinology under his leadership—has focused on many other hormones besides insulin, looking at the genes responsible for hormone production and how they express themselves at the molecular level. This work took a giant step forward in 1980 when, through the intercession of John Potts and General Director Charles Sanders, MGH signed its first major research contract with a pharmaceutical company, the German life sciences giant Hoechst AG. Seeking early expertise in the field of molecular biology, Hoechst had previously agreed to sponsor groundbreaking work by Howard Goodman at the University of California, San Francisco. On offer was $70 million; all Goodman had to do was find a nest on which to settle this golden egg, that is, a place to work. Potts got wind of the deal, and Sanders soon agreed that this could be a watershed deal for MGH. (More on the Hoechst deal in chapters 6–8.)

In 1978, meanwhile, the Mallinckrodt Ward, site of much early endocrine research, became the MGH General Clinical Research Center (GCRC), a new designation of the National Institutes of Health, which provided funding for it. Within 30 years there would be nearly 80 such centers nationwide, usually located within academic medical centers. The MGH GCRC was among the first. Like the Mallinckrodt Ward, the GCRC was meant to encourage clinical research by providing the specialized resources needed, such as research nurses, computer hardware and software, and sophisticated laboratories.

David Nathan has served as codirector of the MGH GCRC along with the chief of the Neuroendocrine Unit, Anne Klibanski. Neuroendocrinology's focus is the pituitary gland, the master chemical organizer within the brain that in many ways directs the activities of the endocrine system and, through the hypothalamus and brain, coordinates its workings with those of the nervous system. A graduate of the NYU School of Medicine, Klibanski landed a fellowship at MGH in 1978, where, after her clinical year, she went to work first under Janet McArthur and then under Chip Ridgeway, chief of the Thyroid Unit.

Anne Klibanski.

"From the start," said Klibanski, "my interest was in the pituitary, and the only work on the pituitary at MGH at that time was being done in the thyroid unit." Klibanski's fellowship was dedicated to investigating hormone regulation in pituitary tumors. This focus on the thyroid-pituitary axis brought Klibanski's work back to an old MGH topic from the days of Captain Martell: bone metabolism. Bone composition is regulated to a large degree by reproductive hormones; the reproductive glands fall under the command of the pituitary; ergo, as Klibanski discovered, tumors of the pituitary affect bone metabolism. In the 1980s Klibanski's work also zeroed in on how pituitary tumors arise at the molecular level. In 1985 she was made director of a new neuroendocrine clinical center at MGH.

In 1989 Klibanski was asked to head up a new freestanding Neuroendocrine Unit, a position she continues to hold. MGH's Neuroendocrine was the first such unit in the nation. Like so many other physician-scientists at MGH, Klibanski has divided her time and attention among patient care, investigative research, and teaching. Klibanski further divided her time—and in some ways unified it—by administering the MGH GCRC.

Reproductive Endocrinology

At least since 1939, when Nan Forbes took a seat at the bench

William Crowley.

alongside Fuller Albright, women have played significant roles in endocrinology at MGH. At midcentury Janet McArthur was the yin to Forbes's yang. Where Forbes was outgoing and highly collegial in her lab work, McArthur was scholarly and quiet to the verge of hermitic.

Trained as an endocrinologist, McArthur turned her attention early in her career to female reproductive endocrinology. McArthur made several important contributions, "including the development of a procedure to measure pituitary lutenizing hormone (LH), which triggers ovulation in women. McArthur's novel technique led to the discovery that women in menopause have higher levels of LH and another hormone called follicle-stimulating hormone than those in their childbearing years. McArthur also found that LH abnormalities were characteristic in women with polycystic ovary syndrome."[125] There was no medical division at MGH that did work on female hormones, so McArthur became associated with the Gynecology Service under Howard Ulfelder.

William F. Crowley Jr. arrived at MGH as an intern in 1969. John Potts wanted to jump-start an investigative approach to reproductive endocrinology, one that would not be a poor cousin of gynecology, a surgical service. Potts advised Crowley to work with Janet McArthur, who became the young doctor's reluctant mentor in endocrine research. Said Crowley: "We worked together for a full year before having a formal lab meeting. Fortunately, others took pity on me. George Richardson knew Janet McArthur well, and he and his postdoctoral fellow, David

MacLaughlin, gave me advice each day, setting up assays, thinking up projects. It took me a while to realize that there should be regular meetings and to figure out Janet's retiring personality."

It seems that Crowley took several lessons from this uneasy early mentorship. Mentoring and promoting the careers of female colleagues has been a focus for him. Two-thirds of the more than 50 fellows in his department have been women. One of these, Andrea Dunaif, has served as president of the Endocrine Society. In 2000 Women in Endocrinology gave Crowley its annual mentoring award—the first man ever so honored.

Crowley's unit has focused on precocious and delayed onset of puberty. For puberty that comes too early, triggered by the hypothalamic activation of the pituitary gland, researchers have developed a stimulating agent that "locks down the pituitary in a paradoxical way." For delayed puberty (or puberty that never arrives), they have developed a way to administer the natural hypothalamic hormone GnRH by portable infusion pumps. On the molecular level, this same group of investigators has been isolating genes that control reproduction.

"We published our first article about a new puberty gene in 2003," said Crowley. "Now there are 150 labs around the world working on the problem. It's a thrill to see how one observation can light up research fires around the globe."

Lipids

Until recent years the study of lipids has not been a strength of the Boston-area medical establishment. Lipids are fats packaged in particles moving in the bloodstream from liver and intestines to wherever they are needed. Cholesterol is the best-known lipid, and the lipids specialty is most often focused on understanding the so-called good and bad cholesterols, HDL and LDL, and their relevance, predominantly to cardiovascular disease.

Mason Freeman studied at Harvard, then attended medical school at the University of California, San Francisco, where Holly Smith was his mentor. It was there that Freeman became interested in lipids. Freeman chose to continue his training at MGH, but MGH did not have a true molecular biology lab at the time. So Freeman talked with co-Nobelists Mike Brown and Joe Goldstein at University of Texas Southwestern Medical Center about working with them. (Brown and Goldstein both trained at MGH during the 1960s.) For personal reasons Freeman opted instead to work with one of Brown and Goldstein's trainees, Monty Krieger at MIT. There, in 1989, investigators cloned "the holy grail," according to Freeman, the so-called scavenger receptor by which lipids are deposited in the artery wall, causing cardiovascular disease.

During his years in the Krieger lab, Freeman continued his clinical work at MGH, founding a lipids clinic in 1986. In 1992 he returned to MGH full-time and with the blessing of Chief of Medicine John Potts started a new endocrine unit focused on lipid disorders. A focus of his lab's work has been the movement of cholesterol into and out of cells, and in particular a class of proteins called ABC transporters, proteins responsible for cholesterol traffic control.

MEANS CARRIES THE TORCH

A few words should be added here about Chief of Medicine James Howard Means, known to his colleagues as Howard. It was David Edsall, the fresh face from Philadelphia and St. Louis, who shifted clinical research forward into the modern era at MGH, but it was Means, Boston bred and educated, who maintained the forward momentum. While Edsall went on to serve as dean of Harvard's medical instructors, Means, one of his first interns, stayed behind at MGH as the instructor and mentor par excellence—doing more than anyone, including Edsall, to build the intellectual core of MGH within its Department of Medicine. The Edsall-Means transition happened in 1923, when Means succeeded Edsall as Jackson professor of medicine and chief of the medical service at MGH. But the effects of this transition would be felt beyond World War II. Medical leaders recruited and supported by Means in the 1920s, 1930s, and 1940s would be the foundation for clinical and investigative successes throughout the twentieth century.

Means was born in Boston's Dorchester neighborhood in 1885 and raised in Boston's Back Bay. A childhood interest in science was nurtured by his father, "who, though not a trained scientist himself, had science deeply at heart."[126] Young Means attended Noble and Greenough School, took a postgraduate year at MIT under the great biologist William T. Sedgwick, a friend of his father, and went on to Harvard College, where he studied the sciences within a broad liberal arts curriculum. He read philosophy with George Santayana and William James, learned rocks from the grand old man of geology, Nathaniel Southgate Shaler, and studied the new field of experimental psychology with Robert M. Yerkes, which may have opened his mind to the notion of a psychiatry department within MGH 30 years later. English with Professor Barrett Wendell was a course Means would remember as "intellectually titillating."[127]

Means started his postgraduate medical education on the new Longwood Avenue campus of Harvard Medical School in 1907, Harvard's answer, he would later recall, to "the new and glamorous Johns Hopkins Medical School in Baltimore [that] had for fifteen years or so been putting the older medical schools in the shade."[128] Elected to the honor medical society, Alpha Omega Alpha, upon his 1911 graduation from HMS, he became a house pupil at MGH from 1911 to 1913, was made a Walcott fellow, and worked on calorimetry at the Carnegie Laboratory in Boston before going to Copenhagen to study blood flow with the zoophysiologist August Krogh. Krogh would win

James Howard Means.

the Nobel Prize in 1920 for his studies of capillary blood flow in skeletal muscle. Hearing Eugene F. DuBois read a paper on basal metabolism at a "Young Turks" gathering of the American Society for Clinical Investigation in Atlantic City in 1914 "was a pivotal event for [Means]."[129] He returned to Boston to work with the Benedict Respiration Apparatus while also pursuing studies of basal metabolism with DuBois in New York. As mentioned earlier, this steered Means toward the thyroid gland, a lifelong interest.

Means's personal investigative contributions were considerable, but what matters most in the history of MGH is his nurturing of other, younger talents. John Stanbury and Earle Chapman noted, "The casual reader may fail to appreciate the cohesive force of Means in those brilliant investigations by a highly competitive and goal-oriented group of younger physicians. Much of his genius lay in his ability to nurture the creative enterprise of the staff. He believed in and encouraged the 'fecundity of aggregation.'"[130] Someone had to coordinate and muster financial and institutional support for all of the investigations in Ward 4, and that someone was Means. While pursuing his own work with the thyroid clinic, he supported the development of other medical specialties on his watch, including endocrinology (Fuller Albright), cardiology (Paul Dudley White), and psychiatry (Stanley Cobb; see chapter 4).

As Means saw it, Edsall's most important initiative, which Means furthered, was an entirely new or "middle" estate in the field of medicine, the full-time academic, salaried clinician. Means had come into medicine on the cusp of a new age. Previously, there had been two distinct groups of HMS medical professors. Teachers in years one and two had been the "preclinical scientists," viewed by practicing physicians as mere "lab men." Yet these lab-based instructors looked down in turn on the third- and fourth-year clinical instructors, those who taught students at the bedside, as practitioners of "largely unscientific guesswork." According to Means, these clinicians taught and attended hospital patients "for love or kudos, or a mixture of the two, and made their livelihoods in private practice."[131]

Edsall instituted what came to be known as the Harvard full-time system, effectively an honor system in which full-time clinical professors were permitted to collect fees from private practice, but "not more than was consistent with doing a fair measure of full-time work."[132] This system, although it allowed clinically based research to gain a foothold at MGH, was still an odd compromise compared with the Johns Hopkins full-time system, where a huge grant from the Rockefeller Foundation allowed staff to live off their salaries, as their professional fees were applied to departmental budgets within the hospital.

When Edsall moved to Harvard full-time as dean in 1923, Means confessed to being "rather astounded" at having the Jackson mantle as well as the chiefdom of medicine laid on his young shoulders. But from this time forward, following in Edsall's footsteps, he made it his "primary, all-inclusive objective . . . to promote the development and evolution of a modern university medical clinic of the best quality possible." As Means explained: "I use 'university' here in a spiritual rather than organizational or pedagogical sense. . . . Although the objective was essentially the same as [Henry] Christian's at the Brigham Hospital, the problem at MGH differed sharply, in that, instead of creating everything *de novo*, one had to deal with a venerable institution and mold it to a modern purpose. . . . There were plenty of entrenched mores which had to be dealt with understandingly if peace was to be preserved."[133]

The mission called for humility on Means's part: "There was no call, as I saw it, for dominating leadership. . . . If the chief could establish conditions that would attract people and, having got them, keep them content in their work and promote their growth, his main function would be fulfilled."[134]

It was a slow, incremental process: "Edsall started with a corps of old-style volunteer physicians plus a skeleton force of full-time people. As time went on, more funds for full-time salaries from both the hospital and the medical school gradually became available. Also, a new category of workers, research fellows, made its appearance—and has grown prodigiously of late [in the 1950s and 1960s]."[135]

There is a seemly Brahmin sense of noblesse oblige about the mature Howard Means, who wrote these words while looking back on his career from retirement. There is quite a bit of Richard Cabot, too, in the Means who furthered the Social Service Department at MGH.[136] For the 50th anniversary of the founding of the department in 1955, Means said, "I would like to stress that the Medical Social Worker, because of her intimate knowledge of the patient's whole family background, is one of the most important integrating persons in the whole medical care team."[137] As was true of Cabot, one gathers that economic self-interest was never Means's primary motive. The Jackson professor "became a strong proponent of group practice and medical insurance at a time when these concepts were bitterly opposed."[138] In his 1953 preface to *Doctors, People and Government*, Means wrote words that still might add fuel to the fiery debates over health insurance reform: "The American people are entitled to the best medical service which science and art permit, and which they can afford to buy. They are entitled to get it at the lowest price consistent with high quality, or to have it given to them if they cannot pay. . . . The health of the citizen is his concern, but it is also his neighbor's. . . . The affairs of medicine, therefore, are the affairs of the people no less than of the medical profession."[139]

James Howard Means lived on Beacon Hill, walking to and from work at both MGH and HMS before and after his retirement in 1951. For his contributions in Boston and beyond, Means received the highest honor of the Association of American Physicians, the Kober Medal, in 1964. His many contributions to MGH may be read between the lines of the success stories in the chapters that follow.

WORLD WAR I

The Great War had begun in Europe with the German assault of the summer of 1914, but at Massachusetts General Hospital life rolled on with barely a hitch. Courageous, public-spirited souls like Walter Dodd went "over there" early to help out, two years before George M. Cohan wrote a song about it. But the medical reign of David Edsall continued, along with the firm leadership of "Colonel Washburn," the resident physician Frederic A. Washburn, who would write the official volume of the hospital's history covering that period. Washburn would be remembered with trembling awe by the professional staff who grew up under him,

Col. Frederic Washburn in his
World War I uniform.

a group that in later years included the surgeon Claude Welch:

Three of us [interns] were walking down a corridor one day laughing about some trivial matter. Suddenly a hand was clapped upon a shoulder and the director of the hospital—Colonel Washburn—thundered, "Young man, there shall be no levity in the Massachusetts General Hospital!" . . .

He topped six feet and, stiff as a ramrod, never lost his military bearing nor his sense of essentially divine authority. Every Tuesday he inspected the entire hospital. Nurses quaked in terror when he, with his retinue, marched through their wards. Short girls were particularly at risk because some dust might be hiding on the top of a cabinet at the exact level of his eyes. House officers rarely saw him except to receive some dire warnings if they committed minor peccadilloes. His gimlet eyes missed nothing.[140]

It was Washburn who decreed that young doctors' lab coats should have no pockets, because young doctors' hands should be occupied with their work![141]

Once it appeared that American troops might become engaged in the conflict, the MGH made a major commitment to the war effort. A proposal that American field hospitals be affiliated with American medical schools was squelched in part by "officers of the Massachusetts General Hospital," who argued that "such units should appertain to hospitals, not to medical schools."[142] In 1913 Washburn had initiated a meeting with U.S. Surgeon General William C. Gorgas to discuss the organizing of military hospitals in the event of war. By a vote of the trustees on March 17, 1916, Washburn was authorized to create a mobile hospital unit, drawing on the manpower resources of the hospital and funds from the Massachusetts Red Cross, "together with such contributions from outside the Red Cross Chapters as may be offered."[143] With war experience in both Puerto Rico and the Philippines, Washburn was an obvious choice to head up Base Hospital No. 6 A.E.F. (American Expeditionary Force), which swung into active service in April 1917. On May 24 Paul Dudley White went on active duty to sign up noncommissioned personnel. Also serving in leadership roles were Richard C. Cabot as chief of medicine, Lincoln Davis as chief of the surgical service, and, fresh from the theological seminary, the Reverend Henry Knox Sherrill as chaplain. Named an MGH trustee in 1928 and elevated to chairman in 1935, Sherrill would become presiding bishop of the American Episcopal Church in 1945 and grace the cover of *Time* magazine on March 26, 1951. Sara Parsons was chief nurse of Base Hospital No. 6.

This was a genuine army unit, which underwent six weeks of training at Fort Strong on Long Island in Boston Harbor before sailing for Liverpool aboard the

Aurania on July 9. On board were 28 officers, 1 chaplain, 64 nurses, 6 secretaries, 1 dietitian, and 153 medical men with all the materiel for a 500-bed hospital. After the fact, Washburn confessed that this had not been anywhere near enough: "The inadequacy of this equipment and the lack of conception of the problem will be apparent when it is said that Base Hospital No. 6, when in full activity, had 4300 patients at one time." A destroyer accompanied the ship for the last leg of its journey into Queenstown Harbor, where it arrived July 21. From England the unit crossed the Channel into France, traveling to the town of Talence, south of Bordeaux, in southwestern France, where they settled. A complete hospital was installed on the campus of the Petit Lycée de Talence, and here the sick and wounded were brought, away from the front lines northeast of Paris. Bordeaux was a key port of debarkation for American men and materiel en route to the front, and for the hospital's first months of operations the only patients were sick American personnel moving in and out of the port.

A stream of American troops in 1917 became a flood by early 1918. The majority of fresh men flowed into France and Flanders through England, and on April 25, 1918, Washburn was ordered back to England to manage service hospitals there; Warren L. Babcock took his place in Talence. At Base Hospital No. 6 there were 1,800 beds and 864 patients by June 1918, and in the first six months of that year the unit performed 874 surgeries. "The laboratories were extremely busy during the winter and spring, especially in work on meningitis, of which there were a number of cases very difficult to treat because of the weakness of some of the anti-meningococcus serum."[144] One MGH nurse, Lucy Fletcher, succumbed to meningitis and was buried in Talence with full military honors. Work

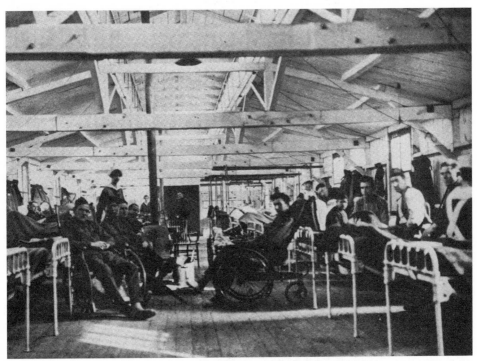

A ward at Base Hospital No. 6, near Bordeaux, France.

accelerated through the summer and fall of 1918 as the American wounded and gassed began to pile up. October was the cruelest month: there were 4,378 admissions and 528 surgeries, as the American effort and the war itself reached their climax. On November 12, the day after the armistice, there were 4,319 patients in a hospital with a capacity of 3,000.

Meanwhile, the situation in England became extremely demanding after the outbreak during the summer of the worldwide influenza pandemic, known to that generation as the Spanish flu. Though the horrors of AIDS and smaller-scale panics over SARS and swine flu continue to command our attention in the twenty-first century, the mortality statistics from 1918 and 1919 take one's breath away: at least 20 million died worldwide as a result of the flu, considerably more than the 16 million soldiers and civilians who died as a direct result of the war. By mid-1918 American troop ships began arriving in England laden with flu-stricken soldiers, 2,000 on one ship alone, and Washburn's medical personnel in England were charged with caring for countless men even before they saw battle. Howard Means was working under Washburn when the flu hit Allied troops in England. He recalled the onset with excruciating detail: "Its fulminating course, high mortality, early anoxemia, extreme moisture in the lungs, and watery bloody sputum made a unique picture—nothing at all like classic pneumococcus pneumonia. Our helplessness in treating this disease was appalling."[145] By the armistice, there were 14,000 patients in American hospitals in England and 5,000 in British hospitals.

Back home in Boston, Joseph B. Howland served as acting MGH administrator in Washburn's absence, and he and the staff who stayed behind (too old to serve or too young to be trained medically in time) had their hands full. On December 6, 1917, a French cargo ship, the *Mont Blanc*, collided with a smaller vessel in the harbor of Halifax, Nova Scotia. The *Mont Blanc* was loaded to the gunnels with military explosives, and the result of the collision was the greatest man-made accidental explosion in world history. There were 2,000 killed and 9,000 injured in the Hiroshima-like concussion. In his history of MGH, Washburn noted only, "A number of doctors and nurses responded to the call at the time of the Halifax disaster."[146]

The following August the flu outbreak nearly broke Boston, as a particularly virulent strain appeared in the Massachusetts capital, as it also did for reasons unknown in Brest, France, and Freetown, Sierra Leone. Thomas D. Cunningham, an MGH intern at the time, would recall:

> The Surgical wards were turned over to Medical cases. Each Medical interne was put in charge of a ward, and the two senior Medical internes took alternate turns in the Emergency Ward, never leaving, as the cases poured in so fast. Meningitis was a favorite disease to come under the name of influenza, and I remember we had five at one time. . . . During the first week of the epidemic, 57% of the admissions died. Bodies were piled in the students' rooms near the laboratory. The morgue was completely filled, and the undertakers could not begin to keep up with the number of dead. Many patients were brought to the emergency ward dead in the ambulance. Others would die an hour after admission. It was not unusual to pass two or three of your patients

being carried out the back door as you were going up to make your midnight visit.[147]

Colonel Washburn and the others returned home after the armistice with deeply ingrained experience and more than a few lessons. In his account of Base Hospital No. 6 imbedded in his history of MGH, Washburn wrote:

> Horrible as war is, there are by-products of value. Lifetime friendships are formed. Men who have campaigned together know one another thoroughly. Fine traits of character are brought out, and in contrast the less admirable ones fail of concealment. Men learn the relative importance of things. A man who has parted from his home and risked his life has learned the comparative unimportance of social position and riches. He values accomplishment, service to others, his home life, his chance to raise a family in comfort and security. He intends to keep his liberties. Much as he loves peace, for these things he will again go to war if need be.[148]

It was easy to imagine that MGH and the world had seen the worst of it by then, that the Great War truly was the war to end all wars, that nothing worse than the war and the influenza pandemic could possibly happen in its wake.

Worse was ahead: an economic collapse as great as any in American history, followed by a second war that was truly worldwide, a war of horrors unimaginable only 20 years earlier. MGH would be tried in the double crucible of the Great Depression and World War II, while battling one extraordinary tragedy in its own backyard, the Cocoanut Grove nightclub fire of November 1942, still the worst nightclub fire in U.S. history. Meanwhile, the rules of the hospital game itself would begin shifting with the advent of Blue Cross in 1935. Through this trying period for world, nation, and hospital, Mass General would continue to emerge from its nineteenth-century complacency, while in fields as diverse as cardiology, psychiatry, and the treatment of burn victims, it would lead the way forward for American medicine.

The White Building under construction.

CHAPTER 4

DEPRESSION AND WAR, 1930–1945

*In 1935 such matters as understanding human disease in
terms of molecular mechanisms, looking for the responsible
gene or its absence, still lay far in the future. Massive federal
financing of research was not even a dream. And at the
same time, such nightmares as a plague of malpractice suits,
open-ended government payment systems leading to excessive
billing, paperwork by the forestful, insurance companies telling
physicians what to do, were unheard of. Changes such as
these were to start with a rush after World War II.*

—Francis D. Moore, A Miracle and a Privilege

AFTER SURVIVING THE GREAT DEPRESSION, *the United States was hit
with the greatest war in history. Yet Massachusetts General Hospital
emerged from this trying period revitalized, with new leaders and new
expertise.*

*Among the leaders was Edward Delos Churchill, one of the hospital's first
full-time surgeons who, in 1948, became chief of MGH's newly combined surgical services. Although Churchill emphasized general surgery over specialization,
he did encourage clinical research, which led to breakthroughs in thoracic surgery, vascular surgery, pediatric surgery, parathyroid surgery, and other surgical
areas. He also established a new form of surgical residency that would become
a national model.*

*Meanwhile, the hospital continued to expand in new directions under Chief
of Medicine James Howard Means and General Director Nathaniel Faxon. Old
buildings were torn down to make way for new facilities, including the White
Building; and new services such as psychiatry emerged. In the 1930s Blue Cross
began to change the way Americans paid for health care. Beginning in 1937 the
hospital's nursing school was reorganized. Volunteers, including the Ladies Visiting Committee, have always played important roles at MGH, but their volunteer services became particularly critical in keeping the hospital lit during the war.*

*The staff was tested by fire during the 1940s. Not only did more than 640
hospital personnel serve in World War II, but also the horrific Cocoanut Grove
nightclub fire of 1942 proved the hospital's disaster readiness. The inferno,*

killing 492, led to breakthroughs in treatments for burns, lung injuries, and psychological trauma.

Departmental histories in this chapter look at psychiatry, burns and trauma, and the role of volunteers in the 200-year history of Mass General.

THE STOCK MARKET CRASH OF OCTOBER 1929 and the financial depression that swept the nation also engulfed Massachusetts General Hospital. Salaries and wages were slashed across the board (5 to 10 percent in 1932). Deficits piled up as day rates in Baker and other fees had to be cut because of slumping demand. In 1934 "the working hours of special-duty nurses were shortened to eight per day in order to spread the work and so relieve unemployment. Two floors in the Phillips House (2 and 8) and one in the Baker Memorial (10) remained closed, while the ward patients of the General Hospital overflowed into the second and third floors of the Baker Memorial." The economy began to recover in 1936, allowing a 50 percent restoration of pay cuts made in 1932. All 102 beds in Phillips House were reopened in 1936 as well. Baker occupancy rates grew to about 80 percent of capacity, but it was not until 1938 that the freestanding hospital for middle-income patients turned a modest profit of $11,000.[1]

Never was philanthropy needed more. Among the gifts was a 1930 bequest made by Mrs. Harriet J. Bradbury, which made possible the construction of the George Robert White Building, named in honor of her brother. It took a full nine years before the White Building opened, on Ether Day 1939. The history of any long-lived hospital is one of building up and tearing down. To make way for the White Building, several nineteenth-century buildings, including the Bigelow surgical amphitheater and the old Outpatient Department, or Gay Ward, were demolished.

Rosemary Stevens, a historian of American hospitals, wrote about the 1930s: "Overall, despite the increased burden of free care, hospitals fared less badly than many other sectors of the economy. To some extent, the Depression provided a shake-up and consolidation of the hospital system, emphasizing the advantage of concentrating the fixed costs of radiology, pathology, and other technical services in larger institutions."[2] Stevens noted that most closings occurred among small proprietary hospitals and single-specialty operations. Large general hospitals like MGH fared relatively well.

WHEN SURGEONS WERE KINGPINS

The hospital industry was not the only institution to weather the Depression handily. By the 1930s the doctor with hospital privileges—particularly the surgeon—emerged as a figure of major stature in the American landscape. "A student graduating from medical school in 1932," wrote the MGH surgeon Claude E. Welch, who did graduate from HMS in 1932, "was guaranteed few external controls,[3] adulation by a public blissfully ignorant of medical facts, and a reasonable living. It is no wonder that many doctors considered themselves to be at least minor gods in the pantheon."[4]

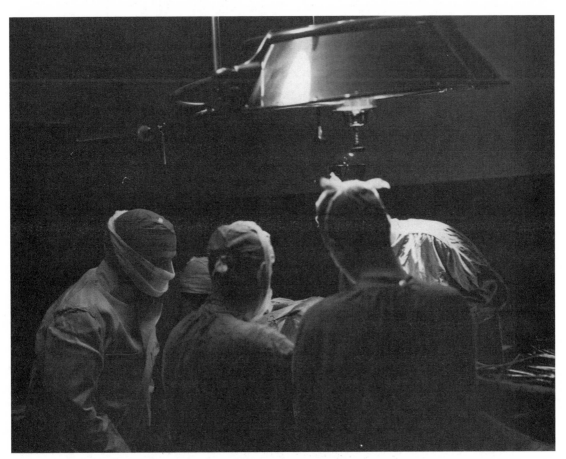

An operating room, 1938.

Despite some notable advances in recent years, there was relatively little that medicine could do for patients. (Three exceptions were the development of a vaccine for typhoid fever in 1897, Behring's vaccine-antitoxin for diphtheria in 1913, and the discovery of insulin in 1921.) Still ahead lay the quantum leaps in pharmacology that would radically improve prognoses, beginning with the first sulfa drugs of the mid-1930s and mass-production of penicillin during World War II.

More than half of the Harvard Medical School class of 1932, which included both Welch and Henry Knowles Beecher, opted for surgical careers. In the 1930s surgeons were the kingpins of hospital operations and prestige, according to Stevens. A surgeon had the idealized image of someone "in control of the workplace, wielding power within the hospital by virtue of his ability to bring in paying patients, and undertaking interventionist procedures whose results were evident in satisfied patients."[5]

MGH's leadership had attempted to unify the Surgical Service before World War I. Maurice H. Richardson's brief reign as surgeon in chief had ended with his untimely death in 1912, and Charles A. Porter had a one-year stint as overall chief in 1925–1926. But it was really the elevation of Richardson's son Edward P. to chief of a third surgical service (1922–1925) that marked the beginning of a "full-time" service. (For the next 47 years a full-time surgical service meant that the individuals had full-time appointments at Harvard Medical School, did research, and yet remained in private clinical practice. Not until W. Gerald Austen became chief of surgery in 1969 did surgeons begin to become full-time employees of the hospital.) The younger Richardson's novel position was eventually merged into the West Service, which became home under him of a full-time group; visiting surgeons in private practice continued to operate on the East. As Edsall had already done in medicine, Richardson sought to deepen the investigative work of the surgeons under him by allowing them the freedom and modest financial support to pursue their investigative interests. In this Richardson may have been following through on the vision of his own father, Maurice, who wrote to Harvey Cushing at Johns Hopkins in 1909: "I feel that my men, although they make splendid practitioners of surgery, failed to get from me any inspiration towards so-called research work. . . . [It] seems that the coming generation needs a broader field in which to work; that the men should be more than purely clinical observers. . . . I feel, too, that we get to be very narrow in Boston. . . . I hope later to have my son, Edward, get the inspiration from your example."[6]

Cushing would return to Boston in 1913 to begin a surgical service at the newly opened Peter Bent Brigham Hospital. MGH would wait another decade for such a service. In the 1920s Edward Richardson began searching for promising young men who had the potential for investigative success. These included Munroe McIver, James C. White, Robert Linton, Oliver Cope, and the future chief of surgery Edward Delos Churchill. Like the young physicians Howard Means, George Minot, and Paul White, whose stellar careers were jump-started by David Edsall before the Great War, several of these young surgeons recruited by Richardson *fils* did tours of study at home and abroad before returning to full-time duty at MGH. James White spent seven months in 1927–1928 working in a clinic in Strasbourg, training that "found clinical expression in the surgery of the sympathetic nervous system." Another young surgeon in training, Champ Lyons, studied under Sir Samuel Phillips Bedson at the London Hospital. Henry K. Beecher (see chapter 2) studied with the Nobel laureate August Krogh in Copenhagen before making the switch from surgery to anesthesia; Oliver Cope studied the pathology and physiology of endocrine glands with Ludwig Pick in Berlin in 1933 and with Sir Henry Dale in London the following year. Edward D. Benedict toiled in Edinburgh under D. T. D. Wilkie and subsequently turned his attention to endoscopy, bronchoscopy, and esophagoscopy.[7]

In this constellation of young stars Edward Churchill was arguably the brightest. Born in Chenoa, Illinois, Churchill earned a master's degree in biology at Northwestern University in 1917 before going to Harvard Medical School, where he graduated cum laude in 1920. A member of the house staff at MGH in 1920–1924, he became the first surgical resident on the West Service under Edward Richardson's new full-time system. Thus marked for future greatness, he won a Dalton Scholarship in 1925 under Cecil Drinker and a Moseley Traveling Fellowship in 1926, which took Churchill to the Krogh lab in Copenhagen. With this breadth of postgraduate education he returned to MGH in the summer of 1927 to join Richardson's full-time staff. In 1928 Churchill and the cardiologist Paul White created a surgical sensation, carrying out the first pericardiectomy for constrictive

Edward Churchill.

pericarditis in the United States. "This pioneering and spectacularly successful effort in the field of cardiac surgery—a demonstration of bringing the physiologic laboratory to the operating room—together with his accomplishments in thoracic surgery . . . very early projected [Churchill] into a position of national leadership," according to the MGH surgeon Gordon Scannell, who wrote the lead profile of Churchill for a book of MGH history published after Churchill's death. Thoracic surgery of all kinds would become Churchill's clinical focus for the next 25 years, or until a minor stroke made him set aside the scalpel in 1952. Key clinical contributors in his thoracic clinic included Frederick T. Lord, Donald King, and Helen Pittman. Richard Sweet of the East Service, where he served a "clinical indenture to Daniel Jones," took charge of thoracic work during World War II while Churchill was overseas.[8] Sweet's esophageal anastomotic technique was legendary.[9]

In demand as a young surgical pioneer, Churchill moved to Boston City Hospital to begin a surgical service in 1928. He considered competing offers from Columbia Presbyterian and New York Hospital but decided instead to return to MGH, where, on April 21, 1931, he was made chief of the West Surgical Service. The appointment was held up for six months while Harvard Medical School dragged its heels about making him Homans professor of surgery, usually a concurrent appointment. According to Scannell, resistance to this appointment for Churchill may have come from Harvey Cushing, chief of surgery at the Brigham: "To establish a full-time university department outside the Quadrangle ran counter, perhaps, to Cushing's grand scheme of things. After six months the academic smoke cleared, and the designation of Churchill as Homans Professor then facilitated his appointment as chief of the West Surgical Service." Scannell noted that in this awkward transition one might read the essence of "the relationship that survives to this day between [MGH] and the Harvard Medical School."[10] It is a relationship that Joseph Garland, editor of the *New England Journal of Medicine*, captured:

> The relations between the Massachusetts General Hospital and the Harvard Medical School have been based, like the government of England, on certain unwritten conventions. By a tacit gentlemen's agreement both parties recognize their interdependence, and the representatives of both parties being

gentlemen (frequently the same gentlemen!), mutual good will usually prevails. Other good hospitals have come into the field to serve the growing population—just as other good medical schools have been founded in the community—but the Massachusetts General Hospital and the Medical School of Harvard University stand unique as the still robust pioneers.[11]

Churchill's appointment marked "the beginning of thirty years of leadership that sees the integration of a research-oriented full-time staff into a clinically oriented matrix of unusual depth," according to Scannell. "As the Warrens, Bigelows, and Richardsons had done before him, he left an indelible mark on the growth and development of the Surgical Services and, indeed, of the hospital as a whole."[12]

Surgery had come far in the first three decades of the twentieth century. One of the hospital's historians, Nathaniel Faxon, noted the changes and growth that had occurred at MGH:

> In 1906, there had been listed 1,922 major surgical operations; in 1936 there were 5,640. Analysis of the types of operation reflected not only the progress surgery had made during this period but the changes the Hospital had made in meeting the needs of the community. In 1906, the majority of operations had been for appendicitis and for hernia. In 1935, the actual number of operations for these conditions had remained practically the same in spite of a fourfold increase in the total number of surgical procedures. The increase in the total was in the more complicated operations for goiter, brain tumor, for cancer in all parts of the body, and in chest operations.[13]

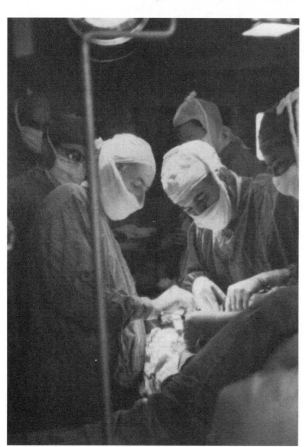

Edward Churchill (left) performs a general thoracic surgical procedure, assisted by Thomas Gephart, circa 1940.

The Meaning of East and West

Until 1948, when Arthur Allen retired as chief of the East and the two services were combined under Churchill, surgery at MGH would remain divided between East and West. (In his history, Nathaniel Faxon noted that by 1938 "the old distinctive pattern of the East and West Surgical was gradually breaking down and had now reached the point at which members of the staff often served part of their time on the East Service and part on the West, much to the advantage of Residents and House Officers, who benefited by the varied techniques and methods of the staff members.")[14]

The East Service was traditionally dominated by visiting surgeons such as Daniel Fiske Jones, Richard H. Miller, George W. W. Brewster, Lincoln Davis, Robert Greenough, Charles Scudder, and Beth Vincent (a man, of course, as there were no female surgeons on the Harvard Medical School faculty until the 1970s). These veterans in private practice had come up through the old master-apprentice system. As a house officer in 1932, Claude Welch was awed by this "elite group."

> Their staff room was fitted with leather chairs; ours [for the house officers] had wooden benches. The visiting surgeons oozed Aesculapian authority. In the operating room—and everywhere else in the hospital—each one of them was a "captain of the ship." Interns and nurses who misread a gesture at the operating table were apt to get their knuckles rapped with an instrument. The lowly were supposed to anticipate every demand of the masters; we had to be gifted with extrasensory perception. "Don't give me what I ask for—give me what I need" was supposed to be understood, even by interns.[15]

Each of the surgical masters of the East Service had his own apprentice "waiting in the wings, his star in the ascendant." These included Arthur Allen, Leland McKittrick (with a special interest in the diabetic complications of vascular surgery), Joe Meigs (an early leader in gynecology; see chapter 7), Channing Simmons, Ernest Daland (focused on the Tumor Clinic), "and so on down the list. It was a strong group," according to Scannell, "all clearly products of a master-apprentice system and, as time was to prove, extraordinarily able clinical innovators."[16]

McKittrick was perhaps first among equals in those backing up Allen. After Churchill, he was the second surgeon receiving a profile in the official MGH history of the period. Born in Wisconsin in 1893, he was educated at the University of Wisconsin and Harvard Medical School. After a brief internship at the University of Minnesota, he came to MGH in about 1920 and apprenticed himself to Daniel Fiske Jones. "A person of great integrity, honesty, and judgment" and "a superb clinical surgeon,"[17] McKittrick was considered "heir to the tradition of the East Service"[18] when Allen retired in 1948, but instead the MGH board saw fit to unify surgery once and for all under Churchill. According to Scannell, "McKittrick remained as a clinical tower of strength, of incalculable influence on the training of residents, but clearly his center of gravity shifted uptown to the Deaconess Hospital."[19] It seems that McKittrick's allegiance had been shared by the Deaconess since 1932, since this is where his mentor in the classic master-apprentice relationship of old-time surgery, Daniel Fiske Jones, had become a senior surgeon. Jones introduced McKittrick to the pioneer diabetes practitioner Elliott Joslin, and through that connection McKittrick became a world expert in the surgical treatment of diabetic patients.

Claude Welch was Arthur Allen's principal associate from 1936 to 1941, a five-year apprenticeship. "There was no other period in my life," Welch wrote, "in which I learned more and none that molded my life more firmly." Welch

Arthur Allen in a portrait
by William Draper.

would remember the East chief as "a master surgeon, and a true friend of all of his patients."[20] Born in Somerset, Kentucky, in 1887, Allen was a graduate of Georgetown University and the Johns Hopkins Medical School (1913). Welch recalled:

Dr. Allen's scientific interests and contributions were many, ranging from all aspects of trauma to all organs and lesions in the abdomen to peripheral vascular disease, and from preoperative preparation to postoperative care and complications. . . .

Dr. Allen was *The Chief*. . . . In many respects he was the personification of the Old Testament Jehovah. His underlings viewed him with awe, respect, admiration and, to a certain extent, fear. He also was a jealous god; anyone who attempted to take away one of his patients incurred his everlasting wrath.

Dr. Allen first and foremost was concerned with patients' care. He often said that the surgeon who did not wake up at 2 A.M. and worry about his patients did not deserve to be a surgeon. . . . Every morning after I had finished rounds, he arrived at 8:30 for the first operation. His opening sentence always was "What is the BN?" BN, of course, stood for bad news, and that often was a long story. In those days, major abdominal operations were followed by serious complications in nearly thirty percent of the cases and by postoperative mortality in nearly ten percent.[21]

Welch had the memorable experience of caring for his mentor at the end of Allen's long career: "On March 15, 1958, I operated on Dr. Allen for the final time. He asked, and I told him the findings. He said, 'That is that.' As far as I know they were the last words he spoke. He died quietly three days later."[22]

Edward Churchill's own career was known not only for his investigative work but also for the clinical research he encouraged in others. In association with Reginald Smithwick (an expert in the autonomic nervous system), James White charted his course in neurosurgery (see chapter 7). Working closely with Fuller Albright and other physicians of Ward 4, Oliver Cope became renowned for his parathyroid surgery, significantly advancing the reputation of MGH in the investigation and treatment of this endocrine system with "a superb . . . cooperative effort on the part of a strong medical service with its Means, Aub, Albright, and Bauer."[23] His contributions with Francis Moore to burn therapy would be notable before and especially after the devastating Cocoanut Grove nightclub fire of November 1942, detailed below.

Robert Linton, "an individual of uncommon force and positive imagination,"[24] was a pioneer in vascular surgery—although that seems too narrow a category for even an abbreviated list of his accomplishments: interested in gastrointestinal and biliary tract surgery, he also "greatly enjoyed pediatric surgery" and performed the first blue-baby operation at MGH. Linton was direct with his patients. "Lose forty pounds or don't come back to see me," he would tell an obese person facing surgery. "If you don't care about your life, I have to care about mine."[25] His official MGH biographer records an entry from Linton's log that is hard to top:

> Operation: December 8 and 9, 1970. Mr. F____ B____—resection of thoracoabdominal aneurysm from left subclavian artery to both groins with grafts to all visceral vessels: 13 anastomoses, gastrostomy—the record documents *seven* different scrub nurses, *five* different anesthetists, *three* different residents, one of whom developed phlebitis during the case, and one Dr. Linton who carried on for 23 straight hours. Patient did well and subsequently presented at the Grand Rounds as noted by Earle Wilkins, "At the conclusion of the presentation and the ensuing discussion, something happened which was unique and unprecedented, at least in my recollection. The audience, including the usually reserved and chary surgeons present, arose and applauded. Bob Linton was 70 years old.[26]

Bradford Cannon, son of Walter Cannon, an HMS professor of physiology and nephew of the social service leader Ida Cannon, developed the field of plastic and reconstructive surgery first brought to MGH by Varaztad Hovhannes Kazanjian. Also noted by Scannell as important associates of Churchill were John Stewart (metabolic problems and the liver), Champ Lyons (surgical infections), Fiorindo Simeone (vascular surgery and shock), and Edward Benedict (endoscopy and bronchoscopy).

Churchill Alone at the Top

In the operating rooms of the West Service, Churchill was king. His own specialty (odd that one who preached the wisdom of *general* surgical training did have a specialty) was thoracic surgery, beginning with that pericardectomy in 1928 and focusing on "management of bronchopulmonary suppuration, bronchiectasis, lung abscess, and cancer of the lung. In these areas Churchill was an acknowledged leader, and he attracted a succession of clinical fellows which included John Gibbon, Howard Bradshaw, Gus Lindskog, Ronald Belsey, Max Chamberlain, and Ralph Adams."[27]

"[Churchill] handled tissues with the utmost delicacy," according to Welch, "and his technique was meticulous. He was particularly proud of his thyroidectomies. Three days after operation, an observer could barely see the operative incision."[28] Scannell noted that Churchill's "sensitivity to the human needs of his patients was exquisite. Scannell borrowed from Kipling to illuminate this facet of a surgeon's life: 'And, meanwhile, their days were filled, as yours are filled, with the piteous procession of men and women begging them, as men and women beg of you daily, for leave to live a little longer, upon whatever terms.'"[29]

Outside the OR, Churchill developed a new form of surgical residency, one that would become the national standard. Scannell explained the Churchill system, launched in 1940, as "a matter of geometry, a rectangular structure instead of a pyramid."[30] In other words, it dispensed with the old hierarchical master-apprentice system of teaching surgeons, with its emphasis on technique, and opened the resident to a wider field of influences. The Churchill system took men (still only men) in their final year of medical school and plugged them into a five-year continuum of resident training. Welch wrote that the system

> guaranteed that all residents could obtain the necessary qualifications for Board examinations. . . . He gave his residents great responsibility, particularly in the operating room. In his opinion the visiting surgeons should serve as consultants and called by residents only at the residents' option. Many visiting surgeons at that time believed that residents learned best by watching well-trained older surgeons at work and assisting them. Today [1992], Churchill has been proved correct; his point of view was rendered tenable in large part by improvements in anesthesia. Many of us believe the MGH surgical residency program is the best in the country.[31]

"Unwillingness to fragment General Surgery into its component specialties was the Churchill way," according to Scannell. "For example, before the American Association for Thoracic Surgery in 1941 he warned that other special societies had often become preoccupied with technical proficiency and operative experience which could lead to 'an encouragement of myopic regional technical surgery.'"[32] In the tents of the Italian campaign of World War II Churchill's prejudice against specialization became intransigent. Under the pressures of wartime, Churchill was appalled at how few physicians and surgeons could adapt to whatever crisis they faced. This convinced him that a young surgeon must be able to do it all.

In the 1950s, still under Churchill's leadership but championed by Marshall Bartlett, the first attempt at a surgical group practice, the Surgical Associates, was established at MGH. Though not a true group practice, it was the first of several moves in that direction. Churchill would claim that the first conversations leading to the Surgical Associates were had on the battlefields of Italy. Yet Scannell noted that "Churchill—while approving in principle and obviously an important factor in the development [of the Surgical Associates]—nevertheless avoided direct commitment of the department."[33]

"Lonely at the top" is an expression that would seem to define Edward Delos Churchill, especially when one reads Welch's tribute to him. "Churchill was an extremely proud, reserved person," Welch wrote.

> He was quite jealous of many men on the clinical ladder. Eminent surgeons such as Robert Linton and Grantley Taylor never obtained an academic appointment above that of assistant professor of surgery. Even some of his closer associates were not awarded titles that many would have considered appropriate.
>
> I would not wish to imply that he was wrong. Instead I am certain he believed that the title of professor of surgery was a mark deserving the highest respect and that there were very few persons who could qualify. . . . His

attitude did conspire to produce a sort of loneliness of power. But his influence has not diminished.[34]

As the 1950s wore on, Churchill remained nominally in control of the department, though his attention was often focused elsewhere, and a new generation of surgical hotshots named Raker, McDermott, Waddell, Nardi, Shaw, Russell, Grillo, Burke, Malt, Huggins, Constable (and the list goes on) were chomping at the bit. All, noted Gordon Scannell, "were to be involved in the time of succession." When Churchill had all but retired to Vermont in the 1960s, the question of succession came front and center. Scannell would note that this was "a difficult period in the department."[35] But that is a story for later (see chapter 6).

PSYCHIATRY IN A GENERAL HOSPITAL

The redoubtable Frederic Washburn was replaced by George Hoyt Bigelow as the hospital's general director on February 23, 1934. Washburn, who had guided MGH for 26 years, became director emeritus and soon set about compiling a history of Mass General for the period from 1900 to 1935, the third of six installments issued before the present volume. Bigelow, who had been commissioner of public health for Massachusetts before coming to Mass General, died of apparent suicide before the year was out and was succeeded by Nathaniel W. Faxon after a short interlude when Bigelow's assistant, Norman C. Baker, took the reins. A graduate of Harvard Medical School, an assistant to Colonel Washburn (1919–1922), and a former director of the Strong Memorial Hospital of the University of Rochester, New York, Faxon was formally hired on July 1, 1935, and served for 14 years, until being replaced by Dean A. Clark in 1949. Lawrence Martin, hired as a cost accountant that same year, would remember Faxon as "a very strict, military type individual who used an old-fashioned roll-top desk. If you went into his office, it looked like something out of the Victorian era."[36]

It was during this interregnum that Stanley Cobb arrived at Massachusetts General Hospital to establish a psychiatry department. Cobb's goal was to establish psychiatry in a general hospital setting, with support from the Rockefeller Foundation, and to innovate at the borderland among psychiatry, psychology,

Stanley Cobb.

and neurology. The department was also a bold experiment to bring psychiatry out of mental hospitals, where the chronically mentally ill continued to be treated, and to link the field more closely with treatment of ambulatory psychoneuroses. The department would also bring psychiatry into closer contact with the other departments of modern medicine, while addressing the psychological components of physical illness. An interest in psychology had flourished at MGH in the Departments of Social Service (see chapter 3) and Neurology (see chapter 7), but it had gone through a long hiatus after World War I.

The experiment succeeded admirably because of the skills and training that Cobb, Harvard's second Bullard professor of neuropathology, brought to bear on his new task. After graduating from Harvard Medical School in 1914, Cobb had worked as a surgical intern at the Peter Bent Brigham Hospital. He then moved to the Henry Phipps Psychiatric Clinic at Johns Hopkins, one of the first psychiatric clinics in a general hospital, where he studied under Adolf Meyer. Meyer's integrated psychobiology would leave an indelible mark on Cobb's approach to psychiatry. Meyer urged the need for a systematic collection of empirical data on patients, such as heredity, cultural background, nutrition, education, exercise, habits, temperament, and intellectual capacity. He insisted that his protégés have a firm grasp of neuroanatomy and construct a three-dimensional model of the brain. He also gave them the task of writing their own psychiatric life history.

Following in the footsteps of his mentor, Cobb was a monist: he believed in the unity of mind activity and brain activity. He valued both neuroanatomy and psychoanalysis, practicing each to varying degrees over the course of his career. Cobb wrote, "No biological process takes place without change of structure. Whenever the brain functions, there is organic change. The brain is the organ of the mind. Therefore, all function is organic, and mind and body are one."[37]

Cobb would be pleased to know that today at MGH an entire institute is dedicated to the inseparable connection between mind and body: the Benson-Henry Institute for Mind Body Medicine. The institute was founded by the mind-body medicine expert Herbert Benson, a cardiologist by training, and opened at MGH in 2006.

Benson first made headlines in the 1975 book *The Relaxation Response*, which shared his findings that through meditation or simply by sitting quietly and emptying the mind of everyday thoughts while focusing on breathing, research subjects experienced decreases in metabolism and breathing and heart rates, as well as slower brain waves. On the basis of this discovery, Benson developed a view that disease should be approached as a three-legged stool: surgery constitutes one leg, pharmaceutical medicine another leg, and mind-body medicine the third. In line with this vision, the Benson-Henry Institute's clinical programs treat patients through a combination of relaxation-response techniques, proper nutrition and exercise, and the reframing of negative thought patterns. Staff members conduct research on the relationship between mental and physical health and seek to educate caregivers on the mind-body connection. In 2011 Benson serves as director emeritus of the Benson-Henry Institute, and Greg Fricchione, an associate chief in the MGH Department of Psychiatry, is its current director.

Although the work conducted by the Benson-Henry Institute closely relates to psychiatry and mental health, in striving to integrate the mind-body connection into all medical disciplines it collaborates with departments across the hospital. The integration of mind-body medicine into clinical care has proven to be a valid and important effort: Benson's most recent research suggests that relaxation techniques can alter an individual's gene activity, deactivating genes that trigger inflammation and others that prompt cell death.

A lifelong struggle with a severe stammer stoked Cobb's interest in neurology and psychiatry while providing persistent frustration. Having observed the emotional component of his own stammering and having undergone analysis himself, Cobb grew increasingly interested in psychoanalysis and the role of psychic factors in certain diseases. In the early 1920s Cobb had dinner with Carl Jung and Harry Murray, Cobb's doctor friend, who also stammered. Murray and Cobb described their stammering problems at length to Jung, hoping he might provide some solution or insight. Jung replied, "Don't at all costs give up stammering. It is most attractive to women."[38] Murray laughed and Cobb blushed. Cobb's speech impediment did not keep him out of the lecture hall, however, and his neuropathology course became very popular. When Cobb lectured, he would use both hands to write on the blackboard at the same time, recalled Chester Pierce, now professor emeritus of psychiatry for Harvard Medical School. "The medical students, of course, were all just overwhelmed by that."[39]

In the spring of 1916 Cobb, who had been attending lectures at the Phipps Clinic, was appointed assistant in neurophysiology with a stipend of $500 and a lab of his own, later called the Neurological Laboratory of the Henry Phipps Psychiatric Clinic. He worked on the wards at Phipps as an intern from 1917 until the fall of 1918, when he left for active duty in the military. Upon his return, Cobb and his wife, Elizabeth, settled in Boston, and he received a $500 Dalton Scholarship. He maintained an office at MGH to see private patients, a financial necessity rather than a labor of love. His main interests lay in teaching and research. In the spring of 1920 Richard C. Cabot requested that Cobb teach an elective neurology component of a graduate course.

After the untimely death of the HMS Bullard professor of neuropathology, Elmer Southard, in February 1920, David Edsall asked Cobb to suggest a potential successor. Cobb replied with a few suggestions, noting the need for a professor with an approach broader than Southard's. He wrote, "We should get a good man to put his whole time into neuropathology at the School and give him the hospital connection in order to get material, but we do *not* want a man interested merely in pickled brain sections."[40] (Southard notoriously kept myriad crocks and battery jars full of pickled brains in the neuropathology lab at HMS.) In June 1920 Cobb was promoted to assistant professor of neuropathology, without a full professor above him. Five years later he was appointed to the Bullard Professorship.

Through his old cadaver mate, Carl Binger, Cobb met Alan Gregg at a cocktail party, who introduced him to Simon Flexner. Both Gregg and Flexner were officials of the Rockefeller Foundation. Impressed by Cobb and his work, they furnished him with the funds for a two-year study with European leaders in neurology and psychiatry. In August 1925, upon Cobb's return to the States, the General Education Board of the Rockefeller Foundation gave Harvard a $350,000 grant, the income from which would support an academic department of neurology at Harvard Medical School, headed by Cobb, with its wards at Boston City Hospital. Cobb began work at Boston City Hospital in January 1926, effectively shifting the focus of neurology at Harvard from MGH, where it had been since the late nineteenth century (see chapter 7).

Howard Means had informed Cobb in the fall of 1924 that he wished to expand neurology at MGH, and he asked how he could induce Cobb to leave Boston City Hospital for MGH.[41] Ten years later Cobb finally returned to MGH to establish the Department of Psychiatry. In the beginning the new liaison service met with some resistance, and Cobb was faced with "the monumental task of organizing a psychiatric service at that conservative institution where he encountered doubts and some overt hostility about the place of psychiatry in a general hospital. . . . Some colleagues resented the number of Jews on the psychiatric service, and the neurologists, most of whom looked upon themselves as neuropsychiatrists, felt threatened by the competition from a new department of psychiatry."[42]

The MGH Psychiatry Service had 12 beds also associated with the neurology and neurosurgery departments, as well as two outpatient services, one for adults and one for children. (A child psychiatric clinic had existed since 1931 in the outpatient clinic under the aegis of the Neurology Department.) Most of the early members of the department began as practitioners of the approach espoused by Adolf Meyer at Johns Hopkins, though over the first few years many underwent psychoanalytic training, which inaugurated the practice of long-term psychoanalytic therapy. In a first for the Rockefeller Foundation, funds were made available for patient beds and for psychoanalytic training for residents.[43]

Although many departments initially resisted, a few were open to early collaboration, including the Department of Rheumatology in 1938. Soon afterward, the cardiologist Paul Dudley White requested that the Psychiatry Service collaborate with his unit, which resulted in seminal work on neurocirculatory asthenia. The Psychiatric Consultation Service eventually helped manage mental health issues throughout the hospital's departments and wards, in collaboration with physicians and surgeons.[44]

In the early years of the department, psychoanalysis was an important focus. The neurologist James Jackson Putnam was an early follower of Freud (see chapter 7). He encouraged Louville Eugene Emerson, the first clinical psychologist at MGH after 1911, to teach and write about psychoanalysis and to incorporate it into his psychotherapeutic practice. Emerson said, "I was a philosopher who taught people how to live."[45] His entire career as a clinical psychologist, however, was carried on as a member of the Department of Neurology, until his death in 1939.

Cobb gave the psychoanalyst Erik Erikson his first job when he came to MGH in 1933.[46] Erikson would be celebrated as the author of *Childhood and Society* (1950), *Young Man Luther* (1958), and *Gandhi's Truth* (1969). Cobb also set up a lectureship for Hans Sachs, a lawyer who had trained in psychoanalysis under Freud himself and who wrote *The Creative Unconscious: Studies in the Psychoanalysis of Art* (1942). Cobb, who had personally undergone analysis with Sachs, allowed Sachs to walk the wards and consult with the other physicians about the patients. In 1934 Cobb helped organize the Boston Psychoanalytic Institute, where Sachs was established as a training analyst.[47] Bill Herman, Cobb's longtime friend, was a remarkable analyst, though he died young, in 1935. Jacob Finesinger was a talented psychoanalyst, although first and foremost a pioneer in psychosomatic medicine. As a psychoanalyst, he was known for his espousal of "minimal activity," an analytic practice of saying very little apart from artfully timed grunts as a patient spoke.[48] Finesinger also directed the Inpatient Service of the Psychiatric Department.

Beyond psychoanalysis, Cobb extended psychiatry and neurology to incorporate psychologists from the very beginning of patient care. For example, in the 1930s he commissioned Robert Young to found a camp for neurotic boys as part of their treatment. Indeed, throughout the entire history of the Psychiatry Department, psychologists have always been a part of the service, setting the stage for a unique collaboration.

Cobb was legendary for his devotion to the department. For example, he treated a member of an old Boston family, who lived in Boston's Back Bay, with the expectation that upon his death, there would be a bequest to the Psychiatric Department. But when the will was read, all the man bequeathed to the department was his brain. Dismayed but enterprising, Cobb asked the MGH trustees to accept the brain; he would stain it, section it, study it, and send a report to the estate. This he did, with a $50,000 bill, and the estate paid it.[49]

Cobb's Legacy Carried On

Erich Lindemann was a psychoanalyst with an interest in the psychological and social aspects of psychosomatic diseases. His vision of a "hospital community" and a "therapeutic human environment" was before its time. Later he helped launch the community psychiatry movement, and his work continues to inform both social psychology and social psychiatry. Lindemann received a Rockefeller Fellowship to join the MGH Psychiatric Service part-time in 1935, and shortly afterward he assumed full-time responsibilities. As a young psychiatrist, Lindemann accomplished important collaborative research with members of other departments, including Chester Jones of the Medical Service (psychosocial causes of ulcerative colitis), Walter Bauer (arthritis), and Oliver Cope (the psychological effects of loss of bodily integrity from, for example, hysterectomy or mastectomy).

In the wake of the Cocoanut Grove nightclub fire of 1942, Lindemann published a groundbreaking paper, "Symptomatology and Management of Acute Grief."[50] The article, his biographer explained, "laid the groundwork for subsequent studies and treatment of acute grief as distinct from chronic melancholia. It also gave Lindemann a model for the

Erich Lindemann.

new field of community psychiatry: disruption of social networks as a contributor to mental illness."[51] The latter-day chief of psychiatry Jerrold Rosenbaum would comment that Lindemann's work enabled mental health experts to "improve the ability to respond to the psychiatric consequences of traumatic events."[52]

From the 1950s through the building of the Wang Ambulatory Care Center in 1982, the Psychiatry Department's main assets on campus were the three clinical services: a 21-bed inpatient unit in the Bulfinch Building (to become a 24-bed elite med-psych inpatient unit in the Blake Building); a high-intensity psychiatric emergency room, the APS (Acute Psychiatry Service, founded in the 1950s by the alcohol research pioneer Morris Chafetz); and the Consultation Service. But the service moved off-campus during this period as well.

Lindemann was an important figure in the national movement to bring health care, especially mental health care, to the entire population to improve social conditions. After President Harry Truman signed the Mental Health Act of 1946, creating the National Institute of Mental Health (NIMH), Lindemann instituted an NIMH-funded program for three residents in psychiatry. In 1948 he was appointed associate professor of mental health at the Harvard School of Public Health, where he founded the country's first department of mental health in a school of public health. Lindemann's vision of health care called on health professionals to broaden the understanding of their work, including the community outside the hospital, patients' families, and other disciplines in health care. The ad hoc committee comprising representatives from MGH, McLean, and HMS unanimously elected Lindemann psychiatrist in chief in 1954 after Stanley Cobb's retirement.

During his tenure as chief, Lindemann continued his work in bringing mental health treatment and research out of the hospital and into the community. With Laura Morris and, for a time, the MGH psychiatrist Peter Sifneos, Lindemann established the Mental Health Unit at MGH, which collaborated with community leaders for the accomplishment of their mutual goals. Lindemann and his colleagues soon realized that a major community crisis was right outside their doors. A compulsory relocation of working-class families in Boston's West End became the topic of a classic study in community mental health research: "Relocation and Mental Health—Adaptation under Stress" ("The West End Story").[53] The study included an analysis of working-class community structure, and it urged the need to exclude compulsory relocation of entire communities from the process of urban development.[54]

David Satin remarked on Lindemann's gifts as a teacher and shortcomings as an administrator:

> In personal style Erich Lindemann was more comfortable as "guru"—teacher and humanist, encouraging patients and colleagues to broaden and realize themselves—than as wielder of power in institutional battle—comfortable with successful conflict. He rose to the former with skill and warmth, and avoided the latter with discomfort and distaste. . . . There were those who revered his grasp of social issues and contributions to individuals and projects. A group of these . . . lobbied successfully to have the MGH-affiliated

mental health center named for him in recognition of his outstanding contributions to psychiatry. On the other side there was the phenomenon of a circulated petition, signed by selected members of various MGH services (but not psychiatry), asking that the new Chief of Psychiatry be "free of dogma" (psychoanalysis), avoid "inquiries into the hypothetical cause or causes of psychiatric illness" (preventive psychiatry), and "encourage the use of physical and chemical methods in the treatment of psychiatric illness" (not social and psychological ones).[55]

The Lindemann Center, guided by Lindemann's vision of community mental health, opened on Staniford Street near the main MGH campus in 1971 with 50 beds. Gerald Klerman, the first superintendent, made the center's pool and gym available to the surrounding communities, to integrate the center into the community rather than isolate its patients. Since the opening of the Lindemann Center, the care of the chronically mentally ill has generally shifted from state hospitals to communities. The center has adapted to the new model by creating halfway houses, cooperative apartments, day treatment programs, social clubs, and active medication monitoring for the chronically mentally ill.[56] The Freedom Trail Clinic, an outpatient clinic at the Lindemann Center run by Donald C. Goff and staffed with MGH doctors, serves as an MGH research outpost for schizophrenia. The MGH Psychiatry Department is also responsible for community outpatient clinics in Charlestown, Chelsea, Revere, and the North End (see chapter 6).

After Lindemann retired in 1965, John C. Nemiah served as interim chief for two years. In 1967 Leon Eisenberg, a pioneer child psychiatrist, came from Johns Hopkins to become chief of psychiatry at MGH. In response to the attitude expressed in the circulating petition regarding Lindemann, and the opinion of some doctors that psychiatry had become unscientific, Eisenberg was assigned the "task of bringing psychiatry back into medicine and strengthening clinical services and research." Under Eisenberg, the Psychiatric Department's psychoanalytic component diminished, and biological psychiatry received more emphasis. He recruited Seymour S. Kety from the NIMH to start a research program in the genetics of psychosis, psychopharmacology, and the neurosciences and expanded the residency program to 24 residents. Funding came from MGH, not NIMH.[57]

At the age of 20, Eisenberg had applied to a number of medical schools, but was turned down because of restrictive quotas for Jewish students. When a Pennsylvania state legislator intervened in the young man's behalf, Eisenberg was admitted to the medical school at the University of Pennsylvania, from which he graduated as valedictorian. During his time at MGH, Eisenberg worked to increase diversity as part of an affirmative action committee at HMS, which succeeded in increasing the number of African American medical students. Eisenberg

Leon Eisenberg.

went on to serve as chairman of the HMS Admissions Committee and of the HMS Commission on Black Community Relations.

Psychopharmacology had begun in the 1950s with the advent of reserpine, chlorpromazine, and lithium. In 1971 Matthew Friedman, a doctor of pharmacology who had returned to school for a medical degree, established the Psychopharmacology Clinic (PPC) at MGH. Friedman brought in 50 chronically psychotic people, saw them in groups, and provided them with support and medication.[58] In 1975 Robert Hicks took over direction of the PPC, where he arranged for Ross Baldessarini and a few other young doctors to teach, make rounds, and see patients. The group met patients weekly in the old upper amphitheater of the Clinics Building. An outpatient psychopharmacology unit was initially established in 1978 when Jerrold Rosenbaum became the director of the Psychopharmacology Clinic, later known as the Clinical Psychopharmacology Unit. The unit's activities in the 1980s moved toward subspecialized outpatient clinical and research units such as the Depression Clinical and Research Unit headed by Maurizio Fava; the Anxiety Disorders Unit directed by Mark Pollack after early years of research led by David Sheehan; the Bipolar Clinic and Research Program under the direction of Gary Sachs; the Perinatal and Reproductive Psychiatry Program founded by Lee Cohen; and several other disorders-based clinical and research programs. Charles Welch took over the Somatic Therapies Service from Michel Mandel, and Joseph Biederman founded the Pediatric Psychopharmacology Program.[59] The Biederman group grew to comprise a team of more than 160 faculty and support personnel; Biederman himself was cited as having the most highly influential papers of any researcher in the world of psychiatry.[60]

Thomas Hackett.

From Snakes to Psychiatry

The integration of psychiatrists throughout MGH resulted in findings that could not have come out of an isolated department. Thomas Hackett, who served as chief of psychiatry from Eisenberg's departure in 1974 until his own untimely death in 1989 from a heart attack at age 59, was a leader in the delivery of psychiatric care to medical and surgical inpatients, known as consultation psychiatry. For example, working with Edwin H. "Ned" Cassem, Hackett identified depression as a predictor of mortality in cardiac patients. On one occasion, while walking through the Myocardial Infarction Unit, where patients were hooked up to heart monitors, Hackett heard a monitor's loud and shrill noise and wondered what the emotional effect of such a startling noise might be to a heart patient.

Hackett was the first psychiatrist to examine and address the unique stresses involved with the new environment of intensive care. His success as a psychiatrist in intensive medical settings derived from his pragmatic approach to helping patients, as well as his engaging, charismatic manner punctuated by a booming laugh.

Born 1928 in Cincinnati, Ohio, Hackett had entered the world of biology through a boyhood interest in snakes. He began a correspondence at age 13 with the famed physiologist Gustav Eckstein at the University of Cincinnati, visited him, read all the books Eckstein suggested, and was soon hired to work in Eckstein's laboratory, where he became an

Edwin Cassem.

instructor in physiology. Hackett finished high school a year early, and college in three years. By age 23 he had graduated from the University of Cincinnati's Medical School. He worked for the U.S. Public Health Service in several federal prisons, including Alcatraz, before winning a residency under Avery Weisman at Massachusetts General Hospital. He became a clinical and research fellow at MGH in 1955. He served as chief of the MGH Consultation Service (1967–1973) before taking over as interim chief of psychiatry in 1974. In 1977 Hackett was named Eben S. Draper professor of psychiatry at Harvard Medical School.

To this day, the department's Consultation Service provides psychiatric support for patients in the hospital's other surgical and medical departments. Edwin H. "Ned" Cassem, the Consultation Service's third chief, after Avery Weisman and Tom Hackett, and chief of psychiatry from 1989 until 2000, started the Optimum Care Committee in 1973. The committee addresses some of the most difficult questions on critical care that confront doctors, in particular, when to continue dramatic, invasive medical treatment and when to halt treatment and let a patient ease into death. Cassem modeled the committee on observations of daily rounds in one group: "The cardiologist would ask the head nurse, the residents and the attending physician: Does this patient require A, B, C or D? A is the works; anything goes to save him. B is still the works, but we will see how he does today. C means some treatments are outlawed, like CPR or putting the patient on a ventilator. D means stop everything now and let him die a comfortable death."[61]

Cassem's background informed his interest in such difficult issues. A Jesuit from the age of 18 and ordained a priest 13 years later, Cassem meanwhile pursued a medical career and served duty in Vietnam. He considered himself both a psychiatrist and a priest and saw no conflict between the two roles, explaining:

> From the very start of talking to patients, I asked, "Is faith important in your life?" and as church attendance began to get thrown under the bus I changed it to: "Is spirituality important in your life?" And still about two-thirds of them said yes and then immediately qualified why they had gotten fed up

with their church-going experiences. There were many who said they were agnostics, but only rarely did someone say they were an atheist. It takes a lot of faith to be an atheist. In short, my perpetual answer to the question, "Are you priest or doctor?" has always been IT IS EXACTLY THE SAME, doctor of body and doctor of feelings and spirit.[62]

Cassem's holistic approach made for new perspectives on medical problems. A colleague recalled the time Cassem was treating a man who had come to this country for cardiac surgery. After the surgery the patient became delirious. The colleague recalled: "In the course of treating this man, he became catatonic. I called Ned in and he said, 'Oh my gosh this isn't a good thing.'" But Cassem calmly administered an intravenous anti-anxiety medication. Soon after, "the patient rose up out of bed and said, 'I have to go to the bathroom. And I'm hungry.'" Amazed, the nurses asked, "'Dr. Cassem, Dr. Cassem, what did you give the man?' As he walked out of the room, he said, 'Holy Water.'" This led to a study of lorazepam use in catatonic states, and the drug is now the first line of defense in treatment of this condition.[63]

The collaboration with other fields that makes clinical psychiatry so effective at MGH permits researchers to use the tools available in psychiatry and other disciplines to approach mental illness from many angles. For example, in 1994 Hans Breiter was a young MGH staff member at an obsessive-compulsive disorder (OCD) clinical unit in Charlestown. While eating lunch with a neuroradiologist who had access to the latest functional MRI (fMRI) equipment (see chapter 3), Breiter wondered if he could use the technology to study a patient with OCD. With the patient's consent, he put a germ-phobic patient in the fMRI and placed a glove on the patient's hand, which he told the patient had been wrapped around a mop that had been sweeping the hospital. Areas of the prefrontal cortex lit up. Breiter published the first paper on the psychological processes measurable in the frontal lobe of the brain.

Michael A. Jenike and Scott Rauch established the Neuroscience Division of the Department of Psychiatry at Charlestown, which led to the array of basic and translational science that is now accomplished by MGH's Psychiatry Department, a quality of collaboration and resourcefulness that would have been impossible in a non-biomedical setting. For example, in 1979 Mike Jellinek became chief of the Child Psychiatry Division in partnership with Don Medearis, who was recruited as chief of pediatrics. Jellinek developed an outpatient clinic, and beginning with one resident, together with Eugene Beresin, developed the nation's most selective child psychiatry fellowship program. It now has 18 child psychiatry fellows, part of the more than 100 current MGH psychiatry trainees, including adult residents and subspecialty fellows.

Advancing Research in Psychiatry

Having arrived at MGH as a trainee in 1974 and serving later as Hackett's chief resident on the Consultation Service, Jerrold Rosenbaum succeeded Ned Cassem in 2000 as chief of psychiatry, a position he holds in 2011. Together, Cassem and now Rosebaum have elevated MGH psychiatry to an enviable level. Beginning in 1996 and for 14 years running, the department has earned the number-one ranking in psychiatry in the *U.S. News and World Report* survey of America's best hospitals.

Rosenbaum's leadership, in particular, has dramatically expanded the research effort in psychiatry. Before the 1990s MGH psychiatry did relatively little research; today research is the department's largest division. Psychiatry boasts the largest clinical trial research program at MGH, and its fifth-largest research portfolio. Stretched over three football fields of space and with more than $50 million of annual federal, industrial, and other grant money, psychiatric research spans three major domains of therapeutic, genetic, and neuroimaging research. The executive vice chair of the Department of Psychiatry in 2011 is Maurizio Fava, and Jonathan Alpert, Greg Fricchione, and John Herman serve as associate chiefs of the department. Joy Rosen is vice president for psychiatry.

Under Rosenbaum's leadership, major clinical trials and dozens of subspecialty clinical and research programs were launched and developed. As one example, Rosenbaum and Maurizio Fava helped design the largest and longest study ever to evaluate treatments for depression, the Star*D Study (Sequenced Treatment Alternatives to Relieve Depression). Funded by the NIMH, the study enrolled more than 4,000 outpatients, aged 18–75, and studied their responses to medication and cognitive therapy over a seven-year period.

Gary Sachs similarly led the STEP-BD (Systematic Treatment Enhancement Program for Bipolar Disorder), a $26.8 million clinical trial funded by the NIMH. The study conducted primary treatment studies and long-term follow-up of persons with bipolar disorder; the final enrollment was 4,361 participants across 19 clinical centers and associated community partners. The tradition continues with national leadership in psychiatric neuroimaging and psychiatric genetics.

The department has leveraged its clinical and research expertise and its national reputation to extend its teaching missions to colleagues across the United States and the world, initially through continuing medical education programs in the Boston area. The first courses were given in Boston in 1975 and 1976 on psychiatry and psychopharmacology. Over the past five years, under the direction of Robert Birnbaum, the Massachusetts General Psychiatry Academy was launched to provide an array of seminars, courses, and Web-based educational offerings; it currently has more than 40,000 clinician members participating nationally. In the last 10 years the department has undertaken a major philanthropic campaign that has raised nearly $100 million, in large measure owing to the recruitment of a major-gifts officer, Carol Taylor, dedicated to psychiatry. With those resources, cutting-edge and innovative clinical and research programs have been launched, including the

Jerrold Rosenbaum.

Center for Addiction Medicine directed by Eden Evins and Tim Wilens. The exemplar of this division is its ARMS (Addiction Recovery Management Service), a 24/7 wraparound care service for youth aged 15–25.

The most recent of the 45 ongoing programs in the department today is the LEAP (Learning and Emotional Assessment Program), offering comprehensive neuropsychological assessment and follow-up of children with learning problems and emotional issues. Rosenbaum compares its potential research implications to those of the Framingham Heart Study of 1948 (see chapter 3), as it offers the capacity to understand the longitudinal course and outcomes of various early cognitive and emotional differences in children.

In addition to carrying on Thomas Hackett's legacy of returning psychiatry at MGH to its original function of integrating the profession into general medical practice, Rosenbaum, like other chiefs of service, has continually promoted the integration of psychology and psychiatry. As Putnam fostered the clinical psychology career of Emerson, and Cobb worked with Murray to bring psychoanalysis into the HMS curriculum and onto the wards of the hospital, so did Lindemann work closely with psychologists in the School of Arts and Sciences on social problems. Eisenberg carried on the tradition into the Hackett era. Under Hackett and Cassem, clinical and research programs in psychology thrived.

Dennis Norman, the present director of the Psychology Program, who has overseen several generations of fellows in a nationally known program of postdoctoral clinical training approved by the American Psychological Association, began under the leadership of Richard Peebles in the Child Division. Lee Baer and later Michael Otto helped bring subspecialty programs in therapy and research to national prominence; examples include Anne Alonso in psychodynamic psychotherapy, Sabine Wilhelm in OCD, Steven Safren in behavioral medicine, and Dina Hirshfeld-Becker and Aude Henin in childhood anxiety disorders. A child psychologist, Bruce Masek, became the clinical director of the Child Outpatient Service. MGH psychology internships and postdoctoral positions are now among the most competitive in the country. Further, the integration of clinical and research psychologists in the MGH Psychiatry Service is a critical factor in the department's success, and doctoral-level psychologists represent more than one-third of the department's 700 faculty and trainees.

These endeavors, combined with many others, underscore the department's commitment to practice as well as theory. "We're not just here to absorb what we were taught, apply it, and pass it on. We've got to make the world better. That's always been the tradition of this hospital," Rosenbaum said. One of Rosenbaum's favorite quotes is a couplet by Johann Wolfgang von Goethe: "Whatever you can do or dream you can, begin it. Boldness has genius, power, and magic in it."

"That's the whole story there in a nutshell," Rosenbaum said.

REORGANIZING AND REBUILDING

Economic downturns are times of realignment. At MGH and in the hospital industry at large, the 1930s were a period of major changes. General directorship at Mass General changed, from Washburn to Bigelow to Baker to Faxon, and the General Executive Committee changed as well. So did the MGH campus. Old services were terminated and new services added, as closings were mixed with mergers. By the end of the decade the most unsettling shift of all had taken place—a major change in the way hospitals were reimbursed for their services. The name of the change was Blue Cross.

Like the construction of Baker Memorial, the emergence of Blue Cross was a response to a fundamental inefficiency in the hospital industry that provided high-quality care to the wealthy, who could pay top dollar, and free care to the poor, who had few dollars. Meanwhile, little provision was made for the middle-income patient. As this problem became more pressing, alternatives to pure free-market allocation of medical services were proposed, from suggestions that hos-

Nathaniel Faxon.

pitals be regulated like utilities to calls for the federal government to take over the country's medical system. A national committee on the costs of medical care was convened in 1927; it was chaired by Stanford University's President Ray Lyman Wilbur, also its dean of medicine, 1911–1916, and Herbert Hoover's secretary of the Interior, 1929–1933. The accepted solution, however, came from the grass roots rather than the top: prepaid health insurance. The most influential model was a prepaid insurance plan originated in the late 1920s by Baylor University Hospital in Dallas, Texas, as hospital-only coverage for Texas schoolteachers. Between 1929 and 1939 similar loosely organized voluntary plans spread across the nation, growing from 1,300 covered individuals to 3 million. As a voluntary system, Blue Cross meant "a balancing of power between doctors and hospitals, locally and nationally, which avoided control by either group," according to the historian Rosemary Stevens. "Thus the hospital remained, formally at least, the practitioners' workshop, not their employer."[64] (In time, physicians' fees were covered by a companion program, Blue Shield.) Few worried then that Blue Cross and other third-party payers would wield extraordinary power in medicine.

Stevens pointed out another consequence of Blue Cross and then Blue Shield: "Separating hospital and physician services through the new prepayment arrangements imposed a major structural division into U.S. health services that created long-lasting ripples in American hospital practice."[65] Before long, doctors were at odds with hospital administrations. At MGH, the Mass General Physicians

The lobby of the White Building.

Organization (MGPO), founded in the 1990s, finally gave doctors the negotiating leverage and administrative power to form a true working partnership with the hospital. In 2011 this close partnership is embodied by two MDs: Peter Slavin, a Harvard Medical School and Harvard Business School graduate, as president of the hospital; and David Torchiana, an HMS grad and cardiac surgeon, as CEO and chairman of the MGPO (see chapter 8).

A committee of MGH trustees appointed in 1932 reviewed the reports of the Wilbur Committee while watching the development of Blue Cross. They voted to support an insurance plan at MGH, and in 1934 a group of Boston-area hospitals agreed that such a plan would be workable. Approved by the hospitals, it was shot down by county medical societies.[66] Finally, in August 1937, MGH joined Blue Cross with the formation of the Associated Hospital Service Corporation of Massachusetts. The contract was signed August 20, and the first Blue Cross patient was admitted to Phillips House two weeks later.[67]

During the 1930s the MGH staff underwent several levels of reorganization. The hospital's General Executive Committee noted in 1935 a "definite tendency for a more closely united staff with an increased singleness of purpose." This was most notable in clinics (thoracic, fracture, renal stones, and so on) where physicians and surgeons, often from different departments, put their heads together over patient care and clinical study. Also in 1935 the Surgical Executive Committee was formed, and two years later the Medical Executive Committee, which had lapsed after 1911, was re-created. On it were Chief of Medicine Howard Means, General Director Nathaniel Faxon, and the heads of the Dermatology, Pediatrics, Neurology, and Psychiatry departments. That year the GEC itself was reorganized to include representatives from the Radiology and Pathology departments, "thus recognizing the growing importance of the Laboratory Services."[68]

The MGH campus had grown since the sprawling of the pavilion system across the west lawn in the nineteenth century. In 1898, 1908, and 1909 the hospital had purchased three parcels of land to fill in its holdings south of Bulfinch to Fruit Street (leaving only the southwesternmost corner of Fruit and Charles streets to the Massachusetts Eye and Ear Infirmary, which would remain independent of MGH—although today the two are closely aligned). The old Harvard Medical School building was razed to make room for a new outpatient building fronting Fruit Street (1903) and the Moseley Memorial Building (1916), which consolidated administrative offices and officially moved the hospital entrance from Bulfinch to a courtyard on Fruit Street.[69] But like the old asylum property that had been encircled and finally strangled by railroads, the core campus bounded by Fruit Street to the south, Charles to the west, Allen to the north, and Blossom to the east was besieged by the city around it. Through the twentieth century the hospital would push its landholdings doggedly north of Allen Street and south toward Cambridge Street, but the sprawl was slowed to a crawl.

The immediate solution was the George Robert White Building. After the economic slowdown of the first half of the 1930s, MGH trustees appointed a committee in 1936 to enact the bequest of Harriet Bradbury. The vision was for "a central building which would bring together wards at that time scattered in small pavilions . . . [also] to place all surgical patients in the George Robert White Memorial Building . . . and all adult medical patients in the Bulfinch Building." The teardown took place in 1937 and 1938.[70] Demolished were the Gay Ward (dating from 1884), the old operating building (1867), and the newer Bigelow operating rooms (1900), as well as smaller structures. A temporary operating room had to be set up until White opened and surgery was consolidated there. Excavation work was completed January 14, 1938, leaving a large depression in front of the west end of Bulfinch and setting the stage for a memorable prank:

> A sizable pond collected in the excavation, leaving only a few iron rods projecting from the caissons showing. One morning a wooden fisherman complete with pole and line appeared on one of the caissons. The next morning he was joined by a rainbow collection of live ducks: purple, green, red, blue, brown, and white. What breed could these be? Speculation ran rife and it was anybody's guess. . . . Cautious detective work finally solved the mystery, by working backwards. The night of the disappearance coincided with the "Change Day" of a certain surgical service. The *pièce de résistance* of the Change Day dinner was roast duck. Ergo, the ducks belonged to that service. The varied colors—oh, those were stains from the Pathological Laboratory, methylene blue, carbol fuschin, and other dyes, liberally applied before release in the pond.[71]

Construction of the White Building began May 1, 1938. The cornerstone was laid December 23 and the building dedicated October 16, 1939, the 93rd anniversary of Ether Day. The final cost was $2.546 million, all but $46,000 of which was provided by the Bradbury bequest. The initial occupants moved in from October

North End Diet Kitchen, 1909

19 through January 22, 1940. All surgical patients were moved to White, thereby vacating Bulfinch West for medical and psychiatric patients who had been taking up needed space in Baker. Simultaneously, pediatric patients were moved to "more commodious quarters in old Ward E, which was remodeled for their accommodation." With the opening of White, the total bed count at MGH was 852.[72]

Meanwhile, there were other restructurings. The North End Diet Kitchen was dissolved in 1938. Founded in 1874 to serve food to the poor "as a specialized charity of the City of Boston," it had become a diet clinic of the Outpatient Department in 1923. Its funds were turned over to MGH in February 1938 and were thereafter used "for the purpose of teaching diets to patients and of giving special food orders to enable the sick and needy to follow their prescribed diets."[73]

While the diet kitchen was closing and the White Building opening, other hospitals were merging into Mass General. Each of these will be taken up in greater detail elsewhere.

The Vincent Memorial Hospital, founded in 1890 to care for women patients, found itself increasingly handicapped without the labs, radiology, pathology, and other services found at a general hospital. In 1941 it entered into a close, mutually beneficial affiliation with MGH. Vincent's chief surgeon, Joe V. Meigs, became the head of the new Gynecology Service at Mass General, which agreed to build a new Vincent Hospital on the grounds. Construction was delayed by the war; during the interim Vincent patients were housed on White 7 and 8 and supported by funds from the Vincent Club, a Boston women's charity founded in 1892 to support the health and well-being of women and still active in 2011 at 71 Brimmer

Street. In 1948 the Vincent Burnham Building finally opened, combining women's care with a pediatric service. (For more on the Vincent and OB/GYN at MGH, see chapter 7.)

The Collis P. Huntington Memorial Hospital of Harvard University, specializing in cancer and located on Huntington Avenue in Boston, was purchased by MGH; the transaction became effective on January 1, 1942. (For more on cancer treatment and research at MGH, see chapter 7.)

Finally, the Hall-Mercer Hospital was created in July 1941 as a joint venture of MGH and the Pennsylvania Hospital, each of which would care for and study psychiatric patients in their wards. The MGH division of Hall-Mercer opened in the Bulfinch Building on December 1, 1941.

THE SIXTH GENERAL HOSPITAL

World War II marked the fifth time in its history that MGH had been directly affected by war. The hospital's inception was delayed by the War of 1812. It provided medical staff for and treated casualties of two engagements in the nineteenth century, the Civil War and the Spanish-American War; and Base Hospital No. 6 was a significant contribution to the Allied effort in World War I. By 1940 what came to be known as World War II was still referred to in the United States as "the European War," and few suspected the role that America or MGH would play. In the trustees' minutes for 1939 the only hint was a request for permission to purchase extra supplies, such as gauze, "not only to avoid price increases but also to be assured of delivery." After Britain and France declared war on Germany on September 3, 1939, however, "the war clouds gathered." On March 20, 1940, the surgeon general of the United States asked MGH to organize the Sixth General

The medical staff of the 6th General Hospital.

Hospital, "to be an affiliated unit of the United States Army Medical Corps, such unit to be called into service in case of war or similar serious situations."[74] Thomas R. Goethals was named organizing officer and later made commanding officer. By the end of the year 26 officers had been commissioned from the ranks of MGH doctors. A national draft was instituted September 16, 1940.

The Japanese bombed Pearl Harbor on Sunday, December 7, 1941. "The effect upon the country and upon the MGH was instantaneous," wrote Faxon. "By Wednesday night a defense organization against fire and sabotage, which could be called to duty at any time, day or night, had been set up under the direction of Dr. W. T. S. Thorndike and suitable equipment for defense against incendiary bombs was in place on every roof."[75] The thinking was that if Pearl Harbor could be bombed, why not Boston? Blackouts went into effect, as blue and black curtains were mounted on every window. A committee under Edward Churchill planned ahead for triage in the event of large civilian casualties. Incoming patients were to be classified in five categories—slightly injured, seriously injured, burns, shock or resuscitation, or immediate surgery; the hospital was thus unwittingly preparing itself for an unexpected nonmilitary tragedy in November 1942. One classification would have to be added for the Cocoanut Grove fire: dead on arrival.

By the end of 1941, 92 members of the medical staff had been commissioned in the army or navy medical corps and called to active duty. Beginning in April 1942 an intern's term at the hospital was cut from two years to one, to speed preparation for war service. During 1942 a Civilian Defense Program was elaborated at MGH, which included practice drills and a manual of organization in the case of disaster.

Activated on May 15, 1941, the Sixth General Hospital was ordered to Camp Blanding, Florida, on May 15, 1942.[76] The unit shipped out in January 1943 and arrived in Casablanca on February 19. In September 1944 the Sixth moved from Africa to Italy and operated out of Rome until late December. Following a period of inaction and reorganization, it was moved to Bologna on May 1, 1945, functioning there until August 10, 1945, five days before the Japanese surrender that ended the war. On September 15, the Sixth General Hospital was formally deactivated at Livorno, Italy, 40 months to the day after its arrival at Camp Blanding.

Six hundred forty-four MGH hospital personnel served in the war with the Sixth General Hospital and elsewhere; seven lost their lives, and many were wounded or taken sick. Meanwhile, back home, MGH leadership operated on the belief that "the very best in healthcare must go on, no matter the calamities occurring outside our walls." The stay-at-home staff comprised mostly men over 45 years of age, a small cadre of women physicians (for whom the doors of discrimination had finally been forced open), and a few younger men. Discrimination ended in nursing as well: the MGH School of Nursing admitted its first African American student in 1944.[77]

Faxon named some of those who performed extraordinary wartime duty at home:

The hospital policy of not reappointing doctors to the Active Staff beyond the age of sixty was suspended during the war. That the Hospital was able in large measure to carry out its obligation during the war was due to the willingness of the remaining staff to make the necessary extra effort, aided by the return to active service of many of those who had retired. Drs. George Gilbert Smith, James B. Ayer, and C. Guy Lane continued as Chiefs of their respective services, although over the retiring age. When Dr. J. C. White was called to full duty in the Navy, Dr. W. Jason Mixter returned as Acting Chief of Neurosurgery. Dr. George W. Holmes likewise returned to act as Chief of Radiology when Dr. Hampton left. Drs. R. H. Vose, J. D. Barney, Andrew P. Cornwall, and Willard S. Parker returned to their former services. Dr. Harold Giddings devoted much time and effort in keeping the Surgical Out-Patient Department going.[78]

Leland McKittrick served as acting chief of the West Surgical Service in the absence of Churchill. Benjamin Castleman replaced Tracy B. Mallory as acting pathologist, and Wyman Richardson replaced Francis Hunter as clinical pathologist.

What a difference 10 years had made! In the early 1930s working hours had been shortened because of slack demand for hospital services. By the end of the war just the opposite happened, and there was a marked shortage of nurses, orderlies, and other staff. In 1943 Faxon wrote that the hospital's greatest challenge "has been the struggle to maintain the usual quality and quantity of hospital service to this community in spite of decreasing professional and non-professional personnel, rising wages, fluctuating governmental regulations and restrictions on supplies." In 1944 shortages were so severe that whole floors of White, Phillips, and Baker had to be closed temporarily, reducing bed count by about 100.[79]

Volunteers helped take up the slack, working in every department except maintenance. In 1943, for example, "a total of 1248 volunteers gave 148,577

Baker Memorial volunteers, 1946.

hours of service, or the equivalent of 50 people working 8 hours a day." Paroled federal prisoners helped out as orderlies, in the kitchen, and elsewhere. Also providing help were a group of conscientious objectors under the direction of Rufus Jones of Philadelphia and the Society of Friends. Faxon noted that the group was, if unconventional, very helpful.[80]

By 1944 the situation was dire: "The hospital was getting disgracefully dirty. This condition has been greatly improved by a group of fifty business men under the direction of Mr. Howard Haywood" serving "as cleaners, washing walls, scrubbing and polishing floors, and tidying up in general." Materials were in short supply, as sugar, coffee, meat, butter, canned goods, and oils were all rationed and "pharmaceutical supplies were unpredictable." General food rationing began in March 1943, a challenge for the chief dietitian, Marion Floyd.[81]

Shortages usually mean inflation, and wages and prices jumped dramatically during World War II. In 1945, as costs rose sharply and capacity was reduced by nearly 100 beds by the nursing shortage, the hospital recorded its highest operating deficit in history, more than $1 million. The General Fund was depleted "to a dangerous low."[82] Against such a backdrop began one of the greatest growth surges in the history of Massachusetts General Hospital, to be chronicled in the following chapter.

Although the world may never see the like of the global conflict that ended in 1945, one condition of World War II will be familiar to today's reader: "Wartime restrictions by the Boston Traffic Commissioner placing a one-hour limit on parking in the street resulted in many of the staff receiving parking tickets."[83]

VOLUNTEERISM BEFORE, DURING, AND AFTER THE WAR

The outpouring of volunteer support from Pearl Harbor to V-J Day seems exceptional, but Massachusetts General Hospital began as a volunteer operation. John Collins Warren, James Jackson, and their many successors of the nineteenth century were volunteers, at least in their direct service to the hospital and its patients. The trustees were volunteers, and as early as 1821 a Men's Visiting Committee began visiting wards on a rotating basis to observe and help out where possible. By the 1860s the need was felt for female volunteer visitors, and in 1869, by vote of the trustees, the first contingent of what became the Ladies Visiting Committee (LVC) was elected by ballot.[84] The following year a gift of $200 was assigned to the LVC for hanging pictures on ward walls. In June 1870 the LVC was authorized to visit male wards as well as female. The work was not always cheery: the LVC was given one particularly grim task, that of authorizing the official hospital register of autopsies. Trustees saw many benefits of female visitors in the wards, according to one official report. Women could be counted on for "their more acute perceptions; their greater power over details; their better knowledge of housekeeping; their natural aptitude for care of the sick; their better judgment of the character and conduct of the female nurses; but chiefly their power of giving the female patients a degree of personal aid and sympathy which the trustees cannot give."[85]

Soon the LVC was providing such amenities as rocking chairs in the wards,

The first gift shop, 1943.

men's and women's dressing gowns, carriage rides around town for convalescing patients, and new shades of paint for ward walls—"light-green, pink-buff and peach" instead of "monotonous white." The Warren Library, founded before 1850 with an original gift of $1,000 from John Collins Warren, provided patients first with Bibles and other religious books, then, beginning in 1855, with such popular fare as Dickens, Cooper, and Irving. This too became the domain of the LVC.

Moving into the twentieth century, the LVC provided significant financial support to hospital services including the Social Service Department, Occupational Therapy, and a Patient Activity Center. (When Richard Cabot initiated social service in 1905, the path-making department was staffed by two paid social service workers, supported by volunteer assistants.) In 1941 the LVC supported the opening of a chapel; 70 years later it still provided altar flowers for an increasingly ecumenical room for prayer and meditation. The Red Basket Service was inaugurated to perform errands during World War II; formally this was part of nursing, but the LVC infused it with cash and enthusiasm. In 1953 it became a dispatch service under nursing, serving all departments.

With the surge of volunteerism during World War II, and with the management of volunteerism becoming a professional pursuit, MGH appointed its first formal chief of volunteers, Eleanor Greenwood, in 1941. Eleanor Wilson served as chief for 1945–1946, and Mrs. Paul G. Courtney for 1946–1953. Mary Ruth Wolf—with significant public health experience overseas in World War II; at the U.S. Naval Hospital in Chelsea, Massachusetts, for six years following the war; and, during the Korean War, at Murphy Army Hospital in Waltham, Massachusetts—took over in October 1954. The timing was dramatic: Wolf's first summer at MGH, in 1955, was spent managing an overtaxed volunteer force through the horrible epidemic of poliomyelitis that killed many and saw up to 43 patients at a time confined to iron lungs. Wolf would remember "an awful silence" in the polio ward, "except for the slight hum and swish of respirator machines."[86] In her reminiscences she also noted that, as MGH had not offered an obstetrics service for some time, the first three babies delivered here "in years" were born to mothers in iron lungs. (For more on the polio epidemic, see chapter 5.)

The LVC, which developed a liaison relationship with the MGH Volunteer Department, continued to sponsor its own fund-raising service activities, including a coffee shop (1964), a relocated general store (1969), a flower shop (1977), and beauty services (1981). The first general store had opened on March 4, 1941, "in the old cashier's cage in the Moseley Building, under the direction of Mrs. R. K. Crouch," according to Faxon's history of the hospital. By December 31, 1941, all indebtedness was paid off and the store had a cash balance of $97.66.

In 2010 the LVC ran six shops, including the MGH General Store in its latest location on the corridor to the Warren Building. Beyond the store is a hairdressing salon and farther on the left is MGH Outfitters, which supplies work clothing and supplies to staff, including scrubs, stethoscopes, and appropriate shoes. There is a smaller gift shop in the Yawkey Center, and on the ninth floor of Yawkey those recovering from cancer can visit Images, a boutique offering wigs, breast prostheses, and other items, including jewelry, skin lotions, and additional products to help patients feel better about themselves. Images is a spinoff of the hair salon, where cancer patients used to come looking for wigs. The LVC and the hospital together help subsidize wig purchases for some patients whose insurance plans don't cover them. In 2010 the LVC launched its sixth shop, Images Northshore, at the Mass General / North Shore Center for Outpatient Care, opened in Danvers, Massachusetts, in 2009. Mimi McDougal, president of the LVC, said: "When you're recovering from cancer, anything we can do to make you feel better is really worthwhile. I just got a letter yesterday from a woman who's in Colorado who had ended up somehow at MGH for her care and she's gotten a wig. By the time she got here and had her treatment she had no money, so the LVC paid for her wig, and she just had to write. Never had a letter like that. That's a really feel-good thing that we do."

All the LVC shops are professionally managed, although the committee helps select the general manager of the shops and some staffing is provided by LVC volunteers. At the end of the year, net proceeds of each shop are turned over to the LVC and used to fund projects around the hospital. Hospital staff are encouraged to submit "grant" proposals. "For a long time," said McDougal, "among the many good things we did, a lot of our money went to decorating the hospital and putting pictures around, but we're trying to get out of being the hospital decorators. The space is too expansive and we don't have the resources, so we're easing out of that. It's the feeling of the LVC that our resources are better spent on the broad range of needs throughout the MGH community." LVC members used to assemble during the winter holiday season to decorate the entire hospital. "It was a very big deal," said McDougal, "but then the hospital grew and it became impossible to do it all."

Other LVC services have evolved over the many decades since the committee

Mary Ruth Wolf.

began—from patient carriage rides in the 1870s to bus rides to see the Tall Ships in the 1970s. For many years, a needlepoint wagon and an art wagon made the rounds under LVC auspices, allowing patients to do needlework while bedridden and even to decorate their rooms to personal taste. In the twenty-first century, however, inpatient stays are dramatically reduced, so these activities have gone by the wayside. The LVC does have many other committees serving MGH on a wide front, including the Archives Committee (headed in 2011 by Patricia R. Austen), the Chaplaincy Committee (responsible for the upkeep of MGH's multidenominational chapel), and the Pediatric Services Committee (which keeps in touch with the many areas serving children, from the main hospital campus to satellite areas like Chelsea, Revere, and Charlestown).

Mary Ruth Wolf and her successors professionalized and expanded volunteer services at MGH. From 1961 until 1970 Wolf offered a course for directors of hospital volunteer organizations, a four-week training totaling 175 classroom hours. This coincided with the founding nationally of the American Society of Directors of Volunteer Services, in which Wolf played a role.

Wolf was succeeded by Maeve Blackman in 1976, and she in turn gave way to Patricia "Pat" Rowell, who came aboard first as assistant director of volunteers in 1984, then as director at the end of 1985. In 2009 Rowell retired and was succeeded by Paul Bartush, as director, Department of Volunteer, Interpreter and Ambassador Services—which itself shows the expanded definition of "volunteers" at MGH. Perhaps most remarkable is the MGH Medical Interpreter Program, which began as a volunteer service when it was founded with eight languages offered in 1976, but is anything but volunteer today. State and federal laws now mandate that *every* patient, no matter what language he or she speaks, must have competent medical interpreter services provided at no cost to the patient.

Said Rowell, "We hired a medical interpreter coordinator in the late 1980s [before the state law], augmenting her efforts with employees and volunteers who were bilingual." Once medical interpretation became mandatory, MGH continued to lead the way by establishing its own language testing process. "We have one of the most sophisticated departments anywhere," said Rowell, and "our testing is known across the city as rigorous. We are mindful of the MGH standard."

MGH now has 35 medical interpreters on staff and contracts with Pacific Interpreters, a firm in Oregon, to provide telephone interpretation

Maeve Blackman.

Patricia Rowell.

for all languages. Blazing trails again, MGH has introduced video interpreting: a patient walks into a clinic and begins speaking a foreign language. Clinic staff seat the patient in front of a video device, push a button, and immediately an interpreter is there, off-site but on-screen. "That, more than anything, has catapulted us to the next level," said Rowell. By the end of 2011 the hospital planned to have every inpatient unit wired for video interpreting.

Meanwhile, volunteerism has never been stronger. So many well-intentioned people are prepared to volunteer at a place like MGH that the hospital must screen applicants carefully. Somewhere between 1,000 and 1,500 volunteers serve in any given year; total volunteer hours in 2008 were 86,175, provided by 1,403 people. "We are successful," said Rowell, "not only because volunteers know the reputation of Mass General and want to work here, but also because they see that we are organized and prepared, ready to take them on. We want them to be glad they came in." In recent years many individuals, even those who work full-time, have found the time to volunteer each week. It's a way for very busy people to balance their lives, give something back, and make new connections and friendships.

Long before Rowell's time, a name was given to the award for exemplary volunteers: Jessie Harding. The original Jessie Harding, a volunteer who died in 1961 at the age of 81, was "a veritable little volunteer department in herself," according to Wolf.[87] She worked three days a week from 9 A.M. to 1 P.M., logging 11,698 volunteer hours. It is likely that few have matched those numbers since Harding's

MGH Pet Therapy Program volunteers (courtesy Paul Bartush).

day, but Rowell cherished anecdotes of several volunteers who stood out in her memory. Evening volunteers may be wondering if they made the right career decision and are "trying out" health care. Others have different motives:

A young woman attorney new to Boston had a grandmother who was dying in the Midwest. The attorney was so new to her job that she could not return home to be with her grandmother, deciding instead to save any personal days for visiting just before and after her death. Instead, she offered to volunteer at MGH, saying, "I have my own need but there must be elderly patients here who don't get visitors. Maybe I can fill in that way." I think this helped her process her feelings about her grandmother.

We had a gentleman volunteer in the emergency department named Oscar. Oscar was here forever. I spoke with him once when the Ellison and Blake Buildings had just been built and the Emergency Department [ED] had become bigger and more impersonal. People were saying that communication was harder in the new ED. "Oscar," I said, "I don't see you frustrated." "What's to gripe about?" he answered. "We have patients, nurses, docs, and there's work to do."

I accompanied Oscar one night, and in between assignments he just walked around the ED. Walking, walking, he came into the pediatrics section, and he said, pointing to an examination area that was curtained off, "Do you notice anything, Pat?" No, I didn't. "See those sneakers," Oscar asked, pointing to a pair of sneakers, apparently belonging to a parent at a child's bedside, visible beneath the curtain. "Those sneakers haven't moved since the last time we walked by." Oscar pulled the curtain open, and there was a very anxious mom. He looked in and said, "I'm ready to do a coffee run. How do you like yours?" He took her order, closed the curtain, and went to get her coffee.

The same night, we transported an elderly lady who was accompanied by her sister. Both had been crying. Apparently, the news was not good. We were out by the elevators heading up to Ellison 7 when Oscar turned to the ladies—and how did he know just the right moment? He said, "We're going upstairs now, but first we're going dancing." The two women roared with laughter. How he knew when to intervene—that came from years of being in that environment. One of the sisters said, "Oh, if we only could." Those interventions are so important.

Arriving patients and visitors should not assume that every "volunteer" really is a volunteer. Information Associates is an employee volunteer program that provides greeters at hospital entrances. At busy hours, the information desks can be overwhelmed with traffic. Employees asking "Can I help you?" are able to handle most questions, directing visitors toward the proper building and floor. All 12 managers in Bartush's department participate in this program, as do the

Paul Bartush.

hospital president, Peter Slavin, and senior officers such as Joan Sapir, Jeff Davis, and Gregg Meyer.

Since taking over for Rowell, Bartush has created a number of new positions for volunteers, such as serving lunch to chemotherapy patients and helping patients get to their cars after same-day surgery. Bartush says the structure of such jobs is simple, but the significance "huge." "I'm thankful that we have an institution that understands this. Mass General has a pretty open mind about applying volunteers in these scenarios. I don't have to ask permission to start a volunteer program. People might say, I'm surprised volunteers would want to do that. It shocks me that people are shocked. People want to volunteer, but they want that connected moment of impact. They don't want to be three people removed from the situation."

It's all about "enhancing the patient experience," according to Bartush, "softening the interface between the institution and the patient."

BURNS FROM COCOANUT GROVE TO SBI BOSTON

It was the last weekend of the college football season of 1942, a weekend of traditional rivalries and battles for bowl berths. In his room above the Emergency Ward at MGH, Francis D. Moore, a surgical resident, was listening to football on the radio. Across town, at the Cocoanut Grove nightclub, located in the Bay Village neighborhood near downtown Boston, an overflow crowd was partying in the aftermath of a college football upset. The College of the Holy Cross in Worcester, Massachusetts, had upset Boston College that afternoon by the stunning score of

Tending victims at the scene of the Cocoanut Grove fire (courtesy Boston Herald).

55–12. Everyone had thought BC was headed to the Sugar Bowl. Fans of the local (Chestnut Hill) college may have stayed home to mourn, but fans of Holy Cross more than compensated for their absence, swelling attendance at the Grove to about 1,000. Legal capacity was 600.

The sound of a siren broke in on Franny Moore's consciousness as he listened to the radio. Nothing unusual about that, he would recall years later; you heard ambulances all the time in the Emergency Ward.[88] Then there was a second ambulance, and a third. Soon all Boston was wailing. A fire that began in a basement lounge of the Cocoanut Grove when a match or spark set the paper-and-cloth decor on fire soon engulfed the entire nightclub. The final death toll reached 492, and hundreds more were injured, some scarred for life. The grim toll did not equal that of the December 3, 1903, Iroquois Theater fire in Chicago, which killed more than 600, but to this day the Boston inferno of November 1942 remains the deadliest nightclub fire in U.S. history. Locked emergency doors and overcrowding were a killing combination.

By the time Moore and his fellow resident Charles Burbank had pulled on their white coats and run downstairs, holding onto stethoscopes in their pockets so that they did not fall out, "dead bodies were lined up in rows in the hall. The smell of burnt clothes and hair permeated the entryway and the hall."[89] The scene in the Emergency Ward was "wild," Moore recalled, as panicked friends and relatives frantically searched and screamed for loved ones. The dead fell in three categories. Those with lips and skin turned blue had died of asphyxiation. Those turned cherry pink were victims of carbon monoxide poisoning. A third group frothed at the mouth, killed by poisonous gases released by the combustion of chemicals in the Grove's decor. Of the 114 casualties received at MGH, 75 were either dead on arrival or gone within a few hours. Of the 39 remaining patients, 10 had severe burns and 29 suffered from lung injuries. Seven of these died within three days, all of lung injuries. Despite panic at the nightclub, there were no reported fractures. (The Boston City Hospital emergency room, closer to the scene, received the most casualties of the fire, about 300. Smaller numbers were rushed to other hospitals in Boston.)

The Cocoanut Grove victims were unlucky: they had been far from the only doors that worked, stymied by the stampede, in the wrong place at the worst possible time. Yet there was a kind of luck in all this for MGH, as luck was defined by Seneca the Younger: a meeting of preparation and opportunity. Out of the tragedy Mass General would develop the world's finest burn treatment and research organizations, largely because by November 28, 1942, the hospital was prepared for a large-scale tragedy involving burns. Fortuitous developments in the preceding 14 years provided the preparation.

Coping with Disaster

The story really began in 1928. A fourth-year Harvard Medical student, Oliver Cope, was on hand in the MGH Emergency Ward when 30 people burned in a fire at Beacon Oil in Everett, Massachusetts, were brought in. Cope would write: "Staff, house officers, and surgical students were down in the EW, stripping the burns of the dead epidermis and squirting the wounds, soaking the patients in

Oliver Cope.

tannic acid. As the tannic acid was being applied, the patients were dying for want of attention to the developing dehydration. It was evident then that the priorities were off balance."[90]

As his career evolved through the 1930s, in cooperation with Joe Aub, Walter Bauer, and Fuller Albright's work in the Medical Service, Cope developed an expertise in parathyroid surgery (see chapter 3). But the Beacon Oil disaster was lodged in his memory. In 1940 Cope returned to burns, studying their physiology and treatment with the plastic surgeon Bradford Cannon, orthopedic surgeon F. W. Rhinelander, and Francis Moore, then a first-year surgical resident. Together they developed a treatment regimen for burns that included not tannic acids but "bland ointments, carefully protecting the blebs [blisters] so that they would not rupture."[91] They would conclude that "prompt removal of all dead tissue and immediate repair of the wound," as well as fluid resuscitation, were keys to survival and infection-free healing. "These theories [not fully understood by the time of the Cocoanut Grove fire, but developed over several decades] completely changed the philosophy and methods of burn treatment and now routinely govern the treatment of burned patients," wrote John F. "Jack" Burke, MGH burns chief, in 1980.[92]

In 1941 Edward Churchill convened his committee to develop triage techniques in case of a large-scale civilian disaster.[93] After Pearl Harbor it seemed ever more likely that an attack, perhaps by German U-boats, might be launched on continental U.S. territory. The hospital ran a disaster drill only a few days before the Cocoanut Grove fire, and extra burns dressings and "a stockpile of fluids" were on hand the night of the tragedy.[94] This stockpile included 391 units of sterile frozen plasma, 38 flasks of whole blood, 106 units of dried plasma, in addition to 76 units of frozen plasma held in reserve at the Faulkner Hospital. No one expected the Grove fire, but everyone was prepared. As Cope summarized the remarkable MGH effort in a dedicated edition of the *Annals of Surgery:* "The war had made us catastrophe-minded. The hospital was well prepared, partly as a result of the foresight of Dr. N. W. Faxon, Director, and of Dr. E. D. Churchill, Chief of the West Surgical Service, who had given careful thought to the problems of the hospital faced with a disaster; and partly to the good fortune that an active research program in burns was in progress at the hospital."[95]

The fire started at 10:15 P.M., the first victims were received in the EW around 10:30, "shortly thereafter the hospital was notified of the disaster,"[96] and by 11:15 an entire team was assembled. A floor of the White Building, totaling 40 beds, was evacuated for the surviving victims. Harvard undergrads, Red Cross volunteers, private nurses from Phillips House, and more than 100 nurses from outside hospitals pitched in for this heroic effort.

Fifteen articles published just seven months later in a special edition of the *Annals of Surgery* suggest the total commitment of the hospital staff. Leading off were three write-ups on the administrative and psychiatric problems of coping with a large-scale civilian disaster: Faxon wrote as general director, Ida Cannon as director of Social Service, and Stanley Cobb and Erich Lindemann as psychiatrist and neuropathologist. Four articles on lung injuries were written by the anesthesiologist Henry Beecher, by Joseph C. Aub and his colleagues, by the radiologist Richard Schatzki, and by the pathologist Tracy B. Mallory, who teamed with the Boston city coroner. Five articles on burns were authored by Cope (two, including one coauthored by Rhinelander), Bradford Cannon, the surgeon Champ Lyons, and physical therapist Arthur Watkins. Closing out this remarkable group report were articles on the newly installed MGH blood bank by Lamar Soutter and on thrombophlebitis by Moore, as well as metabolic observations by Cope and his colleagues, and protocols on all 39 patients who arrived alive. Cope headed the treatment team, and from this time forward burn surgery would be a focus for him, while he continued as the hospital's chief endocrine surgeon.

John Burke.

In the late 1940s "Cope drew on the experiences of Churchill and Henry Beecher in military medicine to study the surgical excision of full-thickness burns, a practice that was demonstrated to reduce the incidence of infection and accelerate the healing of deep wounds."[97] Ten years later Jack Burke founded "a laboratory investigating nonspecific host defense and methods to prevent surgical infection."[98] A graduate of the University of Illinois and of Harvard Medical School, Burke took more than a year of postgraduate training as a Moseley Traveling fellow at the Lister Institute of Preventive Medicine in London, working with Sir Ashley Miles on the general question of infection. His "initial driving force," he said in an interview years later, was "my interest in finding a way of not having an infection at all after surgery—rather than treating infections that occur after surgery":

> The reason I concentrated on burns was that that was where the most infections occurred. In general surgery, infections occur in a very small proportion of cases, while in burns cases virtually every patient has some bacterial contamination, and the rate of invasive infection is much higher. The death rate from these was relatively high, especially when the burn was extensive. So if you were interested in preventing infection, as I was, and you wanted to look at a patient population that had a lot of customers you were interested in, you would naturally want to look at burns.

By 1963 the young investigative surgeon and his team had developed a six-pronged approach to understanding and treating burns:

1. Development of techniques for prompt excision and immediate grafting
2. Development of a frozen skin bank (cadaver skin for temporary grafting, until the body has healed enough to permit an autograft, or graft from the patient's own skin)
3. Development of artificial skin for grafting
4. Development of bacteria-free nursing units for burn victims, to minimize infection
5. Development of immunosuppression techniques so that the patient does not reject grafts of cadaver skin or artificial skin
6. Development of optimal nutrition for burn patients (since an open wound dramatically shifts the body's metabolic balance)[99]

This plan unfolded under Burke's direction and was taken up by Ronald Tompkins when he succeeded Burke as chief of the MGH Burn Service in 1986. Said Burke, "Our original ideas are now in place everywhere I know of in the world, namely, actively doing something about the burn wound rather than leaving it to God and hoping for the best."

A Key Partnership

In the 1960s this six-point program proved to be another case of preparation meeting opportunity. In 1920 the Shrine of North America (the "Shriners") began developing American hospitals for the free treatment of crippled children. By the late 1950s, with 17 Shrine hospitals created, the need for such hospitals was diminished, especially after a polio vaccine was developed by Jonas Salk in 1955. The Shrine was financially as strong as ever and began looking for a new, underserved set of child patients. Judge Robert Gardiner Wilson Jr. of the Shrine consulted with the U.S. Army Medical Research Command and concluded that the greatest need was for the treatment of serious burns, "especially in this atomic age." The Shrine's vision was for what amounted to a teaching hospital for burned children, one that would combine treatment with research and education. "When the MGH's long preoccupation with burn problems came to his attention, [Wilson] arranged for a conference in Cope's office at the hospital [on] December 27, 1961. . . . The judge was astonished to discover the walls of Cope's office papered with maps and diagrams of a proposed burns research unit for which the doctor was hoping to raise federal grant support"—apparently Burke's six-point program in embryonic form.[100]

Seven years later the Shriners Burns Institute (SBI) Boston opened on Blossom Street across from the Edwards Research Building and the main MGH campus. In those seven years lay a tale of organizational politics and devoted persistence on the part of Cope, Burke, and others. In a nutshell, MGH General Director John Knowles (see chapter 6) decided that, like many things within his field of vision, he wanted control of the burns hospital. He wanted it on the MGH campus. He wanted it headed by hospital administration and staff. And he wanted the Shriners' financial gift made to MGH rather than to an institution of its own.

Judge Wilson and the Shriners effectively said, "No, thank you, this is our charity and our money, we'll spend it as we please." But Cope and company persisted against what Burke characterized as "plenty of headwinds," and with the intercession of, among others, the Boston Redevelopment Authority (BRA) and an MGH trustee, Elliot Richardson (later lionized as President Nixon's independent attorney general), a solution was found. A space across Blossom Street, controlled by the BRA, became available. The hospital held out for an underground tunnel, connecting the Shriners' facility with the main MGH campus, in order to move sick children back and forth easily. The first children were transferred from MGH to the newly opened SBI Boston on September 17, 1968. To this day the lead clinicians and investigators at SBI Boston are MGH staffers and Harvard professors.

Although Ronald G. Tompkins replaced Burke as burns chief in 1986, Burke remained active at MGH as late as 2009. Tompkins praised Burke as "a superb surgeon." "All you have to know is that when my favorite MGH surgeon, Claude Welch, needed a thoracotomy, he chose Burke to perform it. Early in his career, Burke chose to invest serious effort in research, and he did a superb job, becoming a very special role model for anyone who would come after him. I've never known anyone with more insight into people than he still has. He can tell you what people will do and why long before they do it."

With his medical degree from Tulane, Tompkins arrived at MGH in 1979 as a surgical resident. Between then and 1986 he earned an ScD (doctor of science degree) in medical and chemical engineering at MIT. When he returned permanently to MGH in 1986, he took an office with Claude Welch. "PCs [personal computers] were just beginning," Tompkins recalled, "and I taught Dr. Welch how to use a computer. It was remarkable in a man his age that he learned to use a computer and even wrote his last articles on a PC."

Tompkins was chief of Trauma Services at MGH from 1990 to 2000, at which time trauma and burns were split into separate services and Tompkins became burns chief. He also served as John F. Burke professor of surgery at Harvard Medical School. When the entertainment mogul Sumner Redstone, badly burned in a Boston hotel fire in 1979, made a record gift of $35 million to MGH, a new chair in surgery was named for him. Tompkins became the first holder of the Redstone Chair, while George Velmahos, chief of the Division of Trauma Surgery, took over the Burke Chair.

Bioengineering, so important in the development of artificial skin, has been a career focus for the MIT-trained Tompkins. Together with Martin Yarmush and Mehmet Toner, both of the Department of Surgery, he has done groundbreaking work in quantitative biology, funded mostly by the NIH. Tompkins said, "These are areas that are important to serious injury and burns, but if you do this research it can have other applications as well."

Such an application is the microchip developed by MGH doctors for isolating tumor cells circulating in the blood stream.[101] This was the fruit of a remarkable collaboration of MGH departments, including the Burns Service of the Department of Surgery under Tompkins and the MGH Cancer Center under Daniel A. Haber (see chapter 7). Meanwhile, two applications have borne fruit. Diana Bianchi and a team at Tufts have shown that it is possible to capture fetal cells in the first trimester and that these cells can determine both the sex of the fetus and the presence or absence of such conditions as Down syndrome. This application eliminates

Ronald Tompkins.

the need for amniocentesis. Another venture company has had success counting CD4 cells (the cells that the HIV virus invades and kills), and this technology promises to replace previous cell-sorting technologies that are simply too expensive to use in the places where AIDS is most prevalent, Africa and southeast Asia.

In 2001 Tompkins was named leader of a $37 million "glue grant" issued by the National Institute of General Medical Sciences (NIGMS). Drawing together investigators from 10 institutions, including the University of Texas, Stanford, and Washington University, the project began a five-year effort to tease apart the immune system's response to traumatic injury. According to NIGMS at the time of the grant award: "The researchers seek to study the complex interplay between the acute events that take place after a serious injury and how the body's immune system responds. An important goal of the project will be to develop standard operating procedures, called SOPs, for burn and trauma patients. Establishing such standards will encourage collaborations across multiple trauma centers nationwide. Currently, physicians have a limited number of standards to follow in the immediate care of burn and trauma patients."[102]

Although Tompkins and his associates have cast a broad net far beyond the MGH and Shriners' Burns Services, burns remain the focal point. In 2009 there were four other successful Shriners' hospitals for burned children built on the Boston model. Tompkins was asked how it is possible to control one's emotions when confronted with a horribly disfigured child and weeping parents. With emotion in his voice, Tompkins demonstrated that, though it may be impossible to avoid such emotions, there is some solace in knowing that the outcomes are often quite good. Noting that excision of burn wounds and grafting techniques—the approach advocated by Cope, Burke, and others at MGH since the 1950s—have great survival value, even for patients burned over 70 to 90 percent of their bodies, Tompkins said that he and others were eventually forced to ask themselves whether they weren't "playing God." Is it not possible that a devastatingly injured person, a child especially, who is "destined to a tragic outcome" by impairment or disfigurement, might have been better off in the "the dark ages," when death came quickly? Are burn specialists saving children who will only suffer?

Such hard questions led to an extraordinary series of outcomes studies: interviewing burned children and their parents about their experience after successful treatment (that is, treatment that led to survival and as much function as possible). In one of these studies, children and parents were asked to rate the patient's recovery in 12 categories:

- Upper extremity function
- Physical function and sports
- Transfers and mobility
- Pain
- Itch
- Appearance
- Compliance
- Satisfaction with current state
- Emotional health
- Family disruption
- Parental concern
- School reentry

One general and remarkable conclusion of these studies was that, though a typical patient's parents may have a glass-half-empty perspective ("My child is damaged"), the child looks at the glass as half full. One might expect a burned, disfigured child to "become a hermit," according to Tompkins, but in fact, the child usually is ready to get as much out of life as possible. Tompkins remembered in particular one patient who said to him, "I'm not a monster inside, I'm just a little boy." Tompkins admitted that it is "hard to keep your emotions in check when you hear something like that, but it is still better than treating children with cancer in cases where you know the child will die. Many of our patients are going to have hard lives, but many if not most get jobs, they get married—it's amazing how strong the human spirit is."

RESEARCH BEGINS LIFTOFF

By the mid-1930s some at the MGH thought that research was getting out of control. Following a 1937 study ordered by the General Executive Committee, laboratories were divided into three categories: clinical, research, and combined (where clinical and pure research were "so closely associated that they could not be separated," as in the case of Ward 4). A Hospital Research Council was authorized in 1938 "to keep all investigators in the Hospital constantly informed of the activities of their colleagues—a clearing house and censor of all reports prior to publication."[103]

The extraordinary nationwide effort to muster resources in wartime included a newly founded Office of Scientific Research and Development (OSRD) and its Committee on Medical Research. One of this committee's greatest accomplishments was the mass-production of penicillin.[104] By the end of the 1950s, Faxon could write, "Penicillin and other antibiotics are now commonplace but 1944 may be remembered by a few older men as making the transition from 'B.P.' ('before penicillin') to 'A.P.' ('after penicillin'), so great has been the therapeutic effect of these compounds."[105]

Other remarkable outcomes of accelerated wartime research included resuscitation therapy and the wholesale development of blood plasma supplies. Scientific research was placed at the center of medical efforts, setting up a postwar boom in biomedical research. "For medical schools, knowledge production became an end in itself, with an increasing number of faculty members holding doctoral (rather than medical degrees) in the basic research fields of anatomy, physiology, biochemistry, pharmacology, and bacteriology."[106]

The first OSRD contract for MGH was awarded in 1941 to Champ Lyons "for the study of the chemotherapy of contaminated wounds," and beds on White 12 were set aside. By 1943 contracts included research on trauma, shock, healing of wounds, treatment of burns, survival at sea, neurocirculatory asthenia (also known as soldier's heart, or effort syndrome), and selection criteria for pilots. Work also proceeded on antimalarial drugs and the metabolic aspects of convalescence.[107]

Yet this remarkable wartime research effort was only a humble preamble to what followed V-J Day and the return of the troops. America got down to business again, and medicine got down to research.

CHAPTER 5

. . . .

A POSTWAR SURGE, 1946–1960

*In 1950, a confluence of forces propelled MGH onto a
remarkably steep growth curve in research. Those forces can
be boiled down to three things: the NIH, Walter Bauer,
and David Crockett.*

—John Potts

BY THE TIME WALTER BAUER *became chief of medicine in 1951, the
physician-scientist was coming to the fore at MGH. Postwar funding
for biomedical research from the National Institutes of Health and other
sources began as a trickle but was soon a spate. With a keen ability to select the
right person for the right job, Bauer increased the number of medical subspecialties from six to 12, giving research ever-greater prominence. In choosing new
unit heads, Bauer inevitably preferred investigators over clinicians.*

*Not all Mass General trailblazers wielded a stethoscope or scalpel. In 1946
David C. Crockett was hired to run the hospital's centennial celebration of Ether
Day and stayed on as chief fund-raiser. His role would prove indispensable. A
post–World War II slump hit MGH hard; the budget ran into the red and wards
were closed amid a nursing shortage.*

*Other nonmedical giants included trustees Henry Knox Sherrill and John
E. Lawrence, who guided the hospital through economic and ethical challenges.
Dean A. Clark, general director from 1949 to 1961, arrived with an activist
agenda that included comprehensive planning, a focus on rehabilitation, and improved outpatient care. Under Clark, outpatient care, long neglected, came back
into focus, although a new ambulatory care center would not open on campus
until 1982, long after his departure. The Warren Building, named in tribute to
MGH's first family, was opened in 1956, providing significant space for physicians' offices on campus for the first time.*

*The astonishing success of antibiotics after World War II led many to hope
that infectious diseases would soon be conquered, but those hopes were dashed
by the devastation in 1955 when poliomyelitis reached epidemic proportions.
Although vaccines halted this scourge, other epidemics would follow. A section
in this chapter examines the development of the Infectious Diseases Division at
MGH. Other sections trace the histories of pediatrics and dermatology.*

Celebration of the ether centenary, Sanders Theater, Harvard University.

From monday through wednesday, october 14–16, 1946, Massachusetts General Hospital gave itself a party unparalleled in its history. Exactly 100 years had elapsed since the first public demonstration of ether for surgical anesthesia on the fourth floor of Bulfinch. A three-day ether centenary "had been planned by a committee of Trustees and staff with Dr. James Howard Means as chairman. . . . [A] distinguished group of men and women presented a wide range of subjects, dealing with surgery, medicine, degenerative joint disease, anesthesia, war wounds, and the social and financial problems of hospitals." An enormous tent was set up on the Bulfinch Lawn, and 2,000 people came to listen and applaud. The final event took place at Sanders Theater at Harvard, where the rostrum was crowded with dignitaries, including the president of the Rockefeller Foundation, Raymond B. Fosdick, and the president of MIT, Karl Taylor Compton. No doubt the annual house pupils' dinner on Monday evening had added "much social happiness," as the hospital historian Nathaniel Faxon reported.[1]

MONEY TROUBLES

The success and optimism of the ether centenary presaged dramatic growth in the years ahead. A key link between the three-day celebration and events to come can be summed up in two words: David Crockett. In 1846 a frontiersman and American folk hero of that name was 10 years dead, a martyr of the Alamo. In 1946 another pioneering Crockett began to emerge at MGH as one of its nonmedical heroes, and all because he ran into Ralph Lowell on Hereford Street in Boston's Back Bay.

Born and raised in Ipswich, Massachusetts, and the Back Bay, Crockett attended Milton Academy and graduated from Harvard College in 1932. His father, Eugene A. Crockett, had been chief of staff at the Massachusetts Eye and Ear Infirmary, but he died just as Crockett was finishing college. David wanted to be a surgeon himself, but his father's death during the Depression forced him into the job market to help support his family. He worked as a clerk at a First National grocery store. According to his son Christopher, "In daytime, he would deliver groceries to the back doors of people his family knew socially. At night, he would go through the front door to attend their parties."[2] For some time before the outbreak of World War II, he worked for Boston radio station WRUL, while getting his feet wet with fund-raising. He helped support the city's Emergency Relief Fund as well as the Boston Symphony's concerts on the Esplanade. According to Benjamin Castleman and S. B. Sutton, his coauthors of an MGH history of the period, "[Crockett] went from door to door on Beacon Street, soliciting the lady of the house in the upstairs parlor over a cup of tea—or drink, if he was lucky (Prohibition was in force)—and then went downstairs to ask for contributions from the cook and the maids."[3]

"Asking for money can be very good fun if you like people, if you listen to them say their piece," Crockett would say in his low-key way. "They have the money, you're just trying to get it, and they like to have a little fun. They don't want to just sign a card or answer a mail appeal. There's nothing duller than that."[4]

Crockett served in the Office of Strategic Services (OSS) during World War II: "One of Mr. Crockett's clandestine duties as a lieutenant in the OSS, his son said, was to take gold to Lisbon because Portugal was a neutral country. There, it would be converted to Italian currency, which he would take to Italy to give to the Italian Free Army, the resistance movement fighting the Germans."[5]

He earned the Legion of Merit for his work with the OSS. After the war Crockett found himself newly married and out of work when, in early 1946, he ran into Ralph Lowell. The MGH trustee said he had been looking everywhere for Crockett and had just the job for him. Crockett was hired to organize and run the ether centenary. He knew Boston and MGH's place within it. In an interview years later he would say, "Harvard, the MGH, the Boston Museum of Fine Arts, and the Boston Symphony were the institutions that the city

David Crockett.

supported. They always said that the proper Bostonian has a card at the Athenaeum, membership in the Somerset Club, is a contributor to the Massachusetts General Hospital, and has an aunt in the McLean."

After the ether centenary, Crockett's employment agreement expired and his status with MGH was unclear. He asked for a meeting of the trustees' committee that had hired him: Lowell, Phillips Ketchum, and Henry Guild. Crockett would recall: "We met in Mr. Lowell's office at the Boston Safe Deposit and Trust Company. Mr. Ketchum got rather excited and inquired what the problem was: What was the trouble? Was I unhappy? Didn't I like my job? Did I want a contract? I said I just wanted some assurance that I was employed by the hospital. After a great deal of shuffling about, Mr. Ketchum professed to be frightfully busy and rather annoyed that he had been called to this meeting. I was informed that if I was content, they were happy, and I could go along as I wanted to, but it wasn't a very specific arrangement."[6]

In the years before World War II, fund-raising in Boston had been a gentleman's pastime. After the war it became a profession, and Crockett was one of its first practitioners. Before the war a trustee's idea of financial urgency might have been a shortfall in the annual operating accounts of $100,000. Hospital legend pictures a board member walking the Back Bay and Beacon Hill with his briefcase, collecting checks in an afternoon of tea and biscuits and returning home by dinner with enough to cover the need. Crockett had his briefcase, the same one he had used to carry gold for the OSS, but after the war two factors made money a far bigger matter: deficits that threatened the hospital's very survival, and a mandate for research.

John E. Lawrence, who became a trustee in 1947 and achieved his own status as an MGH legend, would recall that up to this point, "There had been no concerted effort or any real interest on the part of the board in raising money. . . . I really knew nothing about raising money in the sense that it was necessary. Ralph

Francis Gray.

Lowell expressed the idea to the board saying, 'All you have to do is use an up-country method of scraping the bottom of the well in the spring time. As the water will flow, so will the dollars.' Fortunately, along came David Crockett, putting his hands in everybody's pockets! That was a whole new era that came into the board at that time."[7]

Lawrence recalled the immediate postwar period as "an appallingly serious time." He remembered Chairman Francis Gray intoning ominously, "We are facing the possibility of having to close the doors of the Massachusetts General Hospital."[8] There might have been hyperbole in this dire warning, but there is no question that a combination of national postwar inflation and local personnel shortages had created unusual financial stresses, catching most by surprise. The 1945 annual report reflected what must have been an almost universal sense of optimism: "Today, with the war brought to a victorious end, there is reason to expect the beginning of a return to normal sometime in the near future."[9]

Of the 644 MGH personnel who had entered the service, only seven lost their lives.[10] But the losses to the hospital were greater. Of 174 nurses who had served, only three had returned to work at the hospital by the end of 1945.[11] The forces that had turned Rosie into a riveter had changed roles for American women everywhere. Of the 100 MGH nurses who had served in the Sixth General Hospital overseas, 40 had married. Another 20 decided to attend college after the war instead of resuming their prewar duties, and 15 remained in the military service.[12] Those women who wanted a career in nursing were now demanding a broader education. Until 1934 MGH had cooperated with Simmons College, providing instruction in nursing to complement a degree program at Simmons. But that agreement had ended and it was not until September 1946 that MGH joined forces with another partner, Radcliffe College. This partnership gave students a choice: a three-year course leading to a nursing diploma only, or a five-and-a-half-year course that included a bachelor's degree.[13] In 1949 Simmons reaffiliated with MGH.

But this was not enough to stanch the loss of nursing talent from MGH or from hospitals nationwide. Trustees would express their surprise in the 1946 annual report, referring to the nursing shortage as "the most outstanding and perplexing problem in the administration of the hospital," adding that it was "a national hospital problem."[14] National enrollment in nursing schools fell from 51,000 in 1945 to 24,300 a year later. It took several years for MGH to upgrade compensation and work conditions enough to reverse this trend. A nurse's week was reduced to 40 hours, and for the first time she received overtime and paid holidays; nurses were included in a retirement plan; sick leave was liberalized. By 1950 there were five applicants for every opening in the nursing school.[15]

Meanwhile, however, the shortage had forced the closing of floors and wards at Phillips House, Baker Memorial, and the general hospital, amounting to 88 beds for several months, or an estimated 5,000 patient days per year. This cut into revenues and created a long patient waiting list. The shortages were not limited to nursing. Doctors were in demand, as well. Some staff physicians retired after the war, and others worked until their posts could be filled by younger men (and now the occasional woman).[16] The bed shortage forced some physicians to move to other hospitals.[17] It would take 10 years before all patient care units reopened. Credit for the resumption of full operation was given to, among others, Ruth Sleeper, "the distinctive director of nursing at the MGH."[18]

With all these forces at play, MGH recorded its highest annual deficits to date in the years just after the war, exceeding $1 million in each of the years 1945, 1946, and 1947.[19] Nearly $6 million of the deficit that had accumulated since the start of the war was made up from income on investments, but more than $1 million had to be withdrawn from the general fund, which began to run dry. This drain on the hospital's finances would be reduced to just $53,000 in 1948,[20] though "it was obvious that the pattern of increasing salaries and the rising cost of supplies would continue."[21]

Further analysis, continuing into the 1950s, would blame nonnursing factors for these poor financial results after the war. In 1948 it was calculated that the general level of wages and prices in the economy had increased approximately 160 percent in the nine years since 1939. Reimbursements from third-party insurance did not keep pace.[22] Average length of stay also fell dramatically in the 10 years before 1951, a result that was only fully analyzed at the end of the period.[23] Although admissions *rose* during the decade from 16,806 in 1941 to 16,934 in 1951, shorter stays yielded a 14 percent decline in patient days. The trustees concluded, "The drop in services provided is a serious matter, not only for the financial picture (nearly $750,000 in [annual] income is at stake), but most especially for medical teaching and House officer training."[24] Financial pressure in the 1950s would also result from the increasing cost of medical education and the eternal hospital problem of funding capital improvements.[25]

To meet these fiscal needs, beginning in 1946 David Crockett and the board ran an advertisement in special sections of the Boston daily newspapers appealing to the community. "We weren't allowed, by the restrictions of the community fund, to raise operating money because the community funds were tending to that," Crockett said. "All we could do was raise unrestricted capital—a little word which I invented which meant that it was capital, but it could be spent at any time, just like income."[26]

Crockett told wonderful stories of sorties on Beacon Hill and along Commonwealth Avenue in search of unrestricted capital. When Mrs. Henry Vaughn read the newspaper ad appealing for funds, Crockett said, she was in a hospital bed at Phillips House. She promptly summoned her State Street banker so that she could scratch the Museum of Fine Arts from her will and leave everything to Mass General. "That," said Crockett, "was the first visible evidence that I had of how we could utilize publicity, which had never been done before, to stir up monies which you never expected to receive."

Crockett's office raised funds through direct mail as well, targeting patients pleased with their health care who might respond favorably to a call for help. He created his mailing list by deciphering the longhand sign-ins on the Phillips House register. "We never knew if [the patients had] survived. Some old log books were *extremely* old. . . . I used to get [Francis] Gray to sign these letters. He would sign them all by hand, sometimes a thousand letters at a crack, and he would put little personal notes, and on one he put down, 'This is indeed a grave situation.' And the person wrote back and said, 'It is *indeed* a grave situation. My husband died in the hospital 30 years ago."

Crockett spent a great deal of effort cultivating relationships, one on one. Among many philanthropic souls was Amelia Peabody. Crockett enjoyed tea with her at her home on Commonwealth Avenue two or three times a year, and each visit harvested another check. After just two or three years Peabody wrote to Francis Gray to say that she would give MGH $25,000 a year as long as Crockett was on payroll. "I was getting paid $7,500 [a year]," Crockett explained, "so it was a pretty damned good investment."

Not all of Crockett's targets enjoyed his attentions as much as Peabody. As the former general director Charles Sanders recalled in 2008, there was one potential donor in Rhode Island who had never given a dime to the hospital. Crockett paid this man a visit and overstayed his welcome. Finally, the Rhode Island gentleman said, "Okay, I will give you $50,000 if you will just go home!"

ALWAYS THE TRUSTEES

The 12 low-key, conservatively tailored gents on the MGH Board of Trustees—and primly dressed ladies, beginning during World War I—have always played a major part behind the scenes. There were still only 12 trustees at the end of World War II, eight elected by the hospital corporation and four appointed by the governor of Massachusetts, as had been done for more than 130 years. By 2009 the board had expanded to 16, but four were still state appointees. Such a small board is unusual in the nonprofit arena, where trustees often multiply because they are viewed as donors. At MGH the trustees traditionally have been a working board, one perceived as advocates for both patients and doctors. The presence of state appointees on the board, together with Mass General's community roots in Brahmin Boston, gives the hospital a sense of public trust.

In 1946–1947 one legend passed from the scene and another arrived. In the transition from Henry K. Sherrill, Episcopal bishop, to John Lawrence, cotton merchant, the old bloodlines of MGH stewardship were in evidence, but Sherrill and Lawrence are more than representative men in this narrative. They were paragons of trusteeship. Their combined tenure—from Sherrill's advent in 1928, through his chairmanship (1935–1946), to the end of Lawrence's chairmanship in 1978—covered a critical half century in the hospital's development. And the reins were handed on: after the chair passed from F. Sargent "Sarge" Cheever (1978–1982) to Francis H. "Hooks" Burr (1982–1987), it was taken over first by Nicholas Thorndike and then by John Lawrence's son-in-law Ferdinand Colloredo-Mansfeld, who served until 1997. Succeeding "Moose" (an apt nickname for the towering Colloredo-Mansfeld) was John Lawrence's nephew Edward P. Lawrence, a partner at the venerable Boston law firm of Ropes and Gray. Ed Lawrence continued to serve as chair through 2008, when the first female was chosen to head the board: Cathy E. Minehan, former president and CEO of the Federal Reserve Bank of Boston.

"The Hospital has been able to command the service as Trustee of the best type of man and woman in Greater Boston," wrote Frederic Washburn in his history. "They have as a rule esteemed their selection for this position as a high honor, and have devoted their best abilities to their task. They serve without pay. Many of those who have had the means to do so have given generously for the relief of the financial needs of the Hospital. The Chairman of the Board is usually its outstanding member."[27]

Bishop Henry K. Sherrill.

Outstanding was the word for Sherrill and Lawrence. Born in Brooklyn, New York, in 1890, Henry Knox Sherrill prepped at Hotchkiss and went on to Yale, where he came under the influence of the Episcopal clergyman Henry Sloane Coffin.[28] After his ordination Sherrill served as assistant pastor at Trinity Church in Boston's Copley Square before beginning his first formal engagement with MGH and its staff, as chaplain of Base Hospital No. 6 in France. After the war Sherrill served as pastor of the Church of Our Saviour in Brookline, near Boston. In 1923 his clerical star status was acknowledged when he returned to Trinity Church as pastor, filling a pulpit once graced by Phillips Brooks. It was in the 1920s that Sherrill attracted the patronage of Bishop William Lawrence (1850–1941), a member of the Harvard Corporation and "one of the most influential men in Massachusetts."[29] (Descended from the nineteenth-century Boston merchant Amos Lawrence, the bishop was a first cousin, twice removed, of MGH's trustee John Lawrence. The latter was descended from Amos's brother and partner, Abbott Lawrence.)[30]

Elected an MGH trustee in 1928, Sherrill became board chairman in 1935. The Depression played out and war came on. What sort of man guided the hospital through these years of crisis? "As an administrator he was a model of unruffled efficiency; in coping with complex and incendiary human relations, he never started an unintentional fire."[31] That tribute, from a cover story on Sherrill in *Time* magazine on March 26, 1951, described his church leadership, but these qualities were brought to bear too as MGH dealt with the aftershocks of economic depression, challenging wartime shortages, and matters as tragic as the Cocoanut Grove fire.

The youngest man ever to be made Episcopal bishop of Massachusetts, at age 39 Sherrill was chosen presiding bishop of the Protestant Episcopal Church of America in September 1946, which forced him to step down from the MGH board that November. The following year his fellow trustees thanked him for his "consecrated devotion, his tempered judgment and his gracious and benign nature, as well as a natural gift of leadership."[32] Sherrill served as president of the National Council of Churches, 1950–1952, and resigned his episcopacy in 1958.

John E. Lawrence.

John E. Lawrence, legendary for exploits and energy, was mourned by the *Boston Globe* on April 7, 2007, following his death at 97. Lawrence was Boston-born and Groton- and Harvard-educated. He was captain of the Harvard crew and qualified for the U.S. Olympic Downhill Ski Team in the 1930s, but instead he stayed in law school on his mother's orders. Rather than practicing law, Lawrence entered his father's business as a cotton merchant trading in India, Pakistan, Egypt, and elsewhere. In his twenties John Lawrence interviewed Adolf Hitler; 50 years later, in his seventies, he was one of a six-man crew who sailed a sloop across the Atlantic. In World War II he served on the staff of Admiral William

"Bull" Halsey. The *Boston Globe* editor H. D. S. Greenway characterized Lawrence as "charming beyond belief."[33]

If charm had been his only endearing quality, though, he would not have been John Lawrence. His chairmanship of the MGH board (1964–1978) coincided with the tenure of two dynamic general directors, John Knowles and Charles Sanders (see chapter 6). There were critical decisions to be made: about expanding MGH's reach beyond the core campus to surrounding neighborhoods; whether to enter the field of heart transplantation; and, at the end of Lawrence's term, about research alliances with major industrial partners. Along the way there were bumpy transitions in medical and surgical leadership to manage, as the legendary Walter Bauer and Edward Churchill left the scene and a new generation of chiefs was tried by fire.

Lawrence's retirement from the board in 1978 did not slacken his commitment to MGH or diminish his élan. In 1983 he, General Director J. Robert Buchanan, and Chief of Surgery W. Gerald Austen went to Bombay (now Mumbai) to help the Hinduja Foundation, a public charitable trust, build and staff a new hospital. "With his keen legal knowledge, John Lawrence worked out an agreement in two or three sentences," Buchanan said. Together, Lawrence and Buchanan would visit India about 20 times. Lawrence played golf into his nineties on a prosthetic leg attached following an amputation.

With the understated manner for which Bostonians are famous, John's nephew Ed Lawrence shrugged off the suggestion that the Lawrences are as much an MGH dynasty as the Warrens. An early trustee, Amos Lawrence, was "sort of an ancestor," he said, and a Grandmother Lawrence did help start the Ladies Visiting Committee. But who keeps track of such details? What the younger Lawrence was more comfortable talking about was how different the role of a trustee had become by the twenty-first century. "Those trustees in the old days," he said, "had extraordinary responsibility for making it work financially. They really ran the hospital."

Today, though, MGH is far more complex organizationally and financially, and there are many layers of administration to handle operational matters that trustees once shouldered. But to assume that the trustees have a less central or forceful role in the direction and year-to-year management of MGH would be wrong, Ed Lawrence said. To make the trustees more effective, the younger Lawrence as chairman encouraged the creation of trustee committees to oversee finance, development, quality and safety, and other matters. As chairman, Lawrence placed a strong emphasis on quality and safety, a major theme at MGH from the 1990s forward (see chapter 8). "I tried to send the message that this was important at the highest levels," he said.

In recent years the MGH board has also been supplemented by the President's Council, a group that Ed Lawrence categorizes as "successful people who have a sense of the hospital." In many cases these are individuals who may be contemplating significant gifts to MGH. "It's an interesting time because we're in a new era," Lawrence said. "Today, people give for reasons other than patient gratitude. There are people who have made a tremendous amount of money and would like to make a difference. Maybe their child did not have AIDS, but they have seen the effects of AIDS in Africa, and they want to change the world."

Cathy Minehan.

Marking that new era was another first for MGH in 2008, the elevation of Cathy E. Minehan to the position of chair. Upon taking over, Minehan spent a lot of time in one-on-one meetings with administrators and service chiefs to understand the hospital better. She discovered "how multilayered and complex an organization it has become. That has motivated me," she added, "to see that others on the board understand this complexity and have a chance to weigh in on the bigger issues facing the hospital at all levels." A member of the board since 2002, when she still headed the Boston Fed, Minehan leads a remarkable group that includes former Bank of America Chairman Charles K. "Chad" Gifford, Boston Red Sox principal owner John W. Henry, MIT's Nobel Prize–winning Institute Professor Phillip A. Sharp, and Henri A. Termeer, chairman and CEO of Genzyme Corporation. "Like me," said Minehan, "they didn't agree to join the board because they were going to be part of a corporate, for-profit organization. They came because they were interested in the public, community role of Mass General, and the good work that gets done here."

RESEARCH FUNDING

Not all the money raised in the postwar period was to cover deficits. With the constant clamor of tearing down and building up that is a hospital campus, there is always a need for construction funds. The biggest building projects of the 1950s, the new Edwards Research Building and the Warren Building, will be discussed below in their respective places. But there was a third need for funds. In the postwar years, *research* was the word of the day.

Organizing biomedical research and raising funds for it became a rigorous exercise at MGH. The Committee on Research (COR) and the Scientific Advisory Committee (SAC) were both formed in these postwar years to solidify MGH's commitment to research. Originally named the General Research Committee, COR was formed in 1947. It was composed of three trustees (Francis C. Gray, Phillips Ketchum, and Ralph Lowell); General Director Nathaniel W. Faxon; and 10 members of the medical staff, including Chief of Medicine Walter Bauer (the first COR chairman) and Chief of Surgery Edward Churchill. "All applications for grants-in-aid had to have its approval, and monthly meetings were held to hear reports on research proposed and in progress."[34] The focus of research was changing. The advent of antibiotics during the war seemed to lessen the dangers from infection, and a population that was living ever longer meant that degenerative and metabolic diseases were coming into focus. Cancer, arthritis, cardiovascular disease, and other later-life ailments began to command the most research dollars.

The Scientific Advisory Committee, meanwhile, consisted of eminent scientists from outside institutions who advised the hospital on the direction of research. The first committee included Karl T. Compton, president of MIT; Carl F. Cori, professor of biochemistry at Washington University; Herbert Gasser, director of the Rockefeller Institute for Medical Research; and Eugene M. Landis, professor of physiology at Harvard Medical School. More than 60 years old at this writing, the SAC has always included one representative from Harvard and one from MIT. Board Chairman Ed Lawrence pointed out the significance of the MIT connection in the modern era: "The relationship to MIT has been extraordinarily important in collaborative research; in many cases, MGH has been closer to MIT than to Harvard." Lawrence identified a number of innovations detailed elsewhere as fruits of the MGH-MIT marriage, including the Center for Integration of Medicine and Innovative Technology (CIMIT); the Martinos Imaging Center in Charlestown; and the Broad Institute, a collaboration of Harvard and MIT driven by the vision that genomics can change medicine.

David Crockett credited Churchill with the idea behind the SAC, but Crockett added that he himself "pushed it very hard with him that we should have an outside review committee. . . . It was all very well for us to tell everybody that we were the greatest, but who was going to believe us after a certain point? We needed to have some outside scientists tell us and give us advice on how to proceed. . . . We asked them at the first meeting, should the hospital accept funds from the National Institutes of Health and other federal agencies for research, and their reply was, yes, provided that the control was maintained by the hospital on the use of the funds and that there was no federal interference."

The second question asked of the SAC was whether MGH should accept funds from the American Cancer Society. "Both of the questions seemed elementary," said Crockett, "but you have to remember that the trustees in the hospital had no experience with either of the federal agencies and they had never heard of the American Cancer Society . . . so they were very suspicious of it and again, the Scientific Advisory Committee said the hospital should, providing the control was maintained in the hospital.

"And then we asked them the other $64,000 question," continued Crockett, "which I always thought was such fun. Should the hospital build new research facilities? . . . That was also quite a shock for the trustees who were still fighting deficits." In fact, Crockett realized that having a specific fund-raising objective, such as a new research building, would ensure an influx of donations. "We would never be able to raise money to support the hospital on just a deficit-financing basis. Everybody would say it was badly run, that they don't know what they are doing with the money." Crockett understood the mentality of the Proper Bostonian, a breed to which he belonged.

So an early goal of the COR was the creation of a new research building that would centralize the laboratories that had grown up in cellars, attics, and scattered quarters. Compared to 2011, when more than $600 million in research funds annually flowed into MGH, the dollars raised for research in the immediate postwar period may seem minuscule. Crockett launched a $2 million campaign on August 1, 1946—$1 million designated for "current research" and $1 million for the new building.

Francis W. Hatch, one of the trustees, had a way with doggerel, and at a meeting of the corporation on December 5, 1949, he captured the new approach to research, while alluding to Crockett's role. Charged with running a factory where the "workers" (the researchers and clinicians) were in certain respects the intellectual superiors of the "bosses" (the board), Hatch said that the bosses had to find a new role for themselves, and that role was fund-raising:

> Consider the fate of the layman trustee
> who got his degree, a simple "A.B.,"
> with the help of a "C" and the fear of an "E,"
> a modest soul who dodged on the run
> courses exacting like "Chemistry I,"
> he feels inferior, desperately
> when chatting with stalwarts from M.I.T.;
> he knows a little of Shelley and Kipling
> (he read "The Brushwood Boy" as a stripling.)
> yet should you ask him, he knows to the fraction
> Where G.E. sold in the closing transaction. . . .
> but science, NO, science go hang!
> leave that field to the slide-rule gang.
> His knowledge of medicine, bless his heart,
> ranks in depth with a raspberry tart. . . .
> and here we find him, lost in a daze,
> trying to cut through the technical haze
> of what is discussed by clinicians and others
> he finds by mere chance are his MGH brothers.
> this talk about isotopes, antibiotics, hormones
> and sedatives good for neurotics,
> of Cortisone, miracle drug for Arthritis,
> a new unpronounceable cure for Nephritis!
> he learns that a doctor in far-away Sydney
> has found how to make a mechanical kidney:
> centrifugal action, it works like a rotor.
> (to "A.B." it sounds like a new outboard motor.)
> a doctor in Hartford will take you apart,
> and right on the table shake hands with your heart.

After a poetic list of more modern medical marvels, Hatch declared:

> Small wonder, then, that "A.B. Trustee"
> speculates what his role should be.
> lost in the maze of the test-tube era
> he feels so alone, yes queerer and queerer,
> 'til suddenly tinkles a faint little bell
> deep in his brain in the loneliest cell:
> "see here, just remember, not one of these guys,
> no matter how M.I.T.–totally wise

can synthesize the thing called dough,
the stuff that makes the hospital go."[35]

The funds for the Edwards Research Building were amassed from sources public and private. A grant for $700,000 came from the National Cancer Institute for cancer research facilities, and $485,000 was given by the National Heart Institute. In December 1950 the Kresge Foundation of Detroit provided a grant for $200,000. The total raised for the new building reached $2.4 million. Ground was broken on December 30, 1949, at the northeast corner of the hospital grounds and immediately to the east of the Bulfinch Building.[36]

Dedicated in May 1951, the Edwards Research Building was significant not only as a symbol of MGH commitment to postwar biomedical research but perhaps most of all because it provided an entire floor for Fritz Lipmann. Other floors were allocated to cardiovascular disease, cancer, and arthritis. Lipmann was a pure scientist; he was head of the Biochemical Research Laboratory, without reference to any medical service or disease. A native of Königsberg, Germany, Lipmann had earned an MD in Berlin in 1924, but since that time had focused primarily on biochemistry, earning his PhD in 1927. After a distinguished decade in Europe in the 1930s, he was recruited by the Department of Biochemistry at Cornell Medical School in 1939. He joined MGH in 1941 as a research fellow in surgery on the recommendation of Churchill and Cope. Later appointed a research chemist at MGH, he became a Harvard Medical School professor of biological chemistry.

Someone at MGH had good instincts. Lipmann's research, conducted at Mass General from 1941 until he left in 1957, earned him the Nobel Prize for Medicine in 1953, which he shared with Hans Adolf Krebs of England, for "fast and significant contributions to the research into the functions of the living cell."[37] Lipmann's discovery was coenzyme A and its significance to the metabolism. The annual report for 1953 noted: "It is a pleasure to record that one of the reasons for our new research building . . . was to provide adequate space for Dr. Lipmann's work and laboratories."[38] The prize must have encouraged everyone, from the trustees to the lowliest lab assistant. In the latter half of the twentieth century five more MGH-trained physician-scientists would win the Nobel after moving on to other institutions.

Fritz Lipmann.

In 2009 another MGHer, Jack Szostak, won the prize while active at the hospital and Harvard Medical School (see chapter 8).

Morton N. Swartz, an infectious disease expert, remembered Lipmann as a refugee from Nazism whom "Oliver Cope had the wisdom to bring here. Ironically, he was sort of an outcast over here: the Biochemistry Department at the medical school didn't like the idea of someone doing biochemistry off the medical school campus, so his promotions were advanced very slowly. Then, when he won the Nobel Prize, suddenly the medical school whipped him up several notches!"

As unequivocal as Lipmann's achievement was, it provoked questions. How was such basic research to be funded within the walls of a teaching hospital, where funding for professional staff flowed from patients and their third-party insurers? The second question came up after Lipmann unexpectedly departed for the Rockefeller Foundation in 1957: Who would replace him? The fifth floor of the Edwards Building stood vacant until Herman M. Kalckar arrived from Washington University—four years later—to work in biochemical genetics.

As Kalckar set up shop in the Edwards Building, David Crockett was preparing to celebrate the hospital's 150th anniversary on October 16, 1961. In all, Crockett would serve MGH for a quarter century, and about $300 million was raised on his watch. Yet while others won Nobels, he enjoyed his challenging, rewarding role largely in anonymity. Annual reports acknowledged major gifts and grants, but he was rarely credited publicly with making them happen. There is a chromosome for humility in the MGH genotype. Or perhaps it is a recessive gene for arrogance, a trait that crops up with surprising infrequency. Crockett was typical. He devoted himself to the mission and retired quietly. He saw himself as a facilitator and was truly convinced that MGH's ability to attract support came from its own stellar reputation.[39] "Backing me," he would say years later, "was an illustrious hospital with a devoted staff. Someone simply had to mobilize them."

PEDIATRICS FROM BURNHAM MEMORIAL TO MGHfC

As late as 1910, child mortality was terribly high by today's standards. Infectious diseases such as gastroenteritis and pneumonia, made more deadly by poor nutrition, particularly threatened the young. Yet pediatrics did not exist as a medical specialty until well into the nineteenth century. Thomas Morgan Rotch is credited with founding the first pediatrics practice at MGH in 1876, when he began limiting his Boston practice to children age two and younger.[40] Children's Hospital of Boston,[41] founded in 1869, had been incorporated by that time, and children were also being treated at Boston City Hospital (founded 1858), at the Carney Hospital in South Boston, and at the House of the Good Samaritan on McLean Street in Boston.

MGH has cared for children from its inception, but until 1902 children were treated with adults and had no separate wards or dedicated staff. In the 1870s, 14 percent of the patients treated in the Bulfinch wards were children. The annual report of 1881 stressed the mutual advantages to adult and child patients sharing quarters:

The interest and sympathy [children] excite among the adult patients, their own buoyant spirits, if suffering is even for a moment allayed, and the power they exert in banishing from their fellow sufferers that listlessness and depression which are often the worst foes to recovery,—constitute sufficient reasons why they should always be welcome as among the best of curative influences. They become the petted and indulged favorites of the ward; and the kindly attention they receive reacts upon their own condition, and encourages their recovery.[42]

In 1902 a small children's ward was established in cramped, sunless quarters on the third floor of Bulfinch. The new Outpatient Building (1903) had rooms dedicated to children on its second floor. Still, MGH did not recognize pediatrics as a specialty until June 1910, when Fritz B. Talbot became the first chief of the Pediatric Service. He appointed Richard M. Smith to head the Children's Outpatient Department, but, as Talbot later recalled, "the Children's Medical Department was organized with no salary or budget. All the work was carried on *gratis*."[43] Nevertheless, there may have been benefits to a less structured approach, according to Faxon: "Having no traditions to hold it back, [the pediatric service] developed without inhibitions."[44]

Talbot had no previous training in pediatrics, so he apprenticed himself to John Lovett Morse, a 35-year pediatric specialist and instructor. Despite his lack of early training, Talbot would become "a pioneer in determining energy requirements for children and adults," in the estimation of Ronald E. Kleinman, who headed the MGH children's service a century later.

A 1913 visitor to the MGH Children's Outpatient Department was sufficiently impressed to file the following editorial in the *Archives of Pediatrics*:

The patients are seen as soon as possible, adequately examined, even to laboratory methods, and carefully treated by *interested physicians*. . . . It is greatly to the credit of those directing this dispensary that the work is made likeable by dividing up the cases into classes and assigning certain of cases to one physician or to another, with the expectation that some investigation will be undertaken by each doctor. . . . There is a second point of excellence at the Massachusetts General Hospital, the social worker's desk is cheek by jowl with that of the physician. It is not subordinate work the social service worker does but coordinate. . . .

But the lasting impression of the Massachusetts General Children's Department is the *spirit of the place*, a spirit of friendliness, a spirit of service, a spirit of conscientious medical work.[45]

Talbot was alarmed by conditions just outside MGH's campus: the West End had become congested with immigrants, and their children suffered from all the health problems associated with poverty. Even if he successfully treated children in the hospital, he realized they would return to potentially dangerous conditions at home. So Talbot took the unusual step of appointing Edith Terry, a social worker, to accompany him on his rounds and to conduct home visits to ensure that instructions were being carried out. Terry would later develop the "In-Bed Club" to bring teachers to homes to instruct sick children so that they wouldn't fall behind their classmates. Also long remembered was Isabelle Whittier, known as the "Play Lady," who "spent twelve years of unselfish devotion in the children's wards, sharing their joys and sorrows, and surrounding them with love and affection."[46] Whittier was appointed by Talbot, who recognized the importance of play in children's health, and her work was a forerunner of many children's social services today.

Talbot also made strides in medical research that benefited children; he was particularly interested in understanding somatic growth from early infancy onward. Talbot's metabolic studies "by the calorimetric methods" coincided with similar work in what would become the early Endocrine Division (see chapter 3).[47] He pioneered the use of a ketogenic (high-fat, low-carbohydrate) diet to reduce the incidence of seizures in children with epilepsy and pushed for longer periods of breast-milk feeding to improve children's health. Other early pediatric research focused on rickets and heart disease in children. In 1914 the Allergy Clinic was founded under the direction of Edward O'Keefe. This would evolve into an independent Allergy Unit founded in 1919 by Francis M. Rackemann.[48] In 1916 the Nutrition Clinic began serving underfed children, and in 1920 a small second ward was created in the room that had served as the Treadwell Library (which moved to the Moseley Building in 1916). The Children's Medical Service was home to the first female intern anywhere at MGH. Mary Wright, a house pupil in 1918, subsequently served seven years in the Children's Outpatient Department before dying of a strep infection in 1927. During the 1920s the department pursued studies in idiopathic epilepsy, acidosis, cretinism, and what was then referred to as "Mongolian idiocy," now Down syndrome. Studies in basal metabolism continued.

Tents used as pediatric wards on the hospital grounds.

Although MGH began overseeing care of children at Mass Eye and Ear in 1927, the children's service had no permanent home. "Owing to the building program of the Hospital which included remodeling the Centre and West Wing of the Bulfinch Building, [it has] suffered various vicissitudes along with the surgical service," the General Executive Committee reported in 1925. "During the summer the ward was once more placed in tents, as in years past, and with the onset of cold weather moved into the emergency wards." There was a silver lining to this ad hoc arrangement: "Both of these changes . . . have given the Service an increased number of beds." And there was a certain tradition to the tents: "Before the building of the Phillips House [1917], rows of tents were used for children along the Charles Street end of the Hospital Yard on several occasions. Later they were in the main garden of the Hospital."[49]

In 1930 Beth Vincent (a male) became the first MGH surgeon specializing in pediatrics. Robert Linton and John Steward continued his work after Vincent's retirement in 1935. Meanwhile, Paul Dudley White, the cardiologist (see chapter 4) who first worked in the Children's Clinic in 1917, began offering a children's cardiac clinic one day a week in the early 1930s. Infantile paralysis was treated by placing patients in the newly developed Drinker respirator, or "iron lung." Harold L. Higgins replaced Fritz Talbot as chief of the Children's Service in 1932. His annual salary of $3,000 was paid by the chief of Children's Hospital, and he struggled to secure research funds and to recruit physicians.

The Vincent Burnham Building

It would take a large bequest—from Maria Theresa Burnham Hopkins, a stalwart of the Ladies Visiting Committee for 50 years, who died October 25, 1935—for MGH to build a facility dedicated to the treatment of children. It would also take a war, and it would take women. Plans for the Burnham Memorial, intended solely for children, were not ready by the time hostilities flared in Europe. Then, in 1941, MGH made an agreement with the Vincent Memorial Hospital for Women that brought this important women's service in Boston under Mass General's wing and effectively made it the MGH GYN service. (For more on the Vincent and gynecology and obstetrics at MGH, see chapter 7.) A six-story building was planned, to house the Vincent service for women on the bottom three floors and the Burnham for children on the top three. Allan M. Butler and Nathan B. Talbot became chief and associate chief of the MGH children's service, but not until 1948 did the Vincent Burnham Building open, adding 84 beds to the Children's Inpatient Service at MGH. The total was 110, including emergency and isolation wards.

Once settled into its new quarters, the MGH pediatric service could boast "a staff caring for infants and children exceeded in number or quality by few pediatric services in the world: 3 full-time salaried physicians, 1 tenured professorship, 1 associate professorship, 8 part-time salaried physicians, 31 staff physicians without salary, 10 house officers (interns), 15 clinical and research fellows, 7 research technicians, 8500 outpatient and 1550 inpatient visits per year."[50] The MGH Surgical Service had no one specializing in pediatrics until the arrival of W. Hardy Hendren in 1960.

Allan Butler led the pediatric service from 1941 until 1960 and is credited by

Allan Butler.

some, including Lewis B. Holmes, with revitalizing it. Nathan B. Talbot, who would succeed him, told Butler's back story at an American Pediatric Society gathering in 1969:

In 1912 [Butler] entered Princeton and, upon graduating, was slated to become a bond salesman on Wall Street. His desk in that institution happened to be next to that of James Forrestal. On a Saturday morning following New Year's Day in 1917, Allan said to him, "Jim, I have decided that I am not going to have an eighth of a point on the stock exchange as a major interest in my life, so I am resigning today." Forrestal indicated that he didn't want this as a major interest either, but said he was going to stay on the job until he made a million. He stayed, made his million, became the first secretary of defense, had a mental breakdown, and took his own life just before the end of World War II. Butler never made a million, but he did receive the Howland Award of the American Pediatric Society in 1969.[51]

Though Fritz Talbot had hired the first woman intern, Butler hired women from the start, and by the end of his tenure nearly one-third of the pediatric physician staff and trainees were women. Butler's interests frequently looked beyond pediatrics, as he was a vocal critic of American Medical Association policies while an associate editor of the *New England Journal of Medicine*, and he worried early and often about escalating health care costs.[52] Butler's advocacy on behalf of democracy and peace and against America's China policy landed him in the crosshairs of the Communist-hunting Senator Joseph McCarthy, and he was cited for disloyalty in 1951. Butler was exonerated by the U.S. State Department in 1953 after three days of congressional hearings.

The pediatric chief focused on finding treatments for severe diarrhea, often caused by cholera, which dehydrated adults and children to the point of death. Doing research on mock life rafts—floated from property in Marstons Mills, Massachusetts, owned by Chief of Psychiatry Stanley Cobb—his team discovered that carbohydrate and salt must be ingested together in fluids to achieve maximal water uptake by the intestine. This discovery permitted the development of modern oral rehydration solutions. Butler's interest in treating malaria helped identify chloroquine as an antimalarial, still in use today. With Gano Benedict, Butler developed techniques for predicting body development in boys and girls, and their work served as reference standards for energy requirements and expenditure in children.

Butler recruited John "Jack" Crawford, a pioneer in pediatric endocrinology. Crawford became a medical student only after his mentor, an entomologist, warned, "You can't make a living on bugs." While a Harvard Medical School student early in World War II, he volunteered to help care for victims of the Cocoanut Grove fire of November 1942. Inadvertent overdosing with the new antiobiotic streptomycin "caused permanent damage to Jack's inner ear and the loss of his vestibular sense of balance. . . . Using vision, Jack compensated for his loss of balance to a degree that exceeded the expectations of his doctors."[53]

With Nathan Talbot, Janet McArthur, and Edna Sobel, Crawford coauthored the second major textbook in pediatric endocrinology.[54] He was tapped to head the Pediatric Endocrine Unit in 1963. His list of contributions is impressive. His research focused, often in association with W. Hardy Hendren and Patricia Donahoe, on disorders of sexual development. He also took an interest in chlorothiazide in the treatment of diabetes insipidus and in how growth is controlled by hormones. Studying the descendants of Nova Scotian settlers of the eighteenth century who had suffered from diabetes insipidus, he became known for the Hopewell hypothesis, named for the ship that had brought the settlers to the New World. Other areas attracting Crawford's interest included using radiation therapy to treat hyperthyroidism in children; treating precocious puberty with the neurohormone GnRH; and the causes and treatment of Prader-Willi syndrome.

Crawford took an early interest in the Shriners Burns Institute (see chapter 4) and was its director of pediatrics from 1967 to 1986. Upon his death in 2006, one of the eulogies was by chief of the MassGeneral Hospital *for* Children (MGH*f*C) at the time, Alan B. Ezekowitz, who said: "Dr. Crawford was the quintessential pediatrician and scientist. His incredible intellect, warm sense of humor and great humanity inspired respect, admiration and adoration among colleagues, families and especially the children who were his patients."[55]

When Butler left MGH, Nathan B. Talbot, now a leading pediatric endocrinologist focusing on the field of adrenal physiology, became chief. Talbot promptly changed the name of the department to "The Children's Service" to emphasize that it would focus on both medical services and surgery.

Pediatric Surgery

As noted above, Hardy Hendren was the first MGH surgeon to specialize fully in pediatric surgery, beginning in 1960.[56] William Hardy Hendren III (to give him his full due) was born in 1926 in New Orleans and transplanted to Kansas City at age seven. Enrolled as a freshman at Dartmouth College in the fall of 1943, he quickly jumped ship for the navy for the duration of the war. He returned to Dartmouth, graduated in 1948, and entered the two-year medical program in Hanover. To complete his medical training, he moved his young family to Boston and Harvard Medical School. He interned at MGH, where Chief of Surgery Edward Churchill became a beloved mentor. From 1955 to 1957 he studied pediatric surgery and heart surgery under the legendary Children's Hospital surgeon in chief Robert Gross. In 1957 he was a senior surgical resident at Mass General, in 1958 an American Cancer Society fellow and Churchill's chief resident on the East Surgical Service. In 1959 Hendren returned to Children's and Gross, a reunion that ended badly. He walked out a year later, went across town to see Churchill, and was hired to concentrate on pediatric surgery at MGH.

Hardy Hendren was a one-man gang. Not until the arrival of Samuel H. Kim in 1970 did Mass General have a second pediatric surgeon. But Hendren was a clinical giant who put in such long hours in the OR that he earned the

W. Hardy Hendren.

nickname "Hardly Human," and in the 1960s he did pioneering work, especially in pediatric urology. During this decade he learned to repair two major congenital deformities: megaureter syndrome and cloaca. Megaureter occurs in either a male or female child, in whom at least one ureter (leading from kidney to bladder) is blocked, a potentially deadly condition owing to the high incidence of infection. Cloaca, which occurs only in females, is a horrible deformity in which the child is born not with three normal openings—urethra, vagina, and anus—but one. Because so many organs and systems are involved, cloaca had proved previously unsolvable, until Hendren stepped in to sort everything out. Rebuilding a child's plumbing and reproductive organs, by untangling them first of all, was in some ways more complicated than separating conjoined twins, another area of specialty for Hendren as his career progressed.

With all of his clinical brilliancy, Hendren had little time for the laboratory. That was remedied in 1973, when the Pediatric Surgical Research Laboratories were established at MGH under the directorship of Patricia K. Donahoe, an appointee of Chief of Surgery W. Gerald "Jerry" Austen and notably the first female professor of surgery in Harvard Medical School history.

After graduating from Boston University and teaching for two years at Indiana University, Donahoe attended medical school at Columbia College of Physicians and Surgeons. By the year of her graduation, 1964, MGH had yet to accept a single woman as a surgical house officer; so though Donahoe would have preferred a Harvard-affiliated hospital, she began a surgical residency at New England Medical Center, and five years later she completed a chief residency there. She went to work in Judah Folkman's lab at Children's Hospital, where Folkman, who had trained at MGH, was developing his groundbreaking hypothesis that much of tumor growth is angiogenesis-dependent (dependent on the growth of new blood vessels from existing blood vessels). Folkman, who doubled as surgeon in chief at Children's, was the inspiration and mentor who launched Donahoe's career in pediatric surgery. She came to Mass General in 1971 and worked with Hardy Hendren as a research and clinical fellow. After a subsequent year in England as a senior registrar in neonatal surgery, Donahoe returned to MGH in 1973 to set up a pediatric surgical research laboratory while spending about half of her workday in the operating room repairing newborns with genetic birth defects. Much of this work built on Hendren's surgical genius, working especially with children with ambiguous or malformed reproductive organs.

Donahoe's first lab—about 400 square feet on the fifth floor of the Edwards Research Building, alongside the neurosurgical lab—began to investigate Müllerian inhibiting substance (MIS), a hormone that inhibits the growth of the female reproductive tracts in a male fetus. For the next three decades, MIS would be the holy grail of her investigative work as she followed up on a fundamental question: If this hormone inhibited female reproductive cells, could it be used to inhibit tumors emanating from female reproductive organs? In other words, clinical work performing surgery on affected newborns led to laboratory work that might elucidate cancer therapies in their mothers, or in any woman, for that matter. The work, she commented, was "very inspiring. Trying to repair critically ill children made me realize we had to work harder at the bench."

Through the late 1970s and on through the 1990s, Donahoe would credit considerable support from Austen and consistent grants from the National Institutes of Health. She and her longtime collaborator David T. MacLaughlin painstakingly proved their hypothesis by purifying MIS and developing antibodies against and assays to detect MIS. They cloned the MIS gene in collaboration with Richard Cate at Biogen, then scaled up production of recombinant MIS. MacLaughlin and Donahoe detected receptors for MIS in tumors of Müllerian

duct origin (certain female reproductive organs) and cloned the receptors with their colleague Jose Teixeira. They then discovered MIS's downstream transduction pathways (genes that signal to the nucleus to turn on genes). By 2008, with a new state-of-the-art laboratory in the Simches Research Center, Donahoe was planning preclinical and clinical trials that could lead within a few years to a novel biological therapy for ovarian cancer, and there are many other applications of the MIS work still in prospect. Since MIS works on the male fetus, the Donahoe laboratory also has found that MIS can be effective against prostate cancer, since the prostate is exposed to secreted MIS, as well as against breast cancer. Time and clinical trials will tell whether these tumors might also be effectively treated with MIS in the clinic.

Meanwhile, Donahoe pursued a new holy grail. Given that fully one-third of

Patricia Donahoe.

all pediatric beds are taken by children with congenital defects, she and her colleagues saw great potential in focusing on the genetics of these congenital anomalies to head them off at the pass, instead of doing one repair at a time. Work in 2008 focused on congenital diaphragmatic hernia (CDH), which results in a child with undersized lungs and a high probability of death. Donahoe spoke with irrepressible enthusiasm about this new tack: "We wrote a grant with Children's Hospital Boston, focused on kids with CDH, discovered a gene that is causative, and are now setting up a program to find other genes involved so we can determine whether a molecular pathway involving both lung and diaphragm development can be used to find a rescue treatment strategy for these babies either in utero or early in life." Such strategies were being applied by other research groups at Harvard and elsewhere to birth defects involving heart, brain, gastrointestinal tract, maxillofacial deformities, and skeletal and hearing disorders.

Donahoe replaced Hendren as chief of pediatric surgery in 1982, when Hendren took the crosstown shuttle one more time and became chief of surgery at Children's. For more than two decades Donahoe continued operating on newborns and children, while raising three children of her own. "My family," she noted, "was very supportive." None of her three children has entered her line of work. ("They told me I worked too hard.") There comes a time in every surgeon's career to give way to younger practitioners, and by 2006 Donahoe had reached it. Donahoe missed the operating theater, but she relished having more time to devote to investigative work: "I feel happy as a dog rolling in mud every day."

Joseph "Jay" Vacanti replaced Donahoe as chief of pediatric surgery in 2003. A self-described "city boy" raised in Omaha, Nebraska, Vacanti trained at MGH from 1974 to 1981 after receiving his medical degree at the University of Nebraska. From that time on his career would be closely linked to two mentors: Hardy Hendren and the man who had preceded Hendren as surgeon in chief at Children's Hospital, Judah Folkman. During this seven-year period of postgraduate training, Vacanti spent two years in Folkman's lab at Children's. Then,

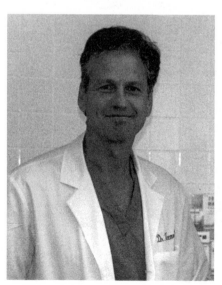

Joseph "Jay" Vacanti.

returning to MGH as a senior surgical resident, he spent six months as Hendren's chief resident in pediatric surgery. Said Vacanti: "I figured that was the last time I would have contact with Dr. Hendren. I thought I would go to Children's and he would stay here. So I imprinted on every single move that Dr. Hendren did, like an apprentice; then I went to Children's to train in clinical pediatric surgery, and within a year, he had been selected to move there, so I became his first chief resident at Children's Hospital."

After completing his clinical training at Children's, Vacanti stayed on the staff there as Hendren's first appointment as chief. The young surgeon began to focus on transplantation in children, particularly of the liver, a new procedure in the early to mid-1980s. Liver transplantation in Boston was highly regulated by the state, which mandated a single center to coordinate procedures: the Boston Center for Liver Transplantation. Four sites participated: MGH, Children's, New England Medical Center, and New England Deaconess. (For more on transplantation efforts at MGH, see chapter 6.)

Vacanti remained on staff at Children's during Hendren's entire tenure there. When Hendren stepped down, Vacanti decided to move on, and Chief of Surgery Andrew Warshaw recruited him back to MGH in October 1998. Donahoe would remain chief of pediatric surgery for another five years, but meanwhile Vacanti was given the Homans Chair, the oldest chair in surgery at MGH and the second oldest in the entire Harvard Medical School.

In the five years before he took over from Donahoe, Vacanti used his freedom of motion to develop pediatric transplantation further at MGH while building research efforts in tissue engineering and regenerative medicine. *Tissue engineering* did not exist as a medical term in 1985 when Vacanti settled in at Children's. With Robert Langer, an MIT chemical engineer, Vacanti effectively invented the methodology, although originally Vacanti wanted to give it an unwieldy name: *neo-morphogenesis*. "It didn't catch on," he admitted. But the approach did, as Vacanti explained: "The major problem I experienced trying to transplant organs in small children was an organ donor shortage. It was the problem then, it's the problem today. My solution was straightforward: if you need something, you design and build it. I began by saying, 'Let's build livers,' but within a year we began to think we could build any living object. That was a radical notion, but it was based on others' work. In fact, our inspiration was Jack Burke's work on an artificial dermis. He had been doing that creative work when I was a resident here, and it stuck with me."

Stem cells were a decade away from being described, but Vacanti and Langer concluded that the fundamental building block of tissue engineering must be the cell. Cells know how to manipulate their environment almost continuously. In the event of a wound, they know how to repair the damage locally. The central idea, then, was to take advantage of genetic rebuilding programs already inherent in the cell and provide a scaffold on which to build tissue. It was like putting up a building with "smart bricks"; give them the scaffolding to follow, and the bricks would do the work.

Where did stem cells, once described, fit in? Vacanti explained: if you draw a Venn diagram of tissue engineering and stem cell technology (as two overlapping circles), the area of overlap is what we now call regenerative medicine. To date, about 10 tissue types in the human body have been studied in this field; some are in clinical trials, some are commercially available. Tissues include skin, cartilage, bone, corneas, bladders, blood vessels, airways, and others. Did Vacanti see engineered gray cells on the horizon? "Not yet," he said. "But we're trying to get there before ours are gone!"

Two measures of Vacanti's influence in tissue engineering are his patent count (about 85) and the number of tissue engineers who have trained in his lab and gone on to leadership positions elsewhere.

Donald Medearis.

A Comprehensive Children's Service

Through the last half of the twentieth century, the MGH Children's Medical Service grew and ramified dramatically, as the need for countless subspecialties in pediatrics was recognized, while treatment and diagnostics took enormous leaps forward. Said Lewis B. Holmes, who interned at MGH beginning in 1963 and was chief of the genetics and teratology unit here 46 years later: "When I was an intern we had children contracting meningitis from *Haemophilus influenzae*. Since then a vaccine has been developed. When I was an intern, about the only thing we could do for a patient with acute childhood leukemia was to counsel his or her parents on how to deal with the child's death."

In 1999 MassGeneral Hospital *for* Children was established to encompass children-oriented clinical facilities within MGH, in three community hospitals, and in four health centers. By 2011 the two largest pediatric programs in Boston were the MGHfC and Boston's Children's Hospital. In research dollars as well as in bed count, Children's was approximately four times the size of the MassGeneral Hospital *for* Children in 2009. Holmes and others credit Donald N. Medearis Jr. (chief of pediatrics, 1977–1994), Alan Ezekowitz (1994–2005), and Ronald Kleinman (2006–present) with building and strengthening MassGeneral Hospital *for* Children in the face of this stiff competition. Said Holmes, "Alan got a lot of support from the hospital to make MGH the tertiary pediatrics care center for the entire Partners network."

Here are some landmarks in the last half century of pediatrics at MGH:

- Mass General's close collaboration with the Shriners Burns Institute (see chapter 4) began in the 1960s. It has given MGH a preeminent position in this highly specialized form of intensive care.

- In 1970 Daniel C. Shannon founded at MGH what seems to have been the second neonatal and pediatric intensive care unit anywhere.[57] Shannon spent six months on Gray 3A studying the adult Respiratory ICU (RICU), then opened one unit for infants and another for children. When it became clear that the workload was more than one doctor could handle, Shannon recruited I. David Todres from Mt. Sinai Hospital in New York. Todres took over the Pediatric ICU (PICU) from Shannon in 1979.

- W. Allan Walker and Ronald Kleinman have shepherded many scientific and clinical efforts in pediatric gastroenterology that have helped advance understanding of the field and identify improved treatment approaches. This work includes Walker's important research in developmental mucosal immunology in infants, children, and adolescents, and Kleinman's studies demonstrating the significant physical and psychological effects of hunger on children.

Alan Ezekowitz.

- In research, Donahoe has led the way for nearly four decades, and more recently exciting investigations are under way in mitochondrial disease (Katherine Sims and Marcia Browning) and its genetic basis (Vamsi Mootha). Ron Kleinman and his group helped identify the physical health and psychosocial implications of hunger in childhood, and he has renewed the commitment of the department to community and global health and advocacy, in part by establishing the first Division of Pediatric Global Health, led by an internationally known investigator, Patricia Hibberd.

- Jonathan Winickoff identified the dangers to public health of second- and third-hand smoke.

- Lew Holmes identified the consequences of a number of commonly used medications on the development of the fetus.

- Dan Shannon and the PICU staff pioneered the use of methylxanthines to prevent apnea of prematurity, high-frequency jet ventilation to support ventilatory failure in infants, as well as use of land and air transport of critically ill infants and children.

Reintroducing a full obstetrics service at MGH in 1994 at the direction of Isaac Schiff (see chapter 7) allowed pediatrics to create a truly complete service.

Ronald Kleinman.

A new facility was organized to manage high-risk pregnancies on three floors of the Blake Building; Frederic Frigoletto served as chief of obstetrics and Elizabeth Catlin as chief of neonatology. If OB/GYN and pediatrics are combined, as they frequently are in practice, MGH may be considered the leading, unified "family-oriented" care center in New England. Brigham and Women's (OB/GYN) and Boston Children's (pediatrics) are closely allied but technically separate institutions.

The Vincent Burnham Building was torn down in 2005 to make way for the enormous Lunder Building, but by then MassGeneral Hospital *for* Children had spread its wings far beyond its original confines. Inpatient care had moved to the new Ellison Building in the early 1990s, and the outpatient area had long since moved from the old Clinics Building to the Wang Ambulatory Center in the early 1980s and then to the Yawkey Center in 2004. In 2008 pediatric research activities were spread among Charlestown and numerous locations on the main campus.

Today MGH*f*C is the third-largest admitting service in the hospital, representing about 10 percent of total admissions—a far cry from the day when children were cared for in tents. With Children's Hospital Boston, it remains one of only two pediatric units affiliated with Harvard Medical School. MassGeneral Hospital *for* Children has regional reach. The most acute cases are treated on the main Boston campus. Others are treated at Newton-Wellesley Hospital, at North Shore Children's Hospital in Salem, at the new MGH outpatient facility in Danvers, and at nearly 20 other community institutions in eastern Massachusetts and southern New Hampshire.

This pediatric hospital with a general hospital approach to the care of children has enabled the full resources of MGH to benefit the youngest patients through both clinical care and research. MGH*f*C represents the hospital's steadfast commitment to lifelong, family-centered care.

A LEADER AHEAD OF HIS TIME

A farewell party for General Director Nathaniel Faxon, complete with bagpipes, was held in October 1949 in MGH's dining rooms and Moseley Auditorium. Poems were read, among them another bit of doggerel:

> "Remember those days," Nathaniel said,
> "When the annual balance was black, not red?
> When the staff was small and there wasn't any Crockett
> Putting his hand in other people's pocket?"
> "Those days," said trustee Francis Gray,
> "Like dinosaurs are passed away.
> We have rising costs and heavy taxin',
> But thanks to Nathaniel W. Faxon,
> The MGH future is bright, not dark."
> "You said it brother," said Dean A. Clark.[58]

The background of Dean A. Clark, the new general director upon Faxon's retirement in 1949, was not in clinical practice or research, or even in hospital administration. He was not a Harvard man, either. A graduate of Princeton, a Rhodes scholar at Oxford, a Johns Hopkins Medical School man, he came to Mass General directly from a stint as medical director of the Health Insurance Plan of Greater New York. Previously, he had held the positions of associate professor of public health practice at Columbia University and lecturer in medical economics at the University of California School of Public Health. In an MGH culture revolving around private practice—independent medical entrepreneurship—Clark favored group practice.

Clark's concern for community was sincere and deep. In Sunday school camp as a young boy he had shared a bunk bed with Roy Wilkins, the future director of the National Association for the Advancement of Colored People (NAACP).[59] One night Clark asked Wilkins about his plans for the future. Wilkins replied that he wanted to find a way do something for his people. This comment and Clark's own Presbyterian upbringing had an effect. Clark remained interested in the problems of the underprivileged and in government programs to meet human needs. In 1937 he and his wife, Kay, conducted a six-month study and follow-up report entitled "Medical Care in Selected Areas of the Appalachian Bituminous Coal Fields." This triggered a larger study that led to a comprehensive national health and welfare program for the members of the United Mine Workers. When increasing numbers of Jews were fleeing the Third Reich, the Clarks investigated potential locations where physician refugees from Nazi Germany could practice in the United States.[60]

Dean Clark later committed himself to the field of public health by joining the U.S. Public Health Service as a commissioned officer. He served as chief of the hospital section of the U.S. Office of Civilian Defense, then as chief medical officer in the Office of Vocational Rehabilitation, and after that as a medical survey officer of the American National Red Cross. Each position broadened his understanding of American medical needs and sharpened his problem-solving skills. But it was his experience as medical director of the new Health Insurance Plan of New York that would finally mold him:

> It combined a new approach to the actual delivery of care with a unique form of prepayment. A comprehensive range of services was to be provided by physicians and associated personnel organized into group practices rather than by a series of solo practitioners. Each group practice would undertake to provide medical care to a population specifically enrolled with it. The medical group would be paid for its services through annual capitation payments based upon the size of the enrolled population. Support for the entire program came from insurance premiums paid by, or in behalf of, the enrollees. . . . [Clark's] crucial leadership role in the pioneering program is acknowledged today [in the early 1980s] by students of health care.[61]

Who recruited Dean Clark? According to John Stoeckle, some of the trustees, encouraged by some of the staff, were committed to instituting a form of group practice at the hospital, and they saw Clark as the man for the job. Said Stoeckle: "Dr. Means was very active at that time and so was Alan Butler, head of pediatrics. Butler got called a socialist for supporting a White Cross plan here in Boston, a prepaid insurance plan. He

Dean A. Clark.

was a member of a group of physicians, mostly academics on the East Coast, who were scapegoated by physicians aligned with the AMA. Those two, especially Butler, were very interested in the idea of group work, and Means wrote about it himself. They had some influence over the trustees."

Clark brought an activist agenda with him. Upon arrival in 1949, he outlined a comprehensive planning effort for MGH. He proposed the establishment of a group practice that all staffers would be invited to join—the primary purpose of which was to bring medicine to all, no matter their income level. Such a practice would group medical activities on the MGH campus (most professional offices remained off campus) and provide continuity and coordination of care for patients. In 1951 the trustees noted, "It is believed that the establishment of a means by which the full and part time staff may center all their activities at the hospital is highly desirable. The Massachusetts General Hospital Staff Association . . . may be the answer to this need."[62] In 1954 MGH Staff Associates was formed, a forerunner, if a toothless one, to the Mass General Physicians Organization (MGPO), which came into being 40 years later. Charter members included Daniel S. Ellis, Marshall K. Bartlett, Otto Aufranc, Daniel Holland, Edward F. Bland, Earle Chapman, Joseph S. Barr, and Stanley Wyman.

Just back from World War II, many doctors were nervous about restarting their private practices, and the notion of joining forces in group practice received some physician backing. But once the dollars started flowing again and doctors of the 1950s began to be envied for their incomes, the hue and cry for group practice died. Stoeckle remembered a straw vote of 75 to 80 percent in favor of group practice, but when the question was finally put to them, doctors couldn't muster majority support, and "the trustees didn't think they had the push to get it through its early phases."

An architectural rendering of the Warren Building.

For there to be any kind of group practice on the hospital grounds, on-campus offices were needed, and while Clark and others were pushing the Staff Associates forward, the Warren Building came slowly into being. The project had been conceived and advocated for before Clark's arrival. The MGH annual report for 1945 cited the major postwar building needs at MGH: space for pathology and physiology labs, "offices for the Doctors on the Staff, conveniently near to the hospital," nursing residences, and a "chronic hospital."[63] The Warren would provide the doctors' offices and pathology lab, which had been left out of the Edwards Building for lack of space. Ground for the Warren Building was broken on November 8, 1954. Named in tribute to one of MGH's first families, it officially opened December 3, 1956, with a luncheon and dedicatory exercises. The 12-story structure housed the James Homer Wright Pathological Laboratory, the Edwin S. Webster Research Laboratory for neurology (the site of MGH's first electron microscope), additional laboratories for dermatology and psychiatry, five floors of offices for the 72 members of the MGH staff, and a 12th floor for patient care. The significance of the Warren was that it finally brought most of the hospital's private practitioners on campus. It did not, however, create or foster group practice. It simply made private practice more convenient, for both doctors and hospital.

Dean Clark also recommended that the hospital open a rehabilitation center to provide continuing care for patients after their critical needs had been met, along the lines of a "chronic hospital" advocated in 1945. In June 1951 the Bay State Medical Rehabilitation Clinic (BSMRC) opened on the hospital grounds, organized as an independent nonprofit organization. It occupied the old orthopaedic building, Ward I, and served patients from the surrounding community regardless of financial condition. Staff appointments were jointly approved by MGH and BSMRC. Set up by Richard Clark, the rehab clinic lasted only until 1963.

Clark also lobbied for an improved Outpatient Department, or ambulatory care. His objectives, according to Sheps, "were almost revolutionary for hospitals at that time, i.e., to organize medical care services around the needs of the patients and to provide an atmosphere that took into account their convenience and personal sensibilities."[64] Here Clark's goals meshed with those of John Stoeckle.

THE HUMAN FACE OF THE
OUTPATIENT DEPARTMENT

The Outpatient Department of the Massachusetts General Hospital had formally opened on October 16, 1846, the day of the first ether operation, but in a way outpatients, the "walking sick," had been the raison d'être of MGH since its first admission in 1821. Outpatients were the undoctored poor, who in the nineteenth century could not afford to visit practitioners in their private offices and so wandered through the gate on Blossom Street and into a consultation with a volunteer professional. The hospital's first "Physician-to-Outdoor Patients" was appointed in 1858, and between 1863 and 1887 eight special clinics were developed to further serve walk-ins and those with special needs not requiring a bed stay. By 1900, 17 part-time volunteer staffers saw more than 100,000 outpatients a year. From 1846 to 1887 the physical premises of the Outpatient Department (OPD) were "but a small crowded space of two offices and a waiting room on the first floor of the 1821 Bulfinch Building."[65] In 1887 the OPD moved, with six clinics, into the three-story Gay Building beside Bulfinch. In 1903 the Proctor Outpatient Building opened, with 120 office-exam rooms and two large auditoriums. The improvement was significant but the hours were odd: the Proctor Building was all but empty in the afternoons, because the OPD staff was all-volunteer and usually worked mornings only.

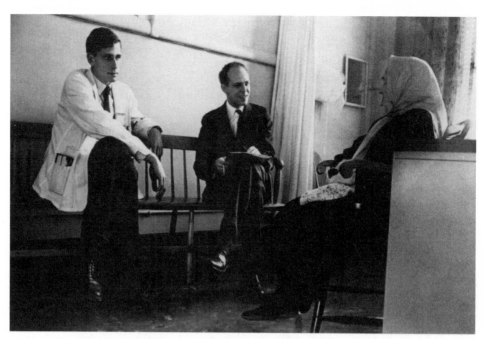

*John Stoeckle (center) and an unidentified medical student interview a patient
in the Outpatient Department, 1953.*

In 1948 the General Executive Committee identified the OPD as a "major problem" and recommended investigating it "to see if its scope could be broadened so that it would be of more service to the community and would give a better example of the practice of medicine to the students and house staff who work in the OPD." One idea proposed was a West End dispensary, separate from the formal OPD, to serve members of the surrounding West End community. A dispensary did open on February 10, 1949, as "a place to handle minor injuries and infections, to sort patients whose admission interviews do not disclose a proper clinic, to give intramuscular medications . . . or to dismiss the patient with inconsequential symptoms."[66] Admission fees were $1.00 for the dispensary, which was staffed by two assistant residents, and $2.25 for the clinics. John Stoeckle recalled that the dispensary had closed by the time of his appointment as the first full-time OPD physician in 1954.

The Proctor Building had hardly changed in half a century, and the Outpatient Department was a pretty sad affair, according to Stoeckle. A native of Sturgis, Michigan, a graduate of Antioch College, and a member of the Harvard Medical School class of 1947, Stoeckle would remember being one of four or five graduates that year who were in favor of national health insurance. "I came to the MGH as an ordinary guy who just wanted to be a doctor," he said. The two truly formative influences in his life, he said, were growing up in a small town, where he knew "everyone," and a year-and-a-half bout with tuberculosis that made him think more about the importance of chronic disease. After his residency at MGH, Stoeckle moved to the Pentagon for service during the Korean War, from which he intended to embark on a fellowship in thyroid research. Then one day he got a call from Walter Bauer:

He said to me, "Stoeckle, I'd like you to come back to Mass General. . . . Do you want to be chief resident or do you want to run the clinic [the Outpatient Department]?"

I said, "No one has ever run the clinic."

"That's right. Now, why don't you do it?"[67]

Dean Clark had brought E. Michael White, trained as a lawyer, with him from the Health Insurance Plan of Greater New York to administer the OPD. Ruth Farrisey, director of nursing and assistant director of clinics, was a key contributor—"always around," according to Stoeckle, "always looking to make things better. Operationally she really ran the clinic, because the nurses ran admissions." John Stoeckle's role initially was as the first full-time staff member in the department.

Why would this career track have appealed to him? Stoeckle had an answer to match his midwestern roots: the patients in the OPD were the ordinary folks he had known back home in Sturgis, "only they happened to be Italian and Catholic in Boston, for the most part, instead of German and Lutheran." And most of them suffered from chronic disease: arthritis, bronchitis, emphysema, and so on. "I enjoyed the homespun quality of this place, you might say, and felt comfortable with it." Stoeckle walked into an outpatient department that was

> old and rundown while public expectations were rising, bringing staff criticisms of its poor amenities, old equipment, drab décor, hard benches, creaky floors, crowding and lack of privacy when compared to their private practices. Even so, patients still came, most as self-referrals coming on their own, some with spouse or children, by public transport to the Charles Circle Red Line stop, then walking down (and, after their visit, back up) the 52 steps of its stairs, then past the Suffolk County Jail to the OPD on Fruit Street. Others came by car, parking it in an open lot next to Boston's mortuary that was but a block away across Fruit Street on Grove, and a few walked from their tenement apartments in the North and West End, arriving 8–10 AM which were the hours for admission that included the 9 AM beginning of scheduled visits.[68]

Stoeckle's vivid memories reflected his concern for the way the less privileged were cared for in the OPD of the early 1950s: "At the Medical Clinic, patients would then wait on the hard benches lined up as church pews in the waiting room or along the wall until called by the nursing staff or student nurses, numbering some 6, who informed them of clinic procedures, 'took' their weight, height, blood pressure, and, in the case of new female patients, had them

Ruth Farrisey.

redress in white hospital gowns and their "slips" for the physical exam, place their clothes in lockers, and then escorted them to the waiting room to sit alongside the dressed waiting patients."

Everything about the OPD was outdated, even the patient medical records, which "came up on an overhead noisy chain shuttle from the record room in the basement, but records were often missing."[69] The OPD had "a declining census, an inefficient, irregular operation of morning sessions, limited resources, a persistent annual deficit, and a part-time staff whose voluntary ethic of free service was faltering as, everywhere else, professional work was paid."[70] Stoeckle would add that the educational result was not good: "There was no staff support for outpatient education until Walter Bauer encouraged us to go ahead with it."

In 1955 a committee chaired by Dana L. Farnsworth began meeting at MGH to consider improvement in outpatient care. Farnsworth had been an internist at Williams College and MIT before heading up Harvard University Health Service. According to Stoeckle, Bauer and Clark recruited Farnsworth to head the committee "because he was a neutral person already running a small group health service." The Farnsworth Committee met for nearly two years, from mid-1955 to mid-1957, and came up with many recommendations, published in 1958. A memo from Michael White enclosed with the report made the important distinction between putting up a new clinics building and improving outpatient service with or without a new building.[71] The politics were intricate, and the immediate results were few. Stoeckle recalled: "Farnsworth suggested a new center with separate office for private staff and a clinic center, but with common diagnostic services. I was at the meetings. You can't believe staff reaction: They did not want their private patients coming in the same door or sitting around in the X-ray room with clinic patients!"

Resistance to a true group practice was strongest among the Surgical Service, according to Stoeckle, "since it might undermine residents' authority to hospitalize their clinic patients for operations."[72] The Farnsworth Committee, backed by the trustees, recommended an ambulatory care center built so that office space could be added later for private practice—a compromise with the doctors in private practice who wanted nothing to do with group organization.

To construct a new building for ambulatory care would take 24 years, from the time of the Farnsworth report in 1958 to the opening of the Wang Ambulatory Care Center in 1982. In 1961 Dean Clark was replaced as general director by the dynamic chief of the pulmonary unit, John Knowles, and Knowles's agenda (see chapter 6), while activist, did not emphasize outpatient care, at least not on campus. The new buildings that went up in the Knowles era were dedicated to inpatient care (Gray) and research (Jackson). Outpatient outreach occurred mainly in community health clinics at Logan Airport and in Charlestown, not on Fruit Street.

Factors contributing to the lack of interest in an ambulatory care clinic, according to Stoeckle, were the retirement of Alan Butler and the passing of Walter Bauer, both of whom had advocated strongly for outpatient care. It was not until Knowles was replaced by the cardiologist Charles Sanders as general director in the 1970s that a new building for ambulatory care reappeared on the radar

Groundbreaking for the Wang Ambulatory Care Center.

screen. Then, in 1972, a true salaried group practice in medicine came into being on campus, Internal Medicine Associates (IMA), founded by Jerome Grossman and headed by Stoeckle, with strong backing from Chief of Medicine Alexander Leaf. Four goals were established for IMA: (1) build a primary care practice, (2) integrate clinic and private patients with one standard of care, (3) educate young doctors in primary care, and (4) conduct research in the practice of primary care. At last, MGH had a committed group of full-time professionals to take over the outpatient medical clinic and fully integrate it with private practice. Similar groups followed in OPD clinics and other departments. A medical residency in primary care was instituted in 1973.

Stoeckle noted that IMA was not in fact the first MGH-related group practice in the Department of Medicine; these had been instituted at the community health centers opened at Logan Airport in 1963 and in Charlestown in 1968 (see chapter 6). A factor in the creation of IMA was the founding in 1969 of the Harvard Community Health Plan, the grandfather of managed care in New England, conceived and founded by Robert Ebert, dean of Harvard Medical School and a former chief of medicine at MGH.

According to Stoeckle, IMA led finally to the renovation of the old OPD building, including removal of the hard, pewlike benches and installation of carpeting, X-ray view boxes, a new, flexible examination table, and pictures on the walls. Planning for a new ambulatory care center began in earnest in 1974. To be effective, this had to be more than another doctors' office building. There needed to be a single standard of effective care. In 1979 the Moseley Building and Walcott House were removed to make way, and three years later the Wang Ambulatory Care Center opened with a complex of 900 offices, including ones for ambulatory surgery.

Still, Dean Clark's dream, backed by Stoeckle, for a true full-time outpatient service at MGH was never entirely realized. Said Stoeckle: "OPD fizzled. They built a building, which then housed group practices. There were some remaining clinics, as the surgeons never converted their clinic into a group practice but instead had their own private group, Surgical Associates, leaving the surgical clinic running for the residents. What Clark and others envisioned was a prepaid group practice plan for everybody, but it never happened."

The Mass General Physicians Organization (MGPO), formed in 1994, might seem to be just such a group practice, but Stoeckle demurs: "The MGPO brought the doctors together for administrative purposes and the better to negotiate with insurers, but it did not affect how they served patients. Converting part-time charitable OPD clinics into full-time salaried group practices for everyone became possible, as many patients became insured either privately or with Medicare and Medicaid."

To those less invested in outpatient care than Stoeckle, this might seem a fine point. As will be seen in subsequent chapters, one of the great themes of MGH from the 1960s onward is how it has reached out to surrounding communities, and its definition of community has become the world. With the 1994 merger with Brigham and Women's Hospital to form Partners HealthCare, a true regional health system, including eight member hospitals and 20 individual group practices, is now in place—realizing hopes for an integrated outpatient service. But according to Stoeckle, ever the proponent of medical care for the ordinary folks, the health care system in general is in need of reform.

WALTER BAUER AND THE RISE OF THE PHYSICIAN-SCIENTIST

Dean Clark, Edward Churchill, and Walter Bauer were a sort of triumvirate that ran MGH through the transitional 1950s, with able assistance from the trustees and David Crockett. Clark's visions as general director may have gone largely unrealized, but Churchill was unquestionably a force to be reckoned with (see chapter 4). Yet if there was one man who changed the face of MGH in the first full postwar decade, it was Chief of Medicine Walter Bauer.

In 1947, 35 years after David Edsall arrived at MGH to shake things up, research had moved ahead sporadically, but there were still only four medical doctors on the full-time service: Chief of Medicine Howard Means, Bauer, Joe Aub, and William W. Beckman. Sixty years on, virtually everyone on staff would be full-time. This shift began in earnest after Bauer replaced Means as chief of medicine and Jackson professor of medicine on July 1, 1951. MGH physicians from the Bauer era still alive in 2010 revered their former chief's memory, acknowledging him as one of the true giants in the hospital's history and as a character nonpareil. He brought the physician-scientist to the fore in a way that Edsall never had, and he did it with color and character.

"If I can't build a strong basic research unit at the MGH," Bauer reportedly said, "I am going to quit and raise chickens!"[73] It seems Walter Bauer was always coming out with statements like this. He was the antithesis of the reserved Means.

Although quite scholarly (he was selected late in life to write the 75-year history of the Association of American Physicians), Means did not relate comfortably with the house staff, whereas Bauer knew them all by name and treated them as sons. According to an article by two of the young doctors who trained under him,

> Walter Bauer's greatest interest lay in the careers of the younger physicians at the MGH—the members of the medical house staff and the new staff physicians whom he personally chose. The medical house staff was Bauer's particular pride and concern until the day of his death. Despite his many responsibilities, he found time to be remarkably conversant with each of the diverse and talented physicians who served under him during 12 years. . . . None doubted the sincerity of Bauer's interest in him as physician and as a human being, even when in disagreement with his conclusions.[74]

Bauer treated patients with the same universal concern and respect. "I admired him a lot," said John Stoeckle. The ultimate proponent of plain, old-fashioned doctoring, Stoeckle has a good eye for physicians with the human touch. (With George Abbott White, Stoeckle coauthored a remarkable photographic study of doctors in ordinary settings during the New Deal era.)[75] Bauer had the human touch. "He was a wonderful person," Stoeckle said, "and in caring for patients he was terrific. He could care for low as well as high. He had a moral view of outpatient care too. He thought that we owed something to patients who had spent their lives sitting on the hard benches of the OPD and taught us while we cared for them."

Raised on Michigan's Upper Peninsula and educated at the University of Michigan, Bauer was an outsider of German Lutheran stock, who liked to say that if his people had never left Germany he would have become "the best damn cobbler in Würzburg." Some were offended by Bauer's nonstop profanity; others said he "swore to perfection."[76] Bauer suffered from mood swings. He was mercurial, said Paul Russell, appointed chief of surgery near the end of Bauer's life. "He sometimes bellowed at meetings." Said one of Bauer's chief residents, "When manic he was fun. Once I disagreed with him on ward rounds and damned if he didn't kick me in the ass!" Bauer also smoked virtually nonstop, a habit that probably speeded his death in 1963.

A colonel in the U.S. Army during World War II and director of the medical activities of the Eighth Service Command, Bauer headed up the Arthritis (rheumatology) Unit at MGH, where he was among the first to treat rheumatoid

Walter Bauer with Eleanor Roosevelt and an unidentified child.

arthritis with cortisone. Bauer would serve as chief of medicine for a dozen years, from 1951 until his passing. Under Howard Means, identified by Edsall as a rising star in 1913 and named chief only 10 years later, a handful of specialty medical units had come into being: thyroid (Means), cardiac (Paul White), gastrointestinal (Chester Jones), endocrine (Fuller Albright), and arthritis (Bauer). In a write-up on Bauer, Lloyd Hollingsworth "Holly" Smith and Daniel Federman referred to Means's Department of Medicine as a "Hanseatic League of specialty units" over which Means "presided benignly and with a loose hand, secure in the knowledge of MGH preeminence."[77] The only significant appointment of Means's final decade was John Stanbury to replace Means himself as chief of the Thyroid Unit.

Bauer pushed the specialty envelope. By 1966, when Alexander Leaf took over from Robert Ebert, Bauer's successor, there were 12 units within the Department of Medicine, doubling Means's number. Leaf continued what Bauer had begun. When Leaf gave way to John Potts 15 years later, the number had climbed to 23.[78] It was during the Bauer-Ebert-Leaf era that scientific medicine zoomed to the forefront at MGH.

By force of personality and academic reputation, Bauer had big-money connections that allowed him to build the Department of Medicine in a significant way. He had friends at the Commonwealth Fund in New York and was involved in setting up the Helen Hay Whitney Foundation, where he served as chairman of the scientific board. Thus, he had the resources to make his trademark appointments.

Bauer had a gambler's hunches about where to bet that big money. The classic Bauer appointment was to take a young, scientifically oriented physician whom Bauer had known previously as an intern or resident and to install that young man as chief of a unit *in which he had little or no clinical experience.* The same instincts and confidence that would lead Bauer to give two newly minted assistant residents charge of the great polio emergency in the 1950s (see below) led him to install Kurt Isselbacher as head of gastroenterology, Mort Swartz as head of infectious diseases, Holly Smith as head of endocrine, and Edgar Haber as head of cardiology. The case of Isselbacher and gastroenterology was typical:

> One Friday afternoon [Bauer] visited Isselbacher in his laboratory and posed the question: "Which do you want to head up? Endocrinology or gastroenterology? Let me know your decision by Monday."
>
> Isselbacher agonized over this unexpected opportunity throughout the weekend and then told Bauer, "I think I would choose gastroenterology even though I have worked primarily in the area of metabolism, which would be closer to the field of endocrinology. However, the problem in suggesting gastroenterology is that I really don't know any."
>
> Without hesitation Bauer replied, "I am perfectly aware of that. But people aren't born gastroenterologists, so you will just have to learn to become one."[79]

Stephen Krane and rheumatology is another example of Bauer playing a hunch and winning. Krane was a product of New York City, where his father had been a high school English teacher—instructing most notably Lionel Trilling, one of the great literary critics of the twentieth century. It wasn't easy sending a son to an Ivy League school on a public school salary, and when Krane's older brother was accepted at Harvard and Columbia, the only affordable choice for the Krane family was Columbia. They moved to 114th Street and Riverside Drive so that Steve's brother could live at home. Four years later, Steve Krane himself matriculated at Columbia. The war was on, and the U.S. Navy called. "I took care of the clap on a hospital ship," said Krane, "then did some lab work. They put me in the marines for a while, but I was a 116-pound marine and they didn't think much of me."

Stephen Krane.

After discharge from the service, Krane attended the Columbia College of Physicians and Surgeons (familiarly, "P&S"). To his surprise, med school was easier than college had been. Toughest of all, Krane felt, had been the Bronx High School of Science: "*That* was the most competitive academic environment I had ever been in. P&S was a breeze; I was tops in my class." He was accepted as an intern at MGH, the year Walter Bauer took over as chief of medicine. Also in his class was John Knowles, named general director in 1961.

Magnetized by the legendary example of Fuller Albright ("I had read Albright's book while a med student"), Krane became interested in calcium metabolism and worked in John Stanbury's thyroid lab. Krane recalled: "Then Stanbury went on sabbatical and I worked alone. I worked with radioactive isotopes of calcium to understand how calcium was turned over. I did it all: made up the solution, injected it in humans, autoclaved it. We calculated the doses as being inconsequential, but I've never been certain of that. I got a paper out of it, and I sort of thought bone was where I was going to work."

Instead, Bauer asked him to take over rheumatology, the study of connective tissue in which the most common clinical application is arthritis. It was Bauer's own field. In 1961 Krane took charge of the Robert W. Lovett Memorial Laboratories for the Study of Crippling Diseases from Evan Calkins and began building rheumatology into a true scientific discipline at MGH. With humility, Krane would say only: "In rheumatology during my time, we had good people and discovered some interesting things. We were looking for how joints get destroyed in rheumatoid arthritis and bone disease, and we discovered the enzymes that are involved in breaking down the joint structure, collagenases. At the time it was a big discovery."

In 2009, well into his eighties, Krane remained a *distinguished* professor at HMS, and decidedly not *emeritus*. "*Emeritus* means retired," he explained. "I refuse to retire." In the intervening years, rheumatology has been combined with allergy and immunology as an important medical division at Mass General.

There was a method to Walter Bauer's madness. Bauer knew that as medicine became ever more specialized during the latter half of the twentieth century, one doctor would not be able to do it all—care for patients, teach students, and conduct groundbreaking research. Any medical department would have to combine men and women who showed excellence in one or two of these areas, but rarely all three. This was strategically sound. Exciting research is more likely to attract brilliant young talent than is clinical expertise alone, especially in medicine. Bauer's approach was to build a medical staff around brilliant physician-scientists, confident that clinical expertise would follow.

Not everyone would say that Bauer had this knack alone. Krane himself said, "Means picked some good people, too. Alex Leaf, as well." And there were those fiercely opposed to Bauer's methods. When Bauer picked Isselbacher to replace Chester Jones as chief of gastroenterology, according to a chief resident of that era, Jones stormed into Bauer's office and told him he had ruined gastroenterology at MGH with this "idiotic" appointment. A Brahmin favorite in the venerable MGH tradition of private practice, Jones wanted Perry Culver, one of his apprentices, named instead. In fact, the Isselbacher appointment—also the first appointment of an openly Jewish chief at MGH—was a great success. Isselbacher established himself as such a presence at MGH that when he got a notion to switch to cancer research in the 1980s, the hospital accommodated him (see chapter 7).

Holly Smith would say in later years that during the 1950s, the Bauer era, MGH was "the preeminent academic medical center in the country. They got their pick of the interns." The list of chief residents under Bauer, the cream of the cream, is a testament to his remarkable leadership. It includes:

- Isaac Taylor, who became dean of the medical school at the University of North Carolina, Chapel Hill. Krane noted that "Ike" was "most famous for having sired musicians James, Livingston, and Kate Taylor."

- Evan Calkins, who turned over rheumatology to Krane in 1961 and went on to become chairman of medicine at the University of Buffalo.

- Mort Swartz, whose national eminence in infectious diseases is detailed below.

- Fred Goetz, who would head the diabetes unit at the University of Minnesota.

- Richard Field, who went on to Beth Israel Hospital in Boston and did early work on diabetic retinopathy.

- Holly Smith, arguably "the one that got away." After five years as chief of endocrinology at MGH and a year of research abroad, he was recruited by the University of California, San Francisco, to be chief of medicine and built that institution into what might be, in 2011, the best academic medical center west of the Mississippi.

- Steve Krane.

- John Knowles, who headed up the pulmonary unit at MGH before replacing Dean Clark as general director in 1961. Always a player on the national medical scene, Knowles would leave MGH for the Rockefeller Foundation after a decade.

- Donald B. Martin, who went on to the NIH and was in the vanguard of diabetes research.

- Ralph C. Williams, who became a distinguished immunologist working at Rockefeller University, did some of the early work on rheumatoid factor. Williams then became a chair at the University of New Mexico Medical School in Albuquerque.
- K. Frank Austen, brother of Jerry Austen and the last of Bauer's chief residents. He would move to a distinguished position at the Robert Breck Brigham Hospital in 1966, which later became part of Brigham and Women's Hospital. His role in fighting the polio epidemic of the 1950s follows.

INFECTIOUS DISEASES, FROM SYPHILIS TO HIV/AIDS

The astonishing success of sulfonamides and penicillin during World War II led many to think that infectious diseases might soon be a thing of the past. The 1947 MGH annual report reflected this optimism when it reported that penicillin "has practically eliminated chronic osteomyelitis. It has also produced a marked decrease in treatments for syphilis and gonorrhea."[80] Wasn't it only a matter of time before all disease would be eradicated by antibiotics? After World War II medicine shifted its attention from infectious diseases to chronic ones, such as cancer, arthritis, and cardiovascular disease. But then came polio, then came salmonella, then came Asian flu, then came HIV/AIDS.

In fact, the very first patient at Massachusetts General Hospital, in 1821, had an infectious disease, syphilis. From 1900 to 1910 the major diseases causing admission to MGH were also infectious: tuberculosis, pleurisy, malaria, pneumonia, and meningitis. Every fall in the early twentieth century there was a wave of typhoid fever. By the middle of October about four-fifths of the beds in the Medical Service were patients with typhoid, who stayed about six weeks on average. There was no treatment for them, other than bed rest, a nutritious diet, and prayer—mainly prayer. Typhoid had a mortality rate of 10 to 20 percent. Meanwhile, between 65 and 100 patients were visiting the syphilis clinic each day.

Jump ahead to 1941. Sulfonamides having been available since the mid-1930s, an MGH surgeon, Champ Lyons, received a National Research Council grant for the study of chemotherapy in the treatment of contaminated wounds. Some beds were set aside on White 12 to study these cases, and, in effect, MGH had its first infectious disease unit. When the survivors of the Cocoanut Grove nightclub fire came to MGH with infected wounds, Lyons became, in Morton N. Swartz's felicitous phrase, "the maître d' of sulfonamides." But then Lyons went off to war, and that was the end of an infectious disease department at MGH, though it had never been called that.

In 1944 the first penicillin became available in civilian life, and in Boston Chester Keefer of Massachusetts Memorial Hospital oversaw distribution of the drug, still scarce because the Allied military needed most of the available supply. In 1951 Louis Dienes, head of bacteriology at MGH for about two decades, stepped down from his leadership position because of age, and a replacement, Lawrence Kunz, was appointed. At about the same time Thomas F. Paine was selected to head the new Bacteriology Unit at MGH. Paine had been a house officer at Boston City Hospital; spent two years as a fellow with Maxwell Finland, the father of modern chemotherapy; and worked a year in the MGH lab with Fritz Lipmann, of 1953 Nobel fame. Paine would soon leave MGH to head the Microbiology Department at the University of Alabama.

In 1955, poliomyelitis staged a climactic outbreak in the United States. This one started like previous outbreaks, according to Frank Austen, then a resident at MGH. Patients reporting in to MGH, Brigham and Women's, New England Medical Center, the Deaconess, and elsewhere in Boston complaining of stiff neck and fever were referred immediately to Boston City or Haynes Memorial Hospital at Boston University, the last true infectious disease hospital in Greater Boston, in the tradition of isolation hospitals for smallpox established more than two centuries previously. But Boston City and Haynes ran out of beds for polio patients. Austen recalled what happened next:

> MGH to its great credit said that somebody had to take care of these patients and that they would. Nobody else did, not the Brigham, not Beth Israel, not the Deaconess. But MGH had no experience with polio. So in July, as I was about to go on holiday, Walter Bauer said that he would like me *not* to go on holiday at that time but to start admitting polio patients representing the Department of Medicine, along with Jan Kochweser, another resident and a running mate of mine. We were both first-month assistant residents. Nobody thought this was going to be as big as it was, and Dr. Bauer said Dr. Louis Weinstein from Haynes would make rounds with us once a week.[81] There was no specific drug for polio; all we could supply was supportive care.

But within two weeks, the volume of patients became so great that Bauer and the hospital made two additional decisions. The first was that no private doctor would be allowed to write orders on polio patients; all orders had to be

Frank Austen.

made by Austen and Kochweser, because they were the ones developing on-the-job experience with the disease and they were in direct touch with Louis Weinstein, the acknowledged regional expert. Raymond D. Adams, head of neurology at MGH, also pitched in. Said Austen: "We began admitting patients who had lost control of their respiratory systems, either because of weak respiratory muscles, especially the diaphragm, or because of weak larynx. The latter, with so-called bulbar polio, couldn't swallow without getting food into airways. For respiratory weakness we needed iron lungs. For bulbar without respiratory, we needed a tracheostomy for breathing, plugged off when they wanted to eat."

The second "remarkable" decision

by MGH, according to Austen, was turning over the entire ninth floor of the White Building to polio patients and simultaneously reducing surgical activities at the hospital to accommodate this responsibility. Said Austen, "This was a decision made for the right reasons. It is what an institution ought to do. They took responsibility for the episode and made substantial internal adjustments to optimize patient care." No other hospital in Boston did likewise.

Over the course of the six-month outbreak, Mass General treated 428 patients, including 52 children; of these numbers, 73 adults and 8 children had to be put in respirators, an acute emergency that began waning by year's end. A good number were cured or released with relatively minor impairment, but tragically 30 were still in respirators, and likely to remain there, at the beginning of 1956. Like the Cocoanut Grove catastrophe 13 years before, the polio scourge pulled the MGH staff together, drawing on all necessary resources.[82] The injected polio vaccine developed by Jonas Salk in 1955 and the oral vaccine by Albert Sabin in the early 1960s removed polio as a serious threat thereafter, but for those patients who spent the rest of their lives in iron lungs, the damage was permanent.

At MGH there are almost always research and education components to patient care, and in the case of one young resident, Austen, still effectively in training, the polio incident was a career changer. "In the end," he said, "I authored three papers in the *New England Journal of Medicine* [about polio at MGH], which subsequently profoundly influenced my life."[83]

When Walter Bauer became gravely ill with end-stage pulmonary disease, Austen was on a third fellowship at Johns Hopkins, but Bauer requested that he come back to MGH to help with his care, and Austen gladly complied. Austen called it "an incredible privilege." He remembered Bauer as "the kind of person who wouldn't spend two minutes talking about himself. Right away, he wanted to know about me, my family, my wife. He was simply a wonderful mentor who played a wonderful role in my career and the standards that I brought to my career. He left me his desk from the MGH." Asked if Bauer had been a second father to him, Austen said, "I wouldn't blame that on him. But he was an inspiration, and tolerant of my shortcomings."

After Robert Ebert, Bauer's replacement as MGH chief of medicine, moved to Harvard Medical School as dean in the mid-1960s, he convinced Austen to move to the Peter Bent Brigham Hospital to establish a program for immune diseases. As Austen recalled, it was "closer to the medical school so that I could do more teaching." Now the AstraZeneca professor of respiratory and inflammatory diseases at Harvard Medical School, and a member of both the American Academy of Arts and Sciences and Britain's Royal Society of Medicine, Austen is still active in his eighties, leading research into bronchial asthma.

An MGH Legend Arrives

Born in a triple-decker in Dorchester, Massachusetts, Mort Swartz was the son of a Boston dermatologist whose father had wanted him to be a rabbi or, second best, a kosher butcher. But that wasn't what Jacob Swartz had in mind, and he threatened Mort's grandfather that if he tried to force him into rabbinical school, he would go to a Protestant theological seminary instead. So Jacob attended Tufts College

Morton Swartz.

and Harvard Medical School, and he later had appointments at Boston City Hospital, Beth Israel, and MGH, and a downtown practice in Kenmore Square. His son Mort would attend grade school and high school in Brookline and go to Harvard College, where he entered the navy V-12 program. This accelerated wartime program allowed Swartz to complete his undergraduate premedical studies at Harvard in two years, serve in the navy as a medical corpsman, and enter HMS in 1944 as a naval ensign.

An MGH intern in medicine in 1947, Swartz would be named chief resident by Walter Bauer in 1953. Next the young doctor moved to Johns Hopkins, where he looked forward to a long career doing research in biochemistry. In 1955 the phone rang. It was Walter Bauer. Back in Boston the polio epidemic was under way. Swartz didn't know it at the time, but Bauer had been trying for two years to find a replacement for Chief of Bacteriology Thomas F. Paine, who had resigned in 1952. He had tried to lure high-profile names but with no luck. Bauer thought the world of Mort Swartz; according to Holly Smith, Bauer would come to view Swartz as a "secular saint." Smith said, "I was walking with Bauer down the hall once in the old Bulfinch. 'Holly,' he said to me, looking at Mort, 'there goes Jesus Christ.'" Mort later joked that Bauer got his Testament wrong.

The admiration was mutual. "There will never be another Walter Bauer, in my view," said Swartz in 2009. "He had so much insight, so much charisma and energy—when he was in the 'up' phase. He called me one day and said I was going to be the next head of infectious disease (ID) at MGH. I was aiming for another career, but he was so dominant, I had no choice." Swartz tried to bargain: "I said, 'I have no training specifically in infectious disease,' and he said, 'That's all right, you're going to start fresh.' I asked if I could have a couple of years to train with Max Finland or someone equally prominent. He said no. My heart sank because I was thinking of the patients—and treating them while learning on the job."

Swartz reported to Bauer the following February (1956). Polio had subsided. Swartz arrived without any specific knowledge or skills in ID, but he did have a keen interest and brilliant mind for research. He was, in other words, a classic Walter Bauer hire. "But unlike the others—Kurt Isselbacher, Holly Smith, Steve Krane," said Swartz, "there was no underpinning in infectious diseases here. There was *nothing!* I hardly ever saw my wife for five years after that."

It started out as a three-person unit: Swartz, his secretary, and a research technician, whom Swartz would claim he never saw because he was always seeing patients instead. Within two months of Swartz's 1956 arrival, a clinician, Rita M. Kelley, approached him in the corridor one day and said she had a patient with a case of diarrhea that she could not diagnose. This was the sort of thing Swartz would do all the time from here on, consult with other physicians about their mystery cases. Swartz recalled:

> It turned out that there were in all more than 50 cases of diarrhea, and they all occurred in a short period of time, and they all occurred in the Baker, the Phillips House, and Burnham (pediatrics), but not in Bulfinch or White. How was that possible? The first presumption was *Salmonella*, which is usually passed through undercooked meats and the hands that handle them. We thought of this in part because the food in Baker, Phillips, and Burnham was prepared in a separate kitchen than food for the wards. So we brought all of the food handlers into the clinic, had them bend over, and took a swab culture from their rectums. All of them were negative! How could that be possible? It turned out, however, that one person was absent from work that day, with fever and malaise. I went to her house, obtained a culture, and found *Salmonella heidelberg*. Her job in the kitchen was to prepare salads and highly nutritious fresh foods that generally were not cooked. The funny thing was, three house officers came down with *Salmonella heidelberg* infection too, but they ate in the White cafeteria. Explanation? They were *sneaking* meals from the kitchens on the patient floors of the Baker and Phillips House!

In 1957 came a serious outbreak of so-called Asian flu—the most widespread flu outbreak since the Spanish flu pandemic of 1918. "For the next five years," said Swartz, "I was immersed, seeing patients, consulting with surgeons and physicians, giving the infectious disease portion of the postgraduate course in medicine with Louis Weinstein's help. At the end of the five years, I was pretty bushed. I was young, fortunately, but I was married and our first child was already born."

Swartz went to Walter Bauer and said he needed a respite from total immersion in patient care. Bauer agreed and Swartz left for Stanford, where he spent a year in the lab of Arthur Kornberg, who had won the 1959 Nobel Prize in Medicine for discovering the enzymatic synthesis of DNA. Rejuvenated after a year on the West Coast, Swartz returned to MGH and began building the Infectious Disease Department in a big way, just as one of the most fascinating cases was developing. Documented six years later in an "Annals of Medicine" piece in the *New Yorker* by Berton Roueché, the mid-1960s outbreak of *Salmonella cubana* was a real puzzler. Unlike the *S. heidelberg* outbreak of 1956, this one was so sporadic as to be barely perceptible. It was first noted at a monthly meeting of the MGH Committee on Infection Control in early 1966, as Roueché would report. At the meeting, an assistant pediatrician, David J. Lang, weighed in "on the incidence of *Salmonella cubana* on the Burnham floors." Five pediatric patients had been affected since October 1965; one infant had died. In the six months before that, seven additional cases had been noted, including two children and five adults. If this was indeed *S. cubana*—and lab tests at the New York Salmonella Center, at Beth Israel Hospital in Manhattan, confirmed it—this was rare indeed. Since it was first observed in Cuba in 1946, it had been seen only rarely outside that island nation. And why was the bug being found sporadically, as if at random, around the MGH campus?[84]

The solution came after long work and an odd chain of circumstance. No other Boston hospitals were seeing *S. cubana*, so this outbreak was limited to MGH at this time, meaning patients were probably catching the bug *here*. One possible source for a bug that was appearing randomly around the hospital was the special-diet kitchen, which served all buildings. The workers there were cultured: all negative, a dead end.

The next lead came from Santa Claus. MGH has a long-standing tradition that a Mr. S. Claus is admitted to the Emergency Ward every Christmas, usually in the Surgical Service. An empty bed is assigned to him, a history is written up, blood and urine specimens are sent to the lab for analysis. Lo and behold, in 1965, Santa Claus was demonstrated to have *salmonella!* (The infection was subsequently shown to be *S. cubana*.) But the specimen wasn't even urine! The pranksters (house officers) had mixed up "water, an intravenous multiple-vitamin preparation, a pinch of powdered carmine dye for coloring, and a throat swab from one of the patients on the floor" and sent the culture to the lab. Several months later, when the 21st patient was observed with *S. cubana*, Lang decided to take the child as a case study. Looking over the chart, he saw "carmine red transit-time test," and, he told Roueché, "That lit me up like a light bulb. . . . It made me think of the Santa Claus specimen."[85]

Working with others, Lang demonstrated that the bug had been carried by carmine red dye, which was manufactured by a mom-and-pop operation in New Jersey. Carmine red is made from dried and crushed coccus cacti, an insect indigenous to the Canary Islands, Mexico, Peru, and Central America. Carmine red is used in thousands of applications as a dye. By tracking this outbreak of *S. cubana* to its source, the MGH infectious disease team had warded off what potentially could have been a worldwide outbreak.

Building the Unit

Through his first 20 years as chief, Mort Swartz built the ID unit at MGH into a powerhouse, while extending his own influence nationally. One of Swartz's innovations was to develop intracity rounds, among the Harvard hospitals, in infectious-disease training. These continued during his 34 years as chief of the ID unit at MGH. Said Swartz:

> That worked out well, except once, when I was driving a carload of people from here to Tufts. I have a notoriously poor sense of direction. When I was in the army in 1950–1953, I was the only officer in 5th Corps who failed map reading—because I got lost trying to get to where the exam was given. So one day I took off toward Tufts with a load of people. I usually go by Yogi Berra's dictum, "When you come to a fork in the road, take it." But I go Yogi one better. I always take the bigger fork, which introduced the Mass Turnpike into my itinerary that day.

Swartz told this story in typically self-deprecating fashion. But talk with just about anyone else who has been around the MGH faculty long enough, and you will hear acclaim for Swartz as teacher and clinician. His successor, Stephen B. Calderwood, would call him "one of the most miraculous men you'll ever meet."

He is not just smart. His knowledge is across all human knowledge. He knows more about philosophy, physics, sports than you'll ever imagine. Ask him something and he'll know it better than you do, even if it's your area of specialty.

Mort has this intuitive ability to take the same information everybody else has and put it together to solve a puzzle. You can give him the most complicated case that 50 people have thought through for hours. He'll hear it and say, Most likely, it's the following.

One of the fun things in training with Mort is, not only can he tell you what the problem is, but he can explain what it was about the information that led him to that—to help students learn clinical reasoning.

Headed by a genius in the clinic and in teaching, infectious diseases also saw an uptick in research during Swartz's years of leadership, beginning with Swartz's own inquiries into DNA synthesis in bacteria and the biochemistry of DNA structure. Paul H. Black worked on the role of viruses in tumor induction; Martin S. Hirsch on the role of interferon in transplantation, among other things (more on Hirsch below); Robert H. Rubin on the treatment of infections in immunocompromised hosts; Robert C. Moellering Jr. and Arnold N. Weinberg on the mechanism of antibiotic synergism against enterococci; George A. Jacoby on bacterial genetics; and A.W. Karchmer on the clinical features and outcome of treatment of bacterial endocarditis.

When Legionnaires' disease broke out in a Philadelphia hotel during a convention in 1976, Mort Swartz was one of a small panel of experts called in by the Centers for Disease Control (CDC), such was his professional reputation and the reputation of MGH in the field. From a standing start so much had been learned in 20 years. As in all successful departments of medicine and surgery, one of the main things Swartz learned was to recruit good people. Enter Steve Calderwood. Enter Marty Hirsch.

Stephen Calderwood.

The ID Unit in Recent Years

A native of Hohokus, New Jersey, Calderwood was in George W. Bush's class at Andover, went on to Harvard, then spent three years in the U.S. Army at the height of the Vietnam War. A Harvard Medical student beginning in 1971, he first met Swartz while doing his fall clerkship in 1973. Calderwood recognized something special in Swartz right away: "He was probably the smartest man I had ever seen in medicine, not only in what he knew but in how he interacted with people and was able to interact with people to get relevant information. I thought to myself, 'Boy, I've got to work with that man.'" Calderwood's first major research work, after a fellowship, was with Robert Moellering on antibiotic resistance.

Calderwood was John Potts's first chief resident in medicine at MGH in 1981, after Potts replaced Alexander Leaf as chief of medicine. Potts encouraged Calderwood to get serious about research, so Calderwood returned to HMS for a postdoctoral research fellowship in microbiology under John Mekalanos. When Swartz stepped down as chief of ID in 1990 to become one of the three so-called firm chiefs, focused on mentoring interns and residents, Calderwood was tapped to replace him in ID.

The ID unit developed a distinctly international look under Calderwood. His own work has focused on enteric, or diarrheal, diseases, especially cholera—diseases that don't occur with any frequency in the United States. Calderwood's lab works in close collaboration with the International Centre for Diarrhoeal Research in Dhaka, Bangladesh, funded by an International Collaborations in Infectious Disease research grant from the NIH.

How does a Boston hospital justify spending so many resources studying and treating "offshore" problems, which also include drug-resistant strains of tuberculosis? Calderwood counted the ways:

> First, there is no good in vitro or animal model of cholera. You can do lots of studies, but if you want to study cholera, you have to study it in humans. And the only place that cholera occurs in humans is outside of U.S. So to bring modern tools to study cholera, you have to take those tools outside the U.S. Same with malaria.
>
> Second, many of these are wonderful model systems for understanding other illnesses. So if you can solve a problem that's primarily offshore, you can bring findings to bear on other diseases that aren't as easily studied. Cholera is a wonderful example: we can't make a good oral vaccine for an organism that works through the gastrointestinal tract. We fundamentally don't understand the immunology of that system. We have good vaccines that we give by shots; but to be widely effective a cholera vaccine will have to be an oral vaccine. There are many other diseases that we contract through the oral route but we have few vaccines for them. Cholera is probably the most advanced model for that kind of illness.

As we have learned with SARS and other infectious diseases making news in recent, offshore instances, if a disease is easily transmissible, it can come onshore, given the amount of international travel today. That's why the ID unit has set up the Travelers' Advice and Immunization Center. Edward T. Ryan runs this, as he does the related Tropical and Geographic Medicine Center. Ryan is principal investigator on a CDC travel grant, learning to track disease outbreaks around the globe, including who is contracting the disease, and how the afflicted are being treated.

Finally, there are compelling humanitarian reasons for attacking offshore diseases from a Boston base. Said Calderwood: "If you look at what people are dying of around the world, they are dying of the things we don't see here anymore or as much. We've solved many of our diseases by vaccines and treatments, so if you really want to apply science to IDs and human health, you will have your biggest impact if you do it with diseases that aren't really represented here."

The Great Epidemic of Our Times

The most significant infectious disease of the past three decades is HIV/AIDS. This is where Martin S. Hirsch reenters the story. Hirsch studied medicine at Johns Hopkins and took his residency at the University of Chicago Hospital. He came to his interest in IDs "sort of by accident," he admitted. The Vietnam War was being fought and "I wanted to stay away from killing or being killed, so I ended at CDC, where I got interested in IDs and virology." Hirsch moved on to the National Institute for Medical Research in London, followed by a fellowship at MGH in 1969. "Expecting to spend two years here," he said in 2009, "I have spent 40."

Until 1981 Hirsch's research focused on viruses and immune responses, primarily with the herpes group and particularly with the cytomegalovirus (CMV). Then young men with "crashed" immune systems began showing up in emergency rooms across the country, including the one in Boston's West End. Said Hirsch: "When I read about the first cases of what came to be known as AIDS, reading CDC reports, I saw that all of the early patients had a CMV infection. I had been studying for the past decade how CMV could suppress immune responses, so I thought AIDS might be caused by a super strain of CMV. Like many of my great ideas, this was wrong!"

Acquired immune deficiency syndrome (AIDS) was first diagnosed in 1981 and traced definitively to the human immunodeficiency virus (HIV) in 1984. By 1985, according to the MGH annual report for that year, there had been "not a single recorded cure,"[86] and mortality was nearing 100 percent within three years of onset. But already MGH researchers under Hirsch were making their mark. Earlier than most, Hirsch had started a small lab to study HIV, which initially included two key colleagues: Robert T. "Chip" Schooley, later head of ID at the University of California, San Diego, and David Ho, who would move on as director of the Aaron Diamond AIDS Research Center in New York. Ho was nothing less than *Time* magazine's Man of the Year for 1996 for his pioneering work in using protease inhibitors to treat HIV-infected patients.

Said Hirsch: "That was our group in the early 1980s. We were lucky enough to get into the field at the beginning. That was particularly exciting, and we made a lot of observations that have stood up."

In 1982 Hirsch and Schooley started a prospective study on the hunch that AIDS might be an infectious disease and

Martin Hirsch.

caused by a virus. They started collecting blood samples from men who were perceived to be possibly at risk. "We didn't know who was infected or who wasn't," said Bruce D. Walker, then a resident at MGH but soon to be a key contributor in the effort here against HIV/AIDS. In the 1980s "an explosion of contributions came from MGH," Walker said. "I don't think anybody realizes how many of the fundamental advances related to HIV came from Mass General." Among MGH firsts were the identification of neutralizing antibodies (David Ho); identification of cytotoxic T cells[87] (Schooley and Walker); the first identification of HIV-specific T-helper cells in infected persons (Walker and Rosenberg); and the first laboratory demonstration of combination chemotherapy (the now-familiar "cocktail" of drugs used to thwart AIDS in HIV-infected patients) (Hirsch). MGH investigators were the first to isolate the HIV virus in semen, in the female genital tract, and in the central nervous system—demonstrating how broad its effect was. MGH was also one of the first places where AZT was tested and shown to be effective. Said Walker: "Marty Hirsch is a bit soft-spoken, but he is a giant in the field and played a really critical role in mobilizing global research efforts against HIV. MGH was the preeminent place for this kind of translational work in those early days. Dozens of MGH papers on HIV/AIDS have appeared in *Nature* and *Science*."

Walker, a native of Colorado, by way of Case Western Medical School and the Swiss Federal Technical Institute in Zurich, began to emerge on the Hirsch-Schooley team by the mid-1980s. A fellow in Hirsch's lab, mentored by Schooley, Walker built an investigative career by repeatedly demonstrating that though the patient's immune system may appear to crash in the face of HIV, it actually puts up a remarkable fight; in some cases, in fact, the patient's immune system wins the fight.

In 1987 Walker was an author of a paper in *Nature* demonstrating that people with HIV make cytotoxic (virus-killing) T cells.[88] The conclusions of the paper were counterintuitive: here was a disease that seemed to destroy the immune system; yet the paper said that the body's initial immune response to the disease was more powerful than any previously identified. How could that be? It wasn't until 2006 that Walker and his colleagues published a paper showing that T cells are turned off by the body when the infection becomes active. Walker said, "The body prematurely gives up and tells these killer T cells to stop fighting."

Walker's early work caught the attention of the medical community, and in 1988 he was named Burroughs Wellcome investigator in virology of the Infectious Diseases Society

Bruce Walker.

of the United States, a prestigious award for young researchers. Around 1993 a hemophiliac who had been infected with HIV in 1978 was referred to Walker. The patient was feeling fine, 15 years later. Somehow, Walker and his colleagues deduced, this patient had the upper hand on the virus. The patient was the subject of a 1997 paper in *Science* and the start of Walker's work on what came to be known as "elite controllers," patients who showed a unique ability to control the effects of the virus. There was a lesson here not only about HIV/AIDS but also about MGH. Said Walker: "What's great about Mass General is the emphasis on clinical care. The same people who are doing clinical care are also doing the research, and that keeps the research focused on really critical issues facing patients. Part of our daytime job is seeing patients so we see the manifestations of disease and we get the clues from the way disease manifests itself in different people—and that is what leads us to various discoveries." In 2010, despite heading a phenomenal research effort, Walker was still working one month a year on the MGH floor, between trips to Africa.

The Ragon Institute

By the mid-1990s, according to Steve Calderwood, Walker had become a hot commodity. Said Calderwood, "We didn't want to lose him." So the Partners AIDS Research Center (PARC) was founded and organizationally split off from the Infectious Disease Department at MGH. (*Partners* is Partners HealthCare, the regional health system formed in 1993–1994, detailed in the final two chapters.) Walker was PARC's first and only chief.

"I wasn't really that interested in going," Walker would say nearly a decade after his first trip to South Africa, "but we had a scientific question that needed an answer: Why do children do so much worse than adults when they become infected with HIV?" Walker had recruited Philip Goulder from Oxford expressly to work on infected newborns. Following a definitive 1996 trial of the drug azidothymidine (AZT) on HIV-infected pregnant women and the finding that AZT significantly reduces the risk of transmission to infants born of these women, AZT began to be administered widely in such cases throughout the developed world. As a result, far fewer children were born with the virus; so there were few cases to test. Africa did not have AZT or wasn't using it. To get blood samples from a large number of children who were infected from birth, Africa was then the place to go.

Goulder returned from his first trip to South Africa reporting on a disaster of unimaginable proportions—a disaster and an opportunity. He convinced Walker that an AIDS effort in South Africa might have unimaginable effects. Walker agreed to go to the city of Durban, epicenter of the AIDS epidemic in a country where 20 percent of the population was infected. It was, he said, a life-transforming experience:

> The burden of the disease was just staggering. I went to a local mission hospital and took a tour with Sister Christa Mary. We went through the emergency room and she pointed out the countless stretchers with people on them. They were all young people. As I was trying to absorb this, she said, "Watch this." There was a person lying on a stretcher and a woman came over with a big

bucket of something like oatmeal with a bowl, took a ladle out of oatmeal and put it in the bowl and handed it to the person. The patient was clearly close to death. A big smile came across the patient's face, and Sister Christa Mary said, "That's what it's all about; that's what we can do here."

I was not prepared for the epidemic there. It was everywhere, in all aspects of life. I wasn't prepared for the enormity of the disease, but I also wasn't pre-pared for the number of people who wanted to get involved in doing some-thing about it—to begin to do research on AIDS because they were living in the midst of it and everyone there was dying. It was emotionally wrenching and yet at the same time strangely exhilarating, because I met more people per unit of time than I'd ever met in my life who were devoting their lives to doing something to help other people. Again and again you'd hear stories of people who had gone over there to spend six months and ended up spending their life there. Or people from South Africa who had an option to go else-where but were staying there because that was where they were needed.

Walker and Goulder began to think they could make a major difference in the fight against AIDS. Said Walker, "If we really wanted to have an impact, we had to think about how science gets done. As far as I was concerned, science advances by the way it is done at MGH. You put research and care next to each other and good things happen. And so the idea was, let's go to the center of the epidemic, and try to do just that."

For a clinic and a research lab, funding was needed. Initially, some flexible funding from an MGH donor was amplified by gifts from the Elizabeth Glaser Pediatric AIDS Foundation and then the Doris Duke Charitable Foundation. By 2003, together with their South African collaborators, Walker and Goulder opened the Doris Duke Medical Research Institute at the Nelson Mandela Medi-cal School at the University of Kwazulu-Natal in Durban. Facilities at the med school were run-down; nary a new building had been erected since the institution was built in 1950. Said Walker, "We were initially given a small little room to set up a lab. There was no better place. We were studying disease. This was a medical school. It was the only one in Durban." A companion clinic was opened to care for the patients who were being entered into their studies. "We felt we could not conduct research unless we were able to give something back to the patients, and at that time there was no HIV treatment available to people." Walker and Goul-der eventually envisioned something even bigger: a cure for AIDS. That would take funding on a far bigger scale. Through a personal friend, Walker made a pitch to several prospective well-heeled donors, but there was no immediate response.

Meanwhile, an electronic medical records salesman in Durban named Henry Adams was bugging Walker. The mission hospital with which Walker worked used medical records software from a vendor Adams represented named Track Health. Adams repeatedly asked to meet with Walker, but Walker resisted, thinking he was trying to sell him more software. Finally, he agreed to meet in the Johannes-burg airport on a day when each was waiting for a connecting flight. Over cof-fee, Adams explained that he simply wanted Walker to tell the owner of Track Health, Phillip T. "Terry" Ragon, that the system was saving patients' lives, so that Track Health would continue to provide the system in South Africa. The company was threatening to pull out of South Africa because of government regulatory excesses. Walker was happy to talk with Ragon. "They had a better system at this hospital in South Africa then we did here at Mass General," he said.

Ragon lived in the Boston area; he had an office in Cambridge not only for Track Health, but also for the parent company, Intersystems. He agreed to meet with Walker for

Terry Ragon addresses a group of South African children during his first visit to the country in 2007.

half an hour. Walker described the scope of the AIDS epidemic in South Africa and ended the meeting by suggesting that Ragon might want to make a contribution to the effort. Within a day, Ragon had made arrangements to accompany Walker on his next trip to Durban. On the flight over, Ragon told Walker not to get his hopes up about a contribution. According to Walker, Ragon said, "I see a lot of different programs but it's rare that I ever give money because I like my donations to have leverageability." Walker found that this lightened his own attitude about having Ragon along and decided to "farm him out" to other people who would show the businessman around Durban and environs. Firsthand experience of AIDS patients on the ground in South Africa had the same effect on Ragon it had had on Walker: it was transformative.

At the end of the week, Walker and Goulder drove Ragon to the airport. According to Walker, Ragon said, "I don't know how anybody could have the experience I've had this week and not want to get involved." Over coffee at the airport, the scientists laid out a wish list for funding—everything from $5,000 for a lab instrument to a grand plan of seven-to-ten years' funding for a program that would aim at creating an HIV vaccine. Ragon said that such a grand plan sounded very expensive, and the scientists agreed. Upon their return to Boston, Ragon and his wife, Susan, agreed to give $4 million for clinical studies of a trial vaccine.

Over the course of the following year, Ragon brought up the "grand plan" a couple of times. Walker's thinking had evolved. Since the early 1980s, HIV had been studied in "an isolated silo," Walker said. "You had to have access to patients and access to containment facilities to work on it. Most of the basic immunologists didn't leave their fields to come work on HIV. It was a field that grew up out of nothing from people like me who had no formal immunology training. I was a physician motivated because of what I was seeing in the clinic."

Instead of the "silo" approach, Walker and Goulder envisioned a collaborative network of investigators from many fields—not only immunology, but also physics, mathematics, engineering, computational biology—and from multiple institutions. Where better to create such a network than in Boston and Cambridge, with Harvard, MIT, and MGH? With backing from Dennis Burton, from the Scripps

Research Institute, and Wayne Koff of the International AIDs Vaccine Initiative, Walker approached Ragon again. A meeting in Ragon's office was inconclusive, but a week later Ragon's office called to say he wanted another meeting. He and Walker sat down in Walker's office. Walker recalled the exchange:

> Terry came in and sat down and said, "I want to hear some more about that project that you and Dennis were talking about." I started blabbing again about this thing and after about five or 10 minutes, he leans forward and says, "Let me interrupt you. Let me see if I understand. It sounds as if you don't think we're going to get a vaccine the way we're doing it right now but you think it's a solvable problem. And you think you need to bring people from other fields into the HIV field and you think that Boston and Cambridge is the right environment in which to do this. And my guess is that you're talk-ing about something like $10 million a year for 10 years to make something like this happen. Is that about right?" I said, "Yeah, that's about right." And he said, "Well, my wife and I would like to do it."

The size of the Ragons' commitment was staggering. In December 2008—just as the economic downturn was gathering steam and investigators everywhere were beginning to worry about funding—a deal was inked in a private gathering at the Charles Hotel in Cambridge, attended by Harvard's President Drew Faust, MIT's President Susan Hockfield, and Peter Slavin, president of MGH. Said Walker, "Afterward, I went to Harvard Square, bought a bunch of bottles of Champagne and came back to the lab, and in the hallway we popped corks and got the whole lab together. I said, 'This is going to happen! In fact, it's actually just happened!'"

The funding and founding of the Ragon Institute were formally announced in February 2009. The story made the front page of the *Boston Globe* on February 4:

> The hunt for an AIDS vaccine, a scientific quest that has stumped infectious disease researchers for two decades, is receiving a $100 million boost from a Massachusetts technology magnate, whose gift will create a Boston institute fusing the expertise of doctors, engineers, and biologists.
>
> Stunned by scenes of desperation he witnessed in HIV-ravaged South Africa, Phillip Terrence Ragon is spending a considerable chunk of his for-tune to accelerate research for a vaccine that would slow the relentless spread of the virus that causes AIDS and now infects more than 33 million people worldwide.
>
> The money, $10 million a year for the next decade, will go to Massachu-setts General Hospital but be shared with other research powerhouses, includ-ing Harvard University and the Massachusetts Institute of Technology.[89]

"It was like an out-of-body experience, the whole thing," Walker said a year later. "And it's continued to be that because it's been the most exhilarating period of my entire scientific career: the new people that are coming in—the new ideas that are being generated—and this very clear demonstration, day after day, that we have not begun to put the full scientific arsenal towards solving HIV/AIDS."

As one of the first fruits of the collaborative effort made possible by the Ragon Institute, Walker cited a paper in *Nature* published in May 2010 showing that the use of statistical physics to analyze experimental data offers new insights into how an effective immune response happens.[90] Walker and the other lead author on the paper, the MIT statistical physicist Arup Chakraborty, "never would have had a conversation" if not for this new approach, according to Walker. The steady march forward in the war against HIV and AIDS continued at the end of 2010, when Walker and his colleagues at the Ragon Institute published a landmark paper in *Science* showing that of the three billion nucleotides in the human genome, just a few amino acids in a protein called HLA-B dictate whether individuals infected with HIV will develop full-blown AIDS or whether their immune systems alone can control the viral levels.

Walker observed that this was all also made possible by having taken place at MGH, "where they allow you to think outside the box. It's not the bureaucracy of a university, which never would have allowed us to build that research institute in South Africa. You would have to take me kicking and screaming to get me to leave MGH."

On the road ahead, Walker has a number of top colleagues working on HIV/AIDS alongside him at MGH. These include:

- David Bangsberg, with a major HIV research project in Uganda
- Nesli Basgoz, associate chief of the infectious disease unit and former head of the MGH HIV/AIDS clinic
- Rajesh Gandhi, new head of the HIV/AIDS clinic.

Walker laid final credit at the feet of Martin Hirsch, who had godfathered the HIV/AIDS effort at MGH from the beginning: "It all goes back to Marty. Marty

A lab technician at the HIV Pathogenesis Program in Durban, South Africa, founded by Bruce Walker and Philip Goulder.

was the one who had the vision. In the beginning, quite frankly, the hospital didn't want to have an AIDS program because they were afraid it would drive the patients away. Marty insisted."

In 2010 Hirsch's mentor, Mort Swartz, had a tiny one-man office tucked in a corner of Bulfinch, still a contributor well into his eighties. Like Hirsch, Swartz could take pride in what the Infectious Diseases Division has accomplished at Mass General.

DERMATOLOGY FROM SYPHILOLOGY TO MOLECULARLY TARGETED THERAPIES

The grandfather of dermatology at Massachusetts General Hospital was James C. White, a native of Belfast, Maine, and America's first academic dermatologist. In 1863 he was appointed Harvard Medical School's first professor of dermatology. In the early 1870s White led a dermatological inpatient service at the hospital. The "skin ward" was met with intense opposition from hospital surgeons, led by the senior surgeon Henry Jacob Bigelow, who, as we saw in chapter 2, did not believe in specialization. In 1872, after the surgeons protested twice, the trustees heeded their complaint and voted to close the skin ward.

Mass General had no inpatient dermatology service until after White's retirement in 1902, when a private donor funded the creation of a new ward in honor of White's career. The ward, which opened in October 1903, had 22 beds, 18 of which were for skin patients. James White's son, Charles James White, complained in the *New England Journal of Medicine* that "all these long years the progress of Boston dermatology had been forced to suffer by the willfulness and short-sightedness of certain selfish men."[91] The surgeons' concerns about a dermatology inpatient service were not entirely unwarranted: the mean duration of a dermatology inpatient stay in 1906 was 32 days. Most dermatology inpatients were treated for conditions that would now be treated in an outpatient setting.

Part of the controversy surrounding the establishment of an inpatient dermatology clinic at the hospital was the stigma associated with syphilis, a common disease among the dermatology patients of the day. Although the hospital's first patient had syphilis, the MGH trustees voted in 1839 to refuse admission to syphilitics unless their situation was urgent *and* they paid twice the normal rate of board. This restriction was dropped in 1900, but distaste for the disease must have remained.

In 1906 the attending Dermatology Ward physicians were Charles White and John Templeton Bowen, a Bostonian who began

James C. White.

work as a physician at MGH in 1889 and was appointed the first Wigglesworth professor of dermatology at Harvard Medical School in 1907. Bowen, who described "precancerous dermatosis" in 1912, now called Bowen's disease, had a scholarly and introverted nature that sharply contrasted with Charles White's extroverted personality. Bowen never married, became a recluse later in life, and died at the age of 84 in December 1940. Both Bowen and White served as president of the American Dermatological Association in the later years of their careers.

In these early years, dermatology treatment consisted mostly of washes, baths, powders, lotions, pastes, ointments, soaps, and oils. Topical treatments were used as astringents, keratolytics, emollients, antiseptics, and antipruritics. Dermatologists also prescribed systemic drugs, including Fowler's solution (potassium arsenite) for psoriasis and mercury injections for syphilis. Radiotherapy was used to treat lupus vulgaris. X-ray therapy was used, and sometimes overused; Walter Dodd (see chapter 3) would understand. Light therapy was administered to patients with eczema, psoriasis, and Raynaud's disease. In dermatological surgery, curettage (the use of a curette to scrape or scoop tissue) usually sufficed, but lesions were sometimes excised.

Dermatology in the Modern Era

Several distinguished dermatologists headed the service between James White's retirement in 1911 and what might be viewed as the beginning of the modern era, when Thomas B. Fitzpatrick assumed leadership in 1959. These were:

1911–1913	John T. Bowen
1913–1925	Charles J. White and Harvey P. Towle
1925–1929	Charles J. White
1929–1935	E. Lawrence Oliver
1935–1948	C. Guy Lane
1948–1958	Chester N. Frazier
1958–1959	Maurice Tolman (acting)

A graduate of the Harvard Medical School, a PhD in pathology from the University of Minnesota, a fellow in chemistry at Oxford, and a resident in clinical dermatology at Minnesota's Mayo Clinic, Thomas B. Fitzpatrick became chairman of dermatology at the University of Oregon at the young age of 32. Seven years later, in 1959, Fitzpatrick moved east to head the MGH service, where he served for 28 years. Fitzpatrick himself recalled: "In 1959 the Rockefeller Foundation agreed to provide funds for five years in a second attempt to build a department. [The previous chief, Chester North Frazier, hired in 1948, had come with a 10-year grant from the foundation.] Furthermore, it was a fortuitous time for the enlargement of research facilities because the NIH had awarded a dermatology training grant which provided stipends for trainees and staff from 1960 onwards. The grant enabled the department to find and train a large number of investigators between 1959 and 1980."[92]

During his tenure Fitzpatrick trained dozens of academic dermatologists, 12 of whom went on to become chairs of departments. Howard Baden, a leader in hair diseases and the genetics of skin disease who celebrated his 50th anniversary at

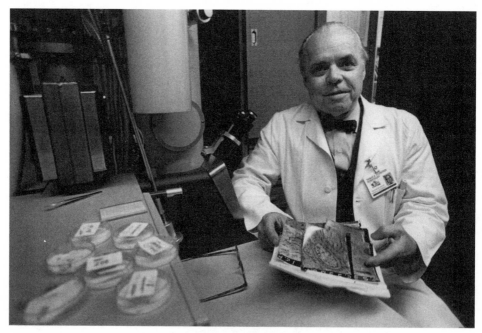

Thomas Fitzpatrick.

MGH in 2009, was Fitzpatrick's first resident. In 1971 Fitzpatrick led the effort to publish the first comprehensive multi-author dermatology textbook, *Dermatology in General Medicine,* of which a seventh edition was published in 2007, four years after Fitzpatrick's death. Today the Dermatology Department at MGH trains 16 to 18 residents annually, as well as fellows in dermatology, dermatopathology, lasers, photobiology, Mohs micrographic surgery, and basic and clinical research.

In addition to his significant contributions to teaching, Fitzpatrick dramatically improved the quality of dermatology research. His own work focused on the biology of melanin. Irvin Blank, a pioneer in understanding water content in the dead outer layer of the skin (and the father of the skin moisturizer), and Walter Lever, a leader in blistering diseases of the skin and author of an earlier dermatology textbook, were two significant figures in dermatology already working at MGH when Fitzpatrick arrived. Fitzpatrick consolidated research in a laboratory on the fifth floor of the Warren Building. Projects included the barrier function of the skin, keratinocyte biology, melanocytes and melanoma, and photochemistry. The group's work in the pathology of the skin increased when Fitzpatrick brought in Wallace Clark, a dermatopathologist. Martin Mihm, a senior pathologist and an expert on pigmented lesions, lymphoma, and cutaneous inflammatory diseases, carried on the tradition of cutting-edge dermatopathology at MGH.

No More Inpatients

John Parrish was a resident training in internal medicine at the University of Michigan, married with two children, when he was drafted into the military. It was the late 1960s, the Vietnam War was not going well, and battlefield doctors were desperately needed. After just two weeks of basic training in the U.S. Marine Corps, Parrish was sent to the front lines in Vietnam, where he treated 20 to 30 casualties a day for the next year—"totally immersed in the cost of war," as he recalled. During the Tet Offensive of January–February 1968, the hospital where he worked was taken over by the Viet Cong and Parrish narrowly escaped. Others were not so lucky; nurses were executed, and the North Vietnamese chopped off the hands of a barber who had worked with Americans.

Once discharged, Parrish came to MGH to practice and do research in dermatology in 1969. Admittedly, Parrish said, dermatology does not usually involve life-saving procedures, as his wartime work had, "but the problems can ruin a life and almost always can be treated. So dermatology is rewarding, if not necessarily heroic, like cancer surgery." Parrish served in the department for more than 30 years and for his last 20 as chairman of the department, following Fitzpatrick's retirement in 1987. In his time on the Dermatology Service, Parrish noted two major developments: an end to inpatient care for dermatology patients and the development of a whole new form a treatment, in the form of ultraviolet light and lasers. The two developments are related.

When Parrish arrived at MGH, the service had about 20 inpatient beds assigned to it for patients with disabling skin diseases who would be hospitalized for up to four weeks at a time. Treatments often involved wrapping diseased skin with cloths soaked in ointments. Parrish's primary research beginning in the 1970s focused on ultraviolet light. Early in his tenure, Fitzpatrick had begun with Madhu A. Pathak to study a disease, vitiligo, known for millennia in Egypt and India. According to Fitzpatrick, "A traditional treatment in North Africa and Asia had been the use of psoralens, a naturally occurring group of plant photosensitizers, in combination with exposure to the sun." With Parrish and Lewis Tanenbaum,

John Parrish.

Fitzpatrick and Pathak "began using psoralens and long-wave ultraviolet light (UVA) as a therapy for intractable cases of psoriasis."[93]

Parrish eventually took over this research, developing the use of PUVA (psoralen plus UVA) therapy. When PUVA treatment was introduced into the clinic, it proved so effective against skin disease that patients who would previously have been inpatients could be treated in an outpatient setting. By 1980 the Dermatology Service no longer needed inpatient beds, and today it offers exclusively outpatient care. Patients who require hospitalization are treated under the Medical Department or in the Burns Unit. PUVA therapy is now widely used to treat psoriasis, eczema, vitiligo, and mycosis fungoides.

Research in Parrish's lab soon also included lasers and their effect on skin. Translational research on lasers led to innovative therapies for skin lesions, abnormal skin coloration, hair removal, and blood vessel removal. Parrish's Wellman Laboratory grew to include other departments that use lasers in therapy, including surgery, OB/GYN, and ophthalmology. Now the Wellman Center for Photomedicine is the world's largest multidisciplinary research center for the effects of laser on tissue. The Wellman is directed by R. Rox Anderson, a Harvard professor of dermatology and a leader in photothermal and photochemical skin treatments and in vivo optical diagnostics.

Another research development with clinical implications began under Parrish's departmental leadership: the Cutaneous Biology Research Center (CBRC), a basic science research center focused on skin treatments, which came into being thanks to major funding from Shiseido, a Japanese cosmetics company, in 1989. When the grant was received, Parrish recruited Jerry Gross, emeritus professor of medicine, to work on oncology in the deeper skin, while Howard Baden investigated the more superficial skin. The CBRC is now located in the Charlestown Navy Yard, where it functions as a basic science research center and the Dermatology Department's strongest link with both industry and academia. Pigment, skin cancer, melanoma, and basic research in the immunology of skin diseases are its primary areas of investigation. Its mission is to enhance the understanding of fundamental biological processes that underlie the formation and homeostasis of the skin and its appendages.

The Molecular Era

David E. Fisher, who succeeded John Parrish as chief of dermatology in 2008, began his career at MGH as an intern and resident in internal medicine in 1985–1988. He subsequently trained in both adult and pediatric oncology at the Dana-Farber Cancer Institute and Children's Hospital, followed by postdoctoral research training with the Nobel laureate Phillip Sharp at MIT. He served on the clinical and research faculty at Dana-Farber and Children's for 15 years, during which time he became known as a leading expert in melanocyte and melanoma molecular biology. He made seminal discoveries regarding the MITF transcription factor, which is a master regulator of melanocyte development, skin pigmentation, and the survival of melanoma cells. He also delineated the pathway through which ultraviolet (UV) radiation triggers skin pigmentation (in tanning).

Recruited to MGH at the end of 2007, Fisher now directs the CBRC. In that position he has overseen a transition from a research unit dominated by support from Shiseido to one in which all investigators hold independent funding from the NIH. Fisher also directs the multidisciplinary Melanoma Program at the MGH Cancer Center, which includes dermatologists, dermatopathologists, medical oncologists, radiation oncologists, and surgical oncologists. One key component of the MGH Melanoma

David Fisher.

Program is the Melanoma and Pigmented Lesion Center, a clinical service of the MGH Dermatology Department that was begun under Fitzpatrick and operates as a large referral center for patients from MGH and around the world who come to have their lesions classified. Arthur Sober, a leading expert in melanoma and pigmented lesions, served for many years as the director of the Pigmented Lesion Center, which is now run by Hensin Tsao, an authority on the genetics of melanoma. The Dermatological Surgery Unit focuses on treating skin cancers while leaving a maximum of healthy tissue. The unit uses the Mohs technique, a microscopically controlled surgical method that has proven highly effective against skin cancer.

Melanoma, of course, is a deadly cancer. During the Fisher era a number of major clinical breakthroughs have occurred, emanating from either his own research or that of his faculty. Most notable among these were the discoveries that therapies using kinase inhibitors (targeting mutated oncogenes) are capable of producing predictable and dramatic remissions in patients with metastatic melanoma if their tumors harbor a mutation in the drug-targeted oncogene. These discoveries are expected to lead to a new standard of care for advanced melanoma patients; they have largely transformed advanced melanoma from a disease of enormous clinical frustration to a poster child of molecularly based clinical progress.

CHAPTER 6

. . . .

MUCH ADO ABOUT SURGERY,
1961–1981

*In 1965, with the advent of Medicare, a new era dawned for
me and my colleagues. It was one in which the socioeconomic
features of medicine became more and more prominent and
adaptation was necessary. It was characterized by frequent
change rather than by stability. . . . New directives appeared
with increasing frequency, statutes were changed, and
disciplinary bodies became more active.*

—Claude E. Welch, A Twentieth-Century Surgeon

A S THE 1960S BEGAN, *General Director Dean Clark faced health issues
that would lead to his resignation, Chief of Medicine Walter Bauer was
dying from emphysema, and Chief of Surgery Edward Churchill was
slowing down. As one generation of leadership was leaving the scene, a dynamic
35-year-old, John Knowles, took over as general director in 1962.*

*Lauded by many for his energy, criticized by some for his ambition, Knowles
restructured the hospital's administration, improved its public relations arm, and
spearheaded advancements in outpatient care, including, most important, the
establishment of community clinics. He also oversaw the opening of the Gray
Building, with the adjacent Jackson and Bigelow towers.*

*Concurrently, under Paul Russell and then W. Gerald Austen, Churchill's
successors, surgeon-scientists made strides in transplantation, in cardiac surgery,
and in other emerging specialties. In a controversial decision, hospital trustees
twice squashed efforts to branch into heart transplantation, deeming the procedure
too risky and expensive; the decision would finally be reversed in the mid-1980s.*

*As computers began to take over clerical work, and as Medicare and Medic-
aid transformed the financial landscape of medical care, Knowles used MGH as
a bully pulpit for speaking out on national health issues; he left in 1972 to head
up the Rockefeller Foundation and was succeeded by Charles Addison Sanders,
another forceful leader. Although the consensus-building Sanders employed a
less flashy management style, he successfully guided MGH through the inflation
of the 1970s and into a game-changing deal with a German chemical giant.*

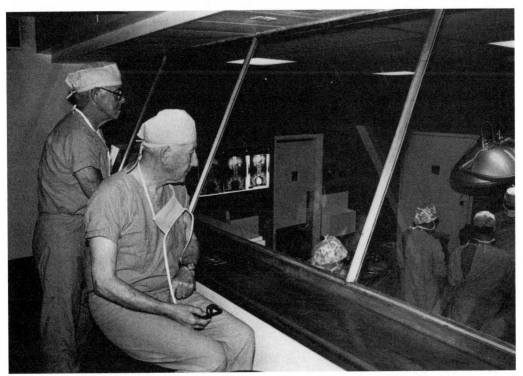

Senior surgeons Marshall Bartlett (left) and Claude Welch observe an operation.

With a focus on the Surgical Service as it developed under Russell and gained additional prominence under Austen, this chapter looks at Russell's field of specialization (transplantation) and Austen's (cardiac surgery), as well as two surgical services that stand apart organizationally: oral and maxillofacial surgery, and urology.

TO HEAR VETERANS TELL IT, Massachusetts General Hospital had a collective crisis of confidence at the beginning of the 1960s. The general director, Dean Clark, had health problems that were common knowledge, and his visionary goals, developed previously in a public health setting, had proven ahead of their time. Clark formally resigned on September 29, 1960, and Ellsworth T. Neumann was named acting administrator, while John H. Knowles, head of the small Pulmonary Medical Unit, was appointed director for medical affairs.[1]

John Stoeckle remarked that Clark's premature departure was "sad. I liked him very much, and he and I got along very well. But he didn't accomplish what he came here for." Despite the good work and intentions of Neumann, an able administrator during this period of transition, the hospital staff worried about everything from possible cuts in research support to the fate of their jobs.

Mass General had long been run largely by its chiefs of service, however; so the vacancy in the general director's chair might have been a minor matter. But in surgery and medicine, two additional voids were opening. Chief of Surgery Edward Churchill was no longer operating and was probably holding back the

Ellsworth Neumann.

service by insisting on training generalists at a time when specialization was called for. The equally revered Walter Bauer was ending his days in severe pulmonary distress, thanks partly to a smoking habit that, in those days, before the warnings of the U.S. surgeon general, was widespread.

Bauer's long illness was noted in the Medical Service report for 1963: "Overshadowing everything, and casting a pall over every activity of the Medical Service, was the prolonged and serious illness of Dr. Walter Bauer, . . . suffering from crippling pulmonary emphysema."[2] Admitted in June 1962, transferred to a hospital in New York, then returned finally to Phillips House, Bauer died on December 2, 1963.

The official MGH history of the period recalled additional difficulties: "Superficially the MGH continued to function so that patients did not notice anything amiss, thanks largely to the attentions of Ellsworth Neumann, who kept the administrative machinery in motion. But the staff worried about shifts in priorities, research programs that had received support from the old regime failing to find favor with the new, and the fate of clinical projects and jobs. Uncertainty generated gossip, vague rumors, and general unease until even the maintenance crew felt demoralized."[3]

A NEW GENERATION OF LEADERSHIP

The city surrounding the hospital, however, had plenty of reason to cheer. Massachusetts' native son John F. Kennedy was elected president in November 1960 and sworn in the following January. Among his first official acts was a televised observance of Massachusetts General Hospital's 150th anniversary, aired on January 31, 1961.[4] Kennedy had been a member of the MGH Corporation since 1947.[5] America had its new generation of youthful leadership. Would Mass General follow suit?

The hospital had seen significant growth in the decade just completed. The expense budget had increased from $7.8 million to $17.2 million, while research nearly quadrupled, from $1.4 million to $5.2 million. The growth of research was also measured by the percentage of square footage allotted to it: 4.9 percent in 1950, more than 15 percent by 1960. Major buildings had gone up: the Edwards Research Building had been followed by Bartlett and Warren. But medicine was entering its boldest era, and bolder leadership would be needed.

The poster boy for *bold* at MGH in the 1960s proved to be the hospital's recently appointed director of medical affairs, John Knowles. He was formally appointed general director on February 16, 1962,[6] and the annual report would remember the year 1962 as a transitional one, in which uncertainty was replaced by "buoyant optimism."[7] Knowles drove a dark blue Mercedes coupe bearing a low-number vanity license plate (28), which was usually seen parked beside the emergency entrance to the hospital.

The symbol of a newly dawning technological age was the computer; the ever-bold Knowles oversaw the first in-house use of computers by Mass General. In 1963 the National Institute of General Medical Sciences contracted with MGH and the firm of Bolt, Beranek, and Newman to develop "the first prototype of a Hospital Computer System."[8] Seminars were held for staff members to explain the possible uses of computer technology.

More innovative leadership would emerge in the 1960s. In medicine a string of fine chief residents brought in by Bauer in the 1950s would become the unit leaders of the 1960s. After a transitional period in which Robert Ebert was named chief of medicine, only to leave for Harvard Medical School, where he was hired as dean a year later, Alexander Leaf would emerge as a quiet but effective chief of medicine, serving for 15 years. The surgical side also saw a transition from the transplantation specialist Paul Russell, who replaced Churchill, to W. Gerald "Jerry" Austen, first a leader in heart surgery, then Russell's successor as chief of the Surgical Service in 1969.

John Knowles was already two steps ahead of Dean Clark when he assumed the general director's chair in 1962: he was a practicing physician, not a public health official, and he was "one of us." This phrase, heard often in the corridors of Mass General, meant not *Harvard-trained*, but instead *veteran of the house staff* (a former MGH intern). Paul Russell, who began as a surgical intern in 1948, explained the culture in which this criterion of membership was important: "After World War II, it was a close-knit operation, and the house staff was the core of it. The house staff was here all the time. They were devoted very much to the institution. There was a feeling of being in the trenches together. I was part of a group

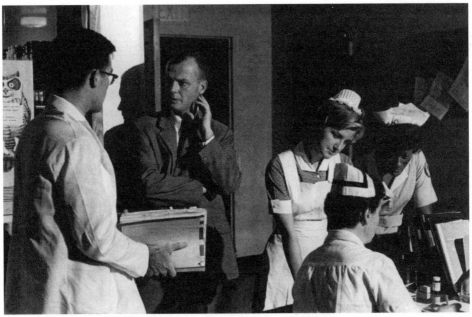

John Knowles surrounded by hospital staff.

of six people who were surgical interns, and we supported each other, and worked very closely together."[9]

"Here all the time" is not an exaggeration. The house officers lived on campus (being married was frowned on), and during this period there were no limits set on the number of hours a house officer could work. "We were all Stakhanovites!" Russell said, and proud of it. This sense of solidarity, this criterion of being "one of us," would continue to weigh in the respective abilities of leaders to gain institutional confidence. It will come up again in this history.

John Knowles was born in Chicago in 1926; his family eventually settled in Belmont, Massachusetts. He graduated from Harvard College, where he was roommates with the actor Jack Lemmon. Knowles was not accepted at Harvard Medical School, however, so instead he attended medical school at Washington University in St. Louis, graduating at the top of his class. He arrived at MGH as an intern in 1951, the same year Walter Bauer succeeded Howard Means as chief of medicine. Climbing the ladder quickly and, by all accounts, aggressively, Knowles progressed from assistant resident to resident to chief resident by 1958. In 1959 he became chief of the small Pulmonary Unit, then director of medical affairs two years later. In 1962, at 35, he was made general director of Massachusetts General Hospital. Along the way, he met his bride-to-be, Edith Morris LaCroix, a lab technician, over a stomach pump in the Emergency Ward.

The official MGH history noted that Knowles was chosen because of the prevailing malaise: "The trustees' selection of Knowles was a deliberate response to this domestic crisis. They perceived a need for a home-grown product who knew the hospital intimately and was already known by the staff. Knowles had demonstrated administrative acumen—not to say eagerness—and was immensely popular. Whereas Clark had come from public health administration, Knowles was a hospital-based practicing physician."[10]

While still a resident, Knowles had been heard to tell his mates that, although they might be content with being doctors at MGH, he had higher aspirations.

One observer said that Knowles wanted to be president of the United States, not an absurd conjecture, given the way Knowles later would project himself onto the national scene. Katherine Walker "Kay" Boling began her MGH career in the endocrine lab, but in 1969 she became administrative assistant to the general director. Later, as Kay Bander, she was promoted to director of staff services. She described Knowles as "very positive, self-confident, some would say brash. People were quite ready for his energy and vibrancy. Whatever Dr. Clark was like, it seemed he was lacking in these qualities, lacking in leadership capacity toward the end of his career."

Charles Sanders added these adjectives

Kay Boling Bander.

when describing his predecessor: charismatic, profane, feisty, controversial. Sanders recalled a trustee, John Lawrence, telling him after Knowles had left the hospital, "When I got a call Saturday morning, I knew John had done something, had got himself into trouble." According to Sanders, another trustee characterized Knowles as "high risk, high gain."

Claude Welch was both admirer and detractor, characterizing Knowles's arrival as "the next major move in the modernization of the MGH," yet simultaneously describing him as brash and egocentric.[11] Robert Ebert, who served as chief of medicine under Knowles, was all positive, writing that Knowles

> was truly a remarkable administrator of a large and complex institution. . . .
> He was into everything and knew everyone from the janitors to the professors.
> But he was not simply a gadfly. He had a burning need to know everything he
> possibly could about the institution he had been called to lead, and, remember, he was the youngest general director ever chosen to head the MGH. John
> had succeeded a brilliant but erratic man as general director, and the hospital
> was in substantial disarray when he took over. Patiently he rebuilt not only
> the physical plant and the administration, but also the spirit of the place. He
> was a marvelously cohesive force.[12]

Holly Smith, who was Knowles's chief resident in 1956 and later served as chief of endocrine under him for a couple of years, offered this broad outline of the Knowles persona: "I liked him, everybody did. He had a good sense of humor, was very political, smart, charming. I always considered him a friend. He moved in country club circles, had big ambitions, good public speaker, charming. He carried out a survey to see how many people in Massachusetts knew him, thinking of running for U.S. senator. I'd say as a scholar he was not deep, but he had breadth and charm and good sense."

On balance, Knowles's accomplishments and reputation during a decade-long tenure were far more positive than negative. Those who wrote the history of the period noted that "he guided the institution through a complicated phase of growth and change," and MGH benefited from this. "Knowles was undeniably one of those rare creatures: a true leader of men."[13]

One of Knowles's signature achievements was to broaden the base of power within the hospital beyond the old triumvirate of general director–chief of medicine–chief of surgery, in which the general director was usually least powerful of the three. The chiefs controlled the agenda, while the general director acted as secretary of the General Executive Committee (GEC), taking notes. In 1966 the GEC was expanded from a small, 10-person group to a larger one in which each clinical service, as well as the Departments of Nursing and Social Service, was represented.[14] The general director's secretary (Kay Bander after 1969), rather than the general director, kept the minutes. Charles Sanders would recall: "It meant he controlled the minutes. It was really inspired the way he did it. He or she who writes the minutes does have power. John Knowles understood how to wield power."

The profile of Knowles in the official history of the era, coauthored by his widow, confessed, "It is true that during his tenure power gravitated towards the

Martin Bander.

office of the general director. . . . Knowles was an ambitious man who liked to control."[15] When Charles Sanders took over as general director in 1972, the enlarged GEC allowed him "to expand communication links throughout the institution," according to Bander. "He brought other people along, with a view to involving people. If you involve people in decision making, that was acceptable. [Sanders] reenergized the spirit of cooperation while not losing the benefit of competition."

"The actual result [of Knowles's restructuring of the GEC] was a far more open and democratic structure," according to Leon Eisenberg, former chief of psychiatry. "In the past, those who had been excluded felt paranoid about what was happening behind closed doors."[16]

To knit together a growing organization, Knowles needed clear, effective communications. This led to the hiring in 1968 of the award-winning *Boston Herald-Traveler* science writer Martin Bander to improve the hospital newsletter, *MGH News*, and to enhance relations, internal and public. Bander had served in the U.S. Army as an editor of its periodical *Stars and Stripes* before moving to the *Herald-Traveler*. In 1969 Bander launched a publication for staff called the *Hotline*, published regularly ever since. In 1974 Bander added media relations to his responsibilities, and he became the first and last stop for members of the press seeking information from or about MGH. "A serious and relentless pursuer of the truth,"[17] he was intellectually fascinated by the intricate relationship between medicine and the press, and he published two articles in the *New England Journal of Medicine* about physicians, science, and the news media.[18]

At the hospital Bander came into daily contact with Kay Boling, administrative assistant to Knowles and Sanders. According to her, "Dr. Knowles informed Martin that he should investigate me for nonprofessional reasons." The investigations were conclusive. At this writing, Kay Bander continues to be an important contributor to the MGH community—most recently as a volunteer on the Ladies Visiting Committee. Speaking proudly of her husband's contributions to the hospital, she said:

> Martin was an expert science writer and an unusual person to bring in to head public affairs because he was a journalist first and foremost, and he never lost that edge, but that edge is also what gained him a great deal of respect. In today's political environment, that probably wouldn't play as well, but he was highly respected by both trustees and general directors. Some of the service chiefs would just as soon not have encountered him because he didn't do their bidding. The researchers always wanted publicity, and he would say, "It's not ready yet. There's not enough data." He could understand and translate medical science.

Martin Bander succumbed to a long illness in January 2009. The hospital's president, Peter Slavin, eulogized him, citing both his expertise and his intense loyalty to the institution: "Martin's dedication to his hospital was legendary. He loved the place, tackling his job each day with boundless interest, deep curiosity and great tenacity. He relished being part of the energy and vitality of the MGH. . . . He sought perspectives from people who were walking down hallways, working in labs or dining in the cafeteria. He made it his business to know what was going on."[19]

THE GRAY BUILDING

Hospital leaders are often remembered for construction projects. The most visible effort of the Knowles era was the Gray Building and the adjacent Jackson and Bigelow towers. High occupancy rates were straining the capacity of the hospital in the late 1950s and early 1960s, making the creation of more space a top priority. The new complex would provide centralized operating rooms for the entire hospital; for years, surgery had been dispersed inefficiently over three locations: Phillips House, Baker Memorial, and the White Building. The Gray also would provide postsurgical care units, research laboratories, medical wards, and other facilities. The old Domestic Building (1901) was demolished in the summer of 1965 to make way, and the purpose of the Bulfinch Building changed significantly for the first time in the hospital's history.

Hospital leaders met at John Knowles's house in Brookline in the spring of 1965. Kneeling, from left: David Weisberger, William Sweet, Howard Ulfelder, Thomas Fitzpatrick, Raymond Adams, Sidney Rabb, Paul Russell, John Knowles, Francis O. Schmitt, and Francis Hatch. Standing, from left: Henry Meadow, Francis H. Burr, Benjamin Castleman, Robert Ebert, John Lawrence, Phillips Ketchum, George Berry, Francis Gray, Henry Guild, Ralph Lowell, Henry Knowles Beecher, Laurence Robbins, Edward Bigelow, Ellsworth T. Neumann, George Phillips, Nathan Talbot, Thornton Brown, and Erich Lindemann (courtesy Paul Russell).

During planning and construction the new structure was known simply as the North Building, as it was on the north side of the campus. The 1964 annual report projected its total cost at $12 million.[20] When bids were opened in December 1965, it was learned that "costs would be considerably higher than expected."[21] By 1967, with the total at $22 million, the hospital found itself forced to borrow for the first time in more than 130 years. The First National Bank of Boston made a significant loan, and the hospital sold its accounts receivable, as well.[22] Finishing the building would eventually require another first-time financing strategy, issuance of long-term bonds backed by the Massachusetts Health and Education Facilities Authority (HEFA).

Expectations for the new building were as high as its costs. Chief of Surgery Paul Russell's report for 1964 noted that the OR suite in the new complex would be "the largest single operating room area in the world, to our knowledge, and will be fully equipped for the most complicated new surgical operations now foreseeable."[23] Planning for this suite was a complicated business pursued with devotion by F. Thomas Gephart and Oliver Cope, at Russell's request. The trustee report for 1966 trumpeted North as "our largest building and, indeed, we believe the largest hospital building ever built in New England."[24] The location of the new complex, abutting White, Baker, and, Bulfinch, would permit centralized admitting and surgery, while bringing many new labs into the mix.

In 1968 the principal structure of the North Building was renamed the Gray Building when a generous donor, Reginald Gray, father of a trustee, Francis C. Gray, left about $2 million to MGH. The labs on floors 6–13 were named for Dr. James Jackson, first chief of medicine.[25] The adjacent tower of the new building would not be named until 1976, as apparently the hospital was waiting for a significant donor to step forward. Finally, the tower was named for a leading family in MGH history, the Bigelows. Three generations— Jacob Bigelow, his son Henry Jacob Bigelow, and his grandson William Sturgis Bigelow—had served through most of the nineteenth century.[26]

The scale of the Gray-Jackson-Bigelow complex was a bet on the future of MGH; when it opened in 1968, the top nine floors were still unfinished. The east wing would increase MGH research space from 110,000 to 160,000 square feet, including lab space for the following units: renal (Alexander Leaf), gastroenterological (Kurt Isselbacher), arthritis and connective tissue (Stephen M. Krane and Jerome Gross), bone chemistry (Melvin Glimcher), physical chemistry (Roger W. Jeanloz), and biochemistry (Herman M. Kalckar and Paul C. Zamecnik).

As floors of the new building opened, featuring the private and semiprivate rooms that were the way of the future, the old Bulfinch wards were abandoned; the final ward patients left Bulfinch in 1977. (Select services, including psychiatry, continued to see patients in Bulfinch after the wards were dispensed with.) By this time the Medical Service had formally moved semiprivate facilities onto Bigelow 6–9.[27] Eighty-seven beds were moved and distributed over three times the floor space previously allotted in Bulfinch. The move "was not accomplished without a few tears and ruptured sentimental ties," according to Alexander Leaf, "but it really was time for a change." It all confirmed Mass General's "efforts to bring patient care up to one single high standard of care"[28]—and marked the end of an era, 156 years after the first patient was admitted to Bulfinch.

Another key building project falling at the end of the Knowles years was the Cox Cancer Center, named for William C. Cox. In 1965 Paul Russell and Paul Zamecnik headed an ad hoc oncology planning committee to map out future cancer facilities and programs. This led to the opening of the Cox Center in 1971, a development that will be detailed in chapter 7.

EXPANDING THE DEFINITION OF COMMUNITY

In the 1960s Massachusetts General Hospital began to see itself as part of a larger world. By 2011 that self-definition would encompass the entire globe. Chartered to serve the poor of Boston and staffed by volunteers for its first century, the hospital was in the process of becoming a big business, where the practitioners were well compensated for their services. Who needed to look beyond the comfortable confines of Fruit and Blossom streets? But social trends were pushing outward.

In the aftermath of World War II, America's population poured out of cities into suburbia. Leadership of Mass General was aware of this trend, while its own city campus was severely constrained by real estate limits. At times a major Boston developer, Jerome Rappaport, seemed to represent a one-man chain-link fence around Mass General's property, as he led the crusade to raze and then redevelop Boston's West End, beginning in 1956. The thought of spreading its wings, however, did not come easily to MGH. Consider this note in the annual report for 1961: "A trial balloon was floated at the autumn dinner of the MGH Corporation proposing that a pilot study in the form of an experiment be undertaken which would extend MGH standards into some segment of suburbia. It met with a cool reception in some quarters."[29]

That attitude began to change under John Knowles. As Kay Bander recalled, expanding into the surrounding community was not only the right thing to do, it was the only thing to do if MGH was going to continue to grow: "I think there was a sense that outreach was going to be necessary to keep the patient flow for the inpatient side of the institution, and it was an expectation of the communities that they would not always have to come to Boston for their care. Other medical schools were beginning to look more at community medicine, and there was some concern that if you didn't enlarge your catchment area, you wouldn't be able to maintain and grow your patient population."

Following a news-making airplane crash at Logan International Airport on October 4, 1960, the hospital agreed to open a small clinic at the airport. The terms were favorable; the airport provided the clinic space. On January 3, 1963, the Logan International Airport Medical Station of the Massachusetts General Hospital, a cooperative venture with the Massachusetts Port Authority, opened to patients with Kenneth T. Bird as director.[30] Within a few years, the clinic was seeing about 100 patients a day.[31] It moved into the control tower at Logan on April 1, 1970. Nurses were central to the clinic's operation; physician coverage was limited to five hours per weekday, 8–11 A.M. and 4–6 P.M., high-traffic hours.

This was the first use of telemedicine, a technique widely used now to allow a physician to consult on a patient's care from any distance. A TV room on the first floor of the White Building linked MGH physicians with the Logan clinic.

President John Kennedy was assassinated on November 22, 1963, and his vice president, Lyndon Johnson, assumed office. With the mandate of a landslide 1964 victory over Senator Barry Goldwater, Johnson began to roll out the pieces of his Great Society program. One goal of this costly vision was an ongoing "war on poverty," which included delivering health services to the poor. Grants became available from the U.S. Office of Economic Opportunity to help promote an expansion of community health services.

Concurrently with this national initiative came a local one: the 1965 Sackett Plan of the Boston Department of Health and Hospitals (named for Commissioner Andrew Sackett). Boston hospitals, including MGH, were advised that they would be considered responsible for expanding health services in designated areas. For Mass General, these were the West End, Beacon Hill, the North End, Charlestown, East Boston, Chelsea, and Revere. The hospital already effectively served Beacon Hill (the carriage trade filling Phillips House), as well as the West End (outpatient and ward patients, mostly). In the years ahead, it would expand its reach to each of the other communities assigned to it by the Sackett Plan.[32]

Another major impetus was the Social Security Act of 1965, which mandated Medicare (federal health coverage for the elderly) and Medicaid (coverage for the impoverished). John Knowles, attuned to the national picture, would recognize this as "a social and economic revolution which in this century can only be equated in importance and significance to the Social Security Act itself of 1935."[33] Lawrence "Larry" Martin, comptroller since 1951, worked overtime to figure out the ramifications of Medicare and Medicaid.

Lawrence "Larry" Martin.

Martin liked to say that he had graduated from Boston University twice, once with a BS in business administration in 1943 and again, after the war, with an MBA in 1947. He began his career as a cost estimator at the venerable Boston book publisher Houghton Mifflin, where his last project was costing Winston Churchill's *The Gathering Storm.* "I knew I could do better somewhere else," said Martin, and answering a blind ad in the classifieds, he signed on as a cost accountant at MGH in 1949.[34] Assigned to develop a cost-accounting system for the hospital, his first memorable job was measuring each room on campus with a tape measure. Martin was promoted to comptroller in 1951, associate director in 1961, and associate general director in 1974. He would not retire until the end of September 1989, by which time he was senior vice president of the hospital, and he did not fully retire from part-time duties until five years later. Along the way, he also played Santa Claus for five years at holiday parties for employees' children. Larry Martin was a central thread in the fabric of MGH for nearly 45 years and remained a loyal spokesperson in 2011.

In 1966 the trustees reported that "the Hospital began to exhibit all the pressures and frustrations that inevitably occupy initial efforts towards bureaucratic implementation of a massive Federal program." The report cited strain on facilities, finances, and personnel. "Our Accounting Department has coped manfully and effectively with the mountain of paper work and Mr. Martin has been of great assistance to the government in the establishment of workable procedures."[35]

Years later, Larry Martin would say, "The most frustrating change [during my career at the hospital] is the interference by the third-party payers and the federal and state governments." There were massive accounting and compliance headaches.

As the cost accountant for a leading academic medical center, Martin was called to Washington by the Social Security Administration to help implement Medicare. While there, he had the idea of developing a per diem rate, one all-inclusive Medicare formula for reimbursing hospitals. Said Martin: "We really got bounced around when it came to measuring laboratory tests, X-rays, and ancillaries that go along with patient care. You can't take a stopwatch and measure how much time it takes to do each individual laboratory test. You're dealing with averages . . . , and that is when I came up with the idea of the per diem rate."[36]

With the help of a government grant Martin began to test the concept at three hospitals in Denver, Colorado. Unfortunately, the government did not implement Martin's idea. "It failed essentially because people thought they were paying for things they didn't get. They wouldn't deal with averages. . . . So my grand idea went up in smoke."[37]

Federal regulations were not the only burden, as Martin recalled:

> The state had a law passed, Chapter 176a, which was adopted in 1952. It stipulated that hospitals must adopt uniform accounting and cost analysis under the direction of the Department of Public Health. This further created what is known as the Division of Hospital Cost and Finances. . . . It was very difficult to set your own rates to try to break even on a budgetary basis. A further expansion of state authority came when they established the Rate Setting Commission, which actually set the rates for the hospital. This, we felt, was an interference with the hospital prerogatives. They didn't set rates for the private patient. They set rates for the welfare patients. The rates for welfare patients to this date aren't adequate.[38]

There were still more intrusions into hospital affairs in the 1960s. A new Heart Disease, Cancer, and Stroke Law encouraged planning among medical schools, teaching hospitals, and government agencies. New federal funds were mandated to train health professionals. The Hill-Burton Act was extended to help build more hospitals, as well.

MGH's Social Service Department, led by Eleanor Clark, was forced to grow to accommodate rising patient counts and referrals into community-based care programs. The elderly and those on limited incomes could finally address their

Eleanor Clark.

health concerns, and they did. But meanwhile, Medicaid patients appeared with a multitude of health issues, including substance abuse, depression, unwanted pregnancies, and other problems. This all put additional pressure on MGH's social services.[39] The trustees reported for 1967, "Of the more than 12,000 patients served by social workers this year, an increasing number present themselves to the hospital with social difficulties so complicated that these issues present more hazardous conditions than the medical problem which admits them to our system of care. . . . Obstacles in the community are great. The social systems of the community are so hampered by bureaucratic burdens that delays in obtaining services are common and often involve weeks."[40]

To help deal with the increased numbers of elderly turning to MGH for help, the department devised the Family Care Program. Elders without families who were not candidates for nursing homes could live with a host family. Client and family were reimbursed by Medicaid.[41] The program continues at this writing.

Despite the administrative and accounting headaches, Medicare was initially a financial boon to the hospital industry because reported costs were fully reimbursed. This led to a swelling of hospital and professional fees; and Medicare caused price pressures for another reason. Because both the elderly and the indigent were covered by federal insurance, everyone could afford hospital care. This meant higher occupancy rates, capacity constraints, and demand-driven price increases.

Given the Sackett Plan, Medicare, and Medicaid, an expansion of MGH services into underserved, low-income communities made compelling sense at this point. So though Dean Clark can be credited with envisioning community health centers run by MGH and the John Knowles administration began building them, these developments were heavily driven by external influences.[42] Knowles recognized community health as a drum worth beating. In his 1967 report he wrote that hospitals, while traditionally considered "health centers," in fact had a more limited function as "citadels of acute curative, scientific, and technical medicine."[43] Knowles said that medicine would have to "develop a holistic concept of a community's health, if it is to prevent disease and maintain health and thereby enhance the quality of life, to say nothing of the national welfare. . . . It is the intention of the MGH to develop such a holistic plan."[44]

In 1965 the Committee on Community Programs was created to form a comprehensive community health plan for the 16,000 residents of Charlestown, across the Charles River. A community health center in Charlestown was, Knowles continued, "a most important new functional departure of the M.G.H."[45]

In his report for 1968, Knowles carried the theme of community health forward: "In the not-too-distant future, we will see similar extensions to the sub-urbs where the middle and upper income people live."[46] Knowles did not live to see Mass General expand its reach to such communities as Danvers, where the Mass General / North Shore Center for Outpatient Care opened in the summer of 2009.

Charlestown, Chelsea, and Revere

The Bunker Hill Health Center in Charlestown opened in 1968 with John Connelly as its "passionately committed director."[47] He would be replaced by Andrew D. Guthrie Jr. in 1973. Established in an old school building leased from the city, the center offered "first-line caretaking in teams of pediatricians, internists, nurses, nutritionists, dentists, mental health and social workers." Two teams became operational in late 1969, offering "family-centered, continuous, comprehensive, unfragmented and coordinated care." The center was open 365 days a year.[48]

John Stoeckle noted: "These were the first salaried docs at the Mass General doing [work in clinics], not looking in test tubes—a group of salaried pediatricians and internists who worked in the community [while they] had privileges at a downtown teaching hospital. So we [shed] the identity of MGH as an elite downtown practice and gained more identity as a community-centered practice. . . . That was a big step in the identity of the hospital internally, and on a public level too."[49]

Bunker Hill Health Center.

Stoeckle analyzed some of the other forces that caused the shift: "Things aren't done just out of pure goodness. The idea was that Medicare and Medicaid had come in, taking patients who typically had been ward patients into private channels. The ward patients were being admitted by the private service. So the ward was decreasing in numbers. This was a way to keep capturing the referrals."[50]

In March 1972 Daniel D. Federman, acting chief of medical services, presented a plan for a similar center in Chelsea, to serve that city as well as Everett, Revere, and Winthrop, all low-to-middle-income communities immediately north of Boston. The trustees reported that Eleanor Clark, "our nationally recognized Director of Social Service, . . . has consented to take an additional responsibility as Administrative Director of the Chelsea Health Center."[51] The Chelsea Health Center began in the basement of the Horace Mann Baptist Church but moved in 1973 into the former nurses' residence at the Chelsea Memorial Hospital. Subsequently, Chelsea Hospital trustees asked MGH to take over Chelsea Memorial Hospital in its entirety. MGH agreed to convert the Chelsea facility into an ambulatory care center while also maintaining 24-hour emergency service and a 10-bed inpatient unit. The facility was renamed the Chelsea Memorial Health Care Center of MGH.[52]

In February 1981 MGH opened another community health center by assuming responsibility for the Revere Health Center (RHC), set up in 1973 on the initiative of the Revere city government, the Permanent Charities Foundation, and the community. Roger Sweet, medical director of the MGH Neighborhood Health Care Groups, said, "The RHC is not as yet a high-volume operation. We are currently projecting 15,000 visits annually, compared to 60,000 at Chelsea and 55,000 at Bunker Hill. But the project will grow."[53] It did so. Only a year later the RHC purchased condominium space in the Revere Post Office building at 500 Broadway. The 4,200 square feet of floor space tripled the size of the old clinic. The new quarters opened in 1984, with staff that included internal medicine, pediatrics, obstetrics, gynecology, podiatry, nutrition, and social service. The Revere center saw about 14,000 patients a year in the 1980s.

Within 15 years of the opening of the first community clinic, Charlestown, Chelsea, and Revere accounted for roughly 30 percent of all patient visits to MGH-owned facilities.[54] Those served included a high percentage of lower-income immigrant groups who would not have had easy access to MGH-quality care without this move beyond Fruit Street.

In time the community health centers became fully integrated into the educative mission of MGH. In 1973 a new medical residency track was implemented in which medical training was based on 50 percent experience in the clinics and 50 percent at the hospital—"a major departure from the standard medical residency that was almost exclusively hospital-centered," according to John Stoeckle. "For the first time in MGH history, ambulatory training was integrated with a staff practice. The primary care program, which became a model for other institutions, emphasized the learning of skills and techniques important for general medicine and developed a tradition of rounds on ambulatory patients as a major teaching exercise."[55]

When, in 1994, the Massachusetts attorney general's office established new guidelines mandating that hospitals take responsibility for the care of underserved groups in their areas, Mass General was well positioned to respond. In fact, the hospital was already in the process of building magnificent new health centers in Chelsea and Revere. In response to the attorney general's guidelines, a new Community Benefit Program was established at the hospital, and Joan Quinlan was its first director and only staffer. (Renamed the Center for Community Health Improvement in 2007, the CCHI now has 50 staff members.) A Boston College graduate, Quinlan had worked as Governor Michael Dukakis's advisor for women's affairs until 1987. In 1990 she was hired as administrator for the Boston Health Care for the Homeless Program, a landmark effort headed up by James J. "Jim" O'Connell III (see chapter 8).

Quinlan began a process of assessing underserved community health needs, particularly in the three MGH health center communities of Charlestown, Chelsea, and Revere initially. What were the health problems that these communities were most concerned about? The answers—including substance abuse and domestic violence—fell outside the normal boundaries of "conditions" treated by academic medical centers like MGH. Quinlan acknowledged that there was at first some resistance to her program from certain quarters at MGH. "It was not entirely clear that this is what an academic medical center should be concerned with," she said. Richard Clarke Cabot, founder of the Social Service Department at MGH in 1905, would certainly have understood both Quinlan's initiatives and the institutional inertia that met them.

Fifteen years later, however, the CCHI has 35 programs, each of which involves partnership with community agencies. Quinlan calls the attitude changes at Mass General "exciting," noting that in 2007 the hospital's mission statement was formally changed to include "improving the health and well-being of the diverse communities we serve." Each of the 19 clinical departments was formally enjoined by President Peter Slavin to understand how it can contribute concretely to this mission. The hospital has made it clear that a patient visiting a community health center should have the same experience, beginning in the waiting room, as a patient on the main campus.

"Today [in 2011] you hear a great push for global health," Quinlan says (a push that will be documented in chapter 8). "But increasingly we understand that global health is local. Given the resettled immigrant communities that make up a large portion of our patient populations at the community centers, when you go to Chelsea, you might as well be going to another country."

A NEW CHIEF FOR SURGERY

In 1962 a 12-year-old boy and his severed arm were rushed into an MGH operating room. Trying to hop a freight train, Everett "Red" Knowles had been thrown against an abutment and his arm had come off at the shoulder. (The boy was unrelated to John Knowles.) A human arm had never before been replanted, but as the Cocoanut Grove fire had done 20 years before, Knowles's injury proved that in emergency medicine, readiness is all. Ronald A. Malt was the chief resident on duty the afternoon Knowles was brought in, and he is commonly credited with the

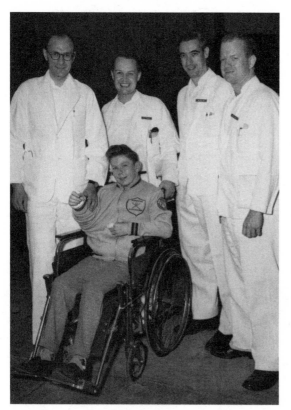

Everett "Red" Knowles's arm was replanted in 1962 by the team of (from left) Ronald Malt, John B. Herrmann, Lucian Leape, and John Lewis, all residents at the time.

miracle operation that reattached the boy's arm and all the internal connections, leading to a remarkable recovery. When Malt died in 2002, the lead line of his *New York Times* obituary called him "a Boston surgeon who made medical history 40 years ago when he oversaw the first successful reattachment of a human limb."[56] The results *were* historic: After therapy and several follow-up operations, Knowles could raise 50 or 60 pounds to waist level and work 88 hours a week as a mail clerk (one full-time job) and a security guard (another).

To read a contemporaneous account of the procedure in what was then America's leading news magazine, *Time*, is to realize, however, that "Malt's miracle" was really a team effort. If Knowles had been brought in the following night, another resident might have been on duty, yet the same basic team might have done the work. *Time*'s detailed report of June 8, 1962, credited all of the following:

- L. Henry Edmunds, the duty surgeon who "promptly spotted a chance for a historic operation"

- Malt, who "gave the go-ahead order that called in all the specialists who would make the operation a major team effort"

- John Herrmann, who "took the arm to the operating room [and] flushed out the whole artery-vein system with a special saline solution combined with antibiotics, an anticoagulant and a radiopaque dye. X rays promptly showed that the arterial tree was open all the way to the fingertips. Relieved, Dr. Herrmann picked up the arm, carried it carefully to the operating table on which Ev Knowles had just been wheeled in, all draped except for his torn and bloody shoulder."

- A "many-surgeon team, . . . specialists in blood-vessel repair"

- "M.G.H. Spokesman Dr. Robert Shaw."

In fact, as Paul Russell recalled for this history, Shaw, a brilliant vascular surgeon, led the surgical team that saved Knowles's arm and was "very generous" in allotting credit to Malt. "He backed him up," said Russell, "didn't take the patient into the private service, but spent all night with Ron Malt putting everything together. Bob Shaw should be very prominent in any account of this event."

The historic operation took place one month before Paul Russell replaced Edward Churchill as chief of surgery, an event that marked a change in emphasis at MGH, from the general to the specific. To his last years, Churchill held fast to the generalist approach, especially in training surgeons, but all the while a new generation of surgical specialists was emerging at MGH—people like Shaw, with expertise in vascular surgery, and Russell, the hospital's pioneering leader on the bold frontier of organ transplantation. Gastrointestinal, thoracic, plastic, cardiac, endocrine, and other specialties joined vascular surgery as nodes of interest within the general surgical service. As we saw in chapter 4, burn surgery was another emerging discipline of importance,

Robert Shaw.

under John Burke. Outside the general service were those specialties that, for a complex of reasons, arose independently, such as orthopedic surgery (see chapter 2), gynecology and neurosurgery (see chapter 7), and oral-maxillofacial surgery and urology (later in this chapter).

Veteran leaders of the general service included Oliver Cope, Claude Welch, Marshall Bartlett, and Robert Linton, but none of these ranked above associate professor at Harvard Medical School, as Churchill apparently believed that there should be only one full professor, himself. Churchill made an exception only for Henry K. Beecher, head of anesthesia, whose career he had promoted since the 1930s (see chapter 2). But a young star rose in the midst of these veterans, Paul S. Russell, and another specialty began to emerge, transplantation. After Russell became chief of surgery in July 1962, he saw to it that Cope, Welch, Bartlett, and Linton received the academic promotions that Churchill had long withheld.

A Chicago native and a graduate of Groton School, one of New England's old-line prep schools, Russell returned to the Midwest for undergraduate education and medical training at the University of Chicago. There he studied with the urologist Charles Huggins, who went on to win a Nobel Prize in 1966. Russell decided to go into surgery and arrived at MGH in 1948 as a surgical intern:

> We revered the people we worked for. There were some marvelous people here with strong principles. They watched us pretty closely, and we wanted their approval. We wanted to be like them. For me, Richard Sweet was very important as a technician. He was a beautiful operator, and an elegant person. The way he operated was something that influenced all of us. When I got a little approval from him, I felt very good. Dr. Churchill was also very important to all of us. He was in charge of the surgical training program and of the department. He was a somewhat austere person. He had had military experience, and I think he gloried in that. I respected him a lot.[57]

The Surgical Service, as Russell found it, was divided in three locations: Phillips House for the carriage trade, Baker Memorial for middle-income patients, and four floors in the White Building apportioned to the "East" and "West" ward services, a throwback to the day when charity patients were housed in the east and west wings of Bulfinch.

Although clinical activities were central to his life as an intern, Russell began hungering for a research career, and one night in Treadwell Library he made his find:

> I started reading papers on a wide range of subjects to get some notion of what were current subjects of interest to others. I came across a paper in a journal called *Nature*, which described what was termed "immunological tolerance" to transplanted tissue in mice. This work originated from University College in London by a team of three people in a department of zoology. I had never heard of any of them or indeed, of University College itself. The senior member was a man called Professor Peter Medawar. I thought, What a fascinating finding! Normally when one transfers living tissue from one person to another, or one animal to another when the subjects are genetically dissimilar, the grafted tissue doesn't survive. It lives for perhaps 10 days. But Medawar's group had found that if an intended recipient had encountered cells from a donor as an embryo or a fetus or in the neonatal period, its response is turned upside down. Instead of rejecting that tissue, it will then accept the tissue from that donor, not any other.

From such discoveries careers are born, and Russell's was now. *Immunological tolerance* is central to the success of transplant surgery, where the constant danger is host rejection of the transplanted organ. Russell could not see this at the time, as human organ transplantation lay in the future.

Although it took some doing (he was the first American to be accepted),

Paul Russell.

the year 1954–1955 found Russell at Medawar's lab in London. In 1955 he returned to MGH as chief resident in surgery, doing thoracic and general surgery. Two years later he and Hermes Grillo scrounged up lab space over a storeroom in the Huntington Laboratory and a grant from the NIH, and began work in endocrine transplantation, a subject Russell had explored with Medawar. Said Russell, "There was reason to believe endocrine cells might survive transplantation more easily than other tissues, and I set out to investigate this."[58] Ruben F. Gittes, a medical student, became a major contributor. Together they learned how to transplant parathyroid glands from one rat to another. The pace of discovery would continue to race forward: a dozen years later, the South African surgeon Christiaan Barnard would make world news by transplanting a human heart.

Russell's career took a geographic detour in 1960. The chief of surgery at Columbia Presbyterian Hospital in New York City, George Humphreys, came to Boston and offered him a tenured position there. The family moved to New Jersey, and Russell expected that he had reached his career's final destination. He continued to study immunological tolerance and rejection, following a fascinating question: Why are babies not "rejected" by their mothers' bodies? "We're genetically dissimilar from our mothers," Russell said, "yet somehow the placenta, which is closely applied to the uterine wall in a similar way to a transplant, is not rejected. We found that the placenta in the mouse had special immunological qualities."

Then, again, a detour: "To my surprise, in 1962 people came to visit from Harvard and asked me all about what I was doing. I was first invited to come for a visit and then was interviewed by the selection committee, chaired by Francis Moore of the Peter Bent Brigham Hospital, that was looking for a successor to Churchill as chief of surgery. I was only 37, and very inexperienced in the ways of the world. I wasn't particularly ambitious to be head of a department and was truly absorbed in what I was doing. But I was given a remarkable opportunity."

In July 1962, just two years after moving his family to the New York area, Russell succeeded Churchill and plunged into the "piles of administrative work" such a position demands. His connection with Harvard Medical School became far more extensive, and in the mid-1960s, when Harvard was looking for someone to replace Dean George Berry, Russell's name came up again. Clearly, he was highly regarded throughout the Harvard system. "Nathan Pusey, president of Harvard, liked to pick young people. I thought about this invitation for a week or so, and finally decided that I was reluctant to change my life that much at my young age. By that time, we were on a whole new path of research, which I thought was terribly interesting. So, I decided not to become dean."

Instead, Harvard selected the MGH chief of medicine, Robert Ebert, whose contributions will come up again later in this chapter. Russell continued in his double role as chief of surgery and de facto chief of transplantation. By this time, the first effective immunosuppressive drug had been developed by the Burroughs-Wellcome Company, and in 1963 Russell began clinical trials of kidney transplantation in humans.

Through the rest of the 1960s, Russell and his colleagues at MGH developed kidney transplantation in tandem with the hospital's first hemodialysis program. John Knowles wrote with his customary flair that MGH was "well-prepared to move into the new era of reconstructive surgery (the 'spare-parts' era) and the surgery of transplantation," but the MGH Board of Trustees wasn't so sure.[59] It took a long time to move beyond kidneys. Heart transplantation would run into institutional reluctance in 1975 and again in 1980, and not until the decade of the 1980s would transplantation reestablish itself as a strength at MGH. That would require a new generation of leadership.

MEANWHILE IN MEDICINE

Robert H. Ebert, former chief of medicine at Western Reserve, was named chief of medicine and Jackson professor effective January 1, 1964, although he was formally on leave until July 1. Another double graduate of the University of Chicago (BS, MD), Ebert was a Marine Corps medic during World War II and entered the Japanese city of Nagasaki shortly after the atomic bomb was dropped to treat survivors of the American attack. He taught at Chicago before moving to Western Reserve, now Case Western Reserve, in Cleveland. His *New York Times* obituary in 1996 picked up the story: "[In] Cleveland, he helped overhaul the curriculum of American medical schools. Under the changes, first-year students were required to see sick patients in addition to their theoretical training, and case studies were introduced into what had been more abstract instruction."[60]

After his hiring by MGH and Harvard in 1964, Ebert had a memorable first encounter with General Director John Knowles:

> I had made arrangements for a laboratory to suit my needs, and, believing everything had been settled, I was startled and more than a little angered to receive a letter from John saying the arrangements we had made were too expensive. He suggested that I write him saying how my needs might be scaled down. Impulsively, I wrote back suggesting that instead of negotiating, I would stay in Cleveland, where I had a good job and an excellent lab. By return mail, I received a letter from John saying, "Spoken like a true MGH tiger," and, of course, I could have the lab we had originally planned.[61]

Ebert lasted just a year before moving to Harvard Medical School as dean, but his short tenure at MGH is remembered for the start-up of the hospital's first computer science lab, under G. Octo Barnett.[62] Ebert also assumed interim chiefship of the Pulmonary Unit, vacated by John Knowles when he became general director. In 1965 he would turn over the position to K. Frank Austen, who yielded to Homayoun Kazemi in 1967, when Austen was recruited by the Robert Breck Brigham Hospital, later folded into Brigham and Women's Hospital.

Robert Ebert.

At Harvard, after 1965, Ebert's leadership skills would guide the medical school through a turbulent time. He sided with students in peace rallies against the Vietnam War; simultaneously, he courted industry sponsorship of research, even though this drew the ire of many of the same students and colleagues who joined him in opposition to the war. In 1969 he founded the first academic health-maintenance organization, the Harvard Community Health Plan, precursor of today's HMOs.

Upon Ebert's departure for Harvard Medical School, Alfred Kranes was named interim chief of medicine, pending the appointment of a permanent chief and new Jackson professor. The man selected, Alexander Leaf, chief of the Renal Unit, was mild-mannered to a fault, but he had a streak of adventurousness that may have been traceable to his father, Aron Lifschitz. Born near Odessa, Russia, and trained as a dentist, Lifschitz deserted the demoralized czarist army in World War I, jumped the Trans-Siberian Railway to Vladi-

Alexander Leaf.

vostok, found his way to Japan, and then joined a traveling opera company as a stagehand to reach Seattle. He tried to return to Russia when the revolution broke out there, but he made it only as far as Japan, where he met Leaf's mother, Dora, also a dentist. After more adventures, and Leaf's birth in Yokohama in 1920, the family finally settled in the United States, where his father trained at the Columbia College of Physicians and Surgeons and became a doctor in Seattle.[63]

Alex Leaf attended the University of Washington and entered medical school at the University of Michigan in 1940, then began an internship at Mass General in January 1944. He would recall the liveried doorman for Phillips House making a distinct impression.[64] He took his residency at the Mayo Clinic, then served in the military after the end of the war. A research fellowship at Michigan narrowed his focus to nephrology. A second fellowship brought him back to MGH and under the influence of Fuller Albright (see chapter 3). The following year Chief of Medicine Howard Means asked Leaf to set up the first renal lab at MGH. Leaf began with four rat cages on the fifth floor of the Domestic Building. A Howard Hughes Fellowship followed in 1953, and in 1954–1955 he studied ion transport in Copenhagen and Oxford.

Charles Sanders said, "Alex Leaf was the ultimate result of the post–World War II effort to build biomedical research capability at MGH and across the country, and he was promoted throughout his career based on his intellectual capacity and research accomplishments."

Leaf used toad bladders as a model system for his studies. It was not clear to everyone why this qualified him to serve as chief of cardiovascular research; maybe he was another counterintuitive appointment by Walter Bauer, made in 1955. Leaf admitted: "I had difficulty convincing the Howard Hughes Foundation administrators that ion transport across the toad bladder had any relevance to human biology or disease." Still, he published copiously, and in 1962 Bauer, near the end of his era, made Leaf his second tenured appointment at Harvard Medical School. Roger Jeanloz had been the first. By the time Leaf became Jackson professor in 1966, there was a third, Paul Zamecnik.

By 1981, when Leaf stepped down from heading the department, there were 13 full professors in medicine at MGH. Specialization, which had been limited under Howard Means and accelerated somewhat under Bauer, came into full flower under Leaf. Leaf was also a strong proponent of neighborhood health centers, which began under John Knowles. But where W. Gerald Austen would succeed in gathering surgeons into a group practice in the 1970s, Leaf was frustrated in his attempts to do the same with the physicians. He lobbied Knowles and Sanders, but they were unsympathetic.[65] According to Leaf's memoir, Sanders said, "Well, [group practice] may be a good idea; but it depends on your charisma in selling this to your staff. Look what Dr. Austen has done in organizing the surgeons into a group practice."[66]

Sanders recalled: "Alex wanted a group practice, but he never practiced medicine, to speak of. So there was a fundamental lack of trust among the clinicians. There has always been a division between those who do research and those practicing medicine. Alex's appointment as chief of medicine emphasized that divide."

The chief of medicine approached the chief of surgery about cross-subsidization (since surgeons were significantly better paid than physicians), but he received only a token gesture of assistance from Austen.[67] The two men were as different as night and day. Sanders said, "Jerry is the ultimate people person, Alex the ultimate introvert." It is hard to read the record of this period without sensing mild friction between the reserved student of toad bladders and the assertive heart surgeon. That friction would heat up when the subject of heart transplantation came up in the 1970s.

But by then Leaf had visited Vilacabamba, Hunza, and Abkhazia. Troubled by the fact that as many as half the inpatient beds on the Medical Service were taken up by patients over 65, Leaf became intrigued with the problems of aging and, in particular, why in certain isolated populations people are known to live past 100 in remarkably good health. Leaf had already visited one such village, Vilacabamba in southern Ecuador, when, in 1971, while on sabbatical at Oxford, he was asked by the National Geographic Society to travel to the remote kingdom of Hunza, wedged into the Hindu Kush region bordered today by Pakistan, Afghanistan, Tajikistan, and China. A third trip took him to the Caucasus region of the Soviet Union and the district of Abkhazia. A story in *National Geographic* magazine in January 1973 about his findings, with photographs by John Launois, was, almost to Leaf's chagrin, the publication for which his career would be famous. His conclusions were not earth-shattering: when people *did* live extraordinarily long lives (reliable records in these places were usually nonexistent), several factors seemed to weigh: a largely vegetarian diet, an extremely active lifestyle, and a culture in which the elderly are highly respected and often ceremonially honored. Back at MGH, Leaf would make a more significant medical contribution, publishing widely on the health benefits of omega-3 fish oils.

John Potts, chief of endocrinology (see chapter 3), replaced Alexander Leaf as chief of medicine on May 1, 1981. Leaf took on new responsibilities in preventive and social medicine as the Ridley Watts professor of medicine.[68]

A HEART SURGEON TAKES OVER

As mentioned previously, an academic medical center is often referred to as a three-legged stool, supported by clinical care, research, and teaching. But for an academic who becomes an administrator while remaining a doctor, the stool becomes four-legged and sometimes requires a tough balancing act. That may suggest what happened to Paul Russell as the 1960s wore on. By all accounts, Russell was a genial clinician and inspiring teacher, and in the field of transplant surgery he belonged to the generation of pioneers. But to do all that and simultaneously to administer a department of surgery that needed to shake free of the constraints of the Churchill years, at a time when the medical landscape was shifting seismically, was very difficult.

Being a chief was becoming a far more complex task than it had been even 20 years before, when Churchill and Means (then Bauer) had ruled as a virtual duumvirate. By expanding the GEC, John Knowles had distributed power more broadly among the medical staff, while increasing research budgets, the ramification of specialties, and new administrative headaches from Medicare and Medicaid added complexity. These developments all made "chief" a full-time executive position, one that left little time for a doctor like Russell to work in his own field.

The trustees reported in their report for 1968 that Paul Russell had "expressed a desire to be relieved of his duties in charge of the Surgical Services," in order to focus his work on transplantation. Russell had just been chosen as president-elect of the Transplantation Society, and the move was "enthusiastically endorsed" by the trustees.[69] In 1973 Russell would also become chairman of the MGH Committee on Research (COR), predecessor to the Executive Committee on Research (ECOR) of today.[70] John Potts would be appointed to replace Russell as COR chairman in March 1976.[71]

There were mixed feelings about Paul Russell's stepping down, and not for Russell alone. Nicholas Thorndike, who became an MGH trustee in 1969, after the changeover, had come to appreciate Russell's humanity and professionalism. Thorndike noted that "Paul took it amazingly well when he had to step down from chief of surgery. Paul Russell is a prince." The trustee recalled a Thorndike family emergency: "I was in New York, and our youngest son came down with appendicitis back in Boston. At 3 A.M. the pediatrician decided it was appendicitis, and who did we call but Paul Russell? Paul arrived at our house in suit and tie to take my wife Joanie and the boy to the hospital. The operation took place at 4, and at 6 Joanie was going home. Paul said, 'I've got to stay here in the OR, but I'm going to see you to your car, because I don't trust that garage.'"

When Russell gave way to the veteran surgeon Oliver Cope as interim chief of surgery, MGH had only three full professors on its surgical staff: Russell, Cope, and W. Gerald "Jerry" Austen. How Austen became a full professor at age 36 and how he emerged as the logical candidate to replace Russell—which he would after the Cope interim—involves a perfect coincidence of the right man in the right field at the right time. Charles Sanders, who ran the cardiac catheterization lab during this period, said, "It was a confluence of technology and the dynamism of somebody like an Austen that made it happen. Let me be clear," Sanders went on. "I think Jerry Austen is the most important figure in the Mass General in the past 50 years. No question. He has done more to make it what it is than anybody else. Not only has he made things happen individually but he has stayed the course. He has always been there."

Heart Surgery since the War

In 1948 Gordon Myers and Gordon Scannell were charged with developing cardiac surgery at Mass General, and they were given an initial priority: the establishment of a cardiac catheterization laboratory. The lab, located in Radiology, studied pulmonary hypertension and congenital heart disease. By 1951 the first closed-heart mitral valve procedure was completed at MGH: with the heart beating and without cardiopulmonary bypass, the surgeon's finger was inserted into the left atrium through a purse-string and the narrowed mitral valve was enlarged by finger pressure. By 1955 there was another national first—the removal of an intra-atrial myxoma (noncancerous tumor) with the patient under total body hypothermia. From 1955 to 1962 there were several important advances in cardiac surgery that "allowed the hospital, in sailing terms," according to J. Gordon Scannell, "to maintain a 'safe leeward position' on the national scene."[72] Jerry Austen would interpret this to mean that MGH was a significant participant in cardiac surgery but not yet one of the leaders nationally.

Born and raised in Akron, Ohio, Austen received his BS degree in mechanical engineering from the Massachusetts Institute of Technology and his MD degree from Harvard Medical School. Going from MIT to the medical school across the river was something he was always proud of. "Almost nobody from MIT went into medical school at that time," he said. "I was the only one in my class of 1,000."

Austen came to MGH as a house officer in 1955. By the time he began his residencies in general surgery and cardiothoracic surgery, he was up to his elbows, already working with some of the surgical faculty. Even before he had put on his white house officer's coat, the surgeons J. Gordon Scannell and Robert Shaw had asked him to help them build a cardiopulmonary bypass machine that could take over the function of the heart and lungs while surgeons worked on the stopped heart—an unusual challenge and opportunity for an intern. Two years earlier the Philadelphia surgeon John Heysham Gibbon, who had begun his cardiac work as a research fellow at MGH, performed the first open-heart operation on an atrial septal defect by supporting his patient with a heart-lung machine built by IBM.[73] Austen recalled: "Other places around the country were beginning to think of open-heart surgery with cardiopulmonary bypass. But there was no gold standard, and the pioneers were developing their own machines."

On duty as a house officer every other night, Austen, together with Shaw, was creating a heart-lung machine on his nights off, working in the basement of the White Building and in the basement of Shaw's house. "We built one for a very modest price," said Austen, "paid for it ourselves. Nobody gave us any money. It seemed complicated to doctors, but not for an engineer—particularly when someone else had already done it!" They bought many of their parts at plumbing and building supply stores. When ready, the team began using what Austen himself called a

"Rube Goldberg" machine on dogs, again on Austen's nights off. John Burke assisted Scannell in surgery, while Austen and Shaw ran the bypass machine.

In 1956, without a single canine success—all the dogs died—Scannell and John Burke performed the first successful open-heart procedure with cardiopulmonary bypass at MGH, to correct an atrial septal defect.[74] Shaw and Austen ran the cardiopulmonary bypass machine. Austen admitted that such a fast track for such experimental surgery is unthinkable today. "All I remember is how scared I was that morning," he said. "We talked ourselves into believing that dogs were a special case." The human clinical trials were performed only on desperately ill patients who would have been dead in days or weeks without a radical intervention. And many died.

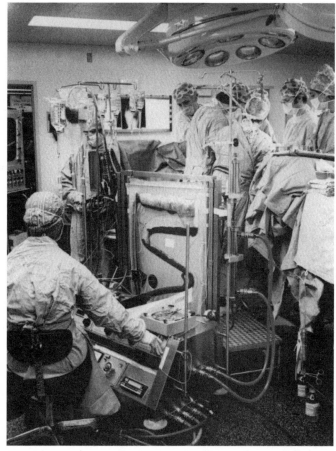

Jerry Austen (center rear) leads a team performing open heart surgery in 1976, using a heart-lung bypass machine (foreground) that he helped design.

But roughly half of the early patients lived. "We proved our machine worked," said Austen, "and it seemed a good direction to go if you had the intestinal fortitude for it."

One of many challenges for the team, as it evolved, was determining the right dosage of the blood-thinning drug, heparin, and the antidote, protamine. They worked by trial and error, which often led to postoperative bleeding that needed immediate attention. "In those days," said Austen, "we had no clue as to how much of either drug to give. We would set up an operating room immediately following surgery in case we needed to reexplore a patient who was bleeding postop. About half the time I would call Gordon Scannell in the evening of surgery and tell him we were losing a pint or two of blood an hour. With the patient still asleep from the first surgery, we would reopen the incision and cauterize the bleeding areas."

Two-thirds of the way through Austen's surgical residency, in 1959, Austen said, "Churchill, whom I loved dearly, offered me the opportunity to go to England, because he had been head of U.S. medical forces in the Mediterranean and had become friends with his English counterpart, who needed a resident for his service in London. He commented to his secretary, 'Austen may be the most con-servative and deliberate person I know.'"

Austen did go to England, doing general surgery at King's College Hospital in London, then heading to the General Infirmary in Leeds, where he did an enor-mous amount of cardiac surgery: "There was tremendous volume in England, with no one to do it. Leeds was a very important part of my experience; I did nothing but heart surgery, and there was a long waiting list of patients who needed help. By the time I got back I probably had done more mitral valve surgeries than Dr. Scannell, the senior heart surgeon at the MGH. I had a great experience." By the time he had finished his residency at home and abroad, Austen had published 15 original papers in peer-reviewed journals—without taking any formal time off to do research.

In those days the highly sought-after job of super-chief resident generally went to an individual who had completed five years of clinical training and two or more additional years of full-time research. Uniquely, Austen became super-chief resident upon his return from England, after a total of only four and a half years. Austen then spent two years doing clinical and research work at the National Heart Institute in Bethesda, Maryland, and in 1963, the newly appointed chief of surgery, Paul Russell, brought Austen back to MGH to concentrate on modern cardiac surgery.

By this time the cardiac surgical services operating room was seeing three open-heart surgeries a week, and cardiac surgery began to emerge as a vibrant spe-cialty at MGH. Said Austen: "We were very lucky here because when I came back in 1963, the other heart surgeons in town were getting older: Dwight Harkin at the Brigham was about 60; Bob Gross, a famous pediatric heart surgeon at Boston Children's Hospital, was in his late fifties. One of the reasons I came back instead of going other places was, I thought there was a real opportunity here, and that proved correct."

In 1964 the number of open-heart surgeries was 159. By 1970 that number had more than tripled. Austen proved adept at obtaining research funding, which fueled activities in the cardiovascular physiology research lab. A cooperative study between Austen and Mortimer Buckley for MGH and the engineering firm Avco led to the development of the intra-aortic balloon pump, "a form of circulatory support that was to achieve major significance in the next decade, the age of the coronary bypass."[75] It is still employed around the world in thousands of patients each year. In 1967, the year of the first heart transplant, the Argentine surgeon René Favaloro would perform the first coronary bypass.

In 1965 Austen was promoted from instructor to tenured associate professor of surgery at Harvard Medical School, bypassing assistant professorship entirely. One year later, after only three years on the HMS faculty, he was promoted to full professor at the age of just 36. Simultaneously, Paul Russell named Austen chief of cardiac surgery at MGH. In cardiac surgery, Austen recruited successfully (Mor-timer Buckley, Eldred Mundth, and Willard Daggett were his first three super-chiefs, all keepers). "They all joined me in cardiac surgery," said Austen. "We had by far the largest heart program in New England, and it wasn't just us. It was Roman DeSanctis and Charlie Sanders, and older cardiologists, terrific people. We were really aggressive," Austen said in 2009 with a glint in his eye. Caseloads grew.

When Austen was named president of the American Heart Association in 1977, it confirmed what everyone in Boston had known for a decade and further solidified Mass General's leadership position in the field of cardiac care. In fact, Austen eventually would become president of every major professional society related to his fields of interest.[76] He also would be elected a member of the Institute of Medicine of the National Academy of Sciences and a fellow of the

Cartoon of MGH cardiac surgery faculty, 1970, from left: W. Gerald Austen, Eldred D. Mundth, Mortimer J. Buckley, Willard M. Daggett (courtesy Willard M. Daggett).

American Academy of Arts and Sciences. Said Sanders: "We worked very hard. We became the go-to place. We really took good care of people, and followed up, taking care of people outside. Jerry was a very active publisher in the surgical world. I give Jerry full credit for putting the place on the map in cardiac surgery. He became a national figure quickly, at a very young age."

Austen Replaces Russell

So it was no surprise when Austen was named to succeed Russell as chief of surgery on April 1, 1969, although the cardiac surgeon was only 39. On June 6, 1974, he would become the first holder of the Churchill Chair in Surgery, named for his mentor.[77] Meanwhile, Austen made Buckley and Mundth coheads of cardiac surgery, and when Mundth left MGH to be chief of cardiothoracic surgery at Hahnemann University Hospital in Philadelphia, Buckley took sole charge. Buckley was an excellent surgeon and a demanding leader and mentor. Because of his competitive nature and intense demeanor, he earned a reputation for being difficult. Under his leadership, MGH cardiac surgery functioned at a high level of clinical excellence and was responsible for starting new programs at four other Boston-area hospitals. MGH cardiothoracic trainees went on to important leadership positions throughout the country in this new and exciting field.

Jerry Austen would prove to be one of the most durable and important forces in MGH history. Serving as chief for almost 29 years, he also would make his mark in philanthropy and in two major changes of the 1990s: the development of the Massachusetts General Physicians Organization (MGPO) and the creation of Partners HealthCare. Capping this string of achievements, in 1997 Austen would become the first trustee of MGH in modern times to be an MGH staff MD.

But those are stories for the next chapter. In surgery, Jerry Austen moved quickly to bring his service into the full-time world of group practice. In 1969 most of the faculty at MGH, including those in surgery, were in private practice. Austen felt that it was essential to create a full-time group practice in surgery: the intention was that everyone would join together in a common mission to create the best academic department of surgery possible. The mechanism of a group practice is that physicians assign their fees to the group and are then compensated with a salary in proportion to their contributions; some funds are held aside for research and education. This setup gives power to the chairman, with everyone's approval, to use a portion of fees to support the general purposes of the department.

A rudimentary surgical group practice, the Surgical Associates, had been formed in January 1961 by several veteran surgeons, including Marshall Bartlett and Claude Welch, but it was purely a voluntary affair, and most did not volunteer. This arrangement made group benefit programs possible for those participating, but it did not remove the old private-practice model, which continued to hold back surgery throughout the 1960s.[78] The economics of the academic medical center can be simplified as follows: if every surgeon (or physician) is operating as a private practitioner, billing and collecting from his own patients, where will the money for research, for education, and for recruiting new outstanding faculty

Senior faculty in the Department of Surgery, mid-1970s. Front row, from left: Earle Wilkins, Grant Rodkey, Jack Burke, Chair Jerry Austen, and Hardy Hendren. Middle row: Tom Green, Frank Ingersoll, George Nardi, Paul Russell, and John Raker. Back row: Frank Wheelock, Gordon Scannell, Ronald Malt, and Gordon (Butch) Donaldson. Missing (out of town or in the OR): Marshall Bartlett, Mortimer Buckley, Hermes Grillo, and Claude Welch.

come from? Furthermore, some surgical specialties are better compensated than others, which leads to imbalances. In the 1960s and 1970s heart surgeons were very well compensated, so Austen's move toward group practice became acceptable to the rank and file. No one took a bigger hit to his compensation than the star of heart surgery at one of the nation's leading heart surgery hospitals. That was the argument Austen made and won.

"I felt strongly that if you want to have a great department, you need to have everybody together," Austen said. "You need to pool funds. You need, to the best of your ability, to be fair to people and give them incentives—but there are going to be some areas that because of the vagaries of health insurance are going to bring in a lot more money per unit of work than others."

Said Russell, "Jerry was very smart about using new categories of appointment set up by the medical school, along with special emoluments like deferred compensation, to make the group practice a very strong vehicle. And that's what the entire MGPO would be based on years later."

Since joining a group practice was not the norm and was totally voluntary, Austen spent his first six or seven years as chief convincing established members of the department to join, while insisting that all new recruits of the department join, at least for a trial period. Eventually, all members of the department joined, with the exception of one veteran surgeon, Robert Linton, a vascular surgeon who soon retired. No one left the group once in it. The Surgical Associates was a success, and all future group practices at MGH have been modeled after it.

Austen determined that his next priority as chief of surgery was to accelerate the trend toward specialization that Churchill had resisted. Austen wrote in 1980, "The MGH General Surgical Services, to my way of thinking, had tremendous strengths, but there were some deficits, too. I felt that we had to find a way to develop emerging specialties of surgery such as cardiac, general thoracic, and plastic surgery as well as such areas as transplantation, vascular, and cancer surgery without jeopardizing the traditional strengths of general surgery."[79]

In an interview given in 2004, Austen enlarged on this:

> I felt that we ought to have people who got up every morning thinking about thoracic surgery, or thinking about cardiac surgery, or thinking about cancer surgery. They would be better surgeons if they did that and only that. They would be better teachers, and they would do better science because they would know everything about their field rather than knowing the broad field of surgery. I would say that was one of the important, strategic decisions that I made on the day that I took the job. So, over the course of a few years, we went from no divisions to 10, with a chief for each. That has basically continued ever since.[80]

Specialization probably would have come with or without Austen, but not as forcibly. The body of knowledge across surgery was just too vast for any generalist to cover, techniques and technologies were becoming far too sophisticated, and certification boards and third-party payers all but demanded a higher degree of specialized care. Churchill had not wanted it; Russell had not pushed it; Austen insisted on it.

By 1980, when the last official history of the hospital was compiled, the following surgical specialties (and chiefs) were in place:

- thoracic surgery (Hermes C. Grillo)
- cardiac surgery (Mortimer J. Buckley)
- plastic surgery (John P. Remensnyder)
- pediatric surgery (W. Hardy Hendren)
- vascular surgery (William M. Abbott)
- burns and trauma (John F. Burke)
- general and gastrointestinal surgery (Ronald A. Malt)
- endocrine surgery (Chiu-an Wang)
- cancer surgery (William C. Wood and Alfred M. Cohen)
- transplantation (Paul S. Russell)

Hermes Grillo.

Making this major organizational change pleased some, particularly those who were made chiefs of their specialties. But there were others who were not pleased, particularly older general surgeons who saw specialties like gastrointestinal and cancer surgery as poaching on their domain. Further, there were three specialties in which a senior surgeon was passed over for a younger, more active practitioner and investigator. As he had with the surgical group practice, Austen showed remarkable diplomacy in carrying out the reorganization.

Thirty years later, as this book was being prepared for press, the organization chart of the Department of Surgery, under its chief, Andrew Warshaw, listed the following clinical chiefs:

- cardiac surgery (Douglas J. Mathisen)
- thoracic surgery (Douglas J. Mathisen)
- plastic and reconstructive surgery (William G. Austen Jr.)
- pediatric surgery (Joseph Vacanti)
- vascular and endovascular surgery (Richard Cambria)
- burns (Ronald Tompkins)
- general/GI surgery (David Rattner)
- surgical oncology (Kenneth Tanabe)
- transplantation (James Markmann)
- trauma, emergency surgery, and surgical critical care (George Velmahos)

In addition, several physician-investigators headed their own surgical research units, including:

- Knight Surgical Lab (Hasan Alam)
- Center for Laryngeal Surgery and Voice Rehabilitation (Steven M. Zeitels)
- Codman Center for Clinical Effectiveness in Surgery (Matthew Hutter)
- transplantation biology (David H. Sachs)

Detailing accomplishments in each of these specialties is too broad a task for this history. Instead, we will look at two surgical services that have for years been separate services at MGH: oral-maxillofacial surgery and urology.

ORAL AND MAXILLOFACIAL SURGERY

The Department of Oral and Maxillofacial Surgery is a mouthful, but it's a name worth committing to memory. This department at MGH is the finest in the country, by almost any measure or standard. Leonard Kaban didn't gloat when a writer visited his office, but he could have. In 2009 the department chief occupied the corner office on the top floor of the Warren Building, and the best corner at that, with a view of the Charles River, the Museum of Science, Fenway Park, and, on the Fourth of July, Boston's biggest fireworks display.

Kaban noted that dentistry and oral surgery have been performed at Mass General since its earliest days. As we saw in chapter 2, the use of ether for general anesthesia was first demonstrated at MGH by William Morton, a Boston dentist, during a neck and jaw operation. The first Harvard Dental School building opened in 1869 on Grove Street, across Cambridge Street from the hospital campus.

The MGH Outpatient Department added a dental service in 1868, and in 1872 Charles Wilson was appointed to the newly created office of "dentist."[81] At Wilson's request, this title was changed to "dental surgeon." The dental clinic soon served a growing number of patients, free of charge except for the cost of gold foil filling material. After 1883 the clinic was moved to the building recently vacated when the medical school moved to Boylston Street in the Back Bay. Both schools relocated to Longwood Avenue in 1909, and the dental clinic at MGH moved to the Out-Patient Building, built in 1903 on Fruit Street. The old medical school–dental school building was razed.[82]

In 1911 Leroy M. S. Miner was listed by the hospital as dental surgeon. When Miner and his associates opened the clinic to general dental cases, they were soon overwhelmed, and a decision was made that "the work of the Dental Department of the Hospital [be] restricted to the relief of pain, and extractions and surgical treatment." In 1932 clinic service was expanded from three days a week to five.[83] Four years later Miner made the cover of *Time* magazine as president of the American Dental Association.[84]

The career of Kurt H. Thoma, appointed chief in 1942, illustrates the close connection between anesthesiology and dentistry at MGH. Born in Basel, Switzerland, Thoma graduated from Harvard School of Dental Medicine in 1911 and subsequently taught anatomy, histology, anesthesia, oral surgery, and oral pathology there. A 1959 article in the *Journal of the American Dental Society of Anesthesiology* noted that Thoma was "rarely regarded as a contributor to anesthesiology because he has become so well known in the fields of oral surgery and oral pathology; but he wrote one of the first texts in the field and contributed many articles to the early anesthesia literature in dentistry."[85] Thoma's text *Oral Anaesthesia*, published in 1914, had a second edition in 1920.[86] Thoma also wrote the most widely used oral surgery textbook and was editor in chief of the most prominent oral surgery journal of the time: *Oral Surgery, Oral Medicine, Oral Pathology*. The section in the journal called "Case Records of the Massachusetts General Hospital" paralleled the Case Records in the *New England Journal of Medicine* instituted by Richard C. Cabot.

Thoma was succeeded by David Weisberger, who served until his death in 1966

from a ruptured thoracic aneurysm.
A professor of oral medicine, Weisberger changed the name of the service to the Department of Dental
Medicine, placing less emphasis on
surgery and more on the oral manifestations of systemic disease and
the effects of oral disease on the rest
of the body. "His interest in precancerous and cancerous oral lesions
and his work on salivary gland
function and radiation therapy was
reflected in his involvement in the
Tumor Clinic."[87] Weisberger established a two-year residency program
with three residents per year, or six
at a time.

Kurt Thoma.

Walter C. Guralnick replaced
Weisberger as acting chief in 1966
and was selected as permanent chief
in 1967. A native Bostonian and
the son of a Boston pediatrician, Guralnick graduated from Boston Latin School,
the University of Massachusetts at Amherst (then known as Massachusetts State
College), and Harvard School of Dental Medicine, earning his DMD in 1941. He
served his residency in oral surgery at Boston City Hospital, then went into military service in 1942, originally assigned to an air base in North Carolina, then to
the Seventh General Hospital, affiliated with Boston City Hospital, stationed in
England, France, and Belgium.

After the war Guralnick settled into private practice in his own office on Bay
State Road in Boston. When the oral surgeon Harold Kent died at a young age,
Guralnick took over his practice at 29 Commonwealth Avenue. In 1951 he joined
the staff at MGH. While serving under Weisberger, Guralnick followed Weisberger's thematic research into salivary function. But once he took over as chief,
Guralnick was so busy he had to turn research over to others and encourage them
in their own investigative pursuits.

Like Thoma, Guralnick never pursued an MD degree, but he appreciated the
added dimension that this education and general surgical training would provide
for oral surgeons. According to Kaban, Guralnick was "really the father of oral-
maxillofacial surgery as we know it today." Notably, he changed the department's
name back to Oral Surgery, then to Oral and Maxillofacial Surgery (OMFS) in
1979. He has been involved in the training of more than 100 residents at MGH
and influenced countless Harvard Dental School students who trained elsewhere
to become oral surgeons.

To read Guralnick's own write-up in the official MGH history of the period,
you would think that his success was due primarily to coincidence. It begins by
saying that "Guralnick's tenure coincided with an overall national growth in the

field of oral surgery."[88] This makes his success seem a matter of good timing alone. Kaban said that it was also a matter of vision: "Walter Guralnick maintained that OMF surgeons should take their place alongside all other surgical specialists."

The contribution Guralnick is most noted for, according to Kaban, is the formal establishment of dual-degree training for oral surgeons. Guralnick believed that for OMF surgeons to become full members of the surgical community, they had to have the same medical training as other surgeons, including an MD degree *and* a general surgery background. Said Guralnick: "I had long been convinced of a deficit in the education of oral surgeons—both in medical knowledge and in general surgical training. I always felt all surgeons should have that general training. My brother was a general surgeon and my father a physician, so I had the advantage of learning a lot of from them and other contacts in the medical community. Of course, this was not as good as formal education."

The board certifying OMF surgeons required only a DMD and a three-year "hospital-based program." No MD was required. Under the Guralnick plan, an oral-maxillofacial surgeon became one of the most highly trained professionals on the hospital campus. The dual degree program involved five years for Harvard dental students and six for non-Harvard students, who had not had the benefit of attending the first two years of Harvard Medical School. These non-Harvard students, then, had to invest 10 years, including the four years previously spent on earning a DMD elsewhere. Said Kaban: "That was very controversial in 1970, because the national oral surgery infrastructure was very much against it. Many OMF surgeons didn't like it; it was threatening." Guralnick added: "People in my own specialty thought they were being demeaned and would not have the same

Walter Guralnick with an administrative assistant, Melody Hess.

privileges as our people had. I didn't have an MD and it made no difference to *my* stature! That controversy eventually died down to a good extent."

Today nearly half of all major programs and more than half of all oral surgery trainees follow such a plan. Why only half? One reason is that not all oral and maxillofacial surgery programs are university-affiliated and therefore do not have access to a sister medical school with which to collaborate. In addition, Guralnick explained: "If you get down to the nitty-gritty of economics, when people get through dental school and find they can be periodontists or the like and make a very comfortable living, they often do it. The five- or six-year program is a big investment. Some of our people have $250,000 in debts when they're done with all their training."

Guralnick's second innovation was to move oral surgery at MGH to a full-time faculty model. Most American oral surgery programs at the time had no full-time faculty, but were staffed by part-time professionals who came out of private practice one or two days a week. At some personal sacrifice Guralnick made a commitment to close his private practice and move it on campus. The facility opened with the Wang Ambulatory Care Center in 1982. But even before 1982, Guralnick pushed his oral surgeons to a full-time model, encouraging all of them to join, as he did, the surgical group practice that Chief of Surgery Jerry Austen was setting up. These changes enhanced the stature of OMFS within the hospital, as did Guralnick's participation on the General Executive Committee when John Knowles expanded its membership. In fact, Guralnick served two years as chairman of the GEC, from 1974 to 1976, the only dentist to have been appointed to this position.

An off-campus initiative of Guralnick's led to the formation of the Delta Dental Plan. He recalled:

> I had a great interest in seeing to it that people should have access to health care, and one of the things I did early on, when quite young, was getting Massachusetts Blue Cross and Blue Shield to pay for oral surgical procedures under Blue Shield. This had never been done anywhere in the country. At the time, dentists were not living the life of ease and luxury that they presently do live, and most people didn't have access to dental care, so it seemed to me there ought to be some form of dental insurance that would give many more people access. After ten years of convincing dentists, who were not thrilled about the plan, and getting help from Blue Cross, where I was on the board, we did get a bill through the state legislature, establishing Dental Service Corporation of Massachusetts in 1966.

This corporation became Delta Dental about 10 years later.

Guralnick resigned as chairman of OMFS in 1982, whereupon Austen asked him to consider being medical director of the MGH operating rooms. Guralnick accepted this new assignment and continued to see patients on a consulting basis into his eighties.

R. Bruce Donoff replaced Guralnick in 1983 and served as chief until 1992, when he was appointed dean of the Harvard School of Dental Medicine. Born in New York City, Donoff attended Brooklyn College as an undergraduate; he received his DMD from Harvard School of Dental Medicine in 1967 and his MD, also from Harvard, in 1973. Editor of the *Massachusetts General Hospital Manual of Oral and Maxillofacial Surgery*[89] and a member of the editorial boards of the *Journal of Oral and Maxillofacial Surgery* and the *Journal of the Massachusetts Dental Society*, Donoff has received numerous honors during his academic career. His research interests have included wound healing, bone graft survival, sensory nerve repair, and oral cancer.

R. Bruce Donoff.

A primary care dental service was established during Donoff's tenure, and, upon his arrival at MGH as Donoff's successor in January 1994 (after Guralnick served a short interim), Leonard Kaban committed to expanding this service. He worked with Agnes Lau, director of the practice. With the help of the Massachusetts General Physicians Organization (MGPO), it was expanded into the MGH Dental Group Practice, housed in a newly built 10-chair facility at 165 Cambridge Street. It now includes three full-time and 13 part-time dentists who represent specialties including pediatric dentistry, orthodontics, and prosthetic dentistry. In 2008, with the approval of Mass General Hospital and the MGPO, a formal Division of Dentistry was established in the department, and Agnes Lau was appointed its first chief. In the summer of 2010 a full-time, 10-chair facility opened at the Mass General / North Shore Center for Outpatient Care in Danvers, Massachusetts, serving both adult and pediatric patients. Plans were in place to add subspecialties to this practice over the coming five years.

The Kaban Years

Under Kaban, the OMFS Service at MGH has grown and thrived, while focusing on three core themes. Kaban arrived at Harvard's dental school in 1965, two years after Donoff, and he graduated in 1969. Born in New York City, Kaban had attended Queens College as an undergraduate. When he began his internship at MGH in 1969, Donoff was chief resident. In 1972, upon graduating from the three-year OMFS program, Kaban decided to go to medical school and was accepted at Johns Hopkins. He was "all packed" when Guralnick offered him and three others (Donoff, Steven Roser, and Edward B. Seldin) an opportunity to attend Harvard Medical School on the new combined five-year plan. Kaban completed work for his MD at Harvard in 1973 and did a general surgery residency in 1973–1974. John P. Kelly, an HSDM graduate, was the first to be enrolled in the combined MGH–Harvard Medical School MD-OMFS program, entering in 1971.

Before 1974 Children's Hospital Boston, another Harvard-affiliated hospital, had never had an oral surgery service. Guralnick sent Kaban there to work with Joseph E. Murray of the Peter Bent Brigham Hospital, better known for his work in transplantation. (Murray would win the Nobel Prize for his transplantation work in 1990.) Kaban recalled: "When I finished my training in 1974, I ran into General Director Charlie Sanders on the elevator, and he said, 'Hi, Lenny, how are you doing?' I said, 'Great.' He said, 'What are you going to do next year?' 'Going to help Joe Murray start a craniofacial clinic at Children's and Peter Bent Brigham.' Charlie put his arm around me and said, 'I'm glad that someone from MGH is going to a small community hospital!'"

A joint division of plastic and OMF surgery was established and MGH oral surgery chief residents rotated for six months. After eleven "great" years at Children's, Kaban was recruited by the University of California, San Francisco (UCSF), as professor and chairman of OMFS and associate dean for hospital affairs. He said:

> I had no administrative experience or interest. Joe Murray always used to ask us young associates our goals, and I said I had one goal: I wanted to be a professor. So when I was recruited by UCSF at age 40, I said during that interview that I would only come if I was made a professor. Their professorships were ranked 1 (lowest) to 7 (highest). I said 7 would be OK. But Julie Krevans, chancellor of UCSF, said the only people who came as 7s were Nobels, so I might have to settle for a 4. I said, "OK, I'll do professor 4!"
>
> They expressed concern that I had no administrative experience. I said I would take that as a plus. I don't think being a topnotch administrator is the most important qualification for being chairman of a surgical department. In surgery, it's all about the credibility you have with the troops, and you can't have credibility if you don't do surgery every day and if you don't have a cohesive and compelling vision for the department. I said, "I have a logical mind, I'm very well organized, I'm sure I can administer the department."

Kaban was hired and moved his family to San Francisco, where he had a successful 10 years. During this time he published (in 1990) the first edition of *Pediatric Oral and Maxillofacial Surgery* (2nd edition 2004) and coedited the book *Complications in Oral and Maxillofacial Surgery* (1997). The pediatric OMFS textbook is the only book on this subject published to date. He started a dual-degree OMFS program at UCSF, patterned after the MGH program and the first of its kind in California. The UCSF residency grew to be one of the premier training programs and OMFS departments in the country.

MGH called him back in 1992. The first time Kaban was offered the chance to replace Donoff, he turned the offer down. But a new Walter Guralnick Professorship had just been created, it was offered to Kaban, and he signed on the dotted line in the fall of 1993.

Kaban's vision for the OMFS service was to begin by recentralizing it and refunding it—to make it the topnotch OMFS practice in the city. In the years immediately preceding Kaban's return, several key contributors had moved the focus of their activities to other hospitals; the Wang practice was underperforming; and the OMFS account at Surgical Associates was in the red. Rectifying this was not easy; professional agreements had to be renegotiated. Once that was accomplished, Kaban set about recruiting a new breed of surgeons.

When Kaban returned, every other faculty member was Harvard- and MGH-trained. "I think I was the first person since Kurt Thoma who had ever been anywhere else," said Kaban. "The service was ingrown." He recruited David Perrott from UCSF to be the program director. Thomas B. Dodson (from UCSF and Emory) subsequently replaced Perrott as program director; Maria Troulis came from McGill and Thomas R. Flynn from Albert Einstein/Montefiore. Bonnie Padwa and Edward Lahey, MGH residents, were subsequently recruited by Kaban and remained. David Keith (who directed the HSDM Orofacial

Thomas Dodson.

Pain Program and OMFS at Harvard Vanguard Medical Associates), Meredith August (the Harvard student externship program), and Edward B. Seldin (OMFS at MIT) all continued on the faculty. A strong fellowship program was developed. Funded by the AO Foundation (Davos, Switzerland), Synthes CMF (West Chester, Pennsylvania), and the department, a fellowship in pediatric OMFS provided the department an excellent group of junior faculty and long-term collaborators who became faculty members in OMFS programs around the country and the world. In 2011, OMFS at MGH was, in Kaban's terms, "a fresh unit, with a vigorous and enthusiastic faculty, fellows, and residents."

With this new generation of surgeons came a new generation of technology. As a result of clinical improvements, the number of outpatient visits per year grew from about 6,000 in 1992 to more than 18,000 in 2008. Kaban cited two other major changes since he took over: a rejuvenation of the resident service and, especially, a dramatic increase in research output. Under the directorship of David Perrott (1995–1997), Tom Dodson (1997–2005), and Maria Troulis (2006–present), the goal of building and revitalizing the MGH resident service was realized. Today there is a busy and growing resident clinical practice that generates many elective cases in the clinic and operating room. This gives the residents a tremendous experience and lets them develop the self confidence required for a successful surgical career. In part for these accomplishments, Kaban received the Donald B. Osbon Award of the American Association of Oral and Maxillofacial Surgeons in 2004. Research in the department is divided into three broad thematic areas and carried out in the department's Skeletal Biology Research Center (Maria Troulis, director) and the Center for Applied Clinical Investigation (Tom Dodson, director).

The first theme is distraction osteogenesis—the lengthening of bone in, for example, the underdeveloped jaw of a child. By making a cut in the bone, putting a device across the bone cut, and turning the device gradually, the jaw can be lengthened as bone spontaneously forms in the widening gap. This procedure, popularized by Gavriel A. Ilizarov, a Russian orthopaedic surgeon in the 1950s, means avoiding bone grafts. Related research involves better understanding how

Leonard Kaban and Maria Troulis with a happy patient after successful distraction osteogenesis surgery to enlarge her jaw. This procedure made it possible to remove a permanent breathing tube from the child's trachea.

the body forms bone, as well as device design and 3-D imaging. The goal ultimately is to treat distraction cases with an automated implanted device that can be remotely controlled. In 2011 work on such a device was ongoing. OMFS is one of the bigger users of high-tech imaging. Said Kaban: "With a buried device, you cannot make midcourse corrections of the vector of movement. Therefore, the device demands very accurate three-dimensional treatment planning and accurate intraoperative placement. So we have a 3-D treatment planning lab working on software to tell surgeons exactly where to make the bone cut and to implant the device."

The second theme of OMFS research at MGH is minimally invasive surgery. Maria Troulis is the director of research, development, and clinical application of minimally invasive techniques for OMFS. Using a combination of laboratory research, simulation, and clinical trials, Troulis has established the use of minimally invasive techniques for treatment of jaw fractures, congenital and acquired jaw deformities, and salivary gland obstructive disease. She has also developed educational programs to teach these techniques.

The third theme, driven by Tom Dodson, is epidemiologic research on common problems that have been treated for generations, like impacted wisdom teeth. What are the risks of removing them? What are the risks of leaving them in? How can we prevent complications such as infection? Dodson and his team have access to a national database of many thousands of patients. By analyzing these data, and by pursuing clinical outcomes research, the Center for Applied Clinical Investigation hopes to answer some of these fundamental questions.

By MGH standards, oral and maxillofacial surgery is a small service, with 13 full-time faculty, only seven of whom are on the MGH campus. (The others are at the dental school, Harvard Vanguard Medical Associates, and Children's Hospital.) Though the average length of stay for OMFS patients is short and the service therefore fills relatively few beds, Kaban's department is a high user of sophisticated imaging equipment and its OR cases are high-tech, so the hospital generally earns high fees for these. "We definitely contribute to margin," said Kaban, who clearly had learned to be an administrator and relished the challenge. "For an OMFS service like ours, the MGH is unique and we are very lucky, because dating back to John Knowles and Charlie Sanders and then Sam Thier and Jim Mongan and Peter Slavin today, the administration has been very supportive of our service. We've never been discriminated against just because we're small. That's not to say we get everything we want. But if we can make our case well, we usually get what we need."

Kaban added that the mission of OMFS is more important to the educational mission of the hospital than its size would indicate. Mass General provides the principal hospital experience for Harvard School of Dental Medicine students. The dental school sends all 40 of its senior students to MGH each year for a four-week OMFS rotation; the OMFS faculty supervises six to 10 students per year doing research projects. The OMFS residency program has 19 residents and rotating residents from the Harvard Plastic Surgery Program, Harvard General Practice Dentistry Program, and Harvard Orofacial Pain Program, among others. Said Kaban, "We are the dental school's equivalent to the medical school's Department of Surgery, though on a much smaller scale."

Guralnick spoke very proudly of the OMFS service in the past few decades: "I think the service here has expanded the dimensions of the specialty as they should have been expanded, by people who have been keen observers, excellent surgeons, good researchers, and fine teachers. As the specialty has expanded, I'm proud of the fact that the people who originally trained under me have reached the pinnacle of the profession, both here and elsewhere." Some of the success stories who moved on to leadership positions elsewhere include Charles Bertolami, who became chairman of OFMS at UCLA, then dean of the dental schools at UCSF and NYU; Steven Roser, chief of OMFS at Columbia, and subsequently chair and chief at Emory; John Kelly, chief of OMFS at St. Francis Hospital in New Haven; Harry Schwartz, chief of OMFS with Kaiser Permanente in southern California; and Bonnie Padwa, section chief of OMFS at Children's Hospital Boston.

UROLOGY SINCE HUGH CABOT

Another surgical service that, like OMFS, has traditionally stood free of the Department of Surgery at MGH is urology. Like oral surgery, urological surgery was performed at MGH long before the discipline was formally recognized as a specialty, primarily to remove bladder and kidney stones and to treat infections and obstructions of the kidney and bladder. Stones have been a major problem since ancient times. The original Hippocratic oath states, "I will not cut for stone, even for patients in whom the disease is manifest; I will leave this operation to be performed by practitioners, specialists in this art." Urologists claim the hero of the French tune "Frère Jacques" as one of their own, although some historians think *that* Brother Jacques may not have been the famous French lithotomist (stone cutter) Frère Jacques Beaulieu. As we saw in chapter 2, the MGH surgeon Henry J. Bigelow devised a method of litholapaxy, a technique for crushing bladder stones and flushing them from the patient's urological tract.

It was not until 1911, however, that the Genito-Urinary Department was formally created within the Mass General Outpatient Department, and Hugh Cabot was appointed its first chief.[90] W. Scott McDougal, who served as chief of urology

Hugh Cabot
(courtesy Wellcome Images).

100 years later, said Cabot's service was the first stand-alone urology service at an American hospital. As a member of one of Boston's leading families, a relative of Samuel and Arthur Tracy Cabot, and the younger brother of Richard C. Cabot, all physicians, Hugh Cabot had the clout to make this happen. At MGH syphilis had been the concern of dermatology since the 1870s, and until Hugh Cabot came along, urological surgery had been handled by the general surgeons like Bigelow and Arthur Cabot, who had done some pediatric urology, including the treatment of bladder exstrophy (a condition in which a child is born with part of its bladder open to the outside of the body. Hugh Cabot began his surgical practice as a junior partner of his cousin Arthur, for whom he would name his fourth child. It was from Arthur that Hugh Cabot acquired his interest in urology.

In 1911 Cabot admitted his first inpatient to the newly formed department, a man with urethral stricture. This would become a topic of interest for Cabot, who wrote four papers on the subject. "His 1912 paper on the training of the urologist helped set the stage and the standard for residency education," according to a profile authored by Scott McDougal and others. "He carefully defined the field of urology, making an interesting distinction between the old-time genitourinary surgeon/venereologist and his new vision of a larger field of urology." Cabot broadened the service by surrounding himself with other physicians who had a particular interest in urology, including J. Dellinger Barney, Richard O'Neill, and George G. Smith. In 1916 the department consisted of six faculty members. McDougal commented on how extraordinary it was to find such a team in a general hospital as early as World War I. Like others on staff, Hugh Cabot left the hospital to serve in France in 1917, and O'Neill was named acting chief. When O'Neill left for war service, too, Smith replaced him. Cabot returned at the end of the war, but only for a short time. By this time the first edition of his *Modern Urology* had appeared. McDougal wrote: "Although Cabot was never short on opinion and personal experience, he was strongly committed to weighing his observations against other published opinions, experiences, and data. In this sense, one might look at his book, true to its name, as the first modern urologic text."[91]

Subsequent editions of *Modern Urology* followed in 1924 and 1936. By then Cabot had left MGH (in 1920) because of what McDougal suspected was a conflict about caring for indigent patients and teaching versus devoting himself full-time to the care of private patients. The latter was not consistent with the highest ethical standards, at least according to Cabot. Hugh Cabot became chief of surgery and then dean of the medical school at the University of Michigan. His entry in the *Dictionary of American Biography* notes that Cabot enjoyed the "undivided allegiance assured by his full-time position" at Michigan:

To integrate and humanize the medical curriculum, he introduced comprehensive examinations and substantial reductions in lecture and laboratory hours required for some courses. To obviate conflict of interest in the faculty, he placed members on a modified full-time basis, entirely forbidding private practice; each man's salary, however, was supplemented in a manner roughly commensurate with his care of patients, who, if they could afford to pay, were charged on a sliding scale . . . To ensure academic autonomy, Cabot and the university's president, Clarence Cook Little, refused legislative appropriations contingent on the hiring of homeopathic faculty members.[92]

Each of Cabot's reforms in Michigan met opposition. A family saying has it that "Cabots have customs but no manners." This seems to have applied to Hugh Cabot in Michigan, where a lack of diplomacy eventually alienated many and created enemies, according to the same source. Asked to resign, Cabot refused, whereupon he was relieved of his duties as dean in February 1930. His friend William James Mayo asked him to join the Mayo Clinic, where he finally enjoyed full-time practice for the next nine years. Cabot was invited back to speak at a Harvard Club dinner celebrating the MGH Urology Service's 25th anniversary, on March 28, 1936.[93]

The endocrinologist Fuller Albright took a medical interest in stones (see chapter 3), and in 1935 the Departments of Medicine and Urology teamed up to form a renal stone clinic.[94] Also in 1935 the hospital established the Surgical Executive Committee, comprising the chiefs of general surgery, orthopedics, neurosurgery, and urology. "Thus, from its inception," wrote McDougal, "Urology played a dominant role in the Surgical Service at the Massachusetts General Hospital."[95] By that time Dellinger Barney's second tenure as chief of urology was drawing to a close. Reaching retirement age in 1938, he was replaced by Smith. Smith gave way in 1945 to Fletcher H. Colby, who served until 1954. In 1948, 480 patients were admitted to the urology ward and 441 operations were performed, the most common operation being a prostatectomy. Mortality was just 3.9 percent (17 of 441 patients).[96] Another important contributor during this period was Howard Suby, whose Suby's solution G became the standard for washing out pulverized bladder stones and was still in some use into the twenty-first century.

Wyland F. Leadbetter, named chief in the fall of 1954, advanced the clinical side of urology in a big way. The official MGH history of the period noted that during his 15 years of leadership, "the census in both clinic and private admissions rose prodigiously while many innovative modes of therapy, chiefly surgical, were developed."[97] A native of Maine and a graduate of Bates College in Lewiston, he went on to medical school at Johns Hopkins. In private urological practice in Boston before and after World War II, Leadbetter taught at Tufts Medical School and had an appointment at New England Medical Center Hospital before accepting a Harvard appointment in 1954.

Leadbetter was famous for 12- and even 14-hour days; rounds began at 6 A.M. He worked many Saturdays in the OR and Sundays in the office. "Patients responded positively. . . . His surgical technique was aggressive, clever, and meticulous."[98] Such dedication by a doctor often leads to grateful patients, but it can also

Wyland Leadbetter.

lead to a strain in private life. Here Leadbetter was fortunate: "Without the encouragement and support of his dedicated wife, Lois, Leadbetter never could have accomplished what he did for the development of urology. She seemed to devote her whole life to the comfort and success of her husband. Whether he got home from his evening rounds at 9 P.M. or at 1 A.M. she always had a hot meal waiting for him. In the morning it was the same story; at 5:30 she would start Wyland off with a substantial hot meal in preparation for another arduous 15-hour day."[99] McDougal credited Leadbetter and his fellow urologist Walter Kerr with "bringing legitimacy of major surgery to urology at MGH." "They moved from abscesses and other minor surgical treatments to being competitors to the best in general surgery. They didn't cure cancer or develop major innovations, but they brought legitimacy to urologists performing major operations: the thoraco-abdominal incision (going through the chest cavity to get to the kidneys) was popularized here. Leadbetter spawned a whole group of residents who became chairmen elsewhere and disseminated this approach."

Though training under Leadbetter was first-rate, it would take the arrival of George R. Prout Jr. as chief in 1969 to push forward research activities in urology. Prout began "a laboratory activity" in 1972, and he "held firmly to his conviction that clinical services in a teaching hospital have no excuse for being if they are not used for research and teaching." He raised funds from the American Cancer Society to allow each house officer to spend six months in clinical research, which required these residents to add six months to their stay at the hospital.[100] Also in 1972 he formed Urological Associates, a full-time group practice. The National Cancer Act of 1971—and Prout's involvement in national urology organizations and committees—was a great impetus for all of this.[101]

McDougal would say that Prout's legacy, both clinically and in the lab, revolved around issues related to bladder cancer. "He established a basic science lab with credibility, established bladder cell lines (keeping cancer cells in culture and studying them), and he made advances in the area of bladder sparing, in cooperation with medical and radiation oncology."

In 1981 the Urology Service at MGH consisted of Prout as chief, one urologist, two associate urologists, four assistant urologists, and three assistants in urology, in addition to an associate in biochemistry heading the Urological Research Laboratory. All had Harvard appointments. Prout would continue as chief for another seven years, whereupon an interim chief was appointed and a search for a new chief was launched. By this time most of the clinical work in urology was being done in the private sector, and the hospital looked for a new leader to bring urology into the twenty-first century. That proved to be W. Scott McDougal.

The son of a surgeon in Grand Rapids, Michigan, McDougal said, "My father always regretted not going into academic medicine." So son did what father had not. The younger McDougal took his undergraduate studies at Dartmouth, went to Cornell Medical School, and then proceeded to Case Western Reserve for his surgical training and Yale for postdoctoral training in physiology. It was at Case Western that he became interested in urology. Following the completion of his training, McDougal, on the Berry Plan (which deferred military service for doctors in training) during the Vietnam War, was assigned to and then directed the clinical activities of the U.S. Army's burn research unit in San Antonio,

George Prout.

Texas. Research there in tissue reconstruction would provide a unique background for a career in urology. He returned to Case Western as a member of the faculty, was recruited to Dartmouth as chairman of urology, then was recruited to a similar position at Vanderbilt. "I loved Vanderbilt," McDougal said. "I wouldn't have left Vanderbilt except for a job like this." He accepted the position of chief of urology at MGH in June 1990 and arrived in Boston later that year.

Much has been accomplished in McDougal's two decades of leadership. Urology was one of the last services at MGH to move to full-time practice. In 2011 the service had 14 full-time faculty and just one "quasi-full-time." Said McDougal, "Being part-time held our service back enormously. The resources were directed into private practice, whereas in a department like this, one needs some of these resources for training and research." The service in 2009 sent eight of its 12 residents to a national urological meeting, where they and the faculty presented an estimated 20 percent of all the papers.

Urology has also been subspecialized in a big way under McDougal: faculty have focused on oncology, stones, infertility, female urology, geriatric urology, neurourology, and general urology. On the clinical side, MGH urology is particularly well known for preserving bladders in patients with bladder cancer and for treatment of (and reconstruction involved in) penile cancer. "We do less-invasive surgery," said McDougal, "and are able to preserve function. This goes back to my experience in the army burn unit with tissue grafting and so on."

In the last 20 years the average length of stay for urology patients has been reduced remarkably, from 8.6 days to 2.4. Admittedly, there has been a trend toward more outpatient treatment in virtually all fields, but, said McDougal, "I don't think anyone has been more aggressive than we have, with a lot of minimally invasive surgery. Also, we've moved an enormous number of cases to OPD [Outpatient Department] without general anesthesia—some local bladder tumors, for example. Patients love it; they don't have to be put to sleep, can drive themselves in, and drive themselves home. We've been on the forefront of moving surgical procedures from OR to OPD."

Research in urology, jump-started by Prout, has zoomed ahead under McDougal, who in 1996 became the first Walter S. Kerr, Jr., professor of urology at Harvard, the first endowed Harvard chair in the field. Major areas of interest include:

W. Scott McDougal.

- Device development. McDougal joked that he would be remembered for two innovations here, the Twisted Piece of Steel and the Blob: "I developed the McDougal prostate clamp, which facilitates doing a radical prostatectomy, although now we're moving away from open surgery and more to the minimally invasive approach. Then there's the Blob, a polymer you can put in the ureter, which, like Jell-o, goes in as liquid and gels. It holds the stone in place so that you can break it up. Squirt cold water on it, the Jell-o dissolves, and you flush the stone!"

- Metabolic abnormalities in patients with reconstructed bladders. When a bladder is removed, an alternative to urostomy is to rebuild the bladder from intestinal tissue. Since intestines weren't meant to store urine, these patients develop abnormalities, and this lab, headed by McDougal, has defined these abnormalities.

- Molecular genetics. This effort studies some of the genes responsible for bladder cancer and prostate cancer and markers determining the relative aggressiveness of kidney cancers. Chin-Lee Wu, jointly appointed by the Pathology Department, is an important contributor here.

- Bladder dysfunction in diabetics. Aria F. Olumi heads up this new effort; she also has published extensively on genes and pathways involved in developing and destroying prostate cancers.

KNOWLES MOVES ON

John Knowles usually seemed to be looking for his next opportunity. As the 1960s wore on, he projected a larger profile on the national health scene. Samuel O. Thier, a chief resident in the mid-1960s who would return to lead the hospital 30 years later, described Knowles as a "a thoughtful leader nationally on health policy," one "who used the MGH as a bully pulpit."

Kay Bander recalled: "There were all kinds of political things in the air, he liked politics, and he began to choose people who were capable of interacting on behalf of the institution on a national level. I think he was distinctly interested in moving on to Washington, had he been selected."

Knowles's politics were pro-Democrat, and he was pointedly against the Vietnam War, the conflict that sank Lyndon Johnson's hopes for reelection. Knowles made long pronouncements on such national political issues in the MGH annual reports.

Knowles's report for 1966 included a lengthy analysis of Medicare that may have been a sort of personal policy platform. While acknowledging that there would be more public scrutiny of medical fees and procedures, Knowles predicted that, with equitable reimbursement from state agencies now mandated by federal law, "our difference and long battles with the State seem to be nearly over." In hindsight, that outlook was probably overoptimistic. Knowles also predicted:

- Increased utilization of hospitals and doctors.
- Hospital facilities and manpower stretched to the limit.
- Cost inflation ("Doctor fee inflation is occurring around the city").
- Increased importance of after-care. (MGH soon created a new Transfer Office within the Social Service Department under Eleanor Clark.)
- Changes in medical education.
- Changed relationship of radiologists to the hospital and medical school.
- Demands for regional planning and control of hospitals.[102]

Since 50 percent of Mass General's operating budget was coming from federal sources by 1968, it made sense for a general director to keep his eye on hospital-related regulations coming out of Washington.[103] It helped to have Ellsworth Neumann ably filling the role of administrator as Knowles's "Mr. Inside," and Larry Martin counting the coin as Mass General's comptroller. With these two covering his back, Knowles could step out on the national stage.

Having established the fact that he thought about health care from a national perspective, Knowles was under consideration, then turned down, for the position of assistant secretary of health at the Department of Health, Education, and Welfare (HEW) in the incoming Nixon administration in 1969. According to Sanders, Knowles knew Robert Finch, a former lieutenant governor of California, who was Nixon's Cabinet appointee for HEW and who recommended Knowles. But Knowles battled openly, before and after the appointment, with the American Medical Association over such issues as fee for service and health insurance, and the AMA opposed his appointment.

Larry Martin recalled the political controversy: "Leading the opposition to that appointment was Everett Dirksen, who was the Senate Minority Leader. This went on for 162 days. On June 27 Secretary Finch said that Dr. Knowles was not to be appointed. The interesting thing about all of this is that two weeks later the hospital had two investigators from the Internal Revenue Service arrive at the hospital. They were to audit the MGH."[104]

Martin remembered two IRS agents remaining on campus for two years, allegedly under orders to find "something wrong" with MGH accounting. A minor matter involving a tuition aid program resulted in a fine of $74,000—which seemed a small price to pay, at least to Martin, who said, "That's how we finally got rid of them."

Knowles continued to speak out on the national scene, making sweeping statements about the present and future state of health care and society at large. He was something of a futurist, and a prescient one. In his report for 1970–1971, he quoted the sociologist Max Weber and perhaps alluded to other social thinkers while writing, "I believe we are approaching the end of a cycle of massive industrial development. We are now passing into a 'post-industrial' 'technotronic' society which will be oriented increasingly to the rational development of human services."[105]

In his final report, knowing that he would soon be moving on, Knowles returned his focus to MGH, capturing his enthusiasm for the hospital, which he had joined as an intern in July 1951: "I was constantly inspired by the excellence of the individuals—now some 6,000 strong—who comprise the MGH. No day opened without a feeling of eager anticipation or without that inner warmth and strength an individual experiences when he is associated with the best and shares common hopes and aspirations with so many strong and dedicated people."[106]

Knowles resigned in 1972 to grab the brass ring, the presidency of the Rockefeller Foundation. Knowles had been "a very good general for the hospital at that time," said Nicholas Thorndike, who joined the Board of Trustees in 1969. Thorndike added that Knowles "would not have fit in any other period. The hospital was smaller, he called everyone by name—but the hospital has become a much different business in the 40 years I've been there. Now, it's a multibillion-dollar business. When the Rockefeller Foundation came to take him away, everyone said, He's perfect for the job, and we're sad to see him go, but God bless. He was very good at what he did, but he was also very ambitious for himself."

The two decades since Knowles entered MGH as an intern had seen tectonic shifts in the way hospitals were organized and reimbursed; it had also seen remarkable growth.[107] In 1951 the inpatient budget had been $5.6 million. In 1971 it was $53.7 million. Meanwhile, the hospital's daily cost of keeping one patient in a bed had increased nearly sevenfold, from $23.88 to $155.01. The house staff had increased in number from 105 to 352, fellows (clinical and research) from 84 to 288. Only the school of nursing had stagnated. Student count over those 20 years actually fell from 358 to 327.

Sadly, Knowles's career at the Rockefeller Foundation was cut short. In 1979, suffering with pancreatic cancer at the age of only 52, he returned to MGH for treatment. There was nothing to be done, and he died, "cruelly cut in full flower."[108] Following his death, a well-attended memorial service was held at Memorial Church in Harvard Yard. When the service ended, those attending moved to the exit. As they did so, they heard the tinkling sound of a grand piano playing popular tunes of the 1940s. The pianist was the actor Jack Lemmon, an old friend of Knowles.[109]

The first responsibility of the MGH trustees has always been to choose the next general director of the hospital. Said Ed Lawrence, board chairman from 1999 to 2008, "There are points along the way where the trustees really make a difference. Picking heads of the hospital is one of those." Who would replace John Knowles, the always charismatic, John Knowles, the often controversial?

The board was also in transition during this key period. John Lawrence had become chairman in 1967 and Thorndike, a future chair himself, joined in 1969;

coming along in the 1970s would be such key contributors as F. Sargent "Sarge" Cheever and Jane Claflin. Cheever would replace Lawrence as chair in 1978; Claflin would become a major force in fund-raising. All along, Hooks Burr would provide continuity, as John Lawrence's right-hand man, his car-pool partner from the North Shore, and eventually, after turning down the post once, chairman of the trustees for much of the challenging 1980s. One eyewitness said that through this period, "Burr was the practitioner, the structural person, and Lawrence was the visionary."

The trustees named Benjamin Castleman, chief of pathology, to serve as interim general director during the search for a permanent replacement for Knowles. Charles Sanders recalled:

> They first identified a former chief resident in medicine, Hibbard Williams, who had gone to UCSF and was later dean of the med school at UC Davis. He had been chief resident here at MGH. John Lawrence particularly liked him. Hibbard came and interviewed, and John Lawrence went out to see him in San Francisco. I heard that Hibbard Williams made the mistake of saying, "Mr. Lawrence, I'm just not sure that I really want to do that right now." And Lawrence said, "Well, if you're not sure, I'm not sure we really want you." And the field was wide open again.

Nick Thorndike, who was on the search committee, did not remember exactly why Sanders himself emerged as a leading candidate for the general director's job. Jerry Austen would recall suggesting Sanders to John Lawrence, after Lawrence said that Austen himself would be a strong candidate. Near the end of his life, John Lawrence spoke of the selection to Sanders's wife, saying, "When I saw him, I liked the cut of his jib. But he was totally unqualified, totally unqualified!" Sanders agreed, admitting, "I wouldn't have hired me if I had been on the search committee. Nowadays, chief executive officers are usually prepared for a job like this. John Knowles wasn't prepared for this job. I sure as hell wasn't."

A native of Texas who did his undergraduate work at the University of Texas and attended Southwestern Medical School in Dallas, Sanders had interned at Boston City Hospital, on the Harvard service. In 1958 he came to MGH as a fellow in cardiology, "much to the chagrin of my basic-science friends at Boston City," he recalled. "They were the have-nots and MGH were the haves, the people who made money practicing medicine. Both were Harvard faculty, but Boston City was a different crowd." Sanders arrived at Mass General "with the idea of staying two years and returning to Texas. Instead, one thing kind of led to another."

"Reasonably good" with his hands, Sanders effectively ran the cardiac catheterization lab in the second year of his fellowship. Enrolled in the Berry Plan, Sanders was required to enter the Air Force once his training was completed, in 1960. Sanders had thought that the idea of the Berry Plan was to allow medical trainees to practice in the military what they had been trained for. Instead, he found himself in the outpatient department on a military base. Then he moved to the head of a women's ward. "Air Force wives can be a mixed-up bunch," Sanders said, "so I was dealing more with psychological and social issues than with organic

Charles Sanders (left) and John Knowles.

disease." In 1962 he returned to Mass General to run the cath lab on a full-time basis.

Sanders was formally approved on May 12, 1972, to succeed Benjamin Castleman. Despite his limited experience, the trustees determined that Sanders had "proved [his] ability as an administrator of large programs reaching into various departments of the hospital."[110] Sanders would serve as MGH's 17th general director through 1981.

Kay Bander would remember one boss, Charles Sanders, in distinct contrast with the previous one, John Knowles: "Dr. Sanders was very laid-back, subtle in his way, quite capable of wielding power but totally different in the way he did it. He was a consummate politician in his capacity to interact with people. He enjoyed it, and his wife, Ann, also from the South, was particularly good at being the wife of a chief executive."

Bander went on: "Sanders was not the flashy leader. Knowles had politics. Buchanan would have buildings. Sanders was a consolidator, in my opinion, and extremely good at it. He was also a very good conceptualizer of what the health care environment needed."

Sanders himself was aware of the strong contrast: "Johnny was charismatic and did a lot to put us on the map. It wasn't very sleepy when he was here! He talked in four-letter words and was irreverent, and that worked in his favor because he intimidated those around him. My style was entirely different. I am inclusive and ask people to help and listen. And one of the things I feel you have to do is listen, and then you try to do what you can to be responsive. So that style was a contrast to Johnny, but that did not diminish his effectiveness."

SANDERS TAKES THE HELM

The 1960s would be remembered as a youth-driven decade, worldwide as at the Massachusetts General Hospital. In the 1970s the hope of the 1960s would meet resistance. Fortunately, MGH had a steady hand at the wheel. Charles Sanders completed several projects that John Knowles had left unfinished. In addition, Sanders put his own stamp on the history of the institution. At the time of his departure in 1982, there was still plenty of work to do, but in two decades Mass General had forged boldly into the spotlight of American medicine. A *Ladies' Home Journal* article of 1967 was framed and mounted on walls around the campus: it declared MGH the finest hospital in America.[111]

Sanders recalled his feeling upon assuming command: "Implicit and explicit was to maintain the strength of the institution. Johnny had been very bright about bringing the hospital onto the national scene. Obviously, I wanted to continue that while strengthening research, teaching, and patient care."

Sanders continued to practice medicine, seeing patients on Wednesday afternoons and covering for colleagues about every fourth weekend. "It wasn't a high-pressure practice," Sanders said, "but it was a way of keeping my hand in and seeing what people had to say out on the floor. It allowed me to manage by walking around, and who knows but I might have had to go back to treating patients full-time someday?" During his tenure as general director, Sanders was made a full professor of medicine at Harvard Medical School.

Sanders had to deal with far more challenging extraneous circumstances than did Knowles. A combination of Great Society and Vietnam War spending, exacerbated by Federal Reserve policy, sent wages and prices soaring through the 1970s. This trend became a distinct crisis each time the Organization of the Petroleum Exporting Countries (OPEC) turned off the oil spigot. Those were days of long lines at the gas pumps and "stagflation," a buzzword meaning a deadening combination of inflation and unemployment. In medicine, the easy-money days of Medicare ended, as a national focus on inflation—from Richard Nixon's price controls to Gerald Ford's WIN buttons (Whip Inflation Now)—forced belt-tightening in all industries. Locally, Sanders saw operational costs rise faster than at any other time in MGH history. Capacity utilization was usually more than 90 percent during this period, so there was pressure on MGH costs even without general inflation.[112]

Sanders's report as general director in 1975 was typical: "The major story and the major problem in the hospital industry for the year continued to be the economy." Wage and price controls had "failed utterly," and the state of Massachusetts was as much as $11 million in arrears on its Medicaid bill, which led to predictable cash-flow shortages for the hospital.[113] The result was what Sanders would refer to as "Robin Hood socialism . . . by overcharging in areas such as the Phillips House."[114]

Government-hospital relations were put under additional strain when, in the fall of 1975, a Massachusetts bill was filed that "virtually gave the power to manage hospitals over to the Rate Setting Commission by empowering them to approve, modify, or delete specific budgets within hospitals."[115] Malpractice cases, almost unheard of at the end of World War II, were now a big enough concern that MGH began in April 1976 to participate in a malpractice insurance program with 10 other Harvard-affiliated institutions.[116]

There would be no respite from macroeconomic woes for Sanders during his tenure as general director. In 1981, his last full year in the post, he wrote, "The subject of finances has recurred like a tiresome refrain in MGH annual reports." Among the litany of economic woes, Sanders cited a national inflation rate of 15 percent.[117] It may be hard for some to imagine, or recall, that in 1982 the Dow Jones Industrial Average made a long-term bottom under 800, just as Sanders was leaving the hot seat. Sanders added, "During the 1950s and 1960s, the MGH—along with the other medical and educational institutions—acquired habits of growth in facilities and technology which the economic structure of the 1970s could not sustain."[118] Growth would resume its bullish course in the 1980s.

In the administrative offices on the main White corridor, ground level, Sanders found a solid core in place: Kay Bander, assistant to the general director; Ellsworth Neumann, "Mr. Inside"; Larry Martin, managing hospital finances; Martin Bander, the PR guy with a passion for science; and at least one unsung hero, or heroine: Mary E. MacDonald, director of nursing.

"She made me appreciate the importance of nurses," Sanders said, "and to the extent I didn't appreciate it, she beat it into my head!" MacDonald ran a daily meeting known as Morning Report. "That was the best way to find out what was going on in the hospital," Sanders said. "Mary was a force. She fought for her nurses and they knew it. I still feel that American medicine is not putting nurses in the proper position, because they're the ones who make it all work, and if you're not working as a team, you may not be giving the very best care you are capable of."

Sanders would credit another key contributor on the General Executive Committee, Eleanor Clark, "a real power in social service." Referring to an advertising campaign for a former brokerage powerhouse, Sanders said that MacDonald and Clark together were like E. F. Hutton. When they said something, you listened.

Hospital administration was becoming more complex by the year. Computers were becoming essential tools; financing was no longer all-cash, as the case of the Gray Building showed; *personnel* was on its way to being redefined as *human resources*. Sanders's first official charge was to hire the consulting firm of McKinsey and Company and commission an analysis of his own shop. The McKinsey report gave Sanders a plan for creating a more corporate structure. In the transition, Neumann left to work with John Knowles at the Rockefeller Foundation. "That worked fine for me," Sanders said, "because he was Johnny's creature." Neumann's inside function was distributed across several positions.

In 1974 Sanders asked Larry Martin to assist him in the management activities of the hospital. This resulted in a new title: associate general director. To replace Martin, Joseph P. McCue was appointed director of fiscal affairs and functioned as the CFO of the hospital. Sanders called Martin "the go-to guy on all things finance. I was go-to on all things medical. We complemented one another. The trustees trusted Larry, leaned on him. I think Larry was recognized among his peers as one of the national leaders in hospital finance, not only in terms of professional competence but in terms of creative ways of how to deal with a changing system. It was a good team."

TRANSPLANTATION BECOMES A REALITY

A. Benedict Cosimi's MGH career has spanned nearly the entire history of clinical transplantation at the hospital; yet it could have been sidetracked at least twice— once when Paul Russell stepped down as chief of surgery and again, a decade later, when Cosimi, Russell, and Russell's replacement, Jerry Austen, proposed that the hospital enter the field of heart transplantation. This initiative put Cosimi and the Department of Surgery on a collision course with the MGH trustees, with the administration, and with the Department of Medicine, thus demonstrating the delicate balance of power in an academic medical center.

A. Benedict seems an odd moniker for an unassuming kid raised by a farmer and a school principal in rural Adams County, Colorado, off Interstate 25 about 15 miles north of Denver. That's probably why Cosimi was and is known as Ben. "My mother was a strong believer in education," he said. "She would do chores late into the night so that my brother and I could do our homework. Our father died at 98, still active on the farm, our mother at 96. My brother and I still have the farm."

A medical student at the University of Colorado from 1960 to 1964, Cosimi came into contact there with Thomas E. Starzl, a surgeon who had already performed successful kidney transplants and was moving on to livers. The Nobel laureate Joseph E. Murray had performed the first successful human kidney transplant at the Peter Bent Brigham Hospital in 1954. Starzl is credited with the world's first successful liver transplant, though his early patients died; none survived until 1967.[119] Starzl asked Cosimi to work with him after graduation, but the farm kid was accepted for an internship at MGH in 1964, so he headed east. Here he immediately began interacting with Paul Russell as well as Judah Folkman, later chief of surgery at Children's Hospital, but then Cosimi's chief resident in surgery at Mass General. Folkman had a patient who was dying of renal failure. Under a grant from the NIH, Paul Russell had an early hemodialysis machine to support kidney transplant patients, but according to the terms of the grant, the machine could not be used for nontransplant patients. So, a bit like Austen with his bypass device in the 1950s, young Cosimi built a dialysis machine "from spare parts, including an old washing machine," he said. For years afterward, as a result, dialysis at MGH would be part of the surgical service—a puzzle to people in other programs,

where dialysis is managed by the renal unit. But then when Cosimi built his machine to meet the need of Folkman's patient, he met resistance from Alexander Leaf, the chief of renal medicine, who believed that there was no need for further expansion of this new procedure beyond the unit already in place at the Peter Bent Brigham Hospital.

When Austen replaced Russell as chief of surgery, Cosimi "drifted away" from transplantation to reconsider neurosurgery as a career choice "because it wasn't clear to anyone that Russell would remain at MGH." Cosimi asked himself, "What would happen to the program?" But Russell stayed, and he and Austen apparently agreed that the future of transplantation at MGH bore the odd name A. Benedict Cosimi. So Cosimi was prevailed on and resumed his work.

A. Benedict Cosimi.

Years later Cosimi, as chief of transplantation surgery at MGH, would lecture on the four limiting factors to advances in the field.

1. Surgical technique—"By 2010 we've pretty well figured these out."
2. Rejection of the donated organ by the recipient's immune system—"Still a problem."
3. The donor source—"We don't have enough."
4. Cost—"When the day comes that we've solved the first three, we'll face this one."

In the early days of transplantation, the first two factors ruled: surgeons worked to master technique, but approaches to suppressing the recipient's immune system lagged behind. During his residency Cosimi worked in Russell's lab to develop antibodies against human lymphocytes as a specific approach to quieting a patient's immune response. Investigative work included injecting human lymphocytes into a horse. According to Cosimi, Russell said to him, " 'You're from the West, you know horses, go buy a horse.' I found an old ragpicker in South Boston who had a horse, and I bought the horse from him and stabled it in his home. I immunized the horse and bled him right there." These early "polyclonal" agents proved to be highly effective and, in fact, continue to be widely used today.

The Vietnam War was grinding toward its inconclusive finale, and Cosimi, like many young doctors, was on the Berry Plan. This gave him a deferment from military duty while in surgical training but obliged him to serve two years once his training was completed. Finishing his residency in 1970, he enlisted in the U.S. Air Force and was "on my way" to Da Nang as a medical officer when President Nixon began winding down the war. So, instead, Cosimi was sent to the Air Force's hospital in San Antonio, Texas, Wilford Hall Medical Center, to start a transplant facility. "I resumed the research I had been doing here, working with horses."

A Debate over Heart Transplantation

When Cosimi joined the Harvard faculty, returning to MGH in 1973, Russell was doing kidneys, only kidneys. But Cosimi was appointed chief of clinical transplant surgery while Russell withdrew somewhat from the operating room to focus on administration and research. So moving forward in patient care was Cosimi's responsibility. Jerry Austen asked Cosimi what other organs MGH might do. At the time, liver transplantation had only a 10–15 percent survival rate, and heart transplantation was on many minds. According to Cosimi, Christaan Barnard, who got the press in 1967, had "stolen" techniques created by Norman Shumway, a Stanford University surgeon who performed the first American heart transplant in 1968. Austen liked the idea of entering the heart field, so Cosimi went to California to learn Shumway's technique. Said Cosimi: "Those early transplants—the problem was, the world wasn't ready to go ahead with mass production. It was a disaster, as all patients died. Norm figured out the limiting factors, including immunosuppression. He also developed better surgical procedures. But after the bad press of the late sixties, some were hesitant to take it on."

Austen, Russell, and Cosimi, together with the cardiac surgeon Bill Daggett, presented a proposal to the MGH trustees in 1975 that the hospital consider initiating a clinical heart transplantation program. The case was "impressively presented," wrote General Director Charlie Sanders. "Although it was fully appreciated that no institution in the world has people better qualified than those at the MGH to perform such surgery, it was reluctantly recommended that clinical transplantation should not be undertaken at the present time. Continued research basic to cardiac transplantation was thought to be desirable."[120]

Russell recalled: "It was felt that this kind of surgery would take up valuable resources, and we'd have a lot of patients in terminal heart failure, which would also take too much of the resources of the hospital. I think many . . . also felt that it was an example of too extreme an effort in medicine, too expensive, way out on the edge and not the kind of thing that medicine should be doing. That was a logical feeling, I suppose, on the part of some, a feeling which I didn't share."

In 1980 a second attempt to win approval for heart transplants was approved by the General Executive Committee, 14 to one. The one dissenting voice was that of Chief of Medicine Alexander Leaf. Said Russell, "Alex is a zealot. I think he felt that heart transplantation was a case of extreme medicine, a tremendously expensive enterprise that would benefit a very small number of patients."

Despite the GEC's backing, however, heart transplantation was again rejected by the Board of Trustees. Said Russell: "Board Chairman Sarge Cheever and Charlie Sanders called me down and told me that they didn't think we should do heart transplantation. I'm not going to scream and rant and rave. I told them I thought they were making a mistake. But I said I would continue to work and I would find something else to do. We turned our attention to liver transplantation and became the first place in New England to do livers."

Jerry Austen was more vocal in his dismay over the board's rejection of heart transplantation. Charlie Sanders would remember: "Paul Russell was very gentlemanly about it, but Jerry Austen wasn't happy." In fact, Austen believed that in presenting the issue to the trustees, Sanders had not made a strong enough case, and this caused friction between the two for a short time. The trustees' report for 1980 would refer only to "this year's difficult decision that the hospital would not do heart transplantation surgery."[121] When interviewed for this book 28 years later, Austen said, "I still think it was a mistake. The MGH has great clinicians and scientists, and on this occasion we should have been prepared to lead rather than follow." Sanders, speaking in 2009, was gracious: "I know that for Jerry it still smarts. He may well have been right."

Sanders added that there were good reasons for opposing heart transplantation. The hospital in the 1970s, he said, was full to capacity: "It was hard to get people admitted, and we didn't want to set aside a particular area for something where the outcomes had been very uneven. Transplant patients had to be isolated; we'd need extra nurses. I felt we would have to set up a special unit in a hospital that was already overloaded. And I felt we were not making a big contribution to science because other hospitals were doing these, too."

Kay Bander offered a dispassionate perspective. She said that the decision to wait on heart transplantation was dictated by "the MGH DNA: we don't have to be first, but let's be the best. Timing is less important than quality." Bander pointed out that, once approved, Mass General's heart transplantation service developed a good reputation for success and innovation. "The whole affair had a happy ending," she said.

Upon the trustees' turndown in 1980, the *New England Journal of Medicine* published an article ("MGH Says No") which was widely reported in the Boston papers. "It was embarrassing to me and Jerry," said Cosimi, "and it was embarrassing to Norm Shumway, who had looked forward to another institution verifying his work. I don't want to be a cowboy and do something crazy, but I don't believe the MGH doesn't have to be first. If you're pretty sure this is the right thing, you should do it."

The primary reason for low survival rates for heart transplant patients in the 1970s was the lack of effective immunosuppressive drugs, and this is where Cosimi focused his efforts. Monoclonal antibodies, a Nobel Prize–winning improvement on the earlier antilymphocyte antibody preparations made in horses, were first described in 1973–1975, and in the latter half of the decade, Cosimi worked to develop one of these to suppress the immune response in transplant patients. He started putting monoclonal antibodies in monkeys in 1978, and two years later he and his lab developed one for use in human transplantation, named OKT3, which proved to be remarkably effective in reversing acute rejection of transplants. At the time, Cosimi published a paper saying that OKT3 probably would eventually be replaced by other monoclonal antibodies. It is still in use 30 years later. Together with another drug, cyclosporine, approved for longer-term treatment of transplant patients in 1983, these agents emerged as the immunosuppressive therapy of choice for the majority of cases. Said Cosimi, "I had debates with Tom Starzl, who argued that cyclosporine was better; I thought OKT3. Together, they made a big difference, from 50 percent survival in kidney allografts[122] to 75-plus. Livers went from 10–15 percent to 65."

Cleared for Takeoff

With this sudden progress in immunosuppressive treatment, transplantation could move ahead smartly at MGH in the 1980s. The kidney program rapidly expanded. Said Cosimi, "When I came to MGH in the 1970s, Brigham and Women's Hospital was doing about 100 kidneys a year, and MGH was doing about 15. We turned that around."

Paul Russell, Hardy Hendren, and Ronald Malt had performed one liver transplant in the late 1960s, while Cosimi was a resident, but it was not successful. The first success with livers did not occur until 1983. By 1986 MGH was doing transplants with five body parts: kidney, liver, pancreas, bone marrow, and (finally) heart. There were some miraculous moments. Cosimi performed the first pancreas transplant at MGH using techniques perfected by a former MGH resident, Robert J. Corry at the University of Iowa.[123] Said Cosimi, "As soon as we connected the few blood vessels to the pancreas, [the patient's] blood sugar fell to normal and has remained there ever since."[124] The patient celebrated the successful pancreas transplant by eating his first piece of blueberry pie in 20 years. In 1990 MGH added lung transplantation to its list of surgical services. The first procedure was performed on a 52-year-old man suffering from severe emphysema.[125]

Other Boston-area hospitals ramped up transplantation, and the matter became political. Should everybody do transplants, and, if so, would there be excessive competition, especially for scarce donor organs? One compromise of several was the Center for Heart Transplantation, founded in 1985, which included all competing Boston-area sites. Cosimi noted that although this did not completely eliminate competition, it did lead to regular meetings that enabled the development of clear, objective grounds for including a patient as a candidate and rapid accumulation of experience for the relatively small individual centers.

Paul Russell formally headed transplantation research during the 1980s, although several innovations came from Cosimi's lab. In 1990 Russell stepped down; Cosimi assumed overall leadership of transplantation; and a former MGH resident-turned-NIH star was recruited back to Boston.

From Boston to Bethesda and Back

David H. Sachs likes to say that he is MGH's oldest resident, because he never finished his residency. He is another early follower of Paul Russell to lead the second generation of transplantation at the hospital. A native of Yonkers, New York, Sachs was educated in New York public schools and arrived at Harvard College inspired by Sputnik and dreaming of a career in astrophysics. Medicine had been on his mind since a brush with polio at age four, however, and within a few months he switched majors from physics to chemistry, a decision reinforced by the excitement of studying organic chemistry with Louis F. Fieser. Sachs worked in Fieser's lab during his final two years at Harvard, then took a year in Paris studying organic chemistry on a Fulbright Fellowship. In 1964 Sachs entered Harvard Medical School, while resuming work in Fieser's lab. He was inspired by a lecture in his second-year course in microbiology and immunology by an HMS instructor, Hugh O. McDevitt. McDevitt explained how Ray Owen's findings about fraternal cattle twins had inspired Peter Medawar to graft donor blood cells into neonatal mice, which then demonstrated tolerance to skin grafts. Sachs wrote: "As a medi-

cal student listening to this lecture, I immediately became excited by the prospect of extending these findings to the field of transplantation. If one could induce similar tolerance between individuals in adult life, patients might be able to accept transplanted organs without major ablation of their immune system. This possibility fulfilled the two criteria I had set for myself in choosing an area of research: 1) that the problem be important; and 2) that there be a reasonable chance of success."[126]

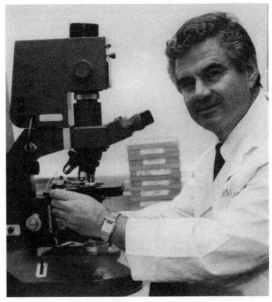

This nascent interest led him to Paul Russell. Sachs wrote of Russell: "He was extremely kind and

David Sachs.

encouraging, telling me that this field was just getting started and could really use enthusiastic young students like myself." Henry Winn, hired by Russell to head up transplantation lab efforts, took Sachs on as a part-time and summer research fellow.

With an interest in transplantation, Sachs entered the MGH surgical residency program in 1968. At the end of his second year he interrupted his residency to accept a two-year research fellowship as a clinical associate at the NIH. Two years later he stretched his leave of absence from MGH when the NIH offered him his own lab. It would be almost 20 more years before Sachs returned to Mass General, and no longer as a resident. By the mid-1970s Sachs had become chief of immunology at the National Cancer Institute of the NIH. Said Sachs: "I went to the NIH thinking I would come back to MGH and finish my residency but I got into an exciting opportunity there and asked MGH for a one-year extension. Then we discovered class-2 antigens, an important molecule in the field, and I decided to stay at NIH for the foreseeable future. Down deep I must have realized my real contribution was going to be in research." Russell said: "Sachs is bright and enthusiastic, and we always wanted to have him come back to MGH, but by that time he was too much of a big shot at the NIH."

For 20 years at the NIH and since 1988 at MGH, as the first Paul S. Russell / Warner-Lambert professor of surgery, Sachs has focused on two of the critical issues facing transplant scientists and surgeons: tolerance and the shortage of donors.

Immunologic tolerance, he said when interviewed in 2010, took up about two-thirds of his investigative time. Here the emphasis has been on *mixed chimerism*, a state in which the hematopoietic system (the system that creates new blood cells in the host) contains a mixture of cells derived from both the host and the donor—harking back to Medawar's mice. This cell mixture is created by a bone marrow transplant. By 1988 Sachs was ready to put his findings to clinical trials, but the NIH had no clinical transplantation program. His search for such a program was part of what led him back to Mass General. Chief of Surgery Jerry Austen was also instrumental in enticing the NIH "big shot" back to MGH.

The timing was fortunate: as is explained in the following chapter, 1988 was the first full year of MGH's new research facility in the old Charlestown Navy Yard, without which there probably would have been no space for Sachs. Though MGH had no clinical bone marrow transplant program before Sachs's return, the hospital assured him of its interest in starting one; and one of his first moves upon returning to Boston was to recruit Thomas Spitzer from Georgetown to run the program. Tatsuo Kawai, a research fellow in Cosimi's laboratory, began working with Sachs, translating his work with mixed chimerism in mice to monkeys. After a landmark paper in 1995, marking the success of this endeavor, the next step was to translate it to humans. A paper in the *New England Journal of Medicine* in 2008 reported the first positive results from human trials. The summary from that paper is hard reading for the layperson, but its main idea is clear. Four of five patients given bone marrow transplants before kidney transplantation were able to go off immunosuppressive drugs within 14 months of surgery (some sooner):

Five patients with end-stage renal disease received combined bone marrow and kidney transplants from HLA single-haplotype mismatched living related donors, with the use of a nonmyeloablative preparative regimen. Transient chimerism and reversible capillary leak syndrome developed in all recipients. Irreversible humoral rejection occurred in one patient. In the other four recipients, it was possible to discontinue all immunosuppressive therapy 9 to 14 months after the transplantation, and renal function has remained stable for 2.0 to 5.3 years since transplantation.[127]

Roughly one-third of Sachs's research effort is now focused on solving donor shortages. "As excited as we are about the possibility that this tolerance approach will improve the quality of life for [transplant] patients," Sachs wrote, "it will unfortunately do nothing to increase the availability of organs, a problem that is increasingly becoming the most critical limitation to the field of transplantation."[128] To this end, Sachs's team worked apace on xenotransplantation, using donors of another species. His laboratory has devoted considerable effort to a pig-to-primate model, using special inbred, genetically modified miniature swine, which are exactly the right size to provide organs to human beings. Success in this endeavor could eliminate waiting lists and bring the field of transplantation to its full potential.

In addition to Russell, Cosimi, Spitzer, and Kawai, Sachs cited the important contributions in transplantation by Nina Rubin, medical director of the MGH Renal Transplant Program, and Megan Sykes, whose laboratory efforts have been key to the design and interpretation of tolerance protocols.

Ben Cosimi stepped down as administrative chief of transplantation at MGH in 2010, giving way to James Markmann, a leader in pancreas transplantation. Because of the donor shortage, which remained unsolved, Cosimi said, "We're not bringing on new staff because you can only do so many transplants each year."

A GAME-CHANGING DEAL WITH INDUSTRY

As the decade of the 1970s began winding down, Mass General saw a flurry of activity, symbolized by the most memorable snowstorm in recent memory, the blizzard of February 1978. In 48 hours, beginning Monday, February 6, 30 inches of snow accumulated; high winds created towering drifts. Greater Boston was paralyzed, Massachusetts Governor Michael Dukakis declared a state of emergency, heavy construction equipment was called in to relocate mountains of snow, and on officially closed city streets and highways the only traffic was pedestrian, punctuated by the occasional emergency vehicle or cross-country skier. The trustees reported, "Those who could forced their way through the drifts on foot, on skis, in emergency four-wheel-drive vehicles, and once inside the Hospital remained on duty for the duration of the emergency. . . . Although the storm cost the Hospital over $1,000,000 in increased costs and decreased revenues, the demonstration by our staff and volunteers of their courage and their devotion to the Hospital was a heartening one."[129] Kay Bander was on-site, keeping the administration up and running and sleeping on a couch in the office.

Under Sanders, the hospital launched its first major capital campaign at the end of the decade, a development detailed in the next chapter. Sanders also shepherded plans for a new ambulatory care center, finally opened in the year of Sanders's departure and named for An Wang, the founder of Wang Laboratories, and his family, who made the lead gift. Sanders pressed for a corporate reorganization, made official on September 22, 1980. The original charitable corporation, The Massachusetts General Hospital, chartered in 1811, retained its endowment and spun off its operating assets into two new nonprofit subsidiaries, The General Hospital Corporation and The McLean Hospital Corporation. The original entity, which came to be known familiarly as "the 1811 Corporation," remained a holding company, legally the sole "member" of both new corporations.

Ernest M. "Ern" Haddad, who became general counsel of the three corporations in January 1981, was strongly of the view that no further corporate entities be created without compelling legal or financial reason. But within just a few years he found it necessary to create The MGH Institute of Health Professions, Inc. (essential to obtain accreditation of the Master of Nursing program), The MGH Professional Services Corporation (later reorganized as the MGPO) (essential for Medicare payment purposes), and The Spaulding Rehabilitation Hospital Corporation. (A discrete governing board was one of the Spaulding family's conditions of selling the Massachusetts Rehabilitation Hospital to MGH, further detailed in the following chapter.)

In 1994 another layer of organization would come into being with the formation of Partners HealthCare, which then became the sole member of the 1811 Corporation.

Dr. An Wang and his family at the dedication of the Wang Ambulatory Care Center, 1985.

Roll these changes up in a ball, however—the capital campaign, the Wang, the new corporation—and they don't match the significance of an initiative that can be credited squarely to Sanders, a game-changing alliance with a major chemical and pharmaceutical firm. Until this period, academic medical centers like MGH had kept their distance from industry, believing that too many conflicts of interest threatened. If industry "owned" a lab within a university hospital, what would happen to cherished academic freedom? Furthermore, academics tended to look down on the more commercially minded. Sanders had a different perspective, at least looking back from 2010, after his own second career in industry:

> If you looked at industry from MGH, particularly in the 1970s, you had a monocular view. But get on the other side and you find that industry is something more than a bunch of people following a recipe: they do have to take risks and they do have to be accountable. Those qualities are not always found in the academic environment, where you may take risk, but you have no hard time line, no accountability. The whole creativity of the academic world is based on the ability to do pretty much what you want to do. Any result is a good result as long as it is repeatable and appears to advance a particular field.

Sanders may not have been quite as active or self-promotional on the national scene as John Knowles had been, but he did earn recognition beyond New England. He was elected to the Institute of Medicine of the National Academy of Sciences, where he headed two high-profile committees; the first addressed the new technology of CT scanning, and the second focused on health care technology in general. Committee reports attracted national attention, because of which in 1977 Sanders was offered the position of assistant secretary of Health, Education, and Welfare by Jimmy Carter's incoming secretary, Joseph Califano. "After thinking about it for three weeks, and consulting with Hooks Burr, among others, I decided to turn it down," Sanders said, "because I simply had not finished the things I had started out to do at the MGH. Later, I headed the National Council on Health Care Technology for HEW."

In addition, Sanders was the first general director of Mass General to become active in outside business directorships. He sat on several boards, including the First National Bank of Boston and the New England Life Insurance Company. "I think that MGH had more of a presence in the Boston community because of my involvement with these boards than it had had before," said Sanders. These activities sensitized Sanders to the potential partnerships that could be forged between academic medicine and the business community.

At the University of California, San Francisco, by the end of the 1970s the molecular biologist Howard Goodman was blazing new trails. Molecular biology was the coming thing in biomedical research, and Goodman's lab was one of the most visible exponents of it. Goodman spoke "the arcane language of molecular biology with the distinctive twang of Brooklyn, where he was born, and Long Island, where he grew up."[130] A Williams College graduate with a PhD in biophysics from MIT, Goodman had done postdoctoral work in Cambridge, England, and Geneva in the late 1960s, then was hired at UCSF in 1970 as a junior faculty member. He was made a full professor in 1976, and the following year he, William

J. Rutter, and other UCSF colleagues transplanted the genetic code for making insulin from a rat cell to an E. coli bacterium, which led to a commercial process for manufacturing insulin. It was the first time genetic code had been transferred for any hormone.

Goodman's work caught the attention of Hoechst AG, a venerable German chemical company with a smaller presence in pharmaceuticals.[131] At the time there were three commercial manufacturers of insulin in the world: Eli Lilly, Novartis, and Hoechst. The molecular biology revolution promised fast profits for companies that could clone hormones like insulin. To accomplish this, Eli Lilly partnered with Genentech and Novartis developed its own capability, leaving Hoechst looking for a pathway into the field. Goodman proved to be the pathway.

On June 2, 1977, Hans-Hermann Schöne of Hoechst sent a letter to Howard Goodman congratulating him on an article in the *International Herald Tribune* entitled "Insulin Gene Is Transplanted in Bacteria for Reproduction." Schöne wrote: "Our vivid interest in your findings is based on the fact that we have a group in our pharmaceutical research division who are engaged in similar problems. As you may know, Hoechst AG is a leading company in all problems connected with the therapy of diabetes (insulin and oral blood-sugar lowering substances). . . . We assume that . . . a discussion might be of mutual interest."[132] Schöne was on the West Coast visiting Goodman in July and subsequently invited the UCSF scientist to Germany.[133]

Such a link between German industry and American academe would prove thorny for both sides. For Hoechst's part, the company had no choice because it had no in-house capability in molecular biology. If it wanted to compete against Lilly and Novartis, it needed American know-how. In a revealing statement, Professor Hans-Georg Gareis of the Hoechst Board of Management shed light on this. "When we at Hoechst started working with gene technology connected with our traditional interest in insulin," he said, "we quickly found this would be difficult to do all by ourselves in Germany. We found a large gap in this area of science in our country. There were many reasons for this gap." Gareis particularly cited the "Hitler period [which] practically eliminated the Jewish scientific community."[134] World War II, he said, also destroyed German cities and scientific institutes, and it took Germany many years to restart scientific life.

Before 1980 such a collaboration of industry and academe would have been unthinkable in the United States. Academic researchers prided themselves on their independence from commercial interests. In the university, the quest was said to be for knowledge, not profits. But in 1980 the Bayh-Dole Act was passed, granting intellectual property rights for research discoveries to the institutions and investigators who made them. Before Bayh-Dole, once a paper was published from a lab at MGH, the intellectual property was legally in the public domain.

But why did Hoechst not simply make a deal with UCSF, allowing Goodman to remain in his lab there? According to a journalist who covered the story, "The bureaucracy of a public university proved too much of an obstacle."[135] And there were other suitors, including Washington University in St. Louis, home to a major academic medical center, as well as Massachusetts General Hospital.

Charlie Sanders was alerted to the Hoechst possibilities by MGH Chief of

Medicine John Potts. Handling negotiations for Hoechst was Hansgeorg Gareis. Sanders characterized his Hoechst counterpart as "a Bavarian, a lovely man, a command-and-control German, very sophisticated, who knew how Americans thought. He and I hit it off."

Not everyone at Mass General was as positive on a deal with Hoechst and Goodman as Sanders was. He recalled:

> We had internal discussions about having this grafted onto our already existing research enterprise, and there was a lot of concern, if not opposition: here was a not-for-profit hospital considering a relationship with industry. Would that taint the academic enterprise by restricting publication and controlling research—either of which would have been anathema to the academic enterprise? From my point of view, it was a wonderful deal for the MGH: they would give us the money, we would do the research, and they would have right of first refusal. Basically, we were going to have a molecular biology facility with faculty and space funded by industry, with virtually no questions asked.

Ern Haddad became general counsel at MGH in January 1981, just as negotiations were heating up. "I was on the job for two or three weeks," Haddad recalled, "and Charlie Sanders walked into my office and said, 'I've got a project for you.' It was Hoechst." There were two highly problematic issues, Haddad said, both falling under the "rubric of academic freedom." What access would Hoechst have to the intellectual property coming out of research at MGH, and would there be any restriction on MGH publication of research results before Hoechst had a chance to secure commercial rights to them?

Kay Bander recalled untold hours of negotiations, both externally and internally: "Every time you looked up there was someone coming in the door from Hoechst, or a lawyer for the hospital. It was extremely tricky not only to design and develop the agreement, but then to sell it internally. Some of the staff thought the hospital was selling its soul. Dr. Sanders took the lead. He believed there was a potential there if it was handled properly. The Hoechst deal was a big part of his legacy. If you had to single out one thing as his legacy, I would have to say that."

Gareis visited Boston, and the chemistry seemed good. He then flew to San Francisco. Said Sanders: "I can't remember who I was talking to, but I said, I want to call George [as Gareis was called] and tell him we're going to give him the space. I called him, got him out of the shower in the Saint Francis Hotel in San Francisco, and I said, 'George, we're going to do everything we can to make this happen for you. We really want you to come, and we think this is the kind of environment where things will prosper.' George Gareis later told me my call was what made the difference in their decision to come to Boston."

In the lead-up to a deal and in the final negotiations, another major player was one of the MGH trustees, Hooks Burr. In Boston and Cambridge Burr was a powerhouse as managing partner at Ropes and Gray, senior fellow (governing board member) at Harvard, and director of several of America's largest corporations; but at MGH, according to Sanders, he suffered somewhat from being in the shadow of John Lawrence. "But if you look at the Hoechst agreement," Sanders added,

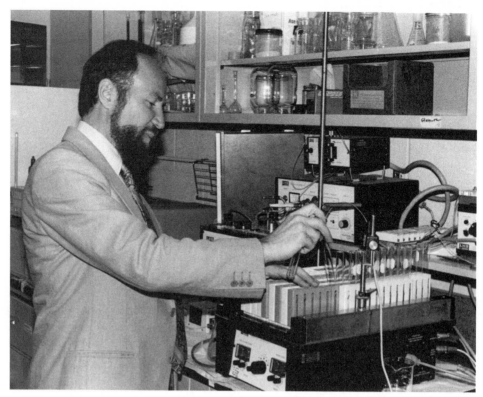

Howard Goodman.

"he's the one who chose the lawyers to work on it and oversaw their work. Also, he never put on his Harvard hat. If he had done so, he might have had reservations about the Hoechst deal. But with his MGH hat on he was very supportive."

The MGH Committee on Research advised on the contract to ensure ethical boundaries and prevent conflicts of interest. Haddad also credited a trustee committee, headed by William McCune, CEO of Polaroid, for having the "spine" to protect MGH's academic interests. In the end, a contract was signed with Hoechst under which MGH retained ownership of patents while Hoechst obtained a right of first refusal to license those patents. The contract also gave MGH academic freedom to publish without embargo and guaranteed an initial flow of $50 million in research funding to the hospital.

The molecular biologist Gary Ruvkun, who would be one of Goodman's early hires at MGH in the early 1980s and win a Lasker Award for his work in 2008, commented on the Hoechst deal: "What's most interesting is how MGH had the wisdom to do it. It was bold for them to take the Hoechst money. UCSF wouldn't take it. It was too close to the sixties. It smelled funny. They're worried about academic freedom. MGH was willing to work it out—though you could figure out 100 reasons not to do it."

Mass General was not the only academic institution to accept commercial investment immediately following Bayh-Dole. Harvard Medical School accepted a $6 million grant from DuPont and MIT $8 million from W. R. Grace, and Monsanto invested $23.5 million in protein and peptide research at Washington

University.[136] But at what finally amounted to $70 million over 10 years, the Hoechst-MGH deal was far and away the biggest of its time.[137]

Why did MGH finally win the deal? Gareis noted that it is "a private institution and therefore can act quickly and unbureaucratically. . . . But there is one more thing of great importance. That is people." Gareis cited Howard Goodman, Charlie Sanders, Hooks Burr, and Robert Buchanan, Sanders's successor, as playing key roles in landing the Hoechst investment. "During the very first hours of [our] meetings," he said, "we found a personal atmosphere of understanding."[138]

The deal proved to be a watershed in the history of Massachusetts General Hospital as a biomedical research institution. It opened the door to other major deals with industry, such as a 1989 agreement with the Japanese cosmetics company Shiseido, which was patterned on the Hoechst agreement. As the final chapter of this book will show, Howard Goodman's molecular biology department conferred unarguable star power on MGH as a major biomedical research institution.

SANDERS MOVES ON

Sanders spent some time in Iran in 1974, helping an American team design a medical school for the Iranian government. Later in the decade another Middle Eastern connection was forged through Roger L. Nichols at Harvard Medical School. He was contacted by the Saudis to help start a medical school there, and Sanders spent time with that team on the Arabian Peninsula helping conceive the design.

In 1979 Robert Ebert, former chief of medicine and recently retired as dean at Harvard Medical School, invited Sanders to join a trade mission to China. The Cultural Revolution was over, the Chinese were restarting scientific investigation and training, and the purpose of the mission was to initiate contact with American academic medicine. Sanders accepted the invitation, which led to a friendship with another person on the trip, Dennis Fill, president and chief operating officer of the pharmaceutical giant ER Squibb.

The China initiative did not yield much fruit for MGH. There were some exchanges of personnel, including a Chinese researcher who worked in Kurt Isselbacher's lab at MGH, but few permanent connections were formed. Sanders would recall one humorous moment, however: "We hosted a dinner for the Chinese here in Boston when they brought their own delegation and threw a party at a new Chinese restaurant on Boylston Street. It went on and on, until about ten o'clock, when trustee John Lawrence got up and announced, 'I've only got one stomach to give for my country. I'm going home.'"

A trip to China the following year, which included several MGH chiefs of service (Chief of Medicine Alex Leaf and Chief of Anesthesiology Dick Kitz, among others), visited much the same territory covered in 1979. Though neither of the China trips led to major results for MGH, the contact with Dennis Fill and Squibb was decisive for Sanders. In 1981 the MGH general director was recruited as vice president for research by Squibb. By 1987 he would be its vice chairman, and in 1989 he moved to Glaxo USA as chairman and CEO.

"I was one of the early 'crossovers' from academia into industry," said Sanders, "which became much more common later on. Roy Vagelos led the way when he joined Merck from Washington University in St. Louis in 1975, to head their R&D. He later became CEO, and his discoveries as well as his leadership resulted in tremendous commercial success for Merck in the 1980s and 1990s."

The MGH annual report for 1981 summarized the achievements of the Sanders years: "It is mainly because of decisions Dr. Charles Addison Sanders made when he first assumed leadership of the hospital in 1972 that we closed the 1981 fiscal year only months away from opening our new Ambulatory Care Center. He brought about the founding of the MGH Institute of Health Professions. He organized and launched last February the hospital's $114 million fund-raising drive. He was the driving force behind the $50-plus million grant from Hoechst AG for the funding of our new Department of Molecular Biology."[139]

Sanders left MGH administration in the summer of 1981, but he never truly left Fruit Street. His allegiance to Mass General has stood the test of time. "When I was at Squibb," he recalled, "Kay Bander and I engineered a $250,000 gift from Squibb to MGH. Kay managed to work the levers in such a way that they didn't have much choice but to give it!" (By this time Sanders had recruited Bander to Squibb.)

Until he was sidelined by a stroke in 2010, Sanders remained a member of the high-profile President's Council and a trusted confidant of senior MGH administrators. "Any success I have had after leaving the MGH is due in large measure to the recognition that my position there gave me, in business management and in the larger field of health care," Sanders said. "I have tried to give back to the hospital through the years, both in terms of time and more tangibly through the establishment of a Harvard professorship in basic science, held [in 2011] by Ken Chien, who heads the Cardiovascular Research Center."

CHAPTER 7

. . . .

QUANTUM LEAPS, 1982–1994

The days of unrestrained growth and unlimited
resources now belong to the past.
—Alexander Leaf, 1982

BY THE 1980S THE MASS GENERAL CAMPUS WAS SHOWING ITS AGE. *Though patient care remained first-rate, the hospital's buildings and facilities were in dire need of renovation, and research space was in short supply. J. Robert Buchanan, who became general director in 1982 after interim leadership by Joseph B. Martin, vigorously addressed these issues with the support of key trustees such as Francis "Hooks" Burr and Ferdinand "Moose" Colloredo-Mansfeld.*

Aided by its first capital campaign, run by a newly professional development office, MGH upgraded both inpatient and outpatient facilities and put up a new research building. The new Wang Ambulatory Care Center opened at the beginning of the period; renovation of the White and Bigelow buildings began early on; and the Ellison and Blake inpatient towers were the capstone of construction. Meanwhile, the Wellman (now Thier) Research Building went up near the east end of the Bulfinch Building. The addition of a helicopter pad on the Blake tower helped turn the MGH Emergency Department into a regional resource. In a daring move, the hospital signed a lease for major research space in the old Charlestown Navy Yard, extending MGH's reach across the Charles River and creating the footprint for what is today America's largest hospital-based biomedical research institution.

Financial pressure brought by managed care helped spur another major move. In 1994, following the December 1993 announcement of the creation of Partners HealthCare System, Massachusetts General Hospital and its longtime competitor Brigham and Women's Hospital merged. With the addition of many smaller "partners" and an integrated network of primary care physicians, Partners, after some growing pains, was soon one of the country's most prominent integrated health care delivery systems. Another far-reaching change was the establishment

Groundbreaking for the Wellman (Thier) Research Building, 1982. Howard Goodman (far right) was not present for the photo session, so his image was pasted in later.

of an effective physicians organization, including a faculty group practice, the Massachusetts General Physicians Organization (MGPO), to represent the interests of doctors in a true partnership with the hospital administration.

Four sections in this chapter look at important clinical specialties: neurology, cancer care and research, obstetrics-gynecology, and neurosurgery.

THERE WAS ONLY ONE PROBLEM WITH THE HOECHST DEAL, at least from Joe Martin's perspective. The three-way negotiations with the German chemical giant and with Howard Goodman at UCSF concluded in the spring of 1981, just months before General Director Charles Sanders's unexpected summer departure from MGH. For two years Sanders had been fending off overtures from Squibb's CEO, Dennis Fill, and its board member Robert Ebert, the former HMS dean; but after the Hoechst deal was inked, he finally agreed to join Squibb as head of the company's science and technology group. The interim general director, Joseph B. Martin, was left with the task of fulfilling the terms of the MGH-Hoechst agreement, and he was not the only nervous one. Howard Goodman was, if anything, more nervous.

The whole deal hinged on providing Goodman, funded by Hoechst, with four floors of new lab space on the Fruit Street campus. Lab space had become a precious commodity at MGH; indeed, 30 years later a leading MGH researcher would say that space remained, if not scarce, then certainly the most valued commodity for the hospital's physician-scientists. Late in the decade of the 1980s, Massachusetts General Hospital would address the shortage of space in a dramatic, game-changing way by moving off-campus and over the river.

The Hoechst deal called for groundbreaking for a new research building by March 1982. Standing on the only conceivable site on campus, to the right of the Bulfinch facade, between the 1951 Edwards Research Building and Bartlett Hall, was the Resident Physicians' House, a nondescript redbrick building. Tear it down? No! Community activists, especially Beacon Hill preservationists, opposed demolition of such a "historic" building, calling it "irreplaceable architecture from the nineteenth century," according to Martin's recollection. Instead, and at the very last minute for the Hoechst deal, the Resident Physicians' House was moved, first to an interim location, then to its current location at the corner of Cambridge and North Grove streets.

Further opposition to the Hoechst deal emerged in the person of Al Gore Jr., then a youthful 33-year-old congressman from Tennessee. Gore called Martin out of the blue, saying such a deal with a German company would skim the cream off the top of U.S. research efforts and give it to a foreign entity. Apparently Martin was persuasive. "As I recall, the conversation lasted about 30 minutes," he said. "I never heard from Gore again."

How the advent of Howard Goodman's lab brought the molecular biology revolution to MGH and affected institutional fortunes into the next millennium is a dramatic story that will be reserved for the next and final chapter of this book.

EMERGING LEADERSHIP IN NEUROLOGY

From his point of view, Joe Martin had little business being in the general director's chair in the first place. He had arrived at MGH only three years before from McGill University, replacing Raymond D. Adams as chief of one of the most venerable and illustrious services at Massachusetts General Hospital, neurology.

The treatment of diseases of the central nervous system had begun in 1872 with electricity. The first MGH physician considered a neurologist, James Jackson Putnam, a house pupil until 1869, was in 1872 appointed to the official position of electrician. There were no lightbulbs to change yet, no wiring to install; Thomas Edison had only just begun to tinker. In Europe Putnam had studied electrotherapy, which was quite the rage through much of the nineteenth century. Putnam's initial duties at MGH were "to take charge and proper care of all the magnetic and electrical apparatus of the Hospital, and administer magnetism and electricity to patients, whenever called upon by the Physicians and Surgeons."[1] According to one historian, Putnam treated patients "with a 'little battery' and a hand-cranked electrical generator, which, along with administration of bromides to reduce brain inflammation, constituted the main bulwarks of neurological therapeutics."[2] In 1873, by a vote of the trustees, Putnam's title was changed from electrician to physician to outpatients with diseases of the nervous system.[3]

The same job description was conferred on George L. Walton in 1889. He

James Jackson Putnam.

and Putnam shared duties, assisted by Henry C. Baldwin and Cyrus F. Carter. Until 1903, when this outpatient service moved into the new Outpatient Building, neurology's quarters were barely adequate. Space was enlarged in 1927–1928 "to accommodate the psychiatrists and the psychologist who were to function with Neurology."[4]

Like other services, neurology encountered the institutional antipathy toward specialization; when a benefactor in 1897 offered $100,000 "for the endowment of a department of nervous diseases at the General Hospital, requiring a new ward, to be under a special staff of Visiting Physicians, Neurologists," the offer was tabled and no action taken.[5] A report from the visiting staff explained its resistance: "The establishment of a special ward should not result in a monopoly of the class of cases for which it is designed, such cases being excluded from the general Medical and Surgical wards. A special ward should be complementary to the general wards. Otherwise the general wards would gradually become specialized, and the Hospital would be converted into a collection of special departments; a result which seemed to this Board inconsistent with the best interests of the Hospital and the community."[6]

James Putnam remained chief of the "Neurological Department" until his retirement in 1912. He had become disenchanted with electrotherapy by that time, having been smitten, as many were, with the teachings of Sigmund Freud. In fact, Putnam traveled to Europe in 1911, the year before his retirement, and submitted to six hours of psychoanalysis administered by the master himself. This encounter between Brahmin Boston and Freudian Vienna was not without its odd moments. In a letter Putnam shared a childhood daydream with Freud: "I used . . . to long for a married life and home of my own and formed a picture in my mind, of myself sitting before an open fire in an otherwise unlighted room, with wife and young children (in my vision I think the children were more prominent) playing around and receiving the usual caresses and attentions—reading aloud, etc." What sense did the father of psychoanalysis make of this benign fantasy? "I see that you are suffering from a too early and too strongly repressed sadism expressed in over-goodness and self-torture," Freud replied to Putnam in a letter.[7]

The closing words about Putnam in the official hospital history of the period reflect the influence of Freud, positioning him as a neurologist *and* a psychiatrist: "[Putnam] was the pioneer neurologist of New England, and to him is due the early recognition of his specialty. His medical writings were numerous and varied, covering many aspects of neurology, both structural and functional. He was perhaps the earliest convert to Freudian psychology in America, and for his efforts in behalf of psycho-analysis he will be long remembered."[8]

Putnam was succeeded by E. Wyllys Taylor in 1912. A General Executive

Committee (GEC) report for 1912 notes the areas of focus during this period: the study of spinal fluids; clinical trials of salvarsan for "syphilitic disorders of the nervous system"; the study of psychoneuroses by the analytic method; and the use of massage for the treatment of some unstated condition(s).[9]

By 1921 the neurology staff was growing, but the hospital still allocated to the department only two beds, "less than any other of equal importance."[10] Finally, in 1926, the year Taylor retired, a joint neurology and neurosurgery ward opened on the first floor of Bulfinch West. The GEC opined that "cooperation between these two departments is vital. . . . To facilitate this union, a combined ward round is made regularly once a week."[11]

James B. Ayer succeeded Taylor in 1927. It was Ayer who formally established the first neurology lab, to study spinal fluid, in 1920. The study of neuropathology had been taken up by the Pathology Department by this time as well. In 1938 a third lab, for electro-encephalography (EEG), opened under Robert Schwab. EEG was used primarily to diagnose epilepsy and locate brain tumors.

Details of the Neurology Department are spotty in the official MGH history written by Faxon covering the years 1935–1955. One development noted was the myasthenia gravis clinic created in 1944. This disease, causing muscular weakness and fatigue, is now known to be an autoimmune disorder. Increased understanding of the pathology and the discovery of the drug prostigmine encouraged MGH to open a myasthenia gravis clinic. This in turn demonstrated the benefits of the drug. MGH pathologists, including Benjamin Castleman, demonstrated a link between myasthenia gravis and the thymus gland. MGH surgeons, including Oliver Cope, began removing the gland to treat the disease.[12]

Ayer stepped down as chief after the war, and Charles S. Kubik was appointed to succeed him in 1946.[13] But it seems that neurology at MGH kicked into a higher gear only after 1951, with the arrival of Kubik's successor, Raymond D. Adams. Adams would live to be 97. When he died in 2008, the MGH neurologist Allan H. Ropper described his contributions to the *Boston Globe:* "What Ray Adams did in essence was establish an American style of neurology and broke it away from the dominant European influence of the 20s, 30s, and 40s. He carved out a much more modern perspective. What he did that really broke the field open is that he made maximum use of neuropathology to study diseases. He established neuropathology as the basic science of clinical neurology."[14]

James B. Ayer.

Using neuropathology amounted to defining diseases of the nervous system by assessing them post mortem. In other words, Adams began leading the charge from bedside to bench— continuing to study patients in the clinic, but also using the microscope and other lab tools to study specimens from diseased patients.

J. Philip Kistler, who would come to prominence in the neurology depart-ment's stroke unit, said that under Adams, MGH became "the place for neurology in the world . . . the place that developed modern thinking about neurology."[15]

There were some major developments in the Adams era (1951–1978):

- The Eunice Kennedy Shriver Center was founded at the Fernald School in Waltham, Massachusetts, in 1959. The fund-raiser nonpareil David Crockett was credited with helping raise money from the Joseph P. Ken-nedy family (Mrs. Shriver was his daughter and the sister of John, Robert, and Ted Kennedy). Mrs. Shriver's interest in neurology was driven by the experience of her sister Rosemary, who had undergone a lobotomy in 1941. Construction began in 1960 on the "Kennedy Building," actually the top floor of the Vincent Burnham Building. Joe Martin said: "Ray Adams was the key person in working with the Kennedy family, and Adams made that a very strong part of the portfolio of the department." Verne S. Caviness Jr. headed the Shriver Center for several years and focused on understanding the development of the nervous system and how, when development goes wrong, it can cause developmental disorders.

- C. Miller Fisher became a world pioneer in the description and diagnosis of stroke. Fisher provided the most complete examinations of the blood vessels and brains of people who had died after various types of clinically studied strokes. He was a master who often stayed overnight at the hospital, remaining with his patients throughout their episodes of illness.

- Other notable achievements, briefly: Maurice Victor and Adams studied alcohol-related illnesses and vitamin deficiencies. Sir John Walton and Arthur K. Asbury made important contributions and became world leaders in the study of neuromuscular diseases and demyelinating neuropathies.[16] Guy McKhann, Richard T. Johnson, and J. Richard Baringer became department chairs at other institutions, and many others went on to lead major programs in the United States and abroad.

Research Accelerates

It's a miracle Joe Martin ever left Alberta, to say nothing of reaching Boston. Born on a dairy farm north of the Trans-Canada Highway, Martin was the son of Penn-sylvania Dutch Mennonites. His grandparents on both sides had been homestead-ers in Alberta. Martin's interest in medicine "goes back as far back as I know: I remember being four or five, walking across a field and deciding I was going to be a doctor." It might have been his church's missionaries, coming back with stories about Asia and Africa, who triggered his interest in medicine as a career.

Getting off the farm was the first step. Of 54 cousins, he was the first to attend college. He took two years of premed courses at the University of Alberta, then earned his BSc from Eastern Mennonite College before returning to the Univer-sity of Alberta for his MD. There faculty told him he would be wasting his time as a family doctor. Through a family connection, he ended as a resident at University Hospitals in Cleveland, where he was impressed with Joseph Foley, a "quintes-sential Dorchester Irishman from Boston City Hospital" and a neurologist at Case

Western. Martin noted that MGH had turned him down as a prospective resident: "They didn't even answer my letter from Alberta."

Martin went on for a PhD at the University of Rochester, where his mentor, Seymour Reichlin, turned him on to neuroendocrinology and particularly the hypothalamic regulation of the pituitary gland. McGill University in Montreal offered him a position, and he rose there to become chair of the Department of Neurology and Neurosurgery. McGill was the only academic medical center in North America where the two disciplines were combined in one department, owing to the university's historical connection to Wilder Penfield and the Montreal Neurologic Institute. Because neurosurgeons do not like being lorded over by neurologists (or vice versa),[17] Martin was soon swimming against the current at McGill.

Neurology faculty, early 1980s. Standing, from left: E. Peirson Richardson, Chief Joseph B. Martin, and Verne Caviness Jr. Seated, from left: C. Miller Fisher and Raymond D. Adams.

In 1978 MGH began a search for a new chief of neurology. Martin was invited to interview and, when offered the position, decided that "a leadership position at Mass General is a once-in-a-lifetime thing." Martin took over in July. At the time Martin was the only neuroendocrinologist in the department, so he was able to make quite an impression on staff and students when he staged grand rounds in the Ether Dome. And whatever doubts veterans may have entertained about the newcomer from Canada, the editors of Harrison's *Principles of Internal Medicine* had none. They soon invited Martin to join their board, and he collaborated with Adams on the ninth edition (1980). The 10th edition followed in 1983. Over the next 15 years, Martin would collaborate with Gilbert H. Daniels as well as Jean D. Wilson of University of Texas Southwestern in Dallas to produce the then-definitive chapter on disorders of the pituitary gland, including pituitary tumors.

Research was clearly a priority for Martin. (MGH would name a prestigious research prize after him.) Renovations to his lab in neuroendocrinology were completed in the spring of 1979.

In 1980 the National Institutes of Health came out with a bold idea—funding disease-focused centers "without walls." This meant multiple institutions collaborating in the study of a particular disease. One of the requests for proposal concerned Huntington's disease, a neurodegenerative disorder that typically comes on a patient between the ages of 30 and 50 and, though not fatal in itself, typically lowers life expectancy dramatically because of complications. It afflicts an estimated three to seven in every 100,000 in Caucasian populations. That translates to 30,000 or more cases in the United States. Said Martin:

> I appreciated that Boston was an excellent place to pursue this problem. There was very good brain pathology at MGH; patients with Huntington's were at BU Medical Center and the Boston VA Hospital, interestingly; and all the genetics was at MIT.[18] So I forged a collaboration across boundaries of BU, MIT, HMS, and MGH, and in 1980 we got one of the two contracts.[19] I hired Jim [James F.] Gusella, a Canadian graduate student working at MIT under geneticist David [E.] Housman, and he came across the river and set up space in my lab. In collaboration with Nancy Wexler of the Hereditary Disease Foundation, we started collecting samples of blood from patients with Huntington's in Venezuela, in the USA, and elsewhere.

Martin was the principal investigator for the Huntington's center without walls from 1980 to 1989. Other key participants at MGH, besides Gusella, included Chief of Neuropathology E. Peirson Richardson. Investigators beyond Boston participated as well; one of these was Anne Buckingham Young of the University of Michigan, who would become chief of neurology at MGH a decade later. Gusella's lab began looking for DNA markers that were linked closely to the gene responsible for Huntington's, thus "providing a guidepost for the search for the abnormal gene itself."[20] The notion of DNA markers may seem old-hat today, in the wake of the Human Genome Project, but in the early 1980s the location of only a few human genes was known. To locate the gene whose mutation caused Huntington's would require at least 300 markers. Said Martin, "Jim concluded that the best he could do was to take whatever DNA markers he could locate from other laboratories working in the field of human genetics and test them one by one."

Blood samples were gathered from affected families and frozen to preserve them for later analysis. Lightning struck in August 1983, as Martin would recall in his memoir:

> I took the phone call in the bedroom. It was a muggy evening in Belmont, Massachusetts. The date was August 5, 1983. "Hello," I said. "Hi, Joe. It's Jim (Gusella). We've got it!" I was stunned. Some moments never delete from memory. "It" was the linkage for the gene causing Huntington's disease to a DNA marker, G8. We had no clue where the marker was placed along the twenty-three chromosomes. It was only the 12th probe that had been tested. "Are you sure?" I asked. "It's linked in both families," Jim replied. "The LOD score is over six!"[21]

Martin wrote: "Never before had a gene for an inherited disorder been located by gene mapping alone."[22] On November 9, 1983, a press conference was called in the Ether Dome to announce the discovery that the Huntington's disease gene had been linked to chromosome number 4.

Work in Gusella's lab would continue throughout the 1980s, narrowing the location of the Huntington's gene. Meanwhile, other achievements mounted. A neuroendocrine clinic grew apace, with collaborations from neurology, neuro-surgery (under Nicholas T. Zervas), and neuroendocrinology (Anne Klibanski). Allan Ropper, Martin's first chief neurology resident, stayed on to establish the first neurological-neurosurgical ICU in the country, with the collaboration of the Neurosurgery Service. John H. Growdon established the Alzheimer's Disease Research Center with funding from the National Institute on Aging. Growdon would lead the program for 25 years, then turn it over to Brad Hyman.

Anne Young Arrives

MGH neurology had not finished making history. In 1991 the hospital appointed its first female chief of service, the neurologist Anne Young. Her only previous visit to the MGH campus before interviewing in 1991 was to attend the press conference in 1983 announcing the Huntington's gene marker as an author on the original paper.

Born in Evanston, Illinois, Young grew up in the Chicago suburb of Win-netka. Her father was a businessman with a yen for chemistry who satisfied his sci-entific interest with photography and a home darkroom. Her mother was a house-wife with more than an idle interest in physics. Louise B. Young had worked in labs at MIT as one of four women among 2,000 men; she was subsequently invited to the University of Chicago for development of the atom bomb, but chose to get married and raise a family instead. As a result, Anne Young said, "there was a lot of science around the dining room table." When her children were older, Louise Young edited science books for lay people and eventually wrote her own, includ-ing *Power over People*, the first book to discuss the effect of electromagnetic fields on human health.[23]

Anne Young attended Vassar College and Johns Hopkins Medical School, where she was mentored by Sol Snyder, a young assistant professor on his way to becoming a world-renowned neuropharmacologist. While at Hopkins, Young

met and married John B. "Jack" Penney Jr., another neurolo-gist. Together they went on to UCSF to train in neurology. They developed a harmonious division of labor, according to Young: "Jack was a good reader, and I'm slightly dyslexic, so he would read everything and rec-ommend what I could focus on. I was a better writer, so I wrote all the grants. He would refer-ence the proposals because he had done all the reading, and he was also good at statistics, so the two of us together made the fig-ures [technical illustrations]."

The couple was recruited to

Anne Young.

the University of Michigan in Ann Arbor and set up labs there studying movement disorders like Parkinson's and Huntington's diseases, tremors, dystonia, and tics. "We hadn't trained in movement disorders," said Young, "but we claimed we were experts. In Michigan you could get away with a lot." Their first daughter, Jessica, had been born during their residency in California; their second, Ellen, arrived after the move to Michigan. (In 2010 Jessica was a mother herself and a teacher of high school science, and Ellen was en route to an MD-PhD and a career in neurology.)

Verne Caviness, who headed the pediatric division within the MGH Neurology Department, had taken over for Joe Martin upon the latter's departure in 1988, an appointment considered interim, pending a worldwide search. By this time Young had been approached for "just about every leadership position that had opened up in neurology," but the Penney family was happy in Michigan and had no intention of leaving. When the MGH search committee headed by Chief of Medicine John Potts called, however, Young knew she had to visit the Boston campus for the second time in her life: "Of all the places that had written me, this was the only thing I would have been interested in."

A self-described "ancient hippie," Young had long hair, which she wore hanging down over one shoulder. She recalled waiting in lobbies at MGH while secretaries looking for "Dr. Anne Young" ignored her, assuming that the youthful (43), long-haired woman waiting patiently couldn't be she. "Since it wasn't my goal in life to be a chief at Mass General, I was very frank in my interviews about how to improve the department, and I guess they liked that." Once given the job, Young instituted those changes. She recalled:

> Joe Martin had brought tremendous science to MGH neurology and expanded the department by having PhDs working in the lab next to other neurologists and scientists, but he didn't emphasize what was going on clinically. Mass General was good clinically, and in fact most in the department, even if they worked in the lab, saw general neurology patients, whatever they presented with. We also had a few subspecialty clinics. But clinicians were overworked and underappreciated, and even though I came in as a scientist, I decided to spend a lot of my effort in building clinical subspecialties and giving clinicians some assistance so they could publish and get grants.

Martin would comment: "The reason clinical development didn't happen until Anne came was because of limited facilities. My office was on Kennedy 9. The Wang had just opened, and we were negotiating some space for the clinic; meanwhile, we were seeing inpatients on Baker 3 and 4, and private patients in Phillips House, while Allan Ropper opened an ICU on Bigelow 12." Neurology was not the only MGH service suffering from a lack of well-organized facilities, a problem that would be ameliorated greatly when the Ellison and Blake towers opened in the 1990s (see below).

Clinical research was a major interest of Young's. She had always participated in clinical as well as basic lab research. Soon after coming to MGH, she set up the Neurology Clinical Trials Unit and appointed Merit E. Cudkowicz and Steven M. Greenberg as codirectors. The unit has thrived and now has about one-third of the Neurology Service research dollars. Cudkowicz is running the biggest clinical trials unit for amyotrophic lateral sclerosis (ALS, popularly known as Lou Gehrig's disease).

Young has actively promoted women in her department. Currently, women constitute one-third of the professors, associate professors, assistant professors, instructors, and clinical fellows.

Many MGH neurologists have gone on to run departments over the course of Young's tenure, including Steven Hauser (UCSF), M. Flint Beal (Cornell), Robert Brown (University of Massachusetts), and Stephen Cannon (University of Texas Southwestern).

By 2010 neurology at MGH included subspecialties in stroke, movement disorders, cerebellar ataxias, neurogenetics, memory disorders, neuromuscular disorders, epilepsies, sleep, behavioral neurology, neuro-oncology, and pediatric neurology. Science has not been neglected. Indeed, Young continued to build on what Martin had started: in 2010 MGH had the largest hospital-based research effort in neurology anywhere.

- Jim Gusella remained a notable contributor in neurogenetics, identifying genes for various neurological diseases, beginning with that first dramatic discovery for Huntington's in 1983. Later discoveries were in neurofibromatosis, Alzheimer's disease, familial dysautonomia, and autism.

- Rudolph E. Tanzi has achieved breakthroughs in the genetics of Alzheimer's disease. As a technician and then graduate student with Gusella, Tanzi worked on localizing the Huntington's gene and subsequently on localizing the amyloid precursor protein gene to chromosome 21. He has been involved in the discovery of all the major genes for Alzheimer's disease to date and in determining strategies for molecular alterations of the course of the disease.

- Bradley T. Hyman has done significant work on the molecular biology and anatomy of Alzheimer's. Recently he has shown that amyloid plaques in Alzheimer's are formed in a day and that antibodies can remove this amyloid. The amyloid can be imaged in the human brain and the effect of the antibodies is now being tested.

- Xandra O. Breakefield focused on molecular neurogenetics and has been involved in gene therapy for brain tumors and dominantly inherited dystonia. She found the first gene involved in dominantly inherited dystonia in 1997 and continues to work on the mechanism of this devastating disease.

- Robert H. Brown Jr. found genes for ALS before departing to head the department at the University of Massachusetts Medical School.

- In the field of stroke research, J. Philip Kistler has been a worthy inheritor of Miller Fisher's mantle. A "third generation" of stroke investigators, including Walter J. Koroshetz, Karen L. Furie, Jonathan Rosand, and Lee H. Schwamm, have done "spectacularly" in the areas of stroke prevention, stroke genetics, and acute stroke care through telemedicine, Young said.

Koroshetz took after Fisher by working in the hospital day and night as he studied the details of stroke and acute neurological disease. In 2010 he was deputy director of the National Institute of Neurological Disorders and Stroke at NIH.

Continuing work started at Michigan, Young's own lab (and Penney's) studied Huntington's, Parkinson's, and Alzheimer's diseases with a particular focus on the basal ganglia, the brain parts governing movement, which are disturbed in movement disorders. They provided the most widely cited model of basal ganglia function, a model that has provided the springboard for testing novel interventions in Huntington's and Parkinson's diseases and related disorders.

According to the Hereditary Disease Foundation:

[Their lab] also studied the role of excitatory amino acids, chemical signals that are necessary for normal brain function, but which, at excessive levels or in unusual circumstances, can become highly toxic and kill neurons. [Penney and Young were] particularly interested in defining the role of the chemical receptors involved with glutamate, one of the most prominent neurotransmitters. Glutamate appears to play a role in killing some nerve cells but not others in stroke, epilepsy, Huntington's, Parkinson's and Alzheimer's. When the gene for Huntington's disease was identified in 1993, [their] lab also began studying how this gene was expressed in tissue from rodents and humans.[24]

In 1999 Jack Penney died suddenly from a heart attack at age 51. The foundation grieved the passing of "a brilliant research scientist and teacher, gifted clinician, loving father and husband, caring and generous friend and colleague, superb skier and enthusiastic fan of the football field."[25] Anne Young carried on, although admittedly "my lab is much smaller, mostly because my husband died and he took care of the lab while I focused on administration."

The lab may be small, but the list of Young's accomplishments in the first decade of the twenty-first century is not. To begin with, she is the principal investigator of the MGH/MIT Morris Udall Center of Excellence in PD Research, which brings together scientists in several laboratories at both institutions to try to understand the molecular mechanisms of Parkinson's disease.

Most recently Young has spearheaded comprehensive drug discovery efforts at the MassGeneral Institute for Neurodegenerative Disease (which she founded soon after her husband's death). The institute has been successful in identifying drug targets for Parkinson's, Huntington's, and other neurodegenerative diseases.

Young's laboratory is examining the role of the protein alpha-synuclein, which plays a key role in the death of dopamine-producing brain cells in Parkinson's disease and other diseases with similar symptoms. Recently the lab has examined the biology of synuclein in a group of Parkinson-like disorders, the multiple system atrophies. These studies suggest novel mechanisms in synuclein turnover, which may be relevant for treatments targeted at this protein.

In addition to her work on Parkinson's disease, Young's laboratory is attempting to elucidate cellular and systems mechanisms underlying the pathophysiology of Huntington's disease. In an effort to help develop therapeutic targets for human movement disorders, she is conducting studies on the vulnerability of neurons to excitotoxic injury and the selective expression of glutamate receptors in these neurons.

Her lab was also among the first to apply the new technology of large-scale DNA micro-array analysis to both Huntington's and Parkinson's diseases, revealing the importance of gene dysregulation in these disorders. Her group is pursuing the role that specific genes may play in the progression of Parkinson's disease.

Young holds membership in the Institute of Medicine, the American Academy of Arts and Sciences, and the Royal Society. She is also the only person (male or female) to have been president of both the international Society for Neuroscience and the American Neurological Association.

Neuroscientists have now identified the genetic causes of most major neurological disorders. Missing are the therapeutics. Joe Martin is skeptical, but Anne Young is convinced that the next 10 or 20 years will see major new therapies for the likes of Parkinson's and Alzheimer's. Her own lab is committed to this.

"The next generation of neurologists," said Young, "will be applying lab work to clinical studies." To that end, the Neurology Service's formidable clinical research unit, directed by Cudkowicz and Greenberg, is focused on bringing new drugs to patients.

(In 2010, as this book was being edited, Young announced that she would be stepping down as chief of neurology, and a search committee was being formed to identify a replacement.)

BUCHANAN THE BUILDER

Like the stock market, Massachusetts General Hospital has shown a long-term uptrend. Also like the stock market, MGH has had its ups and downs. At the beginning of the 1980s the hospital was experiencing a dip.

Several factors contributed, some internal, some external. First, the campus was showing its age. The 1980 annual report noted, "Many parts of the hospital are becoming obsolete and need replacement."[26] In the words of J. Robert Buchanan, who would address this problem as the incoming general director, Phillips House (1917) was "the remains of ancient grandeur." Rooms in Baker Memorial (1930) were too small by 1980 standards, although the hospital was still charging private rates for them. The Vincent Burnham Building, where gynecology and pediatrics were housed, completed a sort of triangle of obsolescence at the western end of the campus. In the children's wards, mattresses were stowed under cribs and pulled out to accommodate parents who wanted to stay through the night with a sick child.

When these problems had been largely rectified, in the early 1990s, an annual report would look back to a time of "tiny infants in their bassinets wedged between the equipment that monitors their heart beats" and "patient rooms so small that a nurse needed 10 minutes to remove the furniture so she could wheel in the equipment to assess a patient's circulation."[27] David Torchiana, who did his first clinical rotation at MGH in 1978, was frank: "In 1980, the MGH physically was pretty tattered, aged, not well organized to implement current technology, dated, tired, shabby. Many of the patient areas and rooms were not air-conditioned and most

Hooks Burr (left) and Robert Buchanan.

did not have their own bathrooms. The Baker and White buildings were disgraceful. Good care was rendered in those physical spaces but the spaces themselves were very antiquated. There was a Quonset hut on the Bulfinch Lawn."

There was an acute shortage of research space. MGH did not approach the standard for lab space per researcher prescribed by the U.S. Department of Health, Education, and Welfare. Treadwell Library, a valuable resource to researchers, was housed in terribly cramped quarters in Bartlett Hall. Two temporary buildings had become "permanent." In the yard in front of the hospital's signature building, Bulfinch, stood Torchiana's Quonset hut, used to house laboratory animals in conditions that would not necessarily have met the highest inspection standards. Another obsolete structure never meant to last stood behind Phillips House—the only one of the old lettered wards remaining, Ward G. When its use for MGH patients ended, it was occupied by the Bay State Rehabilitation Clinic, a separate operation supported by outside funds. Finally, the clinic was merged into MGH for financial reasons.[28]

Onto this checkered landscape strode J. Robert Buchanan, chosen to succeed Charlie Sanders and Joe Martin as the hospital's general director. At six feet, seven inches, Buchanan had quite a stride. Imagine, then, his first meeting with Massachusetts General Hospital in the person of Kay Bander, standing "just under" five feet, two inches, in her stocking feet. As director of MGH staff services and lead staff member on the search committee, Bander was sent to Chicago for a preliminary interview with Buchanan, president of Michael

Reese Hospital and Medical Center and associate dean of the Pritzker School of Medicine since 1977.

Trained as an endocrinologist, Buchanan was a 1954 graduate of Cornell University Medical School and had served with the U.S. Army as chief of medicine of the 121st Evacuation Hospital in Korea. Returning to Cornell as a teacher and an administrator of the ambulatory care program there, he became dean of the Cornell Medical School in 1969 and moved on to Reese in Chicago in 1977.

Years later Buchanan would say that he had had no idea he was a *candidate* for the position of MGH general director on Kay Bander's first visit; he thought Bander was only querying him to build a list of candidates. Said Bander: "My initial impression was that he was an accomplished physician-administrator, proud of his institution and his accomplishments, very articulate and well versed in the local as well as the more global levels of health care issues and opportunities. He seemed confident his institution was rising in prominence and was eager to speak about it."[29]

Bander made a second trip to Chicago as interest in Buchanan heated up. This time she met Buchanan's wife, Susan Carver Buchanan, an accomplished academic cardiologist. The three met in the Buchanan home, "a striking, modern house with circular indoor ramps rather than staircases (à la the Guggenheim Museum in New York) and filled with artwork," according to Bander. "Nestled in an established neighborhood, it stood out for its modern design statement. A bit disconcerting was a large, uncaged macaw roaming about." Talks went well. Buchanan was hired but only after what he described as "a clandestine meeting with a good share of the Board of Trustees in Hooks Burr's office at Ropes and Gray." Until then, Buchanan would maintain, he never thought he was a serious candidate; he thought, rather, that the board was simply pumping him for ideas. Said Buchanan, "I tried hard not to have that meeting. I thought it was more of the same piled higher and deeper. My appointment was then kept incredibly secret until one morning when I was told to come back to Boston and I was put on show in the Ether Dome." Finally, in the summer of 1982, Buchanan settled into his new position, allowing Joe Martin to return full-time to his chair in the Neurology Department.

To be blunt: Bob Buchanan did not fit comfortably into the MGH culture. That modern house in a traditional Chicago neighborhood and that uncaged macaw should have been tip-offs. Charlie Sanders remembered John Knowles for the dark blue Mercedes coupe he drove. Bob Buchanan would be remembered for the DeLorean he sometimes took out of the garage. (It was secondhand, Buchanan noted, "bought from a lady who wanted to get rid of it after 1,000 miles and buy a Rolls Royce.") Whatever he drove, Buchanan was definitely not "one of us," that clubby criterion of MGH belonging that had allowed John Knowles and Charlie Sanders to slip so comfortably behind the general director's desk.

Another man with an imposing frame and a nickname to match, Ferdinand "Moose" Colloredo-Mansfeld, was appointed to the board the year Buchanan arrived from Chicago. He would remain an admirer of the general director. He noted that Buchanan came onto the scene at a particularly difficult time, when leaders of the medical staff were likely to resent any administrator who saw which way the wind was blowing. Said Moose:

There was a transition that slowly started with Buchanan, as the cost pressures were building up. In the old days the chiefs would come in and talk about their budget, as a wish list—we need this, we need that—and it was the hospital administration's task to meet those needs. As we plowed through the 1980s, the needs went way beyond the means. Nobody knew what anyone else's budget was. So Bob Buchanan started talking with the major chiefs and laid out the budget for the whole enterprise, the total hospital budget. Moving forward, he said, we are going to solve this together as opposed to being individual experts.

In a time that required the utmost in diplomacy between hospital and professional staff, Buchanan could be abrasive. Kay Bander said, "The skill he didn't know he needed was how to communicate and come in as the outsider and become a partial insider." Yet Bander added that Buchanan was "a very genuine figure in his own way. In some ways I think he was happier in the Chicago-type environment—more open, free-spoken, a little less game playing to get to something."

Buchanan seemed to relish his outsider status, pointedly never eating in the doctors' dining room. Asked about this years later, he said that he had not eaten with the doctors "because I was never asked." Initially taking over the general director's office on the main White corridor, where Knowles and Sanders had worked, Buchanan later moved his tent to the periphery of the campus, into the newly built Trustees House on the corner of Cambridge and North Grove streets, across from the new location of the Resident Physicians' House. Buchanan had

Nicholas Thorndike (left) and Robert Buchanan.

352   ~   *Something in the Ether*

good reasons for the move, even if he did not communicate them effectively: "I wanted to create an identifiable main entrance to the campus, and I wanted people to know that they could move away from the flagpole."

Most others at MGH seemed to find this strange. Derisive nicknames for the general director's new digs made the rounds, like the Boboleum and the Little House on the Prairie. Nicholas Thorndike, board chair for five of the Buchanan years (1987–1992), said, "I should have stopped him from doing that." Buchanan would admit 20 years later, "I was wrong in this, there's no question, but my reasoning was, the institution was cramped for space. I thought that by my moving out others might be willing to do the same thing." Buchanan's vision would prove acute when, at the end of the decade, MGH recognized the wisdom of moving much of its research effort not just away from the flagpole but across the river.

Buchanan had big dreams, dreams that he would say "were not for Bob Buchanan but for the Massachusetts General Hospital." These dreams were stamped with the approval of Francis "Hooks" Burr, chairman of the Board of Trustees. Said Buchanan: "In my time, he was the one really strong trustee chairman. He became a very close personal friend. He and John Lawrence were both tremendously bright and effective people who could walk in any company." There's no question that "Moose" Colloredo-Mansfeld, chief executive officer of the commercial real estate developer Cabot, Cabot and Forbes, played a central role in rebuilding the campus, according to the man who followed him as board chair, Ed Lawrence: "As head of the Building Committee, Moose was the guy who did so much to drive the change for Blake and Ellison to be built, which were the core of the new hospital in the 1990s. And he was a key player in taking the enormous risk of Charlestown, which had red ink for a long time, but now looks like a slam dunk."

Upon Buchanan's arrival, Burr wrote the rationale for decisive action on the building front: "The reader might say, 'Why did we permit our plant to decline and become obsolete?' The reason is that over the years when we have been faced with the hard choice of replacing bricks and mortar or using funds to make dramatic advances in medical care, we have chosen the latter course. However, even the most dedicated people accustomed to austere working conditions perform better given adequate surroundings and equipment. The quality of patient care particularly, our greatest pride, is bound to suffer eventually if our buildings and facilities are obsolete and inefficient."[30]

Buchanan embraced this reconstruction mission with abandon. Said he: "I decided to rock the boat. Do I think people like having their boat rocked? No, who does? I don't like it any more than anybody else, but I also know that you don't get things done to prepare you for the next challenge if you don't take vigorous, vital action."

Allen Peckham, senior vice president for development and public affairs near the end of Buchanan's tenure, said: "Bob Buchanan had an edifice complex. He inherited an MGH with woeful facilities: world-class docs, education, and research but woeful facilities. He had the vision and guts to do some things that were non-consensus. But he was much better at asking forgiveness than getting approval. Where Jerry Austen is a master at getting independent entrepreneurs on

The Ellison Building under construction, 1988.

the same page, that was not Bob's way. He saw something and charged up the hill and planted the flag."

Buchanan envisioned removing the temporary buildings from the Bulfinch yard (done), planting additional trees (done), and creating a sort of *grande allée* leading up to the signature 1821 facade (not done, mostly because a key piece of real estate could not be acquired). Much more was done.

Said David Torchiana, "Buchanan is remembered as autocratic, but he did a wonderful job on big programmatic institutional decisions. Patton would not have been a great general in times of peace."

Buchanan led this effort under trying conditions, for he was simultaneously charged by the board with containing costs. In the 1983 annual report Hooks Burr complimented Buchanan on cost containment: "Under the able leadership of our General Director, J. Robert Buchanan, and with the dedicated support of the medical staff, administrators, and indeed everyone at MGH, we have made dramatic and encouraging progress in holding down expenses without in any way lowering the high standard of quality."[31]

An extraneous factor made the general director's job even more difficult. In 1983 Buchanan's first full year on the job, Medicare switched from reimbursement at cost to a prospective payment system. Reimbursement would now be based on diagnosis-related groups, or DRGs. This would prove to be just one grinding step in a national effort to rein in health care costs.

Helping to extricate Buchanan from this tight predicament was the first major capital campaign in MGH history, first described in the annual report for 1979 and launched in February 1981, during Charlie Sanders's last days, with an initial goal of $114 million. By the time it was completed, near the end of the Buchanan era, a second phase had been added and the total had exceeded $175 million. Notable individual contributions to the campaign included a $4 million gift from the Wang family to cap off Phase I; $3 million for Phase I and $6 million for Phase II from the John S. and James L. Knight Foundation of Akron, Ohio, and James Knight personally, in recognition of Jerry Austen (the Knight gifts were targeted to the surgical research floor in the Edwards Building and a new cardiac catheterization lab); and $1 million donations from the Hinduja Foundation of Bombay, the Cabot Foundation Charitable Trust, the Thomas Pappas Charitable Foundation, and the estate of Harlan K. Simonds.

The first phase of the capital campaign was used to renovate the White and Bigelow inpatient facilities, to complete the Wang outpatient facility (which by 1989 was seeing 365,000 patients a year), and to erect the Wellman Research Building and the Knight Cardiac Catheterization Laboratories. In 2005 Wellman would be renamed the (Samuel and Paula) Thier Research Building, thanks to a $5 million dollar gift from Jack Connors, chairman of Partners HealthCare, and his wife, Eileen. The Wellman-Thier building contained the world's largest medical laser research lab and housed "MGH's innovative studies in plant and animal genetics, the neurosciences, metabolism, and the phenomena of aging, growth, and development."[32] This seven-story increase in square footage for research would pale in comparison with another expansion late in the decade. As detailed below in the section on cancer, on December 29, 1986, MGH signed its first lease for space in the Charlestown Navy Yard.

Phase I also supported an upgrade of the Emergency Department and the creation of an intraoperative radiation unit, while establishing an endowment for the Institute of Health Professions. Bartlett Hall was extended northward to provide more generous space for the valuable Treadwell Library collection.

In about 1982, MGH was approached by Josiah A. "Si" Spaulding with an offer to sell what is now called the Spaulding Rehabilitation Hospital. Larry Martin was asked to negotiate the deal for the hospital. Said Martin: "It was a very cordial series of discussions. We agreed on a price; then Si and his family went to Puerto Rico for a vacation. He died while there, and I finished the purchase with Sandy, the Spauldings' eldest son."[33] Ern Haddad remembers the night between the two days of the Spaulding closing as the only night he spent on the couch in his office, "which is extraordinary because I lived right down the street."

In 1984 a new burns center opened on Bigelow 12. In 1990 work began on Fox Hill Village, a retirement and life-care facility in the suburban community of Westwood that resulted from a partnership between MGH and Cabot, Cabot and Forbes.[34] Though a movement had begun to develop such a facility as early as 1980, one that would serve retired Mass General doctors, among others, Buchanan was able to push it forward, believing that MGH should offer "cradle-to-grave" care. The "cradle" part of the vision would be realized at the end of the Buchanan era, when MGH reaffirmed its commitment to obstetrics, as will be detailed below.

During the Buchanan years MGH showed that the Hoechst deal of 1981 did not have to be a onetime event. In 1989 the Shiseido Company, one of Japan's largest cosmetics manufacturers, agreed to provide $85 million in research funding over a 10-year period. The funds were dedicated largely to setting up the MGH-Harvard Cutaneous Biology Research Center in converted space at the Charlestown Navy Yard.

The Buchanan years were capped off by completion of the Ellison and Blake towers, made possible by the second phase of the capital campaign. Moose Colloredo-Mansfeld headed the building committee and would recall working closely with Buchanan and other planners: "When Ellison was being planned, I had a long conversation with Bob about thinking ahead five to ten years: How do you see health care being delivered? We have to think where we're going. My point of view was to make the space in the new building as flexible as possible. Can we remove walls if we need to completely revamp a floor, without getting the dynamite out?"

The Ellison was named for the Eben Ellison family foundation, which completed Phase II with a $10 million donation. It towered 24 stories, and the adjoining tower was 15 stories tall. This was named for Curtis Blake, founder of Friendly's Ice Cream, and his wife, Patricia. The family had never received any care at Mass General but decided nonetheless that it was a preeminent Boston institution that deserved significant support.

Together the Ellison and Blake towers replaced 587 beds in outdated buildings and added a signature feature to the MGH landscape: atop the Blake Building is a helipad for landing emergency helicopters that would help make the MGH Emergency Department the leader in community emergency care in eastern New England. (See the prologue.)

In 1984 *Good Housekeeping* magazine polled 250 experts nationwide, asking a simple question: "Which hospitals—other than your own—do you consider most outstanding in terms of patient care?" The number-one hospital in the country was Massachusetts General.[35] What's more, three hospitals associated with MGH ranked in the top three in their respective specialties: Shriners was the best burn center in the United States; McLean Hospital was second only to the Menninger Foundation in the category of psychiatric hospitals; and Mass Eye & Ear was third among eye hospitals.

By the time it was announced on September 30, 1993, that Samuel O. Thier would replace Buchanan the following spring, a tired campus had been revitalized and, with the move to Charlestown, reimagined. Buchanan—the outsider from the Midwest—may have been exactly what Mass General needed in the 1980s, much like David Edsall, the outsider from Pennsylvania, was in the 1910s. The three chairmen of the board from 1982 to 1994—Hooks Burr, Nick Thorndike, and Moose Colloredo-Mansfeld—certainly played important roles, but Buchanan pushed the big programmatic decisions. New blood was injected into a tradition-bound institution.

Moreover, Buchanan had recruited key chiefs from outside Boston. Anne Young, from the University of Michigan, became the first female chief of service, in neurology. Another Michigan product, James Thrall, took over radiology (see chapter 3). Scott McDougal came from Vanderbilt to head up urology (see chapter 6). In psychiatry, after a long search, Ned Cassem took over from the beloved Tom Hackett and did a superb job by all accounts (see chapter 4).

"I wouldn't have done any of this for Bob Buchanan," said the former general director by way of a final analysis. "I happen to think the Massachusetts General Hospital is a great institution that should be constantly on its guard to be on the front line in leading the way for positive change."

PHILANTHROPY TURNS PROFESSIONAL

David Crockett did many fine things for MGH and raised a lot of money, and by 1986, four decades after he began to manage development efforts at the hospital (see chapter 5), the total amount raised from philanthropy annually was $11 million. In 2008 the total was about 30 times that. In fact, Mass General's first major capital campaign, started in February 1981 at the end of Charles Sanders's tenure as general director, was still under way in the mid-1980s and didn't conclude until gifts from the Blake and Ellison families completed the financing for two signature buildings of the 1990s. Before this campaign, Sanders would recall, philanthropy had amounted to "seat-of-the-pants fund-raising—all ad hoc. John Lawrence and I would go to New York from time to time to talk with people. We never had a capital campaign that I'm aware of. Ralph Lowell used to say, 'Not to worry, it will come,' and in many ways it did." By the time the capital campaign of the 1980s was completed, a newly professionalized and highly energized effort was under way in MGH philanthropy.

Though the MGH Board of Trustees traditionally had taken responsibility for meeting year-end deficits, sometimes working parlor to parlor in Brahmin enclaves on Beacon Hill and in the Back Bay, a board numbering just 12 members by state mandate could never be expected to bear the burden of supplying the needed philanthropic funds.[36] The capital campaign of the 1980s relied less on trustee giving than it did on doctors and their grateful patients. Examples were Chief of Surgery Jerry Austen, first among equals, and Edwin P. Maynard and James J. Dineen (both internal medicine), John F. Burke (burns), and Bertram Zarins (sports medicine).

Allen Peckham, who headed MGH's professional fund-raising efforts from 1992 to 1997, commented on the success of grateful-patient philanthropy within the Mass General culture of private practice: "Harvard is a Darwinian place: very entrepreneurial, very independent, with the smartest of the smart. The focus in fund-raising for doctors is themselves and their departments; so you start with grateful patients who feel loyalty to docs. Roman DeSanctis is a wonderful example, with his own fellows program."

Among DeSanctis's longtime patients is Paul Fireman, founder of Reebok International. Fireman and his wife, Phyllis, have donated generously to MGH over the years, and in 2005 committed $1 million to establish the Fireman Foundation Fund to enhance MGH training, particularly in DeSanctis's field, cardiology. More recently the Firemans committed $5 million to name a floor in the new Lunder Building. Other DeSanctis patients have been generous, as well, including William Schreyer, a former chairman of Merrill Lynch, and Jack Satter, the man behind Fenway Franks.

Such entrepreneurial fund-raising, while always valued, tends to focus in areas that may not match overall institutional objectives. By the mid- to late 1980s the financial pressures on academic medical centers were intensifying; as third-party payers changed reimbursement formulas, it was less clear where funding for research and education would come from. The time had come for a full-time professional fund-raising effort, one that would coordinate well with overall institutional goals.

During this period volunteer philanthropy was formalized with a committee cochaired by Austen and, first, Board Chair John Lawrence, and then, in succession, the trustees Jack Cooper and Jane Claflin. In the new century Austen has shared the chair-

Jack Cooper.

manship with the trustees Ron Skates, Ed Lawrence, and (at this writing) Patty Ribakoff.

In 1986 Bert Dane, Crockett's successor, hired James E. "Jim" Thompson as director of major gifts. Both of Thompson's parents had made a career of fund-raising. His father, Charles "Chuck" Thompson, was a senior development officer at Harvard University and later vice president of development at Babson College. His mother, Marjorie Thompson, headed development at the Buckingham Browne and Nichols School in Cambridge. Jim Thompson said, "Having three of us in the same profession and city was unusual, but we always were each other's advocates."

Thompson began his development career at Bentley College and then at Roxbury Latin School, where he had served as development director for seven years before coming to MGH. Said Thompson: "When I came here in '86, the development program was relatively small, but this was offset by the long-term leadership of David Crockett. David was an exceptional fund-raiser and was an early advocate of direct-mail campaigns. He had great credibility with the faculty and believed strongly in the research mission. David's early efforts in raising funds for research helped simulate the creation of what eventually became the Executive Committee on Research (ECOR). David was at ease in Boston social circles and knew many business leaders in Boston. The heavy dependency on Crockett within development did create some limitations in how the department was organized and structured."

After Thompson's arrival, the board hired William E. Walch as director of resource development, and Dane became director of the capital campaign, reporting to Walch. Another important force in fund-raising during the late 1980s and 1990s was General Director Bob Buchanan. Both Thompson and Allen Peckham, who was hired to replace Walch in 1992, agreed. Said Peckham: "Buchanan was a willing and charming fund-raising partner for us, extremely smart with some great stories, quite good with donors. Jane Claflin and Jerry Austen would close many gifts, but in cases where the general director was important, Bob filled that role gladly and well. Some CEOs don't want to do it; Bob was always willing to tell the MGH story and a joy to be with." Thompson added a personal twist: "Buchanan was charismatic, interesting, controversial, and a bit shy when it came to people. But he had a keen interest in his staff and their families."

Peckham and Thompson had crossed paths at Bentley College earlier in their careers, so they made a compatible team when Peckham came on in 1992. Under Peckham, Thompson quickly became number two in the department. Then in 1997, when Peckham moved over to Partners HealthCare to serve as chief development officer there, Thompson took over the corner office in MGH development. In 2009 Thompson was named vice president for development. Said Peckham, explaining his latest role at Partners: "Development officers within the Partners system report to me and to their CEOs, so it's a matrix. Our mission statement is to make everybody the best at what they do."

By the mid-1990s a second major capital campaign was under way, and by 1995 it was so successful that its initial goal of $160 million had been doubled to $320 million. That total paled, however, in comparison with the new campaign that was under way as this book went to press in early 2011. The goal of the Campaign for the Third Century of MGH Medicine, chaired by Austen and Ribakoff, was set at $1.5 billion. There had been talk about setting the bar at $2 billion, but the flagging economy and its effect on philanthropy nationwide made the lower target more attainable. Still, at $1.5 billion, this campaign is the largest for any medical center in New England.

"To envision a campaign like this means one has a vision of making a quantum leap in the next 10 years," said Thompson. The campaign total included $300 million for facilities, including the Lunder Building (recognizing a $35 million gift from Peter and Paula Lunder and the Lunder Foundation); $100 million for unrestricted research; $100 million for unrestricted annual fund support; $50 million for education; and $950 million for the centers of excellence, including cancer, heart and vascular, neurology, neurosurgery, psychiatry, MassGeneral Hospital *for* Children, and others. "The campaign itself has raised expectations across the board," said Thompson.

A number of factors have propelled the MGH community to this new level of giving. One of these, of course, is the roster of donors, many of whom have become committed long-term supporters of the hospital. Sumner Redstone, chairman of National Amusements Corporation, is a textbook example—someone whose interest evolved from that of a grateful patient to a man who understands MGH's uniqueness.

In 1979 Redstone nearly lost his life in a fire at the Boston Copley Hotel. Rescued by emergency workers, he had severe burns on his hands and legs. He underwent a very lengthy series of operations in the MGH Burn Unit, under the direction of Jack Burke. When his life had been saved and

Jane Claflin.

even his tennis game restored, Redstone gave a $1 million gift to the Burn Unit. Many things about the hospital impressed the businessman, not the least of which was a woman who mopped the floors and repeatedly popped her head in to ask him how he was doing. Redstone cited this woman's kindness at a testimonial dinner many years later.

Redstone followed up his first gift with $1.5 million to name a professorship in honor of Burke. In 2007 Redstone made a gift totaling $35 million to Mass General. This included the funds for an expanded and reconfigured emergency department in the Lunder Building, as well as support for the Burn Unit and a professorship in burn surgery.

The MGH board has become much more active in philanthropy during the first decade of the new century, according to Thompson, and since Peter Slavin became president of MGH in 2003, a new and important fund-raising group has entered the picture, the President's Council. Members are community, government, and business leaders who provide counsel to hospital leadership, serve as ambassadors for MGH, and are active participants in the hospital's fund-raising program. They attend three academic meetings each year to more fully understand the hospital and the breakthroughs being made. They also help host events like the Storybook Ball (the annual fund-raiser for the MassGeneral Hospital *for* Children), the MGH Golf Classic, and international trips. Joseph Ciffolillo, chief operating officer of Boston Scientific Corporation, was the first chairman of the President's Council, serving for two years. Since June 2005 Desmond "Desi" Heathwood, chairman and CEO of Boston Partners Asset Management, has held the position.

In 2008 the MGH Development Office hired the consultants Jan Krukowski and Company to better understand the strengths and weaknesses of MGH from a development perspective and to help define the current ambitious campaign. "You know, Jim," Krukowski reportedly told Thompson, "I've worked for 35 years with great clients at academic medical centers. The reality is that you have something special here. You are in a unique position." Krukowski told Thompson that though everybody in the business professes to have what Mass General has, "no other organization comes close to MGH."

James E. Thompson.

But then grateful patients have been saying that for years. The late Jack Friedman, founder of Florasynth, Inc., was a major donor. About 2002 Friedman told Thompson: "Jim, last year was a tough year for me. I had three separate procedures, one at Mass General and two in New York. The outcomes were all very good. I have no complaint about any of the treatment I received. But the way my family and I were treated here by people at every level was extraordinary. What you have here is what every Fortune 500 CEO strives for and rarely achieves."

In recent years MGH fund-raising has set records: $117 million in 2006, $256 million in 2007, $173 million in 2008, and $237 million in 2009, this despite a weak economy and roiled financial markets beginning in the third quarter of 2008. Said Thompson: "The next few years are going to be transformational. It's extraordinarily exciting to be here. I'm very optimistic about the future of philanthropy at MGH. We are making significant progress in expanding beyond our grateful patient base. This institution has a special culture, and people who come here recognize this—*how* they are cared for. I think being a separate hospital, not part of a university system, has allowed this institution to be much more nimble and flexible."

Another major supporter of Massachusetts General Hospital has been John Bertucci, chairman and former CEO of MKS Instruments, Inc. A diagnosis of prostate cancer led Bertucci to MGH in the mid-1990s. He was cared for by the surgeon Alex F. Althausen, the oncologist Donald S. Kaufman, and the radiation oncologist William U. Shipley, and he was impressed by what he called "a pervasive feeling of competence and compassion, not only from the doctors but also from the staff and nurses." After successful treatment, Bertucci stayed in touch with his MGH team, and after his company went public in 1999, he and his wife, Claire, decided that they would like to help support a new center for prostate cancer where there would be better collaboration among services (surgery, oncology, and radiation) than is the normal practice elsewhere. When the Yawkey Center for Outpatient Care became a reality, that emerged as the logical location for such a center. Today the Claire and John Bertucci Center for Genitourinary Cancer is a centerpiece of MGH cancer care.

Asked what most impressed him about MGH, Bertucci replied, "Here is an institution that has been around for 200 years, based from the beginning on compassionate care and quality of care. Still today that culture is evident. I am a student of organizations. I built up a company from a few people, and I know it is very difficult to maintain a corporate culture as you get larger and more geographically dispersed. I don't know what that magic is, but MGH has been able to maintain that institutional culture for 200 years."

THE CAMPAIGN AGAINST CANCER

Well into the twentieth century, cancer was something to cut out or kill you. When surgery failed, the deathwatch was usually on. Today, in the twenty-first century, cancer remains a dreaded diagnosis, but in the majority of cases, it is not automatically a death sentence. Through cutting-edge translational research there is more hope today than ever before for patients suffering from most cancers, and the Massachusetts General Hospital Cancer Center, founded in 1987, works that edge and provides reasons for hope.

The Cancer Center's growth and success in recent years are reflected in the *U.S. News and World Report*'s rankings. Among major cancer centers in the United States, during the five years from 2005 to 2010 the MGH Cancer Center's ranking advanced dramatically—from 25th to 15th to 10th to 7th. "When I arrived at MGH as a medical intern," said the hospital's president, Peter Slavin, "we were underperforming in the area of cancer. Today our clinical and academic efforts in cancer are going as strong as any other area in the hospital." The MGH Cancer Center has emerged as a role model for programmatic collaboration across the hospital.

This advance stems from a three-part leadership effort over the past quarter century: Kurt Isselbacher brought cancer science at MGH to an exceptional level, beginning in the late 1980s. Bruce Chabner began revolutionizing the clinical operation in the mid-1990s. More recently, Daniel Haber, director of the MGH Cancer Center, has brought the investigative and clinical efforts together in a team effort across disciplines. Medicine, pediatrics, surgery, radiation oncology, dermatology, obstetrics and gynecology, nursing, and other disciplines all collaborate.

Early Cancer Efforts at MGH

Massachusetts General Hospital, or at least Harvard Medical School, had begun a formal effort to study cancer more than 100 years earlier. In 1881 J. Collins Warren (grandson of the founder John Collins Warren) and Samuel Cabot described the need for tumor specimens for systematic pathological study at "the College Museum." In 1910 the hospital established a policy of admitting five inoperable cases at a time "for intensive study"—"provided that something towards the board of these patients can be contributed by [the Cancer] Commission."[37]

In 1919 George W. Holmes, chief of the X-ray Department, called together members of the staff to study cases in which radiation had been used to combat inoperable cancers. Included in the discussions were C. Guy Lane (skin diseases), James Howard Means (thyroid disorders), and Robert B. Greenough (breast cancer). "Until this time there had never been any attempt to segregate groups of cancer patients [at MGH] or to study end results except in a few instances. . . . Dr. Holmes and Dr. Greenough conceived the idea of having certain days for certain groups of cancer patients, with men detailed from various departments to care for them."[38]

From this insight the MGH Tumor Clinic was born in 1925, the first such clinic to be established in a general hospital.[39] By 1955 there would be more than 700 tumor clinics in this country. The MGH clinic, part of the Outpatient Department, did not treat patients with tumors so much as offer them consultation and follow-up (a social service worker was assigned to the clinic in 1930), while providing clinicians and researchers with a focus for study. Over the years it would generate reports reviewing "the case material in cancer of the breast, stomach, colon, uterus, cervix, ovary, vulva, vagina, larynx, pharynx, esophagus, and other sites too numerous to mention," while publishing "papers dealing with disease entities like leukemia, lymphoma, melanoma, and bone and soft tissue sarcomas."[40]

The continuing importance of radiology in the treatment of cancer was reflected in 1939 when the White Building opened and the Tumor Clinic moved to the X-ray Department there. In 1942 Holmes wrote, "The cure of cancer is still largely a surgical problem, irradiation being reserved for patients who have passed the stage where surgery can reasonably be expected to effect a cure."[41] It was an accidental wartime discovery—exposure to mustard gas caused white blood cell counts to drop—that turned attention toward chemotherapy as a treatment for cancer after 1945.

Enter the Huntington

Cancer research came to MGH in a big way after the war with the laboratories of the Collis P. Huntington Memorial Hospital. The Huntington had been founded in 1912 with nearly $300,000 raised largely by J. Collins Warren. This included a lead gift of $100,000 from Mrs. Huntington, widow of one of the nineteenth-century businessmen responsible for the transcontinental railroad. The Huntington Hospital stood at the corner of Huntington Avenue and Shattuck Street in Boston on the future site of the Francis A. Countway Library of Medicine of Harvard Medical School. Dedicated entirely to the treatment and investigation of cancers, the hospital contained six private rooms, as well as 10 ward beds for men and 10 for women. In the same two-story building was the John Collins Warren Laboratory of Biophysics, founded in 1922. Here were gathered under one roof all the activities of Harvard's Cancer Commission, founded in 1899. A generation was trained at the Huntington to treat cancer with surgery and radiation.[42]

On the medical side, recalled Paul C. Zamecnik, who arrived at the Huntington as a resident in 1936 and didn't leave until he had retired as its director

Huntington Laboratories.

in 1979, the hospital principally treated Hodgkins disease, leukemias, and "a few other odd things like pernicious anemia." Until 1928, the director of the Huntington was George R. Minot, who would share the 1934 Nobel Prize in Medicine with William P. Murphy and George H. Whipple for using liver extract to cure pernicious anemia, previously a fatal condition. Said Zamecnik: "Minot left for Boston City Hospital in 1928 and the Huntington looked around for a successor. The noted British gynecologist William Blair-Bell had proposed that lead compounds might be a suitable therapy for cancer, so the Huntington looked around for someone who knew something about lead, and they came up with Joe Aub."

As we saw in chapter 3, Aub had inaugurated Ward 4 with studies of lead poisoning sponsored by the lead industry, but by the time Aub took over at the Huntington, said Zamecnik, "the lead bubble had already burst. So here was Aub, the new director of a cancer hospital and lab, not particularly interested in cancer!" Aub elected "to regard cancer as an aberration in growth control. This was a bold course on which to set an entire laboratory effort, since it involved a search for normal control mechanisms as well, and the short-range relevancy . . . to the cancer problem was not immediately apparent."[43] In his history of MGH from 1935 to 1955, Nathaniel Faxon explained the rationale behind the sort of basic research pursued by Aub's investigators: "If a section of a rat's liver is removed, regeneration will begin and continue until the last portion has been replaced, at which point growth will stop. What starts, controls, and stops the proliferation of liver cells? If this could be explained, perhaps it might help in explaining the action of cancer cells."[44] Aub and company were ahead of their time. Zamecnik wrote: "A generation passed before this forward-looking but difficult point of view met general acceptance among the cancer research laboratories of the world."[45]

Under Aub's directorship, the Huntington became a rather odd combination

Joseph Aub.

of cancer hospital and clinical research facility in endocrinology—drawing on Aub's previous Ward 4 experience. Aub and Ira T. Nathanson, a surgeon, made major strides in treating breast cancer with hormones. But cancer was sometimes an afterthought at the Huntington of the 1930s. After completing Harvard Medical School in 1936, Zamecnik wanted an internship in surgery, but by the time he got around to applying, all the plum positions had been taken. Instead, he stumbled into a residency (bypassing internship) with Aub, who spent most of the interview inquiring about Zamecnik's skiing experience: Could the skinny young doctor-in-training from Cleveland teach Aub's daughters to ski? Yes, he could, and so, as World War II approached, Zamecnik found himself in charge of clinics "for such things as fat ladies and tall men with tumors and other abnormalities of the endocrine system. When the circus came to town," he recalled, "some of the dwarfs used to come to Aub." PZ, as he was still known in his own lab in 2008,[46] would especially remember "The Angel," a pituitary giant who was so strong he was a wrestling champion.

In 1937 the Huntington became home to the first million-volt Van de Graaff generator for use in radiation oncology—two floors high with a great dome above it. The physicist Robert J. Van de Graaff came across the river from MIT to consult on the installation, while Milford Schulz, initially a resident on the Huntington staff, operated the massive machine. It was "air insulated with a high voltage terminal some 10 feet on a side and large enough for a man to walk around in. The continuously evacuated tube was made of multiple porcelain sections 10 feet long to the focusing coil and extended through the floor of the generator room into the treatment room below. A fairly honest one megavolt was achieved by the use of six charging belts, each about a meter wide, driven by three electric motors at a rate of 4,000 feet per minute. The output was 40 roentgens per minute at a distance of 80 centimeters."[47] The Van de Graaff machine found a home in the newly constructed White Building in 1939. Seven years later plans were laid for a 2 million–volt machine requiring 26 tons of lead shielding.[48]

On Monday, December 8, 1941, as America buzzed over the attack on Pearl Harbor the previous day, Harvard and MGH announced the merger of the Huntington into Mass General, though the two organizations had already been interacting for years. On January 1, 1942, the Huntington's patients were transferred to the MGH Tumor Clinic. The Huntington's labs were moved to MGH that May.

Divergences

Basic biomedical research moved ahead smartly in the United States after the war; dramatically increased funding came from the NIH and, in cancer, from the American Cancer Society. At MGH the importance of cancer research was symbolized by the Huntington/Warren labs' move to the Edwards Research Building in 1951. The Huntington Hospital's successes in treating breast cancer with hormones attracted "general internists to the use of hormones and thus to specialize in cancer therapy. Among the first of these was Rita M. Kelley."[49] Though it is not possible to profile every contributor in this or any period, Kelley deserves attention as an early female contributor to cancer research.

After graduating from Boston State Teachers College in 1938, Kelley worked as a research assistant with Ira Nathanson at the Huntington. It was Joe Aub who convinced her to become a doctor. Armed with an MD from Columbia in 1946, Kelley returned to MGH as an intern, then as a research fellow at the Huntington Laboratories, now merged into MGH. She authored papers on treating breast cancer with chemotherapy and endometrial and other cancers with hormones. She rose to become interim chief of medical oncology at MGH for three years, 1973–1976, and a professor of medicine at Harvard Medical School in 1980, one year before her own death from cancer. Upon her death, a colleague wrote: "The care of the patient was Rita Kelley's lifelong concern: a careful diagnostic evaluation; the best available therapy; and, throughout the process, devotion to her

Rita Kelley.

patients—who reciprocated with total loyalty. There lay her interest and there her reward."[50]

After Ira Nathanson's sudden death in 1954, Alan C. Aisenberg was hired to head up the medical oncology unit at MGH. Zamecnik replaced Aub as director of the Huntington after Aub's retirement in 1956. At this midcentury crossroads, when leadership changed almost simultaneously in both lab and clinic, we might begin to see why cancer activities at Mass General would proceed through the 1960s and into the 1970s on parallel but separate tracks. There were four tracks, actually: the surgical theater, the radiation clinic, the medical oncology unit (chemotherapy, such as it was in those early days of drug therapy for cancer), and the lab.

First, the surgical theater: cancer once had meant surgery, nothing more. Until the early twentieth century, when X-rays were developed, operating was all a doctor could do for a patient with a tumor. Since the days of John Collins Warren, MGH had been known for its surgical excellence, and these surgeons had always been and would remain *private practitioners*, at least until the 1970s, when Jerry Austen organized a group practice. In the nineteenth century the Warrens and Bigelows donated their services to all but a few private patients. In the twentieth century, more often than not, the Copes and Welches billed patients directly while benefiting from the privilege, as indeed it was, of operating at MGH.

Until the middle of the twentieth century, surgeons, especially at MGH, were generalists: they could do it all—or tried to. With Howard Ulfelder, the Joe V. Meigs professor of gynecology at HMS; Claude E. Welch, "a titan of surgery," according to Zamecnik; and others, a new generation of surgical oncologists began to arise and thrive at MGH in the 1950s and 1960s. Welch was appointed chief of the Tumor Clinic in 1957, and by the middle of the next decade he was "functioning as a Herculean clinical surgeon whose daily surgical list would often eclipse that of a medium-sized hospital."[51] His associate John W. Raker kept pace. Surgical oncology would become a formal unit in 1974 with the encouragement of Jerry Austen, chief of surgery, and Raker was its first chief. William C. Wood and Alfred M. Cohen would become joint chiefs upon Raker's death in 1979. Wiley "Chip" Souba was chief of surgical oncology from 1993 to 1999 and was replaced by Kenneth Tanabe, who became chief in 2000.

Some surgeons made contributions to clinical research. Ulfelder was a case in point. In the early 1970s he discovered a link between the drug diethylstilbestrol (DES) administered to pregnant women and a rare form of vaginal cancer in their female offspring. By the mid-1950s Ulfelder and others were already pushing for a unified cancer front at MGH, where clinical and investigative activities related to cancer would all happen under one roof and where there would be "one level of care for all."[52] (When the Huntington clinic merged into the MGH Tumor Clinic, it brought private patients with it, and the MGH set up a separate clinic "operating on certain afternoons" to cater to them.)[53] Ulfelder took the lead in raising funds for a cancer center, and in 1975 the Cox Building would open for outpatient cancer treatment and cancer research. The Cox was, in its day, the only building at MGH with a disease-oriented designation.

But even here, supposedly under one roof, there was hardly an all-for-one, one-for-all approach to cancer. Take radiation medicine. From 1942 to 1959 Milford Schulz, a Huntington resident, was the only full-time radiotherapist on the MGH staff.[54] Radiation oncology gained some steam in the 1960s; General Director John Knowles wrote in the 1965 annual report: "For some years we have been concerned with our total effort in the field of cancer. We have felt the need for better diagnosis, radiotherapy, clinical research, . . . basic research and teaching— all of which add up to better care for our patients."[55] In 1968 the consulting firm of Arthur D. Little advised MGH to get serious about radiation medicine and allied research. By then Schultz had been joined by C. C. Wang and George F. Zinninger, but until that year the training program did not distinguish between radiation as therapy and radiation as a diagnostic tool. In 1969 the trustees of the hospital finally approved the new cancer-focused building, made possible in part by Mrs. William C. Cox, a patient of Howard Ulfelder. Radiation medicine became a formal department in 1971 under the chairmanship of Herman D. Suit, recruited from the M. D. Anderson Hospital in Houston, and for the next decade, according to one observer, "MGH bet the ranch on radiation oncology."

It's hard to dispute this assessment when reading the official history "MGH and Cancer," published in 1983.[56] The new Cox Building was all about radiation medicine "and its awesome equipage." The first section of the building to open was "a cobalt unit for radiation therapy chiefly for patients with cancer of the breast; [it was] followed by a second cobalt unit of somewhat different capabilities, and then a linear accelerator. Even with these operating, the installation [continued] of additional high energy units as well as the orthovoltage equipment used for the treatment of superficial lesions."[57] The Cox was a radiation palace.

From 1954, when Aisenberg replaced Nathanson, to 1991, when Thomas P. Stossel moved on to Brigham and Women's Hospital, two chiefs, Aisenberg and Stossel, directed medical oncology (chemotherapy) at MGH, bridged by an interim appointment of Rita Kelley. During these 37 years, national cancer care underwent a revolution. A major New England player (read "competitor") emerged: the Sidney Farber Cancer Center (renamed Dana-Farber in 1983 to honor a major donor). New chemotherapies were being created for countless varieties of cancer. Yet medical oncology at MGH languished. Why?

Daniel Haber, director of the Cancer Center, offered part of an answer:

In the early days, surgery and radiation were leading therapeutic areas (especially at MGH, given the strong history of both), and chemotherapy was seen as poisons given out by poorly trained medical specialists. MGH was slower than some other places to build up the medical component, but certainly not unique among general hospitals in this. If you look at most general hospitals, chemo/medical oncology was quite commonly a private practice shop (and still is in many places). The only respected subspecialty at the time was hematology (hence Stossel's selection as chief of hematology-oncology).[58]

The medical oncology section in the Castleman history is brief. It cites Aisenberg's focus on Hodgkin's disease and lymphomas, management of which brought him "national recognition."[59] Yet when Tom Stossel first arrived at MGH as an intern in 1967, he recalled, "the MGH cancer service, such as it was, was a backwater. There was some chemo but not much." Stossel pointed out that Aisenberg, despite his national recognition, was a PhD in biochemistry from the University of Wisconsin "with some notoriety in the field of lymphomas, not that there was much that could be done for such conditions."

According to Paul Zamecnik, MGH might have done more. MGH's senior scientist cited a Bauer-Churchill decision not to participate in NIH-led national protocols for the experimental applications of new chemotherapies. In a memo to Stossel, Rita Kelley wrote: "It is fair to say that both Dr. Churchill and Dr. Bauer regarded clinical interest in cancer as a manifestation of second-class citizenry."[60] Maybe it all goes back to the MGH tradition of private practice, according to Zamecnik: "Pete Churchill and Walter Bauer said the visiting physicians on a ward should decide what treatment their patients got and that the physicians shouldn't have to follow some national program established by the NIH. 'We are a general hospital,' they said, 'and the senior people who have the privilege of working on the wards are in charge of therapeutics.'" And maybe it goes back to Haber's comment about poisons. Said Stossel: "You had to justify poisoning people."

An Uneasy Alliance

In 1976 Stossel was hired to replace Aisenberg, who would continue his lymphoma work in the Huntington lab. By this time the Farber had been officially designated a national cancer center, the only one on the Boston scene, propelling it into the spotlight and shunting MGH/Huntington to the shadows. The Farber and other major cancer centers like Memorial Sloan-Kettering in New York were successful, in Stossel's opinion, because they were "hierarchical organizations where research could beat back surgical conservatism."

Stossel was an investigative hematologist, a detective of the blood fascinated with how cells crawl. His "internationally acclaimed research on phagocytosis," his "ingenuity and success" were noted in the official MGH history.[61] By the early 1980s he would be named editor of the prestigious *Journal of Clinical Investigation* and was subsequently president of the American Society for Clinical Investigation. Stossel was a scientific heavyweight.

"I wasn't even interested in the oncologic portion of hematology," Stossel admitted. Why then did Chief of Medicine Alexander Leaf propose his name and the hospital recruit Stossel as its new chief of medical oncology? Said Stossel, quick with a quip, "They were applying the old Walter Bauer model: take a pediatrician and make him a brain surgeon." But Stossel was a world-class hematologist trying to rally private practitioners in medical oncology into group endeavor, probably a mission impossible. Still, progress was made. For the first time MGH house staff joined the hematology-oncology training program, and Stossel procured an NIH training grant. Recruitment improved, and a couple of house officers in Stossel's unit went on to leadership positions at MGH, including David J. Kuter as chief of hematology. Other graduates of the training program assumed leading clinical and research positions around the world. Stossel started an academic practice plan. And his research, begun at MGH, led to major insights as to how cells crawl—important for cancer metastasis. These and related discoveries are leading to new supportive treatments for cancer patients, recognized by the American Cancer Society and the National Academy of Sciences.

Then, in the late 1980s and early 1990s, MGH decided to become a major cancer center; Stossel was moved from a joint appointment in hematology-oncology back to hematology alone; and before long he had moved a bit further, to the Brigham as chief of experimental medicine, taking some of his research group and technicians with him. The former chief was left with mixed feelings: "What I accomplished under the circumstances was nothing short of miraculous. Yet in the MGH view, it was too little. And everybody was right."

No Nobel

Paul Zamecnik is arguably the most eminent MGH scientist not to win a Nobel Prize, although for about a day in 1964 he thought it might turn out otherwise:

> It was October, and David Crockett called me one day and said, "Hey, did you know you're supposed to get an important prize?" I hadn't heard. "Well, I just heard that over international radio," he said. "You're going to get a Nobel Prize tomorrow." That afternoon, I began to get telephone calls from the dean of Harvard Medical School, from John Knowles, from the American Cancer Society, and others, but I thought, I'm not going to shake anybody's hand until I get official notice.
>
> Someone told me I would hear at eight o'clock the following morning—a phone call from the Swedish embassy. I had a kind of restless night, and at eight o'clock in the morning, by God, the telephone rang. It was my sister-in-law in Manchester, New Hampshire, who had lost her cat. I went into the lab as usual: no prize. The Nobel Committee doesn't give silver medals.

Zamecnik did win a Lasker Special Achievement Award in 1996 for his many career firsts, most of them achieved while he was director of the John Collins Warren Laboratories of the Huntington Memorial Hospital, a position he held from 1956 until his first retirement in 1979. These included unlocking the "black box" of protein synthesis in the 1950s by effectively discovering transfer-RNA and decoding its chemistry in a cell-free system, that is, in the test tube. The Lasker citation said the award

Paul Zamecnik.

was given him "for brilliant and original science that revolutionised biochemistry and created an entirely new field of scientific inquiry."[62]

In the 1970s Zamecnik had more groundbreaking work to report, the invention of so-called antisense therapies. The chemical code for genetically transmitted disease is sent to cells aboard RNA. Antisense therapy combats such diseases by synthesizing molecules to interlock with and thereby neutralize these messenger molecules.

Zamecnik's scientific career did not end with his retirement from MGH in 1979. His former MGH colleague Mahlon Hoaglund recruited him to the Worcester (Mass.) Foundation for Experimental Biology (which later changed its name to the Worcester Foundation for Biomedical Research of the University of Massachusetts Medical School). Here he continued his investigative work until MGH brought him back as a senior scientist in 1997. In 2009, until shortly before his death at age 96, he was on the trail of a therapy for drug-resistant tuberculosis, using principles and techniques he had helped develop over the preceding 70 years.

The MGH Cancer Center

MGH began to rethink its approach to cancer in the mid-1980s. The Cox Building had opened in 1976, and 10 years later its physicians were seeing more than 3,000 new patients annually. But radiation oncology was still paramount; space for research was chronically short here as in other departments; and a unified approach to cancer remained a dream unrealized, despite the best efforts of Tom Stossel and others. It would take the collaboration of several key individuals and the backing of the trustees to take the next dramatic step.

Kurt Isselbacher's work as chief of the Gastrointestinal Unit for nearly 30 years would not seem the ideal preparation for kick-starting a world-class cancer center. Then again, Isselbacher had received no clinical training in gastroenterology when Walter Bauer asked him to head up that unit in the mid-1950s. "I realized," he said, "that what was happening in cancer at the national level was not happening at MGH." Isselbacher's thinking about a solution led to major changes at MGH, not just in cancer care and cancer research but in research generally. It helped lead MGH research from Boston to Charlestown.

Isselbacher had spent two years, 1984 and 1985, on sabbatical with a Fogarty Scholarship at the National Cancer Institute. This had convinced him that MGH was not doing enough to explore the molecular and genetic basis of disease, especially cancer. Isselbacher recalled:

> When I voiced my concerns . . . to the MGH chief of medicine, John Potts, he said, "I agree things need to change. So, would you be willing to develop a cancer center and become its director?" Because this proposal was made to me over drinks at John's summer home in Wareham, initially I passed it off and didn't respond to the suggestion. However, the more I thought about it, the more the idea appealed to me. After all, by that time I had spent almost 30 years as chief of the GI Unit, and taking on a new challenge seemed to make sense. The fact that I had no formal clinical training in oncology was not

an impediment to me, but, of course, I knew it would be viewed with skepticism by the clinical oncologists on the MGH staff. Nevertheless, I concluded that this would be no different than my having become chief of the GI division without knowing my gastroenterology.

It was about this time that General Director Bob Buchanan met the real estate developer Ted Raymond across the river in Charlestown for a tour of the hulking remains of

Kurt Isselbacher.

the U.S. Navy Yard there. More than 200 navy vessels had been built there since 1800. Once used for ropewalks (long buildings in which the rope for rigging was hand-wound) and most recently used for high-tech missile configurations, the Charlestown Navy Yard had been closed since 1974 and begged for occupancy. "Raymond was getting in trouble," Buchanan said years later. Never shy about charging uphill with the flag, Buchanan urged the hospital board to invest in space in Charlestown.

Jim Thompson, who joined the MGH Development Office about this time, would say years later: "Bob Buchanan receives little credit for Charlestown, for his vision in urging us to move there. There was a lot of concern about the idea: What were we going to Charlestown for? In retrospect, though, you have to say, What a stroke of genius! That was Bob."

Ern Haddad agreed: "I don't think our Charlestown movement would have happened without Bob's strong support and initiative."

MGH's Scientific Advisory Committee weighed in: members thought Buchanan's idea was a good one, and they encouraged Isselbacher to look at labs across the river. Isselbacher became a believer: "I was impressed with the idea that having that much space on one floor would be most conducive to effective scientific interactions, compared with the same amount of lab space on separate floors. . . . But this meant the creation of another hospital campus—something that hadn't been done in the 175-year history of the MGH. What about transportation? (We used shuttle buses.) Would we be able to attract graduate students from Harvard Medical School? (This turned out to be less of a problem than expected.)"

In early 1987 the outgoing chairman of trustees Hooks Burr wrote, "We have just completed arrangements, after lengthy and soul-searching negotiations, for the lease of a large amount of space in the Charlestown Navy Yard to provide additional space for our expanding research community."[63] By the following year any institutional nervousness had been overcome. The annual report boasted that the Charlestown Navy Yard "has a fighting tradition behind it. Ships from all the nation's wars have come here for repair and refurbishing. Our country's first war-ship, the *USS Constitution*, is berthed here. We were mindful of this fighting spirit this year as we leased and occupied 211,481 square feet of this superb old build-ing and prepared to mobilize some of it for war again—this time for the war on cancer."[64]

A few years later, one of the trustees, John Kaneb, among others, suggested that MGH buy the buildings in Charlestown being used for parking (no. 149) and research (no. 199). This may have made sense on the corporate balance sheet, but Haddad noted that a straight purchase by MGH would have caused funding problems in research:

> The research funding agencies would take into account the cost of lab space to the extent that we rented it from an independent and uncontrolled party. So long as we were renting from Teddy Raymond, we would get reimbursed for 100 percent of rental costs. If we purchased and owned the buildings our-selves, the NIH would not reimburse us for debt service on the purchase. So in order to make it financially feasible we had to acquire the properties through an entity that for NIH funding purposes was not controlled by MGH. Furthermore, to make it financially feasible for us, we had to purchase with tax-exempt debt, and to qualify for that, the owning entity had to be suffi-ciently controlled by MGH.

An entity called Massachusetts Biological Research Corporation (MBRC) was created to take title to the property from Raymond—sufficiently controlled by MGH to qualify for tax-exempt debt, but sufficiently outside the control of MGH to qualify for reimbursement of debt service. Haddad led the legal team; Larry Martin supported on the financial end. The entire arrangement was "fully disclosed," according to Haddad, and in fact became the basis for a Harvard Busi-ness School case study.

Of the space in Charlestown, which would grow to more than 600,000 square feet by the end of the 1980s, the Cancer Center would occupy 56,000 square feet, adding to space already dedicated to cancer in the Cox Building and at other sites. Once the river was forded, other departments rushed across, and by 1989 a neuroscience center and an imaging center were opening in Charlestown and others were on the way. The entire facility was formally named the Lawrence E. Martin Laboratories in honor of "Mr. MGH." "As a result," the annual report for 1990 could crow, "the MGH has the largest research program of any independent hospital in the nation."[65] This was quite an accomplishment, given the standing start 45 years before, at the end of World War II.

Kurt Isselbacher was appointed director of the MGH Cancer Center, while William C. Wood of the Department of Surgery continued as its clinical director. Isselbacher realized that it would take a long time to build a first-class research unit from the top down—that is, by first recruiting senior faculty. Instead, he recruited junior colleagues first and senior faculty later. By doing so, Isselbacher created the research base for the MGH Cancer Center, raising funds and recruiting an initial crop of young scientists from MIT and Harvard. These included:

Building 149 at the Charlestown Navy Yard.

- Stephen Friend, who went on to discover p53 mutations in Li-Fraumeni syndrome and became head of oncology at Merck
- René Bernards, who became a major scientific leader in Europe
- Ed Harlow, who cloned the E2F genes and became the chair of biochemistry and molecular pharmacology at Harvard Medical School
- Daniel Haber, who succeeded Isselbacher as Cancer Center director in 2003 and became a pioneer in targeted smart-drug therapies (more on this below).

Haber credited Harlow with "establishing a culture of young investigators working collaboratively at the prime of their careers. He really led the way in establishing the MGH Cancer Center as a top scientific enterprise."[66]

A lengthy search process sought to identify a new clinical chief of hematology and oncology in the Department of Medicine. This took more time than anyone expected, which perhaps reflects that the best candidates, coveted by MGH, viewed the MGH cancer program as second-echelon if also up-and-coming. In 1992 MGH hired the Boston Consulting Group, which concluded that a hospital the size of Mass General had to invest heavily in cancer, that cancer care would be critical to its growth in the near future, and that it would require multidisciplinary care coordinated with research and a significant investment in infrastructure. With this in mind, MGH intensified its search for a clinical director, and in 1994 Bruce Chabner was recruited from the NIH.

The interior of Building 149, Charlestown, after renovation.

Chabner, who had been an effective administrator at NIH, applied that skill with success at MGH. Chabner's accomplishments have included:

- Dissolution of the private practice oncology model and creation of a single academic group practice. Here Chabner had support from the hospital that Stossel had not enjoyed, as well as the talents of MGH Vice President Kate Walsh, who helped formalize the Cancer Center structure under MGH President James Mongan.

- Creation of a single Cancer Center–wide research protocol office. According to Haber, this was a key to furthering clinical trials—a sort of back-office support for frontline clinical investigators.

- The integration of clinical practice into true multidisciplinary teams. This became a reality across the board with the move of outpatient activities to the new Yawkey Center for Outpatient Care, opened in 2002. For the first time, medical, radiation, and surgical oncologists had their offices located together in disease-center units. Major contributions to the multidisciplinary care centers in Yawkey have come from Avon Products and Gillette (both for breast cancer), the Bertucci family (genitourologic cancers), the Pappas family (neuro-oncology), and the Gosnell family (GI).

- Endorsement of supportive and alternative therapies, including the HOPES program (art, acupuncture, massage for cancer patients); the PACT program (Parenting At a Challenging Time), counseling adults with cancer about how to talk to their children, a program run by the pediatric psychiatrist Paula Rauch; and the Schwartz Center, an independent foundation housed at MGH that supports compassionate care and open discussions among caregivers.

In 2001 the Cancer Center established the Northeast Proton Therapy Center, at the time one of only two hospital-based facilities in the United States capable of delivering heavy-particle radiation with unique precision for the treatment of brain tumors. (For more on the proton beam, see chapter 8.)

Bruce Chabner.

It all adds up to exceptional clinical care for cancer patients, now a trademark of the MGH Cancer Center.

The Genetics of Cancer

It is difficult to discern Daniel A. Haber's origins by his accent, especially when he has a head cold, as he did when he was interviewed for this book. Born in Paris, he learned English from British teachers. "Most people think I'm Canadian," he said. His American-born father worked his whole life resettling refugees, first in Paris, then in Geneva, where Haber went to a French-speaking grade school and an English-speaking high school. But not for long: he matriculated at MIT at age 16. "My English was okay," he noted, "but there were some choice idioms that I did not know—not all printable." Originally thinking that he wanted to be an endocrinologist, Haber worked in the Stanford lab of Robert T. Schimke in the late 1970s, while earning his MD-PhD. A major discovery was made while Haber was on the premises—that tumors have the capability of multiplying critical genes within their DNA, thus outwitting chemotherapy that is aimed at suppressing their growth, and Haber was so enthralled that he turned to a career in cancer research. At MIT, following internship and residency at MGH, Haber worked in the lab of David Housman, part of a team that cloned the gene for Wilms tumor, a pediatric cancer. Subsequently, at MGH and HMS, he reported the high frequency of a specific BRCA1 mutation in young Ashkenazi Jewish women with breast cancer. Haber's career-long focus on the genetic underpinning of cancer eventually pushed him to international prominence in the field of targeted therapies.

In 2003, in a collaboration with the MGH oncologist Thomas J. Lynch, Haber came up with a true breakthrough. Noting a *Boston Globe* article about a patient of Lynch's whose advanced lung cancer had melted away following treatment with the experimental drug Iressa (gefitinib), Haber asked whether this patient's tumor might have a genetic abnormality that was different from all the other forms of lung cancer that did not respond to the same drug. Although Haber himself had no expertise in lung cancer, the *Globe* story had reminded him of another drug, Gleevec (imatinib), that had proved effective with a type of leukemia known to be

Daniel Haber.

caused by a mutation in the gene targeted by the drug.[67] Lynch collected the pathology specimens from MGH patients whose lung cancer had responded to Iressa, and Haber's lab soon identified the first mutation in the epidermal growth factor receptor (EGFR) gene. "We held our breath with the first one, then the second one. In the end eight out of nine lung cancers responding to the drug had a mutation, and we didn't find any mutations in tumors that were unresponsive. It all unfolded over a number of days, and it was stunning," says Haber. The finding that a single gene mutation could tell which patients with lung cancer would have dramatic responses to a new treatment was published in a landmark 2004 paper in the *New England Journal of Medicine,* which was the most often cited for that year.[68] It set the stage for worldwide efforts throughout the cancer research and pharmaceutical industries to find such genetically defined targets for new cancer drugs across different types of cancer. Instead of searching for a single billion-dollar drug that might somehow be effective in all cancers, the pharmaceutical industry is increasingly focused on the need to target smaller subsets of cancers with specific drugs that can attack common genetic mutations. Meanwhile, the MGH Cancer Center continues to work on leading the clinical applications of these research findings.

To support these efforts in the lab, Haber has initiated major efforts in translational research within the Cancer Center. The first, created in collaboration with Jeff Settleman, is the "thousand-cell-line project," an effort to match novel drugs with genetics. "It's essential to know what biomarkers you're looking for before you start doing a drug trial in humans," Haber said. So MGH's Molecular Therapeutics Lab cultivates cells from 1,000 different cancers, which can be used to lab-test drugs with robotic technology and match drug responses with genetic markers. The project was so successful that it received major funding from the Wellcome Trust of the United Kingdom, and it now runs in collaboration with the Sanger Center, a major genomics research institute in England. To apply such findings in the clinic, the Cancer Center has embarked on a collaborative venture with the MGH Department of Pathology to test all tumors biopsied or resected at MGH in "real time" for a panel of mutations that could help direct targeted therapies, the first such effort by a hospital in the United States.

Would it be possible to monitor a cancer patient without frequent biopsies? That is the question being addressed in conjunction with the lab of an MGH biomedical engineer in the Department of Surgery, Mehmet Toner. The project, which recently secured a $15 million Dream Team Award from a national "Stand Up to Cancer" telethon, is developing a device that can screen a patient's blood for loose, circulating tumor cells, or CTCs. A teaspoon of blood is flowed through a microfluidic chamber made of silicon and not much larger than a microscopic slide but containing 80,000 columns the width of a human hair that are coated with an adhesive to capture extraordinarily rare cancer cells as they flow by. In addition to replacing invasive biopsies in patients with active cancer, this breakthrough technology may one day allow early detection of invasive cancers before they have a chance to metastasize.

With such a track record, the MGH Cancer Center under Haber has been able to recruit what he called "an amazing faculty, on both the clinical and the research sides, all in their thirties and forties, all coming into their own. It is awe-inspiring." These recruits include specialists in targeted therapies, stem cells, angiogenic inhibitors, genetics and epigenetics, and other key areas. "With our young and energized faculty, we've become one of the most exciting institutions for cancer research," said Haber. There's a flip side to such success, though: both Lynch and Settleman were recently recruited away to leadership positions at other institutions.

In 2010 the MGH Cancer Center landed a prize recruit of its own as its new chief of medical oncology, José Baselga, a preeminent clinical research leader who most recently had headed up the Vall d'Hebron Institute of Oncology in Barcelona, Spain. "He is a spectacular physician, scientist, and human being. When he decided to move to the U.S.," said Haber, "there was a virtual feeding frenzy among all the leading cancer institutions, and the fact that he decided to come here is probably the highest compliment we can have. We are now really poised for making continued important contributions in clinical oncology."

At the 2009 "One Hundred Dinner," the annual MGH Cancer Center event honoring 100 noteworthy contributors to cancer care and cancer research, Haber saw MGH history in a single snapshot. Two honorees sat side by side: Paul Zamecnik, in his nineties and only months before his death, next to Konrad Hochedlinger, a young superstar in his thirties, whose MGH lab has achieved international fame for genetically reprogramming skin cells to become stem cells. "It was a magic moment," said Haber, "the very history of biomedical research, from the very early days of DNA and RNA all the way to the current world of cancer stem cells, and all with the same excitement and passion across generations."

In Haber's first six years as director of the cancer center, 2003–2009, research faculty doubled, and the annual research budget grew to $50 million, or about 8 percent of the MGH total. He said: "I think the theme of collaboration within a 'big tent' cancer center, spanning across research and clinical operations, and inclusive of medical oncology and all the other relevant disciplines, is the key piece that makes us so successful now. Our very leadership structure is 'matrixed,' with regular leadership meetings with the chiefs of surgical oncology, radiation oncology, pediatric oncology, medical oncology, and oncology nursing. We strive for an inclusive and collaborative environment."

It is just what was missing in MGH cancer efforts only a few decades ago. Looking to the future, Haber notes that the MGH Cancer Center now has an outstanding clinical and research faculty, most of them young and filled with exceptional promise.

RECOGNIZING A NEED FOR CHANGE

Peter Slavin returned to full-time duties at MGH in 1990, with an MBA from Harvard Business School in hand. A graduate of Harvard College and Harvard Medical School (1984), Slavin had served as a primary care physician on the MGH staff since 1987. Having interned in the Washington office of Massachusetts Congressman Edward J. Markey during college and worked as a legislative analyst at the NIH, Slavin was politically savvy and had professional ambitions that exceeded those of most primary care physicians. "I've always been interested in a career in health care management," Slavin would tell a Harvard Business School reporter in 2010.[69] When he returned to MGH from HBS ready for a challenge, he got it.

Like others, Slavin recognized that the ground was shifting beneath academic medical centers: "Until that time, people here at the MGH thought, 'We're the MGH, we know how to take care of patients, get out of our way.' Beginning in that era, people in the organization became more receptive of change." Slavin was charged with starting a Clinical Practice Council, a systemwide initiative to understand and improve the way the hospital and its physicians were doing business. He recalled:

> When I started looking at data, looking at where we could improve efficiency, the most dramatic place happened to be in cardiac surgery, where our length of stay was about four days longer than that in other academic medical centers around the country. I went to see Mort Buckley, chief of cardiac surgery, and the first time I met with him, he threw me out of his office. Basically he said, "We know exactly what we're doing; we're cardiac surgery at Mass General. Get out of my face." The next time I went back to see him, he said, "Go talk with Dave Torchiana and see if he is willing to help." That's really how Torch and I met and started working together in the early 1990s. Torch transformed the way care was delivered in cardiac surgery.

Torchiana, referring to Buckley's service, called inefficiencies in cardiac surgery "a compelling case. And that happened in multiple areas in the hospital. Peter's leadership was very important in making something happen, and the external environment all of a sudden became very assertive and a lot of things changed as a result of simply starting to pay attention to some things we hadn't focused on before."

In 2011, the year of this book's publication, Slavin was president of Massachusetts General Hospital and "Torch" was chairman and CEO of the Massachusetts General Physicians Organization. Twenty years before, however, they were

Peter Slavin, early 1980s.

just two physicians watching a rapidly changing,

increasingly hostile environment. New factor number one was the rise of managed care, in the principal form of health maintenance organizations (HMOs). (To think HMOs started with Harvard Community Health Plan, the brainchild of a former MGH chief of medicine, Robert H. Ebert!) Managed care represented a billing nightmare for physicians operating alone or in small group practices. More significantly, it transferred power from provider (hospital or physician) to insurer. In such an environment, doctors could find strength only in numbers. They had to combine, to organize; yet the entire tradition of MGH, the tradition of private practice, militated against combination, even though there had been a few notable successes in the area of group practice.

David Torchiana, about 1990.

Dean Clark, MGH's general director, had seen something coming 40 years earlier, and the MGH Staff Associates was the anemic result. Staff Associates had taken a role since Clark's day in such matters as credentialing and medical policies, but had nothing to say about how individual doctors organized their finances or how they got paid. Mass General had a second organization called the Professional Services Corporation, which provided business support for the medical staff: pension, insurance, payroll, billing, and so on. There was still a third organization, what Torchiana called in parliamentary parlance a "rump group," one that might have been confused for a group practice, the Massachusetts General Physicians Corporation (MGPC). Torchiana credited the MGPC with "taking the bull by the horns that the Staff Associates and PSC were asleep to." The MGPC, formed by practicing doctors, not the chiefs, was incorporated outside the hospital, "just to show the degree of dissatisfaction at the time," according to Jerry Austen. A voluntary organization of relatively entrepreneurial doctors, the MGPC was articulate, aggressive, and motivated, but patently did not speak for the majority of MGH doctors. As such, it was, like the other two organizations, "relatively impotent," again according to Austen.

By 1993, Austen said, "the place was in a lot of turmoil, with tension between physicians and the administration." The trustees and General Director Bob Buchanan decided that something had to change, and with the board's backing Buchanan approached Austen about chairing a group to consider a solution. A committee representing the three organizations began meeting in Austen's office, late afternoons, every two weeks. Deliberations lasted more than a year, "with help from consultants, very laboriously," sighed Torchiana. It was not always easy for the chiefs and the rank and file to agree. Said Austen, "Chiefs initially were viewed by docs a bit suspiciously, but we ended up very much together." After a year or so, they agreed on one organization called the Massachusetts General Physicians Organization (MGPO).

The committee stuck to its guns on one critical point: The PO, as it became known familiarly, had to be equal and parallel to the hospital. "I realized," said Austen, "that the hospital had the money, but the PO had the troops, the doctors. I'm a hospital guy, but I felt it was important that this organization be on an equal footing with the hospital." Since that time, by design, the president of the hospital and the CEO of the MGPO have been the two visible leaders of the MGH community. The PO focused on representing the doctors in all negotiations, and over time it took over a host of other functions, including finance and employee compensation and benefits, physician contracting, marketing, professional billing and billing compliance, improved information systems, human resources, practice improvement and support, quality care improvement, primary care development, specialty care development, and communications.

At midsummer 1994, the proposed PO was overwhelmingly approved by the MGH staff. Regular members had two votes, associates one vote. The tally of 450 voters was 764–27. Austen was appointed founding president and CEO of the MGPO in October. Daniel Ginsburg of Boston Consulting Group was appointed chief operating officer. The MGPO would take over all of the roles of the three previous entities. All former PSC physicians joined the MGPO on October 1, 1994. By November 1994 the MGPO included 105 group practices and 807 professional staff physicians, paid in part or in full by the PO.

Ed Lawrence called the formation of the MGPO "a critical event. Everyone is now working for the hospital, everyone is on the same team. Half of the MGPO board are physicians, and half are trustees. These aren't just people living on the North Shore.[70] They are active in the hospital on a daily basis."

Today the MGPO is the largest multispecialty group in New England, representing more than 1,600 employed physicians not only at MGH but also at other institutions. Said Austen, summing up: "As far as I know, there is no other academic medical center in America where the hospital and physicians work in such harmony. If I look at MGH over the last 25 years, the creation of the PO has been crucially important to the way the community works."

COMPETITORS BECOME PARTNERS

Managed care did not affect physicians alone; hospitals—especially academic medical centers like MGH—were profoundly affected by HMOs, which were especially prevalent in Massachusetts and growing all the time. More important to hospitals like MGH, the method of reimbursement coming into vogue within managed care was capitation.

This approach to insurer reimbursement seems to have originated on a large scale with health plans in California. Instead of setting fixed payment levels for each treatment or procedure, as in the old prospective payment system involving DRGs, capitation meant a fixed payment per covered subscriber per month, whether that subscriber was healthy or very sick. Capitation transferred all risk from the insurer to the provider and changed the rules of the road. If capitation became a reality, it would:

- Force hospitals to concentrate less on quality care and more on lowering cost per patient served, resulting in fewer inpatient days and too many empty beds
- Result in less demand for subspecialists, which is to say most clinicians at tertiary care hospitals like MGH
- Make primary care physicians (PCPs) the darlings of the 1990s
- Threaten academic medical centers that had always relied on billings to help subsidize teaching and research.

The key to success for a health care provider in a capitated environment was what David Torchiana called "controlling enough of the base of the pyramid." That is, the more covered lives a provider had in its system, the more it was paid. PCPs effectively controlled huge revenue flows—and didn't like the consequences. Nor did patients. Nor did the providers. This eventually led to a move away from capitation, but not before major changes on Fruit Street and across town in the Longwood Medical Area, site of Brigham and Women's Hospital and Harvard Medical School.

The solution for hospitals in this newly hostile environment was to contract or consolidate, assuming they could avoid closing, and some did not. Contracting was not in the Harvard genotype. That left consolidation, and in January 1993 Harvard Medical School Dean Daniel Tosteson began testing the waters with affiliated medical centers: Would they consider coming in under one umbrella and merging all five major Harvard teaching hospitals? The Boston consulting firm Bain and Company was charged with working with a 25-person team of top managers from the five hospitals "to explore mutual opportunities."[71] The result of this effort was talk, no action. In the summer of 1993 the two biggest Harvard hospitals began to think the unthinkable: forget about five hospitals joining forces. Could Mass General affiliate with Brigham and Women's Hospital (BWH)— itself formed from the 1975 merger of Peter Bent Brigham Hospital, Robert Breck Brigham Hospital, and Boston Hospital for Women? The idea was first broached between John McArthur, the BWH board chair, and MGH General Director Bob Buchanan in a parking lot "after a particularly frustrating meeting at the HMS library."[72] Said McArthur later, "The probability of merging five institutions was somewhere less than zero."[73]

Eight men, four from each hospital, deliberated long and hard over the idea:

- For MGH: Ferdinand Colloredo-Mansfeld (chairman of the board), J. Robert Buchanan (general director), W. Gerald Austen (chief of surgical services), and Francis H. Burr (honorary trustee)
- For BWH: John H. McArthur (chairman of the board), Eugene Braunwald (chairman, Department of Medicine), H. Richard Nesson (president and CEO), and Richard A. Spindler (trustee).

These eight individuals became the founding trustees of Partners Health-Care. The deal, announced at a December 8, 1993, press conference, was a blockbuster. The 1993 U.S. News and World Report survey of America's hospitals had ranked MGH third and the Brigham seventh in the nation. In 1994 the two institutions, merged into Partners HealthCare System, would become one of the most prominent integrated health care delivery systems in America, featuring two academic medical powerhouses affiliated with arguably the most prestigious institution of higher learning in the world. Outlying community hospitals in Boston and beyond joined Partners, including Faulkner Hospital, North Shore Medical Center in Salem and Lynn, and Newton-Wellesley Hospital. Martha's Vineyard Hospital and Nantucket Cottage Hospital, both of which merged with MGH, also became part of the Partners network.

There were many things to like about the MGH-BWH affiliation. It was said to be a true merger of equals; both hospitals were financially strong, with high patient volume, and both had substantial resources to further the grand vision of an integrated regional health care network. Boston Consulting Group, hired to advise the partners, suggested that costs could be cut 10 to 20 percent by eliminating administrative redundancies and consolidating clinical operations. The merging partners would set their sights on acquiring as many groups of primary care physicians as possible, to control the base of Torchiana's pyramid. "The easy part," said Jerry Austen in a speech after the deal was done, "is to arrange a hospital merger; the hard part is forging a primary care referral base of sufficient size combined with excellent secondary and tertiary care to command contracting clout."[74]

The affiliation was finalized on March 2, 1994, after votes by the two merging corporations. MGH and BWH joined as equal partners in Partners HealthCare System, Incorporated, with one board of trustees (although each of the two would continue to be guided separately by its own board). Combined, Partners had 1,800 hospital beds and more than 80,000 inpatient admissions a year. Later in March it was announced that BWH President H. Richard Nesson was named CEO of Partners and Samuel Thier president. Thier, a chief resident at MGH in the 1960s and most recently president of Brandeis University, left Brandeis in May 1994 to become president of Massachusetts General Hospital and its affiliated institutions. Bob Buchanan—who deserves credit for the name *Partners*, another small part of his enduring legacy—retired as the hospital's general director in June.[75]

Not everyone was thrilled about the new partnership. Specialists worried about cutbacks in specialty care, especially when, in July 1994, a 5 percent reduction in residencies was mandated by both hospitals. According to Ed Lawrence, some doctors worried that they might lose a powerful ally. Lawrence said: "One of the things that allowed MGH to be differentiated from others around town was having a very small board of trustees, very capable people who worked very hard. They were perceived as being advocates of both patients and doctors. When Partners was created, the medical folk at MGH were concerned that their trustees might be stripped of power, because they saw the trustees as their principal advocates. There were crunchy issues to work out, making sure our trustees still had a role to play."

Then there was dear old George S. Richardson, who lamented, "All my life, I've had three enemies: Russia, the Brigham, and Yale, and now I've only Yale."[76] The Berlin Wall had fallen five years before, and now another wall was down.

Competing Harvard hospitals did not take the news particularly well. The *Boston Globe* reported, "Heads of other major Harvard teaching hospitals were aghast at the news, since they thought they'd been in serious talks about building a five-hospital Harvard system. 'It's almost [as if] right in the middle of the [Celtics] season Paul Pierce and Kevin Garnett went off with their agents and decided they could form a better team,' recalled David Weiner, then CEO of Children's Hospital, one of the five."[77]

Within one year of the deal, Partners had achieved cost savings in treasury, finance, investments, human resources, and legal services; and reductions in materials management, pharmacy, central sterile services, invasive cardiology, clinical labs, and laundry and linens were all in progress. Hoped-for savings from clinical consolidations, however, were slow to nonexistent.

Ferdinand "Moose" Colloredo-Mansfeld

Clinically, in the research arena, and in the hunt for the most gifted residents and fellows, the two institutions' competitive instincts would prove indomitable. No chief at either hospital wanted to cede authority to his or her counterpart at the other. One attempt to create an über-chief of orthopaedics fell flat. Although there were significant economies, the goal of 10 to 20 percent savings from the Partners deal would prove elusive.

Ed Lawrence, who became the MGH board chairman in 1999, credited his predecessor, "Moose" Colloredo-Mansfeld, for having the vision to push Partners through. Said Lawrence: "Moose had the guts, the foresight to agree with BWH Chairman John McArthur that they were going to create Partners, and that was an extraordinary decision. The trustees basically moved this institution in a way it had not been moved in 170 years—joining its archenemy, creating a structure that worked."

Making the rounds to address the staffs of both hospitals in 1994, Thier summarized the Partners deal as "an educated leap of faith."[78] But where would this leap land five, 10, 15 years later? We'll leave that question for the final chapter.

AT LAST, A COMPLETE OB/GYN SERVICE

If anyone worried that Partners HealthCare would stifle competition in the Boston medical market, Isaac Schiff quickly put that to rest. In 1993, the very year that MGH and BWH were negotiating their historic combination, Schiff, chief of gynecology at MGH, was firing a shot across the bow of the crosstown powerhouse in obstetrics, Brigham and Women's Hospital. Hiring one of BWH's leading obstetricians, Fredric D. Frigoletto, Schiff and Mass General opened the first full-blown obstetrics service on Fruit Street, at a time of declining births in Massachusetts.[79]

First a little history: Founded in 1891 and named for Boston's most beloved actress of the nineteenth century, Mary Ann (Mrs. J. R.) Vincent—veteran of 444

Mary Ann Vincent.

roles during her career in Boston and known familiarly as "dear old Mrs. Vincent"—the Vincent Hospital had begun life as a modest 10-bed affair on Chambers Street in Boston. To accommodate its growth, it moved to South Huntington Avenue in 1908. That was where Joe Vincent Meigs came on as chief of staff in 1931 after Harvard Medical School, a residency on the East Surgical Service at MGH, and a stint as chief of the Gynecological Division of the Massachusetts State Hospital for Cancer in Pondville. By this time Meigs had come to the forefront in the battle against pelvic cancer in women and had helped establish the gynecologic tumor clinic at MGH.

The Vincent Hospital moved to MGH as its Gynecology Service in 1940, with 20 dedicated beds on the surgical wards. In 1947 the Vincent Burnham Building, housing both Gynecology and Pediatrics Services, was erected off the front left corner of the White Building. (It would be torn down in 2007 to make way for the ambitious Lunder Building.) At the Vincent Burnham, Meigs finally had a proper setting (43 beds, offices, labs, a cytoscopy room, and a conference room) for a full-fledged service in which students and younger practitioners could study and gain experience. Meigs remained joint chief of both the Vincent and the MGH Gynecology Service until his retirement in 1955. By then Meigs had been honored worldwide for his contributions to gynecology.

The branches of George Richardson's family tree wind their way through MGH history. His grandfather Maurice H. Richardson was one of the pioneers in the diagnosis and treatment of appendicitis. His father, Edward P. Richardson, was a surgical chief at MGH. His brother E. Peirson Richardson Jr. created the Neuropathology Service here. Another brother was Elliot L. Richardson, an MGH trustee and the U.S. attorney general who refused President Nixon's order to fire Special Prosecutor Archibald Cox at the time of the Watergate scandal.

George Richardson (born in 1921 in Phillips House when "it was fashionable to be born there") remembers well the early years of the Gynecology Service in Vincent

Joe Meigs.

Burnham, as he was trained in the Surgical Service but devoted much of his career to the surgical treatment of pelvic cancer in women, the one area in which the MGH Gynecology Service rose to the fore in midcentury under Joe Meigs's leadership. One of Richardson's colleagues, Maurice Fremont-Smith, was trained in the use of the Pap smear for the early detection of cervical cancer—trained in fact by the eponymous George Papanicolaou of New York Hospital and Cornell Medical School, who had developed the "Pap" technique and, with Herbert Traut, published *Diagnosis of Uterine Cancer by the Vaginal Smear* in 1943. Fremont-Smith studied with Papanicolaou in New York and brought his diagnostic methodology back to MGH, where it was taught to "the Vincent ladies"—volunteers who assisted the medical staff at Vincent Burnham in administering the Pap smear and other gynecologic procedures. A key assistant to Fremont-Smith was Ruth M. Graham, who founded the Vincent Cytology Laboratory. "In our MGH culture," recalled Richardson, "the Pap cultures were routinely referred to as 'Vincent smears.' "

In 1956 Joe Meigs was succeeded by Howard Ulfelder, coauthor with Langdon Parsons of the definitive *Atlas of Pelvic Operations* (1953). Under Ulfelder's two decades of leadership strides were made in the Gynecology Service. These included:

- The advent of the first female resident in gynecology at MGH (1962), Ann Brace Barnes, who would become one of the hospital's first female surgeons and whose life was tragically cut short by cancer

- The formation, under John W. Grover, of an ambulatory obstetric clinic coordinated with Boston Lying-In Hospital (1966)

- Howard Ulfelder's discovery of the relationship between the pregnancy drug diethylstilbestrol (DES) and a rare form of vaginal cancer in the offspring of these pregnancies (early 1970s), in studies assisted by Arthur Herbst

- Janet McArthur's groundbreaking work in reproductive endocrinology, including studies of the menstrual cycle of the bonnet monkey. McArthur's work was not limited to the Gynecology Service: her core work was in endocrinology; she was an important member of the thyroid clinic immediately after World War II; she made significant contributions to the Pediatric Service; and she published her work over an incredible 60-year span, 1939–1999. In 1972 McArthur became the first woman at MGH to be accorded full professorship at Harvard Medical School, as professor of obstetrics, gynecology, and reproductive biology.

Ulfelder was succeeded in 1976 by James H. Nelson, who, despite his unquestioned surgical skill, did not see the Gynecology Service advance as it might have. By the mid-1980s the department, still preeminent in cervical surgery, was lagging in other areas. "Those were uncomfortable years for me," confessed Richardson, who retired in 1985. There was little in the way of a coordinated research effort, and one leading contributor, Cornelius O. ("Skip") Granai, defected for a leadership role in the OB/GYN department at a Rhode Island hospital. As MGH sought a new start in gynecology in 1987–1988, its service was understaffed and underfunded.

Enter Isaac Schiff. A native of Montreal, Schiff had trained at McGill University and Montreal General Hospital before becoming a resident at Boston Lying-In, where he did a fellowship in reproductive endocrinology. In 1966 Boston Lying-In merged into Boston Hospital for Women, which itself merged with the Peter Bent Brigham and Robert Breck Brigham Hospitals in 1980, becoming Brigham and Women's. Schiff became chief of reproductive endocrinology at the Brigham. When he was

Howard Ulfelder.

recruited by MGH in 1988, at age 44, his division alone at the Brigham was larger than the entire Gynecology Service at MGH. The comparison in obstetrics was even more dramatic: in 1988 the Brigham delivered thousands of babies (the rate in 2008 was about 10,000 per year). MGH delivered none.

That MGH had no obstetrics service in the late twentieth century is not quite as shocking after a look back at the nineteenth century. Then gynecology and obstetrics were separate practices. Gynecology usually meant surgery, performed, like most surgeries of the nineteenth century, by general surgeons. Obstetrics, the care of mother and child from pregnancy through childbirth, was largely a matter for midwives until Victorian squeamishness about sex gave way to twentieth-century attitudes. Mothers most often gave birth at home; those without homes, the indigent and the abandoned, as well as those who experienced prenatal emergencies, were treated at special women's or lying-in hospitals. Harvard Medical School asked for obstetric teaching beds at MGH as early as 1845 but was rejected because, according to a special committee of the trustees, "no decent female would come to a hospital maternity ward for delivery,"[80] particularly if there were students on hand to watch. Nineteenth-century Boston hospitals for women included the Lying-In (1832) and the Free Hospital (1875).

Obstetrics had a formal place at Massachusetts General Hospital beginning in 1917 with the opening of the Phillips House, whose fourth floor was set aside for the practice. As Richardson recalled, in the early days of Phillips House a baby delivered there could claim a certain social cachet. In 1930 Baker Memorial began delivering babies to mothers of modest means. At both Phillips and Baker, babies were typically delivered by obstetricians from Boston Lying-In Hospital, where the chief of service was Frederick C. Irving, "a grand figure" in Richardson's memory. "His own satirical description of OB grand rounds consisted of a procession through the ward led by himself, followed at its tail by 'ward maids, villagers, and peasants.'" Although babies continued to be delivered at MGH until after World War II, in the 1950s the practice dwindled, "chiefly because the obstetricians deplored the lack of residents, specially trained nurses, and multiple practice aids which made such a marked contrast with the quality of care they could render at the Lying-In Hospital."[81]

In 1988 many female patients received their gynecological and prenatal care at Mass General but had their babies delivered at the Brigham—as they had previously, under the 1966 arrangement, at Boston Lying-In and then Boston Women's. But Schiff was not discouraged. "I took a leap of faith," he said. "Perhaps I displayed great naïveté. After all, I am from Canada! But the Mass General is the Mass General, and if you grew up outside of Boston in those days, you read about MGH and all the discoveries, and you had faith—I had faith—that they wanted the best possible department and that if I worked hard the department would be supported."

Schiff had a powerful advocate in Bob Buchanan. The general director "was terrific, outstanding to me," said Schiff. Schiff also had the support of the Vincent board, which, despite the Vincent's 1988 merger with MGH, continued in an independent role, especially in securing funding for the care of women at the hospital.

In the decade that followed, Schiff and his team started the Reproductive Endocrine Division, which led to an excellent in vitro fertilization program boasting one of the best success rates in the country. Critical to this effort was the recruitment of Thomas L. Toth, who continues to head up the Vincent IVF Program. They started a urogynecology division, focusing especially on post-delivery bladder problems. This division was first led by David Nichols, a nationally respected figure and past chairman of obstetrics and gynecology at Brown University. He was succeeded by May M. Wakamatsu, a superb surgeon whom residents named teacher of the year almost annually. Convincing MGH that GYN needed OB, however, took some work; but Schiff had powerful support, including that of Jerry Austen and Pat Donahoe.

There were compelling reasons to create a full obstetrics program. These included the neighborhood health clinics in Charlestown, Chelsea, and Revere. Pregnant women were receiving prenatal care at the clinics, but then had to move to the Brigham or elsewhere to have their babies delivered. "The continuity of care was bad," Schiff said. "Not to mention that in training, MGH docs never saw late-term pregnant mothers. But I wasn't sure we could be successful," Schiff recalled, "and one day I said to Buchanan, 'Bob, do you think anybody will ever come to MGH to have a baby?'

Isaac Schiff.

Fred Frigoletto.

"He answered, 'Your problem will be that you won't have enough room for all the women who want to come here.'"

Buchanan proved right. In 1993 Schiff hired Fred Frigoletto away from the Brigham and started a full-fledged Obstetrics Service. Once Frigoletto and his department were up and running, Schiff predicted 2,000 deliveries a year by the turn of the century. In 2008 the annual rate would exceed 3,000.

The key, Schiff believed, was conceiving of OB as a complete program, and he made sure to enlist the support of anesthesiology and other departments. He attracted a remarkably capable staff. Schiff sought a nursing leader for his department and, with the help of Yvonne Munn, he identified Jeanette Ives Erickson, who would go on to become the hospital's senior vice president for patient care services and chief nurse. Schiff recalls the day MGH President Dick Crater called to say he was "taking Erickson away." Schiff said, "You can't do that, she's too valuable!" Crater said, "That's why I'm taking her." (Ives Erickson's role in building Patient Care Services at MGH will be detailed in the final chapter.) Likewise, Sally Mason Boemer, who came in to run the department's finances, ultimately became senior vice president for finance for the entire hospital.

No hire was as important for Schiff's department, however, as Frigoletto. This itself took time. Frigoletto, who had recruited Schiff for the Brigham in the first place, did not want to leave the Brigham. But when a new chief at the Brigham took away Frigoletto's leadership role there, he called Schiff to determine if the opportunity was still available. "Of course," Schiff replied. Delivery service was inaugurated November 1, 1994. Fourteen years later, MGH would be delivering about 10 babies a day on average.

Said Frigoletto, "It was a unique opportunity to bring OB to an institution that had had hardly any connection or thought of OB in 40 to 50 years—no legacy, no expertise, no baggage. It was a gamble that became a success. I may be wrong, but I don't know of another instance where a brand-new nonexisting OB service has been developed as quickly or as effectively."

Schiff remarked, "I am most proud that in our department there is one standard of care for everybody. If you spent a whole day on the labor floor, you couldn't tell the difference between care for poor women from Chelsea and that for those to whom life has been generous, those, let's say, living on Beacon Hill. They get the same rooms, doctors, nurses, everything. We're very proud of that."

Overall, the OB/GYN Service at MGH has blossomed beyond anyone's expectations—although admittedly Bob Buchanan's expectations were always sky-high. One proof is fellowship programs. There are three subspecialties in which fellowships are offered in gynecology, that is, for which board certification is required: oncology, reproductive endocrinology, and maternal-fetal medicine (treating high-risk pregnancies). For certification, a program must have enough clinical care for its teaching volume and a significant research commitment. The MGH OB/GYN Service now has three formal fellowship programs; the Brigham is the only other hospital in Boston with all three. The research effort has been bolstered significantly by the Vincent trustees, who have supported the Vincent Center for Reproductive Biology.

Medical practice is probably the ultimate meritocracy. Excellent doctors will practice, regardless of gender, race, ethnicity—or age. Frigoletto was 60 years old when recruited by Schiff. Few professions would see the proposed leader of a *new department* brought in at that age. Then factor in Frigoletto's health. The obstetrician had a long history of coronary artery disease, dating at least to 1978, which he had chosen to manage medically with the help of cardiologists, including Roman DeSanctis. In June 2003 Frigoletto began to develop heart failure and was progressively incapacitated. He was admitted for a bypass, "which didn't accomplish much." The choice became dire: have a heart transplant or die. Unfortunately, Frigoletto pointed out, "You don't go to Wal-Mart and get a heart off a shelf." He had to wait four months in the cardiac ICU for a suitable donor, an experience Frigoletto recalled as "harrowing. But I was lucky. I was in my own hospital, and my own secretary kept working the whole time. I was at death's door for a month, but the rest of the time I had my computer and kept working while on a heart machine. My family was there, they visited every day, and two of my daughters began reproducing during my stay!"

Eight days after his transplant, the obstetrician was home and, as of 2010, had not suffered a relapse. "I decided that I wasn't going to be a cardiac cripple. I am very faithful about taking my medicine, but I try to put it out of my mind every other moment of the day." Frigoletto's working days were long: 10 to 12 hours, on average. And the MGH OB/GYN service was stronger than ever.

NEUROSURGERY FROM TREPANNING TO INTRAOPERATIVE IMAGING

In the corridor on White 5 hangs a striking portrait. Painted by Warren and Lucia Prosperi, it shows the neurosurgeon Robert Ojemann at a patient's bedside in the late evening. Iowa born, the youthful-looking senior doctor is shown with thinning hair the color of corn silk and a smile warm as the Iowa sun in summer. The patient lies in the foreground, facing the doctor, and Ojemann has reached out to touch the patient's arm. Behind the doctor, through a wall of windows, is the night skyline of Boston. Reflected in the window is a resident observing the surgeon at the bedside.

When he was interviewed for this book, MGH Chief of Neurosurgery Robert L. Martuza made a point of leading a writer out into the hallway to observe this

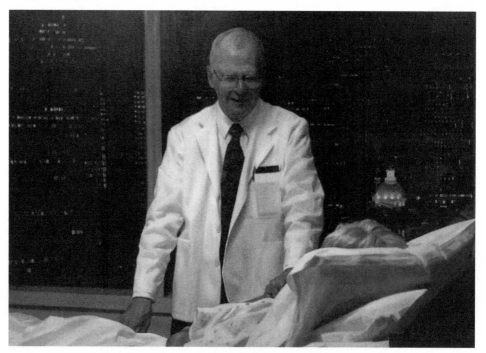

Robert Ojemann, in a portrait by Warren and Lucia Prosperi.

portrait. Martuza said of Ojemann: "He was a spectacular surgeon—not particularly quick (I've seen quicker operators), but he had very good results and was a good *person*. He taught you how to take care of people. He always saw the patients in the operating room before they went to sleep. He would be here late at night seeing patients. He was very patient-oriented, very family-oriented, very good values. He taught me a lot about life, not just about being a doctor."

The writer was struck by this because his own mother-in-law had been treated for brain cancer by Ojemann in 1983 and the family would always remember the surgeon's kindness and attentiveness to "Ruthie." It was a good reminder for the writer, as well—that amid all the high-tech wizardry of MGH specialists and investigators, what matters finally in an academic medical center are the patient, the doctor who attends the patient, and the student who observes. This would seem to be particularly true in the case of neurosurgery, where, as two former members of the MGH department wrote with sublime understatement, "patients do not always do well."[82] In neurosurgery, as much as anywhere, many Bob Ojemanns are needed. The MGH Department of Neurosurgery seems to have been gifted with several.

Early Efforts

Trephination, or trepanning, boring a hole in the skull to relieve pressure, was performed by primitive man, and it was performed seven times in 30 years by MGH's founding surgeon, John Collins Warren. It was usually done only in the case of acute trauma, but in 1832 Warren performed a trephination on an epileptic patient to relieve pressure. Still, as late as the 1890s, operations within the skull were performed almost exclusively in the case of trauma, and the surgeon was whatever visiting surgeon happened to be available. There was no specialty of neurosurgery as such.

The first MGH surgeon with a special interest in the brain was John W. Elliot, who met Victor Horsley (1858–1916), the father of English neurosurgery, during a trip to Europe in 1889 but was not given an appointment at MGH until five years later. When Elliot performed three operations for brain tumor in 1895, the "extern" on duty, who gave the chloroform, was an HMS student, Harvey Cushing, the father-to-be of American neurosurgery. After further training at Johns Hopkins, Cushing made his name at the Peter Bent Brigham Hospital.

Results during the first years of the twentieth century were distressingly poor. The first 36 trephinations for brain tumor at MGH "failed to cure a single patient."[83] Craniotomy for epilepsy gave better results: 9 of 21 cases showed an improvement of symptoms after surgery. Surgical technique was crude:

> The skull was opened with one or more trephined holes; the dura was cautiously opened, and the brain was inspected and palpated. If nothing was found, a cortical incision was made and probed with the finger, extending if necessary under the margin of the craniotomy. Electrical stimulation of the cortex was attempted in several cases with little success, due to failure of the machine or perhaps to the effects of the "antiseptic solutions" (carbolic acid or mercuric "corrosive") continuously poured over the cortex during the operation. The tumor, if found, was scooped out with a finger, and bleeding vessels were tied. Oozing from the brain was stopped with a 10% cocaine solution.[84]

In 1911 a special assignment in the surgery of the central nervous system was given to Samuel J. Mixter (1856–1926), a responsibility he was soon sharing with his son, William J. "Jason" Mixter. Mixter *père* "never abandoned general surgery but did foster the development at the MGH of surgery of the brain and spinal cord."[85] Jason Mixter (1880–1958) grew up in Boston and on his family's farm in the Berkshires, attended MIT as an undergraduate, and then graduated from Har-

vard Medical School in 1902. After a one-year internship, he joined his father in private practice.[86] Assigned to Samuel's South Surgical Service in 1907, "Young Mixter" decided to make neurosurgery his life's work. Upon receipt of the 1911 special assignment, the Mixters were allotted two beds "to try out the procedures being developed by Horsley and Cushing."[87] Jason Mixter spent 1912 with Horsley in England, "and by 1915 he was recognized nationally for his contributions to the treatment of skull fractures, intracranial sepsis, and surgery of the spine and spinal cord." He worked in close consultation with the neurologist James B. Ayer.[88]

Samuel Jason Mixter.

William Jason Mixter.

After the war Mixter and Mixter operated "in the shadow of Cushing's service across town," and most of their work was for trauma.[89] Cushing specialized in brain surgery, but Mixter's interests included disorders of the spine and spinal cord, central nervous system trauma, pain, and disorders of the sympathetic nervous system.[90] In 1934, with Joseph Barr of the MGH Orthopaedic Service, Jason Mixter published his best-known work, which traces lower back pain and sciatica to herniated discs.[91]

While the "Cushing School" of neurosurgery was being created at the Brigham, Mixter labored to develop an MGH school that, he reckoned, might have a longer life since it was related more to an institution than to an individual. About Mixter's character colleagues wrote, "At a time when blatant puerile rudeness in the operating room was the fashionable prerogative of the prima donna surgeon, his behavior was precisely the opposite, and [that] yielded him better support from his operative team." Mixter's was known as "the friendly service."[92]

The White-Sweet Years

The next generation of neurosurgeons that came along between the world wars included John Sprague Hodgson (1890–1979), who was "a superb surgeon, a delightful gentleman, and a humanist scholar," though he had "little taste for research activities—unlike his younger colleague James Clarke White (1895–1981)."[93] White was born in Vienna while his father was studying medicine in Austria. Educated at Groton and Harvard (1917) and with two years as a line officer on a light cruiser during wartime, White graduated from Harvard Medical School magna cum laude in 1923. He interned in pathology at Johns Hopkins, but, impressed by Cushing, he returned to Boston and residency at MGH in 1924.[94] With a Moseley Traveling Fellowship in 1927, he studied the sympathetic nervous system and surgery for pain in Strasbourg and Paris.

A new neurosurgical operating room opened in Baker Memorial in 1933, serving patients not only from Baker but also from Phillips House and Bulfinch. A neurosurgery residency program was established in 1936, and in 1939 the Neurosurgical Service was created, W. J. Mixter serving as its first chief. White succeeded him in 1940 and served until 1961, when he was succeeded by his close collaborator, William H. Sweet. When Sweet stepped down as chief in 1977, he and White had led the service for all but one of its 38 years.

White also resembled Ojemann, according to Ballantine and Sweet:

He not only did not lose his temper, he never even became ruffled. In a day when many distinguished neurosurgeons were paragons of intemperate, even preposterous expression, especially in the operating room, Jim never visibly lost his tact or composure. . . . His description to the patient of the risks and uncertainties of the proposed operation was . . . comprehensive in an age when such emphasis was not the general custom. . . . We learned from Jim how to tread the precarious path between gentleness and discretion. Extraordinarily devoid of formality and pretense, he smoked a corncob pipe, wore reasonable quality, usually unmatching, coat and trousers likely to be of ancient vintage. He had at least one jacket with matching trousers: his naval officer's uniform, dark buttons having been substituted for the regulation brass.[95]

James Clark White.

Together White and Sweet investigated mechanisms of pain and published a classic monograph in 1955, *Pain: Its Mechanism and Neurosurgical Control*. Recognizing psychiatric factors in pain, they included two chapters written with the assistance of two MGH psychiatrists, Stanley Cobb and Frances J. Bonner. White performed the "courageous" first successful operation to cut pain tracts lying deep within the brain stem. A second, more comprehensive monograph in 1969 was titled *Pain and the Neurosurgeon: A Forty-Year Experience*. White was 74 when it came out, and he had done most of the writing with "unflagging industry, honesty, and scholarship."[96]

The attitude of MGH and general surgeons toward neurosurgery saw a shift during the White years, according to Ballantine and Sweet:

In the late forties orthopedic, urologic, and neurologic surgery had such meager appeal to the better medical students that these specialties were described as havens for mediocrity by no less an authority than the late Professor Edward D. Churchill. . . .

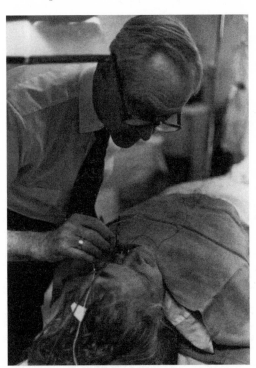

William Sweet.

The allure of neurosurgery to

some of the medical students with superior minds was evident by the mid-fifties, and we have been getting more than our fair share of such applicants. . . .

By the late [1950s] . . . U.S. training centers were turning out more purely clinical neurosurgeons than the country needed [while] the academic posts with an opportunity to combine research and clinical work were often going begging. Hence, at the MGH dual goals for the training and investigative program became more totally basic neuroscience and more such science with potential clinical application.[97]

Asked about this shift in thinking about neurosurgery, Nicholas T. Zervas, chief of the MGH service beginning in 1977, filled in the details:

As late as the 1950s, you had to be a blood-and-guts guy to do neurosurgery because most patients died. Neurosurgery became a desirable field only after four innovations that improved results: Mannitol, a diuretic that dehydrates the brain and prevents it from expanding as it wants to do when CO_2 increases; hyperventilation, which helps reduce the CO_2 level; high-dose steroids used preoperatively, which cause vessels to remain constricted and prevent brain swelling; and the operating microscope. All four things happened within a decade, making virtually any operation safe.

Research got a boost in 1955 when two floors in Warren were devoted to labs for neurology and neurosurgery. David Crockett was credited with raising money for these.[98] The Mixter Laboratories for Neurosurgical Research were formally dedicated on October 16, 1957.[99] The Mixter Neurosurgical Library, funded by

Nicholas Zervas.

a faculty member, Jost Michelson, is still a resource in its current location on the seventh floor of the Wang Ambulatory Care Center.

Sweet succeeded his good friend and collaborator, James White, in 1961. Sweet had grown up in "the timberlands of Washington State," graduated from high school at 14, and studied to be a concert pianist. Concluding that he could not reach the pinnacle in this field, he worked in a sawmill for a year, then entered the University of Washington, graduating in 1930. His career at Harvard Medical School was interrupted by a Rhodes Scholarship that took him to Oxford for two years' research in neurophysiology. Finally graduating from HMS in 1936, he trained in Chicago and Montana before joining the Harvard faculty and MGH staff in 1940. During his career Sweet particularly pushed research combining biophysics, neurophysiology, electron microscopy, neurochemistry, and immunology. He was only the second recipient of the American Association of Neurological Surgeons' premier honor, the Harvey Cushing Medal.[100]

Neurosurgery in Recent Years

In 1911 the MGH provided two beds for the Mixters' neurosurgery patients. Seventy years later the average daily census of neurosurgery patients at Mass General was 70, and the service had 28 neurosurgeons, including 10 residents-in-training. Thirteen investigators worked in the Mixter Laboratories for Neurosurgical Research, including eight PhD's.[101]

Zervas took over as chief in 1977. Born in Lynn, Massachusetts, he was a child pianist who later served as president of the Boston Symphony Orchestra and a trustee of the New England Conservatory of Music. A 1950 graduate of Harvard College, he attended the University of Chicago School of Medicine, interned at New York Hospital, and was a resident in neurology and neuropathology at the Montreal Neurological Institute. After two years in the Army Medical Corps, he began training at MGH.[102]

In 1960–1961 Zervas studied stereotactic cerebral surgery with Jean Talairach at the Hôpital Ste. Anne in Paris and worked with Gerard Guiot at Hôpital-Foche. After five years at Jefferson Medical College, he returned to Boston in 1967 to become chief of neurosurgery at Beth Israel. Coming back to MGH as Sweet's successor in 1977, Zervas believed some changes were critical. At the time, the entire staff was in private practice. Said Zervas, "I felt we all should be in the same group practice, getting rid of competition between people here and allowing subspecialization." Working closely with Ojemann, according to his own account, Zervas "endeavored to give each member of the staff a special area of expertness. [From 1977 to 1982] the number of patients with special problems referred to the Service because of the special knowledge and experience gained through this program has increased considerably."[103]

Zervas and Joe Martin "instituted a plan for unifying many aspects of the Neurological and Neurology Services," combining grand rounds, consolidating personnel and financing of clinical teaching services and research, and creating a pilot program for training residents in neurology and neurosurgery.[104] Zervas would note proudly that at many if not most hospitals neurosurgery and neurology do not always get along. "Here at MGH, there were no arguments, Adams in

Robert Martuza.

neurology and White and Sweet in neurosurgery set a harmonious tone. Where there's harmony, there's a chance for greatness. That remains a very important feature of what happens here."

Robert L. Martuza's father was a coal miner in the northeastern Pennsylvania town of Nanticoke. Martuza's mother had incapacitating migraine headaches. In early life, Martuza began watching the TV drama *Ben Casey*, starring Vince Edwards as a neurosurgeon. He concluded that by following in Casey's footsteps, he might be able to help his mother, or others suffering from head pain. By this time his father had been killed in a mining accident. Martuza finished public high school with honors and went to Bucknell University and Harvard Medical School, and he was chief resident in neurosurgery under Zervas in 1979–1980. He would have been an MGH lifer except for a call from Georgetown University, which invited him to become chairman of its Department of Neurosurgery in 1991. Martuza served there for 10 years. In 2000 he was called up to "the big club" again, as Zervas's successor.

Asked what his charge was as incoming chief, Martuza responded, "This was always a good department, though there were certain undeveloped areas." Among these were complex spine surgery, peripheral nerve surgery, and endovascular neurosurgery. In each case, he sent a promising resident or faculty member elsewhere to train in new techniques, then brought that person back to join the staff at MGH. Christopher S. Ogilvy, an endovascular surgeon, would one day occupy the Robert Ojemann Chair of Neurosurgery.

Martuza also made moves in research, for example, hiring Jeff Macklis to work in stem cell research. Martuza's own investigative area is particularly exciting. Since earning a research fellowship in tumor virology in 1972–1973, he has been interested in exploring new ways of combating brain cancer. In the late 1980s he had the insight that an oncolytic virus, that is, a virus that would attack and kill cancer cells, could be engineered. By 2010 he and collaborators had conducted phase one of a clinical trial for brain tumor and were looking at applying the technique to prostate cancer as well.

Asked to describe the arc of neurosurgery over the 40 years of his career, Martuza pointed to the arrival of CT and MRI imaging as the decisive turning point. In MGH's new Lunder Building neurosurgery will have state-of-the-art operating suites, including two rooms with intraoperative MRI, one with intraoperatve CT, and two with intraoperative angiography. Added Martuza: "The arc of neurosurgery has been ahead of other areas of surgery in being minimally invasive. We still do things really well around the brain but not so well in the brain. We can clip aneurysms or take out an acoustic neuroma tumor. But the future will involve going inside the brain itself in new ways, as with engineered viruses. The arc of neurosurgery will be to modify how brain cells function, treating conditions that you don't usually think of in connection with neurosurgery, like depression and obesity and restoration of neurological functions."

An important feature of the neurosurgical armamentarium at MGH is the proton beam facility built in the 1990s, one of only a handful in the United States. That development will be featured in the final chapter.

Words to Doctor By

To close this chapter, here are a few final thoughts from Bob Martuza about Bob Ojemann, who died March 3, 2010:

> Bob Ojemann means many things to me. He is, of course, the person who taught me how to remove complex tumors and how to take care of patients in a way that I would want to be cared for. But he is much more.
>
> Today we are inundated by committees and "team medicine." Bob was not like that. He was an artist. He took personal responsibility for the patient, for the operation, and for the outcome, and made sure it was the best it possibly could be. He didn't work for the hospital or the system. He worked for the patient. He was the patient's advocate.
>
> Bob knew that the outcome depended not only upon the surgery but also on the postoperative care. It was common to get a call from him at 10 P.M. to go to see a patient with him to take care of a problem. He taught surgeons how to be doctors.
>
> As a resident, Bob Ojemann taught me how to be a neurosurgeon. As a faculty member, he taught me how to be a doctor. When I first joined the MGH faculty, I shared an office suite with Bob Ojemann and got to know him at a personal level, and he taught me how to be a husband and a father. Bob was clearly dedicated to neurosurgery and to patient care. However, he was also very dedicated to his wife and his children. He made many sacrifices to be able to spend what little free time he had with them. For me, he was a great teacher in all aspects of life.

CHAPTER 8

· · · · · · · · · · · ·

A HOSPITAL FOR THE WHOLE WORLD, 1994–2011

Our community is no longer that little neighborhood along the Charles; our community is the world.

—Jeanette Ives Erickson

WITH THE FORMATION OF THE *Massachusetts General Physicians Organization (MGPO) and the advent of a new generation of professional hospital administrators (CEOs with MBAs), the balance of power at MGH has shifted. Where once the chiefs of medicine and surgery effectively controlled the General Executive Committee, the role of hospital president has become more central, while the CEO of the MGPO has become the hospital president's partner in leadership—hospital and doctors sharing power. The chiefs remain important actors in the drama, as do the trustees, but presidents Samuel O. Thier, James J. Mongan, and Peter L. Slavin get top billing here, paired with the first leaders of the MGPO, W. Gerald Austen, Slavin, and David F. Torchiana.*

Women have come to power at Mass General in recent years, and this chapter will feature several. Some, like Senior Vice President Ann Prestipino, have played important roles in administration; others have been prominent in medical, surgical, and patient care services. In 2009 Cathy Minehan, former president of the Boston Federal Reserve Bank, became the first female chairman of the Board of Trustees.

In 1993 another formidable trustee, Jane Claflin, called for an Office for Women's Careers—a signal of a new emphasis on gender diversity in a period when the likes of Jeanette Ives Erickson and Susan Briggs have made major marks.[1] Since then the hospital has diversified across every conceivable borderline of gender, race, and ethnicity, and here such women as Deborah Washington and Carlyene Prince-Erickson play lead roles. As a senior physician was heard to say, "This place used to be white men in Harvard ties. Now it's the United Nations."

This final chapter spotlights several impressive developments (and women who have contributed to them): proton beam therapy (Nancy Tarbell); Patient

The traffic circle at the Wang Ambulatory Care Center, 2010. The Ether Dome atop the Bulfinch Building is barely visible to the left of the large trees.

Care Services (Ives Erickson); and molecular biology, where rising stars like Jeannie Lee work alongside a celebrated group of veterans, including the 2009 Nobel Prize Laureate Jack Szostak. The chapter will conclude with a section on MGH's expanded definition of community, including everyone from Boston's homeless to victims of the latest natural disaster somewhere in the world.

UNTIL THE LATE 1960S THE TRAINING PROGRAM in internal medicine at Massachusetts General Hospital included a dozen new residents a year, usually half from Harvard Medical School, half from other elite medical schools, including Johns Hopkins, Yale, Columbia, and Washington University in St. Louis.[2] An intern and resident formed a team working a ward in Bulfinch, around a central nursing station. Each young doctor was on call every other night, rotating intern-resident-intern-resident for the entire year. Sometime in the 1970s a third trainee was added to the rotation, a more humane setup that trained 50 percent more doctors per year. Though the residents supervised the interns, at MGH, unlike other settings, they did their own admitting on the nights they covered, and the two or three together were jointly responsible for all patients. This team approach, still in practice today, is a hallmark of MGH training, according to the endocrinologist Mason Freeman: "You're expected to know all patients covered by your team. Some don't like this system, thinking they want 'their own' patients. I believe this is why people trained at MGH over several decades have been consistently selected as leaders in medicine—because they know how to get consensus among very bright people about life-and-death decisions."

The team system begins from the moment a prospective intern is interviewed for possible admission to the program. He or she is interviewed by a *team*. Said

Chief of Medicine Alexander Leaf (in black) and Chief Medical Resident Samuel Thier (right of Leaf) with medical residents, 1966. The group included two future Nobel Prize–winners, Joseph Goldstein (third row, far left, with only his head showing) and Ferid Murad (second row, far right) (courtesy Samuel Thier).

Freeman, "In another system, an SOB or a prima donna can be left alone to handle their own patients, but here you have to agree, you have to learn to come to consensus."

Lloyd Hollingsworth "Holly" Smith was chair of the Intern Selection Committee at MGH when Samuel O. Thier arrived for an interview in 1960. Thier hailed from the State University of New York, Syracuse—at that time not one of the elite eastern medical schools that typically fed the MGH training system. Chief of Medicine Walter Bauer reportedly said to Holly Smith: "Syracuse?! We don't take them. Get rid of him!" Smith and his group interviewed Thier, and after 45 minutes Smith returned to Bauer to say, "I've failed you, I can't get rid of this guy."

SAM THIER, ONE OF OUR OWN

Was Sam Thier always in a hurry? Born in Brooklyn, New York, he matriculated at Cornell at age 16 and finished in three years. "I never did get my college diploma," he said. Thier enrolled at the medical school known familiarly as Upstate. He graduated in 1960, before turning 23. An intern at MGH beginning in 1960, he went to the NIH in 1962–1964 and returned to Mass General as a resident in 1964. He was named chief resident in medicine in 1966. His father, a general practitioner in Brooklyn, telephoned his congratulations and asked how Thier felt. His answer: "Terrified." Dad's answer: "Sounds like you're ready." Thier was chief of the Renal Unit by 1967, succeeding Alexander Leaf, who had succeeded Robert Ebert as chief of medicine. Talk about the fast track: Thier was 30 years old.

As a young Jewish man coming to MGH in the 1960s, Thier realized that he was joining an institution long dominated by white, Anglo-Saxon Protestants. "I didn't pay much attention to it initially," he said. "In my intern group, there were several Jewish interns, including Steve Goldfinger, Dave Alpers, Stan Appel. The culture shock wasn't coming to a mostly WASP institution, it was coming from a state university to the MGH. The intellectual depth and breadth here was amazing. My colleagues in the intern group included Rhodes scholars. Whoa! I didn't know if I belonged here or not."

Thier would remember most of his internship well; he contrasted his experience in the early 1960s with the experience of MGH interns in the twenty-first century:

> My wife, Paula, tells the story of me collapsing in my whites on the bed, her coming to ask me if I wanted dinner, me saying, "No, no, what was the blood pressure on that patient?" She said, "Who do you think you're talking to?" We didn't know as much. We didn't know that we didn't know as much. But what the kids now have to deal with, the technology, the new knowledge, is incredible, so being an informed, up-to-date person in this institution is much more difficult. The kids are much broader today. They have lives. They write books. They ski on weekends. The sense of pride in place is the same. If you are selected to be here, you are someone who has done well, and you know that you are part of an important tradition.

Thier remembered sitting at lunch with the chief resident his second year, Frank Austen. "I said to him, 'There are so many spectacular people here! What are we doing here?' He said, 'Oh, you're going to be one of those people, too.'"

Thier's first tour of duty as a member of the staff at MGH ran up against institutional resistance to group practice in the Department of Medicine. He understood, before others, that individual units within an academic medical center needed to join forces and cross-subsidize one another if the overall institution was to remain world-class. He called on Larry Fouraker, a professor at the Harvard Business School, to help develop the idea, but when it was presented to the hospital administration, it was not encouraged.

Thier was recruited to the University of Pennsylvania in 1969, where he was involved with the creation of a faculty practice plan, with help from Penn's Wharton School of Business. He was named vice chairman of medicine at Penn in 1972. He became chairman of internal medicine at Yale in 1975, as well as chief of the medical service for Yale–New Haven Hospital. His father, the GP from Brooklyn, enjoyed visiting his successful son in New Haven. Thier said of his dad, "I thought he was the smartest fellow I ever knew. He came on rounds with me here, and the residents said, 'He's a GP? How does he know so much?' The proud time was when he sat in on some of the postgraduate teaching we had here, and he said to me, 'You're pretty good.'"

In 1985 Thier moved to the Institute of Medicine of the National Academy of Sciences, as president, and in 1991 Brandeis University in Waltham, Massachusetts, appointed him president. He was back in the Boston area. Less than three years later, he was hired to succeed Bob Buchanan as president of MGH. By then, he was aware of the changes under way at Mass General. Harvard Medical School's Dean Dan Tosteson asked Thier about the idea of unifying five major teaching hospitals under the Harvard banner. Thier told Tosteson that he would be fortunate to get any two of the five working together. When MGH turned its recruiting efforts on Thier in 1993, he could not refuse. He had been at Brandeis for so short a time and had promised the university trustees he would not abandon them for *another university*, but this was different. Said Thier, "Being chief resident at MGH was an even better credential than being chairman of medicine at Yale! And I actually like Yale a lot."

One of the trustees, Nicholas Thorndike, was on the search committee that interviewed candidates to replace Buchanan. "I asked him," Thorndike said, "'Why the hell do you want this job? This is the worst job in the world. You have all these prima donnas you have to deal with on a daily basis! Why the hell do you want to be hospital president?' His answer was, 'Because it's a challenge and I think I'm up to it.'"

Thier's appointment to succeed Bob Buchanan as president was announced on December 9, 1993, one day after the press conference trumpeting the affiliation of MGH with Brigham and Women's Hospital. Buchanan's position had been redefined early that year from general director of MGH to president and CEO of the 1811 Corporation (the holding company for the General Hospital Corporation). As such, he oversaw the General Hospital Corporation (MGH), McLean, Spaulding, the Institute of Health Professions, MGH Home Health Services,

MGH Health Services Corporation, and MGH Professional Services Corporation. Thier replaced Buchanan in 1994 and named Richard "Dick" Crater, formerly chief financial officer, as president of MGH proper. Succeeding Crater as CFO was Catherine "Cathy" Robbins, who moved to Partners as vice president for finance in 1995. Thier was hired with the understanding that after a period of two years he would move to Partners as its CEO, succeeding H. Richard Nesson, then president of Brigham and Women's.

It was pure coincidence that brought Thier back to MGH the same year the hospital created the Massachusetts General Physicians Organization (MGPO), including a faculty group-practice plan—one cause over which Thier had left 25 years before. Said Thier, "I thought, maybe this place will finally bring itself into the twentieth century."

Two Years at the Top

Sam Thier was welcomed back to Mass General with open arms. He was making rounds one day, as he would continue to do long after his retirement from MGH and Partners, when a senior surgeon came bursting in and said, "It's so nice to see one of our leaders back at the bedside." Thier said, "The credibility I had as a practicing doc was extremely valuable. And I could learn more from making rounds with the house staff than I could from a dozen meetings."

A reporter for the *Boston Globe* asked the new president how it felt being the first Jewish president "in the center of WASPdom." "I said, 'I think they know who I am, and I don't think that's an issue anymore.'" John Lawrence, board chair emeritus, was one WASP who made Thier feel welcome. Thier visited Lawrence while the latter was recuperating in the hospital. Lawrence said, "Sam, it's so good to see one of our own back in charge." *One of our own* meant a former house officer at MGH.

Thier's wife, Paula, was another person happy with a return to Boston. According to Thier, she said, "Whew! Now that I'm in Boston I can get sick again. I've never felt the same confidence at any place that I've felt at the Mass General." Thier concurred: "There is a sense of excellence here: everybody feels they are responsible for maintaining that sense of excellence. It's a tradition, an absolute performance level, and a sense that you are responsible for it."

Some would credit Sam Thier with inaugurating a new era at MGH, or at least coinciding with one. So many things were changing with the formation of Partners and the PO, and Thier was the man in charge. But then he had always captured notice. The MGH annual report of 1966 had taken note of Chief Resident Sam Thier as "energetic, stimulating, and often provocative."[3] Little had changed 30 years later.

Sam Thier.

Edward Lawrence, a trustee during Thier's tenure as president, called Thier and his successor, James Mongan, "transformative characters. There had been tension between the general director and some of the staff. Sam arrived and moved his office back into the main hospital from Cambridge Street, and that tension started to dissipate. Sam was a very shrewd strategic leader in terms of what he promoted and didn't promote. I think the hospital started to do extremely well."

"More than anyone," the *Boston Globe* would note 14 years after his hiring, Thier "is seen as the architect of the healthcare giant and its aggressive market strategies. He was, and is, formidable by almost any measure—in intellect, charm, and competitive fire." Thier told the *Globe:* "In my view, it was a sacred responsibility . . . to make sure this institution and the Brigham were not done in by the changing environment."[4]

The situation facing Thier upon his arrival was challenging. He recalled:

> By the time I got here they had closed 20 percent of the beds at MGH. It was not a drill, it was really happening. The physicians working with the administration began a review of what they should be doing to sustain the place in the long run. They had decided that they should build a regional network.
>
> The Brigham was facing the same questions but it had a favored relationship with Harvard Community Health Plan (HCHP), and they said, "We don't have to do that. HCHP admits all their tertiary care to us, they have floors at our hospital." But HCHP began to say they wanted to work with other hospitals and began calling the shots more and more with the Brigham and others. And the Brigham began to get the idea.

It took time for the medical staffs of both hospitals to embrace the reality of Partners. The general economy cooperated, however, and hospital economics began improving. By later in the decade, both MGH and the Brigham had

Ann Prestipino.

stabilized and were beginning to reopen the beds they had closed. The reactions of the two hospitals differed, according to Thier: "The Brigham said, Wow, Partners worked! MGH said, See? We didn't have to do it!"

An important move was the hiring of Ellen M. Zane as Partners' network president, charged with securing commitments from primary care physicians in the region who could refer their patients to MGH and the Brigham for tertiary care. The goal was 1,000 sign-ups by the year 2000, and the goal was met. Zane served in this capacity at Partners from May 1994 until 2004, when she was named CEO of Tufts–New England Medical Center (NEMC) in Boston.

Internally, Thier had an equal challenge during his two years as MGH president. The administration that he took over "was not in very good shape," he said. "Over the first year I had to turn over about two-thirds of the administrators." But a new generation of leaders began to emerge, including key female contributors:

- Ann Prestipino had risen steadily through a series of administrative roles since her hiring at MGH in 1980. She was the youngest assistant general director named under Bob Buchanan. Under Thier, she was promoted to vice president, overseeing many services and assisting in the creation of the MGH Cancer Center. She was the only woman asked to serve on the four-person transition team that acted collectively as the hospital CEO after the departure of Dick Crater. In 2010 Prestipino was the MGH/MGPO senior vice president for Surgical and Anesthesia Services and clinical business development, leading the establishment of centers of excellence for both the hospital and the physicians' organization.

- Kate Walsh relocated to Boston from New York to serve successively as an assistant general director for medical services, vice president of medical services and primary care, and senior vice president of medical services and the MGH Cancer Center. In 2010 Walsh left a five-year hitch at the Brigham to become president and CEO of Boston Medical Center.

- Martha Wagner Weinberg served as Thier's chief of staff. In 1995 she moved on to Partners as vice president for project management and chief of staff.

- Jane L. Holtz became vice president for neurosciences in 1994 and clinical vice president for neurosciences and pediatrics in 1996. Key events during her leadership period included the establishment of MassGeneral Hospital *for* Children and the designation of MGH as a Level 1 Trauma Center for Pediatrics. Also during this period Building 114 in the Charlestown Navy Yard was dedicated entirely to neuroscience research.

Meanwhile, Peter Slavin, future MGH president, served as chief medical officer, the key liaison between the hospital administration and the medical staff.

DIVERSITY, WOMEN, AND THE PROTON BEAM

Sam Thier was a bellwether of sorts. He arrived at Mass General as its first Jewish president in 1994, just as diversity—of ethnicity, race, and gender—was becoming an institutional imperative. Once a charity operation funded and run by wealthy white males, MGH today presents a diverse face to the world. In 2011 the 28-member Diversity Committee addresses the hospital's role as an employer, provider of care, and community member, while promoting the integration of diversity into all the hospital's ongoing strategic initiatives.

There was a middle-class community of African Americans in Boston in the nineteenth century—centered on the north slope of Beacon Hill, close to Mass General—but, with one minor exception, they did not work at Mass General. Peter Williams Ray, an African American native of New York City and a graduate of Bowdoin College, was an "interne" at MGH before the Civil War, according to

Chester Pierce with Valerie Stone, MGH's senior African American female faculty member.

many sources.[5] After training in Boston, he returned home to Brooklyn, where he practiced medicine and opened a pharmacy.[6]

The virologist William Augustus Hinton was the first African American full professor at Harvard Medical School. The son of former slaves, Hinton graduated from Harvard College with the class of 1905 and entered Harvard Medical School in 1909. The Wigglesworth Scholarship, which he won, and a part-time job in the lab of Richard C. Cabot and Elmer E. Southard helped put him through school. Not permitted to train for surgery in Boston, he volunteered as an assistant in the Department of Pathology at Mass General for three years. He subsequently became a professor at HMS in 1923 and developed two common tests for syphilis, the Hinton and the Davis-Hinton tests.

Julius Rosenwald, president and chairman of Sears, Roebuck, founded the Rosenwald Fund in 1917, and used it largely to support the education of African Americans. Several doctors appear on the MGH rolls as Julius Rosenwald Fellows, the earliest being Theodore Kenneth Lawless in 1920.

It wasn't until 1931, however, that there was a full-fledged African American physician at the hospital, James L. Guardo, a graduate of the MGH internal medicine program hired to work in the Outpatient Unit. He is listed in MGH records as a graduate assistant, and apparently he did not have admitting privileges. In 1968 Chester M. Pierce became the first African American full professor at MGH, in the Psychiatry Department. He had graduated from the Harvard Medical School in 1952. During his first summer at the medical school, needing a job, Pierce had worked at MGH as a janitor.[7]

It is not always possible to identify firsts on the MGH staff, since members of some groups were known to change their names in order to "pass." The first openly Jewish staff physician at MGH was Harry Linenthal, an assistant to outpatients. He started in February 1913 after being sponsored by Richard C. Cabot and approved by the General Executive Committee. Cabot also brought the next three Jewish doctors to Mass General (Hyman Morrison, 1915; Louis Mendelsohn, 1916; and Solomon H. Rubin, 1918) as well as a Jewish dentist (Fred R. Blumethal, 1915).[8] The first known Native American faculty member was Dennis Norman, chief of psychology since 1989. Norman has worked with Native American nations to bring in more Native students to Harvard.

In 1992, two years before Thier's return as president, Winfred W. "Win" Williams, an African American nephrologist in the MGH Transplantation Unit, founded the Office for Minority Health Professions to increase the number of underrepresented minority trainees at MGH, principally in the Department of Medicine.[9] A native of Baton Rouge, Louisiana, and a Harvard graduate who attended medical school at NYU, Williams returned to the Boston area to begin training at Brigham and Women's Hospital in 1980, then joined the staff of the MGH Department of Medicine in 1987. Williams credited Chief of Medicine John Potts with pointing out the need to develop physicians of color. With Potts's backing, Williams and N. Anthony "Tony" Coles, an African American fellow in cardiology, made a presentation to the Robert Wood Johnson Foundation, which provided $100,000 in funding to the Office for Minority Health Professions. It was slow going at first. Williams admitted that Boston's reputation—"not that far removed from busing and some deep-seated civil rights issues"—could be a detriment to recruiting talented professionals of color. But, he added, Boston "has a density of medicine that is hard to find anywhere else, including a biotech and pharmaceutical infrastructure," and progress was made.

In 2000 the office was renamed the Multicultural Affairs Office (MAO), to reflect its evolution into a hospital- and community-wide resource that now works with virtually all departments at MGH. That August, Elena Olson, a veteran civil litigator in a large Boston law firm, was hired to run the MAO full-time. Under her daily direction, and with the active involvement of Williams and several other physicians and staff members, the MAO focuses on physicians underrepresented in medicine (URMs), including African Americans, Hispanics, and Native Americans.[10] It is specifically aimed at advancing URMs among the MGH faculty and in the pipeline feeding the faculty. Clearly, other groups are underrepresented, as well; for example, though an estimated 15 percent of patients at the Chelsea Health Center are of Cambodian heritage, the hospital does not have a Cambodian-born doctor serving them at this writing.

Win Williams (first row, left), founder of the Multicultural Affairs Office, and Elena Olson (second row, left), MAO executive director, with student participants in the MAO's 2009 summer program.

"I had worked in health care," said Olson, "and on issues like civil rights and human rights. I came in as an advocate, to figure out ways in which we could advance the mission. I developed strategies, along with Dr. Williams and hospital leadership."

One of many MAO programs to assist URM trainees and faculty has been in place since 1993. This is an eight-week summer program bringing in 15 top-level college and medical students and matching them with MGH preceptors who direct their research. Olson said: "We start with the pipeline. The only way to build a workforce for the future is to look at our younger generation. We give them this phenomenal research experience that bolsters their résumé and their desire to get into academic medicine. Our researchers and faculty see that there are a lot of great students out there who could pursue academic medicine." Many participants publish their research with their MGH preceptors. Ninety-eight percent of undergraduate participants in this summer program have gone on to medical school.

Boston is a youthful city with many colleges and universities, but the city can be a turn-off for students of color, particularly those coming from other areas of the country. Olson said, "Boston has a mixed history that has not always been diversity-friendly. It's very far from their families and it's cold, especially if they come from the West or South. It's very expensive, and many already have student loans." Another issue is the social scene and the somewhat mistaken belief that there are few underrepresented professionals here. "Boston has a very diverse community of students, health professionals, educators, business executives, and lawyers," said Olson, "but old images die hard." The MAO helps MGH participants and other URM recruits with networking opportunities. Becoming part of the Mass General MAO community can overcome many ills, according to Olson: "My experience has been that this younger generation is very much about being part of something. That's where we can add value: we invite them to be part of something larger than their specialty training program. Not only are you coming to train in internal medicine in the best possible place to train, but we have a family here who is looking out for you."

MGH faculty have played an important role in MAO programs as champions and role models to young URM professionals. In recent years these have included, in addition to Win Williams, the internists Joseph Betancourt, Ronald Dixon, and Celina Mankey, dermatologist Ernesto Gonzalez, gastroenterologist Andrea Reid, and most recently emergency physician Monique Sellas and vascular surgeon Michael Watkins.

From 1997 to 2010 the percentage of URM employees grew from 16.6 to 19.6 overall. Among physicians and PhD's, however, there was a tripling, from 2.1 percent to 6.1, whereas the percentage of URM nurses on staff grew from 3.4 to 5.0.

Said MGH President Peter Slavin: "Of our incoming residents a greater proportion are minorities than at any other hospital in town. It is an institutional priority. There are two arguments for diversity. The first is obvious: social justice. But it's also good business: we won't succeed at giving the best possible care to all of our patients until our medical staff and other caregivers look like the patients they are serving."

Where faculty is concerned, Olson pointed out that retention is the key, and here there is more evidence of success. In recent years up to 66 percent of eligible URM residents and clinical fellows have been retained on the MGH staff after graduation.

In 2010, Win Williams called the MAO "a success story—the first of its kind in a Harvard teaching hospital and the most robust of its kind still standing."

The United Nations of Health Care

Diversity is an institutional priority from top to bottom and side to side. It extends far beyond the faculty. Patient Care Services (detailed below) runs programs for minorities under the leadership of its director of diversity, Deborah Washington. Senior Vice President for Patient Care Services Jeanette Ives Erickson said of Washington, "She has hit a home run with some unique programs, including an African American pinning ceremony during Black History Month. I don't think anyone else in the country has a celebration like this, a passing of the baton from one generation to the next." During one of the periodic shortages of nursing in America, at the beginning of this century, Washington started a foreign-born nurse program at MGH, to encourage nurses certified in their home countries to qualify for certification here.

About 4,000 non-physician clinical professionals and support staff are employed by Patient Care Services. The full employee count of Mass General is something closer to 23,000, a number that has doubled since 1994. During that time the proportion of minority employees has grown from 21 percent to 30 percent, according to Jeff Davis, senior vice president for Human Resources. James Mongan, as president, put a redoubled emphasis on diversity when he arrived in 1997. The new Diversity Committee took on the work of "fully integrating diversity plans and goals into day-to-day hospital management and making hospital leadership responsible and accountable for the success of ongoing diversity initiatives."[11] Mongan noted: "I came from an institution in Kansas City that was a public hospital serving a very racially mixed population, and I had learned that it was important for hospitals to reflect the populations they served. When I was recruited, both Sam [Thier] and Moose [Colloredo-Mansfeld] suggested that diversity was a priority, and I am very pleased to say that [Peter] Slavin has seamlessly picked up that interest."

Jeff Davis was in on these early efforts. More recently a key leader in the diversity effort, reporting to Davis, has been Carlyene Prince-Erickson. Boston-born, a proud product of Roxbury-Mattapan and "a die-hard Celtics fan," Prince-Erickson came to the hospital in 1995 after working in the administration of Boston Mayor Raymond Flynn on economic development and housing programs. She came to MGH, she said, on a two-year plan: "I figured I would learn what I had to learn and move on. Fifteen years later, I haven't looked back. Professionally, I have never been so challenged or had such opportunity. Here if you have a good idea, there's the flexibility in the room to let you run with it."

Prince-Erickson started working with Joan Quinlan, director of the MGH Community Benefit Program (see chapter 6) (renamed the Center for Community Health Improvement in 2007). She said that at the time, in the mid-1990s,

Celebrating Martin Luther King Day, 2010, were, from left, Peter Slavin, Massachusetts First Lady Diane Patrick, Carlyene Prince-Erickson, Akin Demehin, and Jeff Davis.

despite outreach through community health centers in Chelsea, Charlestown, and Revere begun in the 1960s see (chapter 6), there was still a temptation for MGH to view itself as "a building where all the knowledge was. The hospital thought, 'We have the data, we'll treat you.'" The Community Benefit Program played a big role in helping change that model, creating more of a partnership with the outlying communities served by the hospital.

With an undergraduate degree in journalism, Prince-Erickson was encouraged by MGH to go back to school for her MBA. Then she was offered a human resources position by Jeff Davis. As MGH's director of employee education and leadership development, Prince-Erickson now creates and oversees policies and programs that promote employee diversity and support minority employees as they seek professional education and career advancement. Examples include an on-site ESL (English as a second language) program. Courses follow the academic year, meeting twice weekly in 90-minute sessions, and the curriculum is contextualized for the MGH environment. (For example, forms frequently used in the workplace are used for instruction.) At any time there are approximately 100 employees in the program. Prince-Erickson said it is the longest continually running employer-based ESL program in Greater Boston. She boasted of a native Polish speaker who went through the program, then encouraged his parents to come work at MGH. They did so, and they entered the ESL program themselves.

MGH offers not only a tuition-assistance program for employees who want to continue their professional and vocational training (up to $2,000 per employee per year), but also a grant program that supplements the tuition-assistance program (up to $1,500 per employee for such items as textbooks, uniforms, and lab fees). Said Prince-Erickson, "Employees become our partners in their education."

The full list of programs offered to promote diversity at MGH since 1995 is too long for detailed discussion. A partial list includes:

- MGH-Timilty (Middle School) Science Connection and the related MGH Community Benefit SummerWorks program
- Minority High School Student Research Apprentice Program
- Asian-American Heritage Celebration
- Diversity Awareness Forums
- Steps to Success program for employee career advancement
- Cooperation with local organizations, such as the Latino Professional Network.

One measure of diversity at MGH is the growth of its Latino-Hispanic workforce. Since 1994 the increase has been about 300 percent, to a total count of 1,664 in 2010. Guillermo Jorge Banchiere, MGH's director of environmental services, has been here a good deal longer. The son of a surgeon in Buenos Aires, Banchiere came to the United States one summer in his twenties, fell in love, and stayed on. He started working for ServiceMaster, a firm that provides janitorial and other services to hospitals, and became a manager with the company. Hired by New England Medical Center, one of his client companies, as director of environmental services, he caught the attention of managers at MGH in 1986.

Banchiere confessed that he was very happy at NEMC, but "the cultures of the two are different." He was surprised at MGH that he was interviewed by "eight or nine people. I talked with vice presidents, the director of nursing, Yvonne Munn, the president of the hospital." This interview process demonstrated "an integrated team effort" and showed Banchiere that MGH is not a "top-down culture, where the administration sets the goals and tells you what to do. I was not used to that."

Admittedly, there was a "very small number" of Hispanic employees when he arrived in the mid-1980s. "I was a little surprised," he said, "because you'd figure in downtown Boston you would have more. But then we started attracting more Latinos." Having a Hispanic director of the department made a big difference, and Banchiere diversified his management team. "When people have a problem," he noted, "they like to speak in their native language. They feel comfortable when they can come speak with a manager they can talk easily with."

Banchiere has grown on the job, and his department has grown with the hospital it serves:

We've become a department that provides services, instead of just a cleaning department. Because we are doers, they give us more and more responsibility. My focus was cleaning for the first five years, but our policy was, we never say no. Now we do all the preparation work for the disaster readiness team. We do bookings and set up conferences. I contract for waste removal, a highly regulated area. The hospital gave me $1.5 million for disposing of medical waste. I shut down the incinerator and started an autoclave. We do site contracting, pest control, carpeting, shades, venetian blinds—you start one thing, and when you don't tell people "That's not my job" and you do it well, you grow. We are part of the team.

In 2010 Banchiere was responsible for more than 4 million square feet of facilities, from the main campus to the old Charlestown Navy Yard to community health facilities in Charlestown and Chelsea, Waltham and Danvers. "I do them all," he said proudly. He served on several committees and was a director of the Harvard University Employees Credit Union.

In his primary role as director of environmental services, Banchiere reported to Jean Elrick, senior vice president for administration. "She has a great philosophy," he said. "We go down together, we go up together, there are no stars." Everything has happened, he said, "because it is the philosophy of the hospital. Our goal is to take care of patients and everything serves that goal."

A bit like Prince-Erickson, Banchiere said, "I thought I would get bored after five years here, and I'm busier now than I was when I came here to work. It's a great environment: you can bring ideas, and people will listen to you."

Women and Protons

"Put yourself in the shoes of an African American woman doctor coming here in the late forties," Elena Olson said. "She had two huge hurdles to overcome as both a female and a minority." That was the case with Frances Bonner, a psychiatrist and the first African American woman on the MGH faculty, appointed in 1949. Unlike Chester Pierce, she never made it to full professor.

Earlier chapters have highlighted pioneering female physicians and surgeons at MGH, including the oncologist Rita Kelley, the pediatric surgeon Patricia Donahoe, and the neurology chief Anne Young. But as recently as the mid-1990s, there were only three female full professors on the MGH faculty: Donahoe, Young, and the neuroendocrine chief Anne Klibanski (see chapter 3). Then, in 1993, the same year Isaac Schiff hired the obstetrician Fred Frigoletto to provide more totally for women's health (see chapter 7), the stalwart trustee Jane Claflin did something important for women health care professionals at MGH. She founded the Women in Academic Medicine (WAM) Committee. This led to the formation of the MGH Office for Women's Careers (OWC) and the search for a director. That led across town to Children's Hospital and Nancy J. Tarbell, a woman in medicine who, like so many others, had a complex career path.

A native of Hudson, Massachusetts, Tarbell graduated from the University of Rhode Island in 1973 with no thought of being a doctor. But encouraged by a friend, she entered a 1.5-year premed program at Columbia University. Following medical school at Upstate Medical School in Syracuse and an internship in medicine at Beth Israel, she drew a high lottery number when the time came to choose clinical electives, and so she backed into the undersubscribed field of radiation medicine. Tarbell recalled: "Radiation had a terrible image in those days. But the good you

Frances Bonner.

can do is enormous. The first patient I ever saw was a 25-year-old woman who at three years old had been cured of Wilms tumor with the help of radiation—'in the dark ages.' How rewarding! You can cure patients! When children with cancer go on to have children of their own, you know you've done your job."

At the time, there were only a few places in the United States with full-blown radiation therapy programs and the medical physics to advance them. Stanford, Yale, and Harvard had the oldest and most distinguished training programs. On one side of Boston, in the Longwood Medical Area, was the Joint Center for Radiation Therapy (JCRT). The JCRT was a collaborative effort by Brigham and Women's, Dana-Farber, Beth Israel, New England Deaconess, and Children's Hospital to provide clinical care, conduct research, and offer training to radiation oncology residents. Meanwhile, at Mass General, Chief of Radiation Medicine Herman D. Suit was leading the parade as successor to Milford Schulz (see chapter 7). Raised in the dusty west Texas town of Llano and educated at the University of Houston and the Baylor College of Medicine, Suit was appointed chief of radiation medicine at MGH and professor at HMS in 1970, the year the medical school decided to separate radiation therapy from radiology as an academic department. Suit worked with others to design the "radiation palace" that was the Cox Cancer Center when it opened in 1975.

The Cox Building contained two cobalt-60 therapy machines, two 18-MeV linear accelerators, and one 35-MeV linear accelerator, providing high energy photons (X-rays). By the early 1980s MGH radiation oncologists were treating more than 2,000 patients a year. But Suit was beating the drum for something better: proton beam therapy. In 1946 a young Harvard physicist, Robert Wilson, had published the rationale for using protons for radiotherapy.[12] A beam of these fundamental subatomic particles would deliver the same biological impact as X-rays, but unlike X-rays, they could be made to enter tissue and stop at a target point with no exit, so that every beam delivered a targeted dose of radiation and the effect on surrounding healthy tissue was minimal. This meant the possibility of fewer side effects, which could be particularly valuable for patients requiring high doses of radiation; where the cancerous area adjoined sensitive structures of the central nervous system, as at the base of the skull; or in children, where side effects can be particularly devastating.

Harvard had built its first cyclotron, or particle accelerator, capable of generating a proton beam, in 1937. It took years to develop a beam powerful enough for limited therapeutic use. Beginning in 1961, the neurosurgeon Raymond Kjellberg began using the Harvard cyclotron to treat patients with single-dose radiosurgery. Much of the potential of proton beam therapy—to affect pituitary adenomas, arteriovenous malformations, and other hard-to-reach tumors—had to await the development of CT and MRI scanning technologies in the 1970s and 1980s, which allowed therapists to pinpoint their targets. Still, by the time the facility closed in 2002, the Harvard Cyclotron Laboratory (HCL) had treated more than 9,000 patients. One of these was Ferdinand "Moose" Colloredo-Mansfeld, whose treatments for a neoroblastoma occurred in 1993 while he was chairman of the Board of Trustees of MGH and discussions of a proton beam facility at MGH were ongoing. Suit pursued the holy grail of the proton beam at MGH: "I was appointed

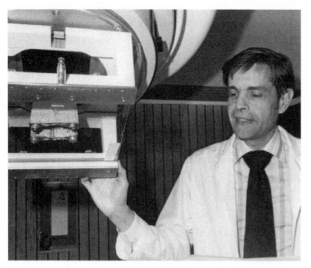
Herman Suit.

Chief of the new department at MGH, effective June 1970. The Job Description essentially was to develop the department, including a physics and radiation biology program. There was no mention of proton therapy. However, I was seriously interested in the potential of proton therapy and visited the Harvard Cyclotron Laboratory."[13]

A nuclear physicist, Michael Goitein (Oxford undergraduate, Harvard PhD), brought on in 1971, was Suit's primary collaborator at HCL. In 1973 the first MGH cancer patients were treated at the HCL with fractionated proton therapy, but the cases that could be handled here were severely limited by the relatively low energy of the proton beam and the lack of a gantry and robotic couches that could optimize the delivery of high-energy beams to a specific location within the patient's body. Instead, the patient was positioned in front of the beam in either a standing or supine position. Also, because the HCL was located miles from the MGH campus, it was not feasible to put the patient under general anesthesia for treatment.

Grants from the National Cancer Institute to MGH for the development of proton beam technology began flowing in 1972. Throughout this developmental period, Suit and his team worked in collaboration with leaders of the MGH Neurosurgery Service, eager to develop new therapies for tumors of the brain and spine. A medical annex to the HCL was provided by a NASA grant to William Sweet (see chapter 7), chief of neurosurgery. When the time finally came in the 1990s to install a proton beam generator at MGH, Sweet's successor, Nicholas Zervas, would be instrumental in convincing the federal government to release a request for funding proposal for a hospital-based proton facility. The MGH proposal was given the highest review scores and was awarded a $6 million planning grant and a $20 million grant for construction by the NCI; MGH was required to match the amount for construction.

By the early 1980s it was clear that MGH needed a proton beam facility of its own; at least that was Suit's appeal to a receptive Bob Buchanan and others. It would take 20 years to happen, however. A facility was formally commissioned in September 1993, but it was another eight years before the first patient was treated, on November 4, 2001.

Meanwhile, in the 1980s and early 1990s, Nancy Tarbell had parallel careers: as a pediatric radiation oncologist at the JCRT and as a wife and mother. Her professional résumé included serving as chief of radiation oncology at Children's Hospital from 1984 until 1997 and authoring hundreds of papers and editing a text on pediatric oncology. Her home life included children born in 1982 (while she was still a resident), 1989, and 1993, the year Jane Claflin was gathering the

WAM Committee at MGH. Side by side with her on both tracks was her colleague and husband, Jay S. Loeffler. Loeffler was the associate chief of radiation oncology at Brigham and Women's and director of the Brain Tumor Center of the Dana-Farber, Brigham and Women's, and Children's Hospital from 1990 to 1996. Said Tarbell, "I found radiation medicine attractive in part because cancer patients are rewarding to take care of and in part because of the ability to balance work and family."

In 1996 Tarbell and Loeffler were preparing to leave Boston. Together, they had been offered the positions of chief of the Department of Radiation Oncology at the University of Maryland and vice president for medical affairs at the University of Maryland Hospital, respectively. Herman Suit knew that they would be an ideal team to run radiation therapy at MGH, especially once the proton beam was up and running—but that was still six years in the future. So Suit, a "stubborn man," according to Tarbell, connected her with Kate Walsh, a senior administrator under Sam Thier and his successor, James Mongan. Walsh offered Tarbell a second position, as director of the new MGH Office of Women's Careers (OWC). Loeffler joined the MGH staff in 1996 as director of the Northeast Proton Therapy Center, and Tarbell came aboard in March 1997 as director of pediatric radiation oncology and director of the Office of Women's Careers. With the addition of a second job and young children still at home, Tarbell found her career becoming more complex. But she found the OWC work gratifying—and Claflin impressive: "Nobody said no to Jane! An elderly woman when I met her, she had such force, she was so dynamic. She would smile with that great big warm southern smile, not abrasive at all the way women in medicine can sometimes be. She was a 'southern magnolia' who convinced Bob Buchanan and others that something had to be done. Only three women professors? That was crazy!"

Jay Loeffler (third from left) and Nancy Tarbell with Andy Warshaw (left) and Jerry Austen.

The WAM Committee, later the OWC under Tarbell, incrementally changed the nature of women's professional work at MGH. Two examples:

- A backup child-care program, begun in 1997 and promoted strongly by Isaac Schiff and Jane Claflin, among others. When the sitter calls a doctor and mother at six-thirty in the morning to say she is sick, what does the doctor do? If she works at MGH, she brings her children to the backup child-care program. Space is such a precious commodity in an academic medical center that Mass General's commitment to this service has meant a lot. "It made a huge symbolic difference," according to Tarbell.

- The Claflin Awards, administered by the Executive Committee on Research. Each female faculty member with children is awarded enough to pay the salary of one postdoctoral fellow. This allows the faculty member to pursue investigative work, while also seeing patients, teaching students, and caring for her children. "It solves a catch-22," according to Tarbell. "You need grant funding to do research, but you have to do research to get funding." For a working mother in academic medicine, the research piece is often the hardest to make time for. One of the first women to receive a Claflin Award was Merit Cudkowicz, now a full professor of neurology specializing in amyotrophic lateral sclerosis (ALS). According to Tarbell, "She now receives significant federal funding for collaborative clinical trials."

In 2009, 38 percent of the MGH faculty were female. Only 15 percent of the full professors were women, but that is an extraordinary improvement since the 1990s. Given that 49 percent of instructors and 34 percent of assistant professors were women, the female proportion of full professors will increase over time. Though it is only one tool in MGH's kit to promote diversity of its medical staff, the OWC is clearly a success.

So is the Francis H. Burr Proton Therapy Center, which occupies a lower corner of the Yawkey Center for Outpatient Care at MGH. The proton center was originally a stand-alone facility in the old athletic yards of the former Charles Street Jail. Within a few years, MGH built the Yawkey outpatient facility above and around the proton center. Other notable developments in radiation medicine during recent years:

- The Edwin Steele Laboratory of Tumor Biology was established by Suit in the early 1970s to study cancers and their microenvironment. Under the leadership of Rakesh Jain (member of the National Academy of Science), the lab has discovered important cytokines that regulate tumor angiogenesis, invasion, and metastases. This has led to groundbreaking translational work for patients with brain tumors, head and neck cancer, ovarian cancer, hepatocellular tumors, and colorectal cancers.

- Intraoperative radiation (IORT) was pioneered at the MGH. MGH installed the first linear accelerator in an operative suite to apply directed radiation during surgical resection of tumors. This allows the surgeons to displace critical structures and apply the radiation directly to the tumor. The IORT suite is now a routine part of the radiation oncology service.

The Francis H. Burr Proton Therapy Center currently treats about 70 patients a day, and pediatric patients represent about 20 percent of the volume. Ongoing studies with the M. D. Anderson Proton Therapy Center are exploring the value of protons for liver, lung, prostate, head and neck, and pediatric cancers.

TRIPLE TRANSITION

As it had in the early 1960s, Mass General underwent a total turnover of top leadership in the years 1996–1997. James J. Mongan replaced Sam Thier as president of the General Hospital Corporation; Chief of Nephrology Dennis A. Ausiello was appointed chief of medicine, replacing John Potts; and a pancreatic surgeon, Andrew L. Warshaw, took over as chief of surgery from his mentor, Jerry Austen, who continued to lead and shape the MGPO.

Unlike the transition in the early 1960s, however, this triple change did not cause the MGH to miss a beat. Continuity was preserved, in part, because power had been dispersed significantly since the day when Walter Bauer and Edward Churchill ran the GEC and General Director Dean Clark kept the minutes. The "chiefs' meeting" now included about two dozen departmental leaders from medicine to finance, surgery to nursing. Hospital administration had become far more corporate, as responsibilities were spread over several levels of staff. Medical and surgical departments had become highly specialized and stratified.

Jim Mongan's father was a county clerk immersed in local politics back home in San Francisco, so it was no surprise that when Mongan decided to become a doctor, he looked at the larger political and economic issues of health care. After training in medicine at Stanford and serving two years in the military, Mongan had an opportunity to work in Washington in 1969, when the Senate Finance Committee needed a young MD to work on the first set of amendments to Medicare. Success at the Senate eventually led to an appointment in the Carter administration as deputy assistant secretary for health at HEW and later as associate director of the Domestic Policy Staff at the White House itself. When Ronald Reagan became president in 1981, Mongan began a 15-year double appointment as executive director of the Truman Medical Center in Kansas City and as dean of the University of Missouri–Kansas City School of Medicine. By the time Mass General called in 1995, the quiet, thoughtful, and effective Mongan had a well-rounded résumé.

Joe Martin, then dean of Harvard Medical School, described the new MGH president: "Jim is one of the finest human beings I have ever met—shy, a little introspective, not chummy, but his ability to take a complicated situation and boil it down into three points, and convince people to go with him, is remarkable."

James Mongan.

Nick Thorndike, the former board chair and a member of the search committee that identified Mongan, remarked: "Sam Thier was very strong on Jim Mongan. He really felt that of all the people he knew, Jim was the person for the job. I didn't realize that Jim's executive skills were as good as they are. He could run anything, and with an MD, he had credibility with the medical staff."

Ed Lawrence, board chair for most of the Mongan years, said: "Sam Thier and Jim Mongan were transformative characters. Mongan was remarkably effective. At 2 A.M. he would show up to shake hands with the graveyard shift. He is fair; he is a razor-sharp thinker."

Edward Lawrence.

Mongan would serve as MGH president for seven years, 1996–2002. During that time, a funny thing happened on the way to the apocalypse. Just when it seemed that Mass General (and the Brigham) were in decline—with waning volume in a challenging economy against a background of intense pressure from insurers—things improved. The economy jumped, capitation receded as patients and employers pushed back against it, and the metrics of economic viability at MGH bounced back sharply. During the Mongan years at MGH:

- Inpatient volume grew an average of 4.2 percent per year.
- Average length of stay declined 12 percent from 6.65 days to 5.86.
- Average daily census increased 13 percent from 616 to 695.
- Outpatient visits grew an average of 4 percent per year.

An important focus for Mongan was working with Jerry Austen to build a better working relationship between the hospital and the doctors, represented by the MGPO. With the advent of a true staff group practice, the veterans of the private practice years were "in mourning over the loss of the old model," according to Mongan. "Doctors wanted a voice in the future of MGH. Jerry Austen was a key player here and establishing a good relation with him was important to me."

Austen said, "Jim really understood that it was crucial for the hospital to have a happy professional staff and crucial for the professional staff to have a successful hospital. He was extremely helpful, bending over backwards to make sure that the MGH community was led by him as head of the hospital and by me as head of the PO."

Daniel A. Ginsburg, hired as chief operating officer of the MGPO in 1994, was a key player in assuring a smooth interface between the PO and the hospital during the early years. Austen could use the help: for his first three years as president of the MGPO he doubled as chief of surgery. "I never worked harder in my life," he recalled, "seven days a week all day. They were two full-time jobs." Austen gave way to Andrew Warshaw in the Department of Surgery in 1997. "After those three years, it took me a couple of years to recover!" Austen said.

"I enjoyed it, but it was a lot of work." In 2000, the year he turned 70, Austen decided it was time to give up the reins of the MGPO as well, and Peter Slavin was recruited back to MGH from Barnes-Jewish Hospital in St. Louis, where he had been named CEO in 1997.

Another focus for Mongan at MGH was to shepherd the evolving relationship with Partners. This relationship would only become smoother after Mongan moved to Partners as its CEO in 2003, carrying forward initiatives systemwide that he had seen begin while head of the hospital. (A key example, a renewed focus on quality and safety, will be taken up below.) Meanwhile, the Mongan era saw the completion of two major building projects, the Yawkey Center for Outpatient Care, housing the proton beam facility, and the Richard B. Simches Research Center, with four new "thematic centers" of research (detailed below). In addition, Mongan participated in some key personnel decisions that would set the stage for continuing improvement.

Ausiello Takes over Medicine

After building an endocrine department that is the envy of most others (see chapter 3), John Potts succeeded Alexander Leaf as chief of medicine in 1981. During the next 15 years the Department of Medicine moved ahead smartly, and Potts participated in several major initiatives previously detailed, including the research move to Charlestown in the late 1980s. He helped identify the opportunity represented by Howard Goodman and molecular biology, and early in his term as chief Goodwin's department was integrated into the MGH culture (more details below). After 15 years, Potts turned his full-time attention to being director of research, a role he assumed in 1995.

Potts's replacement could not have presented a more striking contrast. The smooth-talking, impeccably coiffed Potts was replaced by Dennis A. Ausiello, a bearded, straight-shooting guy from the working-class city of Revere, Massachusetts. Ausiello went to Harvard from Revere High School, a baseball player determined to be a scientist. His tutor (advisor) at Harvard was Jim Orr, a PhD who worked in the old Huntington Labs at MGH, and at Orr's suggestion, Ausiello began working during the summers with Geoff Sharp, a PhD assigned to the Renal Unit of Alexander Leaf. This was in the mid-1960s, at a time when Sam Thier was chief resident in medicine. "Sam took me under his wing," said Ausiello. They were two outsiders: the Italian kid from Revere mentored by the Jewish kid from Brooklyn. "We were both sports addicts, and he knew I loved baseball."

Ausiello called Thier "my godfather." After graduating from Harvard in 1967, Ausiello attended medical school at the University of Pennsylvania. In 1969 Thier

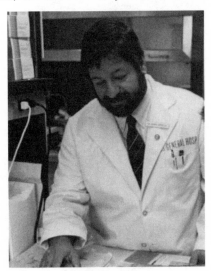
Dennis Ausiello.

was recruited to Penn, but the day soon came when Ausiello told Thier that he was returning to MGH for internship and residency. Then, after two years at the NIH, he returned to Mass General as a kidney fellow, set up a lab, and subsequently took over the Renal Unit from Leaf after Potts became chief of medicine. "What intrigued me about nephrology," he said, "was that it was one of the few medical specialties at the time that was quantitative. Nephrology is not just about the kidney. It's about the salt and water constituents of the body." Ausiello served as chief of nephrology until 1996, when he was tapped to take over for Potts.

Key appointments in the Ausiello years have included Vice Chairmen of Medicine Daniel Podolsky (1996–2008) and Stephen Calderwood (2008–), as well as the following division chiefs:

- Nephrology: M. Amin Arnaout (1997–)
- Rheumatology, Allergy, and Immunology: Andrew Luster (1999–)
- Pulmonary and Critical Care: Charles Hales (1999–2009) and Benjamin Medoff (2009–)
- Cardiology: G. William Dec (2003–)
- Hematology-Oncology: Thomas Lynch (2004–2008), Daniel Haber (2008–2010), and José Baselga (2010–)
- Biomedical Informatics: Henry Chueh (2006–)
- Gastroenterology: Ramnik Xavier (2010–)

Perhaps the most significant development during this period has been the creation of four thematic centers of research at the Simches Research Building in 2002. With Dan Podolosky, Ausiello was a mastermind of the Simches (details below).

Warshaw Takes over Surgery

Andrew L. Warshaw grew up in Queens, New York, where his father was a surgeon in a 35-bed private hospital that he owned himself. A World War II veteran, David Warshaw revered Generals Pershing and MacArthur and emulated their can-do spirit. When Mrs. Warshaw smashed her leg in an accident, her surgeon husband wired the leg back together with what their son called "hardware unusual for that time."

Andrew Warshaw.

Father was a model to his son, but son was a disappointment to his father, at least where his choice of college and medical school was concerned. David Warshaw had been one of the first Jewish scholarship students at both Cornell College and Medical School. Andy Warshaw opted for Harvard College and Medical School, or what his father referred to as "that den of pinkos."

Warshaw trained in surgery at Massachusetts General Hospital, spent two years as a clinical associate in gastroenterology at the NIH, then came back to MGH to finish his surgical training and for a clinical and research fellowship in GI medicine before becoming chief resident in surgery. Moving back and forth between medicine and surgery gave him "an unusual background," and he said it "would lead to a fruitful and unique collaboration with GI. We did a lot of joint publishing, and I taught GI fellows for 20 years."

In 1972, the year he joined the staff and faculty ("Dad considered himself a big fish in a small pond, but he said the way of medicine in the future was to be a small fish in a big pond"), Warshaw opened the MGH Pancreatic Biology Laboratory, because, he joked, the pancreas was "the last organ that wasn't taken." In the early 1970s, before the advent of new imaging technologies like ultrasound and CT scanning, the pancreas was a mysterious organ, and "feared as a ticking time bomb," according to Warshaw. "Relatively few operations were done on it. I got interested in pancreatic function at the NIH; then in my year as chief resident (1971), I found there was a disproportionate number of patients with pancreatic diseases on the service." Using that opportunity, Warshaw led a clinical trial that was written up in the *New England Journal of Medicine*.[14] Then Ronald Malt asked him to write a paper on pancreatic abscesses for the journal.[15] A third *New England Journal* article followed, and a specialist was born.[16] "People thought I was a big expert even though I was still wearing a resident's white suit," he said.

In fact, a so-called "pancreas Mafia" was developing around the country, as others of Warshaw's generation at Hopkins (John Cameron), NYU (John Ransom), UCLA (Howard Reber), and elsewhere began to study the organ and its function. Once "young, opportunistic competitors," the group became colleagues as data about the pancreas began to be collected and analyzed. "John Cameron and I used to fight like crazy," Warshaw said. "Now we're buddies."

The surgeons Marshall Bartlett and Claude Welch were Warshaw's early mentors at Mass General; Kurt Isselbacher was a third, as chief of gastroenterology; and Jerry Austen would become his teacher in the ways of hospital leadership. Warshaw said of Austen, "His role in my career has been instrumental and enormous. From a purely professional point of view, he had his hand on my shoulder early on, and by the early 1990s, he would regularly meet with me and fill me in on what was going on around the hospital." In 1997, after an open search, Austen's protégé became his successor. Warshaw was named the first W. Gerald Austen professor of surgery and chief of the department.

"It's not easy to follow an iconic figure who has done it for 29 years and whom everyone trusts and loves," said Warshaw. But in 13 years at the helm, Warshaw oversaw an almost complete revamping of surgical leadership in his department, and a remarkable growth in clinical activity. From 65 surgeons when he took over, the department grew to 107. The research budget tripled, and clinical revenues more than doubled.

Warshaw announced that he was stepping down as chief in 2009, and he planned to end his clinical activities by the end of 2010. As editor in chief of the journal *Surgery*, with a big role in the American College of Surgeons, as treasurer and head of the Health Policy and Advocacy Group, and with new responsibilities evolving at MGH, Andy Warshaw had little thought of slowing down.

FROM NURSING TO PATIENT CARE SERVICES

Along with Jim Mongan, Denny Ausiello, and Andy Warshaw, Jeanette Ives Erickson was a fourth top leader appointed in the mid-1990s. How much nursing had changed at MGH over 130 years is demonstrated by Ives Erickson's dual title, assumed in 1996: chief nurse and senior vice president for patient care. She negotiated the *chief* in her first title because she wanted her role to be on a par with that of other MGH chiefs, of medicine, surgery, and other services. The term *patient care* requires considerable explanation, as it covers much besides nursing. A third title that Ives Erickson has carried since 2006 is unlikely to have been conferred on her predecessors: instructor in gynecology, obstetrics, and reproductive biology at Harvard Medical School.

Chapter 2 followed the evolution of nursing education at Mass General from the Boston Training School for Nurses of the 1870s to the Institute of Health Professions of today. Here we will look at a short history of nursing leadership at MGH beginning after the Civil War. Georgia Sturtevant was appointed hospital matron on July 31, 1868, upon the death of her predecessor. Sturtevant had joined the MGH staff as an assistant nurse in 1862, receiving a monthly salary of $7.50. Remembered as the last untrained nurse at MGH, Sturtevant was an astute and able woman who took her duties as head nurse seriously during her 26-year tenure.

The life of a nurse in Sturtevant's day offered little enticement for those with any other option. The young women lived in terrible quarters, were allowed very little personal time, completed all the hospital's nonclinical work from laundry to making tea to rolling bandages, and were at the beck and call of doctors, to whom they were not allowed to speak. Most considered it inappropriate for a young woman of breeding to be surrounded by men, whether the men were doctors or patients in varying states of undress, and decades would pass before the nurse was considered a respected and integral member of the medical or surgical team.

Sophia Palmer.

Sturtevant's successor was Linda Richards, the first individual in the country to graduate from a formal nurse training program, which was offered at the New England Hospital for Women and Children. Her certificate of graduation is housed at the Smithsonian Institution in Washington, D.C. Another nursing pioneer at MGH in the late nineteenth century was Sophia French Palmer, who served as head nurse of Wards 29 and C. In 1900 Palmer was a founder of the *American Journal of Nursing* and became its first editor, a position she held for 20 years. In 2010 *AJN* is the oldest and largest circulating nursing journal in the world, with a circulation of 340,000.

The grueling labor and unending hours of the working nurse continued to dissuade many women from the profession. In 1913 California limited working hours of student nurses to eight hours a day and forty-eight hours a week—in addition to class time. In Boston, however, "twelve hours of night duty without a break for a month or more and 62 hours per week of day duty had not passed from the scene."[17] Sara Parsons, superintendent at the Massachusetts General Hospital Training School for Nurses (MGHTSN) from 1910 to 1920, worked to make the exigencies of the nursing life more bearable. In her words, it is "no more right to sacrifice the nurse . . . than it is to neglect the patient."[18]

Sally Johnson.

Sally Johnson took over for Parsons as superintendent in 1920. During Johnson's tenure, nurses began to take on administrative positions in the hospital, and she herself reported directly to General Director Frederic Washburn, who in turn reported to the trustees. Johnson had relatively little direct contact with the trustees, however, so that many of the changes she petitioned for were denied. A movement to standardize nursing across the wards at MGH also took place at this time. When the Baker Memorial Building opened in 1930 to accommodate middle-income patients, the idea was to increase the general standard for nursing, instead of creating a special service for the Baker. Patient fees at the Baker permitted more graduate nurses to be hired, which in turn lightened the burden of the student nurses.

In early years the medical house staff entered instructions in the doctor's order book. "The head nurse transferred these orders to medicine cards or to the treatment sheet. Several of these large sheets were kept on the head nurse's desk, where in the appropriate spaces the students checked off the various orders as they were carried out. Thus all the nurses could see, almost at a glance, what were the orders for each patient, and what had been done or remained to be done."[19] This top-down system, in which nurses literally took orders, would evolve into one of teamwork and two-way communication.

An MGH Nursing Legend

Ruth Sleeper (MGHTSN 1922) began her 33 years of service at the hospital when she was appointed assistant superintendent of the Nursing Service and assistant principal of the Training School in 1933. (Between graduation from the school of nursing and this 1933 appointment, Sleeper had served as a science instructor at the Western Reserve University School of Nursing in Cleveland.) In 1946 she was promoted to head both the school and the Nursing Service.

During her tenure, Sleeper led the MGH Nursing Service through several major crises. One of these, the Cocoanut Grove fire (see chapter 4), occurred during another, World War II, when the nursing staff was stretched thin because

Ruth Sleeper.

so many women served the war effort overseas. After the war, a terrible shortage of nurses led Sleeper to point out that this was largely due to rapid turnover and a changing view of nurses' roles. She understood the big picture. In a 1945 article for the *American Journal of Nursing*, she wrote, "Coordinated planning by national nursing organizations has developed a comprehensive program for nationwide action in the field of nursing. Now let us, through the strength of coordinated effort in national, state, and local organizations, put this plan into action that nursing may progress and contribute effectively to the health and welfare programs of the nation."[20] As the polio epidemic peaked in the early 1950s, it drove the development of critical care and, with it, critical-care nursing. Through it all, Ruth Sleeper not only led the school and hospital service; she also contributed important thinking on the national scene.

Such crises accelerated the development of nursing as a profession because overworked doctors had to delegate ever more responsibilities. An early example was Ada Plumer, the world's first nurse to administer intravenous treatments. She was the only nurse in the first-of-its-kind IV program MGH established in 1940. Plumer's responsibilities included the administration of solutions and transfusions, cleaning infusion sets, and cleaning and sharpening IV needles by hand.

As noted in chapter 6, *Ladies' Home Journal* ranked MGH the number one hospital in the United States in 1967. That was the year Mary MacDonald succeeded Ruth Sleeper. She too was a leader of vision. MacDonald was the subject of a column, "Nursing Service," in the *American Journal of Nursing* in May 1969, "Nursing Service Director Predicts Changed Emphases." The column reads: "There is an imperative need for understanding from all those commonly, but actually inappropriately, referred to as the health team—of how we are all to function—dependently, interdependently, and independently—with the emphasis on who can best do what, rather than who is who. . . . Miss Mac-Donald pointed out the rapid change in health care practice, the redistribution

Tina DiMaggio.

of tasks to nursing practitioners, with some instances of 'downright defection from the primary caretaking role (as opposed to the cure and coordinative role).'"[21]

Mary MacDonald's second in command, Tina DiMaggio, became one of the first two female associate general directors, along with Eleanor Clark, in 1984. That was the year Yvonne L. Munn took over as director of nursing. Munn lit the flame of nursing research at MGH. She promoted patient-focused, outcome-oriented, research-based practice. The speaker at Munn's retirement party was Peter Buerhaus, an expert on the profession whose studies on the nursing workforce and nursing shortages have since become widely known. The talk became the seed of a broad-based research effort in the

Yvonne Munn.

years ahead, culminating in the dedication of the Yvonne L. Munn Center for Nursing Research.

What It Means to Be a Nurse

Munn's replacement, Gail Kuhn Weissman, proved to be a transitional selection, but a new successor was waiting in the wings. Jeanette Ives Erickson had come to MGH in 1988 as a staff specialist after a 17-year career in nursing, but her training had begun even before that because of her extended family's work in service-related jobs in Portland, Maine. As a girl, she lived with her family over a grocery story owned and operated by her great-grandparents, first-generation Italian immigrants. She grew up in a neighborhood where Italian was the language spoken in homes, an ethnic neighborhood that would help inspire her to advance the diversity agenda of MGH years later. Members of her extended family worked together in the neighborhood store and restaurant started by her great-grandfather. Later her mother's brother opened DiMillo's Floating Restaurant in Portland Harbor, helping launch the revitalization of the Old Port section of the community. She said: "I learned from my uncle, Tony DiMillo, how to treat people well. He created a sense of loyalty and had a participatory management style without realizing there was a name for his leadership approach."[22] (An exceptionally polished speaker, Ives Erickson betrays her Maine roots with dropped r's, though she seems to lack nothing else where *leadahship* is concerned.)

Ives Erickson's father was away at sea with the merchant marine most of the time, and, other than her uncle, those who inspired her career were mostly women. Her mother helped run the family restaurant, adding insights on business strategy. Two aunts had business careers elsewhere: one as an insurance executive, the other in the hotel business. A shy child, Jeanette was an active Girl Scout. In high school she helped lead the cheerleaders and volunteered with the Red Cross, reading to children. She loved science and thought of being a psychiatrist, but two more women furthered a growing interest in nursing: "During my senior year in high school, I decided I wanted to go to nursing school, and our next-door neighbor, Mrs. Alice Haskell—a nurse—took an active interest and helped me with my applications. She also introduced me to Sr. Mary E. Consuela White, RN, head of the Mercy Hospital School of Nursing and director of Nursing at Mercy Hospital in Portland, Maine. From my initial interview, Sr. Consuela became a role model."[23]

Another mentor, Barbara Sheehan, the night shift nursing supervisor, took the young woman under her wing while in nursing school: "Her mentorship has always been important to me and truly shaped my career. Barbara embodied what it means to be a nurse. She placed patients and families above all else, and her teachings later drove my decision to become a nurse executive."[24]

As she climbed the ranks at Mercy Hospital (critical care nurse, head nurse, nursing director), Ives Erickson decided to go back to school, first for a BS in nursing at Westbrook College in Portland (1986), then for an MS in nursing administration (1987). For the master's degree, she routinely commuted 200 miles round-trip between Portland and Boston University. The following year she began at Mass General, quickly proving an old career principle: perform the job in front of you excellently and other opportunities will follow. (And continue your education: as this was written, Ives Erickson was enrolled in the Doctor of Nursing Practice program at the MGH Institute of Health Professions.)

Appointed a staff specialist by Mary Connaughton, director of medical nursing, Ives Erickson caught the attention of Yvonne Munn, who asked her to apply for a recently vacated position, director of Nursing Support Services. Responsible for a range of clerical and administrative work at the clinical level, this department was highly centralized. Ives Erickson's mission was to decentralize and integrate it into patient care delivery. Over the following year, she successfully reorganized six service positions (for example, unit transcriber). She recalled: "By 1990 I had integrated all these roles into the units, reporting directly to the nursing directors. I went to Yvonne Munn and said, 'I think I've just worked myself out of a job.'

Jeanette Ives Erickson.

Always a wonderful leader, she said, 'Now, let's see, you just did what we've been trying to do for the last decade and you think we're going to let you go?'"

One challenge, one opportunity followed another over the next five years. Ives Erickson was asked to work with Larry Martin and others to manage the transition of clinical activities into the Ellison Building, opened in 1991. The Blake Building opened next, with parallel responsibilities for the rising leader. When the hospital made the decision to have a full-blown obstetrics program (see chapter 7), Ives Erickson worked closely with Isaac Schiff to make this a reality. And as Peter

Slavin, future MGH president, worked to reorganize clinical practice in the early 1990s, she often teamed with him. An important bond was forged. Ives Erickson recalled:

> Peter brought to the table that wonderful balance of being a clinician with an MBA, to look at how we could become more effective. Peter was identified as the overall leader of the Operations Improvement effort. I was identified as the leader for patient care delivery redesign. We all worked very closely at role redesign, system redesign, enhancements to patient safety, and patient aggregation (utilizing expensive inpatient beds appropriately and moving patients into outpatient settings when appropriate). While there was pressure to reduce costs, we never lost sight of the importance of our mission and the importance of patient care quality and safety. Many of our patient- and family-centered care ideas started to be developed out of that.

Yvonne Munn gave a year's notice of her retirement in 1993, and a national search turned up a replacement, Weissman. Unfortunately, 10 of the 12 directors of nursing reporting to her left over the next 18 months, leaving only two standing: Edward Coakley and Jeanette Ives Erickson. By the time Jim Mongan was on his way to Boston to take over as CEO at the beginning of 1996, the decision had been made to launch a new search for a nursing leader at MGH. The previous year, the unification of non-physician clinicians under the banner Patient Care Services (PCS) had begun with Nursing, Respiratory Services, Physical Therapy, Occupational Therapy, and Speech-Language Pathology. Subsequently, Social Service, the Volunteer Department, Medical Interpretation, and Chaplaincy joined PCS. Ives Erickson was appointed interim director in April 1996. A letter from Mongan told her that her appointment would be no shorter than three months and no longer than a year. It was made permanent on September 18, 1996. Mongan said, "It did not take me very long to come to the conclusion that she had every skill she needed to do the job on a permanent basis."

In accepting the position, Ives Erickson thought of advice given her by the former head of the BU master's program, Muriel Poulin, and negotiated firmly to position herself for success:

> Mentally, I went through a list of things that would not be a problem to ask for, but also included things I knew I wouldn't receive unless I asked for them. So I asked for an office located in a highly visible location. I asked for resources to create a Center for Clinical and Professional Development that would be a critical resource to support our professional practice model. I asked for voting membership at the General Executive Committee and attendance at the Chiefs Council, in addition to the ability to attend monthly MGH Board of Trustees meetings. These forums positioned me to influence decisions impacting patient care and nursing practice.

From the first day on her new job, Ives Erickson said, she had a "mantra," one she never abandoned: that the mission of the hospital was not reserved for the medical staff. The traditional three-part mission of an academic medical center—patient care, education, and research—should be shared by nursing and all related patient care practices, such as physical therapy, social work, and chaplaincy. She knew that whatever strategies she and her colleagues adopted, she herself had to be a nurse before anything else: "I had to make sure that everyone in the organization understood that the leader valued the profession and understood what it was like. I wasn't a C-suite person (CEO, CFO, CIO). I was a nurse, I am a nurse, and I know about nursing practice and I know about the importance of interdisciplinary practice."

She was also clearly optimistic about the future role of nursing at MGH. At a time when MGH and other hospitals were facing intense cost pressures and expected downsizing, Ives Erickson leaned against a national trend toward cutting clinical nurse specialist (CNS) and educator positions and actually added to them. In 2010 the hospital had 69 CNSs who were highly visible outside MGH walls through leadership roles in professional and specialty organizations.

Storytelling

It was vitally important that patient care professionals valued their own roles and communicated the importance of those roles so that the entire institution would become aware of nursing at the center of things. Ives Erickson began hosting staff breakfasts for small numbers of nurses and other practitioners, asking, "What difference did you make in the life of a patient today?"

"It became very powerful," she said. "People didn't have to talk about carrying out the physician plan of care. They talked about their own work, their relationship with the patient, their presence with the patient and with the team."

In the first issues of *Caring Headlines*, a biweekly newsletter published under her leadership, Ives Erickson urged nurses and other practitioners to write down accounts of their interactions with patients and other clinicians so that the practice of nursing could be brought into the spotlight. Over the next decade, *Caring Headlines* began featuring these narratives. She said, "The narrative program allowed nurses to begin to articulate their presence to patients and to help others to see very clearly what impact nurses had on patients, an impact very different from that made by physicians and other disciplines. People began to read those stories, and that silent voice was no longer silent." Narrative programs were being introduced in other organizations around the country, but again MGH was unique, according to Ives Erickson, in that it introduced this narrative culture across the board in Patient Care Services.

Said Mary Ellin Smith, a professional development coordinator within PCS, "Nurses began to examine their own practice in order to be able to articulate it through these narratives. People said, 'I had to stop and to think. This helped me unbundle my practice.'"

One remarkable narrative began as follows:

My name is Meredith Pitzi, and I have been a neurological nurse at MGH for ten years. I work in the Neuroscience ICU where end-of-life discussions are both a difficult and necessary part of my job. Neurological injury strikes at the core of who we are and challenges us to act as advocates for patients who are no longer able to communicate for themselves. One example of the challenges and complexities of this care involves my patient, "Karen." Though we met under unfortunate circumstances, the relationship I developed with her family and friends directly affected the outcome of her hospitalization.

Pitzi's narrative, which appeared in *Caring Headlines* in 2005, documented her interactions with "Karen" (patients are always given pseudonyms in these accounts), beginning with the day the patient was admitted with "severe, closed-head injury with multiple organ system trauma." Riding her bike without a helmet, Karen had been struck by a car. Surgery had been performed, and Karen arrived at the ICU "cardiovascularly unstable, having intercranial pressure issues." She was in a coma. To read Pitzi's entire 2,000-word narrative is to appreciate just how complex the role of a nurse can be. Among Pitzi's duties while treating Karen were stabilizing the patient for transport to CT scanning, initiating a consult with New England Organ Bank (NEOB) for possible organ donation in the event of a poor end result, and meeting with Karen's distraught boyfriend and mother. Along the way, personal details were not lost: "Karen was a Libra just like me, and oddly enough, we shared the same birth date. Karen was an artist who was talented and well-respected among her peers."[25]

Within three days, Pitzi and family members were "engaged in an end-of-life discussion." At a moment that brought her to tears, the nurse introduced Karen's parents to a representative from NEOB. After a day of soul-searching, the parents concluded that, although Karen had never expressed her wishes about the question, "she wouldn't have thought twice about" donating her organs. Pitzi's narrative concludes: "Although I had struggled emotionally with the prospect of presenting the option of organ donation to this family, I went home realizing that it works. The noble decision Karen's family made with the guidance of her friends allowed Karen to live on in two kidney recipients, 50 bone recipients, and two cornea recipients."[26]

A further way to "break the silence" about nursing's influence was to develop an awards and recognition program. A new award for patient care excellence was named for an influential clinical nurse specialist who had died young, Stephanie Macaluso. The day of the first award ceremony, in 1996, the O'Keeffe Auditorium at MGH was standing-room-only. "I was pleasantly surprised by the number of physicians," Ives Erickson said. "I read narratives as part of the ceremony in recognition of the nominees and recipients. . . . This was the first time that nursing practice had been described so publicly within MGH. I walked out of the auditorium with a physician colleague who was in tears because of one of

Stephanie Macaluso.

the narratives I read, which was about one of his patients. He said, 'I wish I worked for the Department of Nursing.' At that moment, I thought, We are doing some good things here. Nursing had a presence that was palpable."

These efforts to formulate nursing narratives from the lives of MGH patient care professionals raised consciousness. But the implementation of clearly defined strategies was needed as well. Ives Erickson was not shy about articulating the end goal: to lead the nation in nursing in the new century. "We put a lens on the patient and the nurse. Everything was about making sure that the integrity of that relationship was solid," she said. "And then we set up systems, infrastructure that supported direct care—and began a journey of clinical excellence." As it had after World War II, the United States would endure a major nursing shortage a few years after she took leadership, but Ives Erickson pushed her vision forward: to be best.

This "journey to excellence" began with the articulation of a professional practice model in 1996. While essentially theoretical and subsequently published in professional journals, the model guided steps forward with its vision of nursing practice as interlocking puzzle pieces, including such elements as standards of practice, professional development, research, entrepreneurial teamwork, and collaborative decision making.[27] The whole "puzzle" was held together by the aforementioned narrative culture, by visions and values, and (in the middle of things) patient-centeredness.

Collaborative governance was central to the vision. Gone were the days when nurses silently took orders from physicians. Ives Erickson's work in the early 1990s decentralizing activities and support for nursing to the unit level had empowered patient-care professionals. Collaborative governance promoted "collaborative decision making between and among the many clinical groups providing care in our high-acuity, fast-paced practice environment."[28]

In 1997 what is now the Norman Knight Nursing Center for Clinical and Professional Development was founded to create what Ives Erickson termed a "learning organization." Marianne Ditomassi was charged with developing an array of professional development activities to help PCS professionals continue their education and advance their practice—while never leaving the bedside.

Under Ives Erickson and Ditomassi—with Carol Camooso, Carmen Vega-Barachowitz, Mary Ellin Smith, Ann Daniels, and others—Patient Care Services created a clinical recognition program, developing criteria for practitioners to demonstrate evidence that they had advanced their practices. Much like a university, with its *instructor, assistant professor, associate professor,* and *full professor,* clinicians were encouraged to see their careers develop along a continuum—from the entry or beginning level to the level of *clinician* (demonstrating excellent practice), to that of *advanced clinician,* and finally to *clinical scholar* (still taking care of patients, but known by their peers to be experts). This was the first multidisciplinary program of its kind in the country, in that it included nurses, therapists, social workers, and other practitioners. The key was finding criteria that applied across all these jobs.

President Jim Mongan said of the clinical recognition program: "I thought it was good judgment on Jeanette's part, the concept of structuring a clinical ladder

The Patient Care Services Executive Committee.

to reward nurses who improved their clinical skills and not necessarily to force them into management positions to raise their pay. One wants to allow people to progress in the same parallel fashion that physicians can."

Nursing research moved ahead as well. Upon Yvonne Munn's retirement, the hospital had instituted an annual Yvonne L. Munn Nursing Research Lecture. Ives Erickson thought that this could become the starting point of a major nursing research effort, so that Mass General might become a national leader in this area, much as it was becoming a leader in biomedical research. "We understood," she said, "that we needed to stimulate the generation of ideas, of problems to be solved through research, and began to give out seed funding." Proposals for this funding poured in and were evaluated by a panel of nurses with doctoral degrees. Four research awards were given annually. This led to an annual Nursing Research Day, and subsequently to the Yvonne L. Munn Center for Nursing Research. Ives Erickson said, "Yvonne herself was so pleased with how we were advancing her basic idea of a research lectureship that she made a significant donation. Peter Slavin, believing that we had the opportunity to lead the nation in nursing research, made a significant investment from his own special funds as well, just as Jim Mongan had made an investment to support the clinical recognition program."

Many initiatives flourished. As one further example, in 1999, under the direction of Patient Care Services, MGH established the Maxwell and Eleanor Blum Patient and Family Learning Center, a multimedia center with more than 500 books, 150 videos and DVDs, and 250 pamphlets, as well as computer resources. The Blum Center serves more than 30,000 visitors a year.

An anonymous donor funded the new Center for Innovations in Care Delivery, launched in 2007. In the same year Patient Care Services launched the Institute for Patient Care, a first-of-its-kind, innovative model for advancing care—a strategic reshaping of systems to better integrate activities. The institute comprises four foundational centers: the Norman Knight Nursing Center for Clinical and Professional Development, the Maxwell and Eleanor Blum Patient and Family Learning Center, the Yvonne L. Munn Center for Nursing Research, and the Center for Innovation in Care Delivery. The institute, which also includes interdisciplinary programs and initiatives such as Collaborative Governance and the Clinical Recognition Program, is designed to foster the work of each center while promoting a synergy across centers. The goal is to provide nurses, therapists, social workers, and other PCS staff with opportunities for growth through knowledge and experiences needed to advance personal and professional goals and patient and family care.

Jerry Austen—chief of surgery when Ives Erickson was appointed senior vice president in 1996 and still active at MGH 15 years later—has had a bird's-eye view of the changes in Patient Care Services since she took over. In 2010 he wrote that Ives Erickson "has transformed the MGH nursing service from being good to being absolutely great. The morale in nursing at the MGH is incredibly high and the nurses have a true dedication to their patients and a love of the MGH. I've never seen a time when the relationship between the physicians and the nurses at the MGH has been better." Austen called Ives Erickson "arguably the most outstanding nurse leader in this country."[29]

Others have been paying attention beyond the hospital walls. In the 1980s, in response to a major nursing shortage, the American Academy of Nursing had noticed that some hospitals had no trouble attracting and retaining nurses, whereas other hospitals were closing beds because of the shortage. The academy asked a small team of nurse-researchers to identify common features of the hospitals that were attracting and retaining nurses (the magnets) and of those that weren't. The researchers articulated 14 "forces of magnetism" in their book, *The Magnet Hospital Study.* As the study showed, the successful hospitals also had lower patient morbidity and mortality rates, fewer patient injuries, and fewer nurse injuries. The original study identified a small number of hospitals that met these criteria.

In 1993 the American Nurses Credentialing Center (affiliated with the American Nurses Association) introduced a formal Magnet Nursing Services Recognition Program, recognizing excellence in patient care, professional practice development, interdisciplinary teamwork, the cultural competence of care, leadership, and documentation. In 2002 the decision was made to apply for Magnet status at Mass General. "We realized we had something special," Ives Erickson said. "The application for Magnet status was simply a validation of that." A total of 2,035 pages of evidence was assembled for the application. The evidence had to meet criteria to qualify the hospital for a site visit; then there was a rigorous weeklong site review by a team of ANCC surveyors.

In September 2003 Massachusetts General Hospital was designated the state's first and at the time only Magnet Hospital, one of about 50 so designated of 5,000 hospitals nationally.[30] "I couldn't have been more proud," Ives Erickson said. "I'd always known that I was working with the greatest nurses in the world, but this made it official. MGH nurses are leaders in their profession and role models for the next generation of caregivers."

MGH President Peter Slavin said, "We've been known for a long time for having the best medical staff; now that's complemented by the best nursing staff anywhere. This reflects our understanding that to be the best hospital possible means not only making correct diagnoses and giving the best treatment but also being very patient-centered and delivering treatment in a thoughtful way. That is the essence of what this place is all about."

MGH has taken its success as a Magnet Hospital into the world arena, working with international hospitals to help them pursue Magnet credentials and achieve Magnet designation. Six hospitals outside the United States had already become Magnets by 2009. MGH patient care clinicians have also had a growing involvement in international relief efforts. As just one example, Ives Erickson helped organize the hospital's response to the Asian tsunami disaster of December 2004 and was among those MGHers who visited the ravaged coast of Indonesia. Upon her return to MGH, in collaboration with colleagues she wrote a proposal to establish the MGH Center for Global Health. She said, "If we could do that amount of good in a disorganized, chaotic situation, think of what we could do if our efforts were organized in a center with a director. We could help MGH staff who wanted to volunteer around the world, train physicians and nurses to care for patients outside the hospital setting, and create fellowships and educational programs." Today the Center for Global Health is directed by David Bangsberg.

When a devastating earthquake struck Haiti in January 2010, PCS administration had its hands full coordinating the response of patient-care professionals and, notably, maintaining adequate staff at home while so many volunteered in Haiti. "There's a huge interest in the world and commitment to the world within this organization," Ives Erickson said. "We began to talk about corralling all this energy." Ann Prestipino and others worked tirelessly to help coordinate shipment of supplies and equipment to Haiti, while Ives Erickson coordinated personnel.

Ives Erickson insists that the hospital has an important core mission "to serve patients in all of the communities that we serve." In important respects, the MGH "community" is now the world, a theme developed more fully at the end of this chapter.

MOLECULAR BIOLOGY IN A GENERAL HOSPITAL

Gary Ruvkun won a 2008 Lasker Award for trailblazing work in micro RNAs.[31] By then his research interests had expanded to include a search for life on Mars. In 2009, having already won a Lasker in 2006, Jack Szostak shared the Nobel Prize in Physiology or Medicine for his pioneering work on telomeres, the "shoelace tips" that protect the ends of chromosomes; but Szostak had not been working actively on telomeres for nearly two decades. By the time he won the Nobel, he was speculating about the origins of life on this planet 13 billion years ago.

Brian Seed set out in the early 1980s to find a cure for HIV/AIDS, only to trip over a pot of gold when he found a treatment for rheumatoid arthritis. Today Seed is back looking for a solution to HIV. Given his druthers, he would also rewrite the mathematical underpinnings of quantum mechanics, a "hobby" of his. In an MGH Molecular Biology Department stocked with geniuses, Seed is acknowledged to be "famously brilliant."[32]

Ruvkun, Szostak, and Seed are three veteran molecular biologists who have worked at MGH since the early 1980s. Asked if any of them does any real work, Szostak replied, "We're all just having fun here."

Starting with Plants

It's not clear that "fun" was what Howard Goodman, Charlie Sanders, and company had in mind when they signed the Hoechst deal in 1981 (see chapter 6), or when Goodman recruited Seed, Szostak, and Ruvkun, in that order; but then one of the messages of pure science in an academic medical center is, you never know where it might lead. You might find a cure for cancer. You might win a Nobel—or two. As this book went to press, the Lasker-winning Ruvkun was said to be "teed up" for a Nobel, in the phrase of Sam Thier. (Winning a Lasker often presages a Nobel; Szostak won the Lasker in 2006 and the Nobel in 2009.)

An early tip-off that something strange was happening in the new molecular biology faculty recruited by Howard Goodman in the early 1980s may have been the greenhouses on the roof of what was then the Wellman Research Building (now the Thier Building). One might ask: Greenhouses in a hospital? Especially where space is the one coveted commodity? In addition to the greenhouses, molecular biology was allotted four floors in the new 11-story research building that went up between 1982 and 1984. To understand the greenhouses, it would be useful to know something about Fred Ausubel, Goodman's first outside recruit and perhaps his secret weapon.

Born in New York City, Frederick M. Ausubel was raised in Illinois, where his father was a psychologist. In 2010, when he was interviewed for this book, Ausubel sat behind his desk studying his interviewer with the wary yet friendly gaze of a veteran people analyst. He attended the University of Illinois, where he began studying to be an engineer. Said Ausubel, "I was a little insecure at that time and wasn't sure if I was smart enough to be a scientist." But he found engineering "extraordinarily boring" and became a chemistry major instead. Next came MIT

Fred Ausubel.

and the study of molecular biology, which is biology viewed at the molecular level, a field that overlaps biochemistry and genetics. After earning his PhD, Ausubel began working in the Cellular and Developmental Biology Department at Harvard. He recalled: "I went to graduate school in 1966, which was really at the peak of the molecular biology revolution. By the time I finished graduate school in 1972, the shine had worn off, and everybody was now thinking about how to apply molecular biology principles to more complex organisms. I had become politicized in those days, and there was a lot of talk in the lab about how to help people and society with this technology. I thought I could make a contribution in agricultural science."

Ausubel studied nitrogen fixation and worked at cloning the genes that accomplish it. Nitrogen is most often the limiting nutrient for plants, so improving the efficiency with which atmospheric nitrogen is transformed ("fixed") into a form usable by plants (ammonia) could improve agricultural yields. Ausubel taught a plant molecular biology course at Cold Spring Harbor Laboratory on Long Island, and one of his first students was Howard Goodman. Ausubel called Goodman "by far our most illustrious student." By this time Goodman and his colleagues at UCSF had cloned insulin, which made his reputation. But like several of the younger scientists he would recruit to MGH, Goodman had a nomadic curiosity, and his investigative interests had already turned to plant biology. By the time Goodman arrived at MGH, in 1981, his new interest had fixated and the greenhouses went on the drawing board.

With "intense blue eyes, sandy hair, a red beard and the energetic, encouraging manner of a college basketball coach,"[33] Goodman was quite a recruiter. Within 18 months of his arrival, he had built a department of 50 faculty, fellows, and staff. One was Ausubel. Another was Ellen Fitzgerald, former administrative assistant to Thomas Durant (whose work will be detailed below). Durant recommended that Fitzgerald apply for an opening as Goodman's assistant, although she had no scientific background.

Said Fitzgerald, "I learned very quickly that Howard was incredibly shy. He's also the most honest, ethical, sweet person you could ever imagine, but he's been misunderstood because he seems up in the clouds. Whenever we had a new secretary, I'd say, 'Now listen, when Howard comes through the door in the morning and he doesn't say hello, don't take it personally. Sometimes I'm in the elevator with him and he doesn't even notice me.'" From her privileged position alongside Goodman, Fitzgerald developed an understanding of his strengths as a leader: "He hired the best people, and he left them alone. He made arrangements with Harvard that they wouldn't have to teach their first year, even though they had appointments over there—no committee memberships, none of that."

Robert E. "Bob" Kingston, one of Goodman's early recruits, and his successor as chief in 2004, said it would be a mistake to underestimate the role Fred Ausubel played in the molding of the department. "Fred had phenomenally good taste in science," said Kingston. "Fred was involved in hiring Jack Szostak, myself, Gary Ruvkun (Fred was Gary's thesis advisor), and everybody else, including Brian."

The Molecular Biology Department became a congenial working environment. Fitzgerald called it "a very unrealistic atmosphere. No one ever leaves here. Howard created that." A key factor was the absence of divisive competition. Fitzgerald said in early 2010: "We had a candidate here yesterday, for assistant professor, a faculty position, a guy who has interviewed 12 places and already has offers from Rockefeller, Cal Tech—every place. I drove him to the airport last night. I said, 'How was your visit?' And he said, 'I don't think I've ever been in a department where the faculty genuinely get along as much as your group does.'"

Kingston agreed. There were two factors, he said, that made the MGH Molecular Biology Department unique: collegiality ("we all get along") and the encouragement provided by Howard Goodman, together with the Hoechst funding, "to go out on a limb scientifically."

Until the Wellman Building was completed in 1984, physical working conditions weren't ideal, no matter how congenial the faculty or farsighted their research. Two floors in the Jackson Building were set aside for Goodman's group while the Wellman was going up on the eastern edge of the campus, and early concerns about microbiology spawning dangerous microbes meant the installation of containment facilities; staffers had to don white "space suits" and walk through connecting clean rooms to reach their work spaces; a Boston city councilor got up in arms over the dangers of recombinant DNA work at MGH. But for new recruits during this era like Brian Seed and Jack Szostak, the pluses far outweighed the minuses.

Seeds of Success

Seed's colleagues marvel at the range and breadth of his knowledge. "If I had a question about something," said Fitzgerald, "I wouldn't call the Boston Public Library reference desk, I'd call Brian, because he would have the answer. Brian's so brilliant that if he tried to write a grant for the NIH, they wouldn't understand what he was talking about."

Others, while acknowledging Seed's brilliance, would not overlook his eccentricity. Said Kingston, "At Harvard, before coming to MGH, he wore ripped T-shirts and torn cutoff shorts, and he went to job interviews looking like that. Nobody thought he was anything other than an eccentric smart scientist that no high-end academic department would want. Why hire such a brilliant nut? But everybody connected with Harvard knew that Brian was special. His coming here was a signal that this was a place that would tolerate great science, no matter how the scientist was perceived."

Brian Seed.

The son of a doctor who trained at MGH, Brian Seed joked that he was the failed product of a long line of physicians, also including an uncle and grandfather. Raised in Westchester County, New York, he was convinced that he would be the next physician in the family, until he turned 12. "We had medical journals at home," he said, "and I read them all. But at about 12, I decided that I was probably going to be bored silly as a physician. Instead, I began looking for something where I could express myself creatively. Science and writing were the two things that came to me."

Writing turned into a hobby for Seed, who has banged out poetry, novels, and short stories in his spare time and talks happily about favorite authors like E. L. Doctorow, Joan Didion, and John Gregory Dunne. Science was the main thing, however: a PhD from Cal Tech was followed by "a peculiar post-graduate career" involving four advisors, which "complicated my résumé," he said. With the last of the advisors, Tom Maniatis, an illustrious molecular biologist, Seed moved to Harvard. He had been there only a year when Goodman called. "I consider myself the first mistake the department made," Seed said, though his colleagues all see through that bit of self-deprecating humor. Maybe it was Seed who had made the mistake? In 1982 it was not at all clear that Goodman's new department was the right spot for such a high-powered investigative talent. Seed said:

> When I arrived, there was very little at MGH in the way of basic research. It was not one of the meccas of biomedical research, like the Rockefeller, Salk Institute, Dana-Farber, MIT (which had very strong biology), or Cal Tech, Stanford. There were a lot of high-gloss places to go and MGH was not one of them. People even advised me that Howard was not my kind of guy. They said, "Don't go there, you won't get along." We got along okay. We didn't have to get along. I went my way and he went his. Howard was not a hands-on micromanager. It all worked out almost unacceptably well.

Seed developed a strategy for attacking the HIV virus by cloning a chimeric (hybrid) immunoglobulin molecule. Think of a centaur, a composite made up of a receptor that the virus needs to attack a cell and something that neutralizes the virus. "Now the virus is stuck," said Seed explaining the concept. "It has to see that receptor, because it needs that to get into the cell, but the virus ends up attacking something that will neutralize it." That was Seed's idea. "I created a technology that I thought would work against HIV," he said, "and it totally didn't work." The chimeric concept did prove ultimately effective, however, against the symptoms of rheumatoid arthritis. In the late 1980s and early 1990s, Seed's lab developed a drug that neutralizes the symptoms of this often disabling auto-immune condition. By a chain reaction that no one could have predicted in 1980, Hoechst's entire investment in MGH was justified. Their money had hired Seed to follow his muse. Seed had set off on the trail of a treatment for HIV/AIDS. The trail had been a dead end, but not before branching. And the drug Seed's lab did develop, etanercept (trade name Enbrel), earned royalties beyond counting for MGH, for Hoechst, for Immunex (a partner that owned necessary technology), and for Seed himself. Seed recalled: "The official stance at Hoechst in Frankfurt, for as long as I knew, was that the MGH agreement had been a waste. I ended on their scientific advisory board, and at every meeting they would shake their heads over MGH. In 2002 or 2003 I stopped everybody cold when I said, 'As of this year, the accumulated royalties you have earned on Enbrel have paid back your entire investment in MGH. And you have 12 more years to the patent.'"

With a personal windfall in the hundreds of millions of dollars (much of which has been reinvested in labs with which Seed is associated), many men might have sailed off into the sunset. In his late fifties, and nearly 30 years after joining MGH, Seed lived 100 meters from the hospital campus, worked seven days a week, and was again searching for a solution to HIV/AIDS. His explanation: "I'm a work-aholic, a lab rat. My whole life is right here. I trundle in, I trundle out."

A Prized Recruit

In contrast to Brian Seed, whose first and last core mission, a treatment for HIV/AIDS, is therapeutic, Jack Szostak has always been interested in basic things, like the structure of chromosomes and the mechanism of recombination. Seed called Szostak's work "absolutely spectacular, consistently really high-quality, innovative, cool stuff." Not bad for a kid from Montreal whose first brush with applied science was a summer job in the lab of a chemical factory where his mother worked. She and Szostak's father, an aeronautical engineer, helped the boy get the chemicals he needed for a lab in the family basement. Szostak took his undergraduate degree at McGill and then did his graduate work at Cornell, where he worked with the molecular biologist Ray Wu. He joined the Harvard Medical School faculty in 1979, at the uncommonly young age of 26.

The experiment that really got him started was transplanting telomeres from a one-celled organism, *Tetrahymena*, into baker's yeast; he was spurred on by a paper presented by Elizabeth Blackburn from the University of California, Berkeley, describing how telomeres help preserve the fraying ends of DNA. Once that initial transplant proved successful, Szostak continued studying telomeres at MGH through the 1980s, while Blackburn and a postdoctoral fellow in her lab, Carol Greider, pursued related tracks elsewhere.

Nobel Prize–winner Jack Szostak (in suit jacket, center) surrounded by fellows and students who help conduct research in his lab.

Why are telomeres important? When most of the cells of our body divide, their telomeres get shorter over time. As a cell ages or becomes cancerous, it eventually loses so much DNA that it gets into trouble and dies. There is an enzyme in the body that fights this natural process, but usually this enzyme is turned off. For most cancer cells to keep dividing, they have to turn the enzyme on. So in the fight against cancer, controlling this enzyme could be decisive. The flip side, Szostak explained, is aging. While we would like to know how to kill cancer cells efficiently, we would rather that our normal cells not die, but replicate. Stem cells are the core building blocks of tissue regeneration, but after they have divided a certain number of times, their telomeres get short and they can't divide any more. Tissue regeneration then starts to slow and the body begins to fall apart. Shoring up telomeres conceivably could slow the natural aging process.

By the late 1980s Szostak had completed his seminal work on telomeres, and other investigators were beginning to flood the field. Said Szostak, "I started to feel like it wasn't going to matter if I was in the field. So, why not go and do something different? So I did."

By the 1990s Szostak was focused on creating life, or its building blocks, in the lab as a way of understanding how life may have started on the Earth. He and his colleagues worked with the commonly held hypothesis that before there were DNA and proteins, there was RNA, the first building block: "We worked on how to evolve RNA molecules to bind to different targets or to catalyze different chemical reactions. That kept our lab busy through the 1990s. We got into ways of trying to evolve proteins, and I started a biotech company, which subsequently went bankrupt, though it was an interesting experience. Today [2010] we continue trying to figure out what was here, how these chemicals got together and made cells. I'm sure once we understand it, it will seem simple, but right now, it's a little confusing."

As the work evolved, the goal was to describe and "build" what Szostak and his colleagues came to call a "protocell" containing two components: RNA-encoded genetic information to tell the cell how to grow and divide, and the liquid contents that would do the growing and dividing.

In 1998 Jack Szostak became a Howard Hughes Medical Institute investigator. By this time the Hoechst funding was slowing and new sources were needed. HHMI is a prestigious independent research institute founded by the famously reclusive aviator-industrialist and dedicated to funding about 350 top scientific investigators worldwide. "Hughes came in as Hoechst was winding down, so I was really lucky. HHMI is actually my employer," said Szostak. "They pay my salary, they lease my lab space from the hospital." Jeannie Lee is another Hughes investigator in the MGH Molecular Biology Department. Her lab studies fundamental differences between the sexes, using state-of-the-art technologies to understand how one X chromosome is turned off in the female but not in the male. Hughes investigators can be found in other MGH departments as well.

But Are There Worms on Mars?

While Szostak worked with a one-cell organism found in freshwater ponds, his colleague Gary Ruvkun made his mark initially with an assist from *Caenorhabditis elegans*, a tiny worm a millimeter long. Again, you never know where something will lead: a control mechanism Ruvkun discovered in that worm, which seemed to be nothing but an oddity for a decade, turned out be important in regulating the expression of genes in mammalian cells. The mechanism is the micro RNA, a strand of RNA as short as 20 molecules long, which helps organisms fine-tune their responses to environments. Ruvkun's pioneering work has led, in the past 20 years, to what he called "a huge micro RNA explosion" and a Lasker for Ruvkun and his colleagues Victor Ambros (University of Massachusetts) and David Baulcombe (Cambridge University).

Ruvkun grew up in Oakland, California, the son of an engineer. Said Ruvkun, "I didn't excel in the things people value around you when you are 10. I liked ham radio, I liked electronics. This was my first case of getting nitty-gritty about how

Gary Ruvkun.

things work. When you're 12 years old and you understand how a radio works, deeply, you're on your way to being a scientist, because you're understanding things that have some pretty deep mysteries to them."

His radio work earned Ruvkun a merit badge from the Boy Scouts—and big disappointment when he matriculated at Berkeley. "I wanted to do electronics and Berkeley didn't teach it. But at Berkeley I discovered physics, which is the mother of everything, so that's where I learned what real science is, and where I learned about intellectual revolutions. Quantum mechanics is as big an intellectual change as ever has happened." Ruvkun marched out of college to his own drumbeat. He did not go straight to grad school but instead lived in his van for a year planting trees in the Pacific Northwest. He traveled in Latin America for another year, then spent a third year off from school working as a technician in a nuclear medicine lab. Why did Harvard accept him as a PhD candidate in biology in year four? "I had spent a summer doing research at Harvard," he explained, "so they sort of knew that I wasn't an idiot." He focused on biophysics and was mentored by a "bow-tied classic Harvard professor," Arthur Solomon, whom Ruvkun remembered as wearing a cape, driving a Porsche, and running "a great program with no requirements." That's where he met his advisor, Fred Ausubel, who would lead him to Howard Goodman. In 2010 Ruvkun and Ausubel had offices side by side.

Ruvkun finished up a postdoc at MIT and interviewed with Goodman in 1984. At the time, he said, there was a renaissance going on in developmental genetics, using recombinant DNA technology to figure out how organisms go from one cell to millions of cells. "The main approach," said Ruvkun, "is to identify genes by getting variants that seem to have defects. For example, if you find a leg growing where an arm is, you've discovered the switch that makes a leg different from an arm." Ruvkun was not working with anything so complex as a biped, however. His focus was *C. elegans*.

"This was a weird place to come," said Ruvkun, "being in a hospital department. Most of us would traditionally have gravitated to a university setting. But full funding for your lab was a unique benefit—coming here and not having to write a grant, not having to get NIH to agree that I was doing interesting stuff." Ruvkun received full funding from Hoechst from 1985 to 1992, then half funding for another five years or so, until other sources took over completely. There was a cultural difference that Ruvkun liked about MGH. Speaking in particular of Ausubel and Seed, Ruvkun said, "Neither of these guys had a Harvard attitude. They did not have a tweedy Ivy League feel to them. They had a lot of IQ and not much attitude—the kind of attitude that you learn to be repulsed by in academia because you run into it so often."

This unique environment offered singular advantages to a young investigator with unusual ideas. Ruvkun said, "If you have enough people around you doing interesting, bizarre things, it enables you to do that. 'That's the norm,' you say, 'so I can do that.' I might have been laughed at for doing my Mars thing in another department, but Szostak's doing even weirder things, so—"

We'll get to the Mars thing momentarily, but first the worm thing. Ruvkun admitted that Hoechst had trouble viewing his work with C. *elegans* as relevant to their core mission of developing profitable pharmaceuticals. But Hoechst seemed to be satisfied with getting access to the intellectual creativity of American bio-medical research. In 1992 Ruvkun and Victor Ambros were working on genes in C. *elegans* that they knew "talked to each other." Ambros figured out that his gene coded a particular micro RNA; Ruvkun then saw that the gene he was working on was the target of the same micro. They then sequenced their genes and saw that the two matched up. The link between them was the micro RNA. That finding, published in *Cell*, was greeted with a yawn in scientific circles, mostly because the scientific establishment couldn't see the relevance of an apparently anomalous discovery. But seven years later Ruvkun and Ambros found a second micro RNA, while Baulcombe proved the concept in plants. People started paying attention, especially when the investigators wrote a paper describing the same micro in a wide range of organisms, from C. *elegans* to pufferfish to cows to humans. How did they collect the evidence? Said Ruvkun, "I'm really good at begging from strangers, so I would e-mail people working on the weirdest organisms I could find and say, 'Please send us an RNA sample. Here's what we're doing. You'll be a coauthor on the paper.' That paper had about 30 authors. One of my postdocs wrote me and said, 'I sharpened your pencil. Can I be an author on your paper?'"

Two papers on the second micro RNA had high visibility; they were published in *Nature*.[34] "It started a gold rush," Ruvkun said, "where people started cloning micros like crazy. Now if you do a reference search on micros you'll find 7,000, where there was one in 1992."

Why are micro RNAs important? Some appear to be at least a billion years old, making them "highly conserved." But there's still much to be discovered about them, as Ruvkun noted: "We know what it does in the fruit fly, we know what it does in the worm, we don't know what it does in us." There is some indication that micro RNAs are involved in growth control and that cancers tend to mutate through micros. By 2010 there was an emerging view that undifferentiated cells, like stem cells, have not yet "turned on" their micros, but as they commit to becoming muscle or brain or some other specific cell type, they turn on one suite of micros or another. Micro RNAs seem to be switches, or as Ruvkun put it, "The reason your body is not just a slimy pile of cells is that a lot of switches got thrown to make bone and muscle. In the same way that a computer program is just a con-catenation of billions of switches, your DNA program is just a series of switches turning off and on various genes."

So, then, the lure of micros is that they might lead to a cure for cancer? Not for Ruvkun: "I constantly harp that laypeople should be more curious than that.

Even if you're not a scientist, you should have awe and wonder at molecular explanations of the world around you. We don't just exist to cure disease, we exist to understand. I hate it when all anybody stresses is the health impact. Yes, that's important, but even more important is to understand what's going on, and the health impact will come out of that."

Ruvkun, Szostak, Seed, and others are realistic enough to know that in the long term investigators at an academic medical center will occasionally have to demonstrate that their work has a "health impact." But that doesn't mean boys can't have fun once in a while. Which is probably the best explanation of Ruvkun's Mars thing. The MGH molecular biologist said that the space race of the 1960s was rocket fuel for his interest in science. Growing up on the West Coast, Ruvkun loved the early and lengthy coverage of NASA's Mercury and Gemini launches, although his heroes were surprising: "As a Jewish kid, I didn't bond with the astronauts. I was into the scientist part of it. I looked at the guys with flat tops and thin ties talking about cool stuff and thought, 'That could be me.'"

So, along with electronics, astronomy was his first love. Then, around 2000, scientists began identifying universal genes, genes that all earthly organisms have—a list derived from comparing all the genomes that had been sequenced. When Ruvkun heard a talk by Norm Pace about work he was doing studying genotypes in the Yellowstone hot springs, Ruvkun's mind leapt to the obvious next step: Let's do that on Mars! In 2010 Ruvkun had a research grant to develop the machine necessary to do Pace-type gene work on the next planet out from the sun. He admitted that the contract was about 3/100s of what he needed, given that it takes about $30 million to build an instrument that can be sent to another planet on a probe. But the work continued.

And not only there. Down the hall from the Mars lab, Ruvkun was working away with C. *elegans* on what he called the "nausea project"—trying to identify the biochemical basis of a worm's feeling ill. Ruvkun was excited about this project, too:

> We think we have a model for how worms feel sick, just as when humans feel sick. We have an instinct to know when we are being poisoned. There is a chemical warfare that goes on between organisms. Bacteria, for example, produce a wide range of chemicals that try to be toxic to our protein. Why is this important? Because there are diseases where people hallucinate chemicals, feel nauseous all the time, like migraines, anorexia, and I think it's going to be important in depression too, because when you're depressed you're inappropriately assigning extreme negative feelings to something. We're getting at that endocrine state in the worm. And I've been totally enthralled with that.

Ruvkun and colleagues were also on the trail of another type of RNA, which they termed the sulfur RNA. But was Ruvkun even sure such things existed? "We have some hints. I think we'll find that they intersect with proteins and are important in the choreography of proteins. It's been fun, a very serious intellectual quest."

"Howard Goodman had a very good ability to choose people, even though he was a little shy himself in interactions with people," said Fred Ausubel. Goodman retired in 2004, but several of his key recruits were still in place at MGH. In 2010 Ausubel was studying pathogens that attack both plants and animals. Seed was encouraging other investigative pioneers, with an assist from Enbrel. Szostak was recovering from six months of adulation following his phone call from Stockholm in October 2009. Watching over this happy collection of dreamers was Bob Kingston, another Goodman hire. If anyone had to be mindful of the practical "health impact" of the MGH Molecular Biology Department, it was Kingston.

Recruiting the Next Generation

A graduate of Harvard College with a PhD in biochemistry from Berkeley, Kingston was a postdoc in the MIT lab of the future Nobelist Phillip A. Sharp when he took the recruiting call from Howard Goodman. He walked into Sharp's office and asked what Sharp thought about going to work in the Molecular Biology Lab at MGH: "I told Phil that the offer gave me enough money to do what I wanted and that Jack Szostak was coming, too. Phil said, 'Take it.' David Baltimore, another of my mentors at the time, said that Jack was one of the best minds anywhere. I realized that if I failed, I would have no one to blame but myself." Kingston found that stressful, but Fred Ausubel proved "hugely helpful as a father figure. He told me that the only way for a young person to do science was to assume that you were going to get tenure." That thought helped Kingston deal with the stress of his new position, as did distance running. He began running with Rhonda Feinbaum, who worked in Ausubel's lab. In 1990 the running partners married.

Kingston credited Jerry L. Workman with the direction of his own lab from the late 1980s onward. Workman convinced Kingston that "the wave of the future" was in understanding the packaging of the genome. DNA is not linear. If the human DNA molecule were stretched out, it would be a meter long. The human cell is microscopic; so, to fit inside a cell, a DNA molecule must effectively coil itself into a yarn-like ball. How the yarn is coiled and how the human body accesses information at the center of the yarn ball are packaging questions. Scientists had been aware of packaging almost since Watson and Crick described DNA as a long double helix in 1953, but the notion that Jerry Workman lobbied for and that Kingston took up was that packaging helps the body work with and regulate the genome. Kingston described one application. Cancer, he said, "is cells forgetting what they are. It turns out that part of that is improper packaging. Jerry Workman dragged me kicking and screaming into this field."

In 2010 Kingston's lab was still working on packaging, particularly in relation to embryonic stem cells, which are *pluripotent,* meaning that they can turn into anything. As stem cells develop selectively into skin cells, brains cells, and so on, they have to be packaged in order to do what they're supposed to do. A goal of

Bob Kingston.

the Kingston lab is to understand how packaging selectively turns off pluripotent cells. Workman continued to work in molecular biology, although at the Stowers Institute in Kansas City, where Kingston called him "very prominent."

By taking over from Goodman in 2004, Kingston took on additional responsibilities. Chief among these was recruiting the next generation of molecular biologists to MGH. At a Scientific Advisory Committee meeting in 2010, the Nobel laureate Joseph L. Goldstein (a house officer at MGH in the 1960s with his co-winner Michael S. Brown) told Kingston that his department was the equivalent of the star-studded Stanford Biochemistry Department of the 1970s. That department contained two Nobels (Arthur Kornberg and Paul Berg), and other luminaries like Robert "Buzz" Baldwin and David Hogness. "You all like each other," Goldstein reportedly said to Kingston, "and you are incredibly accomplished. Stanford had issues going forward. Your job is to deal with the transition."

Among the younger generation coming along under Kingston and those of his generation like Ausubel, Szostak, Ruvkun, and Seed is Jeannie T. Lee. A Howard Hughes investigator, like Szostak, Lee is one of the world's leading experts on sex differentiation at the molecular level. Why do boys and girls have different genetic material? In particular, why is an X chromosome deactivated in human females? In January 2010 Lee won the National Academy of Science Award for a recent notable discovery in molecular biology by a young scientist. Her citation read in part: "By using X-chromosome inactivation as a model system, Lee has made unique contributions to our understanding of epigenetic regulation on a global scale, including the role of long, non-coding RNAs, interchromosomal interactions, and nuclear compartmentalization." The award may bode well: Jack Szostak is a previous winner.

Other notable young investigators in molecular biology include:

- David Altshuler is a leader in the study of human genetic variation and its application to disease, including type-2 diabetes. Altshuler also heads the Broad Institute, a collaboration of Harvard, its hospitals, MIT, and the Whitehead Institute for Biomedical Research, dedicated to the study of genomics.

- Deborah Hung studies the interaction of hosts and pathogens in vivo (in living organisms, rather than in the test tube) with a view to developing new antibiotics in a world faced with new pathogens, increasing antibiotic resistance, and bioterrorism.

- Michael Blower is another investigator of RNA. To quote from his Web page, his lab primarily is "interested in the spatial control of gene expression and how interactions between RNA and the cytoskeleton influence cytoskeletal assembly."[35]

Another important responsibility for Bob Kingston in 2010 was serving as the interface between his brainy bunch on Simches 7 and the leaders of one of the world's finest collections of physicians and surgeons, sitting in offices on the main campus. One might think that with Enbrel racking up royalties and Szostak polishing his Nobel medal, no justification would be needed, but Kingston took his guardianship seriously. Among his broader duties, he spent "at least one early Wednesday a month (scientists don't like early mornings!)" at administrative meetings with other hospital leaders. He added, "It's important for me to understand what the hospital does. My job is a lot easier now, because most people understand that you have to do research in human biology in an academic medical center. Peter Slavin absolutely, positively recognizes it; Daniel Haber, chairman of ECOR [MGH's Executive Committee on Research], recognizes it."

In 2010 Kingston also served as vice chairman of ECOR and was slated to take over the chairmanship when Haber stepped down. Kingston called ECOR "probably the single most effective overall committee running science at any institution that I am aware of." Among the committee's responsibilities was administering about $3 million a year in what Kingston called "Band-Aid money"—funds to sustain MGH investigators while they waited for their next grants to kick in. MGH physician-scientists are responsible for their own funding, but ECOR was there to help them when they hit the inevitable bumps in the road.

So what finally is the raison d'être for this island of pure research in the sea of MGH medicine? Kingston said: "The reason for this department is to have people who think about science first and come up with technologies which, in a perfect world, are then communicated with the people who think about diseases first. Medicine has become too specialized for anyone to be both a world-class clinician and a world-class investigator. The roles have diverged. You don't want your heart surgeon thinking about bench research while he's operating on you any more than you want anyone from my department operating on your heart!"

Externally, with funding sources and even other departments in the hospital, Kingston continued to make this case. Internally, his mission was to further the legacy of Howard Goodman. "There is a joke," he said, "that to be a good chief, follow a lousy chief. But I don't have that advantage. Howard laid the groundwork. My challenge is not to mess that up."

While Kingston worked to maintain the unique chemistry of his department, Ed Kaplan, the finance director, often looked on quizzically. What's it like managing the finances for a bunch of overgrown nerds? "In one sense," said Kaplan, "it's a little bit like when I was training my kids and trying to teach them financial responsibility." The years 2009 and 2010 were especially trying, as the financial calamity that was the end of 2008 meant that many dependable sources of funding and income were jeopardized. In early 2010 Kaplan said: "We've got a whole group of people who have been in this department for 20, 30 years, and whenever they wanted a whiz-bang hunk of equipment and there was funding there to just go ahead and buy it; they didn't really have to think about the financial implications of the purchase. Now they do. What I've been trying to do over the last year and a half is to instill some financial discipline into a group of people who have never really had to worry about it. I keep telling them I'm going to retire if they keep giving me a hard time."

While most credit Howard Goodman—and those at MGH, like Charles Sanders, who recruited him—for MGH's remarkable achievements in molecular biology, Goodman's first recruit, Fred Ausubel, thought he saw a deeper meaning:

I think there has been a long-term traditional commitment to basic research at MGH. That has always been an important idea here: not just clinically related research, but what I call "true basic research." And a hands-off approach. Howard had that. I don't think anybody felt that Howard was our "boss"; we were all equals, we all had our individual labs. Certainly there was no direction from Howard in terms of what projects we would pursue. It was all hands-off. He just let people develop. You choose good people and you set them free to do good science, and that was the goal here. You couldn't do that in just any institution. The institution had to accept that idea and stand back and just let it happen. I guess the people at the top of MGH were insightful enough to let that proceed in a natural, organic way, and it's been very successful.

"I've got one of the best jobs in the world here," Ausubel added. "As a scientist, you can't do better than this."

NEW APPROACHES TO RESEARCH

The 2009 Nobel Prize awarded to Jack Szostak is an honor for one man and a validation for the Department of Molecular Biology begun with Howard Goodman. It is also a triumphant note for the entire biomedical research effort at MGH that began after World War II, as detailed in chapter 5. As it approached its bicentennial year of 2011, Massachusetts General Hospital had become the largest hospital-based biomedical research institution in the United States.

Credit for this development goes to generations of hospital leadership, dating back to David Edsall a century ago, who have encouraged both clinical and pure research. If you ask Richard Bringhurst, senior vice president for research, or Nancy Risser, director of ECOR, whether there is a master plan for research at MGH, they will shake their heads. No, they say, our success is a case of "1,000 flowers blooming." Most physician-scientists at Mass General are responsible for raising their own research funds, and the postwar growth at MGH is the result of thousands of independent minds allowed to pursue their own ends in a highly supportive environment. The Molecular Biology Department of the 1980s was rare in giving Szostak and the others financial carte blanche. The reality for most researchers is a constant round of applications for renewed funding from the NIH on down. That not-so-merry-go-round turned faster and in some cases more desperately late in the first decade of the twenty-first century as the economic downturn and government belt-tightening hit biomedical research as hard as any industry.

The sheer size of the MGH research effort—more than $600 million per annum—is overwhelming, but something else of note has been happening in recent years. Research has left the silo. In 1975, to pick a point in time, most biomedical research was organized according to traditional departmental boundaries within medical schools. A cardiovascular researcher seldom collaborated with a dermatology lab or with a physician-scientist studying anesthesia. In the period 2005–2010 old barriers have broken down, and none more so than at MGH. As

Simches Research Center.

chief of medicine since 1996 and a major force on ECOR, Dennis Ausiello has had a bird's-eye view of this development. Ausiello believes that recent developments at Mass General are attributable in part to the uniquely flexible relationship between the hospital and Harvard Medical School: "Almost all other academic medical centers are scientifically organized around the way their medical schools are organized. Historically, the hard sciences have grown up under those categories—structured with less flexibility. As MGH organized itself over the last 50 to 75 years, people wanted to be here not only to ask questions about disease and to be compassionate distributors of that knowledge, but also to create new knowledge about the human condition. This allowed us to be flexible about how we organized."

As Ausiello looked back over the period since 1975, he saw three symbolic inflection points: the Hoechst deal at the beginning of the 1980s, the addition of enormous research acreage at the Lawrence E. Martin Laboratories in Charlestown at the end of the 1980s, and the opening of the Richard B. Simches Research Center adjacent to the main campus in 2004. The Simches Building is not the only MGH example of research "leaving the silo," but it is the outstanding symbol of this development. The building itself was made possible by the family of a successful Massachusetts businessman. Richard Simches and his wife, Nancy, were touched by the care he received from the staff of the MGH Brain Tumor Center. Simches passed away in 2001, and the research building was named in his memory.

The eight-story, 267,000 square-foot complex was the first major expansion of research acreage at MGH since the development of the Charlestown campus.

Chief of Gastroenterology Daniel K. Podolsky (since 2008 the president of the University of Texas Southwestern Medical Center in Dallas) headed the committee that developed the concept of four "thematic centers" that would grow up inside Simches, and as the chief of medicine and chairman of ECOR during this period, Ausiello could fairly claim to be the Simches "godfather." Ausiello's own experience as renal chief helped him see the value of the new multidisciplinary approach to research: "I had been running a lab in membrane biology where we had everything from orthopaedic surgeons to biophysicists, because we were studying a common issue, the biological membrane." Still, developing the thematic centers—each of which drew on faculty from existing departments—had to be a major collaborative effort involving many. For one thing, there were reportedly department chairs who resisted the idea of their best talents being cherry-picked by the new centers. Many talents gathered here:

- The Center for Computational and Integrative Biology is headed by Brian Seed. It brings together faculty from diverse disciplines to apply a broader scale of inquiry to the study of biology.

- The Center for Human Genetic Research (CHGR) is led by Jim Gusella. Housed in 60,000 square feet, the CHGR brings together faculty from MGH's Departments of Medicine, Molecular Biology, Neurology, Pediatrics, and Psychiatry, as well as HMS preclinical Departments of Genetics and Systems Biology.

- The Center for Regenerative Medicine is focused on understanding how human tissues are formed and particularly on harnessing stem cells to repair or replace damaged tissues and organs. Under the direction of David T. Scadden, it is closely linked with the Harvard Stem Cell Institute.

- The Center for Systems Biology was established in 2007 to analyze ways in which biological molecules, proteins, and cells work together at a systems level to affect health and disease. Though fundamental in its nature, the center's work, under the radiologist Ralph Weissleder, is directly linked to the diagnosis and treatment of cancer, cardiovascular disease, diabetes, autoimmune disease, and renal disease.

- The Wellman Center for Photomedicine, headed by R. Rox Anderson, focuses on investigating the effects of light on human biology and discovering new diagnostic and therapeutic uses of light.

Ausiello noted that it takes "a higher order of organization" to support the work inside the Simches Building. "To take all the information that used to be derived desk by desk, '1,000 flowers blooming,' and reorganize it, has taken wisdom and courage." It takes imagination, as well. Why would Weissleder, with a background in advanced imaging technology, be an obvious choice to lead a center in systems biology? Said Ausiello, "We pushed for Ralph to lead that center because of the importance of noninvasive strategies in interrogating biological pathways."

Joe Martin, the former chief of neurology, watched the Simches concept unfold from his office as dean of Harvard Medical School. He said, "I think MGH has made great strides in integrating its science. The four interdepartmental initiatives in Simches have worked really well." Martin cited the Ragon Institute under Bruce Walker (see chapter 5) as another "very powerful" example of research that cuts across traditional academic boundaries.

CIMIT

Yet another research institute bridging gaps both departmental and institutional is the Center for the Integration of Medicine and Innovative Technology (CIMIT), the brainchild of John Parrish, the former chief of dermatology at MGH (see chapter 5). As a cofounder and director of the Wellman Center, Parrish helped develop new treatments for commercial application, shepherding projects through the maze of funding and government regulations. He said, "I learned how hard it is for someone like me, who's unskilled in law or business, to deal with all the hurdles to get research done." Busy clinicians may have good ideas, but "even if they could find the technician to help them execute the idea, they don't have the time or the energy or the skill to wade through all it takes to get a research project done."

How to speed the path from idea to research to patient care? Parrish wondered. After leading a task force on the future of medicine, he produced a white paper proposing "a place where ideas and people could meet, form teams, and receive financial support to achieve their goals." About this time, a group of clinicians in radiology, obstetrics, gastroenterology, and general surgery found that they shared a desire to advance the use of technology for minimally invasive surgery. Known by their colleagues as the "Four Horsemen," Steven L. Dawson in radiology, Keith Isaacson in gynecology, Norman S. Nishioka in gastroenterology, and David Rattner in general surgery joined forces with Parrish and Ronald Newbower, founder of MGH's Department of Biomedical Engineering, to create CIMIT in 1998. Parrish was named its executive director. Four founding institutions initially took part: MGH, Brigham and Women's, the Charles Stark Draper Laboratory, and MIT.

Now a consortium of academic and engineering research laboratories, universities, and more than 40 private-sector companies, CIMIT fosters interdisciplinary collaboration among world-class experts in medicine, science, and engineering, in concert with industry and government, to rapidly improve patient care. Parrish calls it the 3-F approach: "Find, fund and facilitate."

> We find clinicians with good ideas that can really change and improve health care. Most of them wouldn't know what to do with those ideas. We have a variety of techniques to find people with good ideas. And then we find the correct technological partner for them to execute those ideas. And then we provide seed funds—probably funds that no one else would provide because ideas are so early—there's no preliminary evidence. The third F is facilitation. We have a faculty of six or seven people who are totally committed to the success of the investigators. They are full-time coaches, advisors.

In 12 years, CIMIT has invested more than $120 million in 560 projects and other activities by more than 300 principal investigators. The focus has been on procedures, devices, and systems engineering, rather than pharmaceuticals. Already the research has translated into new clinical practices and, in some cases, a new standard of care for particular problems.

For example, CIMIT aided the work of Leonard Kaban and Maria J. Troulis, of MGH's Department of Oral and Maxillofacial Surgery, in pioneering a new technique for jaw reconstruction and repair. "Minimally invasive distraction osteogenesis" is now a standard treatment for babies born without a lower jaw or those with severe jaw injuries. Without CIMIT's help, the technique "would have just remained a crazy idea," Parrish said.

Another CIMIT-supported project is perfecting a new way to repair the anterior cruciate ligament (ACL). Tears in this ligament are common—more common in girls than boys—and because the ligament will not reattach like other tissue when held together, repair often requires elaborate, open surgery. Could there be, researchers wondered, some kind of biologically safe glue that could hold the ACL together long enough to promote healing? Then the ACL could be repaired with one minimally invasive puncture.

This was a question facing Martha Murray, a Children's Hospital surgeon, who assembled a team to design and test a cell-friendly gel that would clot and form a scaffold or bridge to help the ACL rebuild. It was a surprisingly complex challenge—the glue had to have two components to come together on the spot at the right temperature. CIMIT helped the Murray team with early grants, which enabled her to gather enough data to attract funding from the National Institutes of Health and other sources. She worked with MIT engineers who created a tool that would fit through a small incision and could mix and inject the gel. Animal trials have been promising and now the process is ready for human trials, Parrish said.

A third CIMIT project focused on creating "the operating room of the future." When a group of MIT physicists and architects were brought to evaluate and update an MGH operating room, they took one look at the inefficient design, the wires snaking throughout the room, and the variety of equipment that could not "talk" to each other and joked, "There must be a patient in here somewhere," as Parrish recalled. A CIMIT-supported team that included eight industrial partners was given the task of designing a more efficient operating room: wires and devices were hung from the ceiling; equipment was made interoperable. A surgeon with the right ID badge could walk up to the operating table and it would automatically adjust to his or her preferred height. The operating room of the future has since become the operating room of the present.

TODAY'S LEADERS

Peter Slavin and David Torchiana are often referred to around the MGH campus as "Peter and Torch," like a compound word. Since 2003 the president of the hospital and the CEO of the Massachusetts General Physicians Organization (MGPO) have functioned as an effective, remarkably compatible team. Their excellent working relationship is symbolic of something special about Mass General. In other times and places, hospitals and the doctors who work in them have been opposed camps. Inside the Bulfinch Building, where hospital administration offices are on one side of the central stairwell and MGPO offices are on the other, a harmonious balance seems to hold.

Their personalities differ: Slavin trained in internal medicine, did some legislative work in Washington, became a primary care physician, and then studied for his master's degree in business administration at Harvard Business School before returning to MGH in 1990. As he meets to discuss a book project he listens attentively with a quiet smile, perhaps like a young John Stoeckle working up a case. He sits back in his chair and seems almost reticent, until he offers an opinion. Then his language is clear and thoughtful.

Torchiana, who replaced Slavin in the west wing of Bulfinch when Slavin moved east, is a heart surgeon by trade and cuts right to the point. He hunches forward and says things that sound written in advance, such as, "One of the attributes of doctors is that they are not only unmoved by lofty rhetoric but actually repelled by it." It's hard to miss Torch: he stands six feet, seven inches, and is built like a (retired) power forward.

Medicine and Policy

Slavin grew up in the city of Malden, Massachusetts, in the heart of the MGH catchment area north of Boston. His great-grandfather Louis Tokson, an immigrant from Lithuania, had settled in Malden and gone into the poultry business but was barely able to support his family. He was what Slavin characterized as a Jewish mystic healer: "People from the region would come to see him, the wise man in town, and he would take them into the back room, where they apparently benefited from his healing powers."

David Torchiana (left) and Peter Slavin touring the Lunder Building construction site.

Plagued by a chronic infection caused by a splinter imbedded in his leg, Tokson regularly took the streetcar to Mass General for treatment. "So," said Slavin, "ever since I was a little boy, I heard about this place called Massachusetts General Hospital from my grandmother, where they had provided her father free and technologically advanced care, and where people were so nice to him and to her. That shaped my early experience of the hospital."

When Slavin was five years old, he contracted bacterial pneumonia, and when his hometown pediatrician could not cure him, his mother consulted a Malden doctor who had Slavin admitted to Children's Hospital. That left the boy with "vivid memories of being in an oxygen tent, having fluid drained from my chest. I was dazzled by everything I saw in the hospital, the wizardry of the medicine, the oxygen tent, the thoracentesis [draining his chest]. From that time on, I talked about being a physician."

Slavin attended Harvard College, where he met his future wife, Lori Pearlman: "We lived next door to one another in the dorm at Harvard College and we've been neighbors ever since." As summer work, he volunteered to work for Edward J. Markey in Markey's first campaign for U.S. representative, and when Markey won in 1976, Slavin took a job in his Washington office the following summer. His interest in public policy was kindled. After college, he worked for the director of the NIH in Washington for a year, then entered Harvard Medical School. Internal medicine was the rotation he enjoyed most. "I liked that you developed long-term relationships with patients," he said. "You weren't just involved in some episode of care. In primary care, I also enjoyed the breadth of what you're dealing with. You have to know a lot about a lot of different things."

Slavin was impressed with the MGH community: "I found people here to be very smart and very committed to each patient, dedicated to unleashing the full intellectual and technological know-how of the place, but at the same time to treating people with compassion and dignity, as if they were members of your family. I view that sustaining that culture is in many ways the most important thing that I have to do. This is what's special about the place." While there were many Jewish faculty members by the time Slavin arrived at MGH, he was distinctly aware of his heritage: "When I first arrived, I felt a little uncomfortable being open about the fact I was Jewish. We Jewish residents had a saying we kept to ourselves: "Look British, think Yiddish." I don't think this hospital was any better or worse than other institutions in our society, but there may have been a certain underbelly [of prejudice]. Today I work closely on our diversity effort."

A remarkable encounter with a past dean of Harvard Business School, Lawrence Fouraker, led Slavin to study there: "I had gone to school with his son at Buckingham Browne and Nichols School. One day while I was on rounds, he went into cardiac arrest, and I was able to resuscitate him. A day or two later I stopped by to talk with him. He quickly turned the tables on me and asked me what I was thinking about. At that point, I was actually probably more interested in a policy direction, the Kennedy School or getting a public health degree. It was he who brought management to my attention for the first time. Why not get into health care management?"

Slavin earned his MBA from Harvard Business School from 1988 to 1990.

Observing top managers of the hospital had shown him that by working in administration he could address some of the same issues of access, cost, and quality that had interested him in Washington:

> One thing I didn't like about Washington was that on any given topic, you were one of 10,000 people trying to influence an issue, and the connection between your work and a person's health care was remote. What drew me to management was what draws many physicians to research. They imagine that by doing some great research they can come up with something that will take care of more people than you can by dealing with them one at a time. That's the thought I pursue in health care management: that you can have a very tangible impact on patients and their loved ones.

When Slavin returned to MGH to pursue a career in administration in 1990, John Potts, chief of medicine, helped him do so. Said Slavin, "Ninety-nine percent of chiefs of medicine at that time would have brushed me aside—he couldn't have been more supportive." With Potts's encouragement, Slavin "cobbled together" a position made up of one-third clinical practice in internal medicine, one-third clinical outcomes research, and one-third management. His early work with the Clinical Practice Council is covered in the previous chapter and further detailed in the section on Patient Care Services above. As the prospect of managed care became more of a reality by the middle of the decade, a program entitled Operations Improvement (OI) came into being: multidisciplinary teams focused on reengineering clinical operations, supported by the consulting firm APM (American Practice Management). OI was led first by Jeff Davis, then by Jean Elrick, while Slavin played an important role in quality improvement and cost reduction.

When Sam Thier was appointed president of the hospital in 1994, he asked Slavin to be chief medical officer (CMO), the most senior medical advisor to the president. The chief medical officer works with all chiefs on programs to improve quality and efficiency of practice; the position thus represented a logical arena for Slavin to continue his reengineering efforts. After Jim Mongan succeeded Thier as president in 1996, Slavin was approached by a headhunter recruiting for the newly merged Barnes-Jewish Hospital, affiliated with the medical school at Washington University in St. Louis. "For political reasons," Slavin said, "they didn't think that the president of either hospital should have the combined role, so they looked for someone from outside." Offered the presidency of Barnes-Jewish, Slavin decided to go for it: "It's a great medical center. I had been CMO at MGH for four years, and I saw an opportunity for my learning curve to be steeper there than here." He and Lori moved their family to St. Louis, thinking this was a long-term choice: "I forced myself to make the decision based on the notion that I would never be back to MGH." But three years later, Mass General called again, in the person of Andy Warshaw, chief of surgery, heading another search committee.

Jerry Austen had decided to step aside as head of the MGPO after putting the physicians' organization squarely on its feet, and Warshaw asked Slavin to consider replacing Austen. Said Slavin: "There's no place like home—Boston and Mass General."

When Slavin moved to Barnes-Jewish Hospital, Britain W. "Brit" Nicholson succeeded him as chief medical officer, a position Nicholson continues to hold in 2011, along with serving as senior vice president for medicine. Nicholson had been an MGH staff member since 1982, serving successively as director of the Medical Walk-in Unit, associate chief of the General Internal Medicine Unit and the Department of Medicine, and director for primary care development. Jerry Austen described Nicholson as "an outstanding leader, one who listens attentively to the concerns of others; and as a practicing physician he is very aware of staff members' concerns. I can't think of a better choice for this [chief medical officer] position."

Running Things

"Jerry is Jerry," Slavin spoke knowingly of his predecessor at the MGPO, "and he brought with him all the gravitas to make the PO very real here at MGH and across Partners." There was still work to do, however. Austen had improved the doctors' billing operations considerably, but further improvement took a lot of Slavin's early time and energy, an effort continued by Torchiana when he replaced Slavin in 2003. Today, Slavin said, "the MGPO has one of the best physician billing offices anywhere."

The other emphasis for Slavin in three years heading the physicians' organization was physician contracting with insurers. An analysis demonstrated that MGH physicians had not had significant rate increases in a number of years, and while their costs were going up, the hospital was losing some of its best doctors to other communities and better financial offers. "We couldn't compete on salary," Slavin said. "When we did the analysis, all roads led to contracts with local payers, which were paying docs substantially less than what they were paying in other communities in the region. So the PO became a major force within Partners to make sure physician rates were an important part of our contracting."

In January 2003 Slavin moved from west to east in Bulfinch to replace Mongan as president of the hospital. The new head man spoke less of his accomplishments in his first eight years as MGH president (2003–2010) than he did of his goals. He said he has worked hard to sustain "the culture of the place . . . the spirit around here." He also has made it a major priority to continue work he credits to Mongan: building a superb working relationship with the hospital's physicians. Slavin said: "The hospital recognizes that without a great medical staff, we're not a great hospital. And I think the physicians appreciate the same. We benefit from physician loyalty to the hospital, that cultural thing we can't put our finger on."

Leading the MGPO

For "Peter," that critical hospital-physician relationship begins with "Torch." Born in Evanston, Illinois, David Torchiana said his father's position on the faculty at Northwestern University, as a professor of Anglo-Irish literature specializing in Joyce, Yeats, and Swift, "explains a lot about my subsequent life." He spent most of seven early years in Ireland, following his father's career, and spent two of the happiest summers of his youth working as a boatman at the Royal Irish Yacht Club in Dún Laoghaire, near Dublin. His mother was a teacher, trained in child psychology, who finished "one yard short of her PhD."

As an undergraduate at Yale, Torchiana took a year in Churchill College at Cambridge with a Churchill Scholarship in science and technology, working in the lab of Robert Geoffrey Edwards, the British pioneer of in vitro fertilization (IVF) who would win the Nobel Prize in 2010. Notably, Torchiana worked there the year before the first IVF baby, Louise Brown, was born on July 25, 1978. By then he had become passionately interested in the development of an embryo during the period before it is implanted in the uterine wall. Efforts in Edwards's lab, he said, "presage the stem cell work of today. These embryos are basically all stem cells."

That interest launched Torchiana into medical school at Harvard, where he realized that one of the things about the Edwards lab that had fascinated him was the highly technical nature of it, using micromanipulators and other cutting-edge tools. "In clinical courses in medical school, I saw what doctors do, and it was obvious that heart surgery is the ultimate manifestation of technical challenge." He took his residency at MGH, where Willard Daggett was an important mentor—"a combination clinician-scientist, who thought with great clarity. I was interested in how his brain worked." It was Daggett who asked Torchiana if he had ever considered being a heart surgeon. Torchiana's negative answer had two reasons behind it. First, all heart surgeons seemed a bit crazy to him. Second, the surgery looked so difficult, he wasn't sure he was talented enough. Daggett gave him the decisive answer: "I learned how to do it. You can learn how to do it, too."

As a heart surgeon, Torchiana was an "adult generalist, involved in everything: transplants, valves, coronaries." Meanwhile, he quickly became interested in administration when he saw a new area of need open up, one that had not meant much historically, what he termed the interface between doctors and the hospital involving how the clinical services worked, managing the cost of care, managing patient flow, in an environment of managed care and contracting. "There was an awakening of interest or activity from doctors in this area at that time. The MGPC [Mass General Physicians Corporation] had started forming in response to dramatic developments in the external environment. Because it seemed so important, I put time and energy in that stuff and was involved in reorganizing the cardiac service, identifying critical pathways to simplify the course of management of patients. I was also involved on the contracting side with both the PC and PO."

When Operations Improvement began, Torchiana headed efforts in the cardiac service line as a whole—that is, for both cardiac surgery and cardiology. For the young heart surgeon, these represented "leadership opportunities that I would not have had otherwise. It was not something I had set out to do, but it was apparent that the need was great." With a growing administrative résumé, he replaced Mort Buckley as chief of cardiac surgery in 1997 (interim) and 1998 (permanent). When the search started to replace Slavin as head of the PO, Torchiana was a likely candidate. He was not interested in the job, he would say later, but a number of respected colleagues "came to see me on a recurrent basis, and persuaded me it was something I should take seriously." After taking over for Slavin, Torchiana continued to perform heart surgery for a few years, then gave himself completely to his job as chairman of the PO. He admitted, "I don't have a day job anymore. If I were to go back to the OR, I'd have to be supervised."

Since the mid-1990s service chiefs have reported jointly to the heads of the hospital and the physicians' organization, one of several ways in which power is shared. To an outsider, Slavin and Torchiana now seem joined at the hip. Torchiana said, "We complement each other well. We have similar views, similar personalities, neither of us interested in outshining the other. We tend to have similar appraisals of the people around us, too." Torchiana acknowledged an important leadership role for Jerry Austen, as well, as a "big help and very good compass" to the young leaders of the hospital.

Like Slavin, Torchiana is slow to list "accomplishments" since the pair took over in 2003. In fact, Torchiana suggested that this final chapter of the bicentennial history book be the shortest of all, "since we don't really know what's important yet about recent developments. We're too close to them."[36]

In one important respect, the story of these years remained unwritten as this book went to press. Though both Slavin and Torchiana were seemingly years away from retirement age themselves, an entire generation of service chiefs was entering their mid-sixties. The tale of the period would be told finally in the roll of new chiefs chosen in the 2010s. Said Torchiana, "I hope we can say we've recruited a great batch of chiefs. Five years from now we'll have an essentially new cast."

In 2011 women occupy seven of the 12 senior vice president chairs around Peter Slavin's MGH executive management table. This leadership team, known as "Ops," comprises Rick Bringhurst, research; Jeff Davis, human resources; Jean Elrick, administration; Jeanette Ives Erickson, chief nurse and patient care services; Sally Mason Boemer, finance and cancer; Gregg Meyer, quality and safety; Brit Nicholson, chief medical officer and medicine; Greg Pauly, orthopaedics, oral and maxillofacial surgery, and urology; Ann Prestipino, surgical and anesthesia services and clinical business development; Allison Rimm, strategic planning and information management; Joan Sapir, neurosciences, women's and children's services, dermatology, molecular biology, and physical medicine and rehabilitation; and Peggy Slasman, public affairs.

Over on the MGPO side of the Bulfinch Building, the executive team, led by David Torchiana, includes Deborah Colton, external affairs; Tim Ferris, medical director; Jim Heffernan, chief financial offer and treasurer; Alexa Kimball, service excellence and practice improvement; as well as Davis, Elrick, Meyer, Nicholson, Pauly, Prestipino, and Sapir.

Quality and Safety

A new era in thinking about quality and safety in American health care delivery began in November 1999, and not just at Mass General. That's when the Institute of Medicine (IOM) released a striking, highly influential report titled *To Err Is Human: Building a Safer Health System*.[37] "At least 44,000 and perhaps as many as 98,000 Americans die in hospitals each year as a result of medical errors," the report noted.[38] The primary causes of these deaths were not incompetent or uncaring health providers; they were faulty systems that led to improper transfusions, wrong-site surgeries, falls, burns, accidents, and so on.[39]

MGH Board Chair Ed Lawrence especially found the report compelling, and over the next three years, while Jim Mongan was president of MGH, the two began actively to consider the implications of the IOM report and take the first steps toward a hospital-wide response. Lawrence, who is credited by Mongan and others with leading the way on this issue, created a trustee subcommittee on quality and safety (one of several subcommittees he initiated). That move alone, Lawrence said, gave quality and safety "a momentum of its own." Lawrence also credited a Partners-wide retreat in Chatham, Massachusetts, for taking up quality and safety as a central theme during this period. The combined MGH-MGPO Clinical Performance Management Program for quality improvement was launched, and under the incoming president Peter Slavin the hospital opened a formal Office of Quality and Safety.

Gregg Meyer.

Under Slavin, Senior Vice President Gregg S. Meyer has emerged as the leader in this area. Today Meyer has the corner office in the Edward P. Lawrence Center for Quality and Safety. There are two notable things about the center: its name and its location. Most offices of quality and safety at American hospitals have traditionally been "in the basement," according to Meyer. His center is positioned squarely in the executive suite at MGH, within a few steps of Peter Slavin's office, a clear statement of institutional priorities.

Meyer grew up in northern New Jersey and spent considerable time on his grandparents' farm. He attended Union College and Albany Medical College and was a resident in internal medicine at MGH and a Rhodes scholar. In the U.S. Air Force he served on the medical staff and retired as a colonel. Following his military service, he was recruited as director of the Center for Quality Improvement and Patient Safety at the Agency for Healthcare Research and Quality of the U.S. Department of Health and Human Services—the Clinton administration's response to the IOM report. Called back to MGH in 2002 as chief medical officer of the MGPO by Peter Slavin while he was still heading the physicians organization, Meyer was promoted to senior vice president by Slavin and Torchiana in 2007 and given command of the Lawrence Center. Like other administrators, he still sees patients and had a stethoscope draped over his shoulders when he sat for an interview in 2010. "Patient care is my opium," he said. "If I didn't do it, I would crave it, but if I did too much, I would overdose."

How do you improve quality and safety at an institution like MGH? Paraphrasing Louis Pasteur, Meyer says the key is "not the seed, but the soil." The entire culture has to change, not particular people or programs. Meyer said: "There are many initiatives, but the key is having the culture—the chiefs, the medical staff, the nursing staff, executive leadership—all thinking this is about Q&S. It's a work in progress. MGH cannot be accused of complacency. We don't wear complacency well."

Because quality and safety is an institution-wide effort, Meyer spreads the credit widely: Lawrence gave the push, and Slavin has maintained the momentum, putting enough resources behind Meyer's effort that it is recognized hospital-wide as a central initiative of his administration. Meyer even sees Slavin's hiring of him as medical director of the MGPO as "prescient": "I was a curious choice, and I know he cast a wide net in the interview process. I didn't have extensive experience in the nuts and bolts of being a medical director—negotiating managed care contracts, oversight of physician credentialing, and so on. I had been at a federal agency."

The Agency for Healthcare Research and Quality is not just any federal agency. Slavin promoted Meyer in 2007 because he wanted to know "that there was someone losing sleep over this issue," Meyer said. Meyer was quick to add that he is not the only one losing sleep. "There can't be any solo effort in quality and safety. It wouldn't get very far."

Meyer credits Mongan for having played a central role, not only in laying the foundation with Lawrence at MGH but particularly in pushing a Partners-wide effort once he became Partners CEO in 2003. Ed Lawrence agreed: "At Partners Jim raised the boats enormously. These hospitals are now clearly at the forefront of a quality-and-safety movement in the country. Read the quarterly quality reports: every single procedure you can have is analyzed. This is going to happen nationally. It is already happening here."

Meyers called Mongan's work at Partners "foundational"—particularly in establishing a systemwide electronic records system. Meanwhile, Meyer said, work at MGH is focused on the culture, and on the tiniest details, such as hand hygiene.

Another hero of quality and safety at MGH is Jeffrey B. Cooper, director of the MGH Center for Medical Simulation, who has driven patient safety especially in the area of anesthesia. Said Meyer, "If you want to name the one person who has saved more lives internationally than anyone else at this hospital, it would be hard to win an argument that Jeff is not the one."

Meyer is quick to add, "Our accomplishments are not measured by statistics or captured in data. The single most important accomplishment is the evolution of MGH's culture to one where we feel incredibly accountable for patients. We have taken it upon ourselves to make it right, and when there are mistakes they are shared openly."

Meyer sees Mass General reaffirming the foundational notion that "everyone is our neighbor." "We are a public trust, and those of us who are stewards of this trust owe it to our patients to deliver safe, high-quality health care and to convince our patients that we are delivering it. Quality has been implied and widely accepted here over 200 years, but we recognized over the past decade that that is not enough. We have to be transparent with the community about where we fall short. Our message is, MGH is relentlessly trying to make it better."

A NEW DEFINITION OF COMMUNITY

When the planes hit the towers, Susan Briggs was ready. Three months before the terrorist attacks of 9/11, the onetime San Francisco night nurse turned MGH trauma surgeon was coordinating the response to a simulated civilian disaster at

Hanscom Air Force Base, west of Boston. When the call came to set up a field hospital beside the World Trade Center in New York in September 2001, Susan M. Briggs was the lead doctor in charge at the scene.

Such a coincidence is uncanny. But then Oliver Cope was ready with new ideas about burn treatment when the Cocoanut Grove fire hit Boston in 1942. In fact, the history of Massachusetts General Hospital repeatedly demonstrates a readiness and an ability to serve emergency medical needs—from the streets of the West End in the early nineteenth century to the trenches of France in 1918; from the Cambodia-Thailand border during the Khmer Rouge genocide to the rubble of Armenia after a 1989 earthquake; from a devastated Haiti in 2010 to the streets of Boston again, where a pioneering health care plan for the homeless continues to bring professional medical attention to the city's darkest corners.

A community hospital in an inbred city has expanded its sense of community dramatically. With a professional staff that *is* the world, MGH *serves* the world.

Just One Bigger Neighborhood

Susan Briggs credits Tom Durant with making this vision a reality. If Thomas Stephen Durant were still alive he himself might credit three other factors—neighborhood, Vietnam, and rugby. Durant died seven weeks to the day after the attack on the World Trade Center. In an appreciation in the *Boston Globe*, his friend David Nyhan, a *Globe* columnist, explained the attraction of refugee medicine for the kid from Dorchester: "For Durant, the world was just one bigger neighborhood."

Tom Durant had a lot of friends, beginning and ending in St. Mark's Parish. That's how you knew where you were from if you were a Catholic kid of French and Irish extraction living in a Boston neighborhood. You were from St. Mark's Parish. An only child, Durant graduated from Boston English and Boston College, further markers of belonging in the city. He joined the army in the late 1940s and served in Korea, before America's intervention there began. He befriended a young boy who was receiving inadequate medical care, and this galvanized him. He swore that if he ever got a chance he would go back to Asia as a doctor.

In 1955 he graduated from medical school at Georgetown. Although Durant's devoted wife of 49 years, Fredericka, was said to be more devout than he, "Doc's" faith was always a factor. As he lay in a bed at MGH, weakened from a long battle with prostate cancer, he had the last rites administered by a Jesuit, the MGH psychiatrist Ned Cassem. The

Susan Briggs at Ground Zero in the days after 9/11.

sacrament came early, however; Durant lived another two months after being given up for dead, but then he always was a survivor. He made it through the worst shelling of the 1968 Tet offensive in Vietnam by hiding under a hospital bed; he took up the brutal game of rugby at age 47; he lived the last 13 years of his life with prostate cancer.

Father of three sons, chief resident and then an OB/GYN on the staff at Boston City Hospital, armed with a master's degree in public health from Harvard, Durant volunteered for duty in Vietnam in 1966, leading a U.S. Agency for International Development effort to treat civilians of Saigon and the Mekong Delta, many of them refugees. While MGH was setting up a community clinic in Charlestown, Durant was running a series of clinics in Vietnam. It was there that he befriended the author David Halberstam and *Boston Globe* journalist David Nyhan. There he met MGH General Director John Knowles, while Knowles was on a fact-finding trip. Knowles saw something in Durant and invited him to join the staff at MGH, as a gynecologist and assistant general director. Durant would serve as assistant to five general directors and presidents until his death in 2001.

Durant was politically savvy. He had what few patrician leaders at MGH ever had, credibility in Boston neighborhoods. His son Stephen A. Durant, an MGH psychologist, said,

He's a St. Mark's Parish guy, he's a Boston English guy, he's a BC guy, he's a known factor, and he still lives in Dorchester, so he has absolute credibility. This was a secret of his success and it really helped the hospital, because going forward the Boston politicians, the Billy Bulgers, the Speaker [Thomas] McGees, the Tip O'Neills, they all trusted him—he personalized the hospital for these people; if they had a problem, he would make sure they got the right doc, he would visit them. He would do that whether you were a mucky-muck or not, he'd do the same for a cop's sister from Dorchester.

Durant's office was on White 1, across the hall from the general director's, and it was a scene of happy chaos. Keeping a lid on things was Durant's savvy secretary, Angela D'Arcangelo Sartorelli. Steve Durant called the office Grand Central: "Every homeless guy came in, politicians came in. Angela was a terrific administrative assistant. She protected him, had her ear to ground, could smell a political issue 1,000 miles away, and was a tremendous neighborhood person." But Durant had a knack for getting along with everyone, according to his son: "Even though his last name is French Canadian, and he was three-quarters Irish, he looked Italian. My mother used to tell the story that when he was at the Parthenon, he was mistaken for a Greek guide." Steve Durant added: "What I loved about him was, he was catholic with a small c. He hated it if you big-timed somebody, he had no patience for that. Butcher, baker, candlestick maker, cleaning staff, administrative staff—it didn't matter to him. That's why we lived in Dorchester, same parish he was brought up in. He lived in the same house since 1967."

Durant was also restless, however. His son, the psychologist, thinks he had attention deficit disorder, ADD. Time and again the old man would pull up stakes, leaving Fredericka and the boys at home on Melville Avenue, and head off to some trouble spot, caring for refugees.

In 1979 it was the Thai border with Cambodia, treating Cambodian refugees from Pol Pot's massacres. The Boston journalist Mike Barnicle was there "beneath a huge tent top . . . as the concussion of distant mortar rounds whispered through the humid night air."[40] His sons Joe and Sean were there too, working alongside their dad. Their brother Steve, who did not go, said, "I've never been prouder of our family." Ly Y, one of the refugees and the author of a memoir about the experience,[41] would remember Tom Durant: "He looked like John Wayne, the famous American movie star, only smaller. He was not a tall person, but a person of Cambodian size, except that he was a little husky. Along a red dirt road, in sun that was 90 degrees, he entered a makeshift bamboo tent with palm leaf walls, and a light blue tarp stretched over for a roof. He did not

Tom Durant in Bosnia, 1992.

look afraid of anyone. He would put his feet up on anyone's desk."[42]

Later trouble spots included Afghanistan, Iraq, Sudan, Somalia, Rwanda, Bosnia, Blace. His final "vacation" was to Honduras in 2001, the year he died. Whether he worked with the American Refugee Committee, Concern Worldwide, or the Irish-American Partnership, he learned enough fragments of the local language to get people's attention. He said places like Blace (teeming with refugees from the Serbian regime of Slobodan Milosevic) were "proof of Original Sin, of good vs. evil, of man's inhumanity to man."[43] He railed against the "three B's"—bureaucracy, banditry, and baksheesh (bribery), which he said held back the developing world. He won a humanitarian award from the United Nations. He wore a Red Sox baseball cap everywhere.

The same care and concern for the powerless that took Durant around the world kept him busy in Boston. Barnicle told one story:

> A woman in Dorchester had a husband home sick on a dialysis machine. To care for her husband, she quit her job. She was not an assistant vice president at State Street Bank. She had been a waitress at the Victoria Diner on Mass. Ave., in the meatpacking district. She had no money, huge problems, and a large electric bill that she was unable to pay or even dent. . . . Durant was on the phone early in the day, telling me about the woman, the dying husband, dialysis and the bill. He didn't simply want to relay the story, he wanted to know what time that morning I could meet him so we could both go to the house, talk to the woman and do God's work: fight a huge utility bill.[44]

Tom Durant.

Through the administrations of John Knowles, Charlie Sanders, Bob Buchanan, and Sam Thier, Durant kept his office in the White Building as indispensable assistant to the general director (later termed *president*). Jim Mongan, the last president under which Durant served, would say:

He was a fascinating character whom I first met when I was in Washington years before, when he was down there representing the hospital. He was a wonderful combination of physician, humanitarian, and lobbyist all rolled into one. As president, I benefited from his contacts on Beacon Hill and in the city. I'll never forget Tom shepherding me around on Beacon Hill. It was like being up there with the pope. It was not about political contributions. Over a 30-year period he had arranged for medical care for their friends and family members, and they all remembered that. He was a wonderfully warm and friendly fellow.

Through Tom Durant's last years, Laurence J. "Larry" Ronan, Durant's primary care doctor at MGH, "was Dad's go-to person," according to Steve Durant. "Larry was *always* accessible for my father and for his patients. He was probably, amongst the docs here, as trusted as anyone. If anyone needed a primary care physician, Larry was the first person my dad would send them to." Ronan was a Chicago native, but what impressed Durant about him was that he was one of the few doctors on the MGH staff who lived in a Boston neighborhood. Ronan ministered to Durant during his last years, then took up his torch after he was gone, as director of the Thomas S. Durant Fellowship in Refugee Medicine. In 2006 Ronan was cofounder of the MGH Center for Global Health, an institution-wide effort to coordinate the work of many MGHers around the world. In 2010 Ronan's many other duties would also include senior advisory work with the Red Sox Foundation and Massachusetts General Hospital Home Base Program. He also served as team internist for the Boston Red Sox.

The Next Generation in World Health

The Durant Fellowship is awarded annually to an MGH nurse or physician seeking to work in refugee areas or on the site of acute humanitarian disasters. The first Durant Fellow was Kristian R. Olson, a physician in the Department of Medicine and the MassGeneral Hospital *for* Children whose career was personally inspired by Tom Durant. With an MD from Vanderbilt and a master's in public heath from the University of Sydney, Australia, Olson began a Harvard combined residency in medicine and pediatrics in 1999, which involved work at MGH, Children's Hospital, and the Brigham. After he completed his residency in 2002, his clinical work would focus exclusively at MGH, at least when he was in the United States.

Personally passionate about global health, he was directed by several people to Durant but initially didn't follow up. "I had an impression that he was an administrator without a foot in the field," said Olson, referring to Durant's most visible on-campus role. Then one day Olson received an international cell phone call from Bosnia. The voice on the other end of the line growled, "What the —— are you doing there?! When are we going to meet? I've been told I have to talk with you."

Kristian Olson in Ethiopia, 2010

Olson was "floored," but he later understood that this was typical Tom Durant: "He would make anyone feel they were the only person who mattered." When Durant returned from Bosnia, they had an hour-plus talk in the MGH cafeteria, which Olson called "incredible, a breath of fresh air." The young doctor was on the point of deciding his next career steps. Should he do an internship at the World Health Organization? Durant's response: "—— that! You have to be in the field. You have to get your hands dirty." That, said Olson, "was exactly what I wanted to hear."

Durant helped Olson make connections with the Red Cross and the United Nations. A friendship grew. Then Durant died. When the Durant Fellowship was formulated and the call went out for the first applications in 2002, Olson jumped at the chance. In January 2003, awarded the first fellowship, he headed to the London School of Hygiene and Tropical Medicine for a three-month diploma program, just as Durant had recommended, then traveled to the Thai-Burma border, where he worked in three refugee camps with the American Refugee Committee. Olson's future wife worked there too.

Durant had warned Olson, "Asia will bite you in the ass and never let you go." After a hitch in Darfur, Olson returned to Asia following the tsunami of 2004. He worked in Indonesia off and on for three years, helping develop a primary health care rehabilitation project on the west coast of Aceh, an underdeveloped region he called "their equivalent of South Dakota." One of his main activities was training midwives to resuscitate babies.

Interviewed in May 2010, Olson had spent about 100 days of the preceding 12 months overseas, including four visits to Ethiopia, one to Tanzania, and one to Cambodia. Much of his work now is connected with his appointment at the Center for the Integration of Medicine and Innovative Technology, as program leader of CIMIT's Global Health Initiative. There he and colleagues have developed a baby incubator that can be made out of automotive parts, as well as a number of other technology projects that seek to enhance the capacity of care providers. In June 2009 Olson was named to the Scientific American Top 10 Honor Roll, which recognizes individuals who have demonstrated leadership in applying new technologies and biomedical discoveries for the benefit of humanity.

Tom Durant was sorely missed when he was gone and his laughter was silenced.

Jim Mongan commented for his obituary: "He got the hospital focused on the fact that there is a very big world out there that we are part of. We're going to miss so many things about him—his integrity, his incredible sense of humor, and all those living connections to the city and government."[45]

"He's an American saint," David Halberstam said.

"Yeah," added Martin Nolan of the *Boston Globe*, "except he can curse in ten languages, if that was how he had to make his point."[46]

When Steve Durant gave the eulogy for his father, he witnessed Senator Ted Kennedy in the front row at St. Mark's in Dorchester, "bawling his brains out."

Disaster Relief

On the phone, Susan M. Briggs sounds like a grandmother from Virginia, not a trauma surgeon or one of the world leaders in rapid medical and surgical response to disasters. In fact, Briggs is all these things. Soft-spoken but sharp as a scalpel, Briggs regularly teams with the U.S. government and military, as well as with nongovernmental organizations (NGOs), to treat people injured by earthquakes, tsunamis, or terrorist attacks. She calmly claims that all she is doing is following "the same philosophy as Tom Durant: taking MGH expertise and reaching out to whatever community may benefit." Briggs founded the Durant Fellowship with Ronan, and she sits on the Fellowship Board. "Tom Durant," she said, "was the reason many of us continue our work." Briggs's book *Advanced Disaster Medical Response: Manual for Providers* is dedicated to Thomas. S. Durant, "Humanitarian, Physician, Mentor, and Friend."

Raised in Alexandria, Virginia, Briggs is Finnish on her mother's side, where a grandfather and two cousins were physicians. She attended the University of Virginia and took her first job at Mass General, as a nurse with the General Surgery Service on White 7. Briggs had always hoped to pursue medicine but had no female physician models while growing up in Virginia. Although she loved nursing at Massachusetts General Hospital for two years, MGH physician mentors such as Leslie Ottinger and Ashby Moncure encouraged her to pursue her dream of becoming a surgeon.

Briggs hopped in her car and headed to San Francisco, where she took premed courses at UCSF, while working nights as nurse in charge in the emergency room of San Francisco General Hospital. Donald Trunkey, a famous trauma surgeon in the making, was chief resident in surgery at the time, and he also encouraged Briggs to pursue a surgical career. She would write of Trunkey, "He taught me the importance of good medicine, a sense of humor, and compassion as the keys to a successful medical career."[47] She worked her way through the Stritch School of Medicine at Loyola University in Chicago as an ICU nurse on the side.

A woman surgeon in the 1970s was a trailblazer. As noted previously, the first woman surgeon on the Harvard faculty, Patricia Donahoe, was appointed in 1976. Briggs started her surgical residency in 1974 at MGH and became the first female surgical chief resident in 1979–1980. Briggs said, "My biggest obstacle was demonstrating that females can retain their female identity and still be excellent surgeons. We are unique but equal members of the medical community."[48] In 1998, to further her interest in disaster and humanitarian relief, Briggs earned a master's

Susan Briggs with a crush-injury child in a field hospital, Port-au-Prince, Haiti.

degree in public health, with a focus on international health, from the Harvard School of Public Health.

In her disaster relief work, Briggs and MGH have often partnered with non-profits and have a particularly long history with Project HOPE. Founded in 1958 by William B. Walsh, a Harvard Medical School graduate moved by poor health conditions he had seen in the South Pacific during World War II, Project HOPE began with a U.S. Navy hospital ship transformed into the SS *Hope*. The ship was retired from service in 1974, but the mission has lived on. When Briggs completed her residency in general surgery at MGH in 1980, she was persuaded by John Remensnyder, chief of plastic surgery and a longtime Project HOPE volunteer, to join the volunteer team from MGH. Her first humanitarian project followed a devastating earthquake in El Salvador in 1987, when she helped evacuate 30 crush-injury children to the MGH/Shriners Burn Unit in Boston. Working with Project HOPE, Briggs and her MGH team have deployed to many disasters, including the Armenia earthquake (1989), the gas explosion in Ufa, Russia (1989), the Bosnia-Croatia conflict (1997), the Indonesia tsunami (2004), and the earthquakes in Turkey (1999) and Sichuan, China (2008).

In Armenia there was a partnership between the government (providing transport) and nonprofits (providing medical care). Briggs and her team treated many crush-injury children who could not get medical care in the USSR. She coordinated an air evacuation to nine medical facilities in the United States. Of the 100 children treated, nine were flown to MGH. As noted earlier in the section on Patient Care Services, the early 2005 relief mission with Project HOPE to help victims of the 2004 tsunami disaster in Southeast Asia was coordinated by Briggs and Larry Ronan, codirector of the Durant Fellowship. Following the Sichuan disaster, an earthquake of magnitude 7.9 that killed more than 80,000 individuals, Briggs and the MGH team joined a Project HOPE mission to provide long-term rehabilitation for crush-injured children, many of whom underwent amputations. In addition to their involvement with the acute medical response to the Haiti earthquake, Briggs, Ronan, and the MGH team worked with several nonprofit organizations to provide long-term assistance to Haiti following the January 2010 earthquake there.

In the early 1980s the National Disaster Medical System (NDMS), a federally coordinated system of disaster response, was established by the U.S. government. In 1985 Briggs helped start one of the first NDMS disaster assistance medical teams, the Boston Disaster Medical Assistance Team (DMAT). The team aided victims of many national disasters, including Hurricane Andrew in Florida (1992) and Hurricane Marilyn in the Virgin Islands (1996), and served as a standby unit for events such as the Olympics and U.S. presidential inaugurations. In 1999 Briggs established the first of three regional "civilian MASH units," formally known as an International Medical Surgical Response Team (IMSuRT). Sponsored by MGH, "IMSuRT East" consists of multidisciplinary medical and surgical specialists and a fully equipped field hospital that can be deployed within 12 hours after a disaster. Other IMSuRTs were established at Harborview Medical Center in Seattle (IMSuRT West) and at the Ryder Trauma Center at the University of Miami (IMSuRT South), using the MGH-sponsored team as a model. These units act as the civilian medical partners for U.S. government disaster response, nationally and internationally. The team has gone to the scene of many natural and man-made disasters, including Ground Zero (2001), Hurricane Katrina (2005), the Bam, Iran, earthquake (2003), and the Haiti earthquake (2010).

Ground Zero was the first deployment for IMSuRT East. Three months before 9/11, a mass casualty drill was conducted at Hanscom Air Force Base in Bedford, Massachusetts. The logistical assets of the U.S. Air Force were coordinated with the medical assets of IMSuRT. The focus of the training was a terrorist attack requiring U.S. military and IMSuRT personnel.

On the morning of September 11, Briggs was in an MGH operating room and could not know what was happening in New York City. For years she had anticipated a domestic terrorist attack, although no one could have imagined jets being flown into the twin towers of the World Trade Center. "Even with all the training you do to respond to these events, you never envision something of this magnitude," she said.[49] Briggs was informed that her team was being activated. Within three hours, Briggs had pulled together components of IMSuRT East and the Metro Boston Disaster Medical Assistance Team. By 6 p.m., about 35 team members, complemented by members of the NDMS Pediatric and Burn Specialty Teams in Boston, left MGH by ground for New York. They did not know exactly where they were headed.

When deployed, those from MGH were no longer officially hospital employees but instead became part-time federal employees on a disaster relief mission. Barbara Walsh, a nurse from White 7, credited the hospital and her coworkers with supporting her emergency work: "It makes you proud to work for an institution that will allow you to participate in something like this."[50]

On the night of September 11, the IMSuRT East team slept in tents at Stewart Air Force Base on the Hudson River, north of New York City. There they met other teams from Rhode Island, New York, and Worcester, Massachusetts.[51] The following afternoon they went to a site near the World Trade Center. One of the team members, Tony Forgione, recalled:

> We arrived in the city, working through the night, unloading equipment and setting up. At 7 AM, we were open and saw patients continuously, 24 hours each day. Being disaster team providers, we treated all types of injuries, including respiratory problems, eye irritation, minor lacerations, chest pains, sprains and fractures and fatigue. We also helped with emotional issues. As the perimeter of Ground Zero stabilized, we were able to establish four more satellite medical stations.
>
> For me, the image that I will never forget happened during the last night of our deployment. As I was going back to the main medical station, I saw about eight firefighters silently, and reverently, carrying a basket stretcher. In it was a body bag. They were bringing one of their own back home. That's the image I will never forget.[52]

Though the number of victims rescued from the rubble was sadly limited, Briggs's MASH unit treated about 500 injuries a day incurred in rescue operations.[53] In the heightened atmosphere of patriotic spirit that followed 9/11, they returned to a heroes' welcome at MGH.[54]

When a massive earthquake devastated Bam, Iran, killing more than 30,000 on December 26, 2003, the IMSuRT East team was activated again, and Briggs led the 10-day mission. She witnessed "such miracles as the rescue of a ninety-seven-year-old Iranian woman who was trapped beneath rubble for nine days and the births of several babies." She said, "One of the most wonderful things was to see the spirit of the people around the camp when a new baby came, because life goes on even in the midst of a devastating disaster."[55]

The broad list of MGH personnel serving in Iran was typical of other deployments:

- Physicians Susan Briggs, Edward George, Annekathryn Goodman, David Lawlor, Jay Schnitzer, Tom MacGillivray
- Nurses Jennifer Albert, Sheila Burke, Lin-Ti Chang, Anthony Forgione, Pamela Griffin, Barbara McGee, Leandra McLean, Jackie Nally, Patricia Owens, Joseph Roche, Maryalyce Romano, Joan Tafe, Barbara Walsh, Brenda Whelan
- Respiratory therapists Robert Goulet, Jesslyn Lenox
- Pharmacist Ronald Gaudette

When Hurricane Katrina hit the Louisiana coast in August 2005, Briggs led another IMSuRT mission, treating casualties for one month in New Orleans and surrounding regions. IMSuRT South was on hand for the inauguration of President

Barack Obama in January 2009, in the event of surprise casualties. Nearly one year later, an earthquake caused unthinkable destruction and death in and around Port-au-Prince, Haiti, and again IMSuRT (East, South, and West) was there. "We never know what we are going to get," said Briggs. "On our first deployment in Haiti we did over 300 surgeries and treated over 3,000 victims in six weeks. Our facility was in one of the worst slums, and we were guarded by 82nd Airborne while we were there." Briggs and the MGH team returned to Haiti later, working with nonprofit organizations.

"Being a doctor," she wrote, "is the best way to avoid the constraints of politics, as medicine is apolitical and allows us to treat all victims, regardless of age, race, nationality."[56] Tom Durant would agree. Humanitarianism is often the only victor in a disaster.

The World outside Your Door

If you wanted to know what the Bulfinch Building was like around the time it opened its doors in 1821, you could do worse than stop by Jean Yawkey Place at 780 Albany Street in Boston's South End. That's where the nation's premier health care plan for the homeless has its headquarters. Stand in the Cary W. Akins Pavilion and watch as Boston's dispossessed and dissociated wander in looking for their doctor, dentist, or psychiatrist. Two centuries ago, the same population, in different clothes, would have appeared at the gates of Boston's new general hospital. There is at least one other difference between then and now: today's doctors to the homeless are all full-time professionals, whereas Warren and Jackson volunteered their services to the hospital.

The Boston Health Care for the Homeless Program (BHCHP) was jump-started at Mass General in the mid-1980s by several characters already introduced, including Tom Durant and John Potts, and by one young physician. Jim O'Connell is too tall to be a leprechaun and too tone-deaf to be a priest, but he shares qualities of both. As the founding doctor of BHCHP and as its president 25 years later, he is a secular Franciscan with a stethoscope, a Marcus Welby in dungarees and work boots. How did Durant and Potts ever know, when they called O'Connell in for a conference in 1985, that he was just the man to run a pioneering program of doctoring in the streets? O'Connell said, "I think Tom Durant knew a sucker when he saw one."

James J. O'Connell grew up in Newport, Rhode Island; attended Notre Dame, where he majored in philosophy; and took a master's in theology at Cambridge University in England, thinking he wanted an academic career teaching the philosophy of religion. Instead, he taught high school and coached basketball in Hawaii for two years; was accepted as a graduate assistant by the political philosopher Hannah Arendt at the New School for Social Research in New York; and, when Arendt died three months after his arrival, bought a barn in Smuggler's Notch, New Hampshire, with some friends. The skiing was great, but after a couple of years, with his "60s conscience" eating at him, O'Connell was ready for something more substantial. He had always been interested in medicine but never did his sciences in college, so when the bug proved persistent, he returned to Rhode Island and took premed courses at Brown. Thinking he wanted to be a country doctor, he applied to med school at the University of Vermont and didn't even get an interview, because of his "advanced" age, 30. Instead, he went to Harvard Medical School, where Daniel Federman was his "most cherished mentor." He began a residency in internal medicine at MGH in 1982 and fell under the influence of the "remarkable" John Stoeckle and James J. Dineen. Said O'Connell, "They were the quintessential primary care doctors, inspiring, totally devoted to their patients."

In "Pod 2" of Internal Medicine Associates, O'Connell encountered a remarkably diverse clientele: wealthy patients of Stoeckle, who flew in from thousands of miles away to be treated by the humble doc from small-town Michigan; homeless drinkers who slept along the Charles and raided garbage cans on Beacon Hill; gypsies who would arrive together by the dozens, even if only one child needed care; a group of call girls from a West End escort service, many of whom had infectious diseases; and, because it was 1982–1984, young men with full-blown AIDS.

Stoeckle would muse, "It was kind of a chaotic practice." O'Connell said of these early experiences, "I thought I had died and gone to heaven. I loved the concept of a hospital that opened its doors to whoever was there, but one that was good enough that it would be seen all over the world and people would fly there to be treated. And John Stoeckle was just fabulous, taking care of everyone."

O'Connell wrote about what happened next: "In the fall of 1984 the Robert Wood Johnson Foundation and the Pew Memorial Trust invited major cities across the country to submit proposals for pilot programs to explore the delivery of health care service to homeless persons. Each city was required to have the support of local government, hospitals, shelters and service agencies. Boston was one of 19 cities awarded four-year demonstration grants, and the Boston Health Care for the Homeless Project was conceived."[57]

In order to qualify, the city of Boston, under Mayor Raymond Flynn, teamed with both MGH and Boston City Hospital (now Boston Medical Center). The program needed a guinea pig, a doctor who would head into the streets looking for homeless people to treat. That was O'Connell. He was worried that Mass General would start identifying him with his patients and marginalize his operation, but here's where Durant and Potts made the difference.

According to O'Connell, "Tom Durant was the first person I heard say that global health begins as you step out the door. While he was doing things overseas, you could walk outside and step over bodies getting into the T station who were literally in the shadows of our hospital. He would say, 'This is a *fascinating* problem! We gotta figure out how to fix it. Can you do that?' He was very convincing, as was John Potts." The chief of medicine persuaded O'Connell that the hospital was serious about making this new commitment to the Boston community. Moreover, he assured O'Connell that health care for the homeless would be an integral part of the academic discipline of internal medicine at MGH: O'Connell would attend on the inpatient wards; he would teach and write; residents eventually would rotate through his service.

But not right away. To begin, the Johnson Foundation grant paid for six staff members—O'Connell, three nurse practitioners, and two case workers—but no building, no lab, not even a fancy van. Their job was to go to where the homeless

Jim O'Connell and Jill Roncarati, a physician's assistant, meet with a patient on the street (courtesy Joshua Touster).

were and treat them there. Some homeless people prefer to stay out of shelters, so O'Connell would have to locate them under bridges, in abandoned buildings and cars. Said O'Connell: "As soon as I got out into the community, I realized that these were very sick people, most of whom had not had access to primary or preventive care, and had only seen emergency rooms. I was overwhelmed by complications of severe and persistent mental illness, as well as substance abuse issues, in addition to their AIDS or their emphysema or their cancer. I was overwhelmed by how complicated it was when someone had no home."

Many of the homeless do take shelter, especially in bitter Boston winters, so the BHCHP established a pilot clinic at the Pine Street Inn, a shelter in the South End. O'Connell was sure that the team of nurses who had been treating Pine Street's clientele would be delighted to have a highly trained doctor joining them. The nurses who looked sternly at him as he entered told O'Connell that he would have to begin by soaking the feet of Pine Street's clients in the anteroom to the shelter. This was a hard lesson but a critical one, he said: "Nothing happens with health care and homeless people unless you can have an enduring one-on-one relationship with them. . . . What the nurses were teaching me was, when you soak feet, it's comforting, and you're at a really respectful distance from someone's personal space. It was pretty interesting to learn that."

One of the longtime nurses at the shelter, Barbara McInnis, became a friend and inspiration to O'Connell. After thinking that he would doctor the homeless for a year, then move on to something else like oncology, O'Connell was hooked. Twenty-five years later, he ran a program with a five-story headquarters on Albany Street, eighty clinics citywide, and a $34 million annual budget. The hours, he said, have always been "way too long," but there are now 17 doctors sharing the burden, many of them chief residents from Boston-area hospitals.

Of course, the social justice reasons for what O'Connell does are compelling, but there are interesting reasons, as well, why work with the homeless fits into an academic medical center. The homeless, he said, are "the canaries in the tunnel" of our health care system, showing where the oxygen is lacking: "Homeless people are large users of the system, and they are the ones who usually point out to us where there are weaknesses in our mainstream systems."

An early example was medical record keeping. How do you track a homeless person's health record as he or she stumbles from emergency room to clinic to shelter and is seen by an unconnected list of doctors, nurses, and social workers? In 1993 O'Connell went to MGH's computer guru, Octo Barnett, and said he needed help. Over the next 18 months, Barnett and Henry Chueh created a computerized record system to track homeless patients, one of the first among the Harvard hospitals. Ten years later, developing a systemwide computerized record system was among the highest priorities for Partners HealthCare.

O'Connell offered two other examples illustrating his canary theory. Homeless people suffer more than most from "triple morbidity," that is, multiple chronic medical problems, such as diabetes, cancer, and AIDS, co-occurring with persistent psychiatric illnesses and active substance abuse. Their teeth are often bad, too. But care for each of these problems is funded separately, by different government agencies. So the BHCHP integrated care across these areas early in its history.

Another important way in which homeless care may be leading mainstream care is in an area that has long been O'Connell's "obsession," medical respite care. He opened the first program in the country with 25 beds nestled in a corner of the Shattuck Shelter in September 1985, with a goal of caring for ill and injured homeless people not sick enough to warrant an inpatient hospital bed, but too sick to be on the streets. As sea changes in the health care system shifted the locus of care from hospitals to home, as hospital stays were shorter and there were more outpatient procedures, homeless persons languished. With help from Partners HealthCare and MGH, BHCHP opened a 104-bed medical respite program named for Barbara McInnis in the new Jean Yawkey Place in 2008, although the demand still overwhelms supply: five to 10 times more beds are still needed. O'Connell said:

Jim O'Connell with a patient at the Yawkey Center, headquarters of the Boston Health Care for the Homeless Program (courtesy Joshua Touster).

We need the health care system to give us a place for people who are too sick to be on the street when you kick them out of the hospital. Inpatient stays have been reduced so dramatically that homeless people are discharged to the streets way too early now, when you are not ready to be anywhere but home and recovering. I'm going to bet that as time goes on, respite care will become part of the mainstream, because lots of poor and marginally housed people when they get out of the hospital are still too ill to be home.

O'Connell admitted that it can be frustrating treating people you know are going to relapse into the habits and homelessness that got them sick in the first place:

I struggle with that. But what happens to people who work with us is this. In the first few months, you become radicalized. You say, "I can't take care of someone who's homeless, this is absurd that we as a society are allowing this to happen," and you begin to fight the system. But the people who make it here are the ones who finally put up the white flag and realize, "I'm just a doctor." Alone we cannot change society or eliminate poverty, but we can strive for excellence in the care of our patients and work to minimize suffering and instill hope. We are here to care for people, not to change or judge them, and there is surprising joy and wonder in sharing in the journeys of these courageous people.

"I have a feeling that's not a bad Mass General tradition," O'Connell added, "just taking care of people as best we can." The philosopher-turned-doctor admitted that in addition to Durant and Stoeckle and Dineen and Federman, he has had another inspiration, Richard Cabot, the founder of MGH's Social Service Department a century ago. "Cabot took a real beating for wanting to get involved with the community," O'Connell said. "He was passed over for the Jackson Professorship. But he knew what it was all about: I can't treat my patients well unless I know where they live and understand the struggles of their lives."

Why These Three?

A skeptic might ask: Why highlight these three humanitarian doctors—Durant, Briggs, and O'Connell—here at the end of a 200-year history, when literally thousands of other MGH professionals never doffed their Harvard hats or left the cozy confines of Fruit and Blossom streets? The answer is easy: because this place made way for them. Maybe it took a century, beginning in 1811, for a self-satisfied Brahmin institution to begin stepping out into the world, but even then the likes of Richard Cabot, as Brahmin as they come, showed what could be done when the gates of the main campus were thrown open.

Then in 1912, one century along, came David Edsall, the first non-Bostonian leader. Five years later, when America entered World War I, Massachusetts General Hospital sent a whole mobile hospital to France, and a quarter century later volunteers were needed to keep the Boston campus lit because so many professional men and women clamored to serve overseas again. After the war women and Jews and African Americans and Hispanics came onto the staff and eventually took leadership positions. Meanwhile, community health centers opened in Charlestown, Chelsea, and Revere.

The world pressed in on the old place, forcing it to change. As the 1980s dawned, a German chemical company offered a deal. A terrible new epidemic sent infectious disease experts back to the lab—and one young doc to South Africa to search for an AIDS vaccine. And the third oldest general hospital in the United States took the longest leap of all: across the river to new research facilities in Charlestown. Tom Durant was trotting around the globe by this time, while Susan Briggs was rescuing crushed children in Armenia and Jim O'Connell was searching under bridges for people to care for. When the staff diversified in a big way at the end of the twentieth century and the beginning of the twenty-first, Massachusetts General Hospital was finally a hospital without borders. The world came to Mass General, and Mass General served the world.

So for just a moment, let Durant, Briggs, and O'Connell stand alone here at the end of the story. Who better?

The Lunder Building, under construction.

WHERE NOW FROM HERE?

When in distress, every man becomes our neighbor.
—*Circular letter, 1810*

*Guided by the needs of our patients and their families, we aim
to deliver the very best health care in a safe, compassionate
environment; to advance that care through innovative research
and education; and to improve the health and well-being
of the diverse communities we serve.*
—*MGH mission statement, 2008*

B OSTON IN THE TWENTY-FIRST CENTURY is a city confident of itself. The
greatest municipal engineering project in American history, the Big Dig,
was completed in 2005. Today, instead of an ugly, corroded snake called the
Central Artery curling through downtown, open space and fresh air brighten the
urban community. A once-Protestant enclave, which added Catholic and Jewish neighborhoods in the nineteenth century, is now a world capital, as dozens of
colleges and universities assure a diverse annual immigration. In 2009 Boston's
first Italian-American mayor, Thomas M. Menino, won reelection for an unprec-
edented fifth four-year term, a measure of the city's self-satisfaction. If that weren't
enough to bust Boston's buttons, the Red Sox, so long a bridesmaid, won two
World Series championships in the first decade of the twenty-first century. Somewhere Tom Durant is smiling.

Boston's largest civilian employer and one of its crown jewels, Massachusetts
General Hospital, had plenty of reason for confidence as the millennium dawned.
At the northern edge of a growing network, a new outpatient center opened in
Danvers, Massachusetts, 20 miles north of Boston, in 2009. Scheduled to begin
admitting patients in 2011, the 10-story Lunder Building will add more than a half a
million square feet to the core city campus, with a new emergency department, five
inpatient floors, and three floors of state-of-the-art operating suites that will include
such features as intraoperative MRI. There will also be four floors below ground,
including two for radiation oncology and two for systems supporting clinical operations. A remarkable $1.5 billion development campaign, larger than any previous
effort at a Boston institution, was preparing to fund this and many other lifesaving
initiatives.

The hospital's mission, as formally updated in a 2008 statement, is being fulfilled on every count. MGH is the highest-funded biomedical research facility based at an American hospital; it is the oldest and still the most prestigious Harvard teaching hospital; and for every neighbor in need—from an international patient with a rare condition to a homeless person with aches and pains—it lacks only enough beds to serve core human needs for health and quality of life.

Still, clouds are gathering. U.S. President Barack Obama came to office in 2009 with a mandate to provide health care for all Americans, a challenge not easily met and never without consequences. How would shifts in American medical priorities force change at an institution as complex as Mass General? Would Obamacare be another Medicare, or something out of Dean Clark's visionary playbook? Time will tell; the only certainty is uncertainty. MGH's former president Jim Mongan said it well: "As a nation, we want health care, but we're not sure we want to pay for it. Whether or not we arrive at socialized medicine any time soon, there will be more constraint on expenditures. In my career health care costs went from 7 percent of gross domestic product to 17 percent, and budgets keep going up. The cost squeeze is going to be greater and greater."

In Boston the very success of Partners HealthCare was drawing renewed attention from the media and government watchdogs. Was Partners, formed under intense financial pressures in the mid-1990s, now too successful, too big, too strong? Competitors in the marketplace wanted to make that argument, not without motives of their own. It would be ironic, though not surprising, if criticism of Partners comes to a boil just as economic woes ratchet up the pressure—once again—on academic medical centers.

There are things you can control and things you can't. "The key," said Sam Thier, Mongan's predecessor, "is taking what's best about this place—the quality of its people and its research—and keeping the remembrance." Thier said that he has seen the likes of Mass General at only one other institution: Johns Hopkins. Both medical centers, he said, are actuated by the core belief that "we take better care of patients than anybody else." MGH is in an enviable position as it enters its third century; the challenge will be to capitalize on opportunities while remaining true to the mission.

No one seems more focused on that mission than Thier and Mongan's successor, Peter Slavin, the current MGH president. Slavin has seen many changes in his 30 years at the hospital. "The MGH I knew as a trainee in the 1980s," he said, "was committed to the mission, but there was a certain arrogance about the place, a feeling that patients were fortunate to receive care here. Now it's our privilege to take care of them, not vice versa." Slavin continued: "In the past 10 or 15 years, through many people's efforts, I think we have developed a very cooperative culture here. Everyone seems to get along well and is focused on advancing the mission; collaboration across departments and disciplines is very important."

Slavin concluded by identifying two keys for future success: infectious enthusiasm for the mission of patient care, and cooperation and communication at all levels of the organization. Still a surprisingly young president in 2011, Slavin, together with David Torchiana and the rest of the MGH leadership team, seemed poised to "keep the remembrance" and to advance the mission.

NOTES

. . . .

Prologue

1. Except where noted, all direct quotations from personnel and observers of Mass General are drawn from personal interviews conducted by the authors. A list of interviewees is provided in the bibliography.

2. Earle W. Wilkins Jr., "Emergency Ward," in *The Massachusetts General Hospital, 1955–1980*, ed. Castleman et al. (Boston: Little, Brown, 1983), pp. 149–153.

Chapter 1

1. Behind New York, Philadelphia, and Baltimore, according to the U.S. Census for 1810.

2. For an early history of medical education in Boston, see Henry K. Beecher and Mark D. Altschule, *Medicine at Harvard: The First 300 Years* (Hanover, N.H.: University Press of New England, 1977), chaps. 1 and 2.

3. Edward Warren, *The Life of John Collins Warren, M.D.* (Boston: Ticknor and Fields, 1860), p. 35.

4. Ibid., p. 46.

5. James Jackson Putnam, *A Memoir of Dr. James Jackson* (Boston: Houghton Mifflin, 1905), p. 166.

6. Stephen A. Hoffmann, *Under the Ether Dome: A Physician's Apprenticeship at Massachusetts General Hospital* (1986; repr., New York: Carroll, 1990), p. 257.

7. Putnam, *A Memoir of Dr. James Jackson*, p. 168.

8. Ibid., pp. 161–162. "Potable gold" was a legendary alchemical elixir.

9. Oliver Wendell Holmes, quoted in Justin Winsor, ed., *The Memorial History of Boston*, 4 vols. (Boston: James R. Osgood, 1880–1881), 4:566.

10. H. H. A. Beach, "The Surgical Records of the Massachusetts General Hospital before 1846," in Frederic A. Washburn, *The Massachusetts General Hospital: Its Development, 1900–1935* (Boston: Houghton Mifflin, 1939), p. 546.

11. Ibid.

12. Rhoda Truax, *The Doctors Warren of Boston: First Family of Surgery* (Boston: Houghton Mifflin, 1968), p. 157.

13. Hoffman, *Under the Ether Dome*, p. 255.

14. From the "margins of one of [Bowditch's] books," quoted in Truax, *The Doctors Warren*, p. 156.

15. Hoffman, *Under the Ether Dome*, p. 255.

16. James Jackson, *Letters to a Young Physician Just Entering upon Practice* (Boston: Phillips, Sampson and Co., 1855), p. 2.

17. Truax, *The Doctors Warren*, p. 137.

18. Beecher and Altschule, *Medicine at Harvard*, p. 48.

19. No longer on the Boston map, Leverett Street ran north and east of today's MGH campus.

20. Beecher and Altschule, *Medicine at Harvard*, p. 12.

21. Nathaniel Ingersoll Bowditch, *History of the Massachusetts General Hospital*, 2nd ed. (Boston: Printed by the Trustees, 1872), p. 3.

22. Ibid., pp. 3–4.

23. Ibid., p. 8.

24. Ibid., pp. 3–12.

25. Ibid., p. 17.

26. Leonard K. Eaton, *New England Hospitals, 1790–1833* (Ann Arbor: University of Michigan Press, 1957), p. 52, quoting an article in the *Boston Daily Advertiser*, December 25, 1816.

27. Alex Beam, *Gracefully Insane: Life and Death inside America's Premier Mental Hospital* (New York: Public Affairs, 2001), pp. 10–11.

28. S. B. Sutton, *Crossroads in Psychiatry: A History of McLean Hospital* (Washington, D.C.: American Psychiatric Press, 1986), pp. 37–38.

29. Eaton, *New England Hospitals*, pp. 82–83.

30. Hoffmann, *Under the Ether Dome*, pp. 249–250.

31. Harold Kirker, *The Architecture of Charles Bulfinch* (Cambridge: Harvard University Press, 1998), p. 312.

32. Bowditch, *History of the Massachusetts General Hospital*, pp. 39–40.

33. Hoffman, *Under the Ether Dome*, p. 250. See also Kirker, *Architecture of Charles Bulfinch*, pp. 311–317.

34. Bowditch, *History of the Massachusetts General Hospital*, pp. 46–47.

35. Sutton, *Crossroads in Psychiatry*, pp. 31–32.

36. Nina Fletcher Little, *Early Years of the McLean Hospital, Recorded in the Journal of George William Folsom, Apothecary at the Asylum in Charlestown* (Boston: Francis A. Countway Library of Medicine, 1972), p. 29.

37. Ibid., p. 127.

38. Beam, *Gracefully Insane*, pp. 21–22.

39. Bowditch, *History of the Massachusetts General Hospital*, pp. 73–74.

40. Little, *Early Years of the McLean Hospital*, p. 14.

41. Bowditch, *History of the Massachusetts General Hospital*, p. 77.

42. Sutton, *Crossroads in Psychiatry*, p. 54.

43. "Historical Sketch of McLean," folder, McLean Hospital Archives.

44. Bowditch, *History of the Massachusetts General Hospital*, p. 105.

45. Ibid., p. 121.

46. Ibid., p. 124.

47. Ibid., pp. 365–366.

48. Claude E. Welch, *A Twentieth-Century Surgeon: My Life in the Massachusetts General Hospital* (Boston: The Hospital, 1992), pp. 42–43.

49. Bowditch, *History of the Massachusetts General Hospital*, p. 96.

50. James Jackson, *Another Letter to a Young Physician* (Boston: Ticknor and Fields, 1861), pp. 125–126.

51. Bowditch, *History of the Massachusetts General Hospital*, p. 63.

52. Ibid., pp. 63–68.

53. Ibid., p. 148.

54. Ibid., p. 175.

55. Ibid., p. 181.

56. Ibid., pp. 181–182.

57. Putnam, *A Memoir of Dr. James Jackson*, pp. 307–308.

58. Bowditch, *History of the Massachusetts General Hospital*, p. 140.

59. Warren, *Life of John Collins Warren*, p. 276.

60. Truax, *The Doctors Warren*, p. 183.

61. Bowditch, *History of the Massachusetts General Hospital*, p. 136.

62. Holmes quoted in Winsor, *The Memorial History of Boston*, 4:569.

Chapter 2

1. Julie M. Fenster, *Ether Day: The Strange Tale of America's Greatest Medical Discovery and the Haunted Men Who Made It* (New York: HarperCollins, 2001), pp. 33–76.

2. Ibid., pp. 124–172.

3. Ibid., pp. 81–94.

4. Ibid., pp. 74–80.

5. Ibid., p. 75.

6. Ibid., p. 217.

7. Bucknam McPeek, "Anesthesia before Beecher," in *This Is No Humbug! Reminiscences of the Department of Anesthesia at the Massachusetts General Hospital—A History*, ed. Richard J. Kitz (Boston: MGH Department of Anesthesia, 2003), p. 76.

8. Ibid., p. 78.

9. The discussion of events leading up to and surrounding Ether Day is based largely on information from Bowditch, *History of the Massachusetts General Hospital*, pp. 215–348.

10. *Pup* is old MGH slang for house officer or intern.

11. Washburn, *Massachusetts General Hospital*, p. 352.

12. J. M. T. Finney, *A Surgeon's Life: The Autobiography of J. M. T. Finney* (New York: G. P. Putnam's Sons, 1940), p. 78.

13. The British spelling was favored in the early days.

14. Washburn, *Massachusetts General Hospital*, p. 353.

15. McPeek, "Anesthesia before Beecher," p. 87.

16. Francis D. Moore, *A Miracle and a Privilege: Recounting a Half Century of Surgical Advance* (Washington, D.C.: National Academy Press, 1995), p. 57.

17. Private hospitals like St. Margaret's were often called *nursing homes* in the nineteenth century.

18. McPeek, "Anesthesia before Beecher," p. 91.

19. Curiously, Harvard clings to the diphthong *ae* in the words *anaesthesia* and *anaesthesiology*, perhaps in deference to Oliver Wendell Holmes, who coined the terms in 1846 as dean of the medical school. Today MGH spells them without the diphthong.

20. "Henry Knowles Beecher: Pioneer in Anaesthesiology and Medical Ethics: Faculty of Medicine—Memorial Minute," *Harvard Gazette*, January 13, 1978, reprinted in Kitz, *This Is No Humbug!* p. 106.

21. Bucknam McPeek, "Personal Memories of HKB," in Kitz, *This Is No Humbug!* p. 96.

22. Edward Lowenstein, "A Journey of the Heart: Cardiac Anesthesia," in Kitz, *This Is No Humbug!* p. 270.

23. George E. Battit, "Henry K. Beecher and the Early Years of the Anesthesia Service," in Kitz, *This Is No Humbug!* p. 108.

24. McPeek, "Personal Memories of HKB," p. 96.

25. Ibid., pp. 96–97.

26. Michael Gionfriddo, "Henry K. Beecher—His Life in Part, The Kansas Years," in *Enduring Contributions of Henry K. Beecher to Medicine, Science, and Society*, ed. Edward Lowenstein and Bucknam McPeek (Philadelphia: Lippincott, Williams and Wilkins, 2007), p. 144.

27. Bucknam McPeek, "Pain," in Kitz, *This Is No Humbug!* p. 225.

28. Edward Lowenstein, "A Journey of the Heart: Cardiac Anesthesia," in Kitz, *This Is No Humbug!* p. 270.

29. Henry K. Beecher and Donald P. Todd, "A Study of the Deaths Associated with Anesthesia and Surgery," *Annals of Surgery* 140.1 (July 1954): 2–33.

30. Beecher and Todd, "A Study of Deaths Associated with Anesthesia and Surgery," reprinted in Lowenstein and McPeek, *Enduring Contributions of Henry K. Beecher*, p. 3.

31. John P. Bunker, "The Contribution of Anesthesia to Surgical Mortality," in Lowenstein and McPeek, *Enduring Contributions of Henry K. Beecher*, p. 11.

32. Henry K. Beecher, "Ethics and Clinical Research," *New England Journal of Medicine* (hereafter *NEJM*) 274.24 (June 1966): 1354–1360.

33. David Rothman, *Strangers at the Bedside: A History of How Law and Bioethics Transformed Medical Decision Making*, 3rd ed. (New Brunswick, N.J.: AldineTransaction, 2008).

34. Lara Freidenfelds, "Recruiting Allies for Reform: Henry Knowles Beecher's 'Ethics and Clinical Research,'" in Lowenstein and McPeek, *Enduring Contributions of Henry K. Beecher*, p. 93.

35. Ibid., p. 94.

36. Ibid., p. 97.

37. H. K. Beecher et al., "A Definition of Irreversible Coma: Report of the Ad Hoc Committee of the Harvard Medical School to Examine the Definition of Brain Death," *Journal of the American Medical Association* (hereafter *JAMA*) 205 (1968): 337–340.

38. Edward Lowenstein, "Defining Brain Death: Motivations and Future Directions," in Lowenstein and McPeek, *Enduring Contributions of Henry K. Beecher*, p. 132.

39. McPeek, "Personal Memories of HKB," p. 97.

40. Nathaniel W. Faxon, *The Massachusetts General Hospital, 1935–1955* (Cambridge: Harvard University Press, 1959), p. 22.

41. McPeek, "Personal Memories of HKB," pp. 95–96.

42. Hening Pontoppidan, "The Development of Respiratory Care and the Respiratory Intensive Care Unit (RICU): A Written Oral History," in Kitz, *This Is No Humbug!* pp. 152–153.

43. A condition in which the lips, fingers, and toes appear blue.

44. Pontoppidan, "The Development of Respiratory Care," p. 154.

45. Ibid., p. 159.

46. Richard J. Kitz, "The Early Years, 1970–1980: Toward a More Influential Department," in Kitz, *This Is No Humbug!* p. 33.

47. Bucknam McPeek, "Personal Memories of HKB: Reflections after 50 Years," *International Anesthesiology Clinics* 46.1 (Winter 2008): 221–232.

48. Keith W. Miller, "Unconscious Journey: Molecular Mechanisms of Anesthesia Research," in Kitz, *This Is No Humbug!* p. 358.

49. Kitz, "The Early Years, 1970–1980," p. 29.

50. Richard J. Kitz, "'In The Beginning, 1969, In the Beginning . . . The First Day'—September 1969," in Kitz, *This Is No Humbug!* p. 15.

51. Kitz, "The Early Years, 1970–1980," p. 39.

52. Jeffrey B. Cooper, "Preventable Anesthesia Mishaps: A Study of Human Factors," *Anesthesiology* 49 (1978): 399–406.

53. Atul Gawande, "When Doctors Make Mistakes," *New Yorker*, February 1, 1999, p. 40.

54. Howard L. Fields, "In Memoriam: Patrick D. Wall, DM, FRS, 1925–2001," www.iasp-pain.org /AM/Template.cfm?Section=Home&Template= /CM/HTMLDisplay.cfm&ContentID=1267.

55. Persistent pulmonary hypertension of the newborn.

56. Letter shared with the author by Zapol, June 2010.

57. William Sturgis Bigelow, *A Memoir of Henry Jacob Bigelow, A.M., M.D., LL.D.* (Boston: Little, Brown, 1894), p. 3. Contained in that volume is Reginald H. Fitz, "Henry Jacob Bigelow: A Tribute of Respect Inspired by Affection, Admiration, and Obligation," which originally appeared in *Boston Medical and Surgical Journal*, November 27, 1890.

58. Jacob Bigelow, "A Discourse on Self-Limited Diseases. Delivered before the Massachusetts Medical Society, at Their Annual Meeting, May 27, 1835" (Boston: N. Hale, 1835).

59. Ibid., p. 8.

60. Oliver Wendell Holmes and Reginald H. Fitz, *A Memoir of Henry Jacob Bigelow* (Boston: Little, Brown, 1894), pp. 9–10.

61. Ibid., pp. 10–11.

62. Ibid., pp. 49–50.

63. Ibid., p. 13.

64. Ibid., p. 66.

65. Ibid., pp. 26–27.

66. James C. White, *Sketches from My Life* (Cambridge, Mass.: Riverside Press, 1914), p. 53.

67. Ibid., pp. 53–55.

68. Ibid., pp. 55–56.

69. Holmes and Fitz, *A Memoir of Henry Jacob Bigelow*, pp. 68–69.

70. Bowditch, *History of the Massachusetts General Hospital*, pp. 196–197.

71. Holmes and Fitz, *A Memoir of Henry Jacob Bigelow*, pp. 68–70.

72. Bowditch, *History of the Massachusetts General Hospital*, p. 22.

73. This discussion of the Webster-Parkman murder is drawn largely from Holmes and Fitz, *A Memoir of Henry Jacob Bigelow*, pp. 115–119. Other sources include Robert Sullivan, *The Disappearance of Dr. Parkman* (Boston: Little, Brown, 1971), and

Simon Schama, *Dead Certainties* (New York: Alfred A. Knopf, 1991).

74. Bowditch, *History of the Massachusetts General Hospital*, p. 588.

75. Ibid., p. 619.

76. Ibid., p. 580.

77. Ibid., p. 583.

78. George E. Ellis, *Memoir of Luther V. Bell, M.D., LL.D.* (Boston: J. Wilson, 1863), pp. 68–69.

79. Holmes and Fitz, *A Memoir of Henry Jacob Bigelow*, pp. 126–129.

80. Warren and Churchill, *To Work in the Vineyard of Surgery*, p. 61.

81. Ibid., p. 60.

82. Ibid., p. 57.

83. Ibid., p. 59.

84. Ibid., pp. 59–60.

85. Sara E. Parsons, *History of the Massachusetts General Hospital Training School for Nurses* (Boston: Whitcomb and Barrows, 1922), pp. 17–18.

86. Ibid., p. 4.

87. Ibid., p. 7.

88. Ibid., pp. 6–7.

89. Sylvia Perkins, *A Centennial Review of the Massachusetts General Hospital Training School of Nursing, 1873–1973* (Boston: MGH Nurses Alumnae Association, 1975), pp. 9–10.

90. Grace Whiting Myers, *History of the Massachusetts General Hospital: June, 1872, to December, 1900* (Boston: Griffith-Stillings Press, 1929), pp. 30–31.

91. Perkins, *A Centennial Review*, p. 11.

92. Parsons, *History of the Training School for Nurses*, p. 21.

93. Myers, *History of the Massachusetts General Hospital*, p. 45.

94. Ibid., p. 61.

95. Perkins, *A Centennial Review*, p. 14.

96. Myers, *History of the Massachusetts General Hospital*, p. 58.

97. Ibid., p. 105.

98. Parsons, *History of the Training School for Nurses*, pp. 86–88.

99. Myers, *History of the Massachusetts General Hospital*, p. 56.

100. C. Macfie Campbell, "History of Insanity during the Past Century with Special Reference to the McLean Hospital," in *A Memorial and Historical Volume of the Massachusetts General Hospital*, ed. Justin Winsor (Boston: Massachusetts General Hospital, 1921), pp. 51–52.

101. Myers, *History of the Massachusetts General Hospital*, p. 163.

102. MGH annual report, 1893, p. 8.

103. Perkins, *A Centennial Review*, p. 7.

104. Ibid., pp. 22–23.

105. Much of the information about the Institute of Health Professions is drawn from the program of the MGH Institute of Health Professions 30th Commencement Ceremony, May 8, 2010, pp. 2–3.

106. Warren and Churchill, *To Work in the Vineyard of Surgery*, pp. 75–78.

107. Ibid., p. 76.

108. Finney, *A Surgeon's Life*, p. 83.

109. Ibid.

110. Warren and Churchill, *To Work in the Vineyard of Surgery*, p. 81.

111. Ibid., p. 77.

112. Ibid., p. 128.

113. Ibid., p. 13.

114. Ibid., pp. 145–146.

115. Finney, *A Surgeon's Life*, p. 68.

116. Ibid., p. 73.

117. Ibid., pp. 74–75.

118. Myers, *History of the Massachusetts General Hospital*, p. 159.

119. Warren and Churchill, *To Work in the Vineyard of Surgery*, p. 167.

120. Ibid., pp. 167–168.

121. Carter Rowe, *Lest We Forget: Orthopaedics at the Massachusetts General Hospital and Ward I, 1900–1996* (Dublin, N.H.: William L. Bauhan, 1996), pp. 1–3.

122. Washburn, *Massachusetts General Hospital*, p. 328.

123. Rowe, *Lest We Forget*, p. 36.

124. Ibid., p. 15.

125. Washburn, *Massachusetts General Hospital*, p. 329.

126. Rowe, *Lest We Forget*, p. 56.

127. Ibid., p. 58.

128. Washburn, *Massachusetts General Hospital*, p. 329.

129. Built between 1848 and 1851 just southwest of the MGH campus, the facility remained a jail until 1990. In 2007, redesigned, it opened as a 300-room luxury hotel.

130. Material on Codman is drawn from Bill Mallon, *Ernest Amory Codman: The End Result of a Life in Medicine* (Philadelphia: W. B. Saunders, 2000).

131. Rowe, *Lest We Forget*, p. 5.

132. Ibid., p. 4.

133. Mallon, *Ernest Amory Codman*, p. 57.

134. Washburn, *Massachusetts General Hospital*, p. 83.

135. Mallon, *Ernest Amory Codman*, pp. 62–63.

136. Ibid., pp. 3, 71–82.

137. Ibid., p. 165.

138. Rowe, *Lest We Forget*, p. 72.

139. Ibid., pp. 49–50.

140. Ibid., p. 22.

141. As this book was going to press, Herndon was completing a comprehensive history of the Orthopaedic Department, and the authors had the benefit of his generous input.

142. Rowe, *Lest We Forget*, p. 90.

143. Ibid., p. 65.

144. Ibid., pp. 84–86.

145. Ibid., pp. 90–91.

146. Ibid., p. 88.

147. The history of sports medicine at MGH is drawn from Bertram Zarins, "History of the MGH Sports Medicine Service," www2.massgeneral.org/sports/history.html.

148. Harry E. Rubash, *Orthopaedic Journal at Harvard Medical School* 5 (2003), www.orthojournalhms.org/volume5/mgh/index.asp.

149. Bowditch, *History of the Massachusetts General Hospital*, p. 637.

150. Myers, *History of the Massachusetts General Hospital*, pp. 28–29.

151. Ibid., pp. 35–36.

152. Ibid., pp. 36–41.

153. In his memoir Francis D. Moore noted that as late as 1935, when he entered Harvard Medical School, "sent to Allen Street" still connoted patient death. In 2010 some active MGH employees recalled this usage.

154. Welch, *A Twentieth-Century Surgeon*, p. 335.

155. The full text of "Allen Street" was found in the footnotes to Claude Welch's memoir, *A Twentieth-Century Surgeon*, pp. 336–338. It was first published in *Aesculapiad*, the Harvard Medical School yearbook, in 1937.

156. Myers, *History of the Massachusetts General Hospital*, p. 74.

157. Ibid., pp. 63–64.

158. Ibid., pp. 72–84.

159. Ibid., pp. 97–98.

160. Ibid., p. 110.

161. Ibid., pp. 129–134.

162. Ibid., pp. 160–161.

163. Ibid., p. 167.

164. Ibid., p. 170.

165. Ibid., p. 43.

166. Ibid., p. 65. See also Sutton, *Crossroads in Psychiatry*, pp. 129–131.

167. Myers, *History of the Massachusetts General Hospital*, p. 76.

168. Ibid., pp. 86, 91.

169. Beam, *Gracefully Insane*, p. 175.

170. Myers, *History of the Massachusetts General Hospital*, pp. 143–144.

171. Beam, *Gracefully Insane*, pp. 64–66.

172. Sutton, *Crossroads in Psychiatry*, p. 131.

173. Holmes and Fitz, *A Memoir of Henry Jacob Bigelow*, pp. 74–75.

174. Warren, *Life of John Collins Warren*, 2:359.

175. Myers, *History of the Massachusetts General Hospital*, p. 161.

176. Washburn, *Massachusetts General Hospital*, p. 118.

177. "Pathology," in Benjamin Castleman, David C. Crockett, and S. B. Sutton, eds., *The Massachusetts General Hospital, 1955–1980* (Boston: Little, Brown, 1983), p. 316.

178. Ibid., pp. 313–315.

179. Holmes and Fitz, *A Memoir of Henry Jacob Bigelow*, p. 37.

180. Ibid., p. 61.

181. Ibid.

182. Ibid., pp. 59–60.

183. Ibid., p. 40.

184. Henry Jacob Bigelow, "Fees in Hospitals," *Boston Medical and Surgical Journal* 120.16 (April 18, 1889): 377–378.

185. Holmes and Fitz, *A Memoir of Henry Jacob Bigelow*, p. 66.

186. Ibid., pp. 57–58.

187. Ibid., p. 170.

188. Ibid., p. 172.

Chapter 3

1. Washburn, *Massachusetts General Hospital*, p. 77.

2. Ibid., p. 78.

3. Ibid., pp. 80–81.

4. Ibid., p. 81.

5. Finney, *A Surgeon's Life*, p. 88.

6. Maurice Richardson to William Sturgis Bigelow, December 26, 1893, in Vogel, *The Invention of the Modern Hospital*, p. 78.

7. Winsor, *The Memorial History of Boston*, 4:569.

8. This section is based largely on Robert J. Allison, *A Short History of Boston* (Beverly, Mass.: Commonwealth Editions, 2004).

9. Cleveland Amory, *The Proper Bostonians* (New York: E. P. Dutton, 1947), pp. 40, 39.

10. Robert J. Allison, *A Short History of Boston*, pp. 87–89.

11. Vogel, *The Invention of the Modern Hospital*, p. 31.

12. Ibid., p. 30.

13. Ibid., p. 103.

14. Ibid., p. 129.

15. Ibid., p. 130.

16. Ibid., p. 88.

17. Ibid., p. 92.

18. Ibid., p. 83.

19. Washburn, *Massachusetts General Hospital*, p. 137.

20. Ibid., p. 175.

21. Ibid., p. 140.

22. Ibid., p. 139.

23. Otha W. Linton, *Radiology at Massachusetts General Hospital: 1896–2000* (Boston: General Hospital Corp., 2001), p. 10.

24. Ibid., p. 99.

25. Washburn, *Massachusetts General Hospital*, p. 140.

26. John Macy, *Walter James Dodd: A Biographical Sketch* (Boston: Houghton Mifflin, 1918), 54–56. See also Linton, *Radiology at Massachusetts General Hospital*, pp. 6–17.

27. Washburn, *Massachusetts General Hospital*, p. 140.

28. Ibid., p. 179.

29. Linton, *Radiology at Massachusetts General Hospital*, p. 14.

30. Ibid., p. 17.

31. Laurence D. Robbins, "The Department of Radiology," in Faxon, *Massachusetts General Hospital*, p. 288.

32. Ibid., p. 290.

33. Linton, *Radiology at Massachusetts General Hospital*, p. 48.

34. Ibid., p. 21.

35. "Radiology," in Castleman et al., *Massachusetts General Hospital*, p. 324.

36. Linton, *Radiology at Massachusetts General Hospital*, p. 117.

37. Ibid., p. 111.

38. Ibid., p. 118.

39. Ibid., p. 139.

40. Ibid., p. 159.

41. J. W. Belliveau, D. N. Kennedy Jr., R. C. McKinstry, B. R. Buchbinder, R. M. Weisskoff, M. S. Cohen, J. M. Vevea, T. J. Brady, and B. R. Rosen, "Functional Mapping of the Human Visual Cortex by Magnetic Resonance Imaging," *Science* 254 (November 1, 1991): 716–719.

42. Linton, *Radiology at Massachusetts General Hospital*, p. 211; R. Weissleder, "Molecular Imaging: Exploring the Next Frontier," *Radiology* 212.3 (September 1999): 609–614.

43. Washburn, *Massachusetts General Hospital*, p. 82.

44. Ibid., p. 83.

45. Ibid., p. 84.

46. Ibid., p. 90.

47. Ibid., p. 92.

48. Ibid.

49. J. Gordon Scannell, "Edward D. Churchill," in Castleman et al., *Massachusetts General Hospital*, p. 204.

50. *Boston Evening Transcript*, April 21, 1876, quoted in Vogel, *The Invention of the Modern Hospital*, p. 10.

51. Washburn, *Massachusetts General Hospital*, p. 240.

52. Ibid., p. 241

53. See ibid.: "[The Trustees] speak of their concern at seeing salaries provided for physicians on full-time duty at other hospitals by one of the great Foundations and their fear that by these means the best of the Hospital's young men would be drawn to other cities."

54. Vogel, *The Invention of the Modern Hospital*, p. 114.

55. Washburn, *Massachusetts General Hospital*, p. 242.

56. Ibid., p. 243.

57. Ibid., p. 244.

58. Ibid., p. 243.

59. Haven Emerson, *The Baker Memorial* (New York: Commonwealth Fund, 1941), p. 3.

60. Ibid.

61. Ibid., p. 9.

62. Ibid., p. 4.

63. Ibid., p. 14.

64. Biographical details of Richard Cabot's life are drawn from T. Andrew Dodds, "Richard Cabot: Medical Reformer during the Progressive Era (1890–1920)," *Annals of Internal Medicine* 119.5 (September 1, 1993): 417–422.

65. Richard Cabot, "Diagnostic and Prognostic Importance of Leucocytosis," *Boston Medical and Surgical Journal* 130 (1894): 277–282.

66. Details of Richard Cabot's practice are drawn from Christopher Crenner, *Private Practice: In the Early Twentieth-Century Medical Office of Dr. Richard Cabot* (Baltimore: Johns Hopkins University Press, 2005).

67. "Cabot," in *Dictionary of American Biography* (*DAB*).

68. Richard C. Cabot's notebooks, Harvard University Archives, as quoted in Dodds, "Richard Cabot," p. 417.

69. Ibid., p. 419.

70. Washburn, *Massachusetts General Hospital*, p. 115.

71. See Jeffrey L. Cruikshank, *A Delicate Experiment: The Harvard Business School, 1908–1945* (Boston: Harvard Business School Press, 1987).

72. Richard C. Cabot, *Social Service and the Art of Healing* (New York: Moffat, Yard, 1909), quoted in Dodds, "Richard Cabot," p. 419.

73. "Cabot," in *DAB*.

74. Aub and Hapgood, *Pioneer in Modern Medicine*, p. 129.

75. Dodds, "Richard Cabot," pp. 419–420.

76. Richard C. Cabot, "The Physician's Responsibility for the Nostrum Evil," *JAMA* 47 (July–December 1906): 982.

77. Paul Dudley White, "Obituary, Richard Clarke Cabot, 1863–1939," *NEJM* 220.25 (June 22, 1939): 1049–1052.

78. Crenner, *Private Practice*, pp. 189–195. The story of Ted's death is told in beautiful, excruciating detail.

79. Ibid., pp. 194–195.

80. Aub and Hapgood, *Pioneer in Modern Medicine*, p. 138.

81. Welch, *A Twentieth-Century Surgeon*, p. 55.

82. Dodds, "Richard Cabot," p. 421.

83. Aub and Hapgood, *Pioneer in Modern Medicine*, p. 130.

84. Ibid., p. 133.

85. Ibid., p. 131.

86. Ibid., p. 2.

87. Ibid., p. 7.

88. Ibid., p. 8.

89. Ibid., p. 17.

90. Ibid., p. 21.

91. Ibid., pp. 24–25.

92. David L. Edsall, "The Clinician, the Hospital, and the Medical School," *Boston Medical and Surgical Journal* 167 (February 29, 1912): 315–323, quoted in Aub and Hapgood, *Pioneer in Modern Medicine*, p. 104.

93. Aub and Hapgood, *Pioneer in Modern Medicine*, p. 168.

94. Ibid., p. 105.

95. *Boston Transcript*, May 11, 1912, quoted ibid., p. 124.

96. Aub and Hapgood, *Pioneer in Modern Medicine*, p. 125.

97. Means quoted in Washburn, *Massachusetts General Hospital*, p. 124.

98. Means quoted ibid., p. 127.

99. James Howard Means, *Ward 4: The Mallinckrodt Research Ward of the Massachusetts General Hospital* (Cambridge: Harvard University Press, 1958), p. 14.

100. Washburn, *Massachusetts General Hospital*, p. 379.

101. Paul Dudley White, *My Life and Medicine* (Boston: Gambit, 1971), pp. 19–20.

102. Ibid., p. 14.

103. Washburn, *Massachusetts General Hospital*, p. 377.

104. Ibid., pp. 380–381.

105. Ibid., p. 378.

106. White, *My Life and Medicine*, p. 218.

107. J. Gordon Scannell, "Cardiac Unit," in Castleman et al., *Massachusetts General Hospital*, p. 240.

108. Edgar Haber, "Cardiac Unit," in Castleman et al., *Massachusetts General Hospital*, p. 101.

109. L. Bu, X. Jiang, S. Martin-Puig, L. Caron, S. Zhu, Y. Shao, D. J. Roberts, P. L. Huang, I. J. Domian, and K. R. Chien, "Human ISL1 Heart Progenitors Generate Diverse Multipotent Cardiovascular Cell Lineages," *Nature* 460.7251 (July 2, 2009): 113–117.

110. Francis M. Rackemann, *The Inquisitive Physician: The Life and Times of George Richard Minot* (Cambridge: Harvard University Press, 1956), p. 94.

111. Much of the material on Ward 4 is drawn from Means, *Ward 4*.

112. Washburn, *Massachusetts General Hospital*, pp. 128–129.

113. Today a completely different disease bears this name—neurofibromatosis type 1—which has nothing to do with parathyroids or calcium.

114. "Fuller Albright," in Castleman, pp. 88–89.

115. Means, *Ward 4*, pp. 92–93.

116. Ibid., p. 95.

117. Ibid., p. 97.

118. Ibid., p. 98.

119. Ibid., p. 101.

120. Ibid., p. 80.

121. Ibid., p. 140.

122. Ibid., p. 148.

123. Ibid., p. 150.

124. Ibid., p. 158.

125. See "In Memoriam: Janet W. McArthur, MD, ScD," MGH Hotline Online, October 20, 2006, at www2.massgeneral.org/pubaffairs/issues2006/102006mcarthur.htm.

126. Dwight J. Ingle, *A Dozen Doctors: Autobiographic Sketches* (Chicago: University of Chicago Press, 1963), p. 174.

127. Ibid., p. 177.

128. Ibid., p. 178.

129. John B. Stanbury and Earle M. Chapman, "James Howard Means," in Castleman et al., *Massachusetts General Hospital*, p. 63.

130. Ibid., p. 65.

131. Ingle, *A Dozen Doctors*, p. 180.

132. Ibid., p. 189.

133. Ibid., p. 192.

134. Ibid.

135. Ibid., p. 196.

136. Stanbury and Chapman, "James Howard Means," p. 66.

137. Ibid.

138. Ibid.

139. Ibid.

140. Welch, *A Twentieth-Century Surgeon*, p. 60.

141. Ibid., p. 61.

142. Washburn, *Massachusetts General Hospital*, p. 530.

143. Ibid., p. 531.

144. Ibid., p. 11.

145. Ingle, *A Dozen Doctors*, p. 188.

146. Washburn, *Massachusetts General Hospital*, p. 536.

147. Ibid., pp. 187–188.

148. Ibid., p. 536.

Chapter 4

1. Faxon, *Massachusetts General Hospital*, pp. 13, 7, 14, 28.

2. Rosemary Stevens, *In Sickness and in Wealth: American Hospitals in the Twentieth Century* (New York: Basic Books, 1989), p. 148.

3. According to Welch, *A Twentieth-Century Surgeon*, p. 72, any surgeon *or physician* could practice surgery immediately upon being licensed until 1937, when the Board of Surgery established by the American Surgical Association upgraded its standards. Welch added (p. 73) that only in the mid-1980s, when malpractice premiums soared, did general practitioners fully and finally withdraw from the OR.

4. Ibid., p. 38.

5. Stevens, *In Sickness and in Wealth*, pp. 180–181.

6. J. Gordon Scannell, "Edward D. Churchill," in Castleman et al., *Massachusetts General Hospital*, p. 201.

7. Washburn, *Massachusetts General Hospital*, pp. 132, 133.

8. Scannell, "Edward D. Churchill," pp. 202, 206.

9. Earle W. Wilkins Jr., "Richard H. Sweet," in Castleman et al., *Massachusetts General Hospital*, p. 219.

10. Scannell, "Edward D. Churchill," p. 202.

11. Joseph Garland, "Harvard and the Massachusetts General Hospital," *Harvard Alumni Bulletin* 48 (July 6, 1946): 761, quoted in Faxon, *Massachusetts General Hospital*, p. 248.

12. Scannell, "Edward D. Churchill," p. 201.

13. Faxon, *Massachusetts General Hospital*, pp. 14–15.

14. Ibid., p. 27.

15. Welch, *A Twentieth-Century Surgeon*, p. 63.

16. Scannell, "Edward D. Churchill," p. 203.

17. "Leland S. McKittrick," in Castleman et al., *Massachusetts General Hospital*, pp. 214–216. The article was "adapted from an obituary by Frank C. Wheelock, Jr., and a Memorial Minute, *Harvard University Gazette*, December 14, 1949, with the assistance of Francis D. Moore."

18. Scannell, "Edward D. Churchill," p. 207.

19. Ibid.

20. Welch, *A Twentieth-Century Surgeon*, pp. 86, 85.

21. Ibid., pp. 86–87.

22. Welch, *A Twentieth-Century Surgeon*, p. 90

23. Scannell, "Edward D. Churchill," pp. 204–205.

24. Ibid. p. 203.

25. R. Clement Darling, "Robert Ritchie Linton," in Castleman et al., *Massachusetts General Hospital*, pp. 217, 218.

26. Ibid., p. 219; emphasis in original.

27. Scannell, "Edward D. Churchill," p. 205.

28. Welch, *A Twentieth-Century Surgeon*, p. 120.

29. Scannell, "Edward D. Churchill," p. 209. Kipling's remarks, made at the annual dinner of the Royal College of Surgeons in February 1923, were reprinted in Rudyard Kipling, *A Book of Words: Selections from Speeches and Addresses Delivered between 1906 and 1927* (London: Macmillan, 1928), chap. 23, "Surgeons and the Soul."

30. Scannell, "Edward D. Churchill," p. 205.

31. Welch, *A Twentieth-Century Surgeon*, p. 123.

32. Scannell, "Edward D. Churchill," p. 204.

33. Ibid., p. 209.

34. Welch, *A Twentieth-Century Surgeon*, p. 125.

35. Scannell, "Edward D. Churchill," pp. 208, 209.

36. Lawrence E. Martin, MGH oral history interview, July 2004, MGH Archives.

37. "Stanley Cobb," adapted from a Memorial Minute, *Harvard University Gazette* 64.38 (June 7, 1969), in Castleman et al., *Massachusetts General Hospital*, p. 166.

38. Benjamin White, Richard Wolff, and Eugene Taylor, *Stanley Cobb: Builder of the Modern Neurosciences* (Boston: Countway Library of Medicine, 1984), pp. 118–119.

39. Chester Pierce, quoted in "75th Anniversary Symposium: Celebrating 75 Years of Research, Teaching, and Clinical Care," MGH Department of Psychiatry, October 24, 2009.

40. White et al., *Stanley Cobb*, pp. 87–88.

41. Ibid., p. 138.

42. Ibid., pp. 206–207.

43. Ibid., pp. 290–302, 177–178.

44. Ibid., p. 223.

45. E. I. Taylor, "Louville Eugene Emerson: Psychotherapy, Harvard, and the Early Boston Scene," *Harvard Medical Alumni Bulletin* 56.2 (1982): 42–46. See also E. I. Taylor, "James Jackson Putnam's Fateful Meeting with Freud: The 1909 Clark University Conference," *Voices: The Art and Science of Psychotherapy* 21.1 (1985): 78–89.

46. Erikson worked half-time for Cobb, and the other half for Henry A. Murray at the Harvard Psychological Clinic in Cambridge.

47. White et al., *Stanley Cobb*, p. 173.

48. Thomas Hackett, with Avery Weisman and Anastasia Kucharski, *Psychiatry in a General Hospital: The First Fifty Years* (Boston: Massachusetts General Hospital, 1987), pp. 12–13.

49. John Herman, quoted in "75th Anniversary Symposium."

50. E. Lindemann, "Symptomatology and Management of Acute Grief," *American Journal of Psychiatry* 101 (1944): 141–149. See also S. Cobb and E. Lindemann, "Neuropsychiatric Observations during the Coconut Grove Fire," *Annals of Surgery* 117 (1943): 814–824.

51. David G. Satin, "Erich Lindemann: The Humanist and the Era of Community Mental Health," *Proceedings of the American Philosophical Society* 126.4 (1982): 327–346.

52. Jerrold Rosenbaum, quoted in "75th Anniversary Symposium."

53. *Relocation and Mental Health: Adaptation under Stress* (NIMH Study No. 3M 9137-C3). The study was conducted under the auspices of the Center for Community Studies, affiliated with the Department of Psychiatry, Harvard Medical School, and Massachusetts General Hospital. "The West End Story" is now a small museum on Staniford Street, just around the corner from MGH.

54. Satin, "Erich Lindemann," p. 3.

55. Ibid., pp. 5–7.

56. Hackett et al., *Psychiatry in a General Hospital*, p. 59.

57. Ibid., pp. xviii, 30, 5.

58. Ibid., p. 43.

59. Ibid., p. 44.

60. See, e.g., T. P. Hackett, N. H. Cassem, and H. A. Wishnie, "The Coronary-Care Unit: An

Appraisal of Its Psychological Hazards," *NEJM* 279.25 (December 19, 1968): 1365–1370.

61. Rachel Gotbaum, "A Beautiful Death," *Proto: Dispatches from the Frontiers of Medicine*, Fall 2005 (http://protomag.com/assets/a-beautiful-death).

62. Edwin H. Cassem, e-mail to author, June 2010.

63. MGH Department of Psychiatry, DVD, "75th Anniversary Symposium: Celebrating 75 Years of Research, Teaching, and Clinical Care," October 24, 2009.

64. Stevens, *In Sickness and in Wealth*, pp. 172, 187.

65. Ibid., p. 190.

66. Washburn, *Massachusetts General Hospital*, pp. 263, 265.

67. Faxon, *Massachusetts General Hospital*, p. 19.

68. Ibid., pp. 9, 21.

69. See the maps ibid., pp. 146–147.

70. Ibid., pp. 13, 17.

71. Ibid., p. 24.

72. Ibid., p. 35.

73. Ibid., pp. 25–26.

74. Ibid., pp. 33, 34.

75. For the time line of the Sixth General Hospital, see ibid., pp. 34–73.

76. For a complete discussion of the Sixth General Hospital, see ibid., pp. 364–386.

77. Ibid., p. 67.

78. Ibid., pp. 69–70.

79. Ibid., pp. 57, 63.

80. Ibid., pp. 58, 64, 55.

81. Ibid., pp. 65, 55, 60.

82. Ibid., p. 69.

83. Ibid., p. 44.

84. Mary Ruth Wolf, *The Valiant Volunteers: The Beginnings, Growth, and Scope of Volunteerism at the Massachusetts General Hospital* (Boston: MGH, 1980), p. 12.

85. Ibid., pp. 13, 14.

86. Ibid., p. 31.

87. Ibid., p. 38.

88. Moore's memories of the fire aftermath are drawn from Moore, *A Miracle and a Privilege*, pp. 60–67. See also John Esposito, *Fire in the Grove: The Cocoanut Grove Tragedy and Its Aftermath* (Cambridge, Mass.: Da Capo Press, 2005).

89. Moore, *A Miracle and a Privilege*, p. 60.

90. "Oliver Cope," in Castleman et al., *Massachusetts General Hospital*, p. 221.

91. Ibid.

92. John F. Burke, "Burn Unit," in Castleman et al., *Massachusetts General Hospital*, p. 254.

93. Faxon, *Massachusetts General Hospital*, p. 42.

94. Moore, *A Miracle and a Privilege*, p. 65.

95. Oliver Cope, Foreword, "Symposium on the Management of the Cocoanut Grove Burns at the Massachusetts General Hospital," *Annals of Surgery* 117.6 (June 1943): 801.

96. Nathaniel W. Faxon, "Problems of the Hospital Administration: I—The Cocoanut Grove Disaster," *Annals of Surgery* 117.6 (June 1943): 803.

97. "Oliver Cope," pp. 221–222.

98. Burke, "Burn Unit," p. 254.

99. Ibid., p. 255. Burke noted in an interview that "in the dark ages," patients with extensive burns most often died of malnutrition because the body used so much protein and other nutrients to heal the wound.

100. "Shriners Burns Institute," written "with the assistance of John F. Burke," in Castleman et al., *Massachusetts General Hospital*, p. 298.

101. S. Nagrath, L. V. Sequist, S. Maheswaran, D. W. Bell, D. Irimia, L. Ulkus, M. R. Smith, E. L. Kwak, S. Digumarthy, A. Muzikansky, P. Ryan, U. J. Balis, R. G. Tompkins, D. A. Haber, and M. Toner, "Isolation of Rare Circulating Tumour Cells in Cancer Patients by Microchip Technology," *Nature* 450.7173 (December 20, 2007): 1235–1239.

102. "NIGMS Awards 'Glue Grant' to Probe Body's Response to Burn and Trauma Injury," October 2, 2001, www.nigms.nih.gov/News/Results/Tompkins.htm.

103. Faxon, *Massachusetts General Hospital*, p. 27.

104. Stevens, *In Sickness and in Wealth*, p. 202.

105. Faxon, *Massachusetts General Hospital*, p. 62.

106. Stevens, *In Sickness and in Wealth*, p. 202.

107. Faxon, *Massachusetts General Hospital*, pp. 59–64.

Chapter 5

1. Faxon, *Massachusetts General Hospital*, pp. 73–74.

2. David Crockett obituary, *Boston Globe*, June 25, 2005.

3. Benjamin Castleman and S. B. Sutton, "David S. Crockett," in Castleman et al., *The Massachusetts General Hospital*, p. 53.

4. David Crockett obituary.

5. All quotations in this section are from David C. Crockett, oral history interview, April 11, 1995, MGH Archives.

6. Castleman and Sutton, "David S. Crockett," pp. 53–54.

7. John E. Lawrence, oral history interview, April 11, 1995, MGH Archives.

8. Ibid.

9. MGH annual report, 1945, p. 27.

10. Honored in the 1946 annual report (p. 34), the seven who made the "supreme sacrifice" were Theodore P. Robie, East Service; Edward L. Young III, West Service; Robert S. Hurlbut, East Service; Meinolph V. Kappins, assistant obstetrician; Joseph Comeau, orderly; Raymond LeMoine, orderly; and Leonard Feingold, pharmacy employee.

11. MGH annual report, 1945, p. 27.

12. Faxon, *Massachusetts General Hospital*, p. 68.

13. Ibid., p. 71.

14. MGH annual report, 1946, p. 30.

15. Faxon, *Massachusetts General Hospital*, p. 104.

16. Ibid., pp. 68–70.

17. Welch, *A Twentieth-Century Surgeon*, p. 118.

18. Cecil G. Sheps, "Dean Alexander Clark, General Director, 1949–1961," in Castleman et al., *Massachusetts General Hospital*, p. 12.

19. As reported in the annual reports, deficits were $1.16 million for 1945, $1.34 million for 1946, and $1.08 million for 1947.

20. MGH annual report, 1948, p. 38.

21. Faxon, *Massachusetts General Hospital*, p. 96.

22. MGH annual report, 1947, p. 37.

23. MGH annual report, 1951, p. 39

24. Ibid.

25. MGH annual report, 1956, p. 42.

26. All quotations in this section are from David C. Crockett, oral history interview, April 11, 1995, MGH Archives.

27. Washburn, *Massachusetts General Hospital*, p. 1.

28. Sherrill biographical details are from "Religion: The Church and the Churches," *Time*, March 26, 1951 (www.time.com/time/magazine /article/0,9171,805953-4,00.html).

29. Ibid.

30. Lawrence family genealogical information is courtesy of Edward P. Lawrence.

31. "Religion: The Church and the Churches."

32. MGH annual report, 1946, p. 29.

33. Quotations and other biographical details are drawn from John E. Lawrence obituary, *Boston Globe*, April 7, 2007.

34. Faxon, *Massachusetts General Hospital*, p. 87.

35. Ibid., pp. 83–84.

36. Ibid., p. 236.

37. E. Hammarsten, "Award Ceremony Speech," http://nobelprize.org/nobel_prizes/medicine/laureates /1953/press.html#.

38. MGH annual report, 1953, p. 36.

39. Castleman and Sutton, "David S. Crockett," p. 52.

40. From Thomas Morgan Rotch's entry in *Dictionary of American Biography*.

41. Mass General's opposition to the opening of Children's Hospital after the Civil War is adequately documented in G. Wayne Miller, *The Work of Human Hands: Hardy Hendren and Surgical Wonder at Children's Hospital* (New York: Random House, 1993), pp. 67–69. That a fierce rivalry still exists between the two institutions is hardly a secret in Boston medical circles.

42. Quoted in Washburn, *Massachusetts General Hospital*, p. 337.

43. Faxon, *Massachusetts General Hospital*, pp. 266–267.

44. Ibid., p. 264.

45. "The Children's Department of the Massachusetts General Hospital," *Archives of Pediatrics* (May 1914): 321–323.

46. Talbot quoted in Faxon, *Massachusetts General Hospital*, p. 274.

47. Washburn, *Massachusetts General Hospital*, p. 338.

48. Alexander Leaf, "Allergy Unit," in Castleman et al., *Massachusetts General Hospital*, p. 96.

49. Washburn, *Massachusetts General Hospital*, p. 341.

50. Faxon, *Massachusetts General Hospital*, p. 279.

51. "Allan Macy Butler," in Castleman et al., *Massachusetts General Hospital*, p. 187, adapted from remarks by Nathan B. Talbot at a presentation to Allan Butler of the American Pediatric Society's Howland Award, 1969.

52. Ibid., p. 188.

53. "John Douglas Crawford II: Faculty of Medicine—Memorial Minute," *Harvard University Gazette*, May 18, 2006, www.news.harvard.edu/ gazette/2006/05.18/25-mm.html.

54. Nathan B. Talbot, Edna H. Sobel, Janet W. McArthur, and John D. Crawford, *Functional Endocrinology, from Birth through Adolescence* (Cambridge: Harvard University Press, 1952).

55. "John Douglas Crawford II."

56. Though pediatric surgeons, like present-day Chief Joseph "Jay" Vacanti, rightly argue for a historic linkage between their specialty and general surgery, pediatric surgery is discussed here in order to simplify the narrative and keep discussion of child-related services in one place. The existence today of the MassGeneral Hospital *for* Children argues for such an approach.

57. The first was at Philadelphia Children's Hospital under Jack Downes, according to Daniel Shannon.

58. Faxon, *Massachusetts General Hospital*, p. 96.

59. Cecil G. Sheps, "Dean Alexander Clark, General Director, 1949–1961," in Castleman et al., *Massachusetts General Hospital*, p. 8.

60. Ibid., p. 9.

61. Ibid., p. 10.

62. Faxon, *Massachusetts General Hospital*, p. 106.

63. MGH annual report, 1945, p. 29.

64. Sheps, "Dean Alexander Clark," p. 12.

65. Details of outpatient history are drawn from an untitled, unpublished monograph by John D. Stoeckle, provided to author.

66. MGH annual report, 1949, p. 48.

67. John D. Stoeckle, MGH oral history interview, December 7, 2004, MGH Archives.

68. Stoekle, unpublished monograph.

69. Ibid.

70. John D. Stoeckle, "Ambulatory Care Division and Community Medicine," in Castleman et al., *Massachusetts General Hospital*, p. 140.

71. Copies of the Farnsworth Committee reports were provided by John Stoeckle to the author.

72. Stoeckle, unpublished monograph.

73. "The Committee on Research," written "with the assistance of Jerome Gross," in Castleman et al., *Massachusetts General Hospital*, p. 35.

74. Lloyd H. Smith Jr. and Daniel D. Federman, "Walter Bauer," in Castleman et al., *Massachusetts General Hospital*, pp. 70–71.

75. John D. Stoeckle and George Abbott White, *Plain Pictures of Plain Doctoring: Vernacular Expression in New Deal Medicine and Photography* (Cambridge: MIT Press, 1985).

76. James B. Wyngaarden, *An Unimagined Life: An Autobiography* (Durham, N.C.: BW&A Books, 2009), p. 42.

77. Smith and Federman, "Walter Bauer," p. 70.

78. Alexander Leaf, "The Chief's View," in Castleman et al., *Massachusetts General Hospital*, pp. 95–96.

79. Daniel S. Ellis, "Gastrointestinal Unit," in Castleman et al., *Massachusetts General Hospital*, p. 122.

80. MGH annual report, 1947, p. 41.

81. Weinstein was chief of infectious diseases at Haynes and a faculty member at Boston University until he moved to Tufts Medical School in 1957.

82. MGH annual report, 1955, pp. 35, 40.

83. F. K. Austen, J. Kochweser, and R. A. Field, "Cardiorespiratory Problems in Severe Poliomyelitis Observed during the Recent Epidemic," *NEJM* 254.17 (1956): 790–793; W. Berenberg, B. Castleman, D. S. Ellis, J. Hanelin, F. K. Austen, E. B. Benedict, and E. P. Richardson, "Acute Anterior Bulbar Spinal Poliomyelitis—Acute and Chronic Tracheitis and Bronchitis, Severe—Tracheal Stenosis, Severe," *NEJM* 254.17 (1956): 810–815; J. B. Livingstone, F. K. Austen, and L. J. Kunz, "A Study of Intercurrent Bacterial Respiratory Infections in Bulbospinal Poliomyelitis," *NEJM* 257.18 (1957): 861–866.

84. Berton Roueché, "Annals of Medicine," *New Yorker*, September 4, 1971, pp. 66–81.

85. Ibid., p. 77.

86. MGH annual report, 1985, p. 18.

87. Cells arising in the patient in response to infection, known as lymphocytes. These cells defend the host by killing virus-infected cells.

88. B. D. Walker et al., "HIV-Specific Cytotoxic T Lymphocytes in Seropositive Individuals," *Nature* 328 (July 23, 1987): 345–348.

89. Stephen Smith, "$100m Gift Bolsters AIDS Fight," *Boston Globe*, February 4, 2009, www.boston.com/yourtown/newton/articles/2009/02/04/100m_gift_bolsters_aids_fight.

90. B. D. Walker, A. K. Chakraborty, et al., "Effects of Thymic Selection of the T-Cell Repertoire on HLA Class I-Associated Control of HIV Infection," *Nature* 465 (May 20, 2010): 350–354.

91. Charles James White, "The History of Dermatology in Boston," *NEJM* 213.8 (August 22, 1935): 339–345.

92. Thomas B. Fitzpatrick and Irvin H. Blank, "Dermatology Service," in Castleman et al., *Massachusetts General Hospital*, pp. 154–155.

93. Ibid., p. 156.

Chapter 6

1. MGH annual report, 1961, p. 42.

2. MGH annual report, 1963, p. 62.

3. "John Hilton Knowles, General Director, 1962–1972," written "with the assistance of Edith Knowles Dabney, Lawrence Martin, and Ellsworth T. Neumann," in Castleman et al., *Massachusetts General Hospital*, pp. 18–19.

4. MGH annual report, 1961, p. 41.

5. MGH annual report, 1963, p. 45.

6. MGH annual report, 1962, p. 43.

7. Ibid., p. 54.

8. MGH annual report, 1963, p. 73.

9. Paul S. Russell, MGH oral history interview, November 30, 2004, MGH Archives.

10. "John Hilton Knowles, General Director, 1962–1972," p. 19.

11. Welch, *A Twentieth-Century Surgeon*, p. 278.

12. "John Hilton Knowles, General Director," p. 19.

13. Ibid., pp. 17–18.

14. MGH annual report, 1967, p. 66.

15. "John Hilton Knowles, General Director," p. 17.

16. Ibid., p. 22.

17. Joseph B. Martin, private memoir provided to author, chap. 6, "Huntington's Disease."

18. Martin Bander, "Sounding Board: The Physician and the Press," *NEJM* 293.8 (August 21, 1975): 402–403, and "The Scientist and the News Media," *NEJM* 308.19 (May 12, 1983): 1170–1173.

19. Peter L. Slavin, electronic message to MGH community, January 29, 2009.

20. MGH annual report, 1964, p. 72.

21. MGH annual report, 1965, p. 45.

22. MGH annual report, 1967, p. 51.

23. MGH annual report, 1964, p. 72.

24. MGH annual report, 1966, p. 49.

25. MGH annual report, 1968, p. 52.

26. MGH annual report, 1976–1977, p. 60.

27. MGH annual report, 1977, p. 82.

28. Alexander Leaf, quoted ibid., pp. 124, 125.

29. MGH annual report, 1961, p. 51.

30. MGH annual report, 1962, p. 43.

31. MGH annual report, 1970–1971, p. 160.

32. A total of 28 health centers were created during this period by all Boston-area hospitals combined.

33. MGH annual report, 1965, p. 49.

34. Lawrence E. Martin, MGH oral history interview, July 14, 2004, MGH Archives.

35. MGH annual report, 1966, p. 49.

36. Lawrence E. Martin, MGH oral history interview.

37. Ibid.

38. Ibid.

39. "Social Service Department," in Castleman et al., *Massachusetts General Hospital*, p. 378.

40. Ibid., pp. 377–378.

41. Ibid., p. 379.

42. An appreciation of Clark's term as general director appears in the Castleman volume. The authors of a profile of John Knowles agree with Cecil G. Sheps, professor of social medicine at the University of North Carolina at Chapel Hill School of Medicine, that "inspiration for such innovations as the Logan Medical Station, the Bunker Hill Health Center, the Chelsea Health Center, the stations in Boston's North End, expansion of the in-town pediatrics and screening clinics—all developments of the Knowles era—can be traced to (Dean) Clark's concern for public health" (Castleman et al., *Massachusetts General Hospital*, p. 23).

43. MGH annual report, 1967, p. 51.

44. Ibid., p. 57.

45. Ibid.

46. MGH annual report, 1968, p. 55.

47. Ibid.

48. MGH annual report, 1970–1971, p. 151.

49. John Stoeckle, MGH oral history interview, December 7, 2004, MGH Archives.

50. Ibid.

51. MGH annual report, 1973, p. 60.

52. MGH annual report, 1981, pp. 14–15.

53. Ibid., p. 14.

54. Lawrence E. Martin, MGH oral history interview.

55. Stoeckle, "Ambulatory Care Division and Community Medicine," pp. 147–148.

56. Eric Nagourney, "Ronald A. Malt, 70, Is Dead; Innovator in Reattaching Limb," *New York Times*, October 17, 2002.

57. Paul S. Russell, MGH oral history interview, November 30, 2004, MGH Archives.

58. Ibid.

59. MGH annual report, 1965, p. 51.

60. Holcomb B. Noble, "Robert H. Ebert, 81, Who Led Harvard Medical School, Dies," *New York Times*, January 31, 1996.

61. "John Hilton Knowles, General Director," p. 19.

62. Octo Barnett, "Computer Science Laboratory," in Castleman et al., *Massachusetts General Hospital*, pp. 109–110.

63. Biographical details of Alexander Leaf and quotations from him are from Alexander Leaf, "Autobiographical Memoirs and Oral History Interview with Arnold S. Relman," unpublished (1996), on file at MGH Archives.

64. Ibid., p. 89.

65. Ibid., p. 428.

66. Ibid., p. 429.

67. Ibid.

68. "Report of the Trustees," MGH annual report, 1980–1982, pp. 5–6.

69. MGH annual report, 1968, p. 51.

70. MGH annual report, 1973, p. 63.

71. MGH annual report, 1976–1977, p. 60.

72. Scannell, "Cardiac Unit," p. 241.

73. Mary Bellis, "John Heysham Gibbon—Heart Lung Machine—Pump Oxygenator," http://inventors.about.com/library/inventors/blheartlungmachine.htm.

74. Scannell, "Cardiac Unit," p. 242.

75. Ibid., p. 243.

76. In addition to president of the American Heart Association, 1977–1978, Austen was president of the Association for Academic Surgery, 1970; Society of University Surgeons, 1972–1973; Massachusetts Heart Association, 1972–1974; New England Cardiovascular Society, 1972–1973; American Surgical Association, 1985–1986; American Association for Thoracic Surgery, 1988–1989; American College of Surgeons, 1992–1993; as well as chairman, Board of Regents, American College of Surgeons, 1989–1991.

77. MGH annual report, 1975, p. 54.

78. MGH annual report, 1960, p. 45.

79. Marshall K. Bartlett, George L. Nardi, and W. Gerald Austen, "General Surgical Services since 1969: The Austen Years," in Castleman et al., *Massachusetts General Hospital*, p. 227.

80. W. Gerald Austen, MGH oral history interview, June 25, 2004, MGH Archives.

81. Washburn, *Massachusetts General Hospital*, p. 367.

82. Ibid., p. 370.

83. Ibid., p. 371.

84. *Time*, July 27, 1936.

85. "Kurt H. Thoma, D.M.D.," *Journal of the American Dental Society of Anesthesiology* 6.8 (October 1959): 23.

86. Kurt H. Thoma, *Oral Anaesthesia: Local Anaesthesia in the Oral Cavity. Technique and Practical Application in the Different Branches of Dentistry* (Boston: Ritter and Flebbe, 1914).

87. Walter C. Guralnick, "Oral and Maxillofacial Surgical Service," in Castleman et al., *Massachusetts General Hospital*, p. 291.

88. Ibid.

89. R. Bruce Donoff, ed., *Massachusetts General Hospital Manual of Oral and Maxillofacial Surgery*, 2nd ed. (St. Louis: Mosby–Year Book, 1992). The third edition (1997) was renamed *Manual of Oral and Maxillofacial Surgery*.

90. For an early history of urology to 1935, see Faxon, *Massachusetts General Hospital*, pp. 347–352.

91. W. Scott McDougal et al., "Hugh Cabot—1872–1945: Genitourinary Surgeon, Futurist, and Medical Statesman," *Urology* 50.4 (1997).

92. "Hugh Cabot," *DAB*.

93. Faxon, *Massachusetts General Hospital*, p. 15.

94. Ibid., p. 9.

95. W. Scott McDougal, *A History of Urology at the Massachusetts General Hospital, 1810–1996* (Boston: Massachusetts General Hospital Urology Department, [1996]), pp. 21–22.

96. Ibid., p. 23.

97. Wyland F. Leadbetter, "Urology Service," in Castleman et al., *Massachusetts General Hospital,* p. 293.

98. Ibid.

99. Ibid., p. 295.

100. "Urology, 1969–1980," in Castleman et al., *Massachusetts General Hospital,* p. 296.

101. Ibid., pp. 296–297.

102. MGH annual report, 1966, pp. 55–58.

103. MGH annual report, 1968, p. 58.

104. Martin, oral history interview.

105. MGH annual report, 1970–1971, p. 62.

106. MGH annual report, 1971–1972, p. 61.

107. Ibid., pp. 62–65.

108. "John Hilton Knowles, General Director," p. 25.

109. The Jack Lemmon anecdote was provided in a note to the author from Lawrence E. Martin.

110. MGH annual report, 1972, p. 55.

111. R. Tunley, "America's Ten Best Hospitals," *Ladies' Home Journal,* February 1967, pp. 34 ff.

112. MGH annual report, 1973, p. 59.

113. MGH annual report, 1975, p. 60.

114. MGH annual report, 1975–1976, p. 64.

115. Ibid.

116. MGH annual report, 1976–1977, p. 59.

117. MGH annual report, 1980, p. 4.

118. Ibid., p. 5.

119. "Liver Transplantation," http://en.wikipedia.org/wiki/Liver_transplantation.

120. MGH annual report, 1975, p. 67.

121. MGH annual report, 1980, p. 5.

122. *Allograft* means a transplant from one person to another who is not his or her identical twin, whereas *isograft* is a transplant from one twin to another, that is, between humans with identical genetic makeups. The first kidney transplant in 1954, by Joseph E. Murray, was an isograft.

123. Robert J. Corry, who had trained as a resident at MGH, pioneered pancreas transplantation at the University of Iowa.

124. MGH annual report, 1986, p. 11.

125. MGH annual report, 1990, p. 24.

126. David H. Sachs, "The Lure of Transplantation," *Clinical Transplants* (2008): 290.

127. T. Kawai et al., "Brief Report: HLA-Mismatched Renal Transplantation without Maintenance Immunosuppression," *NEJM* 358.4 (January 24, 2008): 353–361.

128. Sachs, "The Lure of Transplantation," p. 298.

129. MGH annual report, 1978–1979, p. 63.

130. Katherine Bouton, "Academic Research and Big Business: A Delicate Balance," *New York Times Magazine,* September 11, 1983.

131. Hoechst became Aventis in 1999, following its merger with Rhône-Poulenc, SA. In 2004 it became Sanofi-Aventis.

132. Hans-Hermann Schöne to Howard Goodman, June 2, 1977, on file in MGH Molecular Biology Department.

133. Hans-Hermann Schöne to Howard Goodman, July 22, 1977, on file in MGH Molecular Biology Department.

134. Hans-Georg Gareis, address delivered at the dedication of the MGH Molecular Biology Laboratories, August 28, 1984, text on file in MGH Molecular Biology Department.

135. Bouton, "Academic Research and Big Business."

136. Ibid.

137. Two five-year extensions of the agreement, in 1991 and 1996, increased the total Hoechst investment to more than $100 million.

138. Gareis, address delivered at the dedication of the MGH Molecular Biology Laboratories, August 28, 1984.

139. MGH annual report, 1981, p. 28.

Chapter 7

1. Washburn, *Massachusetts General Hospital,* p. 314.

2. Fred G. Barker II, "Historical Vignettes: The Massachusetts General Hospital, Early History and Neurosurgery to 1939," *Journal of Neurosurgery* 79.6 (December 1993): 953.

3. Washburn, *Massachusetts General Hospital,* p. 315.

4. Ibid.

5. Ibid., pp. 315–316.

6. Ibid., p. 316.

7. Peter D. Kramer, "Adirondack Couch," *New York Times Sunday Book Review,* December 24, 2006, www.nytimes.com/2006/12/24/books/review/Kramer.t.html?fta=y.

8. Washburn, *Massachusetts General Hospital,* p. 318.

9. Ibid., p. 319.

10. Ibid., p. 320.

11. Ibid.

12. Faxon, *Massachusetts General Hospital,* p. 225.

13. Ibid., p. 76.

14. Bryan Marquand, "Dr. Raymond D. Adams, 97," *Boston Globe,* October 26, 2008, C21.

15. Ibid.

16. Walton completed part of his training at MGH in 1953–1954, though he did not do the bulk of his work here.

17. For the same reason, neurology and neurosurgery are being treated in distinct sections in this chapter.

18. In his memoir, unpublished as of 2010 but

generously provided to the author, Martin added, "Interest in neuropathology of HD at Harvard was developing at McLean Hospital under the influence of Dr. Alfred Pope who had recruited Dr. Edward (Ted) Bird from Cambridge University in England to establish a Huntington's Disease brain bank."

19. Another Huntington's disease center was funded in 1980 at Johns Hopkins University.

20. Martin, memoir.

21. Ibid.

22. Ibid.

23. Published by Oxford University Press in 1992.

24. "In Memoriam: John B. Penney, Jr. M.D.," www.hdfoundation.org/bios/penny.php.

25. Ibid.

26. MGH annual report, 1979–1980, p. 5.

27. MGH annual report, 1992, p. 12.

28. Information on Ward G is based on notes to the author by Lawrence E. Martin.

29. Kay Bander, e-mail to author, March 2010.

30. MGH annual report, 1983, p. 3.

31. Ibid.

32. MGH annual report, 1984, p. 13.

33. Lawrence E. Martin, personal note to author, February 2010.

34. See www.foxhillvillage.com/history.html. MGH's board chairman, Ferdinand "Moose" Colloredo-Mansfeld, was a senior officer with Cabot, Cabot and Forbes, having started his real estate career with the firm in 1970.

35. Boston Globe, October 31, 1984, p. 24.

36. Other major hospitals in Boston and New York have trustees numbering in the dozens and in one case 150. In these instances, participating strongly in philanthropy is usually a condition of board membership. By contrast, John Lawrence, the longtime MGH chairman, considered his time donated to MGH to be his contribution and made only token financial gifts to the hospital.

37. Washburn, Massachusetts General Hospital, p. 414.

38. Faxon, Massachusetts General Hospital, p. 292.

39. Ibid.

40. "MGH and Cancer: Cox Building for Cancer Management," in Castleman et al., Massachusetts General Hospital, p. 335.

41. Faxon, Massachusetts General Hospital, p. 294.

42. Early accounts of the Huntington Hospital and quotes that follow are based largely on Paul Zamecnik's interview with the author, December 3, 2008.

43. Paul C. Zamecnik, "Cancer Research: Joseph Charles Aub," in Castleman et al., Massachusetts General Hospital, p. 346.

44. Faxon, Massachusetts General Hospital, p. 223.

45. Zamecnik, "Cancer Research: Joseph Charles Aub," p. 346.

46. Zamecnik passed away in 2009 at the age of 96 and was still active in his lab until several weeks before his death.

47. Linton, Radiology at Massachusetts General Hospital, pp. 101–102.

48. Ibid., p. 103.

49. "Medical Oncology," in Castleman et al., Massachusetts General Hospital, p. 336.

50. "February 2003—Faculty and Staff—Rita Marie Kelley, M.D., 1917–1981," www.countway.harvard.edu/chm/archives/iotm/iotm_2003-02.html.

51. William C. Wood, "Surgical Oncology," in Castleman et al., Massachusetts General Hospital, p. 339.

52. "MGH and Cancer: Cox Building for Cancer Management," p. 332.

53. Faxon, Massachusetts General Hospital, p. 294.

54. "Department of Radiation Medicine," in Castleman et al., Massachusetts General Hospital, p. 341.

55. MGH annual report, 1965, p. 53.

56. "MGH and Cancer: Cox Building for Cancer Management," pp. 332–350.

57. Ibid., p. 333.

58. Daniel Haber, e-mail to author, April 7, 2010.

59. "Medical Oncology," p. 336.

60. Rita Kelley, undated memo to Thomas Stossel, provided to author by Stossel.

61. "Medical Oncology," p. 337.

62. "Hybridon Founder Paul Zamecnik Receives First Albert Lasker Award for Special Achievement in Medical Science," www.prnewswire.co.uk/cgi/news/release?id=15125.

63. MGH annual report, 1986, p. 3.

64. MGH annual report, 1987, p. 3. The Constitution was actually one of six frigates authorized by the Naval Act of 1794 and the third of the six to be launched, in 1797.

65. MGH annual report, 1990, p. 25.

66. Daniel Haber, e-mail to author, April 7, 2010.

67. Haber explained in greater depth in an e-mail to the author, May 24, 2010: "At the time of the Globe article, no one really had a clue where to look for biomarkers. Some were looking for germline abnormalities in patients, rather than in the tumors. (Would the responding patients somehow metabolize the drug differently?) Others were looking at expression signatures of the tumors. (Were there general patterns of gene expression at the RNA or protein level that could identify responders?) What triggered our interest was the genetic argument (I was biased based on my background in genetics). Based on the previous success of Gleevec in leukemias: if the gene that is targeted by the drug is mutated (at the DNA level), it implies that this gene may be 'really important' to the growth of the tumor. Hence, targeting the gene in the subset of tumors marked by the mutation is likely to have

results. We tested that hypothesis by collecting tumors from responders and from non-responders, looking for DNA mutations in the EGFR gene. And there it was. In retrospect, it was totally obvious of course."

68. Thomas J. Lynch, Daniel A. Haber, et al., "Activating Mutations in the Epidermal Growth Factor Receptor Underlying Responsiveness of Non-Small-Cell Lung Cancer to Gefitinib," *NEJM* 350.21 (May 20, 2004): 2129–2139.

69. Gilbert Tang, "Alumni Perspective—Dr. Peter Slavin (MBA '90)," *Harbus*, March 8, 2010, http://media.www.harbus.org/media/storage /paper343/news/2008/04/07/Features/Alumni .Perspective.Dr.Peter.Slavin.mba.90-3305632.shtml.

70. A writer from Beverly might have taken this personally, but Lawrence seemed to be referring to older Brahmin trustees, like his uncle John E. Lawrence, who had homes both in Boston and on the North Shore (Beverly and environs).

71. Gary P. Pisano and Maryam Goinaraghi, "Partners HealthCare System, Inc. (A)," Harvard Business School, case 9-696-062 (1996), p. 12.

72. Ibid., p. 13.

73. Ibid.

74. Jerry Austen, "Mergers, Acquisitions, and the Surgeons," supplied to the author by Austen.

75. Said Buchanan in a personal interview with the author, "After review of many possible names, the group responsible for negotiating returned to the name I had put up initially, which was Partners. Some of them had wanted Greentree. I never did figure that out."

76. According to a story told to the author by several MGH personnel.

77. "A Handshake That Made Healthcare History," *Boston Sunday Globe*, December 28, 2008, page A1.

78. *MGH Hotline*, November 7, 1994.

79. "A Handshake That Made Healthcare History."

80. Howard Ulfelder, "Obstetrics," in Castleman et al., *Massachusetts General Hospital*, p. 265.

81. Ibid.

82. H. Thomas Ballantine Jr. and William H. Sweet, "Neurosurgery: Development of the Neurosurgical Service: William Jason Mixter," in Castleman et al., *Massachusetts General Hospital*, p. 271.

83. Barker, "Historical Vignettes," p. 955.

84. Ibid.

85. Ballantine and Sweet, "Neurosurgery: William Jason Mixter," p. 269.

86. Nicholas T. Zervas et al., *Neurosurgery at the Massachusetts General Hospital, 1909–1983* (Boston: Massachusetts General Hospital, 1984), p. 5.

87. Ibid., p. 6.

88. Ballantine and Sweet, "Neurosurgery: William Jason Mixter," p. 269.

89. Barker, "Historical Vignettes," p. 956.

90. Ballantine and Sweet, "Neurosurgery: William Jason Mixter," p. 270.

91. W. J. Mixter and J. S. Barr, "Rupture of the Intervertebral Disc with Involvement of the Spinal Canal," *NEJM* 211.5 (August 2, 1934): 210–215.

92. Ballantine and Sweet, "Neurosurgery: William Jason Mixter," p. 271.

93. Ibid., p. 270.

94. Zervas et al., *Neurosurgery*, p. 7.

95. Ballantine and Sweet, "Neurosurgery: William Jason Mixter," pp. 271–272.

96. Ibid., p. 272

97. Ibid., pp. 272–273.

98. Zervas et al., *Neurosurgery*, p. 19.

99. Ballantine and Sweet, "Neurosurgery: William Jason Mixter," p. 271.

100. Zervas, *Neurosurgery*, pp. 9–10.

101. Ballantine and Sweet, "Neurosurgery: William Jason Mixter," p. 269.

102. Zervas, *Neurosurgery*, pp. 11–12.

103. Ibid., p. 20.

104. Ibid.

Chapter 8

1. Recent chiefs Patricia Donahoe (pediatric surgery), Anne Young (neurology), and Jeanine Wiener-Kronish (anesthesia) were highlighted in previous chapters.

2. Each year the full complement in the Department of Medicine included 12 house officers (interns), 12 first-year residents, six second-year residents, and one chief resident. Second-year or "senior" residents usually served after a year or two away from MGH, often doing research at the NIH or elsewhere.

3. MGH annual report, 1966, p. 75.

4. "A Handshake That Made Healthcare History," *Boston Sunday Globe*, December 28, 2008, p. A1.

5. Martha Stone, coordinator for Reference Services at Treadwell Library, notes, "Though I have seen 'interne at MGH' noted in many, many sources, I have never found it to have been proven definitively."

6. John A. Kenney, *The Negro in Medicine* (Tuskegee, Ala.: Tuskegee Institute Press, 1912), p. 8, http://pds.lib.harvard.edu/pds/view/6429541?n= 16&imagesize=1200&jp2Res=.25.

7. Information on early appointments of physicians underrepresented in medicine is courtesy of Elena Olson, Multicultural Affairs Office, author interview, August 2009.

8. Arthur J. Linenthal, *First a Dream* (Boston: Beth Israel Hospital and Countway Library, 1990), pp. 372–374.

9. For more on Williams, see www2.massgeneral.org/mao/williams.html.

10. Native Americans include Hawaiian natives. At 7 percent of the U.S. population and 25 percent

of the Harvard medical community, Asians are dramatically overrepresented and so do not fall within Olson's area of responsibility.

11. *MGH Hotline*, May 9, 1997.

12. The history of the proton beam is drawn largely from Richard Wilson, *A Brief History of the Harvard University Cyclotrons* (Cambridge: Harvard University Physics Department, 2004).

13. Ibid., p. 8.

14. A. L. Warshaw and A. F. Fuller Jr., "Specificity of Increased Renal Clearance of Amylase in Diagnosis of Acute Pancreatitis," *NEJM* 292.7 (1975): 325–328.

15. A. L. Warshaw, "Pancreatic Abscesses," *NEJM* 287.24 (1972): 1234–1236.

16. A. L. Warshaw, T. M. Chesney, G. W. Evans, and H. F. McCarthy, "Intrasplenic Dissection by Pancreatic Pseudocysts," *NEJM* 287.2 (1972): 72–75.

17. Perkins, *Centennial Review*, p. 46.

18. Sara E. Parsons, *Nursing Problems and Obligations* (Boston: Whitcomb and Barrows, 1916), pp. 134–135.

19. Perkins, *Centennial Review*, p. 125.

20. Ruth Sleeper, "A Comprehensive Program for Nationwide Action: In the Field of Nursing," *American Journal of Nursing* 45.9 (September 1945): 707–713.

21. "Nursing Service Director Predicts Changed Emphases," *American Journal of Nursing* 69.5 (May 1969): 920–921.

22. Sylvia Rimm, *How Jane Won: 55 Successful Women Share How They Grew from Ordinary Girls to Extraordinary Women* (New York: Crown, 2001), chap. 5.

23. Marilyn Klainberg and Kathleen M. Dirschel, eds., *Today's Nursing Leader: Managing, Succeeding, Excelling* (Sudbury, Mass.: Jones and Bartlett, 2010), p. 11.

24. Ibid.

25. Meredith Pitzi, in *Caring Headlines*, December 15, 2005.

26. Ibid.

27. See, for example, J. Ives Erickson, M. O. Ditomassi, and D. A. Jones, "Interdisciplinary Institute for Patient Care: Advancing Clinical Excellence," *Journal of Nursing Administration* 38.6 (June 2008): 308–314.

28. Ibid., p. 310.

29. Gerald Austen, e-mail communication with the author, June 2010.

30. Beth Israel Hospital in Boston was one of a very small number of hospitals identified as magnets in the original *Magnet Hospital Study* of the 1980s; once the formal Magnet program was started in 1993, however, the original list of hospitals was set aside, and in 2003 MGH was the first Massachusetts hospital formally designated by the American Nurses Credentialing Center.

31. Ruvkun shared the 2008 Albert Lasker Basic Medical Research Award with Victor Ambros and David Baulcombe "for discoveries that revealed an unanticipated world of tiny RNAs that regulate gene function in plants and animals," www.laskerfoundation.org/awards/2008basic.htm.

32. Gary Ruvkun, interview with author, March 2010.

33. Bouton, "Academic Research and Big Business."

34. G. Ruvkun et al., "The 21 Nucleotide *let-7* RNA Regulates *C. elegans* Developmental Timing," *Nature* 403 (February 24, 2000): 901–906; G. Ruvkun et al., "Conservation of the Sequence and Temporal Expression of *let-7* Heterochronic Regulatory RNA," *Nature* 408 (November 2, 2000): 86–89.

35. "Michael Blower," www.hms.harvard.edu/dms/bbs/fac/Blower.html.

36. This chapter is the longest.

37. Linda T. Kohn, Janet M. Corrigan, and Molla S. Donaldson, eds., *To Err Is Human: Building a Safer Health System* (Washington, D.C.: National Academy Press, 2000).

38. Ibid., p. 26.

39. Ibid, pp. 27–40.

40. Mike Barnicle, "Doctor to the World," in *Bantamweight Archangel: The Life and Afterlife of Thomas S. Durant, M.D.*, ed. David Nyhan (Boston: privately printed, 2006), p. 23.

41. Ly Y, *Heaven Becomes Hell: A Survivor's Story of Life under the Khmer Rouge* (New Haven: Yale University Southeast Asia Studies, 2000).

42. Ly Y, "A Pint-Sized John Wayne," in Nyhan, *Bantamweight Archangel*, p. 29.

43. Kevin Cullen, "Proof of Original Sin," in Nyhan, *Bantamweight Archangel*, p. 37.

44. Barnicle, "Doctor to the World," pp. 24–25.

45. Brian C. Mooney, "Attendee of the Dispossessed," in Nyhan, *Bantamweight Archangel*, p. 51.

46. David Nyhan, "Doctor of Decency, Alchemist of Altruism," *Boston Globe*, October 31, 2001, p. A23.

47. "Changing the Face of Medicine: Dr. Susan M. Briggs," www.nlm.nih.gov/changingthefaceofmedicine/physicians/biography_43.html.

48. Ibid.

49. *MGH Hotline*, September 14, 2001.

50. Ibid.

51. *MGH Hotline*, October 19, 2001.

52. Ibid.

53. *MGH Hotline*, October 12, 2001.

54. Ibid.

55. *MGH Hotline*, January 16, 2004.

56. "Changing the Face of Medicine: Dr. Susan M. Briggs."

57. James J. O'Connell, "Health Care for the Homeless," *Harvard Medical Alumni Bulletin*, Fall 1991, p. 32.

BIBLIOGRAPHY

· · · · · · · · · · · ·

Personal interviews with authors, in person or by telephone

Ausiello, Dennis A., MD, November 2009

Austen, K. Frank, MD, September 2008

Austen, W. Gerald, MD, Multiple interviews, 2008–2010

Ausubel, Frederick M., PhD, March 2010

Avruch, Joseph, MD, PhD, December 2008

Banchiere, Guillermo Jorge, June 2010

Bander, Katherine W. "Kay" Boling, MS, Multiple interviews, 2009–2010

Bertucci, John R., May 2010

Briggs, Susan M., MD, May 2010

Bringhurst, F. Richard, MD, March 2008

Buchanan, J. Robert, MD, July 2008

Burke, John F., MD, June 2009

Calderwood, Stephen B., MD, October 2009

Cassem, Edwin H., SJ, MD, June 2010

Chien, Kenneth R., MD, PhD, June 2009

Clark, Christopher, JD, May 2010

Colloredo-Mansfeld, Ferdinand, May 2008

Cosimi, A. Benedict, MD, April 2010

Crowley, William F., Jr., MD, November 2008

Daggett, Willard M., MD, August 2008

Davis, Jeff, June 2010

De Sanctis, Roman W., MD, May 2009

Dec, G. William, Jr., MD, July 2009

Ditomassi, Marianne, RN, Multiple interviews, 2009–2010

Donahoe, Patricia K., MD, November 2008

Durant, Stephen A., EdD, April 2010

Fisher, David E., MD, PhD, July 2010

Fitzgerald, Ellen J., March 2010

Freeman, Mason W., MD, December 2008

Frigoletto, Frederic D., Jr., MD, August 2008

Guralnick, Walter C., DMD, Multiple interviews, 2008–2009

Habener, Joel F., MD, December 2008

Haber, Daniel A., MD, Ph.D, May 2010

Hackett, Eleanor Mayher, August 2008

Haddad, Ernest M., JD, June 2010

Harris, William H., MD, July 2010

Herman, John B., MD, Multiple interviews, 2008–2009

Holmes, Lewis B., MD, January 2009

Isselbacher, Kurt J., MD, February 2008

Ives Erickson, Jeanette, MS, RN, Multiple interviews, 2010

Kaban, Leonard, DMD, MD, October 2009

Kaplan, Edward M., March 2010

Kingston, Robert E., PhD, May 2010

Kleinman, Ronald E., MD, April 2010

Klibanski, Anne, MD, December 2008

Krane, Stephen M., MD, September 2009

Kronenberg, Henry M., MD, PhD, December 2008

Kwong, Kenneth, PhD, May 2009

Lawrence, Edward P., Esq., May 2008

Louis, David N., MD, June 2009

Lowenstein, Edward, MD, February 2008

Lynch, Thomas J., Jr., MD, January 2009

Martin, Joseph B., MD, PhD, February 2010

Martin, Lawrence E., Multiple interviews, 2008–2010

Martuza, Robert L., MD, March 2010

McDougal, Mimi, February 2010

McDougal, W. Scott, MD, January 2010

McPeek, Bucknam, MD, June 2010

Minehan, Cathy E., MBA, September 2009

Mongan, James J., MD, Multiple interviews, 2008–2010

Nathan, David M., MD, December 2008

O'Connell, James J., III, MD, May 2010

Olson, Elena B., JD, August 2009

Olson, Kristian R., MD, May 2010

Parrish, John A., MD, June 2010

Peckham, Allen G., August 2008

Peirce, Georgia W., Multiple interviews, 2009–2010

Potts, John T., Jr., MD, Multiple interviews, 2008

Prestipino, Ann L., September 2009

Prince-Erickson, Carlyene, MBA, June 2010

Richardson, George S., MD, August 2008

Risser, Nancy A., March 2008

Ronan, Laurence J., MD, June 2010

Rosen, Bruce R., MD, PhD, May 2009

Rosenbaum, Jerrold F., MD, June 2010

Rowell, Pat, June 2009

Russell, Paul S., MD, Multiple interviews, 2008–2010

Ruvkun, Gary, PhD, March 2010

Sachs, David H., MD, June 2010

Sanders, Charles A., MD, Multiple interviews, 2009–2010

Schiff, Isaac, MD, August 2008

Seed, Brian, PhD, February 2010

Slavin, Peter L., MD, MBA, Multiple interviews, 2008–2010

Smith, Lloyd Hollingsworth, MD, September 2009

Stoeckle, John D., MD, Multiple interviews, 2009–2010

Stossel, Thomas P., MD, December 2008

Swartz, Morton N., MD, September, October 2009

Szostak, Jack W., PhD, March 2010

Tarbell, Nancy J., MD, March 2010

Thier, Samuel O., MD, Multiple interviews, 2009–2010

Thompson, James E., Multiple interviews, 2008–2010

Thorndike, W. Nicholas, November 2009

Thrall, James H., MD, April 2009

Tompkins, Ronald G., MD, ScD, July 2009

Torchiana, David F., MD, Multiple interviews, 2008–2010

Vacanti, Joseph P., MD, November 2009

Walker, Bruce D., MD, May 2010

Warshaw, Andrew L., MD, Multiple interviews, 2010

Williams, Winfred W., Jr., MD, September 2010

Young, Anne Buckingham, MD, PhD, March 2010

Young, Robert H., MD, June 2009

Zamecnik, Paul C., MD, December 2008

Zapol, Warren M., MD, February 2009 and June 2010

Zarins, Bertram, MD, June 2010

Zervas, Nicholas T., MD, March 2010

Oral History Interviews from the Archives, MGH Office of Public Affairs

Austen, W. Gerald, June 25, 2004

Claflin, Jane, June 1, 2004

Crockett, David C., April 11, 1995

Lawrence, John E., April 11, 1995

Martin, Lawrence E., July 14, 2004

Russell, Paul S., November 30, 2004

Stoeckle, John D., December 7, 2004

Books

Allison, Robert J. A Short History of Boston. Beverly, Mass.: Commonwealth Editions, 2004.

Amory, Cleveland. The Proper Bostonians. New York: E. P. Dutton, 1947.

Aub, Joseph C., and Ruth K. Hapgood. Pioneer in Modern Medicine: David Linn Edsall of Harvard.

Cambridge: Harvard Medical Alumni Association, 1970.

Beam, Alex. Gracefully Insane: Life and Death inside America's Premier Mental Hospital. New York: Public Affairs, 2001.

Beecher, Henry K., and Mark D. Altschule. Medicine at Harvard: The First 300 Years. Hanover, N.H.: University Press of New England, 1977.

Bigelow, Henry Jacob. A Memoir of Henry Jacob Bigelow. Boston: Longwood Press, 1900.

Bowditch, Nathaniel Ingersoll. History of the Massachusetts General Hospital, Second Edition, With a Continuation to 1872. Boston: Printed by the Trustees, 1872.

Castleman, Benjamin, David C. Crockett, and S. B. Sutton, eds. The Massachusetts General Hospital, 1955–1980. Boston: Little, Brown, 1983.

Crenner, Christopher. Private Practice: In the Early Twentieth-Century Medical Office of Dr. Richard Cabot. Baltimore: Johns Hopkins University Press, 2005.

Cruikshank, Jeffrey L. A Delicate Experiment: The Harvard Business School, 1908–1945. Boston: Harvard Business School Press, 1987.

Eaton, Leonard K. New England Hospitals, 1790–1833. Ann Arbor: University of Michigan Press, 1957.

Ellis, George E., and Massachusetts Historical Society, Memoir of Luther V. Bell, M.D., LL.D. Boston: J.Wilson and Son, 1863.

Emerson, Haven. The Baker Memorial. New York: Commonwealth Fund, 1941.

Esposito, John. Fire in the Grove: The Cocoanut Grove Tragedy and Its Aftermath. Cambridge, Mass.: Da Capo Press, 2005.

Faxon, Nathaniel W. The Massachusetts General Hospital, 1935–1955. Cambridge: Harvard University Press, 1959.

Fenster, Julie M. Ether Day: The Strange Tale of America's Greatest Medical Discovery and the Haunted Men Who Made It. New York: HarperCollins, 2001.

Finney, J. M. T. A Surgeon's Life: The Autobiography of J. M. T. Finney. New York: G. P. Putnam's Sons, 1940.

Hackett, Thomas P., Avery D. Weisman, and Anastasia Kucharski. Psychiatry in a General Hospital: The First Fifty Years. Littleton, Mass.: PSG Publishing, 1987.

Hoffmann, Stephen A., Under the Ether Dome: A Physician's Apprenticeship at Massachusetts General Hospital. New York: Scribner, 1986.

Holmes, Oliver Wendell. The Writings of Oliver Wendell Holmes, 13 vols. Boston: Houghton Mifflin, 1891–1895.

Ingle, Dwight J. A Dozen Doctors: Autobiographic Sketches. Chicago: University of Chicago Press, 1963.

Jackson, James. Letters to a Young Physician Just

Entering upon Practice. Boston: Phillips, Sampson, 1855.

Kirker, Harold. *The Architecture of Charles Bulfinch*. Cambridge: Harvard University Press, 1998.

Kitz, Richard J., ed. *This Is No Humbug! Reminiscences of the Department of Anesthesia at the Massachusetts General Hospital—A History*. Boston: Massachusetts General Hospital Department of Anesthesia, 2002.

Linton, Otha W. *Radiology at Massachusetts General Hospital, 1896–2000*. Boston: General Hospital Corporation, 2001.

Little, Nina Fletcher, and George William Folsom. *Early Years of the McLean Hospital, Recorded in the Journal of George William Folsom, Apothecary at the Asylum in Charlestown*. Boston: Francis A. Countway Library of Medicine, 1972.

Lowenstein, Edward, and Bucknam McPeek, eds. *Enduring Contributions of Henry K. Beecher to Medicine, Science, and Society*. International Anesthesiology Clinics, vol. 45, no. 4. Hagerstown, Md.: Walters Kluwer Health/Lippincott Williams and Wilkins, 2007.

Macy, John. *Walter James Dodd: A Biographical Sketch*. Boston: Houghton Mifflin, 1918.

Mallon, Bill. *Ernest Amory Codman: The End Result of a Life in Medicine*. Philadelphia: W. B. Saunders, 2000.

McDougal, W. Scott [ed.]. *A History of Urology at the Massachusetts General Hospital, 1810–1996*. Boston: Massachusetts General Hospital Urology Department, [1997].

Means, James Howard. *Ward 4: The Mallinckrodt Research Ward of the Massachusetts General Hospital*. Cambridge: Harvard University Press, 1958.

Moore, Francis D. *A Miracle and a Privilege: Recounting a Half Century of Surgical Advance*. Washington, D.C.: Joseph Henry Press, 1995.

Mumford, James Gregory. *A Narrative of Medicine in America*. Philadelphia: J. B. Lippincott, 1903.

Myers, Grace Whiting. *History of the Massachusetts General Hospital: June, 1872, to December, 1900*. Boston: Griffith-Stillings Press, 1929.

Nyhan, David, ed. *Bantamweight Archangel: The Life and Afterlife of Thomas S. Durant, M.D*. Boston: privately printed, 2006.

Parsons, Sara E. *History of the Massachusetts General Hospital Training School for Nurses*. Boston: Whitcomb and Barrows, 1922.

Perkins, Sylvia. *A Centennial Review of the Massachusetts General Hospital Training School of Nursing, 1873–1973*. Boston: Massachusetts General Hospital Nurses Alumnae Association, 1975.

Putnam, James Jackson. *A Memoir of Dr. James Jackson*. Boston: Houghton Mifflin, 1905.

Rackemann, Francis M. *The Inquisitive Physician: The Life and Times of George Richard Minot*. Cambridge: Harvard University Press, 1956.

Rimm, Sylvia, and Sara Rimm-Kaufman. *How Jane Won: 55 Successful Women Share How They Grew from Ordinary Girls to Extraordinary Women*. New York: Crown, 2001.

Rothman, David J. *Strangers at the Bedside: A History of How Law and Bioethics Transformed Medical Decision Making*. 3rd ed. New Brunswick, N.J.: Aldine Transaction, 2008.

Rowe, Carter. *Lest We Forget: Orthopaedics at the Massachusetts General Hospital and Ward I, 1900–1996*. Dublin, N.H.: William L. Bauhan, 1996.

Schama, Simon. *Dead Certainties: Unwarranted Speculations*. New York: Alfred A. Knopf, 1991.

Stevens, Rosemary. *In Sickness and in Wealth: American Hospitals in the Twentieth Century*. New York: Basic Books, 1989.

Stoeckle, John D. *Plain Pictures of Plain Doctoring: Vernacular Expression in New Deal Medicine and Photography*. Cambridge: MIT Press, 1985.

Sullivan, Robert. *The Disappearance of Dr. Parkman*. Boston: Little, Brown, 1971.

Sutton, S. B. *Crossroads in Psychiatry: A History of McLean Hospital*. Washington, D.C.: American Psychiatric Press, 1986.

Talbot, Nathan B., Edna H. Sobel, Janet W. McArthur, and John D. Crawford. *Functional Endocrinology, from Birth through Adolescence*. Cambridge: Harvard University Press, 1952.

Thoma, Kurt H. *Oral Anaesthesia: Local Anaesthesia in the Oral Cavity. Technique and Practical Application in the Different Branches of Dentistry*. Boston: Ritter and Flebbe, 1914.

Truax, Rhoda. *The Doctors Warren of Boston: First Family of Surgery*. Boston: Houghton Mifflin, 1968.

United States Army. Base Hospital No. 6. *The History of the U.S. Army Base Hospital No. 6 and Its Part in the American Expeditionary Forces, 1917–1918*. Boston: Massachusetts General Hospital, 1924.

Vogel, Morris J. *The Invention of the Modern Hospital, Boston 1870–1930*. Chicago: University of Chicago Press, 1980.

Warren, Edward. *The Life of John Collins Warren, M.D., Compiled Chiefly from His Autobiography and Journals*. 2 vols. Boston: Ticknor and Fields, 1860.

Warren, J. Collins, and Edward D. Churchill., eds. *To Work in the Vineyard of Surgery*. Cambridge: Harvard University Press, 1958.

Washburn, Frederic A. *The Massachusetts General Hospital: Its Development, 1900–1935*. Boston: Houghton Mifflin, 1939.

Welch, Claude E. *A Twentieth-Century Surgeon: My Life in the Massachusetts General Hospital*. Boston: The Hospital, 1992.

White, Benjamin, Richard J. Wolfe, and Eugene Taylor. *Stanley Cobb: Builder of the Modern Neurosciences*. Boston: Francis A. Countway Library of Medicine, 1984.

White, James C. *Sketches from My Life*. Cambridge, Mass.: Riverside Press, 1914.

White, Paul Dudley. *My Life and Medicine*. Boston: Gambit, 1971.

Winsor, Justin, and Clarence F. Jewett, eds. *The Memorial History of Boston*. 4 vols. Boston: James R. Osgood, 1880–1881.

Wolf, Mary Ruth. *The Valiant Volunteers: The Beginnings, Growth, and Scope of Volunteerism at the Massachusetts General Hospital*. Boston: Massachusetts General Hospital, 1980.

Wyngaarden, James B. *An Unimagined Life: An Autobiography*. Durham, N.C.: BW&A Books, 2009.

Y, Ly, and John S. Driscoll. *Heaven Becomes Hell: A Survivor's Story of Life under the Khmer Rouge*. New Haven: Yale University Southeast Asia Studies, 2000.

Zervas, Nicholas, et al. *Neurosurgery at the Massachusetts General Hospital, 1909–1983*. Boston: Massachusetts General Hospital, 1984.

Periodicals

Anesthesiology
Annals of Internal Medicine
Annals of Surgery
Archives of Pediatrics
Boston Globe
Boston Medical and Surgical Journal
BWH Bulletin
Caring Headlines
Fruit Street Physician
Good Housekeeping
Harbus
Harvard Alumni Bulletin
Harvard Medical Alumni Bulletin
Harvard University Gazette
International Anesthesiology Clinics
Journal of Bone and Joint Surgery
Journal of Neurosurgery
Journal of Nursing Administration
Journal of Shoulder and Elbow Surgery
Journal of the American Academy of Dermatology
Journal of the American Dental Society of Anesthesiology
Journal of the American Medical Association

MGH Hotline
Nature
New England Journal of Medicine
New Yorker
New York Times
Proto: Dispatches from the Frontiers of Medicine
Science
Time
Urology
Voices: The Art and Science of Psychotherapy

Miscellaneous Sources

Ambulatory Clinics Committee of Massachusetts General Hospital. Report (known as the Farnsworth Report). 1958. Provided to author by John D. Stoeckle.

Campbell, C. Macfie. "History of Insanity during the Past Century with Special Reference to the McLean Hospital." In *Memorial and Historical Volume Together with the Proceedings of the Centennial of the Opening of the Hospital*, by Massachusetts General Hospital, pp. 42–57. Boston: Griffith-Stillings Press, 1921.

"Historical Sketch of McLean" Folder, McLean Hospital Archives.

"History of the MGH Sports Medicine Service," www2.massgeneral.org/sports/history.html.

Leaf, Alexander. "Autobiographical Memoirs and Oral History Interview with Arnold S. Relman." 1996. Unpublished; on file in MGH Archives.

Martin, Joseph B. Memoir. Unpublished manuscript provided to author.

Massachusetts General Hospital. Annual reports, 1945–1992.

Pisano, Gary P., and Maryam Golnaraghi. "Partners HealthCare System, Inc. (A)." Harvard Business School, case 9-696-062. 1996.

Satin, David G. "Erich Lindemann: The Humanist and the Era of Community Mental Health." *Proceedings of the American Philosophical Society* 126.4 (1982): 327–346.

"75th Anniversary Symposium: Celebrating 75 Years of Research, Teaching, and Clinical Care." MGH Department of Psychiatry, October 24, 2009.

Stoeckle, John D. Unpublished history of MGH Outpatient Department, provided to author.

INDEX OF NAMES

· · · · · · · · · · · ·

Baldessarini, Ross, MD, 186
Baldwin, Henry C., MD, 340
Baldwin, Robert L. ("Buzz"), PhD, 444
Ballantine, H. Thomas, Jr., MD, 392–394
Balogh, Karoly, MD, 95
Baltimore, David, PhD, 443
Banchiere, Guillermo Jorge ("Bill"), 411–412
Bander, KatherineWalker ("Kay"), 152, 276;
    during blizzard of '78, 329; on Buchanan, 352;
    Buchanan interviewed by, 350–351; on commu-
    nity outreach, 281; as endocrinologist, 276; fund-
    raising activities of, 336; as general director's
    secretary, 276, 277, 322; on heart transplantation
    service, 325–326; on Hoechst–MGH negotia-
    tions, 333; on Knowles, 316, 320; as LVC volun-
    teer, 278; marriage of, 278; on Sanders, 320; as
    staff services director, 276
Bander, Martin, 278, 278–279, 322
Bangsberg, David, MD, 265, 433
Baringer, J. Richard, MD, 342
Barnard, Christiaan, MD, PhD, 291, 324
Barnes, Ann Brace, MD, 385
Barnett, G. Octo, MD, 292, 471
Barney, J. Dellinger, MD, 197, 312, 313
Barnicle, Michael ("Mike"), 461
Barr, Joseph Seaton, MD, 78, 240, 392
Barrell, Joseph, 22
Bartlett, John, Rev., 18
Bartlett, Marshall K., MD, 178, 240, 273, 289,
    300, 421
Bartush, Paul, 201, 203, 203–204
Baselga, José, MD, PhD, 377, 420
Basgoz, Nesli, MD, 265
Bauer, Walter C., MD, 153, 247, 401; as Arthri-
    tis Unit head, 247–248; as chief of medicine,
    150–151, 248, 276, 417; clinical cancer research
    opposed by, 368; connective tissue disease
    research of, 150–151; Cope and, 176, 206; as
    COR member, 222; death of, 244, 272, 274; full-
    time service of, 246; hires of, 141, 156, 254, 293,
    368, 370; human touch of, 247; lead poisoning
    studies of, 148; Lindemann and, 183; medical
    subspecialties increased by, 213, 248–251; as
    mentor, 253; Outpatient Dept. and, 242–243,
    244; polio epidemic and, 252–253; research pro-
    moted by, 246–247; retirement of, 221; signifi-
    cance of, 246; WWII military service of, 247
Baulcombe, Sir David, PhD, 439, 492n31
Baum, Stanley, MD, 116
Beach, Henry Harris Aubrey, MD, 14
Beal, M. Flint, MD, 347
Beaulieu, Jacques, 311
Beaumont, William, MD, 41
Beckman, William W., MD, 246
Bedson, Sir Samuel Phillips, 172
Beecher, Henry Knowles, MD, 45, 279; Anesthe-
    sia Department headed by, 50–51; anesthesia

recruitment efforts of, 48–50; anesthesia research
    of, 46–48, 52; Copenhagen fellowship of, 46,
    172; family background of, 45–46; in HMS class
    of '32, 171; HMS faculty status of, 289; as MGH
    anesthesiologist, 44–45; publications of, 207;
    reputation of, 44; on Smith-Petersen, 77; succes-
    sors of, 51–52; WWII military service of, 46, 207
Belknap, Jeremiah, 26
Belknap, Mary, 26–27
Bell, Luther, 27–28, 28, 90
Belliveau, Jack, 119
Belsey, Ronald, MD, 177
Bendixen, Henrik, MD, 47, 49
Benedict, Edward D., MD, 172, 177
Benedict, Gano, MD, 231
Benson, Herbert, MD, 180
Beresin, Eugene, MD, 188
Berg, Paul, PhD, 444
Bernards, René, PhD, 373
Berry, George Packer, 279, 291
Bertolami, Charles, DDS, 311
Bertucci, Claire, 361
Bertucci, John, 361
Betancourt, Joseph, MD, 408
Bianchi, Diana, MD, 209–210
Biedermann, Joseph, MD, 186
Bigatello, Luca, MD, 50
Bigelow, Edward, 279
Bigelow, Henry Jacob, MD, 58, 99, 280; BTSN
    opposed by, 65–66; Charitable Surgical Institu-
    tion founded by, 58–59; Civil War service of,
    62; death of, 100; ether as anesthetic promoted
    by, 40, 41; family background of, 57; medical
    ethics of, 99–100; as MGH house surgeon, 58;
    microscope as used by, 57; morbid specimens col-
    lection of, 90; patient care as viewed by, 98–99;
    retirement of, 100; skin disease ward opposed by,
    88; specialization opposed by, 72, 266; as surgical
    pioneer, 37, 56–57, 70, 72, 98, 311; as Tremont
    St. Medical School surgery instructor, 60; ward
    named after, 85
Bigelow, Jacob, MD, 34, 42, 57, 58, 59, 280
Bigelow, Jacob, Rev., 57
Bigelow, Luke, 27
Bigelow, William Sturgis, MD, 100, 280
Billings, Mrs. (BTSN superintendent), 66
Binger, Carl, MD, 181
Bird, Edward D. ("Ted"), MD, 490n18
Bird, Kenneth T., MD, 281
Birnbaum, Robert, MD, PhD, 189
Black, Paul H., MD, 257
Blackburn, Elizabeth, PhD, 438
Blackman, Maeve, 201, 201
Black-Schaffer, W. Stephen, MD, 97
Blair-Bell, William, MD, 364
Blake, Curtis, 356
Blake, Francis, 92

early career of, 215; Ether Day centennial coordinated by, 213, 215–216; MGH history edited by, 95; successors of, 358; Zamecnik Nobel possibilities and, 394

Crockett, Eugene A., MD, 215
Crouch, Mrs. R. K., 200
Crowley, William F., Jr., MD, *159*, 159–160
Cudkowicz, Merit E., MD, 346–347, 349, 416
Cullen, David, MD, 52
Culver, Perry, MD, 250
Cunningham, Thomas D., MD, 166–167
Curley, James Michael, 107–108
Cushing, Harvey, MD, 74, 110, 111, 172, 173, 391–392
Cutler, Elbridge, MD, 103, 104, 123

Daggett, Willard M. ("Bill"), MD, 298, 299, 324–325, 455
Daland, Ernest, MD, 175
Dale, Henry, MD, 172
Dane, Herbert ("Bert"), 358
Danforth, Samuel, 16
Daniels, Ann, RN, 430
Daniels, Gilbert H., MD, 156, 343
Davis, Jeff, 409, 410, *410*, 452, 456
Davis, Lincoln, MD, 164, 175
Davy, Humphry, 38–39
Dawson, Steven L., MD, 7, 449
Dec, G. William, MD, 144, *145*, 420
Deftos, Leonard, MD, 154
Demehin, Akinlua ("Akin"), 410
DeSanctis, Roman, MD, 139, 140–141, *143*, 143–144, 298, 357, 389
Dexter, Aaron, 12, 15
Dienes, Louis, MD, 251
DiMaggio, Tina, RN, *424*, 425
DiMillo, Tony, 425
Dineen, James J., MD, 357, 469
Dirksen, Everett, 317
Dirschel, Mark, RN, 6
Ditomassi, Marianne, RN, MBA, 430
Dix, Dorothea, 27
Dixon, Ronald, MD, 408
Dodd, Walter James, MD, 102, *111*, 111–113, *112*, 114, 121, 123, 163, 267
Dodds, T. Andrew, MD 133
Dodson, Thomas B., DMD, MPH, 309, *309*, 310
Dolliver, Pauline, RN, 126
Donahoe, Patricia K., MD, 231, 232–234, *233*, 237, 387, 412, 464
Donaldson, Gordon A. ("Butch"), MD, 300
Donoff, R. Bruce, DMD, MD, 306–307, *307*, 308
Downes, John J. ("Jack"), MD, 486n57
Drachman, Douglas, MD, 143
DuBois, Eugene F., MD, 148, 162
Dukakis, Michael, 329
Dunaif, Andrea, MD, 160

Durant, Fredericka, 459, 460
Durant, Joe, 461
Durant, Sean, 461
Durant, Stephen A., EdD, 460, 461, 462, 464
Durant, Thomas Stephen, MD, 435, 459–464, *461*, *462*, 468, 469, 472, 473
Dwight, Edmund, 129

Ebert, Robert H., MD, *279*, 292; as chief of medicine, 151, 275, 292; as HMS dean, 253, 275, 291, 292–293; on Knowles, 277, 292; managed care prototype founded by, 245, 292–293, 379; Sanders and, 335, 338; successors of, 248, 401
Eckstein, Gustav, MD, DDS, 187
Edes, Robert, 31
Edmunds, L. Henry, MD, 288
Edsall, David L., MD, 87, 101, 124, *133*, 181; assistants appointed by, 137, 172; Benedict Respiratory Apparatus of, 147; clinical research promoted by, 136–137, 146, 161, 446; early career of, 134–136; Harvard full-time system instituted by, 162; as HMS dean, 134, 147; as Jackson Professor, 132–133; as outsider, 472; professional dress of, 133–134; significance of, 128; Thyroid Clinic founded by, 155; Ward 4 and, 148
Edsall, Margaret Tileston, 135, 146
Edwards, Robert Geoffrey, PhD, 455
Ehrlich, Michael, MD, 79
Eisenberg, Leon, MD, *185*, 185–186, 190, 278
Eisenhower, Dwight D., 137, 138, 140
Eliot, Charles W., 105, 109, 129
Elliot, John W., MD, 391
Ellis, Calvin, 91
Ellis, Daniel S., MD, 240
Ellison, Eben, 356
Elrick, Jean, MD, 412, 452, 456
Emerson, Louville Eugene, MD, 182, 190
Emerson, Ralph Waldo, 10, 38, 42, 129
Erickson, Jeanette Ives. *See* Ives Erickson, Jeanette
Erikson, Erik, 182, 484n46
Esposito, Philip ("Phil"), 81
Eustis, Richard, MD, 137
Evins, Eden, MD, MPH, 190
Ezekowitz, Alan B., MD, 231, 236, 237

Farley, Dianne, 5
Farnsworth, Dana L., MD, 244
Farrisey, Ruth, RN, *243*, 243
Faust, Drew Gilpin, PhD, 264
Fava, Maurizio, MD, 186, 189
Favaloro, René, MD, 298
Faxon, Nathaniel W., MD, *191*, 198; on Beecher, 48; as COR member, 222; on early research, 364; on Ether Day centenary, 214; as GEC member, 192; as general director, 169, 179, 206; MGH history written by, 200, 341; on MGH WWII contributions, 196–197; publications of, 211;

Quinlan, Joan, 287, 409

Rabb, Sidney R., 279
Rabkin, Mitchell, MD, 151, 152
Rackemann, Francis M., MD, 146, 228
Ragon, Phillip T. ("Terry"), 262–264, 263
Ragon, Susan, 263
Raker, John W., MD, 300, 366
Randall, John, MD, 34
Randolph, Mark, 81, 83
Ransom, John, MD, 421
Rappaport, Jerome, 281
Rattner, David, MD, 302, 449
Rauch, Paula, MD, 375
Rauch, Scott, MD, 188
Ray, Peter Williams, 405–406
Raymond, Ted, 371, 372
Reagan, Ronald, 417
Reber, Howard, MD, 421
Redstone, Sumner, 209, 359–360
Reichlin, Seymour, MD, PhD, 343
Reid, Andrea, MD, 408
Reilly, Peggy, RN, 131
Remensnyder, John P., MD, 302, 465
Revere, Paul, 11
Reynolds, Edward, MD, 106
Rhinelander, F. W., MD, 206
Richards, Linda, RN, 66, 422
Richardson, Edward Peirson, Jr., MD, 94, 343, 344, 384
Richardson, Edward Peirson, Sr., MD, 124, 148, 171–172
Richardson, Elliot L., 209, 384
Richardson, George S., MD, 159–160, 382, 384–385, 386
Richardson, Henry Hobson, 100
Richardson, Mary Rich, 127
Richardson, Maurice Howe, MD, 88, 91, 104, 105, 123, 124, 171, 172, 384
Richardson, Wyman, MD, 197
Ridgeway, E. Chester ("Chip"), MD, 156, 158
Rimm, Allison Caplan, 456
Risser, Nancy, 446
Robbins, Catherine ("Cathy"), 403
Robbins, Laurence L., MD, 113, 115, 115, 116, 279
Roberts, Brooke, MD, 153
Roberts, Jesse ("Jay"), MD, 54
Robie, Theodore P., MD, 485n10
Roche, Joseph, RN, 467
Rodkey, Grant V., MD, 300
Roentgen, Wilhelm Conrad, PhD, 111, 147
Rogers, William, MD, 79
Romano, Maryalyce, RN, 467
Ronan, Laurence J. ("Larry"), MD, 462, 466
Roncarati, Jill, 470
Roosevelt, Eleanor, 247

Roosevelt, Franklin D., 150
Ropper, Allan H., MD, 341, 345, 346
Rosand, Jonathan, MD, 347
Rosen, Bruce, MD, PhD, 119, 120, 120, 121
Rosen, Joy B., 189
Rosenbaum, Jerrold, MD, 184, 186, 188–190, 189
Rosenberg, Andrew E., MD, 97, 260
Rosenblatt, Michael, MD, 154, 155
Rosenfield, Kenneth, MD, 143, 144
Rosenwald, Julius, 406
Roser, Steven, DMD, MD, 307, 311
Ross, Douglas, MD, 156
Rotch, Thomas Morgan, MD, 226
Roueché, Berton, 255, 256
Rowe, Carter, MD, 73, 77, 81
Rowell, Patricia ("Pat"), 201–203, 202
Rubash, Harry E., 82, 82–84
Rubin, Nina, MD, 329
Rubin, Robert H., MD, 257
Rubin, Solomon H., MD, 406
Rush, Benjamin, 60
Ruskin, Jeremy, MD, 142
Russell, Mary, 86
Russell, Paul S., MD, 1, 279, 290, 300; on Austen, 301; on Bauer, 247; cancer facilities outlined by, 281; early career of, 275, 289–291; HMS faculty status of, 295; on MGH insider culture, 275–276; replacement of, 295, 322; specialization undemanded by, 301; as surgery chief, 247, 272–273, 289, 291, 295, 298; as transplantation pioneer, 295, 302, 323–325, 326; as transplantation research chief, 327–328, 329
Rutter, William J., MD, 331–332
Ruvkun, Gary, PhD, 334, 433–434, 439–442, 440, 492n31
Ryan, Edward T., MD, 258

Sabin, Albert, MD, 253
Sachs, David H., MD, 302, 327, 327–329
Sachs, Gary, MD, 186, 189
Sachs, Hans, 182–183
Sackett, Andrew, MD, 282
Safren, Steven, PhD, 190
Salk, Jonas, MD, 208, 253
Sanders, Ann, 320
Sanders, Charles Addison, MD, 95, 298, 320; achievements of, 272, 336; on Austen, 295–296, 299; capital campaign launched under, 330, 336, 354–355, 357; cardiac cath lab run by, 116, 142, 319–320; community health promoted by, 308; on Crockett, 218–219; GEC and, 278; as general director, 142, 158, 221, 244–245, 278, 320–322, 336; Goodman recruited by, 445; on heart transplantation proposal, 325; Hoechst–MGH deal promoted by, 158, 332–334, 335, 336, 434; IHP and, 68; on Knowles, 276–277, 351; on Knowles's replacement search, 319; on Leaf, 293,

Strauss, H. William, MD, 117
Stuart, Gilbert, 26
Sturtevant, Georgia, 64–65, 422
Suby, Howard, MD, 313
Suit, Herman D., MD, 367, 413–414, 414, 415
Sullivan, Annie, 106
Sutton, S. B., 95, 215
Swartz, Jacob, MD, 253–254
Swartz, Morton N., MD, 226, 248, 250, 251,
    254–257, 266
Sweet, Richard, MD, 173
Sweet, Roger, MD, 286
Sweet, William H., MD, 279, 392–394, 393, 396,
    414
Sykes, Megan, MD, 329
Szostak, Jack, PhD, 226, 399, 433–434, 435, 436,
    438, 438–439, 441, 442, 443, 446

Tafe, Joan, RN, 467
Talairach, Jean, MD, 395
Talbot, Fritz B., MD, 227–229, 230
Talbot, Nathan B., MD, 229, 230, 231, 279
Talbott, John, MD, 151
Tanabe, Kenneth, MD, 302, 366
Tanenbaum, Lewis, MD, 269–270
Tanzi, Rudolph E., PhD, 347
Tarbell, Nancy J., MD, 398, 412–413, 414–416,
    415
Taveras, Juan M., MD, 113, 114, 116, 116–117,
    118
Taylor, Carol, 189
Taylor, E. Wyllys, MD, 340–341
Taylor, Grantley, MD, 178
Taylor, Isaac, MD, 250
Taylor, Rebecca, 30, 30, 64
Teixeira, Jose, PhD, 233
Termeer, Henri A., 222
Terry, Edith, 139, 227–228
Thayer, Mrs. Nathaniel, 130
Thayer, Nathaniel, 66
Thier, Paula, 401, 403
Thier, Samuel O., MD, 311, 400, 403; Ausiello
    and, 419–420; diversity promoted by, 409; early
    career of, 316, 382, 401–402; as first Jewish presi-
    dent, 108; on future success, 476; on Knowles,
    316; MGH recruitment of, 402; on Partners
    merger, 383; as president, 316, 356, 382, 398,
    402–405, 452; successors of, 417, 418
Thoma, Kurt H., DMD, 303, 304, 309
Thomas, Lewis, MD, 85–86
Thompson, James E. ("Jim"), 358–359, 360,
    360–361, 371
Thompson, Marjorie, 358
Thorndike, Augustus, MD, 80–81
Thorndike, Nicholas, 219, 295, 318, 319, 352,
    353, 356, 402, 418
Thorndike, W. T. S., MD, 196

Thrall, James, MD, 117–118, 121–122, 356
Thulborn, Keith, MD, 119–120
Tilden, Bryant, 31
Todd, Donald P., MD, 46–47, 49, 52
Todres, I. David, MD, 236
Tokson, Louis, 451–452
Tolman, Maurice, MD, 267
Tomford, William, MD, 79
Tompkins, Ronald G., MD, 208, 209–211, 210,
    302
Toner, Mehmet, PhD, 209, 376–377
Torchiana, David F., MD, 379, 476; on Buchanan,
    354; on Codman, 76; early career of, 378–379,
    454; family background of, 453; health care
    pyramid of, 381, 382; as heart surgeon, 455; as
    MGPO president/CEO, 76, 122, 192, 378, 398,
    455–456; on outdated facilities, 349–350; Slavin
    and, 192, 450–451, 451, 453, 456
Tosteson, Daniel, MD, 381, 402
Toth, Thomas L., MD, 387
Towle, Harvey P., MD, 267
Townsend, Solomon D., MD, 85, 103
Traut, Herbert, MD, 385
Treadwell, John, 64
Tregear, Geoffrey, PhD, 154
Trilling, Lionel, 248
Troulis, Maria J., DDS, 309, 310, 310, 450
Truman, Harry S., 184
Tsao, Hensin, MD, 271
Tuckerman, Edward, 17
Tully, Susan, 50
Turner, Robert, PhD, 120
Tyler, John, 28, 62

Ulfelder, Howard, MD, 279, 366–367, 385, 386
Upham, George P., 89–90
Upham, George P., Jr., 90

Vacanti, Joseph ("Jay"), MD, 234, 234–235, 302,
    486n56
Vagelos, Roy, MD, 336
Vandam, Leroy, MD, 51
Van de Graaff, Robert J., PhD, 365
Van Lennep, Jacob, 31
Vaughan, Mrs. Henry, 218
Vega-Barachowitz, Carmen, RN, 430
Velmahos, George, MD, 209
Vickery, Herman, MD, 123
Victor, Maurice, MD, 342
Villringer, Arno, MD, 119
Vincent, Beth, MD, 175, 229
Vincent, Mary Ann, 383–384, 384
Vogel, Morris J., 108, 109
Vose, R. H., MD, 197
Vrahas, Mark, MD, 82

Wakamatsu, May M., MD, 387

Walch, William E., 358
Walker, Bruce D., MD, 260, 260–266, 449
Walker, W. Allan, MD, 236–237
Wall, Patrick D., 53
Walsh, Barbara, RN, 466–467
Walsh, Kate, 374, 405, 415
Walsh, William B., MD, 465
Walton, George L., MD, 339–340
Walton, John, 342
Wang, An, PhD, 330, 330
Wang, C. C., MD, 367
Wang, Chiu-An, MD, 156, 302
Wang, Thomas, MD, 145
Ware, John, MD, 34, 103
Warren, J. Collins ("Coll"), 35, 44, 62–64, 69, 70–71, 106, 110
Warren, J. Mason, 35, 84
Warren, John Collins, MD, 13; amputation skill of, 9, 15; assistant surgeons hired by, 103; bedside manner of, 14–15; circular letter drawn up by, 18; family background of, 12; friendship with Jackson, 13–14; full MGH privileges of, 4, 102; fund-raising activities of, 363; HMS relocation suggested by, 60; as medical apprentice, 12–13; MGH duties of, 29; as MGH founder, 9; morbid specimens collection of, 90–91; skeleton of, 91; surgical anesthesia pioneered by, 14, 40, 42; as teacher, 134; trepanning performed by, 390; tumor studies by, 362; as volunteer, 198; Warren Anatomical Museum founded by, 35; Warren Library endowed by, 199
Warren, John, Sr., 11–12, 15–16
Warren, Joseph, 9, 11
Warshaw, Andrew L., MD, 235, 302, 415, 420, 420–421
Washburn, Frederic A., MD: on contemporary hospital care, 125–126; on Dodd, 112, 113; as GEC charter member, 124; as general director, 124; on MGH competition, 101, 482n53; MGH history written by, 163, 167, 219; nurses reporting to, 423; on Stevens, 127; on surgeons and change, 123; on trustees, 219; WWI military service of, 138, 164–166, 167
Washington, Deborah, RN, 398, 409
Waterhouse, Benjamin, 12, 15–16
Waterman, George A., MD, 111–112
Watkins, Arthur, MD, 74, 207
Watkins, Michael, MD, 408
Webster, Edward ("Ted"), PhD, 115, 116–117
Webster, John, 61–62
Wedel, Suzanne, MD, 7
Weinberg, Arnold N., MD, 257
Weinberg, Martha Wagner, 405
Weiner, David, 383
Weinstein, Louis, MD, 252, 255
Weisberger, David, DMD, MD, 279, 303–304
Weisman, Avery, MD, 187

Weissleder, Ralph, MD, PhD, 121, 448
Weissman, Gail Kuhn, RN, 425, 427
Welch, Charles, MD, 186
Welch, Claude E., MD, 273; as Allen associate, 175–176; on Allen St. House, 85; on Churchill resident training, 178; educational background of, 171, 176; HMS faculty status of, 289; on Knowles, 277; on medical school graduates, 170; memoir of, 481n55, 483n3; as mentor, 421; on surgeons and change, 272, 483n3; Surgical Associates formed by, 300; surgical career of, 171; as Tumor Clinic chief, 366; on Washburn, 164
Weld, Charles G., MD, 88, 111
Wells, Horace, DDS, 39
Wendell, Barrett, 161
Wexler, Nancy, PhD, 344
Weyman, Arthur, MD, 144
Wheeler, Edwin, MD, 140
Wheelock, Frank, MD, 300
Whelan, Brenda, RN, 467
Whipple, George H., MD, 364
White, Benjamin V., MD, 150
White, Charles James, MD, 266–267
White, Dorothy, 137
White, E. Michael, 243, 244
White, George Abbott, PhD, 247
White, James C., MD, 59, 172, 176, 197, 266, 266, 267
White, James Clarke, MD, 392–394, 393, 395, 396
White, Mary E. Consuela, 426
White, Paul Dudley, MD, 116, 129; Cabot obituary written by, 132; as cardiologist, 137–140, 248; as celebrity physician, 137, 138, 140; as Edsall assistant, 137, 172; Edsall as viewed by, 134; Framingham Heart Study established by, 144–145; pediatric cardiac clinic offered by, 229; Psychiatry Service and, 182; as surgical pioneer, 172–173; WWI military service of, 138
Whitman, Elizabeth, 39
Whitman, Lemuel, 39
Whittier, Isabelle, 228
Wiener-Kronish, Jeanine, MD, 56, 56
Wightman, Joseph, 40
Wilbur, David C., MD, 97
Wilbur, Ray Lyman, MD, 191
Wilens, Timothy ("Tim"), MD, 190
Wilhelm, Sabine, PhD, 190
Wilkie, D. T. D., 172
Wilkins, Earle W., Jr., MD, 4–5, 7–8, 177, 300
Wilkins, Roy, 238–239
Willard, Joseph, 12
Williams, Conger, MD, 140
Williams, Hibberd, MD, 319
Williams, Ralph C., MD, 251
Williams, Winfred W. ("Win"), MD, 406–407, 407, 408, 409
Wilson, Charles, 303

GENERAL INDEX

. . . .

Korean War, 199, 242
Kresge Foundation, 225
Kubik Laboratory for Neuropathology, 94

laboratory tests, 96–97
Ladies' Home Journal, 320, 424
Ladies Visiting Committee, 169, 198–201, 199, 221
Laing Dispensary, 109
Latino Professional Network, 411
Lawrence (Mass.), 10, 106–107
Lawrence Center for Quality and Safety, 457
Lawrence E. Martin Laboratories, 372, 447
L. C. Elliot Private Hospital (Boston), 44, 109
Lead Industries Association, 148, 364
lead poisoning studies, 364
LEAP (Learning and Emotional Assessment Program), 190
Legionnaire's disease outbreak (1976), 257
Letheon (anesthetic), 40–41
leukemia, 375–376
Lindemann Center, 185
Lipids Clinic, 160
litholapaxy, 70, 98, 311
liver transplantation, 235, 323, 324, 325, 326
Livorno (Italy), 196
Logan International Airport Medical Station, 281, 488n42
Long Island Hospital in Boston Harbor, 101
Lowell (Mass.), 10, 106–107
Lunder Building, 3–4, 55, 359, 360, 396–397, 451, 474, 475
Lunder Foundation, 3, 359
lung transplantation, 326

Magnet Hospitals, 432–433, 492n30
Magnet Hospital Study, The, 432, 492n30
magnetic resonance imaging (MRI), 117, 118, 122, 413; functional (fMRI), 118–120
Magnet Nursing Services Recognition Program, 432
malaria, 88
Mallinckrodt Chair in Anesthesiology, 55
managed care, 245, 292–293, 379, 380, 404, 453
March of Dimes, 50
Martha's Vineyard Hospital, 122, 382
Martin Luther King Day, 410
Martinos Center for Biomedical Imaging, 121, 223
Massachusetts Biological Research Corporation (MBRC), 372
Massachusetts Board of Higher Education, 68
Massachusetts Eye and Ear Infirmary, 88, 91, 95, 101, 108, 193, 229, 356
Massachusetts General Court. *See* Massachusetts Legislature
Massachusetts General Hospital (MGH): Brahmin dominance at, 36, 105–106; capital campaign launched by, 330, 337, 354–355; chartering of, 16, 18–21, 20, 330; circular letter proposing, 18,

19, 475; competing hospitals, 91, 101, 104–105, 108–110, 482n53; early years of, 29–33, 32, 102–103; expansion of, 37, 84–88, 85, 193–195; fees at, 124; finances at, 31–33, 87, 216–218, 418; first patient at, 251; founding of, 9, 11, 15–21; fund-raising for, 21–22, 215–219; future success of, 476; industrial investments in, 332–335, 489n137; inpatient admissions (2010), 4; IRS audit of, 317; as Magnet Hospital, 432–433; mission of, 5–6, 103–104, 287, 475; mummy donated to, 31, 31; nonprofit subsidiaries of, 330; opening of (1821), 28; outdated facilities at, 349–350; power plant for, 88; private services at, 124–128; relationship with HMS, 173–174, 307, 447; relationship with MIT, 348; research budget of, 118; salaries at, 170; sesquicentennial celebration (1961), 226, 274; site of, 22; southernmost branch of, 54, 55; staff at, 29, 409; staff reorganization at, 192–193; as teaching hospital, 134; as volunteer operation, 198; Warren/Jackson legacies at, 33–36. *See also* Partners HealthCare; *specific building, department*
Massachusetts General Hospital (MGH) Corporation, 26–27, 274, 281
Massachusetts General Hospital (MGH)/MIT Morris Udall Center of Excellence in PD Research, 348
Massachusetts General Hospital Center for Medical Simulation, 7
Massachusetts General Hospital–Harvard Medical School MD-OMFS Program, 307
Massachusetts General Hospital Manual of Oral and Maxillofacial Surgery (ed. Donoff), 307
Massachusetts General Hospital Radiology Associates, 118
Massachusetts General Hospital Staff Association, 240
Massachusetts General Hospital Training School for Nurses, 67, 68, 423
Massachusetts General Physicians Corporation (MGPC), 455
Massachusetts General Physicians Organization (MGPO): Austen as CEO of, 417, 418, 454; Dental Group Practice and, 307; founding of, 192, 299, 338, 379–380, 403; as group practice, 246, 301, 338; medical director of, 458; MGH power balance and, 398; PSC reorganized as, 330; relationship with hospital administration, 191–192, 338, 380, 450–451, 456; Slavin as CEO of, 453; Staff Associates as forerunner of, 240; Torchiana as CEO of, 76, 122, 378–379, 454, 455–456
Massachusetts General Psychiatry Academy, 189
Massachusetts Heart Association, 488n76
Massachusetts Hospital Life Insurance Company, 32
Massachusetts Institute of Technology (MIT), 83, 223, 264, 334, 348, 449, 450

Massachusetts Legislature, 16, 17, 18–21, 27
Massachusetts Medical Society, 11, 131
Massachusetts Memorial Hospitals, 101
Massachusetts Port Authority, 281
Massachusetts State House, 10, 23, 108
MassGeneral Hospital *for* Children (MGH*f*C),
  231, 236, 237–238, 359, 360, 405, 462, 486n56
MassGeneral Institute for Neurodegenerative Disease, 348
Mass General North Shore Medical Center for
  Outpatient Care (Danvers, Mass.), 84, 200, 285,
  307, 475
Mass General West Building (Waltham, Mass.),
  83–84
Maxwell and Eleanor Blum Patient and Family
  Learning Center, 431, 432
Mayo Clinic (Rochester, Minn.), 104, 146–147,
  313
McCarthyism, 230
McGill University (Montreal), 343
McKinsey and Company (consulting firm), 322
McLean Asylum for the Insane, 89; Appleton
  Ward, 89; Belknap House for female patients at,
  27, 32, 89; bequests to, 26–27; boarding rates
  at, 27; chartering of, 20; circular letter proposing, 18, 19; finances at, 31–32; fund-raising for,
  21–22; growth of, 27–28; nursing at, 67–68;
  opening of (1818), 24–25, 25; psychiatric treatment at, 25; relocation of, 38, 89–90; renaming of, 26, 28, 89; steward position at, 25–26;
  Upham Memorial Building, 89–90; Wyman as
  superintendent of, 24–26, 27. *See also* McLean
  Hospital for the Mentally Ill
McLean Hospital Corporation, 330, 402
McLean Hospital for the Mentally Ill, 101;
  McLean Asylum for the Insane renamed as, 26,
  28, 89; neuropathology interest at, 490n18; quality of, 356; Wyman as superintendent of, 9. *See
  also* McLean Asylum for the Insane
McMurdo Station (Antarctica), 54, 55
M. D. Anderson Proton Therapy Center, 417
Medicaid, 246, 272, 282, 284, 286
medical apprenticeships, 12
medical assistants, 30
medical education: cardiology, 139; continuing,
  in pathology, 98; at IHP, 68–69; 19th-century,
  59–60; number of schools, 133; in nursing,
  64–67, 65, 66
medical errors, 456–457
medical ethics, 99–100, 131–132
Medical Executive Committee, 192
Medical Intensive Care Unit (MICU), 50
Medical Interpreter Program, 201, 427
Medicare: administrative problems resulting
  from, 295, 354; amendments to (1969), 417;
  community health centers and, 286; financial
  changes resulting from, 115–116, 272, 284;

implementation of, 283; inflation and, 321;
  Knowles's report analyzing (1966), 317; legislative mandate for, 282; MGPO and, 330; OPD
  clinics and, 246
Medicine Department: Ausiello as chief of,
  419–420; CHGR and, 448; diversity in trainees
  in, 406–407; full complement of, 491n2; group
  practice in, 245; heart transplantation and, 323;
  Means as chief of, 161–163; medical ethics and,
  133; significance of, in academic medical centers,
  146; specialization in, 213, 248, 294; training
  program in, 400–401
Medico-Mechanical Department, 73–74
Melanoma Program, 271
Memorial Sloan-Kettering Cancer Center (New
  York), 368
Menninger Foundation, 356
Men's Visiting Committee, 198
Mental Health Act (1946), 184
Mental Health Unit, 184
Merck, 336
MGH-Timilty (Middle School) Science Connection, 411
microscope, 57, 90, 96
midwives, 386
mind-body medicine, 180–181
Minority High School Student Research Apprentice Program, 411
Mixter Laboratories for Neurosurgical Research,
  394
Mixter Neurosurgical Library, 394–395
Modern Urology (H. Cabot), 312
molecular biology: CHGR and, 448; departmental
  collegiality, 435–436; endocrinology and, 154,
  155; faculty of, 433–434; Goodman's research
  in, 331–332; Hoechst AG–MGH research deal
  and, 158, 331–332; research in, 55, 78, 157, 347,
  434–443; young recruits in, 443–446. *See also*
  Hoechst AG–MGH research deal
Molecular Endocrinology Department, 158
molecular imaging, 121
Molecular Pathology and Research Division, 95
Molecular Therapeutics Laboratory, 376
Monsanto, 334–335
Mont Blanc (cargo ship), wreck of (1917), 166
moral management, 22
Morning Report, 143, 322
Morton Chair in Anesthesiology, 55
Moseley Building, 4, 137
Mount Auburn Cemetery, 57
Mt. Sinai Hospital, 109
Müllerian inhibiting substance (MIS), 233
Multicultural Affairs Office (MAO), 407, 407–409
Murphy Army Hospital (Waltham, Mass.), 199
Musculoskeletal Research and Innovation Laboratory, 83
Musculoskeletal Tissue Engineering Laboratory, 83

myasthenia gravis, 341
myocardial infarction, 141
Myocardial Infarction Research Unit (MIRU), 142

Nantucket Cottage Hospital, 382
National Academy of Sciences, 299, 369, 402
National Aeronautics and Space Administration (NASA), 414
National Cancer Act (1971), 314
National Cancer Institute, 328, 370, 414
National Council on Health Care Technology, 331
National Disaster Medical System (NDMS), 466
National Geographic, 294
National Heart Institute, 140, 225
National Hockey League (NHL), 81
National Institute of General Medical Sciences (NIGMS), 210, 275
National Institute of Mental Health (NIMH), 184, 189
National Institute on Aging, 345
National Institutes of Health (NIH), 53, 122, 141, 142, 152, 153, 158, 213, 271, 328, 343–344, 365, 372, 373–374, 450
National Patient Safety Foundation, 52
National Research Council, 251
National Science Foundation, 55
Native Americans, 406, 491n10
Nature (journal), 145, 260, 264–265, 290
Neighborhood Health Care Groups, 286
Nelson Mandela Medical School, 262
Neonatal Intensive Care Unit (NICU), 50
nephrology, 420
Neuroendocrine Unit, 156, 158–159
neuroendocrinology, 343, 345
neurofibromatosis, 347
Neuro ICU, 50
neurology, 338; CHGR and, 448; early developments in, 339–342; faculty of (1980s), 343; first female chief of, 345–349; lab space for, 394; research in, 341, 342–345, 346–349; subspecialties in, 347–348
Neurology Clinical Trials Unit, 346–347
Neurology Department, 180, 192
neuropathology, 341, 490n18
Neuropathology Laboratory, 94
neurosurgery, 338, 345; allure of, 393–394; early efforts, 390–392; lab space for, 394–395; Ojemann as ideal practitioner of, 389–390; operating room for, 392; recent developments in, 395–397, 414; White-Sweet years, 392–395
New England Association of Schools and Colleges, 69
New England Cardiovascular Society, 488n76
New England Hospital for Women and Children, 422
New England Journal of Medicine, 30, 47, 130, 173–174, 230, 253, 278, 303, 326, 328, 376, 421

New England Medical Center, 235, 252, 404, 411
New England Organ Bank, 429
New England Patriots, 81, 81, 82
New England Revolution, 82
Newton-Wellesley Hospital, 238, 382
New Yorker, 52, 255
New York Eye Infirmary, 41
New York Salmonella Center, 255
New York Times, 292
nitric oxide, 53–54
nitrous oxide, as anesthesia, 39, 53–54, 57
Norman Knight Nursing Center for Clinical and Professional Development, 430, 432
Northeast Proton Therapy Center, 375
North End Diet Kitchen, 194, 194
North Shore Children's Hospital (Salem, Mass.), 238
North Shore Medical Center (Lynn, Mass.), 382
North Shore Medical Center (Salem, Mass.), 382
Norton-Brown brace, 74
Novartis, 332
nuclear medicine, 115
Nurses' Associated Alumnae of the United States and Canada, 68
nurses/nursing: as anesthetists, 43–44; in community clinics, 281; at competing hospitals, 108–109; DNP degree in, 69; education of, 64–67, 65, 66, 422, 426; future role of, 427; housing for, 86; importance of, 322, 428–430; at McLean Asylum, 67–68; narratives of, 428–430; 19th-century views of, 29–30, 67, 422; OB/GYN, 388; professionalization of, 423–424, 430–433; racial discrimination ends in, 196; reorganization of, 426–427; research in, 425, 431–432; shortages of, 197, 217, 423–424, 430. *See also* patient care
Nutrition Clinic, 228

OB/GYN, 237, 338, 349, 383–389
obstetrics, 237, 386–389, 426. *See also* OB/GYN
Occupational Therapy, 199
occupational therapy, 427
Office for Minority Health Professions, 406–407. *See also* Multicultural Affairs Office (MAO)
Office for Women's Careers (OWC), 412, 415–416
Office of Quality and Safety, 457
Office of Scientific Research and Development (OSRD), 211–212
Ojemann Chair of Neurosurgery, 396
Olympic Games (Sarajevo; 1984), 81
oncology, 338, 420; Cancer Center and, 361–362; divergent tracks in, 366–368; early efforts, 362–363; genetic research on, 375–377; hematology-oncology training program, 368–369; Huntington Laboratories research, 363, 363–365; proton beam therapy, 413–414; radiation, 412–413, 475; surgery, 302, 366
"One Hundred Dinner," 377

open-heart surgery, 296, 298
Operating Building, 4
operating rooms, *171*, 193, 392
Operations Improvement (OI), 427, 453, 455
Ophthalmological Department, 88
Optimum Care Committee, 187
Oral Anesthesiology (Thoma), 303
oral-maxillofacial surgery, 302; CIMIT and, 450; dual-degree training in, 305–306; early developments in, 303–307; full-time system instituted for, 306; high-tech imaging in, 310; MGH/HMS program in, 307; pediatric, 307–308; recent developments in, 307–311; research themes in, 309–310; residency program in, 304, 309
Oral Surgery, Oral Medicine, Oral Pathology (journal), 303
Orbit (triage system), 5
Organization of the Petroleum Exporting Countries (OPEC), 321
organ transplantation: bone marrow, 326, 328–329; controversies over, 221, 272, 294, 322–323, 324–326; early feasibility of, 47–48; ethics of, 48; heart, 272, 291, 294, 322–323, 324–326; kidneys, 291, 326, 328–329, 489n122; limiting factors in, 324; liver, 235, 323, 324, 325, 326; pancreas, 326, 489n123; pediatric, 235; progress in, 272; research in, 79, 257, 327–329; as Russell's specialty, 273, 275, 289, 290–291; as surgical specialty, 302
Orthopaedic Bioengineering Laboratory, 81, 83
Orthopaedic Fund, 73
Orthopaedic Journal, 84
orthopaedic surgery, 391, 480n141; departmental scope broadened, 78–80; as early specialty, 72–76; headquarters of, 73; modern developments in, 76–80; research funds for, 73; research lab in, 78; subspecialties in, 80–84; Thesis Day in, 80; trauma faculty, 82
Orthopedic Ambulatory Surgery Center, 83–84
Osgood Lecture, 80
osteomyelitis, 76
outcome studies, 75–76, 210–211
Outpatient Building, 73, 227, 241, 245, 303, 340
outpatient services, 138; admissions in, 243; cancer treatment, 367; community clinics, 272; dental, 303; diet clinic, 194; early facilities for, 87–88; integrated, 246; as MGH raison d'être, 241; patient education, 244; shortcomings of, in Proctor Building, 241–244; tumor clinic, 362; urology and, 311, 315. *See also* Wang Ambulatory Care Center; Yawkey Center for Outpatient Care
Ovarian Dysfunctions Clinic, 148
ovariotomy, 72
Overseers of the Poor, 17, 19, 21

Pacemaker Laboratory, 142
pacemakers, 142

Pacemaker Society, 142
Pacific Interpreters, 201–202
PACT program (Parenting At a Challenging Time), 374–375
Pain and the Neurosurgeon (White and Sweet), 393
Pain: Its Mechanism and Neurosurgical Control (White and Sweet), 393
pancreas transplantation, 326, 489n123
Pancreatic Biology Laboratory, 421
Pappas Charitable Foundation, 355
Pap smears, 385
parathyroid hormone (PTH), 148–149, 152–155
Parkinson's disease, 348–349
Partners AIDS Research Center (PARC), 261
Partners HealthCare, 82, 355, 403; AIDS Research Center, 261; BHCHP and, 471; computerized record keeping at, 471; cost savings of, 383; development officers in, 359; formation of (1994), 110, 246, 261, 299, 330, 337; founding trustees of, 381; as integrated health care delivery system, 381–382; MGPO and, 454; naming of, 382, 491n75; pediatrics in, 236–237; Q&S efforts, 458; success of, 476
Pathological Cabinet, 90, 91
pathology: continuing education in, 98; departmental founding, 91–92; growth of, 93–95; informatics in, 97–98; neuropathology, 341; patient care as focus of, 94; residency program in, 93, 98; subspecialization in, 95–98; surgical pathology staff, 97
Patient Activity Center, 199
patient care, 388; clinical recognition program, 430–431; diversity in, 409–412; global scope of, 433; integrated model for, 431–432; narrative culture of, 428–430; non-physician clinicians reorganized into, 427; staff involved in, 409; use of term, 422. *See also* nurses/nursing
Patient Care Services Executive Committee, 431
Pediatric Global Health Division, 237
Pediatric Oral and Maxillofacial Surgery (Kaban), 308
Pediatric Orthopaedic Laboratory for Tissue Engineering and Regenerative Medicine, 79
pediatrics, 192, 213; accomplishments in, 236–237; CHGR and, 448; early facilities for, 226–229, 228; endocrinology, 231; first MGH practice, 226; intensive care unit (PICU), 50, 236, 237; MGHfC established for, 236, 237–238; OMFS services, 307–308; orthopedic unit, 79; psychopharmacology program, 186; research in, 228, 229–231; surgery, 229, 231–235, 302, 486n56; transplantation, 235; trauma faculty in, 405; in Vincent Burnham Building, 229, 349, 384; women in, 230
Pediatric Services Committee, 201
Pediatric Surgical Research Laboratories, 232
penicillin, 171, 211, 251
Pennsylvania Hospital, 16

Ropes and Gray, 333, 351
rotations model, 123
Royal Society, 349
Rumford Chemical Society, 57
Russell/Warner-Lambert Professorship, 328
Ryder Trauma Center (University of Miami; IMSuRT South), 466, 467–468

Sabin polio vaccine, 253
Sackett Plan (1965), 282
Saints Memorial Hospital (Lowell, Mass.), 122
Salk polio vaccine, 50, 76, 208, 253
salmonella, 251, 255–56
Sanger Center, 376
Sanofi-Aventis, 489n131. *See also* Hoechst AG–MGH research deal
SARS, 258
Schwartz Center, 375
Science (magazine), 119, 120, 261, 265
Science Connection, 411
Scientific Advisory Committee (SAC), 222–223, 371, 444
Scientific American, 463
Scripps Research Institute, 263–264
September 11 (2001) attacks, 459, 459, 466–467
Seventh General Hospital, 304
Shattuck Shelter, 471
Shiseido (Japanese corporation), 270, 271, 335, 355–356
Shoulder, The (Codman), 74–75
Shriners Burn Institute (SBI) Boston, 208–209, 210, 231, 236, 356
Sichuan (China) earthquake (2008), 465–466
Sidney Farber Cancer Center, 367, 368. *See also* Dana-Farber Cancer Institute
Simches Research Center, 121, 419, 420, 447, 447–449
Simmons College, 74, 217
Sixth General Hospital, 195–196, 217
Skeletal Biology Research Center, 309
skin disease wards, 88, 109
smallpox, 11, 15, 17
Smith Lecture, 80
Social Security Act (1965), 282
Social Service and the Art of Healing (Cabot), 131
social services, 207; community health clinics and, 286; departmental founding, 101, 130, 131, 287; early developments in, 130–131; funding for, 131; as GEC member, 228; growth of, 283–284; importance of, 163; LVC and, 199; Medicaid and, 284; pediatric, 228; psychology and, 180; reorganization of, 427. *See also* Boston Health Care for the Homeless Program; community health; patient care
Social Work (Cabot), 131
Society of Friends, 198
Society of Magnetic Resonance Imaging, 119, 120

Society of University Surgeons, 488n76
Somatic Therapies Service, 186
Somerville (Mass.), 89
Southern Medical Journal, 41
South Surgical Service, 123
Spanish-American War, 37–38, 88, 129, 195
Spanish flu, 166–167, 255
Spaulding Rehabilitation Hospital, 355
Spaulding Rehabilitation Hospital Corporation, 330, 402
specialization, 213, 248; institutional resistance to, 75, 340. *See also under specific medical field*
Specialized Center for Research on Ischemic Heart Disease, 142
Spectacle Island, 17
speech-language pathology, 427
sports medicine, 80–82, 81
Sports Medicine Center, 82
Sports Medicine Research Program, 81
Sports Medicine Service, 81–82
Spunkers (illicit corpse-procurement club), 11
Squibb, 335, 336, 338
Staff Associates, 240, 379
"Stand Up to Cancer" telethon, 376
Star*D Study (Sequenced Treatment Alternatives to Relieve Depression), 189
START (triage system), 5
Station, The (West Warwick, R.I.), fire at (2003), 8
St. Elizabeth's Hospital, 108
stem cells, 438, 443–444
STEP-BD (Systematic Treatment Enhancement Program for Bipolar Disorder), 189
Steps to Success Program, 411
St. Margaret's Hospital (Boston), 44
Stone Clinic, 148
stroke, 119, 342, 347–348
Structural Heart Center, 144
Structural Heart Disease Program, 143
St. Thomas's Hospital (London), 14, 65
sulfa drugs, 171, 251
surgery, 420–421; abdominal, 72, 88, 91; anesthesia first used in, 40, 42; antiseptic dressing in, 69–72; burn, 289, 302; burns service, 209, 210–211; cancer and, 366; cardiac, 272, 273, 296–299, 297, 378, 455; centralization of, in Gray Building, 279–281; during Civil War, 62–64; departmental division, 174–175, 289–290; departmental growth, 172–174; departmental unification, 171, 175; faculty of, 300; first female professor of, 232; fracture clinic, 77–78; "full-time" service in, 171–172; group practice in, 178, 244, 299–301, 306, 366; HMS/MGH relationship and, 173–174; house staff in, 275, 275–276; infections after, 69, 110; intensive care unit (SICU), 50; neurosurgery, 338, 345; 19th-century milestones in, 37; pediatric, 229, 231–235, 486n56; pre-anesthesia, 37; private hospitals for, 109;

professional standards for, 483n3; residencies in, 169, 172, 177–178, 297–298; specialization in, 72, 98, 123, 289, 301–302; staff reorganization, 123–124; training program in, 289; women in, 175. *See also* oral-maxillofacial surgery; organ transplantation; urology; *specific surgeon*

Surgery (journal), 421

surgical anesthesia, 14

Surgical Appliance Shop, 74

Surgical Associates, 178, 246, 300–301, 308

Surgical Executive Committee, 192, 313

syphilis, 251, 312

systems biology, 448

Tanzania, 463

teaching hospitals, 101, 295, 300–301

telemedicine, 282, 347

telomeres, 433, 438–439

Thayer Building, 66, 86

Thesis Day, 80

Thier Research Building, 355. *See also* Wellman Research Building

Thoracic-Aortic Center, 144

thoracic surgery, 302

"thousand-cell-line project," 376

3-D imaging, 121, 310

thymus gland, 341

thyroid, 147–148, 155–156, 248, 385

Thyroid Associates, 156

Time magazine, 220, 303

tissue engineering, 235

To Err Is Human (IOM report), 456–457

Toronto General Hospital, 50

Track Health, 262–263

Traité médico-philosophique sur l'aliénation mentale (Pinel), 22

transplantation. *See* organ transplantation

Transplantation Society, 295

Transplant ICU, 50

Trauma Services, 209

Travelers' Advice and Immunization Center, 258

Treadwell Library, 64, 124, 228, 290, 350, 355

Treaty of Ghent (1814), 21

Tremont Street Medical School, 59–60

Trustees, Board of: American Cancer Society funding and, 223; appointment/election of, 219; architect hired by, 23; Base Hospital No. 6 authorized by, 164; on blizzard (1978), 329; BTSN and, 66; Crockett and, 216; Edsall and, 146; Ether Day centenary and, 214; ether discovery controversy and, 40–41; Farnsworth Committee report supported by, 244; first female chair of, 222, 222; first meeting of (1813), 21; first staff MD as member of, 299; fund-raising by, 21; general director selection as responsibility of, 318–319, 351; heart transplantation opposed by, 272, 291; LVC and, 198; Martin (Larry) and,

322; McLean relocation and, 89; membership conditions, 490n36; MGH competition and, 482n53; MGH leadership and, 110, 246; MGPO and, 379; Overseers of the Poor as, 17; paragons of, 219, 219–22, 220; Parkman scandal and, 60–61; pathology and, 90, 91; positions created by, 73; private wards and, 126, 127; specialization opposed by, 109, 266; Staff Associates and, 240; staff reorganization supported by, 123; volunteer philanthropy formalized by, 358; as volunteers, 198; Ward 4 named by, 147; White Building authorized by, 193; Wilbur Committee report reviewed by, 192. *See also specific trustee*

Trustees House, 351

Tufts–New England Medical Center (NEMC), 404

tuition assistance programs, 410

Tumor Clinic, 304, 362, 365, 366, 367

Turkey earthquake (1999), 465

Twentieth-Century Surgeon (Welch), 481n155, 483n3

typhoid, 88

Ufa (Russia) gas explosion (1989), 465

Uganda, 265

United Mine Workers, 238

United Nations, 461, 463

United States Agency for Healthcare Research and Quality, 457

United States Army Medical Corps, 196

United States Health, Education and Welfare Department (HEW), 331, 350

United States Office of Civilian Defense, 238

United States Office of Strategic Services (OSS), 214

United States Office of Vocational Rehabilitation, 238

United States Public Health Service, 238

universal genes, 442

University of Helsinki, 83

University of Kansas, 45

University of Kwasulu-Natal (Durban, South Africa), 262

University of Pennsylvania, 134, 135

URMs (physicians underrepresented in medicine), 407–409

Urological Associates, 314

Urological Research Laboratory, 314

urology, 302, 311–316

U.S. Arctic Research Commission, 55

U.S. House of Representatives, 108

U.S. News and World Report, 146–147, 189, 361, 382

U.S. Olympic Team, 81

Van de Graaff machine, 114, 365

Vanderbilt Hall (HMS), 110

Vanderbilt University Medical Center (Nashville), 5